2013
The Supreme Court Review

2013
The

"Judges as persons, or courts as institutions, are entitled to no greater
immunity from criticism than other persons or institutions . . .
[J]udges must be kept mindful of their limitations and
of their ultimate public responsibility by a vigorous
stream of criticism expressed with candor however blunt."
—*Felix Frankfurter*

". . . while it is proper that people should find fault when
their judges fail, it is only reasonable that they should recognize the
difficulties. . . . Let them be severely brought to book,
when they go wrong, but by those who will take the trouble
to understand them."
—*Learned Hand*

THE LAW SCHOOL

THE UNIVERSITY OF CHICAGO

Supreme Court Review

EDITED BY

DENNIS J. HUTCHINSON
DAVID A. STRAUSS
AND GEOFFREY R. STONE

THE UNIVERSITY OF CHICAGO PRESS

CHICAGO AND LONDON

INTERNATIONAL STANDARD BOOK NUMBER: 978-0-226-15873-0

LIBRARY OF CONGRESS CATALOG CARD NUMBER: 60-14353

THE UNIVERSITY OF CHICAGO PRESS, CHICAGO 60637

THE UNIVERSITY OF CHICAGO PRESS, LTD., LONDON

© 2014 BY THE UNIVERSITY OF CHICAGO, ALL RIGHTS RESERVED, PUBLISHED 2014

PRINTED IN THE UNITED STATES OF AMERICA

The paper used in this publication meets the minimum requirements of American National Standard for Information Sciences–Permanence of Paper for Printed Library Materials, ANSI Z39.48-1984. ♾

TO ABR KRASH

Counsel to Clarence Earl Gideon
a half-century ago.
Model lawyer, mentor, and teacher
to generations of lawyers.

CONTENTS

RICHARD H. PILDES

INSTITUTIONAL FORMALISM AND REALISM IN CONSTITUTIONAL AND PUBLIC LAW

Constitutional law, and public law more generally, often entails regulating and reviewing the actions of institutions. Most prominently, in the realm of national affairs, public law oversees the actions of Congress, the President (a mix of an institution and a person), and administrative agencies. In the arena of state action, public law assesses the performance of institutions such as state courts and legislatures. To be sure, public law often involves judging more particularized actions of individual agents of the state—whether law enforcement officers, for example, have conducted a constitutional search or seizure in a specific factual setting. But much of the most important work of constitutional law—and certainly many of the highest-stakes and most visible cases—involves judicial review of the performance of the institutions of government. So it is with one of the most symbolically and politically charged Supreme Court decisions in decades, *Shelby County v Holder*,[1] in

Richard H. Pildes is Sudler Family Professor of Constitutional Law, NYU School of Law.

AUTHOR'S NOTE: For helpful comments and discussions, I am grateful to Daryl Levinson, Adam Samaha, Guy-Uriel Charles, David Golove, Sam Issacharoff, Tom Merrill, Bob Bauer, Helen Hershkoff, Rachel Barkow, Kenji Yoshino, and Barry Friedman. For first-rate research assistance, I thank Alex Kerchner. Support for this research was provided by the Filomen D'Agostino and Max. E. Greenberg Research Fund.

[1] 133 S Ct 2612 (2013).

which the Court concluded that Congress had failed to provide adequate justification for reauthorizing the unique preclearance regime of the Voting Rights Act (VRA).

When courts engage in reviewing the actions of other governmental institutions, such as Congress, they nominally apply, or purport to apply, what I call "institutional formalism." This formalism consists of treating the governmental institution involved as more or less a formal black box to which the Constitution (or other source of law) allocates specific legal powers and functions. Legal doctrine, that is, assimilates the institution—"the Congress," or "the President"—at a high level of abstraction and generality. By design, this institutional formalism blinds courts to any more contingent, specific features of institutional behavior, or to the particular persons who happen to occupy the relevant offices, or to the ways in which the institution actually functions in particular eras in which the institution is embedded within distinct political, historical, and cultural contexts. Instead, the role of judicial review is to assay the powers and properties of the institution at a general, essentialized level that intentionally ignores these fluid features—though these features are central, as we know, to the way the institution actually functions. That this institutional formalism exists is often taken for granted as part, some might say, of what the rule of law entails. How could it be otherwise?

And yet, an alternative does exist, in some form of institutional realism. This form of realism would entail constitutional and public-law doctrines that penetrate the institutional black box and adapt legal doctrine to take account of how these institutions actually function in, and over, time. There are many forms and degrees of institutional realism that legal doctrine could reflect. Such realism could be limited only to certain indicators of institutional change, such as those considered most "objective." For example, the most narrowly legalistic form of institutional realism would take into account only those changes directly reflected in a public institution's formal structure; should the passage of the Seventeenth Amendment, for example, influence federalism doctrines? But the functioning of institutions can change dramatically, of course, even absent any formal structural change. For example, should the way the Court responds to congressional, executive, and administrative action shift at all to reflect that the "Congress" of our era is constituted by hyperpolarized political parties more ideologically unified and more politically distant from each other than throughout the twentieth century?[2] Does the Court's expansive reading of the Clean Air Act, to permit the EPA to regulate greenhouse-gas emissions, already evince this realist view about the Congress of our era?[3] Similarly, institutional realism could operate at higher and lower levels of generality: it could mean taking into account how *this* particular presidency or *this* particular agency is perceived to function. If legal doctrine is receptive at all to institutional realism, where should this form of realism begin and end?

Legal doctrine and judicial decisions, as noted, are typically framed in institutionally formalist terms. This is most obvious, perhaps, with respect to administrative agencies. In the unifying ambition of the Administrative Procedure Act (APA) and administrative law, agencies are legally and formally the same. Regardless of differences in features of how particular agencies are designed or function, courts nominally defer to all agencies to the same extent under the *Chevron* doctrine and apply the same "arbitrary and capricious" or "substantial evidence" tests under the APA. Institutional formalism of this sort is even more consequential, yet ironically less visible, when it comes to "Congress" or "the President." Legal doctrine comprehends these institutions as singular, not just at any moment in time, but over time as well (diachronically as well as synchronically, for fans of structural linguistics). Supreme Court doctrine developed decades or even centuries ago on how much deference Congress is owed in a certain regulatory domain, for example, is relevant precedent today—regardless whether the actual Congress is hindered or empowered in dramatically different ways. "Congress" is always "Congress," for legal purposes. The constitutional powers of "the President" do not ebb or flow with the manifold changes of many forms that make the presidency a radically different institution in the early twenty-first century than the early nineteenth century. The manifestations of this institutional formalism radiate throughout public law.

Despite the rhetorical prevalence and rule-of-law appeal of institutional formalism, this article argues instead that the tension between institutionally formalist and realist approaches is pervasive, even if often obscured or latent, throughout the constitutional (and

---

[2] See generally Richard H. Pildes, *Why the Center Does Not Hold: The Causes of Hyperpolarized Democracy in America*, 99 Cal L Rev 273 (2011).

[3] *Massachusetts v EPA*, 549 US 497 (2007).

public) law of institutions. We cannot understand this law fully without recognizing this fact. Many scholars in discrete areas of law can be understood as grappling with this tension in some form. But I do not think we have appreciated how profound this institutional issue is, nor how it transcends specific areas of law to stand as one of public law's general, defining problems. Notwithstanding the nominal weight of institutional formalism, the pull of institutionalism realism is sometimes irresistible, whether opinions acknowledge so (as they occasionally do) or not. Part of the reason is that, even though some democratic theorists focus on pure procedural democracy,[4] actual institutional designers do not. Constitutional democracies (indeed, all democracies) are institutionally designed with an eye toward substantive performance, based on assumptions about how institutions will function: a single- rather than plural-headed executive to make accountability and decisiveness more likely, separation of powers to achieve an appropriate level of checks and balances, bicameralism to protect minority interests. For those charged with implementing this system, including judges, *not* to take into account how these institutions function in fact would be, at the least, odd (and judges on our most important public-law courts live and breathe, not in Kansas, but amidst the institutions that comprise the national government). Dramatic conflicts within the Court, as well as public and academic debates about judicial decisions, thus are often implicitly fueled by differing stances on how formalist or realist the judiciary should be about Congress, the presidency, or other institutions.

Part I will demonstrate the pervasive presence of this formalist/realist tension across all the main institutions whose actions the federal courts review: the state "courts," the state "legislatures," the federal administrative "agencies," the United States "Congress," or "the presidency." Regardless of the public institution involved, the question of how formalist or realist the federal courts should be about that institution shapes what legal doctrine is, as well as debates about what doctrine ought to be. Part II will then apply this framework to offer a particular perspective on the Court's *Shelby County* decision. I conclude by suggesting that constitutional and public

---

[4] For a recent summary of pure proceduralist theories, see Jamie Terence Kelly, *Framing Democracy: A Behavioral Approach to Democratic Theory* 46–49, 52–55 (Princeton, 2012); see also David M. Estlund, *Democratic Authority: A Philosophical Framework* (Princeton, 2008).

law can neither get rid of, nor solve, the tension between institutional formalism and realism. We cannot make any final choice between formalism and realism regarding institutions. Yet no titration formula (how much realism, how much formalism) exists either. Institutional realism might seem terrifying to contemplate, but public law cannot and does not live by institutional formalism alone.[5]

I. INSTITUTIONAL FORMALISM VERSUS REALISM: THE GENERAL FRAMEWORK

The formalist/realist institutional tension structures public-law doctrine and debates regarding judicial oversight of virtually all the institutions of governance. In the realm of doctrine, the Supreme Court and other federal courts sometimes engage the tension overtly. At other times, we can do no more than speculate, with stronger evidence in some contexts, regarding how much this tension shapes the Court's actions. Indeed, when legal doctrines change, I suggest it is often because the Court has altered its foundational stance toward the particular institution at issue: from a more formal to more realist stance or to a new and altered realist account concerning how the institution now functions.[6] Scholarship, too, frequently turns on judgments and disagreements, explicit or not, on this underlying institutional question.

---

[5] The tension between institutional formalism and realism I develop here bears a distant affinity with Neal Komesar's policy-oriented urgings on behalf of comparative institutional analysis. See Neil K. Komesar, *Imperfect Alternatives: Choosing Institutions in Law, Economics, and Public Policy* (1994); for his own most recent restatement of that work, see Neil Komesar, *The Logic of the Law and the Essence of Economics: Reflections on Forty Years in the Wilderness*, 2013 Wis L Rev 265. Komesar has pressed the idea that legal and policy analysis should focus on a pragmatic, comparative choice between decision-making institutions, with an analysis of the costs and benefits of different decision-making "institutions" (including the market) in light of the likely functioning of these institutions—particularly how their structures make them likely to handle the competing risks of majoritarian and minoritarian bias. But as Gregory Shaffer rightly observes, Komesar analyzes institutions "in ideal-type terms—assessing 'the political process,' 'the market process,' and 'the judicial process' as institutional alternatives." Gregory Shaffer, *Comparative Institutional Analysis and a New Legal Realism*, 2013 Wis L Rev 607, 618 (internal quotation marks added). See also Thomas W. Merrill, *Institutional Choice and Political Faith*, 22 J L & Soc Inquiry 959, 964 (noting that Komesar does not address how to determine the comparative advantage of various institutions in "real-world settings"). My aim here is to reveal the way legal doctrine and scholarship centers on the tension concerning just how much we ought to open up these ideal types to more realist appraisals, and the forms that realism might take, in judicial decision making.

[6] On the issue of doctrinal change, see Adam M. Samaha, *On the Problem of Legal Change*, 103 Georgetown L J (forthcoming 2014), available online at http://papers.ssrn.com/sol3/papers.cfm?abstract_id=2389037.

This tension in how the law should conceive public institutions can be seen as the modern successor to the early twentieth-century tension between formalist and realist approaches to the substantive content of legal concepts, categories, and doctrines. When the more pragmatic and consequentialist vision of legal realism threatened to be too corrosive to legal concepts, categories, and doctrines altogether, the Legal Process school of thought sought to stabilize legal practice by shifting the focus from the substantive content of law to regulating the appropriate processes and institutions through which the underlying substantive conflicts should be resolved. But now the tension between *institutional* formalism and realism reraises the question of how much pragmatism—this time, at the level of institutions and processes—is compatible with certain conceptions of the rule of law.[7] I begin with the field of federal courts.

A. COURTS

The core debate that roiled the field of federal courts for decades (and perhaps still does) was precisely this formalist/realist divide over the stance the federal courts should take toward the state courts, particularly in habeas corpus review of state criminal convictions. The linchpin to all other discrete issues concerning federal habeas review was essentially this: whether a state court is a court like any other court. More precisely, the question was whether the federal courts on habeas review should treat state courts like any other court (i.e., a federal district court) with respect to issues such as whether federal courts had the power and obligation to readjudicate federal constitutional issues fully and fairly litigated already in the state courts.

Doctrinally, this debate was launched with the decision in *Brown v Allen*[8] (decided nearly at the same time as *Brown v Board of Education*), which opened the door wide to routine federal court habeas relitigation of federal questions. During the 1950s and

---

[7] For the critique that scholars adopt realist stances toward governance institutions, but then inconsistently make doctrinal recommendations on the assumption that judges are not motivated in ways similar to the actors in these other institutions, see Eric A. Posner and Adrian Vermeule, *Inside or Outside the System?*, 80 U Chi L Rev 1743, 1745 (2013). In addition to the good rejoinder in Charles L. Barzun, *Getting Substantive: A Response to Posner and Vermeule*, 80 Chi L Rev Dialogue 267 (2014), my claim is that courts already do take institutional realism into account at times, but that it is illuminating to explore how they might and ought to do, whether courts are likely to do so in fact.

[8] 344 US 443 (1953).

1960s, the Court continued to license this expansive federal court review of state criminal convictions—more expansive than that which the Court enjoyed over lower federal court decisions, but starting in the 1970s, the Court shifted direction and began to require the federal habeas courts to defer much more to state criminal proceedings.[9] In the expansive phase of federal review, the Supreme Court did not, of course, expressly belittle the capacities or performance of state courts in general—even as the Court authorized expansive federal second opinions on state court decisions. But there can be little question that disputes within the Court, differences in Court decisions over time, and scholarly analyses and conflicts rested on differing, general institutional views of state courts, including whether doctrine should treat those courts in more formalist or realist terms.

In scholarship, this institutionalist issue was the core of the "parity" debate. For the figures who initially dominated federal courts scholarship starting in the 1950s, the Constitution required that state courts be conceptualized as in parity with federal courts.[10] That followed logically from the original Madisonian compromise that Article III reflects; because Congress was not required to create lower federal courts, the Constitution presumed that state courts would be as adequate as a federal court to adjudicate federal issues. Doctrine over a range of issues had to reflect that constitutional conception; penetrating the black box of "state courts" any further to judge how they generally function or perform in fact is not appropriate. This institutional formalist vein, most elegantly elaborated in Professor Paul Bator's classic article on institutional "finality,"[11] makes further "realist" questions about state versus federal judges legally irrelevant. Institutional formalism also entails consistency over time in the rules that govern federal court oversight of state courts; the same doctrines that applied in one era should apply in another.

"The Myth of Parity,"[12] my colleague Professor Burt Neuborne's

---

[9] Compare, for example, *Fay v Noia*, 372 US 391 (1963), with *Stone v Powell*, 428 US 465 (1976); *Wainwright v Sykes*, 433 US 72 (1977).

[10] Henry M. Hart, Jr., *The Power of Congress to Limit the Jurisdiction of Federal Courts: An Exercise in Dialectic*, 66 Harv L Rev 1362 (1953).

[11] Paul M. Bator, *Finality in Criminal Law and Federal Habeas Corpus for State Prisoners*, 76 Harv L Rev 441 (1963).

[12] Burt Neuborne, *The Myth of Parity*, 90 Harv L Rev 1105 (1977).

influential rejoinder, is a quintessential argument from institutional realism. In essence, Neuborne argued that not all courts are created equal; that to think so was a "dangerous myth";[13] that a more institutionally realist appraisal revealed that federal courts were more receptive to enforcement of federal constitutional rights than state courts; and that legal doctrine in the federal courts area should reflect this institutional realism. Examining the three factors Neuborne invoked to justify this position is important to assessing institutional realism. He argued that (1) state judges are more prone to majoritarian pressures against unpopular federal claims because most state judges are elected;[14] (2) that federal judges are more technically competent lawyers better able to work with complex or novel claims, because federal judgeships are more prestigious and better compensated;[15] and (3) that beyond greater technical legal competence, federal courts had a "psychological set"—a set of cultural and attitudinal characteristics—that made them more disposed to accept federal constitutional claims than state judges.[16]

Notice two distinct aspects of this institutional realism. First, it involves what I call "categorical" or wholesale realism about institutions. The argument is about state courts as a general or categorical matter. That is, the argument is not cast at a more particularist level of realism, such as an argument about how state courts function in a particular moment or era or how particular state courts function. Categorical realism of this sort could therefore still spawn general rules of federal court doctrine applied the same way over time; they would simply be different rules, which gave less deference to state courts on (some? all?) federal claims than the rules generated by the commitment to institutional parity. Second, note important differences between the *kind* of factors Neuborne invokes. His first factor rests on an objective, structural fact about formal institutional design (life tenure versus elections). But his other two factors are more subjective, elusive ("a psychological set"), and, indeed, capable of change over time.

From the perspective of legal doctrine, categorical realism about institutions is more judicially manageable than retail versions, examples of which we will soon see. Categorical realism, as noted,

---

[13] Id at 1105.

[14] Id at 1127–28.

[15] Id at 1121–22.

[16] Id at 1124–27.

still enables courts to craft doctrines of broad and general applicability regarding these institutions. And categorical realism is easiest to justify when based on objective, structural features of an institution. As soon as realism rests on more subjective institutional assessments, as in Neuborne's final two factors,[17] institutional realism will inevitably become more controversial normatively, more contested empirically, and more destabilizing, potentially, to conventional rule-of-law notions. For these less structural justifications for institutional realism open up possibilities such as that the habeas cases of the 1950s and 1960s were correct *and* that the retrenchment from those decisions in later decades was also correct.[18] For if state courts in more recent decades (particularly Southern courts, after the civil-rights revolution) have developed a different "psychological set" than in earlier decades, institutional realism would argue that greater respect for the finality of state court adjudications would be warranted.[19] Indeed, the Justices who led this retrenchment wrote precisely that.[20] This is one area in which judicial decisions explicitly

---

[17] It is true, of course, that interpreting the effects of specific structural features of an institution—such as whether the election of state judges does indeed make them less receptive to federal constitutional claims—is itself a subjective enterprise, absent widely accepted empirical standards and conclusions. Nonetheless, when structural differentiations of this sort do exist (life tenure versus elections) institutional realism based on those differentiations starts from the most defensible premises.

[18] See, for example, Michael E. Solimine, *The Future of Parity*, 46 Wm & Mary L Rev 1457, 1487 (2005) ("Much discourse on parity is characterized by its static nature. . . . The better view is to examine parity as a fluid and dynamic concept, with changes—for good or ill—in both federal and state courts over time.").

[19] As a more "modern," further turning-of-the-realist wheel, Professor William Rubenstein argued that by the late 1990s, state judges had become more on a par with federal judges, though he was writing as a tactical matter for advocates, rather than as a matter of how federal courts doctrine should change. William Rubenstein, *The Myth of Superiority*, 16 Const Comm 599 (1999). For Neuborne's own revisitation of these questions, which concludes that institutional factors continue to make federal courts function better than state courts in resolving close constitutional cases, see Burt Neuborne, *Parity Revisited: The Use of a Judicial Forum of Excellence*, 44 DePaul L Rev 797 (1995). For good summaries of the empirical literature and debates on the "parity" question, see Richard H. Fallon, Jr., et al, *Hart and Wechsler's The Federal Court and the Federal System* 278–83 (Foundation, 6th ed 2009); Barry Friedman, *Under the Law of Federal Jurisdiction: Allocating Cases Between Federal and State Courts*, 104 Colum L Rev 1211, 1221 n 25 (2004).

[20] In *Stone v Powell*, Justice Powell wrote for the Court:

The policy arguments that respondents marshal in support of the view that federal habeas corpus review is necessary to effectuate the Fourth Amendment stem from a basic mistrust of the state courts as fair and competent forums for the adjudication of federal constitutional rights. The argument is that state courts cannot be trusted to effectuate Fourth Amendment values through fair application of the rule, and the oversight jurisdiction of this Court on certiorari is an inadequate safeguard. The principal rationale for this view emphasizes the

and directly reflect changing Court (perceptions) of the arguably dynamic nature of public institutions.[21]

For an example of Supreme Court institutional realism regarding state courts at an even less structural, and more contingent, level, consider an aspect of Justice Ginsburg's dissenting opinion in *Bush v Gore*.[22] Written to mount a challenge to the concurring opinion of Chief Justice Rehnquist, the conflict turned on how much deference federal courts owed to state court interpretations of state law when a federal constitutional issue is at stake. In federal courts terminology, this implicates the "fair support" rule—the doctrine that, even when federal claims are at stake, federal courts should or must accept state determinations of state law as long as those determinations rest upon "a fair or substantial basis" in prior state law.[23] Arguing that the Florida courts had strained the interpretation of state election law beyond any reasonable bound, the concurrence invoked precedents from the 1950s and 1960s for the principle that the Constitution gives the Court a role in ensuring, when federal

---

broad differences in the respective institutional settings within which federal judges and state judges operate. *Despite differences in institutional environment and the unsympathetic attitude to federal constitutional claims of some state judges in years past, we are unwilling to assume that there now exists a general lack of appropriate sensitivity to constitutional rights in the trial and appellate courts of the several States.* . . . In sum, there is "no intrinsic reason why the fact that a man is a federal judge should make him more competent, or conscientious, or learned with respect to the [consideration of Fourth Amendment claims] than his neighbor in the state courthouse."

428 US 465, 493 n 35 (emphasis added) (citation omitted).

[21] Some scholars argue that the Court is the *most* well-positioned institution to evaluate and act on the basis of ongoing institutional reassessment of state court functioning. Barry Friedman, *Habeas and Hubris*, 45 Vand L Rev 797, 819 (1992). For the argument that we should not essentialize the judicial function, and should recognize that state courts differ structurally from federal courts in ways that do or should, for example, lead state courts to apply justiciability doctrines or rationality review differently from federal courts, see Helen Hershkoff, *State Courts and the "Passive Virtues": Rethinking the Judicial Function*, 114 Harv L Rev 1833, 1909–15 (2001); Helen Hershkoff, *Positive Rights and State Constitutions: The Limits of Federal Rationality Review*, 112 Harv L Rev 1131, 1157–69 (1999).

[22] 531 US 98 (2000).

[23] *Demorest v City Bank Farmers Trust Co.*, 321 US 36, 42 (1944). For a comprehensive discussion of this doctrine, see Henry Paul Monaghan, *Supreme Court Review of State-Court Determinations of State Law in Constitutional Cases*, 103 Colum L Rev 1919 (2003). Instead of focusing on how the institution of the Florida courts functioned, the concurring opinion could have been framed around a form of realism about the nature of the claim involved: given the national stakes in a presidential election, federal courts should understand themselves to have much greater power than in ordinary federal cases to make an independent determination of the meaning of prior state law. See id at 1926. In ballot access cases, at least, the Court does seem to apply much greater scrutiny in presidential elections. See, for example, *Anderson v Celebrezze*, 460 US 780 (1983).

constitutional claims are at stake, that state courts have not radically altered state law in the guise of "interpreting" it.[24]

Responding in an institutionally realist vein, Justice Ginsburg argued that those precedents were no longer relevant because they were "embedded in historical contexts" dramatically different from the present: the context of Southern state courts addressing civil-rights claims "in the face of Southern resistance to the civil rights movement. . . ."[25] State high courts in 2000 should not, her dissent argued explicitly, be treated the same as "state high courts of the Jim Crow South."[26] Thus, her opinion offers a temporarily contingent conception of how the Court should treat the institution of a "state court." In contemplation of constitutional law, a state court is not once and always the same institution. Justice Ginsburg was not referring to any specific, identifiable structural change in state courts as institutions; she was appealing to more generalized transformations in culture and politics that should change the way federal courts reviewed state courts. And one consequence of this "realism" was that precedents from the 1950s and 1960s should be confined to that earlier context (the judicially polite way of saying abandoned).

In one sense, who can resist this institutional realism? Of course, far greater reason did exist to be skeptical of Southern courts in civil-rights cases in the era of Jim Crow (but then, the Chief Justice's opinion might reflect perceived institutional realism of its own, albeit more subterraneously: as an elected court Democrats dominated, the Florida court was acting in a partisan fashion). Yet we arrive at a "law of institutions" that varies with perceived changes in how those institutions work—and even when federal judges can point to no specific structural change in the institutions. Indeed, the dissenters in the Court's Eleventh Amendment immunity cases[27] invoked an institutionally realist account of the Court itself in arguing that *Hans v Louisiana*[28] should be narrowly confined; *Hans* should not be taken to reflect any generalizable constitutional prin-

---

[24] *Bouie v City of Columbia*, 378 US 347 (1964); *NAACP v Alabama*, 357 US 449 (1958).

[25] *Bush v Gore*, 531 US at 140.

[26] Id at 141.

[27] See *Seminole Tribe v Florida*, 517 US 44, 85–86 (1996) (Stevens, J, dissenting).

[28] 134 US 1 (1890). For an explicitly realist self-account in this same era of the Court's own limited power, offered as a justification for the Court's decision making, see *Giles v Harris*, 189 US 475 (1903); for discussion of that realism, see Richard H. Pildes, *Democracy, Anti-Democracy, and the Canon*, 17 Const Comm 295 (2000).

ciple about state immunity, but rather the institutional reality that
the Court of the late nineteenth century lacked the power to enforce
any judgment against the states for repudiating their Reconstruc-
tion-era debts. To this the majority responded that realism of this
sort was "a disservice to the Court's traditional method of adjudication."[29]

In the absence of institutional formalism, principles and precedents come and go as judicial perceptions shift of how other institutions function. Institutional realism might be desirable, or irresistible to some extent, but it challenges many of our conceptions
of how law functions.

B. THE PRESIDENCY

Since the Constitution's adoption, the office of the presidency
has obviously undergone vast changes. Some are formal changes
in the Constitution itself, such as the two-term limit embodied in
the Twenty-Second Amendment. Some are structural changes that
have had dramatic practical effects on how much power the President can wield effectively, such as changes in the institutions and
processes through which candidates for the office are selected. For
the country's first forty or so years, party caucuses in Congress
became the de facto method for selecting candidates; as a result,
presidential freedom of action was strongly subordinated to congressional control.[30] Not until the invention of the party nomi-
nating conventions and the ability of Presidents such as Andrew
Jackson to claim a popular mandate did the office come to rest
on an independent basis of support that enabled it, as Corwin
wrote, to be "thrust forward as one of three equal branches of
government...."[31] Some of the changes affecting the actual powers
of the office are technological, such as the advent of television in
the mid-twentieth century, which gave the President a powerful
new capacity to project his views to the country. More modern
technological changes might weaken the office, as it becomes eas-

---

[29] *Seminole Tribe*, 517 US at 69.

[30] For a fuller account, see Daryl J. Levinson and Richard H. Pildes, *Separation of Parties,
Not Powers*, 119 Harv L Rev 2311, 2321 (2006).

[31] Edward Corwin, *The President: Office and Powers, 1787–1957* at 21 (NYU, 4th ed
1957).

ier for dissenters inside government or outside to publicize and mobilize opposition to presidential actions.[32]

Does and should constitutional doctrine on the powers of the presidency take account of developments of these and other kinds that do, realistically, shape and constrain the office's effective power? If the President has greater power to mobilize public opinion once television is invented, should the Court push back by becoming less willing to recognize expansive powers of the President to act without clear, express congressional endorsement? In an era such as ours, when the political parties are so intensely polarized, control of government is divided between them, and enacting legislation has become systematically more difficult than in prior eras,[33] should the Court be more accommodating to presidential uses of other tools to make policy, such as executive orders? Or should the Court adopt an institutionally formalist stance, in which the Court over time construes the powers of the office (both in constitutional terms and in construing statutes) without regard to any of these underlying, dynamic institutional realities? Apart from these normative questions, how much are Court decisions best construed as reflecting this kind of institutional realism?

The Court has issued a small number of opinions on presidential powers. In addition, even if institutionally realist considerations influence the Court's decisions, we might expect the Court to refrain from being explicit about that, given the tension between some conceptions of the rule of law and institutional realism. Nonetheless, institutional realism overtly inspires two of the Court's most significant presidential-power opinions.

The first is the most celebrated opinion in the presidential-powers canon. Justice Jackson's concurrence in the *Youngstown*[34] case insisted that modern separation-of-powers doctrine must reflect the way the effective powers of the presidency had changed over time—with the gap that had come to exist "between the President's paper powers and his real powers."[35] Adverting to

---

[32] Jack L. Goldsmith, *Power and Constraint: The Accountable Presidency After 9/11* (W. W. Norton, 2012).

[33] Paul Kane, *113th Congress, Going Down in History for Its Inaction, Has a Critical December To-Do List*, Washington Post (Dec 1, 2013), online at http://goo.gl/GlatMz.

[34] *Youngstown Sheet & Tube Co. v Sawyer*, 343 US 579, 634 (1952) (Jackson, J, concurring).

[35] Id at 653.

transformations in communications technology by the mid-twentieth century (probably with FDR's "fireside chats" in mind), Jackson pointed out that "[n]o other personality in public life can begin
to compete with him in access to the public mind through modern
methods of communications."[36] Moreover, no judicial assessment
of the lawfulness of presidential action should take place, Jackson
argued, without taking into account the emergence of the modern
system of political parties; the modern dynamics of political parties
across the institutions of government (at the time Jackson wrote)
meant that the President, as the head of one of the two major
parties, held significant parts of Congress (other party members)
under his sway and could potentially wield more power, with less
congressional resistance, than could earlier Presidents or than the
Constitution permitted. In prior work, Professor Daryl Levinson
and I quoted from an arresting passage in Justice Jackson's opinion
that has been virtually ignored, but that expresses vividly this po-
litical-party-based perspective of presidential realism. Justice Jackson wrote:

> [T]he rise of the party system has made a significant extraconstitutional
> supplement to real executive power. No appraisal of his necessities is
> realistic which overlooks that he heads a political system as well as a
> legal system. Party loyalties and interests, sometimes more binding than
> law, extend his effective control into branches of government other
> than his own and he often may win, as a political leader, what he cannot
> command under the Constitution.[37]

We can debate precisely when the party system congealed into
the form it assumed by the mid-twentieth century. But Jackson's
insistence that "the presidency" should not be viewed, by legal
doctrine, as a unitary institution over time puts institutional formalism to the test.[38] Jackson did not take the direct step of stating

---

[36] Id.

[37] Id at 654.

[38] As we explained the significance of this passage more fully:

> Justice Jackson astutely recognized that the separation of powers no longer works
> as originally envisioned because interbranch dynamics have changed with the
> rise of political parties, which by the time of *Youngstown*, had long diminished
> the incentives of Congress to monitor and check the President. Yet this part of
> Justice Jackson's opinion has been ignored entirely. Even after decades of dis-
> secting Justice Jackson's *Youngstown* opinion, neither the Supreme Court nor
> any other federal court has ever quoted this critical insight, nor has it received
> much notice by legal scholars. Justice Jackson's sophisticated realism about the
> workings of government is widely admired by constitutional lawyers, but his

that it was because of these shifting features of presidential power over Congress that he cast his vote to hold President Truman's seizure of the steel mills unconstitutional. But in applying his tripartite framework of analysis, Jackson had to decide whether to put the case in his "zone of twilight," on the view that the relevant statutes did not resolve the issue one way or the other, or in his third category, in which these statutes were read to prohibit the seizure. Jackson placed the seizure in this third category, of course—but he did so not because any express congressional prohibition on seizures of this sort existed, but because Congress had silently refused to grant the President such authority. Is there any doubt that Jackson's decision to locate the case in category three, based on the thin reed of congressional silence, directly reflected his institutional realism about the modern presidency?

Though less baldly, other Justices, too, embraced institutional realism in *Youngstown*. Prefacing an early part of his opinion with the comment that "[i]t is absurd to see a dictator in a representative product of the sturdy democratic traditions of the Mississippi Valley," Justice Frankfurter then did exactly that; as a basis for rejecting President Truman's action, Frankfurter lectured on the incremental steps that paved a path to over-concentrated executive power.[39] Though more tersely than Jackson, Frankfurter, too, suggested it would be feckless for constitutional doctrine not to shape itself around modern institutional facts that appeared to smooth the concentration of greater power into executive hands. Surely the fact that America had just experienced a four-term presidency contributed to the perception of changed institutional realities, against which a more vigilant judicial review had to arise.

As a judicial opinion offering an institutionally realist foundation for constitutional decision making, the most brilliant in this area is surely Justice Scalia's tour de force (initially rejected by most scholars) solitary dissent in *Morrison v Olson*.[40] In upholding the office of an independent counsel, created a decade earlier to investigate and prosecute crimes of high-level executive officials,

---

most penetrating realist insight—recognizing party competition as a central mechanism driving the institutional behavior that separation of powers law aims to regulate—has been missed.

Levinson and Pildes, 119 Harv L Rev at 2315 (footnote omitted) (cited in note 30).

[39] *Youngstown*, 343 US at 593 (Frankfurter, J, concurring).

[40] 487 US 654, 697 (1988) (Scalia, J, dissenting).

the eight-member majority grounded its analysis on the formal properties of the new office, along with the formal relationship of the office to the existing institutions of government. The independent counsel office did not "disrupt[ ] the proper balance"[41] between the branches, for example, because the Attorney General had several means formally available to supervise and control the independent counsel.[42]

Blistering with disdain for the majority's lack of realism, Justice Scalia defined the case as being about the real-world workings of political "Power."[43] He delved into every nook and cranny of the law to conjure a revealing portrait (and a prescient one, as it turned out) of the actual currents of political power the law was too likely to unleash. The realist insights roll out in relentless waves to deluge the majority's focus on formal legal structures and properties: the independent counsel's office will be too zealously focused on one individual; it will lose any of the sense of judgment and perspective that comes with having to internalize budgetary and other constraints that come with a more generalized prosecutorial function; Congress can weaken the presidency not by going after the President in politically accountable ways, through impeachment proceedings, but by hiding behind the independent counsel; low thresholds for triggering public investigations will tie administrations up in knots, and so on.[44] By the end of his opinion, Justice Scalia shifts his institutional realism from the way the independent counsel office is likely to work in practice to a realist's political economy concerning Congress's enactment of the law itself. Thus, he closes by penetrating "Congress" as a black box to provide an account of why members of Congress would be all too likely to vote for such a law (notice the resonance with his views about the nearly unanimous legislation in *Shelby County*), even if many of them believed the law bad policy—and why partisan politics would make it unlikely the law would be repealed even if it did great harm (ultimately Congress did let the law lapse when its sunset provision kicked in).[45]

---

[41] Id at 695 (majority).

[42] Id at 695–96.

[43] Id at 699 (Scalia, J, dissenting).

[44] Id at 713–14.

[45] In full, Justice Scalia wrote:

Whether one nods approvingly or is disturbed at all the modes of institutional realism on display here, the point is to notice this realism and the choice with which it confronts courts. To be sure, the causal linkage between Justice Scalia's legal analysis and his passionate institutional realism is not as clear as in the *Youngstown* opinions. For Justice Scalia, judicial realism about the workings of political power seems offered more as evidentiary confirmation than as legal justification. The main thrust of his legal analysis, in his characteristically formal mode of reasoning, is that a simple syllogism should render the independent-counsel law unconstitutional: the law vests purely executive functions in an official whose actions are not fully within the supervision and control of the President. Case closed, Scalia argues. The work his realist analysis of power is then designed to do is twofold: (1) to explain that there are powerful functional or realist reasons that underlie the Constitution's original allocation of authority (as he sees it) to a unitary executive branch, and (2) to show that when the Court tries to make its own functional judgments of when departures, for seemingly good reasons, from this unitary structure will come at little cost, the Court has a naive appreciation for the currents of real-world political power. Ironically, this most penetrating realist dissection of institutional power thus becomes a brief for the Court to stay out of the institutional realism business, because the Court is not good at it.

Though few presidential-powers opinions overtly speak in institutionally realist language, plausible grounds exist for speculating this kind of realism is silently at work in other cases—such as the Court's Guantánamo Bay detention decisions. By the time these cases started reaching the Court, it was widely understood, particularly among legally attentive audiences, that the administration of President George W. Bush was not just adopting par-

---

I cannot imagine that there are not many thoughtful men and women in Congress who realize that the benefits of this legislation are far outweighed by its harmful effect upon our system of government, and even upon the nature of justice received by those men and women who agree to serve in the Executive Branch. But it is difficult to vote not to enact, and even more difficult to vote to repeal, a statute called, appropriately enough, the Ethics in Government Act. If Congress is controlled by the party other than the one to which the President belongs, it has little incentive to repeal it; if it is controlled by the same party, it dare not. By its shortsighted action today, I fear the Court has permanently encumbered the Republic with an institution that will do it great harm.

Id at 733.

ticular policies it viewed as necessary and appropriate to combat modern terrorism, but also pursuing a consistent, wide-ranging, and independent agenda to redefine the scope of exclusive Article II presidential powers as a more general matter (supporters might say to "restore" the President's rightful powers, critics to "expand" them).[46]

When the Court, through Justice O'Connor, pushed back in cases like *Hamdi v Rumsfeld* with decisions that included statements that "a state of war is not a blank check for the President when it comes to the rights of the Nation's citizens,"[47] the Court might well have been responding not just to one specific policy at issue in a particular case, but to the overall tenor of the administration's conception of presidential powers as a whole: to *this* particular presidency, rather than to the presidency as a formal institution (high-level lawyers who served in that administration certainly view the Court that way[48]). The intriguing question is not whether the Court perceived a need to lecture the particular administration in more rhetorically forceful terms, but whether actual decisions in some or all of these cases about the scope of presidential power were affected. The willingness of other public institutions (as well as the public) to accept novel forms of presidential power is influenced by the extent to which a particular administration builds trust and credibility that suggests its actions reflect sound, well-thought-through judgment and principles;[49] it is no great stretch to believe that similar considerations move the Court as well. To reject President George W. Bush's claims, the Court had to minimize the most relevant precedents, from the World War II era,

---

[46] As a related matter, we can also speculate how much the President's position on executive power in the initial Guantánamo Bay cases was discredited at the Court by release of the vivid, horrifying photographs from Abu Ghraib a mere eight hours or so after the Solicitor General had stated to the Court that "our executive [branch?] doesn't" engage in "mild torture." Joseph Marguiles, *Guantánamo and the Abuse of Presidential Power* 152–53 (Simon & Schuster, 2006) (asserting that the photos' release "proved to be the most powerful amicus brief of all"). As Marguiles notes, there is no evidence that the Solicitor General was aware at the time of the Abu Ghraib facts.

[47] 542 US 507, 536 (2004).

[48] See Jack L. Goldsmith, *The Terror Presidency: Law and Judgment Inside the Bush Administration* (W. W. Norton, 2007).

[49] Richard H. Pildes, *Law and the President*, 125 Harv L Rev 1381 (2012); see also Curtis A. Bradley and Trevor W. Morrison, *Presidential Power, Historical Practice, and Legal Constraint*, 113 Colum L Rev 1097, 1132–49 (2013).

as dissenting Justices pointed out.[50] Of course, much has changed since then, beyond the particular nature of the Bush 43 presidency's claims about executive power; we cannot know whether, and how much, this kind of institutional realism affected the Court's decisions. This is institutional realism at the retail level; were this kind of realism to shape judicial decisions, it could well mean that acts of presidential power invalidated in some or all of these cases might, in contrast, have been upheld in an administration that did not generally invoke an exceptionally expansive conception of unilateral presidential powers. And institutional realism at this retail level might suggest that when related issues arise down the road, the precedential strength of the Guantánamo Bay cases might depend on the Court's "realist" assessment of the kind of trust and credibility on legal issues some future administration in general has (or has not) established.

In our earlier work, Daryl Levinson and I suggested a default rule for separation-of-powers law that might emerge from, and build upon, Justice Jackson's institutional realism about the changing dynamics of presidential power.[51] Jackson is certainly right that presidential power is now strongly shaped by the modern political-party system. One consequence is that the House and Senate cannot be counted on to the same extent as in less party-dominated eras to provide strong institutional checks and balances on presidential power. Instead of being motivated to assert the role of their institutions as such against the presidency (if they were ever so motivated), their reelection prospects and hence motivations are strongly linked to their partisan alliances or antagonisms with the President; a unified Congress of the same party as the President is less likely to challenge his authority, while an opposite-party House or Senate surely will. Thus, in the "twilight zone" in which it is neither clear that Congress has licensed nor prohibited presidential action, we suggested courts should perhaps tilt toward rejecting claims of presidential power when Congress is controlled by the President's political party. Presidents will likely face an open-minded Congress when forced to make their case and gain affirmative legislative endorsement. Conversely, during divided government, the risk that Congress will be more close-

---

[50] See, for example, *Johnson v Eisentrager*, 339 US 763 (1950); *Hamdi*, 542 US at 579 (Thomas, J, dissenting).

[51] Levinson and Pildes, 119 Harv L Rev at 2354–56 (cited in note 30).

minded toward presidential requests, for reasons of pure partisan opposition rather than genuine policy reflection, might suggest that a more generous judicial stance in the "twilight zone" is appropriate.

Even to raise these questions is surely to trigger easily recognizable fears about what institutional realism, particularly at the administration-by-administration level, might mean—including the risk that it opens the door for subjective perceptions about different Presidents to shape the Court's decisions. And yet, is it plausible to believe the Court is institutionally formalist about the presidency or ought to be? The Court has more degrees of freedom in this area than others: many issues on presidential power never reach the Court; the actual cases are relatively few and far between; and the constitutional text is highly specific only on a few issues in this domain. Moreover, the cases often arise in such high-stakes contexts that getting the individual decision "right" can (properly) dwarf considerations of whether the rule of decision is appropriately generalizable across time, contexts, and administrations. We know that widespread cultural views on the presidency have changed over time; it is hard to believe that Supreme Court decision making would be immune, or should be, from the greater skepticism about presidential claims of fact and need (i.e., national security) that emerged after the presidential deceit and abuse of power revealed in the 1960s and 1970s.

As with state courts, institutional realism regarding the presidency is easiest to defend in the form of "categorical" or wholesale realism: judgments that the law should treat the institution differently (less deference on factual issues, or more restrictive readings of congressional delegations) than in a past era because of broad temporal changes that have reshaped the effective functioning of the presidency as a general matter. Categorical realism does spawn law that treats "the presidency" differently over time, but treats the institution in fairly stable ways over the short run. Justice Jackson, for example, points to changes in technology and political parties that justify greater judicial constraint on the presidency as a general matter going forward. Also as with state courts, this categorical realism is itself easiest to defend when proponents can point to objective structural features—such as legal changes—in the institution. The more subjective the perceptions of change that must be invoked, the more threatening this realism will become. But notice that Jackson's institutional analysis, though categorical, relies precisely on these more subjective perceptions (the effect of technology and modern parties on actual presidential power), not hard legal changes to the presidency.

If Jackson's realism about "the nature" of modern presidential power seems hard to resist, though, the boundary between his wholesale-level realism and the kind of retail realism that might have influenced the Guantánamo Bay cases becomes thinner. Once subjective judicial perceptions about the changing nature of the presidency enter decision making, how broadly (several decades?) or narrowly (one administration?) should courts bound the temporal baseline over which this realism is proper? My claim is that, whatever the right answers to questions of this sort, the tension between institutionally formalist and realist approaches to the presidency, and how to apply realist approaches when Justices and the Court do so, is at the foundation of many disputes over how to construe the powers of the presidency. We cannot understand the law of presidential power, or these disputes, without appreciating the work institutional formalism or realism are doing.[52]

C. AGENCIES

Institutional realism might seem most compelling with respect to public-law doctrine that reviews administrative agency action. Indeed, the rise of agency capture theory in the 1970s and 1980s to challenge the expertise vision of agency functioning, with the resulting doctrinal shift to more aggressive "hard-look" judicial review,[53] is itself a form of institutional realism. This defining transformation in modern administrative law reflects judicial re-

---

[52] Institutional formalism and realism in the separation-of-powers arena raise distinct issues from those raised by the conventional debates between "formalism" and "functionalism" in this area. In the latter debate, put most crudely, the question is typically whether national powers should be formally categorized into sharply distinct legislative, executive, and judicial powers—with any such power having to be exercised exclusively by the branch assigned that "kind" of power—or whether Congress should have the power to create more complex institutional arrangements that blur these categorical distinctions in the service of pursuing (Congress's view) of more effective governance. As samples of the immense scholarly literature on those questions, see Peter L. Strauss, *Formal and Functional Approaches to Separation-of-Powers Questions—A Foolish Inconsistency?*, 72 Cornell L Rev 488 (1987); Cass R. Sunstein, *Constitutionalism After the New Deal*, 101 Harv L Rev 421 (1987); Steven G. Calabresi and Christopher S. Yoo, *The Unitary Executive: Presidential Power from Washington to Bush* (Yale, 2008).

[53] For the classic article on this shift, see Richard B. Stewart, *The Reformation of American Administrative Law*, 88 Harv L Rev 1669 (1975).

ceptivity to piercing "the administrative agency" veil and adjusting doctrine accordingly. As new doctrine that functioned as a general matter across all agencies, this transformation reflected a categorical realism, but not one tied to any structural or legal change in agency design. These doctrinal shifts instead embodied a new "realist" political-economy analysis of agency functioning that led courts to shift their stance toward agencies, as reflected in a range of administrative-law doctrines, and to apply that new understanding across the board to agencies in general.[54]

We can ask whether analogous doctrinal shifts should take place today to reflect institutional realities concerning Congress. In numerous policy arenas in which agencies act, Congress has not revisited the issues in many decades, despite dramatic technological, economic, scientific, and other changes. The episodic nature of congressional action in these areas is now exacerbated by the hyperpolarized partisan context, combined with divided government, that cripples the capacity of Congress to act in general. In these areas, such as energy or environmental policy, should courts be more deferential to the relevant regulatory agencies in light of the institutional reality that the agencies alone are likely to be capable as a practical matter of actively updating statutory regimes?[55] Or more broadly, realist accounts of the administrative process today suggested it has changed dramatically over the past decades. Contrasting the "lost world of the APA and administrative law" with "the real world of modern administrative practice"—in which the White House and political considerations play a dominant role; an "agency" often acts in coordination with other agencies, not alone; much of the important decision making is done outside the formal record; and agencies are often led only by acting directors, not Senate-confirmed leadership—Professors Dan Farber and Anne O'Connell have suggested ways in which administrative law should change accordingly.[56]

Just as interesting questions about formalism and realism re-

[54] For a more recent assessment of how judicial review could be redesigned to inhibit agency capture, see M. Elizabeth Magill, *Courts and Regulatory Capture*, in Daniel Carpenter and David A. Moss, eds, *Preventing Capture: Special Interest Influence in Regulation, and How to Limit It* (2013).

[55] For detailed analysis of this question, see Jody Freeman and David B. Spence, *Old Statutes, New Problems*, forthcoming, Penn L Rev (2014).

[56] Daniel A. Farber and Anne Joseph O'Connell, *The Lost World of Administrative Law*, forthcoming, Tex L Rev (2014).

garding agencies operate at a yet more specific level. Agencies vary
in a range of ways, some more visible, others not. Formal structural
differences in agency design are the most obvious, such as the
legal difference between independent and executive agencies, or
whether the agency/commission/board is multiheaded or single-
headed, or whether bipartisan appointment requirements exist.[57]
A categorical doctrinal realism might track these formal differences in agency design. Some agencies are known to reflect partisan political differences more pervasively, and to shift positions
more routinely with changes in administration appointments, than
others. The NLRB immediately comes to mind, as then Professor,
now Judge Winter noted in these pages many years ago;[58] his
argument that the board's distinct mix of political responsiveness
and expertise should lead courts to review board findings of fact
more aggressively than those of other agencies is surely reflected
in the Court's more recent, distinctly assertive "substantial evidence" review in the well-known *Allentown Mack* case.[59] The agencies that administer federal election laws are uniquely headed by
an even number of commissioners, who are also required to be
balanced between the political parties; as a result, they are more
prone to deadlock, and Professor Jennifer Nou has proposed that
unique administrative-law doctrines should govern judicial review
of these particular agencies.[60] Some agencies are required to submit proposed major rules for presidential review through the Office of Management and Budget (OMB) process; other agencies,

---

[57] For good synthesis of the variations in agency design, see Richard Revesz and Kirti
Datla, *Deconstructing Independent Agencies (and Executive Agencies)*, 98 Cornell L Rev 769
(2013); Rachel Barkow, *Insulating Agencies: Using Institutional Design to Limit Agency Capture*, 89 Tex L Rev 15 (2010); Lisa Schultz Bressman and Robert B. Thompson, *The Future
of Agency Independence*, 63 Vand L Rev 599 (2010).

[58] Ralph Winter, *Judicial Review of Agency Decisions: The Labor Board and the Court*, 1968
Supreme Court Review 53. Winter argued for statutory changes that would permit courts
to engage in more aggressive factual review, rather than for courts assuming this power
on their own.

[59] *Allentown Mack Sales and Service, Inc. v NLRB*, 522 US 359 (1998). The Court was
well aware of the view that the NLRB, unlike other agencies, "hides the ball" from the
courts through "obfuscatory techniques" such as significant gaps between articulated standards in adjudication and their application; these claims were developed in Joan Flynn,
*The Costs and Benefits of "Hiding the Ball": NLRB Policymaking and the Failure of Judicial
Review*, 75 BU L Rev 387 (1995), which the Court block-quoted from in its opinion, 522
US at 372–73. The courts also recognize that the NLRB is unique in eschewing rulemaking
and developing all its policies instead through adjudication; that, too, might account for
more aggressive judicial review of the NLRB's findings of fact.

[60] Jennifer Nou, *Sub-Regulating Elections*, 2013 Supreme Court Review (in this volume).

such as those involved in financial regulation, are not.[61] And so on.

How much does, and should, legal doctrine ask and reflect more realist questions (and which ones) about particular agencies in reviewing a specific administrative action? Consider the history of the *Chevron* doctrine. *Chevron*[62] started in exceptionally complex regulatory terrain in the environmental field—an area where Justice Stevens, *Chevron*'s author, admitted he was so confused, he believed he simply ought to defer to the EPA.[63] Yet *Chevron* "gradually displaced formulations about deference developed in other fields [of regulation]," including those, such as labor and tax law, that had preexisting deference doctrines.[64] That is, *Chevron*, as the most important doctrine in modern administrative law, developed into an institutionally formalist rule independent of the particular agency or the nature of any specialized expertise involved.[65] As

---

[61] By the terms of Executive Order 12,866, OIRA review remains limited to the actions of executive agencies (this is unchanged from Executive Order 12,291). See Bruce Kraus and Connor Raso, *Rational Boundaries for SEC Cost-Benefit Analysis*, 30 Yale J Reg 289, 295 (2013); Note, *OIRA Avoidance*, 124 Harv L Rev 994, 998 (2011). In the recent *Business Roundtable v SEC* case, 647 F3d 1144 (DC Cir 2011), the DC Circuit held that SEC's Rule 14a-11, which would have required public companies to provide shareholders with information about shareholder-nominated candidates for their boards of directors, was "arbitrary and capricious" and violated the Administrative Procedure Act (APA). Though decided on procedural grounds, *Business Roundtable* might well be viewed as a decision to apply particularly aggressive "hard look" review precisely because the SEC's rules do not have to go through the OIRA cost-benefit analysis—the court, for example, noted that the SEC failed to conduct a proper cost-benefit analysis of the rule. Kraus and Raso, 30 Yale J Reg at 298, 316.

[62] *Chevron U.S.A., Inc. v Natural Resources Defense Council, Inc.*, 467 US 837 (1984).

[63] Thomas W. Merrill, *The Story of Chevron: The Making of an Accidental Landmark*, in Peter L. Strauss, ed, *Administrative Law Stories* 398, 417 (Foundation, 2006).

[64] Thomas Merrill and Kristin E. Hickman, *Chevron's Domain*, 89 Georgetown L J 833, 838–39 (2001).

[65] Judicial refinements on *Chevron* do suggest differentiations of certain sorts between different forms of agency action. The most significant, of course, is established in *United States v Mead Corp.*, 533 US 218 (2001), in which the Court indicated that *Chevron* deference should apply only to agency interpretations that have "the force of law," though a great deal of confusion reigns about precisely what that does or should mean. To the extent these refinements make deference turn on questions such as how much procedural formality lies behind an agency action (in addition to whether Congress delegated to the agency the authority to act with the force of law when interpreting a statute), these refinements introduce a certain kind of process-based realism: formality serves as a proxy for the seriousness of agency deliberation. This process-based realism remains agnostic about differences between agencies. Similarly, some suggested improvements upon *Mead* also can be seen as efforts to find better process-based proxies for the seriousness of the agency's deliberation or its real-world political accountability for the decision; that is one way to understand the proposal that *Chevron* deference should turn on the "who" of administrative decision making rather than the "how." See David J. Barron and Elena Kagan, *Chevron's Nondelegation Doctrine*, 2001 Supreme Court Review 201, 203–05 (ar-

Professor Tom Merrill notes (speaking from experience), the Department of Justice played a major role in bringing all agencies formally under the protective wings of *Chevron* because doing so (1) simplified defense of agency action and (2) promoted the government's interests through a doctrine perceived to be pro-government.[66] Some scholars argue that *Chevron* should become an even more universal deference doctrine than it formally is already.[67]

Yet here, too, institutional realism pushes back. Indeed, some of the administrative-law experts on the Court itself have divided over just this formalist/realist tension. Justice Breyer, for three other Justices as well, has argued that, to the extent *Chevron* rests on a theory of political accountability, judicial review of the actions of independent agencies—which lack accountability to the President—should be more assertive than that for executive agencies. As he put it in *FCC v Fox Television Stations, Inc.*,[68] "comparative freedom from ballot-box control makes it all the more important that courts review [an independent agency's] decisionmaking to assure compliance with applicable provisions of the law—including law requiring that major policy decisions be based upon articulable reasons."[69] Rejecting this approach, Justice Scalia, writing for four Justices, insisted on adherence to the formalism of the APA, which

guing that *Chevron* deference should apply when the official to whom Congress has delegated statutory responsibility takes personal responsibility for the decision). This suggested adjustment to *Chevron/Mead* again abstracts from institution-specific features of different agencies. Thomas W. Merrill and Kathryn Tongue Watts, *Agency Rules with the Force of Law: The Original Convention*, 116 Harv L Rev 467 (2002); Lisa Schultz Bressman, *How Mead Has Muddled Judicial Review of Agency Action*, 58 Vand L Rev 1443 (2005); Thomas W. Merrill, *The Mead Doctrine: Rules and Standards, Meta-Rules and Meta-Standards*, 54 Admin L Rev 807 (2002).

[66] Merrill, *The Story of Chevron* (cited in note 63).

[67] See William N. Eskridge, Jr., *Expanding Chevron's Domain: A Comparative Institutional Analysis of the Relative Competence of Courts and Agencies to Interpret Statutes*, 2013 Wis L Rev 411, 445. Applying Komesar's "comparative institutional analysis" (see above note 5), Professor Eskridge advocates an even more general (and hence more formal) application of *Chevron*; in his view *Chevron* should be expanded to all statutes, other than criminal ones. As he puts it, "federal courts should defer to all rules adopted by an agency in a public document representing the agency's considered judgment, unless the agency's rule is clearly contrary to the statute or to settled understandings about the statute." Id at 445. As a rule of great generality, this rule willfully blinds itself to any distinct characteristics of any particular agency. Notice that this rule is an institutionally formalist rule of broad generality that emerges from the kind of comparative institutional analysis Eskridge employs; it is based on a realist's view on the general comparative competence of courts and agencies, but without any agency-specific refinement.

[68] 556 US 502 (2009).

[69] Id at 547 (2009) (Breyer, J, dissenting).

makes no distinction between types of agencies, and to the institutional formalism of the Court's administrative-law precedents, which similarly do not distinguish between types of agencies.[70]

In the same vein as Justice Breyer, another administrative law expert on the Court, then Professor Elena Kagan, more than a decade ago, had pursued a similar critique of *Chevron*'s institutional formality. As she noted, administrative law currently tends to ignore whether the President had played any role in shaping the agency's action. Observing that the figure of the President rarely appeared at all in opinions on deference to agency action, Kagan confirmed *Chevron*'s institutional formality by showing that "[c]ourts grant (or decline to grant) step-two deference to administrative interpretations of law irrespective whether the President potentially could, or actually did, direct or otherwise participate in their promulgation."[71]

Cast in the terms of my analysis here, Kagan's article on "Presidential Administration" then sought to change judicial practice by providing a brief for institutional realism in administrative law. Anticipating Justice Breyer in *Fox Television*, she argued that courts should give greater *Chevron* deference to decisions from executive agencies than from independent agencies (presidential accountability and judicial review are substitutes, in this view). At this first stage, this is an argument for categorical realism; it ties judicial review to the formal properties of an agency.[72] But at a second stage, Kagan pursued institutional realism more relentlessly, beyond this categorical level; she also argued for a more penetrating,

---

[70] Id at 523 (plurality). In addition, Justice Scalia observed that, institutional formalism aside, independent agencies were indeed politically accountable, not to the President, but to "Congress"—which presumably means to the committees that oversee a particular agency. When the issue is engaged in these terms, the debate becomes a normative one regarding the modes of "political accountability"—presidential or congressional committee—that *Chevron* should be understood to value insofar as the doctrine rests on a "political accountability" justification.

[71] Elena Kagan, *Presidential Administration*, 114 Harv L Rev 2245, 2375 (2001).

[72] Kagan herself acknowledges that the actual independence of agencies is affected by less "hard" factors other than formal removal control, such as "longstanding (even if psychological) norms of independence. . . ." Id at 2376. And Professor Lisa Schultz Bressman challenged Kagan on realist turf, arguing that independent agencies are in reality subject to "practical control" by both the President and Congress through administrative procedures—both congressionally enacted legal requirements, such as the APA, and legislative oversight. Bressman also pointed out that independent agencies often work together with executive agencies to shape and implement policy, thus further dissolving the formal categorical distinction between these agencies. See Lisa Schultz Bressman, *Procedures as Politics in Administrative Law*, 107 Colum L Rev 1749, 1807–08 (2007).

case-by-case realism that would tie judicial review to the level and nature of actual presidential involvement. If *Chevron* rests on the accountability of agencies to the President, then the doctrine should only apply, she argued, when concrete evidence exists that presidential involvement in an agency's decision rose "to a certain level of substantiality"—as revealed by objective evidence in the decision-making process (executive orders, directives, and the like).[73] In arguing for an analogously realist application of the hard-look doctrine of *State Farm*, Kagan made similar points, descriptively and normatively.[74] Observing that courts currently treated all agency action the same under hard-look review, irrespective of the action's "provenance or pedigree," she argued instead that courts should relax this review when credible evidence shows that the President "has taken an active role in, and by so doing has accepted responsibility for, the administrative decision in question."[75]

Professor Anne Joseph O'Connell presses for a similar turn toward institutional realism in administrative law, but in an even more aggressive style. After perhaps the most extensive empirical study in the legal literature on agency rulemaking, she suggests that a penetrating institutional realism should inform when, and how much, courts should defer to agencies.[76] Instead of relying on the kinds of considerations that *Chevron/Mead* invoke, such as the degree and kind of procedural formality that underlies the agency's action, judicial deference should hinge more on factors like "the type of agency, the agency's track record, the agency's expertise, the level of presidential and congressional control over the agency, and the timing of the agency's action."[77] Moreover, she notes that some of these factors might shift depending on changes in control of Congress and the White House.[78] Seen in light of the more pervasive foundational choices that affect all issues concerning judicial review of public action, both Professors

---

[73] Kagan, 114 Harv L Rev at 2377 (cited in note 71).

[74] Id at 2380; *Motor Vehicle Mfrs Ass'n of the United States, Inc. v State Farm Mutual Automobile Ins. Co.*, 463 US 29 (1983).

[75] Kagan, 114 Harv L Rev at 2380 (cited in note 71).

[76] Anne Joseph O'Connell, *Political Cycles of Rulemaking: An Empirical Portrait of the Modern Administrative State*, 94 Va L Rev 889, 980–81 (2008).

[77] Id at 980.

[78] Id.

Kagan and O'Connell should be recognized to be arguing for bold forms of institutional realism, in more moderate and stronger versions, respectively, as against the institutional formalism they see underlying current administrative law doctrine.

If judicial doctrine rarely invokes this kind of institutional realism, how much does realism of this sort nonetheless inform the pattern of judicial decision making? Getting an empirical handle on that question is, of course, difficult. In a majority of cases, the Court apparently does not even cite the formal deference regime being applied; in a majority of cases, the Court "gave no evidence of deference at all."[79] Studies have shown that courts tend to rely most strongly on precedents involving the particular agency being reviewed, even when the courts are applying general administrative law doctrines, perhaps because counsel tend to present cases in this agency-specific way; thus, "both the articulation and application of the doctrine often beg[i]n over time to develop their own unique characteristics within the precedents concerning the specific agency."[80] This role and effect of agency-specific law might directly or indirectly reflect forms of institutional realism.

With respect to specific agencies, scholars have identified unique patterns of judicial review. Thus, in the antitrust area, Professor Eskridge asserts that the Supreme Court has "almost slavishly" followed the Department of Justice's (DOJ) preferred legal constructions.[81] Whether that is a reflection of the complexity of the economic expertise relevant to these issues, or the Court's special trust in the DOJ as an institution on these issues, cannot be dis-

---

[79] William N. Eskridge, Jr., and Lauren E. Baer, *The Continuum of Deference: Supreme Court Treatment of Agency Statutory Interpretations from Chevron to Hamdan*, 96 Georgetown L J 1083, 1117–20 (2008). The denominator was composed of all cases "between 1984 and 2006 in which an agency interpretation of a statute was at issue and in which the Supreme Court produced a published opinion." Id at 1090 n 33.

[80] Richard E. Levy and Robert L. Glicksman, *Agency-Specific Precedents*, 89 Tex L Rev 499, 500 (2011). The authors examine cases relating to the IRS, FCC, EPA, SSA, and NLRB. See also Kristin E. Hickman, *Agency-Specific Precedents: Rational Ignorance or Deliberate Strategy?*, 89 Tex L Rev (2011). See also 89, 90 (2011) (assessing reasons lawyers engage in agency-specific argument).

[81] William N. Eskridge, Jr., *Expanding Chevron's Domain: A Comparative Institutional Analysis of the Relative Competence of Courts and Agencies to Interpret Statutes*, 2013 Wis L Rev 411, 427. In support, Eskridge cites his own study of antitrust enforcement in William N. Eskridge, Jr., and John Ferejohn, *A Republic of Statutes: The New American Constitution* 120–64 (Yale, 2010), and Douglas Ginsburg and Leah Brannon, *Antitrust Decisions of the U.S. Supreme Court, 1967 to 2007*, Competition Pol Intl, 3, 17–20 (Autumn 2007) (empirical analysis showing the central role of the Department of Justice in setting antitrust policy and persuading the judiciary, 1967–2006).

entangled. Similarly, the unique and well-known tendency of NLRB adjudications to "oscillate between extremes," as the membership of the board changes, has led scholars such as Professors Fisk and Malamud to argue that, as a normative matter, administrative law doctrine should "carve out a category of adjudications [i.e., board adjudications] that will not be entitled to *Chevron* deference."[82] In practice, courts might perhaps be doing so already; some scholars have suggested that despite *Chevron* courts actually review NLRB decisions close to de novo.[83]

More broadly, a recent study of all cases from *Chevron* up until 2006 concluded that the Court afforded agencies considerably greater deference in areas involving "environmental science, energy regulation, intellectual property, pension regulation, and bankruptcy."[84] This differential implementation of *Chevron* suggests the Court is embracing a more grounded, realist's stance on the deference issue; whether that stance is based on the Court's comparative assessment of judicial versus agency expertise, or specific features of the agency applying judgment in these areas—or some mix of the two—is impossible to say. Similarly, there remain contexts in which judicial doctrine directly makes the agency's "expertise" an express factor in judicial review, as when *Skidmore*[85] still applies; in those contexts, courts necessarily are making particularized judgments about the specific agency and issue. Here, too, separating the dancer from the dance—the nature of the agency involved versus some more free-floating concept of expertise regarding the issue—remains elusive.

If there is a great deal of uncertainty about both what courts actually do, and what they ought to do, in the administrative review context, it is in part, I suggest, due to the pervasive tension between

---

[82] Catherine L. Fisk and Deborah C. Malamud, *The NLRB in Administrative Law Exile: Problems with Its Structure and Function and Suggestions for Reform*, 58 Duke L J 2013, 2083 (2009). See also Michael C. Harper, *Judicial Control of the National Labor Relations Board's Lawmaking in the Age of Chevron and Brand X*, 89 BU L Rev 189, 248 (2009).

[83] Jeffrey M. Hirsch, *Defending the NLRB: Improving the Agency's Success in the Federal Courts of Appeals*, 5 FIU L Rev 437, 451 (2010).

[84] Eskridge and Baer, 96 Georgetown L J at 1083, 1173–74 (cited in note 79). A much earlier study had concluded that courts were harsher in reviewing INS interpretations of the immigration laws than other agency interpretations—hardly a surprise and surely a reflection of judicial knowledge of the dysfunctionality of that particular agency. Peter H. Schuck and E. Donald Elliott, *To the Chevron Station: An Empirical Study of Federal Administrative Law*, 1990 Duke L J 984, 1043.

[85] *Skidmore v Swift & Co.*, 323 US 134 (1944).

institutional formalism and realism.[86] Doctrine typically instructs courts to be blind to the particular qualities that differentiate agencies; yet in some contexts, doctrine makes judgments concerning agency expertise directly relevant. Empirical studies confirm what common sense suggests: courts engage in institutional realism at least some of the time. Not all agencies are treated the same. Some move down that path might be unavoidable; surely courts that know these agencies well cannot blind themselves to the differences between the NLRB and the SEC—nor, I would venture to say, would we want them to. And yet, once the Pandora's box of institutional realism is open, questions leap about concerning precisely how far into the black box of "the administrative agency" that realism should penetrate.

D. CONGRESS

In the constitutional sphere, the formalist/realist institutional divide is most immediately recognized, perhaps, in the "political safeguards of federalism" debate.[87] Moreover, the question of how well the national political process actually protects state interests and how to tailor constitutional doctrine accordingly—including whether doctrine should dynamically adapt to (perceived) changes in this political process—has been shaped not just by academic work, but doctrine as well. In the important, precedent-overturning *Garcia v San Antonio Metropolitan Transit Authority*[88] decision, for example, Justice Powell, for four dissenters, argued that "'a variety of structural and political changes occurring in this century have combined to make Congress particularly insensitive to state and local values'"—thus justifying a more assertive judicial role.[89] Rejecting this role, the majority offered a competing realist account to assert that state actors remained practically effective at

---

[86] For the general view that during the Roberts Court the *Chevron* doctrine and related administrative law ones have failed to be applied in any consistent way, and that where Justices differ, the differences reflect ideological preferences about the substantive policies at issue, see Jack Michael Beermann, *Chevron at the Roberts Court: Still Failing After All These Years*, at http://papers.ssrn.com/sol3/papers.cfm?abstract_id=2382984.

[87] Herbert Wechsler, *The Political Safeguards of Federalism: The Role of the States in the Composition and Selection of the National Government*, 54 Colum L Rev 543 (1954). Given the vast modern literature on this issue, I risk offending many if I cite anything other than Wechsler's original article.

[88] 469 US 528 (1985).

[89] Id at 565 n 9 (Powell, J, dissenting) (quoting Advisory Committee on Intergovernmental Relations, *Regulatory Federalism: Policy, Process, Impact and Reform* 50 (1984)).

protecting state interests.[90] More recent federalism cases reprise these realist debates.[91] These outcroppings of institutional analyses otherwise latent are reminders that, even if institutional assessments of this sort are not empirically resolvable, judicial perceptions of political processes are often at work. As the earlier discussion of the separation of powers suggests, judgments about whether, and how, to assess the functioning of national political institutions pervades constitutional law.

Outside the constitutional domain, implicit conceptions of Congress, and the formalist/realist tension, motivate views of appropriate doctrine as well. Many (most?) issues in statutory interpretation reflect this fact. In offering this conceptual framework as a general way to organize specific issues in this area, a few examples should suffice. With respect to the general task of interpretation, should courts interpret ambiguous statutory language to take into account the realistic likelihood that Congress will respond if the Court's interpretation is "wrong"? An institutionally formalist approach suggests not; the courts should provide their "best" interpretation of the statute without predicting the likely congressional capacity to respond. This formalism, which might best fit conventional rule-of-law ideas, treats Congress as an abstraction. In this posture, courts either engage in a formal presumption that Congress will correct erroneous judicial interpretations or treat legal doctrine as indifferent to whether Congress is likely to respond. As with other institutionally formalist approaches, this conception of the judicial role would apply across statutes, without differences tied to the nature of the law being construed.[92]

---

[90] Id at 552–53, 555.

[91] See, for example, *United States v Morrison*, 529 US 598, 616 n 7 (2000); id at 647–52 (Souter, J, dissenting). Interestingly, in defending the role of the congressional political process in adequately respecting state interests, Justice Souter's dissent expressly acknowledges that the Seventeenth Amendment might have reduced the Senate's "enthusiasm" for doing so, but then proclaims this change irrelevant for constitutional purposes. Id at 652.

[92] In his comparative institutionalist approach to legal interpretation (both statutory and constitutional), Adrian Vermeule endorses doctrines of statutory interpretation typically associated with more formalist visions of both Congress and the courts (textualism, strong *stare decisis* effect for statutory precedents, no use of legislative history), but he does so based on a realist, rule-consequentialist comparative assessment of how courts, agencies, and Congress are perceived to function. Adrian Vermeule, *Judging Under Uncertainty: An Institutional Theory of Legal Interpretation* (Harvard, 2006). In arguing that legal interpretation should not be conceived as an attempt to resolve meaning in a vacuum, but instead as a method to determine which potential institutional interpreters are best positioned to interpret the text, and for what reasons, Professor Vermeule argues for a comparative

In contrast, the Court at times adopts an institutionally realist stance toward interpretation based on political-economy judgments of likely congressional response. One clear example is the Court's justification of the rule of lenity in criminal cases as reflecting, among other considerations, the judgment that, if the Court's decision is "wrong," the government will be far more able to overcome the burden of legislative inertia than actual or potential criminal defendants.[93] An extensively worked out generalization of this kind of institutional realism is Professor Einer Elhauge's position that courts should employ "preference-eliciting canons" to resolve cases of statutory ambiguity.[94] Canons of this sort are designed to favor interpretations most likely to trigger a response from Congress, if the Court's resolution of the ambiguity is wrong (by the lights of the current Congress).[95] Moreover, in cases of ambiguity this approach should, he argues, systematically rule against those groups or interests most likely to have "a significant advantage in commanding the legislative agenda compared to those favored by an alternative interpretation. . . ."[96] Public-choice theory completes the analytic process: well-organized groups with intense interests that experience concentrated effects from the Court's interpretation are more likely to mobilize to pressure Congress than large, more diffuse interests that have lost the interpretive battle. Whether Congress overturns the Court's interpretation or not, this pressure is designed to come closest to ensuring that ultimately, the statute will best track current political preferences.[97]

institutional analysis that is "evenhandedly empirical." Id at 18. He contrasts that commitment to institutional analysis that is more of the Weberian ideal type, or what he calls "stylized institutionalism" (which, as he rightly notes, characterizes the Hart and Sacks Legal Process School) and "asymmetrical institutionalism," which takes a highly realistic eye toward some institutions but a more idealized stance toward others.

[93] See *United States v Santos*, 553 US 507, 514 (2008) (Scalia, J) (plurality) ("This venerable rule [of lenity] not only vindicates the fundamental principle that no citizen should be held accountable for a violation of a statute whose commands are uncertain, or subjected to punishment that is not clearly prescribed. *It also places the weight of inertia upon the party that can best induce Congress to speak more clearly* and keeps courts from making criminal law in Congress's stead.") (emphasis added).

[94] Einer Elhauge, *Statutory Default Rules* 151–88 (Harvard, 2008).

[95] Elhauge also emphasizes the ex ante effects of such canons, but I focus here only on their ex post effects.

[96] Id at 182.

[97] For a related argument that the Court should employ similar default rules, motivated by similar "institutionally realist" considerations, in the constitutional domain, see John Ferejohn and Barry Friedman, *Toward a Political Theory of Constitutional Default Rules*, 33 Fla St U L Rev 825 (2006).

Accepting for the moment that this is the proper goal of interpretation in ambiguous cases, is it disturbing or beyond judicial capacity for courts to engage in this kind of political-economy realism about how Congress functions?[98] Descriptively, studies do suggest, not surprisingly, that Congress does override at a higher rate statutory decisions that disadvantage organized business groups or the United States government than those that disadvantage other entities or persons.[99] Moreover, special interpretive rules in antitrust law do include strong presumptions against reading unclear statutes to create exemptions to the law, just as courts maintain that tax statutes should not be read to provide exemptions when text is ambiguous. Various justifications for these doctrines have been offered; Elhauge argues, however, that the best explanation is that, when courts face interpretive ambiguity, they put the burden of overcoming legislative inertia on the politically more powerful because those actors have greater capacity to mobilize Congress's attention to the courts' decisions. In this view, the same institutionally-realist, preference-eliciting approach to interpretation best explains other canons, such as the canon favoring Indian tribes, or the constitutional avoidance canon.[100] And in their detailed empirical survey of how "Congress" actually drafts statutes, Professors Gluck and Bressman conclude that Court decisions already reflect, but in "under-the-radar" ways, the kinds of intricate, institutionally realist insights into the legislative process their work has revealed.[101] Formalist doctrinal principles aside, we cannot

---

[98] For an early reflection on these issues, see William N. Eskridge, Jr., and John Ferejohn, *The Relationship Between Theories of Legislatures and Theories of Statutory Interpretation*, in *the Rule of Law* (Nomos, 1993).

[99] See Michael E. Solimine and James L. Walker, *The Next Word: Congressional Response to Supreme Court Statutory Decisions*, 65 Temple L Rev 425, 446 (1992); William N. Eskridge, Jr., *Overriding Supreme Court Statutory Interpretation Decisions*, 101 Yale L J 331, 348 (1991).

[100] Elhauge, *Statutory Default Rules* at 187 (cited in note 94).

[101] See Abbe R. Gluck and Lisa Schultz Bressman, *Statutory Interpretation from the Inside—An Empirical Study of Congressional Drafting, Delegation, and the Canons: Part II*, 66 Stan L Rev *68 (forthcoming 2014), available online at http://papers.ssrn.com/sol3/papers.cfm?abstract_id=2358074. They suggest that courts should give much greater weight to institutionally realist factors such as committee jurisdictional issues, the way the Congressional Budget Office scores proposed legislation, and the type of statute at issue (whether the court is construing omnibus, appropriations, or single-subject legislation). As they note, they intentionally advocate these factors because they are most "amenable to clear legal rules." Id at 70. In the terms used here, these are "categorical" forms of institutional realism, which is why they are most easy to envision being incorporated into legal doctrine.

dismiss the possibility that courts already undertake interpretation in ways that actually vacillate between an institutionally formalist and realist approach to "Congress."

Demands that the Court embrace institutional realism also course through some critical responses to the *Shelby County* decision itself. Under the Court's decision, Congress retains the power to reenact a preclearance regime tailored more directly than in the 2006 reauthorization Act to areas of the country in which distinct patterns of voting-rights violations have been occurring in recent years. Indeed, that is the significance of the Court not striking down the preclearance regime itself, Section 5, but rather the current coverage formula for that regime contained in Section 4 of the Act. But critics castigate the Court with the reality of today's polarized parties and gridlocked Congress[102] (whether Congress will in fact act in some form, such as on the bill introduced already,[103] the future will tell). To the extent this stark, realist vision of Congress implies that the Court should have given more constitutional latitude to the 2006 reauthorization, *because* a polarized and gridlocked Congress is unlikely to revise the Act, we should recognize this as an argument that constitutional interpretation should reflect a temporally contingent view of how Congress functions (or fails to function) in this era.

At a more specific level, many doctrines or canons (and debates about them) concerning statutory interpretation revolve around whether courts should adopt formalist or realist stances toward Congress. The debate over legislative history has this cast; institutional formalists treat documents such as committee reports as relevant authority regarding congressional intent or purposes, while realists dismiss these documents by asking who actually writes and reads them. Or consider the modern doctrine that *stare decisis* should have exceptionally strong force when Congress reenacts a statute without overturning the Court's prior interpretation[104]—or the closely related acquiescence doctrine, invoked more

---

[102] Kareem U. Crayton and Terry Smith, *Unteachable: Shelby County, Canonical Apostasies, and Ways Forward for the Voting Rights Act*, available at http://papers.ssrn.com/sol3/papers.cfm? abstract_id=2361495.

[103] See the Voting Rights Amendments Act of 2014, HR 3899, 113th Cong, 2d Sess (Jan 16, 2014) and S 1945, 113th Cong, 2d Sess (Jan 16, 2014).

[104] See, e.g., *John R. Sand & Gravel Co. v United States*, 552 US 130, 139 (2008). The doctrine is a relatively modern innovation in the sense that it apparently did not exist before the late nineteenth century and did not take hold until the 1930s. See Thomas

erratically, that even congressional failure to act in response to a prior judicial or administrative interpretation should be taken to mean that "the interpretation of the Act . . . has legislative approval."[105] How much are these doctrines meant to be institutionally realist ones? Should it matter whether any evidence exists that Congress actually considered the prior judicial interpretation, either when Congress reenacts the statute or when Congress fails to act at all (but might debate the judicial interpretation)?[106] Or should these doctrines be understood as institutionally formalist ones, in which courts need not, and should not, take note of anything other than what "Congress" formally did or failed to do?[107] Similarly, should application of doctrines of these sorts vary with changes in the background context more generally in which "Congress" actually functions. As noted earlier, in our era of hyperpolarized political parties and divided government (though the modern filibuster practice requiring sixty votes for much legislation effectively ensures that even a minority party will have blocking power in the Senate) should courts relax any of these or similar interpretive doctrines based on how much more difficult this larger context makes it for Congress to act in general? Or should legal doctrine be blind to these institutional realities?[108]

Preemption issues, too, might well revolve around the formalist/realist institutional tension. Professor Tom Merrill, for example, has suggested that the doctrinal quagmire that is preemption doctrine be sorted out by shifting the inquiry from "the meaning" of federal and state laws to a comparative institutional analysis: which institutions (Congress, courts, or, when relevant, agencies) are best

---

Lee, *Stare Decisis in Historical Perspective: From the Founding Era to the Rehnquist Court*, 52 Vand L Rev 647 (1999).

[105] *United States v Elgin, Joliet & Eastern Ry. Co.*, 298 US 492, 500 (1936). For a modern version of "implicit congressional ratification" of agency interpretation in a significant context, see *Food and Drug Administration v Brown & Williamson Tobacco Corp.*, 529 US 120 (2000).

[106] For consideration of these issues, see James Brudney, *Congressional Commentary on Judicial Interpretations of Statutes: Idle Chatter or Telling Response*, 93 Mich L Rev 1 (1994); William N. Eskridge, Jr., *Interpreting Legislative Inaction*, 87 Mich L Rev 67 (1988); William N. Eskridge, Jr., *Overruling Statutory Precedents*, 76 Georgetown L J 1361 (1988).

[107] David Shapiro defends doctrines like these based on independent, normative legal grounds reflecting the value of continuity. David L. Shapiro, *Continuity and Change in Statutory Interpretation*, 67 NYU L Rev 921 (1992).

[108] For a thoughtful reflection on these issues concerning statutory interpretation, see John F. Manning and Matthew C. Stephenson, *Legislation and Regulation* 175 (Foundation, 2d ed 2013).

designed to apply the range of values that ought to underlie the preemption decision.[109] Having made this institutional turn, he analyzes the properties of the various institutions at a general level; the result, in doctrinal terms, is thus a broad general "rule of law" that allocates decisional responsibility.[110] But Merrill also notes that institutional analysis of this sort "rests ultimately on empirical judgments about the capabilities of different legal institutions."[111] At that point, the level of generality at which those "empirical judgments" ought to be made is inescapable. How rigorously should legal doctrine continuously reflect on these empirical judgments about institutional performance; how much should doctrine, in areas like preemption, adjust the law's allocation of decisional authority accordingly?

Statutory interpretation, like all legal interpretation, is inevitably a matter of implicit political theory as well as legal or linguistic theory. A judge's conception of role responsibility reflects a conception of the proper relationship between courts and legislatures; that conception, in turn, is influenced by judicial views of how much courts are to take into account how legislatures actually function.

E. STATE LEGISLATURES

A final, small window into constitutional law concerning state legislative action (or inaction) reveals that here, too, the formalist/realist tension, and if realism, how much, is inescapably foundational.

The most obvious example is the Court's reapportionment revolution. For decades, the Court adopted an essentially formalist legal stance toward state legislatures—and Congress—in refusing to find malapportionment claims justiciable.[112] Under the Elections Clause,[113] districting was a task constitutionally assigned to the state legislatures, or to Congress should it choose to displace

---

[109] Thomas W. Merrill, *Preemption and Institutional Choice*, 102 Nw U L Rev 727 (2008).

[110] Id at 779 ("Absent resolution of the question by Congress, courts are the best (that is, the least worst) institution to decide whether to displace state law in order to further federal policy objectives, but courts should draw on the expertise of agencies in helping to understand the pragmatic variables that bear on the preemption decision.").

[111] Id.

[112] See, for example, *Colegrove v Green*, 328 US 549 (1946).

[113] US Const, Art I, § 4.

state authority; for the Court, that was the end of the matter, without probing more deeply into how these institutions actually functioned on this issue. If dissatisfaction with that performance existed, change depended "on the vigilance of the people in exercising their political rights," in Justice Frankfurter's memorable phrase.[114] But by the 1960s, the Court had clearly reached the breaking point of its formalist forbearance. Faced with additional decades of legislative inaction, the Court could no longer blind itself to the institutionally realist view that sitting legislators elected under the existing system of massive malapportionment, in the states and Congress, had every incentive to resist change to the system under which they had gained and maintained power. Having all possible political-process avenues to updated apportionment, the Court concluded that "from a practical standpoint"—that is, an institutionally realist perspective—these formal paths were "without substance."[115] Once institutional realism became legally relevant, constitutional doctrine was justifiably adjusted (indeed, revolutionized).

Reapportionment law is the most dramatic example, but legislative regulation of the democratic process always challenges courts about whether they should adopt a formalist or realist foundation for judicial review. Regulation of the process is of course necessary and unavoidable; yet "the state legislature" is not some detached, abstract entity, but a political body composed of incumbents and dominant partisan forces with powerful incentives to act (or fail to act) for narrowly self-interested reasons. How much do courts intentionally blind themselves to these dynamics and take an institutionally formalist stance toward "the state"; alternatively, how much is constitutional doctrine shaped by the courts' willingness to embrace institutional realism?

Given the profundity and intractability of the issues, perhaps it is no surprise that courts are all over the map on this implicit, foundational question. At times, the Supreme Court has been expressly realist. In *Tashjian v Republican Party of Connecticut*,[116] for example, the Republican Party, as the out-of-power party in the state, wanted to broaden its appeal by permitting independents to

---

[114] *Colegrove*, 328 US at 556.

[115] *Baker v Carr*, 369 US 186, 259 (1962) (Clark, J, concurring).

[116] 497 US 208 (1986).

vote in the party's primary. But state law prohibited this. Efforts to change the law produced straight party-line votes in the legislature, then a veto from the Democratic Governor. In holding that state law mandating a closed primary violated the Republican Party's First Amendment right of association, the Court dismissed "the state's" justification for the law with a realist sensibility about the partisan dynamics involved. As the Court wrote: "the views of the State, which to some extent *represent the views of the one political party transiently enjoying majority power* . . . lose much of their force."[117]

A similar willingness to embrace institutional realism sat at the core of the Supreme Court's decision in *Georgia v Ashcroft*,[118] in which the Court accepted some modification of the racial-redistricting regime that the Voting Rights Act (VRA) amendments of 1982 had brought into being. In the 2001 round of redistricting, Democrats still controlled the redistricting process, knew the tides were turning fast against them, and were willing to try whatever they could in the districting process to preserve as much of their fleeting power as possible. Their strategy was to drop the African-American population of some districts modestly, for the purpose of dispersing these voters more widely to foster the electoral prospects of Democrats in the aggregate. Applying conventional VRA doctrine, the DOJ and lower three-judge federal court held that this action violated Section 5. But the Court reversed, held that

---

[117] Id at 244. A similar view is expressed in Justice O'Connor's concurring opinion in *Clingman v Beaver*, 544 US 581, 603 (2005) (O'Connor, J, concurring in part and in judgment):

> Although the State has a legitimate—and indeed critical—role to play in regulating elections, it must be recognized that it is not a wholly independent or neutral arbiter. Rather, the state is itself controlled by the political party or parties in power, which presumably have an incentive to shape the rules of the electoral game to their own benefit. Recognition of that basic reality need not render suspect most electoral regulations. Where the state imposes only reasonable and genuinely neutral restrictions on associational rights, there is no threat to the integrity of the electoral process and no apparent reason for judicial intervention. As such restrictions become more severe, however, and particularly where they have discriminatory effects, there is increasing cause for concern that those in power may be using electoral rules to erect barriers to electoral competition. In such cases, applying heightened scrutiny helps to ensure that such limitations are truly justified and that the state's asserted interests are not merely a pretext for exclusionary or anticompetitive restrictions.

[118] 539 US 461 (2003). For a full account of the decision and its context, see Richard H. Pildes, *Foreword—The Constitutionalization of Democratic Politics*, 118 Harv L Rev 28, 83–101 (2004); for a contrary view on the case, see Pamela S. Karlan, *Georgia v Ashcroft and the Retrogression of Retrogression*, 3 Election L J 21 (2004).

Section 5 should now be read to permit more flexibility in the racial-redistricting regime, and strongly suggested the Georgia plan was legal.[119]

Of central importance for present purposes is that, to justify this conclusion, the Court relied critically on the following kind of "institutionally realist" facts: by this point in time, African Americans had a significant presence in the Georgia legislature; this plan was a Democratic one that had been rammed down the throat of the Republican Party with the joint support of black and white Democratic legislators; that black Democrats had enough power in the legislature to have blocked the plan had they so wanted; and that African American legislators had occupied key positions in the districting process (the Court noted, as one example, that the chair of a key subcommittee was black). The Court did not defer to "the Georgia legislature" in an abstract or formal fashion; instead, these facts served as realist proxies for the judgment that *this* particular political process could be trusted to have made good-faith judgments about the system of districting that would most protect the overall interests of Georgia's minority communities—and hence be consistent with the VRA. Moreover, when the VRA racial-redistricting regime began, almost no African Americans held elective office; by the time that had changed, the Court suggested, legal doctrine ought to adjust accordingly. In other words, the "Georgia legislature" of the 2000s was not the "Georgia legislature" of the 1980s—let alone of the 1960s.

In legal process terms, the underlying substantive issue of how to design districts to best protect minority voters is a difficult one; instead of trying to give a first-order substantive answer, the Court deferred to another institution, the state legislature, as the better forum for resolution. But only because the Court probed the political process deeply enough to convince itself that the "state" indeed warranted this deference. Of course, this institutional realism raises predictable rule-of-law questions (in what other contexts, through what other political processes, is similar flexibility in racial redistricting permissible?).[120] And yet, the Court cannot

---

[119] Technically, the Court remanded for application to the facts of the standards it announced. *Georgia v Ashcroft*, 539 US at 491.

[120] Concerns of this sort played a role in Congress's action to overturn the Court's decision in the 2006 reauthorization amendments. See Nathaniel Persily, *The Promise and Pitfalls of the New Voting Rights Act*, 117 Yale L J 174 (2007). *Shelby County* alludes to this feature of the 2006 amendments but, in light of holding Section 4 unconstitutional, the

avoid institutional realism altogether, with respect to state legislatures and other public institutions.

Current controversies over voter-identification laws are also illuminated through similar formalist/realist tensions. Should constitutional doctrine take into account that these laws almost always pass on straight party-line votes? In the first challenge, to an Indiana law, Judge Evans, dissenting in the Seventh Circuit, certainly thought so; his opinion began by proclaiming that the law had an obvious partisan motivation and was unconstitutional (leaving a strong sense of connection between premise and conclusion).[121] Cutting against this approach, the Court in *Crawford v Marion County Election Board* eschewed realism of this kind or that it had employed in cases like *Tashjian*; the Court found it "fair to infer that partisan considerations may have played a significant role in the decision to enact [the law],"[122] but that such a law should still be constitutional if supported by valid, neutral justifications.[123] In this respect, voter-identification laws are a metonym for all election laws: should courts (1) assess whether an election law reflects a partisan aim and (2) adjust doctrine, and perhaps legal outcomes, in response? When courts suspect that partisan aims have contributed (exclusively? predominantly? in part?) to a law's enactment, for example, should courts apply a more aggressive mode of review?[124]

From a more normative perspective, Professor Sam Issacharoff and I have pointed out that some of the constitutional doctrine and the central public policies in the area of race, rights, and voting were developed in the long era in which the Democratic Party had a complete monopoly on political power in the South.[125] "The state legislature" was not an abstraction, nor an ideal type envi-

---

Court did not have any reason to address the meaning or constitutional standing of this element in the amendment.

[121] *Crawford v Marion County Election Board*, 472 F3d 949, 954 (7th Cir 2007) (Evans, J, dissenting).

[122] 553 US 181, 203 (2008).

[123] Id at 204. In a nod toward realism, the Court did state that if partisan considerations were the "only" justification for an election law, the law would be unconstitutional. Id at 203.

[124] For differing perspectives on these issues, compare Pildes, *Foreword*, 118 Harv L Rev at 55–56, 76, 141 (cited in note 118), with Richard Hasen, *Bad Legislative Intent*, 2006 Wis L Rev 843.

[125] Samuel Issacharoff and Richard H. Pildes, *Politics as Markets: Partisan Lockups of the Democratic Process*, 50 Stan L Rev 643 (1998). See also Samuel Issacharoff, *Is Section 5 of the Voting Rights Act a Victim of Its Own Success?*, 104 Colum L Rev 1710, 1713–14 (2004).

sioned in much of conventional legal doctrine. Constitutional and statutory doctrine concerning the problem of vote dilution, as well as the constitutionally restrictive restraints on political parties in the *White Primary* cases,[126] were designed in this unique, aberrational context of one-party political monopoly. Neither the Court nor Congress could have been oblivious to that. With the dismantling of that one-party system that began with the 1965 VRA and culminated in the emergence of more normal—indeed, robust—two-party competitive politics that came to characterize Southern politics by the 1990s, we have asked whether any of these doctrines or policies should be revisited. Does the modern structure of two-party competitive politics now serve as an adequate (or even better) substitute for the role that doctrine or national policy had to play in the past? Professors Tracey Meares and Dan Kahan launched a related debate in criminal procedure when they argued that constitutional precedents and approaches from the pre-VRA era should be adapted, once African Americans became full political participants.[127] Should certain doctrines and decisions be understood not as general "precedents," but as contingent products—limited to that (or similar context)—of the unique composition of state "democracy" and legislatures in the one-party South?

I have focused on formalism/realism regarding state legislatures in the context of election laws because even the staunchest institutional formalist is likely to find the realist's "distrust" of "the legislature" hardest to resist in this area, as John Hart Ely recognized long ago.[128] Once doctrine opens the door to that institutional realism, though, the familiar anxieties race through, including how far courts can or should take realism. In reapportionment, the realism was at a general, structural level: the design of legislatures makes legislators unlikely to change the systems under which they hold power. In the analysis Professor Issacharoff and I offer, the realism is of an unusual but still categorical nature: law should distinguish at least between long eras of one-party monopoly and more "normal" eras of two-party com-

---

[126] For that tetralogy of cases, see Samuel Issacharoff, Pamela S. Karlan, and Richard H. Pildes, *The Law of Democracy* 220–38 (Foundation, 4th ed 2012).

[127] See Tracey L. Meares and Dan M. Kahan, *The Wages of Antiquated Procedural Thinking: A Critique of Chicago v Morales*, 1998 U Chi Legal F 197.

[128] John Hart Ely, *Democracy and Distrust* (Harvard, 1980).

petition (but, of course, political systems can reside at some point on a continuum, rather than clearly defined poles, so this categoricalism can break down).[129] In cases like *Tashjian* or *Georgia v Ashcroft*, the realism is at the most retail level: judicial decision making should turn on realistic appraisals of the particular political process behind a specific law. Yet if realism in this sphere seems disturbing, would we really prefer a legal order that resolutely takes an institutional formalist stance toward legislative action?

As Part II will now show, this broader framework concerning the formalist/realist tension provides an important perspective on *Shelby County*, the Court's most dramatic civil-rights decision since the modern civil-rights revolution.

II. INSTITUTIONAL FORMALISM VERSUS REALISM: SHELBY COUNTY

Shelby County is a story about how the legal and political system adapts to changes over time in one of the most charged realms of all, the relationship among race, democracy, and politics. In addition to revealing the Court's greater capacity to act as a countermajoritarian institution than some scholars believe,[130] the decision provides a powerful vantage point into the question of how institutionally formalist or realist the Court ought to be about Congress.

In the depressingly characteristic 5–4 divide that recurs on these issues, the Court held unconstitutional the current preclearance regime of the Voting Rights Act (VRA), under which certain states and localities could not make any change in their voting systems without advance federal approval. Nearly fifty years earlier, in initially blessing the constitutionality of this regime immediately after its birth, the Court in *South Carolina v Katzenbach*[131] had expressed a great deal of deference to Congress and called preclearance an "uncommon exercise of congressional power" justified by the "exceptional conditions" obvious to all in the South of 1965. As a signal that preclearance was considered exceptional, Congress al-

---

[129] In the comparative constitutional sphere, Sujit Choudhry similarly argues that constitutional courts should develop a distinct body of law for political systems dominated over long periods of time by one political party. Sujit Choudhry, *"He Had a Mandate": The South African Constitutional Court and the African National Congress in a Dominant Party Democracy*, 2 Const Ct Rev 1 (2009).

[130] For discussion of that issue, see Richard H. Pildes, *Is the Supreme Court a "Majoritarian" Institution?*, 2010 Supreme Court Review 103.

[131] 383 US 301 (1966).

ways designed this part of the VRA, unlike other parts, with an automatic sunset provision. Embodied in Section 5, preclearance first expired in 1970, and Congress then extended it for another five years; in 1975, for another seven; and in 1982, for twenty-five more years. In the 2006 enactment at issue in *Shelby County*, Congress then reauthorized this system for another twenty-five years, until 2031. Thus, from a five-year structure to address the circumstance of American apartheid in 1965, Section 5 became a regime that Congress set into place until 2031.[132]

Shelby County did not hold this preclearance regime itself unconstitutional (Justice Thomas, concurring, would have).[133] Instead, the Court held unconstitutional Section 4, the coverage formula in the 2006 Act. A key element in the 1965 Act,[134] this formula had been designed to identify the particular jurisdictions in which systematic racially-discriminatory voting practices provided strong evidence that justified singling out those areas for federal control. In 1965, such evidence was not hard to come by. In the 1965 Act, that formula was based on whether a jurisdiction (1) had in place as of November 1, 1964, a "test or device" (literacy tests, "understanding" and knowledge requirements, good moral character tests, and the like) and (2) had less than 50 percent voter registration or turnout in the 1964 presidential election. In early reauthorizations of Section 5, Congress updated this formula to include the 1968 and 1972 elections. After that, Congress stopped updating this trigger, including in 2006, when it essentially left in place the 1964, 1968, and 1972 formula from the Act's initial life.[135] The effect, then, was that the areas that had been brought under coverage because they used illegitimate "tests and devices" in 1964, and had low presidential election participation then or no later than 1972, continued to remain covered under the 2006 Act.

The 1965 Act had contemplated that the preclearance regime would unwind from within over time, through provisions that permitted covered areas eventually to "bail out" of coverage. But

---

[132] The Act did include a precatory provision stating that Congress should "reconsider" Section 5 in fifteen years, 42 USC § 1973b(a)(7), (8) (2006 ed, Supp V), but the Act remained in effect without any need for subsequent reauthorization until 2031.

[133] *Shelby County*, 133 S Ct at 2632 (Thomas, J, concurring).

[134] For a good history of how this design came about, see Brian Landsberg, *Free at Last to Vote: The Alabama Origins of the 1965 Voting Rights Act* (Kansas, 2007).

[135] *Shelby County*, 133 S Ct at 2620–21.

for any number of possible reasons, these bail-out provisions never had any meaningful practical effect in unwinding coverage—even after Congress had tried in 1982 amendments to make the bailout process a more practical option.[136] Of all the more than 850 or so counties that the Act originally covered with significant minority populations, fewer than 2 percent had ever emerged from the Act.[137] In the 2006 Act, Congress did not adapt or update the bail-out process.[138] The coverage formula, alone then, had to carry even more weight in showing that the Act was appropriately tailored to current conditions.

Holding that it was constitutionally irrational for Congress to base continuation of the preclearance regime on a jurisdiction's use of voting tests or devices and low turnout from forty or more years ago, the Court announced that Congress could not "rely simply on the past." If Section 5 were to continue, Section 4 had to "identify those jurisdictions to be singled out on a basis that makes sense in light of current conditions."[139] The Court concluded that Congress had failed to do that—though the decision leaves open the possibility that Congress could enact an updated preclearance formula.[140]

A. WHAT WAS SHELBY COUNTY "ABOUT"?

The historical, moral, and symbolic weight of the VRA inevitably entails that the Court's decision cannot be approached in doctrinal terms alone, for a decision so momentous and visible will have "meaning" far beyond anything in the opinion itself. But what is that meaning likely to be?[141]

---

[136] See Paul Winke, *Why the Preclearance and Bailout Provisions of the Voting Rights Act Are Still a Constitutionally Proportional Remedy*, 28 NYU Rev L & Soc Change 69 (2003).

[137] This figure is based on my own calculation.

[138] Congress was urged to do so. See *An Introduction to the Expiring Provisions of the Voting Rights Act and Legal Issues Relating to Reauthorization*, Hearing before the Senate Committee on the Judiciary, 109th Cong, 2d Sess 10, 19–20 (2006) (statement of Richard L. Hasen); id at 14, 26–27 (statement of Samuel Issacharoff).

[139] *Shelby County*, 133 S Ct at 2629.

[140] A thoughtful proposal to do so, modestly bipartisan, has been introduced (whether it will have any traction remains to be seen). See Voting Rights Amendments Act of 2014, HR 3899, 113th Cong, 2d Sess (Jan 16, 2014) and S 1945, 113th Cong, 2d Sess (Jan 16, 2014).

[141] The next several paragraphs are adapted from a blog post of mine. Richard Pildes, *Shelby Commentary: What Does the Court's Decision Mean?* (SCOTUSblog, June 25, 2013), online at http://goo.gl/13sqXl.

I believe the decision will express such radically different meanings to different people for years to come that we will not be able to forge common ground regarding even the threshold question of what the decision is "about." To some, *Shelby County* will be seen as a test of whether the Court believes systematic racial discriminating in voting systems continues in the South; to others, it will be seen as test of the ability of our political institutions, particularly Congress, to grapple with charged issues of race and democracy in an institutionally serious way. These will remain radically incommensurable starting points.

To many critics, the essential question will be whether racial discrimination in voting still exists in the South. Framed this way, the Court's decision will appear to be, at best, a denial of reality.[142] It is not just outside critics who are likely to view the decision this way. Justice Sotomayor, at oral argument, reflected this perspective on "the question" at stake when she pointedly asked the VRA's challengers: "Do you think that racial discrimination in voting has ended, that there is none anywhere?"[143] If the answer to that question is no, as it must be, and if *that* is what the case was about, the Court's decision must look wrong.

Almost as soon as the (metaphorical) ink on the decision was dry, Justice Ginsburg confirmed that this was the starting point for other dissenters. In a remarkable public interview[144] one month after the decision, she proclaimed her dissent to have been right— "I didn't want to be right [in my dissent], but sadly I am"—on the basis that some covered or partially-covered states, particularly Texas and North Carolina, had put back into force or enacted new regulations on voting, including voter identification laws. Accepting Justice Ginsburg's judgment on the legality of these laws (and leaving aside the propriety of her expressing a view on them), this statement further confirms that, to many, the case was "about" whether racially-discriminatory voting policies continue to be

---

[142] For an excellent discussion of how the decision reflects "an end to the racial discrimination consensus" that existed in earlier decades, see Guy-Uriel E. Charles and Luis E. Fuentes-Rohwer, *The Voting Rights Act in Winter: The Death of a Superstatute* 21 (Jan 2014 manuscript, available online at http://papers.ssrn.com/sol3/papers.cfm?abstract_id =2377470).

[143] Transcript of Oral Argument, *Shelby County v Holder*, No 12-96, *64 (US Feb 27, 2013) (available online at http://goo.gl/hEKIQ6).

[144] Mark Sherman, *Ginsburg Says Push for Voter ID Laws Predictable* (Associated Press, July 26, 2013), online at http://goo.gl/Bu1222.

adopted in the South. From this vantage point, as long as it does, Section 4 remains not just justifiable, but essential.

Yet to others, including the Court majority, the case was not about racial discrimination in isolation, but about the way Congress had addressed the issue. In doctrinal terms, that question was whether Congress had met the relevant constitutional obligation to establish that this unique regime of federal control was adequately tailored to where systematic problems with racially-discriminatory voting practices existed. But more generally and symbolically, the question from this perspective was whether our political institutions and culture have the capacity to recognize what has changed, and what has not, at the intersection of race and voting in the decades since Congress last engaged the VRA. As I noted already and will discuss more shortly, the face of the Act did not reflect any change. Congress did not update the coverage formula in any way or make bailout easier; and it reauthorized the preclearance regime for another twenty-five years. This lack of updating led Justice Kennedy, at the oral argument, to say: Congress "should use criteria that are relevant to the existing [conditions]—and Congress just didn't have the time or the energy to do this; it just re-enacted it."[145] That statement reflects disbelief that Congress had engaged in the kind of responsible lawmaking process he thought these issues constitutionally required; even if areas of discriminatory voting practices remain, could they so precisely mirror exactly the areas of which this was true forty or fifty years ago? From this viewpoint, the renewed preclearance structure symbolized that the issues at the intersec-

---

[145] Despite the popular image that Section 5 is about protecting access to the ballot box, Section 5 in practice for many decades had been much more about racial redistricting than access to the ballot box. While the Justice Department in recent decades blocked access changes on average fewer than twice a year, it blocked redistrictings nearly fourteen times as often. Indeed, in the 2006 Act itself, Congress itself did not rely primarily on ballot-box access problems to justify renewing Section 4, but on issues like redistricting. If Section 4 is "about" access to the ballot box in the public imagination, to the Court majority, I suspect, Section 4 is about racial redistricting. This is a further conflict in symbolism regarding what the VRA "represents" that is likely to endure for years to come in debates over the decision. Only in the last few years had Section 5 become significant again with respect to access to the ballot-box issues in responses to changes in state laws that reduced hours of early voting or added additional identification requirements as proof of eligibility to vote. For lengthy analysis of how Section 5 functioned in practice, see Rick Pildes and Dan Tokaji, *What Did VRA Preclearance Actually Do?: The Gap Between Perception and Reality* (Election Law Blog, Aug 19, 2013), online at http://electionlawblog.org/?p=54521; Rick Pildes and Dan Tokaji, *What Did VRA Preclearance Actually Do?: The Gap Between Perception and Reality Part II* (Election Law Blog, Aug 21, 2013), online at http://electionlawblog.org/?p=54638.

tion of race, democracy, and voting rights remain so charged that our political system is paralyzed when confronting them.

Was the case about racial discrimination in voting? Or Congress's lawmaking?

B. THE COURT AND CONGRESS

In deciding whether and how much to defer to Congress, the Court first had to resolve a critical threshold constitutional issue. Yet the two opinions hardly debate this issue—another manifestation of the radically different frames within which judicial perceptions of Congress's action take place. Both opinions largely take their own starting points as given—as a premise, rather than a choice to explain and justify. For that reason, this issue is obscured; it is easy to miss. Yet all other aspects of the case, including deference to Congress and the relevance of the legislative process and record, flow from this threshold question: what should the appropriate baseline be, as a constitutional matter, for judging whether Congress in 2006 had fulfilled its constitutional responsibility in designing Section 4's geographic coverage formula?[146]

Three different possibilities exist for this choice of constitutional baseline.[147] And how the Court "pictured" Congress and the legislative process depended heavily on how this constitutional baseline was set:

1. Does Congress need to establish sufficient continuing differences today between "the covered" and the "noncovered" areas to justify continuing to single out the former for preclearance (taking the covered jurisdictions in the *aggregate*);
2. Does Congress only need to focus on the already-covered jurisdictions in isolation and establish that significant racially discriminatory voting problems continue to exist in *those* areas;
3. Assuming Congress can limit itself to the areas already covered, how much can Congress treat those areas as a group rather than addressing and recognizing any significant differences today *within* the previously-covered areas?

---

[146] The next few pages are adapted from a blog post of mine. See Richard Pildes, *The Supreme Court Response to Congressional Avoidance* (SCOTUSblog, Sept 12, 2012), online at http://goo.gl/4uKaow.

[147] On constitutional baselines, see Daryl J. Levinson, *Framing Transactions in Constitutional Law*, 111 Yale L J 1311 (2002).

First, on which of these understandings of its constitutional responsibility did Congress in fact legislate? Second, on which of these understandings did the majority and dissent decide the case?

As to the former, it is clear, to me at least, that Congress acted on the view that principle (2) defined its constitutional obligations. The legislative process had been designed as if Congress's only constitutional (and policy) responsibility were to establish that race-related voting-rights problems continued to exist *within* parts of the already-covered areas—regardless whether parts of the covered areas no longer differed significantly from parts of the non-covered areas (or whether some noncovered areas were now worse than some covered areas). Most of the legislative record was built in the House, where the legislative process began.[148] After looking at that evidence, I testified before the Senate Judiciary Committee in 2006 to my concern that the evidence in the legislative record did not adequately address whether there continued to be "systematic differences between the covered and the non-covered areas of the United States."[149] Congress simply made a strategic decision

---

[148] James Thomas Tucker, *The Politics of Persuasion: Passage of the Voting Rights Act Reauthorization Act of 2006*, 33 J Legis 205, 233 (2007); Persily, 117 Yale L J at 174, 195 (cited in note 120).

[149] *The Continuing Need for Section 5 Pre-Clearance*, Hearing before the Senate Committee on the Judiciary, 109th Cong, 2d Sess 10, 14 (2006) (Statement of Richard H. Pildes):

> First, I am concerned that the evidence in the record does not address an essential issue to the constitutionality of the proposed bill, and I am not aware that this concern, though I think it may be essential, has been addressed in the House hearings or in the previous hearings before this Committee.
>
> The assumption so far of all of the evidence I have seen, or most of the evidence at least, is that it is sufficient to document continuing instances of problems in the area of race and voting rights in the covered jurisdictions. But I am very concerned that under the congruence and proportionality test that the Court now applies in this area, the Court is going to insist that there be some account of systematic differences between the covered and the non-covered areas of the United States.
>
> There is very little evidence in the record on this, and, in fact, the evidence that is in the record suggests that there is more similarity than difference. . . . Now, I want to be clear about why I raise this point. It is not to assert that the bill as proposed is unconstitutional. But I look at this record as a lawyer concerned about how the courts will respond to it, trying to determine how best to ensure the constitutionality of a renewed Section 5, and I think this is an essential issue that has been neglected until now. . . .
>
> I am more worried than Professor Karlan is about the lack of evidence in the record about the differences between covered and non-covered States. I agree, the power of Congress in the area of voting rights is at its highest, but the Voting Rights Act in Section 5 is also an extremely unusual, indeed unique,

to keep the focus on the already-covered areas and not open up current systematic comparisons with the noncovered areas; for reasons of realpolitik, doing so was thought to be too explosive.[150]

Because Congress chose not to compare in any detail the covered and noncovered areas, it is no surprise that little evidence in the record does so. In her dissent, Justice Ginsburg made a valiant effort to salvage the record by marshaling the one piece of evidence purporting to address this issue, but even that bit of evidence had been undermined before *Shelby County*.[151] But more meaningfully, the larger truth is that battling on this terrain was a losing proposition from the start, given the way the process intentionally bypassed this issue. That is not to say that such differences do not exist; it is to say that Congress did not address that question in any detail.

As to the second question, the majority held that Congress, in essence, had asked the wrong legal question. In holding that Congress was required to "identify those jurisdictions to be singled out on a basis that makes sense in light of current conditions,"[152]

provision, as you know, in Federal law. It singles out part of the country.

   Now, the constitutional jurisprudence has changed greatly since the courts last looked at this singling out of one part of the country. And it seems to me it is one thing, with the Family Medical Leave Act and cases like *Hibbs*, to base national uniform law on evidence from a number of States, but not all the States. It seems to me, constitutionally, it is a very different question to base geographically selective national law, the only one we have, as far as I know, on evidence that does not today show that that targeting is congruent to the constitutional violations that are out there. That is what I am worried about with the evidence in the record so far.

The Court quoted part of this testimony in *Northwest Austin Municipal Utility District Number One v Holder*, 557 US 193, 204 (2009).

[150] Persily, 117 Yale L J at 195 (cited in note 120); Richard H. Pildes, *Political Avoidance, Constitution Theory, and the VRA*, 117 Yale L J Pocket Part 148 (2007).

[151] This evidence, collected by Professor Ellen Katz, is known as the Katz study. Ellen Katz et al, *Documenting Discrimination in Voting: Judicial Findings Under Section 2 of the Voting Rights Act Since 1982*, 39 U Mich J L Ref 643 (2006). In a series of articles, Professors Adam Cox and Thomas Miles argue that Katz's study cannot sustain the weight the dissent puts on it; in strong terms, they conclude "the data provide no meaningful evidence about whether discrimination is worse in one part of the country than the other." Adam Cox and Thomas Miles, *Online VRA Symposium: Social Science Goes to Court* (SCOTUSblog, Sep 13, 2012), online at http://goo.gl/BLbqYd. The dissent does not address these critiques of the Katz study, perhaps because the main briefs did not point the Court to them. For a brief summary of the Cox/Miles critiques, see the blog post just cited; for the academic articles, see Adam B. Cox and Thomas J. Miles, *Judging the Voting Rights Act*, 108 Colum L Rev 1 (2008); Adam B. Cox and Thomas J. Miles, *Documenting Discrimination?*, 108 Colum L Rev Sidebar 31 (2008); Adam B. Cox and Thomas J. Miles, *Judicial Ideology and the Transformation of Voting Rights Jurisprudence*, 76 U Chi L Rev 1493 (2008).

[152] *Shelby County*, 133 S Ct at 2629.

the majority embraced principle (1) as the constitutional baseline required. The Court did not explicitly justify and explain this choice over principle (2). Instead, it treated the Court's prior decision on the constitutionality of preclearance, *NAMUDNO*,[153] in which the Court avoided the constitutional issue, as having resolved that baseline issue already. That is indeed a plausible reading of *NAMUDNO*, which stressed the importance of a coverage formula tied to current conditions and noted that voting problems might "no longer be concentrated in" the covered areas.[154] But even so, *NAMUDNO* itself did not expressly compare these two baselines and offer a considered justification for choosing (1) over (2). Thus, the Court "resolved" this essential issue without any indication that it was making the most important decision in the case. Once this becomes the appropriate baseline, it is unsurprising that the majority would view Congress as not having made a serious attempt to meet its constitutional obligation.

So, too, it is with the dissenting opinion. Justice Ginsburg's dissent paints an entirely different picture of Congress. But in large part, that is because the dissent assumes—more implicitly than not—that the correct legal baseline is (2), not (1). The principal theme of the dissent is deference to Congress; citing the 1966 *South Carolina v Katzenbach* decision, the dissent castigates the majority for not having given Congress "the full measure of respect its judgments in this domain should garner." Justice Ginsburg describes Congress as having approached its task in 2006 with "great care and seriousness";[155] she says Congress "did not take this task lightly";[156] she describes the empirical record before Congress as "huge"[157] and "extraordinary";[158] she characterizes the legislative process as having involved "exhaustive evidence-gathering and deliberative process. . . ."[159] But to what would the Court be deferring? This portrait is based on the assumption that Congress was only required to meet the obligations of principle (2). For if the constitutional baseline is (1), Congress asked and an-

[153] *Northwest Austin Municipal Utility District Number One v Holder*, 557 US 193 (2009).

[154] Id at 203–04.

[155] *Shelby County*, 133 S Ct at 2644 (Ginsburg, J, dissenting).

[156] Id at 2635.

[157] Id at 2639.

[158] Id at 2652.

[159] Id.

swered a different (and in the majority's view, wrong) legal question.

Unlike the majority, the dissent does makes a brief effort to justify (2) as the correct baseline, offering three quick reasons to do so. But Justice Ginsburg's points are more descriptive than legal; it is hard to see how they provide a legal argument as to why the majority is wrong to require Congress to show significant continuing differences between the covered and the noncovered areas.[160] That argument can be made. But in an otherwise lengthy opinion, the dissent, too, mostly assumes that its baseline, (2), can be taken for granted. In addition, the dissent also implicitly rejected (3) as the appropriate baseline. That is, even assuming that Congress could properly avoid comparisons between covered and noncovered areas, could Congress continue to treat the previously covered states as an undifferentiated group without examining in more detail whether they had come to differ in significant ways? Could it be the case that all the areas, and only the areas, that had been covered for decades remained the proper areas to cover today? And did the Court, and Congress, even have to ask that question?

The single most important constitutional issue, then—the legal linchpin—is the one least debated, analyzed, or discussed. Yet the Court's perceptions of how Congress functioned were deeply colored by the answer to this question.

But not only to that question. For as I have written before, in the 2006 VRA amendments, "Congress ha[d], in effect, thrown down a gauntlet to the Court."[161] For nearly twenty-five years leading up to 2006, the Court had been more assertive in limiting the scope of Congress's enumerated powers in the name of federalism; in limiting the scope of Congress's powers to enforce the Fourteenth Amendment; and in limiting the use of race in public

---

[160] See id at 2638–39. She observes that the court should expect the record of violations to be less stark in 2006 than in 1965; she also notes that the sunset provision requires Congress to revisit the scope of coverage. But neither point addresses or explains why Congress should or should not have the constitutional obligation to establish that significant differentiations continue between the covered and noncovered states. The closest the dissent comes is in asserting that "legislation *re*-authorizing an existing statute is especially likely to satisfy the minimal requirements of the rational basis test." But again, this appears to be more of an empirical point—prior bad actors are likely to remain current bad actors—than a legal argument as to why (2) rather than (1) should provide the constitutional baseline (or why (3) is not the more appropriate baseline than (2)).

[161] Pildes, 117 Yale L J Pocket Part at 153 (cited in note 150).

policymaking. The preclearance regime stood at the intersection of all these areas. For many years now, the Court has been more intensely insisting, rightly or wrongly, that legislation in these areas rests on an adequate foundation.

Yet faced with these pivotal developments of the Rehnquist and Roberts Courts, Congress followed the same roadmap it had used when it had last revisited Section 5 in 1982. As in 1982, it did not update the coverage formula; it cemented this regime into place for twenty-five years, rather than the shorter periods that had characterized the pre-1982 preauthorizations; it did not even make bailout easier (as it had tried to do in 1982); and Congress also effectively overruled two Supreme Court decisions with which it disagreed (it had done so for one Court decision in the 1982 amendments). Had Congress narrowed and modified the preclearance regime in any way, the Court might have found it easier to see the reauthorization process as a good-faith effort to honor these shifts in constitutional doctrines at the same time that Congress struggled with a difficult policy and political problem. But even though some of these provisions were not before the Court in *Shelby County*, they all no doubt contributed to the majority's picture of the legislative process. As Chief Justice Roberts wrote about the provisions that overruled prior Court decisions, "the bar that covered jurisdictions must clear has been raised even as the conditions justifying that requirement have dramatically improved."[162] The tone of incredulity is hard to miss. Similarly, the majority concluded that the coverage formula was "irrational in theory" because the existence of tests and devices in the 1960s and 1970s, which had been prohibited ever since, could not possibly be the cause of whatever voting problems remained. How could Congress have left the Act tied to triggering events that dated that far back?

We are left then, among all the other aspects of *Shelby County* with competing pictures of Congress. That is why, for Justice Kennedy, "Congress just didn't have the time or the energy to do this [i.e., to use criteria relevant to existing conditions]; it just re-enacted it."[163] That is why, for the dissent, Congress had acted with "great care and seriousness." What did it mean that Congress has been nearly unan-

---

[162] *Shelby County*, 133 S Ct at 2627.

[163] Transcript of Oral Argument, *Shelby County*, *35 (cited in note 143).

imous in approving the legislation? To Justice Scalia, that was yet another sign that Congress had passed the buck and avoided confronting the serious, difficult issues involved;[164] to critics of the decision, the notion that Justices would probe beneath the surface of a law to ask questions about whether it emanated from a serious, deliberative lawmaking process was itself outrageous.[165] In the legislative processes of the great 1960s civil-rights era that ended Jim Crow, every legislative detail was fought over tooth and nail; the 1964 Civil Rights Act was enacted only after the longest filibuster in Senate history.[166] Was the legislative process in 2006 deliberatively similar—and should that matter, along with the end of Jim Crow itself, to the precedential weight of *South Carolina v Katzenbach*? If the Court showed great deference to Congress then, is it required to do so now? Put in other terms, how formal or realist should the Court be about Congress (or other institutions) and the weight of its own precedents regarding Congress (or other institutions).

Shelby County is "about" many things. But to a significant extent, it is about essential questions that run throughout nearly all of constitutional and public-law adjudication regarding the appropriate role of institutional formalism and realism in judicial decision making.

III. CONCLUSION

The tension between more formalist and realist institutional conceptions is a profound, inescapable, and irresolvable one throughout constitutional and public law. Focusing more directly on this tension illuminates public law and its controversies but can-

---

[164] See this exchange at the oral argument:

JUSTICE SCALIA: . . . What was the vote on this 2006 extension—98 to nothing in the Senate, and what was it in the House? Was—

MR. ADEGBILE: It was—it was 33 to 390, I believe.

JUSTICE SCALIA: 33 to 390. You know, the—the Israeli Supreme Court, the Sanhedrin, used to have a rule that if the death penalty was pronounced unanimously, it was invalid, because there must be something wrong there.

Transcript of Oral Argument at 51, *Nw. Austin Mun. Util. Dist. No. One*, 129 S Ct 2504 (No 08-322), at http://www.supremecourt.gov/oral_arguments/argument_transcripts/08-322.pdf.

[165] See Pamela S. Karlan, *Foreword—Democracy and Disdain*, 126 Harv L Rev 1 (2012).

[166] See Charles Whalen and Barbara Whalen, *The Longest Debate: A Legislative History of the 1964 Civil Rights Act* (1985).

not suggest that any final resolution of this tension can be had. Too much institutional formalism defeats the purposes that animate the constitutional order in the first place; too much institutional realism is perceived to pose a threat to the rule of law. We can try to bound institutional realism in more categorical or generalizable forms, but no rule-of-law-like principles exist to decide just how much institutional realism ought to shape public law. Yet to understand public law fully requires appreciating the powerful role this tension quietly plays.

NICHOLAS O. STEPHANOPOULOS

THE SOUTH AFTER SHELBY COUNTY

For almost half a century, minority representation in America rested on two legal pillars. The first, Section 2 of the Voting Rights Act (VRA), applies nationwide and prohibits practices that "result[] in a denial or abridgement of the right . . . to vote on account of race or color."[1] It is a relatively conventional provision that creates a cause of action for plaintiffs who have been subjected to racial vote dilution or denial. The second, Section 5 of the VRA, applies only to the (mostly southern) jurisdictions specified in Section 4, and bans practices that have the purpose or effect of "denying or abridging the right to vote on account of race or color."[2] Despite its almost identical language, Section 5 is a highly unusual provision that prevents covered jurisdictions from implementing *any* changes to their voting laws unless they first have convinced the Department of Justice (DOJ) or a federal court that the changes will not worsen the electoral position of minority voters.[3]

On the penultimate day of the 2012–13 term, the Supreme Court

---

Nicholas O. Stephanopoulos is Assistant Professor of Law, University of Chicago Law School.

AUTHOR'S NOTE: I am grateful to Josh Douglas, Chris Elmendorf, Dan Freeman, Ruth Greenwood, Bernie Grofman, Dale Ho, Aziz Huq, Ellen Katz, Jennifer Nou, Rick Pildes, Michael Pitts, Eric Posner, Geoffrey Stone, John Tanner, and Dan Tokaji for their helpful comments. My thanks also to the workshop participants at the University of Chicago, the University of Kentucky, and the Chicago Junior Faculty Workshop, where I presented earlier versions of the article. I am pleased as well to acknowledge the support of the Robert Helman Law & Public Policy Fund.

[1] 42 USC § 1973(a).

[2] Id § 1973c(a); see also id § 1973b(b) (specifying coverage formula of Section 4).

[3] See id § 1973c(a).

dismantled the second of these two pillars. In *Shelby County v Holder*, the Court held that Section 4 of the VRA, which contains the formula identifying the jurisdictions that are subject to Section 5's preclearance requirement, is unconstitutional.[4] According to the Court, the Section 4 formula is both obsolete—"based on decades-old data and eradicated practices"[5]—and irrational because covered areas no longer perform worse than their noncovered peers along the formula's metrics of voter registration and turnout.[6] Congress therefore exceeded its enforcement powers under the Fourteenth and Fifteenth Amendments when it reenacted Section 4 in 2006. Section 5 continues to be good law, but it has been rendered a zombie provision, no longer applicable to any jurisdiction, by the demise of Section 4.

An urgent question in the wake of *Shelby County* (and the subject of this article) is what will happen now to minority representation in the areas that formerly were covered by Section 5. The question, in other words, is how large the gap is between Section 2, which continues to apply nationwide, and Section 5. Is the gap quite small, in which case minority representation in the South will be largely unaffected? Or is the gap more like a chasm, in which case the political influence of minority groups will be sharply curtailed? The answer is crucial to determining the electoral implications of *Shelby County* for the minorities who are the VRA's intended beneficiaries. The answer also is highly relevant to whether and how Congress should respond to the Court's neutering of Section 5.

Surprisingly, the existing literature has not explored in detail how Section 2 and Section 5 interrelate. Indeed, some scholars have elided the distinctions between the provisions and argued that they both can be "understood to require the creation of majority-minority districts whenever possible."[7] When academics have explicitly addressed the space between Section 2 and Section 5, they have tended to conclude (without much elaboration) that it is not very large. For instance, Samuel Issacharoff has written that, in the ab-

---

[4] *Shelby Cty v Holder*, 133 S Ct 2612 (2013).

[5] Id at 2627.

[6] See id at 2627–29.

[7] Adam B. Cox and Richard T. Holden, *Reconsidering Racial and Partisan Gerrymandering*, 78 U Chi L Rev 553, 577 (2011); see also, for example, David Epstein and Sharyn O'Halloran, *A Strategic Dominance Argument for Retaining Section 5 of the VRA*, 5 Election L J 283, 285 (2006) (assuming that situations in which Section 2 and Section 5 diverge substantively are "relatively rare").

sence of Section 5, his "suspicion is that the combination of [S]ection 2, . . . the protections of the Fourteenth Amendment, and the fact of being in the process and at the table would afford much protection" to minority groups.[8] Justice Kennedy expressed a similar sentiment at the *Shelby County* oral argument, declaring that "it's not clear to me that there's that much difference [between] a Section 2 suit now and preclearance."[9]

In this article, then, I carry out a conceptual, empirical, and political investigation of the gap between Section 2 and Section 5. I analyze, that is, how the provisions differ in their formal operation, what kinds (and quantities) of practices are permitted by Section 2 but barred by Section 5, and which of these practices are likely to be enacted by the jurisdictions that now are free from Section 5's constraints. My analysis covers both the procedural aspects of voting rights litigation and the substance of minority representation. On the substantive side, I discuss both vote dilution (redistricting in particular) and the recent wave of franchise restrictions that scholars have dubbed the "new vote denial."[10] Throughout my examination, I consider the statutory text, the case law, and the empirical evidence as they stood at the time of this article's writing. Section 2 and Section 5 operated quite differently in earlier periods, and how they will evolve in the future is, of course, unknowable.

With respect to procedure, there are three key differences between litigation under Section 2 and preclearance under Section 5. The burden of proof is on the plaintiff under Section 2 but on the jurisdiction under Section 5. The default is that a challenged policy goes into effect under Section 2 but that it does not under Section 5. And the party that typically invokes the VRA's protections is a private plaintiff under Section 2 but the DOJ under Section 5. These differences mean that certain policies that formerly would have been blocked by Section 5 now will be implemented. Sometimes a plain-

---

[8] Samuel Issacharoff, *Is Section 5 of the Voting Rights Act a Victim of Its Own Success?*, 104 Colum L Rev 1710, 1731 (2004); see also, for example, Bernard Grofman and Thomas Brunell, *Extending Section 5 of the Voting Rights Act: The Complex Interaction Between Law and Politics*, in David L. Epstein et al, eds, *The Future of the Voting Rights Act* 311, 321 (Russell, 2006); Michael J. Pitts, *Let's Not Call the Whole Thing Off Just Yet: A Response to Samuel Issacharoff's Suggestion to Scuttle Section 5 of the Voting Rights Act*, 84 Neb L Rev 605, 627 (2005) ("[T]he gap has been significantly narrowed between what amounts to a section 2 violation and what amounts to a section 5 violation.").

[9] Transcript of Oral Argument, *Shelby Cty v Holder*, 133 S Ct 2612 (No 12-96), *37.

[10] See Daniel P. Tokaji, *The New Vote Denial: Where Election Reform Meets the Voting Rights Act*, 57 SC L Rev 689 (2006) (coining the phrase).

tiff will be unable to satisfy its burden under Section 2 even though, on the same facts, a jurisdiction would have been unable to meet *its* burden under Section 5. Sometimes a plaintiff *will* be able to satisfy its Section 2 burden, but only after a contested policy has come into force for some time. And sometimes private parties will want to challenge particular electoral practices, but will be unable to do so because of limited resources.

How many policies will take effect as a consequence of these procedural distinctions? It is impossible to know for certain, but the available empirical evidence suggests that the number will be substantial. First, the success rate of Section 2 litigation in areas formerly covered by Section 5 has hovered around 40 percent over the last generation.[11] Plaintiffs therefore are likely to lose many of their lawsuits against practices that previously would have been denied preclearance. Second, the proportion of Section 2 suits in which preliminary injunctions are granted is quite small, certainly no higher than 25 percent and probably lower than 5 percent.[12] Many policies thus are likely to go into effect temporarily even if they ultimately are invalidated in Section 2 litigation. And, third, the volume of Section 5 preclearance denials has been about the same, over the past few decades, as the volume of Section 2 suits in covered areas.[13] Accordingly, private parties would need a significant infusion of resources in order to dispute all of the policies that formerly would have been blocked.

Turning next to vote dilution, there also are three major differences between the electoral districts to which Section 2 applies and those protected by Section 5. Section 2 does not extend to bizarrely shaped districts while Section 5 does. Section 2 does not encompass districts that merge highly dissimilar minority communities while Section 5 again does. And Section 2 does not cover districts whose minority voters comprise less than 50 percent of their total population while Section 5 does once more. These differences stem from a series of Supreme Court decisions narrowing the scope of

---

[11] See Ellen Katz et al, *Documenting Discrimination in Voting: Judicial Findings Under Section 2 of the Voting Rights Act Since 1982*, 39 U Mich J L Ref 643, 656 (2006).

[12] See J. Gerald Hebert and Armand Defner, *More Observations on Shelby County, Alabama and the Supreme Court*, Campaign Legal Center Blog (March 1, 2013), online at http://www.clcblog.org/index.php?option=com_content&view=article&id=506:more-observations-on-shelby-county-alabama-and-the-supreme-court.

[13] See *Shelby Cty v Holder*, 679 F3d 848, 872 (DC Cir 2012), rev'd, 133 S Ct 2612 (2013).

Section 2, and they mean that certain districts that previously were shielded by Section 5 now no longer will enjoy legal protection. Jurisdictions now will have the ability to eliminate districts that are shaped too strangely, that have overly heterogeneous minority populations, or that have minority populations that are too small to qualify for Section 2 coverage.

How many districts fall into these categories? To answer this question, I first identified all of the districts that used to be protected by Section 5 in the nine southern and southwestern states to which the provision formerly applied in large part or in full.[14] There are 404 congressional and state legislative districts that meet these criteria. Of these, twenty-two are so noncompact that they likely can be dismantled without violating Section 2. This number is small because jurisdictions seem to have learned from the redistricting battles of the 1990s, when the Court struck down several strangely shaped districts. But a much larger number of districts, 146 in total, contain minority populations that are so heterogeneous that Section 2 may not extend to them. The role of such heterogeneity in Section 2 doctrine is not yet settled, but if it is a binding requirement then minority representation in the South could be slashed in the wake of *Shelby County*. Lastly, only seventeen previously covered districts have minority voter proportions below 50 percent. Here too jurisdictions appear to have taken to heart the lessons of earlier Court decisions—and also to have mastered the art of crafting majority-minority districts while simultaneously advancing partisan interests.

Of course, not all of the districts that populate the Section 2–Section 5 gap will be disbanded. When Republicans are responsible for redistricting (as they now are in almost every formerly covered state), they often will find it politically beneficial to preserve majority-minority districts. Such districts enable them to pack Democrats into a small number of overwhelmingly safe constituencies, thus enhancing Republican electoral prospects. Likewise, when Democrats are in charge, they often will face intense pressure from minority groups not to eliminate minority-controlled districts, even if doing so would help the Democratic cause. But this is not to say that the Section 2–Section 5 gap will not be exploited at all. Republican line-drawers sometimes will be able to reap greater political benefits by concentrating minority voters into a smaller num-

---

[14] These states are Alabama, Arizona, Georgia, Louisiana, Mississippi, North Carolina, South Carolina, Texas, and Virginia.

ber of super-packed districts. Analogously, Democratic line-drawers sometimes will decide to craft more districts in which minority voters are sufficiently numerous to ensure the victory of a Democrat—but not to elect their own preferred candidate.

Finally, the differences between Section 2 and Section 5 are more uncertain in the vote-denial context. The franchise restrictions recently enacted by many states are a relatively new development, and neither the courts nor the DOJ yet have had time to develop concrete standards. Still, it again appears that there is substantive space between the two provisions. Under Section 2, plaintiffs typically need to demonstrate not only that a statistical disparity exists between minorities and whites, but also that a franchise restriction interacts with social and historical conditions to cause the disparity. Under Section 5, on the other hand, a disparate impact alone usually suffices to prevent a restriction from going into effect, as long as the burden imposed by the restriction on voting is material.

Because of the small number of cases to which these standards have been applied, the magnitude of the relevant Section 2–Section 5 gap is unclear. But it is revealing that plaintiffs have yet to prevail in a Section 2 challenge to a photo-identification law, while three such laws were blocked, at least temporarily, under Section 5.[15] Similarly, a recent Florida law that reduced the number of hours for early voting was denied preclearance with respect to the state's five formerly covered counties, but sustained under Section 2 with respect to the rest of the state.[16] If there indeed is space between Section 2 and Section 5 in the vote-denial context, there is little doubt that it quickly will be seized. Unlike in the redistricting context, Republicans' political incentives point unambiguously toward the enactment of additional franchise restrictions. Not surprisingly, in the brief period that has elapsed since *Shelby County* was decided, officials in Alabama, Florida, Mississippi, North Carolina, Texas, and Virginia already have announced their intention to pass or implement photo ID laws and other similar measures.[17]

---

[15] These were a Louisiana law in 1994, a South Carolina law in 2012, and a Texas law in 2012.

[16] Compare *Florida v United States*, 885 F Supp 2d 299 (DDC 2012) (denying preclearance in five covered counties) with *Brown v Detzner*, 895 F Supp 2d 1236 (MD Fla 2012) (upholding law statewide under Section 2).

[17] See Lizette Alvarez, *Ruling Revives Florida Efforts to Police Voters*, NY Times A1 (Aug 7, 2013); Michael Cooper, *After Ruling, States Rush to Enact Voting Laws*, NY Times A9 (July 6, 2013).

Assume, then, that there is both a procedural and a substantive gap between Section 2 and Section 5. Assume, that is, that minority representation in the South in fact will be adversely affected by the nullification of Section 5. What are the implications for Congress and for the Court? If these institutions are unconcerned about minority political influence, of course, the only upshot is that the new status quo should be maintained. If the institutions *are* concerned, however, there exist several options for narrowing the Section 2–Section 5 gap. First, as the Court observed in *Shelby County*, "Congress may draft another formula based on current conditions."[18] Metrics such as the volume of successful Section 2 litigation, the prevalence of racially polarized voting, and the persistence of racially discriminatory attitudes all would result in most of the formerly covered areas once again becoming subject to preclearance. Second, Congress could amend Section 3 of the VRA[19] to make it easier to "bail in" jurisdictions that have committed voting rights violations. Section 3 applies at present only if a *constitutional* transgression has occurred; it could be revised to extend to findings of Section 2 liability as well.

Last, and most relevant to this article, Congress could amend Section 2 to make it more closely resemble the stricken Section 5. On the procedural side, Congress could increase the availability of preliminary injunctions and institute a burden-shifting framework under which the onus would switch to the jurisdiction once a plaintiff makes a preliminary showing of harm. With respect to vote dilution, Congress could expand the scope of Section 2's coverage so that it too applies to districts that are strangely shaped or whose minority populations are heterogeneous or below 50 percent in size. And with respect to vote denial, Congress could make disparate impact alone the standard for Section 2 liability. Moreover, at least on the substantive side, these changes also could be made by the Court. It is the Court that has exercised its interpretive discretion to limit Section 2 in the past. This same discretion could be used to broaden it in the future.

The article proceeds as follows. Parts I–III explore the contours of the Section 2–Section 5 gap in the contexts of procedure, vote dilution, and vote denial. All three include conceptual and empirical

---

[18] *Shelby Cty v Holder*, 133 S Ct 2612, 2631 (2013).
[19] 42 USC § 1973a(c).

assessments of the gap, while the latter two also evaluate the extent
to which the gap is likely to be exploited by political actors. Part
IV shifts from analysis to prescription. It presents a range of actions
that Congress and the Court could take to undo the effects of *Shelby
County*—to make Section 2 minus Section 5 once again equal to
zero.

I. Procedure

Beginning with procedure, then, the crucial difference between Section 2 and Section 5 is that the former authorizes a conventional cause of action while the latter establishes the extraordinary institution of preclearance. In this Part, I probe the
implications of this distinction, focusing on the kind and quantity
of policies that formerly would have been blocked but that now will
go into effect. I first explain, as a conceptual matter, why there are
likely to be policies that fall into the procedural gap between the
provisions. Some previously blocked policies now will not be challenged, some will be challenged but will be upheld, and some will
be struck down but only after they temporarily have come into
force. I then survey the available empirical evidence about the magnitude of the procedural gap. Some rough estimates are that private
parties would require at least twice their current resources to challenge all of the previously blocked policies, that 60 percent of policies that are challenged will be upheld, and that 95 percent of
policies that eventually are stricken still will go into effect temporarily. These figures must be taken with a grain of salt, but they
suggest that the impact of switching from Section 5 preclearance
to Section 2 litigation will be substantial.

A. CONCEPTUAL DIFFERENCES

In its current form, Section 2 creates a cause of action for parties
who allege that an electoral practice "results in a denial or abridgement of the right . . . to vote on account of race or color."[20] The
provision is violated "if, based on the totality of circumstances, it
is shown that" members of a protected racial or ethnic group "have
less opportunity than other members of the electorate to participate in the political process and to elect representatives of their

---

[20] Id § 1973(a).

THE SOUTH AFTER SHELBY COUNTY   63

choice."[21] In contrast, Section 5 bars covered jurisdictions from implementing any changes to their voting laws until the changes have been approved by either the DOJ or the U.S. District Court for the District of Columbia.[22] The DOJ has sixty days to object to a submission, while a three-judge panel of the federal court is convened if a jurisdiction chooses the judicial route for preclearance.[23] Under both the administrative and judicial routes, a jurisdiction must establish that its amendment "neither has the purpose nor will have the effect of denying or abridging the right to vote on account of race or color."[24] "Any discriminatory purpose" is prohibited by this language,[25] as is "diminishing the ability" of members of protected groups "to elect their preferred candidates of choice."[26]

The first important difference between Section 2 litigation and Section 5 preclearance is the allocation of the burden of proof. Under Section 2—as under most causes of action—"the initial burden of proving [a policy's] invalidity [is] squarely on the plaintiff's shoulders."[27] If the plaintiff cannot satisfy its burden, with respect to each statutory element, then the challenged policy comes into (or remains in) force. Under Section 5, on the other hand, "a jurisdiction seeking . . . preclearance must prove that the change is nondiscriminatory in purpose and effect."[28] If the jurisdiction cannot meet its burden, as to both purpose and effect, then its proposed policy cannot be implemented.

Sometimes the allocation of the burden is immaterial. When the illegality of a policy is sufficiently clear, a plaintiff can satisfy

---

[21] Id § 1973(b). According to the statute, minority groups' diminished opportunity to participate in the political process and to elect the representatives of their choice is evidence that "the political processes leading to nomination or election . . . are not equally open to participation" by the groups' members. Id.

[22] See id § 1973c(a).

[23] See id.

[24] Id.

[25] Id § 1973c(c).

[26] Id § 1973c(b); see also id § 1973c(d) ("The purpose of subsection (b) of this section is to protect the ability of such citizens to elect their preferred candidates of choice.").

[27] *Voinovich v Quilter*, 507 US 146, 155 (1993); see also 42 USC § 1973(b) (provision violated only "if . . . *it is shown*" that substantive standards have been satisfied (emphasis added)); S Rep No 97-417, at 27 (1982).

[28] *Branch v Smith*, 538 US 254, 263 (2003); see also *Georgia v United States*, 411 US 526, 538 (1973); Procedures for the Administration of Section 5 of the Voting Rights Act of 1965, as Amended ("DOJ Procedures"), 28 CFR § 51.52(a) ("The burden of proof is on a submitting authority . . . .").

its burden under Section 2 and a jurisdiction cannot meet its burden under Section 5. Likewise, when the lawfulness of a policy is
evident enough, a plaintiff cannot satisfy its burden under Section
2 and a jurisdiction can meet its burden under Section 5. But
sometimes the allocation of the burden is dispositive. There necessarily exist circumstances in which a plaintiff is unable to satisfy
its burden under Section 2 and, on the same facts, a jurisdiction
is unable to meet *its* burden under Section 5. In these close cases,
a policy takes effect if it is the subject of Section 2 litigation, but
is blocked if it is the subject of Section 5 preclearance.[29]

A second procedural difference between Section 2 and Section
5 is that, under the former, a policy typically remains in force
while it is being challenged, while under the latter, a policy never
goes into effect until it has been precleared.[30] The provisions have
opposite defaults, in other words, during the period *before* a decision on the merits has been reached. This distinction means that,
under Section 2, a policy that eventually is declared unlawful still
may be implemented for one or more election cycles, causing harm
to minorities in the meantime.[31] Under Section 5, in contrast, a
policy that is denied preclearance never may be put into operation,
not even for a single election.

However, this difference between the provisions dissolves whenever a Section 2 plaintiff manages to secure a preliminary injunction. In this case, as in a preclearance proceeding, a policy does
not go into effect until it explicitly has been deemed lawful. Of
course, preliminary injunctive relief is not easy to obtain, requiring, at an early stage of the litigation, a judicial finding that a
plaintiff's claim is likely to succeed.[32] But it *is* an available remedy,
and when it is granted, Section 2 and Section 5 partially converge.

---

[29] See Epstein and O'Halloran, 5 Election L J at 284–85 (cited in note 7) (observing
that there exist "proposals whose effects are unclear, so that they would be struck down
under Section 5, but survive under Section 2").

[30] See 42 USC § 1973c(a) ("[U]nless and until [preclearance is granted] no person shall
be denied the right to vote for failure to comply with such qualification, prerequisite,
standard, practice, or procedure.").

[31] See *Shelby Cty v Holder*, 679 F3d 848, 872 (DC Cir 2012), rev'd, 133 S Ct 2612 (2013)
("[D]uring the time it takes to litigate a section 2 action . . . proponents of a discriminatory
law may enjoy its benefits, potentially winning elections and gaining the advantage of
incumbency before the law is overturned.").

[32] See *Winter v NRDC, Inc.*, 555 US 7, 20 (2008). To issue a preliminary injunction, a
court also must find that the plaintiff is likely to suffer irreparable harm in the absence
of relief, that the balance of equities is in the plaintiff's favor, and that an injunction is
in the public interest. See id.

The final procedural differences between the provisions relate to the magnitude and allocation of the proceedings' costs.[33] Litigation under Section 2 is more expensive than administrative preclearance under Section 5. Section 2 plaintiffs must go through some or all of a lawsuit's familiar phases—discovery, summary judgment, trial, appeal, etc.—while jurisdictions covered by Section 5 need only submit a standardized set of forms to the DOJ.[34] Moreover, private parties are the usual plaintiffs in Section 2 litigation, while the DOJ is the key institution involved in Section 5 preclearance.[35] Private parties thus incur much of the cost of litigation under Section 2, while the DOJ shoulders much of the expense of preclearance under Section 5.

The upshot of these differences is that a proceeding's cost rises when it takes place under Section 2 rather than Section 5, and a larger proportion of this higher cost is borne by private parties. Now that preclearance is unavailable, then, private parties would require additional resources in order to challenge under Section 2 all of the policies that formerly would have been blocked under Section 5. If these resources are not forthcoming, then private parties will not be able to contest the full set of policies that previously would have been denied approval. They will need to pick and choose their battles, letting slide some number of policies that they believe (and the DOJ would have agreed) are discriminatory.

But some caveats must be appended to this analysis. First, *administrative* preclearance may be inexpensive, but *judicial* preclearance, which a covered jurisdiction always has the option to request,[36] is not. Full-dress litigation under Section 5 is similar in scope and complexity to a lawsuit under Section 2. Second, while private parties are the most common plaintiffs in Section 2 actions, the DOJ also has the authority to bring suit (and to intervene in

---

[33] One additional procedural difference is that Section 5 requires jurisdictions to notify the DOJ of each electoral change that they wish to make. Section 2 has no comparable disclosure requirement, meaning that sometimes private parties will not *know* about a policy that they would have challenged had they learned about it.

[34] See DOJ Procedures, 28 CFR §§ 5120–28 (detailing procedures for preclearance submission as well as requisite content).

[35] Of course, the jurisdictions whose policies are at issue are the same in either proceeding.

[36] See 42 USC § 1973c(a).

existing suits) under the provision.[37] Now that the DOJ no longer can block policies using Section 5, it can be expected to shift some of its resources to litigating Section 2 claims. Third, while the DOJ always was the indispensable institution under Section 5, private parties played an important role in preclearance proceedings as well. They commonly advised the DOJ in the administrative context and intervened in suits in the judicial context—both costs that no longer will be incurred after *Shelby County*. Lastly, private parties are entitled to the reimbursement of attorney and expert fees when they prevail in Section 2 suits.[38] Thus, in successful cases, the ultimate cost of such suits is not necessarily exorbitant (at least not to the plaintiffs).

One more caveat should be mentioned with respect to this entire Part. In discussing the procedural differences between Section 2 and Section 5, I implicitly am controlling for their differences in *substance*. Their substantive distinctions are addressed at length in the following two Parts, but here I am interested in investigating whether (and how large) a space exists between the provisions even if Section 2 vote dilution or denial is identical to Section 5 retrogression. Having identified the conceptual contrasts between the two kinds of proceedings, then, I turn next to the empirical evidence about the magnitude of the Section 2–Section 5 gap.

B. EMPIRICAL GAP

The empirical evidence, it must be conceded at the outset, is quite limited. Section 5 was in force alongside Section 2 until *Shelby County* was decided, so it is difficult to determine from historical data how many policies that were blocked by Section 5 would have gone into effect had only Section 2 been available to challenge them. The deterrent effect of Section 5—how many policies never were proposed at all because of the provision's existence—is even harder to quantify. Still, a wealth of information exists about the operation of Section 2 and Section 5 over the years, and it is possible to draw several inferences from this material about the size of the gap between the provisions. It also is possible to reach some tentative conclusions from the experiences

---

[37] See, for example, *United States v Blaine Cty*, 363 F3d 897 (9th Cir 2004) (Section 2 action brought by DOJ); *Brown v Bd of School Comm'rs*, 706 F2d 1103 (11th Cir 1983) (Section 2 action in which DOJ intervened).

[38] See 42 USC § 1973l(e).

of jurisdictions that were bailed in under Section 3 but that later were released from their preclearance obligations.

To begin with, a study by Ellen Katz found (and other studies later confirmed) that the success rate of Section 2 lawsuits in formerly covered jurisdictions was approximately 40 percent between 1982 and 2005.[39] This figure suggests that when private parties challenge policies that in the past would have been blocked by Section 5, they will lose a good deal of the time. The figure suggests, in other words, that Section 2's allocation of the burden to the plaintiff rather than the jurisdiction will be dispositive in a substantial number of cases. Of course, the policies that previously would have been blocked by Section 5 may differ in important respects from the policies that were analyzed in the retrospective Section 2 studies. In particular, the former policies may be more clearly discriminatory than the latter, in which case the success rate for plaintiffs challenging the former may be higher than 40 percent. Still, it seems unlikely that this figure will approach 100 percent, meaning that Section 2's burden allocation will be decisive with some frequency.[40]

Next, estimates vary as to how often preliminary injunctions are granted in Section 2 cases, but consistently are quite low. At the *Shelby County* oral argument, Solicitor General Donald Verrilli stated that such relief is obtained in "fewer than one-quarter of ultimately successful Section 2 suits."[41] Veteran Section 2 litigators

---

[39] See *Shelby Cty v Holder*, 679 F3d 848, 875 (DC Cir 2012), rev'd, 133 S Ct 2612 (2013) (citing 40.5 percent figure); Adam B. Cox and Thomas J. Miles, *Judging the Voting Rights Act*, 108 Colum L Rev 1, 54 appendix 1 (2008) (citing 39.4 percent figure); Katz et al, 39 U Mich J L Ref at 656 (cited in note 11) (citing 42.5 percent figure). The success rate was slightly higher, 45.9 percent, for challenges to *changes* in electoral practices—which are, of course, the only policies that can be blocked by Section 5. See Ellen Katz, *Not Like the South? Regional Variation and Political Participation Through the Lens of Section 2*, in Asa Henderson, ed, *Voting Rights Act Reauthorization of 2006: Perspectives on Democracy, Participation, and Power* 183, 221 table 8.6 (Berkeley, 2007) ("*VRA Reauthorization*"). The success rate also has been declining over time. See Cox and Miles, 108 Colum L Rev at 5, 14 (cited in note 39); Katz et al, 39 U Mich J L Ref at 656 (cited in note 11). And the success rate in *noncovered* jurisdictions, 32.2 percent, was lower than in covered jurisdictions despite the unavailability of Section 5 in the former areas. See Katz et al, 39 U Mich J L Ref at 656 (cited in note 11).

[40] An additional caveat is that the 40 percent figure stems from Section 2 suits that gave rise to *published* decisions. See Katz et al, 39 U Mich J L Ref at 652 (cited in note 11). I am not aware of any data on the success rate of Section 2 suits that did *not* generate published decisions. However, former DOJ voting rights attorney (and current law professor) Michael Pitts informs me that the latter rate almost certainly is higher because it would include the many consent decrees approved as a result of Section 2 litigation.

[41] Transcript of Oral Argument, *Shelby Cty v Holder*, 133 S Ct 2612 (No 12-96), *38.

Armand Defner and Gerry Hebert put the proportion at "less than 5%, and possibly quite lower."[42] And former DOJ official Robert Kengle recently testified that "the total *number* of such cases since 1982 is in the range of 10 to 15."[43] Whatever the exact figure may be, the implication is that preliminary injunctions rarely alter the Section 2 default during the period before a decision on the merits is reached. Most of the time, policies that never previously would have gone into effect due to Section 5 now will come into force upon enactment—even if they ultimately are struck down. The nominal availability of preliminary relief does not appreciably shrink the Section 2–Section 5 gap.[44]

Nor is the gap mitigated by the pace of Section 2 litigation. According to testimony by longtime civil rights attorney Anita Earls, it takes "at least two years" to advance a Section 2 action from filing to trial, and "[t]wo to five years is a rough average" of a suit's duration.[45] This period typically is long enough to encompass at least one and possibly multiple election cycles. It indicates that the absence of preliminary relief in most Section 2 cases will have real bite. Litigation will not move quickly enough to produce a decision on the merits before a policy that eventually is invalidated has harmed minorities for an election or two (and allowed incumbents to entrench themselves in office).[46]

Of course, the burden of proof and the availability of preliminary relief matter only if Section 2 litigation actually has com-

---

[42] Hebert and Defner, *More Observations on Shelby County, Alabama and the Supreme Court* (cited in note 12).

[43] Testimony of Robert A. Kengle before the House Judiciary Committee 11 (July 18, 2013) (emphasis added). The reasons why preliminary relief rarely is granted in Section 2 cases include the difficulty of amassing sufficient evidence at an early stage in the litigation, see Testimony of Prof. Justin Levitt before the US Senate Committee on the Judiciary 8 (July 17, 2013) ("Levitt Testimony"), and the aversion of many courts to enjoining elections if alternate remedies can be imposed in the future, see, for example, *Williams v Dallas*, 734 F Supp 1317, 1367 (ND Tex 1990).

[44] Though it should be noted again that the policies that formerly would have been blocked by Section 5 may differ materially from the policies that until now have given rise to Section 2 litigation. It is possible that preliminary injunctions will be granted with greater frequency when the former policies are challenged under Section 2.

[45] Testimony of Anita Earls before the House Judiciary Committee 63–64 (Oct 25, 2005); see also Brief of Joaquin Avila et al as Amici Curiae in Support of Respondents 22, *Shelby Cty v Holder*, 133 S Ct 2612 (No 12-96) ("Avila Brief").

[46] It may be the case, as Michael Carvin has testified, that Section 2 and Section 5 give rise to equally lengthy litigation in complicated redistricting cases. See Testimony of Michael A. Carvin before the US Senate Committee on the Judiciary 7 (July 17, 2013). But during the pendency of the litigation, the district plan typically goes into effect under Section 2 but does not under Section 5.

menced. But such litigation may *not* commence if private parties lack the resources to challenge policies that formerly would have been denied preclearance. Defner and Hebert have estimated that a Section 2 districting case "requires a minimum of hundreds of thousands of dollars,"[47] while Hebert separately has testified that "the cost . . . to bring a vote dilution case through trial and appeal[] runs close to a half a million dollars."[48] Similarly, in a 2005 study, the Federal Judicial Center found that voting rights suits entail 3.86 times more work than the median federal action, and rank sixth in intensity out of sixty-three case categories.[49] The unusual cost and complexity of Section 2 suits mean that private parties will not be able to bring them against all of the policies that previously were blocked by Section 5. As a group of Section 2 litigators has written, "The voting rights bar lacks the numbers and resources . . . to prosecute the . . . Section 2 lawsuits that would be necessary to block all the discriminatory changes that would be implemented without Section 5."[50]

What resources would the voting rights bar need to pursue all of these cases? One way to answer this question (albeit imprecisely) is to compare the volume of Section 2 and Section 5 activity in recent years. Under Section 2, then, there were 653 successful suits[51] in formerly covered jurisdictions between 1982 and 2005,

---

[47] J. Gerald Hebert and Armand Defner, *Shelby County, Alabama and the Supreme Court*, Campaign Legal Center Blog (Feb 28, 2013), online at http://www.clcblog.org/index.php ?option = com_content&view = article&id = 505:shelby-county-alabama-and-the-supreme-court.

[48] Avila Brief at 25 (cited in note 45); see also Levitt Testimony at 9 (cited in note 43) (reporting plaintiffs' fees and costs of $712,027.71 in a representative Section 2 case). In contrast, administrative preclearance usually costs between $1,000 and $5,000 for a major change, and between $500 and $1,000 for a minor one. See Avila Brief at 26 (cited in note 45); see also National Committee on the Voting Rights Act, *Protecting Minority Voters: The Voting Rights Act at Work 1982–2005*, at 55–56 (2006) ("*Protecting Minority Voters*") (noting much greater cost of Section 2 suit challenging at-large voting scheme for Charleston county council than Section 5 preclearance denial of identical policy proposal by Charleston county school board).

[49] Fed Judicial Ctr, 2003–2004 District Court Case-Weighting Study 5–6 table 1 (2005); see also *Shelby Cty v Holder*, 679 F3d 848, 872 (DC Cir 2012), rev'd, 133 S Ct 2612 (2013) (citing this study); *United States v Blaine Cty*, 363 F3d 897, 906 (9th Cir 2004) ("[S]ection 2 cases are some of the most difficult to litigate. . . .").

[50] Avila Brief at 3 (cited in note 45); see also id at 29 (noting that major civil rights groups such as the NAACP and the Lawyers' Committee for Civil Rights have only a handful of attorneys dedicated to voting rights).

[51] See *Shelby Cty*, 679 F3d at 868, 872; *Protecting Minority Voters* at 88 (cited in note 48).

resulting in 160 published decisions.[52] The total number of such suits is unknown, but has been estimated conservatively to be at least 800.[53] Under Section 5, over the same period, there were 626 preclearance denials by the DOJ and 25 preclearance denials by the courts.[54] Another 800 proposed policies were withdrawn or modified after the DOJ requested additional information about them.[55] Accordingly, the ratio of Section 2 to Section 5 activity in the South was between 1:1 and 1:2 over the last generation. Private parties would have had to have launched double to triple their actual number of Section 2 suits in order to have challenged all of the policies that were blocked by Section 5. This larger volume of litigation would have required double to triple the resources as well (assuming that the hypothetical suits would have been similar in cost to the actual suits).[56]

But recall from the above discussion that the DOJ also will be able to shoulder some of the heavier Section 2 burden in the wake of *Shelby County*.[57] Unfortunately, the DOJ's capacity to bring Section 2 suits is relatively limited. Its Voting Rights Section includes a range of demographers, historians, and other analysts who formerly worked on Section 5 matters—but "comparatively few attorneys" who now could turn their attention to Section 2.[58] No-

---

[52] See Katz et al, 39 U Mich J L Ref at 656 (cited in note 11).

[53] See id at 655. A single group, the ACLU Voting Rights Project, brought several hundred of these actions. See ACLU, *The Case for Extending and Amending the Voting Rights Act* 4 (2006).

[54] See *Shelby Cty*, 679 F3d at 866, 870–72; see also Luis Ricardo Fraga and Maria Lizet Ocampo, *More Information Requests and the Deterrent Effect of Section 5 of the Voting Rights Act*, in Henderson, ed, *VRA Reauthorization* 47, 49 (cited in note 39) (finding that DOJ preclearance denials prevented 2,282 individual changes from taking effect).

[55] See *Shelby Cty*, 679 F3d at 866, 872; Fraga and Ocampo, *More Information Requests and the Deterrent Effect of Section 5 of the Voting Rights Act* at 58 table 3.1 (cited in note 54) (identifying 854 such policies).

[56] If Section 5 had a significant deterrent effect in the past, then jurisdictions now may be expected to enact more policies that formerly would have been denied preclearance. In this case, private parties would need even more resources to challenge under Section 2 all of the policies that previously would have been blocked. In terms of actual dollar figures, there were approximately sixty policies per year that were blocked by Section 5 over the 1982–2005 period (including both preclearance denials and withdrawals following requests for more information). If each of these policies would have cost about $500,000 to litigate under Section 2, then the total price tag for challenging the policies under Section 2 rather than under Section 5 would have been roughly $30 million per year.

[57] See note 37 and accompanying text.

[58] Levitt Testimony at 11 (cited in note 43); see also Office of the Inspector General, *A Review of the Operations of the Voting Section of the Civil Rights Division* 9 (2013) ("*Inspector General Report*") (noting that number of attorneys in Voting Section has varied between thirty-one and forty-five in recent years).

tably, the section filed only eighteen Section 2 cases during the eight years of the Bush administration, and has initiated just four cases under the Obama administration (through 2012).[59] These numbers undoubtedly will rise as the section shifts its focus from Section 5 to Section 2, but, as Justin Levitt has observed, "'The Nation's Litigator' should not be expected to meet all of the new need . . . at least given staffing at the current order of magnitude."[60]

Since the DOJ will be unable to play the role of deus ex machina, private parties will need to make difficult choices as to which policies they will challenge (barring a large infusion of resources). The policies they seem least apt to contest are ones promulgated by local governments. In recent years, local practices accounted for more than 90 percent of preclearance denials under Section 5,[61] but only about 70 percent of Section 2 litigation.[62] Suits against local governments also are especially vulnerable to "[t]he unavailability of experienced voting rights attorneys and of sufficient financial resources," according to longtime Section 2 litigators.[63] High-profile statewide laws, such as district plans and franchise restrictions, thus are likely to be the target of future Section 2 litigation. The Section 2–Section 5 gap probably will be largest with respect to less salient local election law changes.

The final evidence about the size of the gap stems from the experiences of the two states, Arkansas and New Mexico, that have been bailed in under Section 3 of the VRA. Section 3 authorizes courts to impose a preclearance requirement almost identical to Section 5's on jurisdictions that are found to have violated the Fourteenth or Fifteenth Amendments.[64] The provision has been used only twice to bail in states, both times for the 1990 redis-

---

[59] See *Inspector General Report* at 24 (cited in note 58). Former DOJ voting rights attorney John Tanner also informs me that since 1976 the DOJ has launched only 112 Section 2 cases, or approximately three per year.

[60] Levitt Testimony at 11 (cited in note 43).

[61] See *Shelby Cty v Holder*, 679 F3d 848, 872 (DC Cir 2012), rev'd, 133 S Ct 2612 (2013); Pitts, 84 Neb L Rev at 612–13 (cited in note 8).

[62] See Cox and Miles, 108 Colum L Rev at 54 appendix 1 (cited in note 39); Pitts, 84 Neb L Rev at 616 (cited in note 8) ("[S]ection 2 cases are much less likely to be filed when it comes to redistricting in smaller jurisdictions. . . .").

[63] Avila Brief at 28 (cited in note 45); see also *Shelby Cty*, 679 F3d at 872 (noting that difficulty of bringing Section 2 claim is greatest "at the local level and in rural communities").

[64] See 42 USC § 1973a(c).

tricting cycle.[65] In both Arkansas and New Mexico, then, the Section 2 litigation in the 1980s that led to the imposition of preclearance was much costlier and lengthier than the proceedings in the following decade. In Arkansas, the *Jeffers* suit in the 1980s necessitated a trial[66] and resulted in the creation of eight new majority-minority districts,[67] while the state's district plans in the 1990s were precleared by the court with relatively little fuss.[68] Analogously, in New Mexico, the *Sanchez* suit in the 1980s led to sixteen districts being invalidated, primary elections being nullified, and federal examiners being deployed,[69] while the state's plans in the 1990s were precleared by the DOJ within four months.[70] This history confirms the much greater expense and complexity of Section 2 litigation relative to preclearance.[71]

Arkansas's experiences *since* the 1990 redistricting cycle—that is, after it was released from its preclearance obligations—also are illuminating. None of the state's district plans in the 2000s was challenged under Section 2, suggesting either that private parties lacked the resources to dispute them or that they were compliant with the VRA.[72] In the 2010s, private parties did bring a Section 2 action against Arkansas's state senate plan, alleging that one of its districts was "not an effective majority-minority district."[73] The

---

[65] See *Jeffers v Clinton*, 740 F Supp 585, 601–02 (ED Ark 1990) (invoking Section 3 for preclearance of majority-vote provisions and court's own equitable power for preclearance of district plans); *Sanchez v Anaya*, No 82-0067M (DNM Dec 17, 1984) (consent decree).

[66] See *Jeffers v Clinton*, 730 F Supp 196 (ED Ark 1989).

[67] See *Jeffers v Tucker*, 847 F Supp 655, 657 (ED Ark 1994).

[68] See id (noting that certain plaintiffs settled with state and upholding state's plan).

[69] See New Mexico Legislative Council Service, *A Guide to State and Congressional Redistricting in New Mexico* 10–11 (2001).

[70] See id at 11–12. The DOJ objected to the original state senate plan, but within five weeks the legislature had passed, and the DOJ had approved, a new plan. See id.

[71] Though the 1980 redistricting cycle also may have been especially laborious for Arkansas and New Mexico because the critical 1982 amendments to Section 2 were passed after the states' districts already had been drawn. Less costly and lengthy litigation might have ensued had the states known in advance about the legal standard with which they later were forced to comply.

[72] See *2000s Redistricting Case Summaries*, Nat'l Conf. of State Legislatures, online at http://www.senate.mn/departments/scr/redist/redsum2000/redsum2000.htm ("*2000s Case Summaries*"). The latter explanation is more likely since the numbers of majority-minority districts in Arkansas's state legislative plans did not decrease between the 1990s and the 2000s.

[73] *Jeffers v Beebe*, 895 F Supp 2d 920, 929 (ED Ark 2012). The district in question had a black voting-age population of 52.8 percent, which according to the plaintiffs' expert

court rejected this claim even though it seemed to concede that the district did not "provide minority voters . . . with the ability to elect candidates of their choice."[74] The court rejected the claim, that is, while apparently admitting that the state senate plan was retrogressive and thus would have violated Section 5. Also of note, private parties did not challenge Arkansas's 2010s state house plan even though it reduced by one the number of majority-minority districts.[75] This plan likely would have been denied preclearance too, but it escaped judicial review altogether thanks to the expiration of the state's Section 3 coverage.

Unfortunately for present purposes, New Mexico's elected branches deadlocked in both the 2000s and the 2010s, forcing courts to design all of the state's districts.[76] While Section 2 supplied one of the principles on the basis of which the districts were shaped, it makes little sense to probe the Section 2–Section 5 gap when courts, not political actors, are the line-drawers. Arkansas's recent history also is suggestive but hardly conclusive; in particular, in the absence of an actual denial of preclearance, it is very difficult to determine whether a district plan in fact is retrogressive. Still, this Section 3 analysis is consistent with all of the other empirical evidence presented in this section about the procedural space between Section 2 and Section 5. If anything, the Section 3 findings are especially compelling because they alone are based on the experiences of jurisdictions that were subjected to—but then released from—preclearance.

II. Vote Dilution

It is no surprise that the Arkansas and New Mexico cases both involved claims of vote dilution arising from redistricting. While the VRA prohibits both vote dilution and vote denial, the former has accounted for the vast majority of activity under both

---

was insufficient to provide African Americans with an equal opportunity to elect their preferred candidate. See id at 932–33.

[74] Id at 933.

[75] The data on the composition of Arkansas's state legislative districts are on file with the author.

[76] See *2000s Case Summaries* (cited in note 72); Justin Levitt, *Litigation in the 2010 Cycle—New Mexico*, All About Redistricting, online at http://redistricting.lls.edu/cases-NM.php#NM.

Section 2 and Section 5.[77] It therefore is the first substantive area to which I turn (and the area to which I devote more attention). I begin by describing the differences between the districts to which Section 2 applies and those protected by Section 5. Thanks to a series of narrowing interpretations by the Supreme Court, Section 2 does not extend to districts that are bizarrely shaped or whose minority populations are highly heterogeneous or below 50 percent in size. Section 5, in contrast, likely shields districts with all of these characteristics.

Next, I use a range of empirical techniques to estimate the *number* of existing districts that formerly were protected by Section 5 but now are beyond the scope of Section 2. No such analysis yet has been conducted even though it is vital to determining the practical impact of *Shelby County*. According to my calculations, only a handful of current districts are so noncompact, or have minority populations that are so small, that they are uncovered by Section 2. However, many more current districts contain sufficiently heterogeneous minority populations that they now may be dismantled without running afoul of the provision.

Lastly, I assess the likelihood, as a political matter, that the districts that populate the Section 2–Section 5 gap will be eliminated. Both parties often will have strong incentives to preserve these districts, Republicans because of partisan advantage and Democrats due to pressure from minority groups. But both parties sometimes will find it beneficial to jettison previously insulated districts. Republicans may be able to win a larger proportion of seats by concentrating minorities into a smaller number of superpacked districts. And Democrats may be able to optimize their electoral position by spreading minorities more evenly across a district map.

A. CONCEPTUAL DIFFERENCES

In its first decision interpreting the current text of Section 2,

[77] See Cox and Miles, 108 Colum L Rev at 11 (cited in note 39) (noting that Section 2 cases are "dominated by decisions involving challenges to at-large elections . . . and challenges to reapportionment plans"); Katz et al, 39 U Mich J L Ref at 656 (cited in note 11) (same); Peyton McCrary et al, *The Law of Preclearance: Enforcing Section 5*, in Epstein et al, eds, *The Future of the Voting Rights Act* 20, 25 (cited in note 8); Rick Pildes and Dan Tokaji, *What Did VRA Preclearance Actually Do?: The Gap Between Perception and Reality*, Election Law Blog (Aug 19, 2013), online at http://electionlawblog.org/?p=54521 ("Redistricting changes generated vastly more objections [under Section 5] than any other category. . . .").

Thornburg v Gingles,[78] the Supreme Court set forth the doctrinal standard for claims of vote dilution arising from redistricting. Initially, a minority group must comply with three preconditions: (1) it must be "sufficiently large and geographically compact to constitute a majority in a single-member district"; (2) it must be "politically cohesive"; and (3) "the white majority [must] vote[] sufficiently as a bloc to enable it . . . usually to defeat the minority's preferred candidate."[79] If these threshold criteria are satisfied, a court proceeds to an analysis of the totality of the circumstances. The most important elements of this analysis are the nine factors identified by the Senate report that accompanied Congress's amendments to Section 2 in 1982,[80] as well as the proportionality of a minority group's existing representation.[81] In order to prevail, a group also must show that there exists a suitable benchmark with which the challenged policy may be compared.[82] A group must show as well that at least one *additional* district could be created in which the group would be able to elect the candidate of its choice.[83]

Section 5, in contrast, almost never requires additional minority-ability (i.e., "ability"[84]) districts to be drawn.[85] Rather, the provision prohibits any *worsening* of the electoral position of minor-

---

[78] 478 US 30 (1986); see also *Growe v Emison*, 507 US 25, 40–41 (1993) (applying the *Gingles* framework to single-member districts).

[79] *Thornburg*, 478 US at 50–51.

[80] See id at 36–37, 44–45. These factors include any history of official discrimination, the extent of racial polarization in voting, the use of election rules that overly advantage the majority, access to the candidate slating process, the impact of discrimination on minorities' political participation, the use of racial appeals in campaigns, minorities' prior success in winning office, elected officials' responsiveness to minority concerns, and the tenuousness of a jurisdiction's justification for a policy. See id.

[81] See *Johnson v De Grandy*, 512 US 997, 1000 (1994).

[82] See *Holder v Hall*, 512 US 874, 880 (1994).

[83] See *LULAC v Perry*, 548 US 399, 437 (2006); *Johnson*, 512 US at 1008 ("[T]he first *Gingles* condition requires the possibility of creating more than the existing number of [minority-opportunity districts]. . . .").

[84] For the sake of simplicity, I use the term "ability districts" to refer to districts covered by both Section 2 and Section 5. But the term "opportunity districts" technically is more accurate for Section 2-covered districts since the provision refers to the "opportunity" rather than the "ability" to elect.

[85] The only exceptions are if the failure to draw additional ability districts establishes discriminatory intent or if a jurisdiction must draw a larger number of districts (due to population growth, for example). See *Texas v United States*, 887 F Supp 2d 133, 156–59 (DDC 2012), vac'd, 133 S Ct 2885 (2013) (*Texas II*); see also note 129 (describing earlier period in which DOJ treated Section 2 violations as grounds for denying preclearance).

ities, that is, retrogression.[86] Retrogression is determined by examining a district plan in its entirety, not by assessing individual districts in isolation.[87] A plan is deemed retrogressive if it reduces, relative to the plan previously in effect, the total number of districts in which minorities are able to elect the candidate of their choice.[88] A plan also is unlawful under Section 5 if it is motivated by any kind of discriminatory intent.[89]

At first blush, Section 2 and Section 5 would seem to have very similar coverage with respect to the elimination of an existing ability district. Under Section 2, a minority group easily would be able to show that an additional such district could be drawn because an additional such district *existed* before it was dismantled. Likewise, under Section 5, the erasure of a district in which minorities previously were able to elect their preferred candidate is the very definition of retrogression. The statutory text confirms the apparent overlap of the two provisions. Section 2 forbids district plans that give minority members "less opportunity . . . to elect representatives of their choice,"[90] while Section 5 bans plans that "diminish[] the ability" of minorities "to elect their preferred candidates of choice."[91] It would take no interpretive gymnastics to construe these passages identically.

But this is not the path the Court has taken. Instead, in a series of decisions spanning two decades, the Court repeatedly has narrowed the scope of Section 2. A clear substantive gap now exists between Section 2 and Section 5, even though neither the provisions' language nor their logic requires that there be such a gap. Below I lay out the three principal ways in which Section 2 and

---

[86] See *Beer v United States*, 425 US 130, 141 (1976).

[87] See *Georgia v Ashcroft*, 539 US 461, 479 (2003).

[88] See *Texas v United States*, 831 F Supp 2d 244, 262 (DDC 2011) (*Texas I*) (noting that Section 5 inquiry "requires identifying districts in which minority citizens enjoy an existing ability to elect and comparing the number of such districts in the benchmark to the number of such districts in a proposed plan"). Under the approach adopted by the Supreme Court in *Georgia*, but rejected by Congress in its 2006 amendments, the retrogression inquiry also would have required consideration of the number of minority *influence* districts, the ability of minorities to participate in the political process, and minorities' legislative power. See *Georgia*, 539 US at 479–85.

[89] See *Texas II*, 887 F Supp 2d at 151–52. Prior to its 2006 amendments, Section 5 had been interpreted to prohibit only *retrogressive* intent. See *Reno v Bossier Parish Sch Bd*, 528 US 320, 328 (2000).

[90] 42 USC § 1973(b).

[91] Id § 1973c(b).

Section 5 diverge in their coverage. These distinctions have not previously been identified, but together they mean that certain districts that used to be shielded by Section 5 now will be bereft of any legal protection.

1. *Geographic compactness.* First, in a line of cases in the 1990s involving allegations that districts were unconstitutional racial gerrymanders, the Court held that highly noncompact districts are never required by Section 2. If minority members are geographically distributed in such a way that only a bizarre-looking district can enclose enough of them to enable the election of their preferred candidate, then there is no liability under the provision. Even if minorities reside in a manner that permits a reasonably compact ability district to be drawn (in which case there is liability), it is an impermissible remedy to create a district that is too strangely shaped.[92] The Court thus declared that a district that tracked highway I-85 through North Carolina "could not remedy any potential § 2 violation."[93] "No one looking at [the district] could reasonably suggest that the district contains a 'geographically compact' population of any race."[94] Similarly, the Court rejected a Texas district that "reaches out to grab small and apparently isolated minority communities."[95] "These characteristics defeat any claim that the district[]" was necessitated by Section 2.[96]

Under Section 5, on the other hand, compactness is largely irrelevant to the dispositive question: whether a district's minority residents possess the ability to elect the candidate of their choice. Whether minorities possess this ability depends on their number,

---

[92] See *Bush v Vera*, 517 US 952, 979 (1996) ("If, because of the dispersion of the minority population, a reasonably compact majority-minority district cannot be created, § 2 does not require a majority-minority district; if a reasonably compact district can be created, nothing in § 2 requires the race-based creation of a district that is far from compact.").

[93] *Shaw v Hunt*, 517 US 899, 916 (1996).

[94] Id.

[95] *Bush*, 517 US at 979.

[96] Id. The case law is ambiguous as to whether it is the compactness of the *district* or of the *minority population* that is relevant under Section 2. The passages from *Bush* and *Shaw* suggest that it is district compactness that matters. This also has been the conclusion of lower courts adjudicating Section 2 cases. See Katz et al, 39 U Mich J L Ref at 662–63 (cited in note 11). However, the original language in *Gingles* that gave rise to the compactness requirement asks whether "the *minority group* . . . is sufficiently . . . geographically compact." *Thornburg v Gingles*, 478 US 30, 50 (1986) (emphasis added). Justice Kennedy also has repeatedly expressed his view that "[t]he first *Gingles* condition refers to the compactness of the minority population, not to the compactness of the contested district." *Bush*, 517 US at 997 (Kennedy, J, concurring); see also *LULAC v Perry*, 548 US 399, 432–33 (2006).

turnout, and political cohesion, but it is not a function of the odd-ness of a district's shape. Not surprisingly, compactness has played no role in the Court's Section 5 decisions (nor in those of the lower courts). It should be noted, however, that during the 2006 debate over Section 5's reauthorization, several Republican senators argued that the goal of the amended provision was to "prevent states from dismantling . . . 'geographically compact majority-minority dis-tricts.'"[97] The DOJ also has stated that one of the factors it considers in assessing retrogression is the "geographic compactness of a ju-risdiction's minority population."[98] These views have not been em-braced by the case law, but they do appear in the legislative history and agency guidance.

The upshot is that when a highly noncompact ability district is eliminated, there is retrogression under Section 5, but there (most likely) is no violation of Section 2. The district's strange shape makes no difference in the Section 5 inquiry, but it clearly means that the district is an invalid Section 2 remedy, and it implies as well that no reasonably compact district could be drawn in the area. Accordingly, in the wake of *Shelby County*, most bizarre-looking ability districts in the South may be dismantled with legal impunity. How many such districts exist is a question to which I turn in Part II.B.

2. *Minority heterogeneity.* The second way in which the Court has constricted the scope of Section 2 is by requiring that a district not combine overly dissimilar minority communities. In the 2006 case of *LULAC v Perry*, the Court held that Texas violated the provision when it disbanded an ability district near Laredo that contained a "cohesive" Latino population with "an efficacious po-litical identity."[99] Had the district *not* contained such a unified Latino community, it likely would not have received Section 2 protection—a claim that can be made confidently thanks to the Court's treatment of the remedial district that Texas created to

---

[97] S Rep No 109-295, at 19 (2006) (quoting testimony of attorney Anne Lewis); see also id at 19 (claiming that new Section 5 language was "designed to prevent legislators from intentionally '"cracking"' or '"fragmenting' geographically compact minority voting communities" (quoting testimony of NAACP president Theodore Shaw)).

[98] Guidance Concerning Redistricting Under Section 5 of the Voting Rights Act, 76 Fed Reg 7470, 7471 (Feb 9, 2011).

[99] 548 US 399, 435 (2006); see also id (noting that "there has been no contention that different pockets of the Latino population in [the district] have divergent needs and in-terests").

compensate for its elimination of the Laredo-area district. The remedial district enclosed a clear Latino majority, but nevertheless was rejected by the Court because it merged "Latino communities . . . [with] divergent needs and interests owing to differences in socio-economic status."[100] As the Court put it, "[t]here is no basis to believe a district that combines two farflung segments of a racial group with disparate interests provides the opportunity that § 2 requires."[101]

Following *LULAC*, it appears that there is no liability under Section 2 when the relevant minority population is highly "spatially diverse"[102] or "culturally non-compact."[103] It also appears that a district including such a population is not a valid Section 2 remedy. This is the case, at least, when the minority groups at issue are both socioeconomically dissimilar and geographically separated.[104] However, the degree of uncertainty associated with this articulation of the legal standard is unusually high. *LULAC* remains the only Supreme Court case addressing this aspect of Section 2 doctrine, and the lower courts have yet to confront many *LULAC*-based defenses to otherwise valid Section 2 claims.[105]

---

[100] Id at 424 (citations and internal quotation marks omitted).

[101] Id at 433.

[102] This is the term I have used in earlier work to describe geographic entities (such as districts) whose spatial subunits are highly heterogeneous. See Nicholas O. Stephanopoulos, *Spatial Diversity*, 125 Harv L Rev 1905, 1912–17 (2012); see also id at 1929–33 (arguing that spatial homogeneity has been an implicit Section 2 requirement for decades).

[103] See Daniel R. Ortiz, *Cultural Compactness*, 105 Mich L Rev First Impressions 48, 50 (2006) ("If the Court were to require that plaintiffs establish . . . cultural compactness, Section 2 claims would be much more difficult."); Richard H. Pildes, *The Decline of Legally Mandated Minority Representation*, 68 Ohio St L J 1139, 1146 (2007) (observing that after *LULAC* "the Act is not violated . . . unless an election district can be created . . . [that is] geographically and culturally compact").

[104] See *LULAC*, 548 US at 435 ("We emphasize it is the enormous geographical distance separating the Austin and Mexican-border communities, coupled with the disparate needs and interests of these populations—not either factor alone—that renders District 25 noncompact for § 2 purposes.").

[105] Lower-court cases that have addressed the heterogeneity of minority populations under Section 2 include *Ga State Conf. of NAACP v Fayette Cty Bd of Comm'rs*, 950 F Supp 2d 1294, 1310 (ND Ga 2013) (finding that African Americans in two nearby towns "share common socioeconomic and political concerns"), *Perez v Texas*, 891 F Supp 2d 808, 836 (WD Tex 2012) (rejecting proposed district that was "nearly identical" to district rejected in *LULAC*), *Fletcher v Lamone*, 831 F Supp 2d 887, 899 (D Md 2011) (rejecting proposed district that combined distinct African American communities in Baltimore and Washington, DC, suburbs), and *Benavidez v City of Irving*, 638 F Supp 2d 709, 722 (ND Tex 2009) (finding that although district contained Hispanic neighborhood that "may differ in some demographic characteristics from the core area," neighborhood was "geographically close to that core" and thus district was valid Section 2 remedy).

Under Section 5, in contrast, the heterogeneity of a district's minority population is extraneous to whether the population has the ability to elect the candidate of its choice. If the population has this ability, then the district that contains it is protected under Section 5—no matter how similar or dissimilar the minority members may be. As with geographic compactness, there is no hint in the Section 5 case law that retrogression is permissible if a district happens to combine disparate minority communities. But as with compactness, Republican senators argued in 2006 that the retrogression inquiry *should* take this factor into account. According to the Senate report they penned, "the [new Section 5] language seeks to protect *naturally occurring* majority-minority districts" that correspond to distinct "'minority voting communities.'"[106] This position has not been adopted by any judicial decision—though the Supreme Court, of course, never had the opportunity to consider how the revised Section 5 should be applied to districts containing heterogeneous minority populations.

The consequence is that when a district that joins dissimilar minority communities is eliminated, retrogression occurs under Section 5 but Section 2 (probably) is not breached. The heterogeneity of the district's minority population is immaterial under Section 5, but it indicates that the district is not a permissible Section 2 remedy, and it also suggests that no district containing a sufficiently homogeneous population could be created in the region. Thanks to *Shelby County*, then, most southern districts that merge disparate minority groups now lawfully may be dismantled. The number of these districts, again, is the subject of Part II.B.

3. *Population size.* The final limitation the Court has imposed on Section 2 involves the size of minority groups. In the 2009 case of *Bartlett v Strickland*, the Court held that in order for there to be liability under the provision, it must be possible to create an additional district in which minority members make up a *majority* of the population.[107] "The special significance . . . of a majority means it is a special wrong when a minority group has 50 percent or more of the voting population and . . . is not put into

---

[106] S Rep No 109-295, at 19 (2006) (emphasis added) (quoting testimony of NAACP president Theodore Shaw); see also Nathaniel Persily, *The Promise and Pitfalls of the New Voting Rights Act*, 117 Yale L J 174, 239 (2007) (flagging Senate report's references to "naturally occurring" majority-minority districts).

[107] 556 US 1, 18–19 (2009).

a district."[108] The Court hinted, however, that districts with minority populations below 50 percent might be relevant on the
remedial side of the Section 2 analysis. "States can—and in proper
cases should—defend against alleged § 2 violations by pointing to
. . . effective crossover districts."[109] After *Bartlett*, it is clear that
plaintiffs must prove that another majority-minority district could
be drawn, but it is uncertain whether a majority-minority district
is the only permissible remedy once liability has been established.

Under Section 5, on the other hand, there is little doubt that
districts with minority populations below 50 percent are protected
if these populations in fact are able (with crossover support from
white voters) to elect their preferred candidates. In the 2003 case
of *Georgia v Ashcroft*, interpreting the preamendment version of
Section 5, the Court held that the provision extends to "coalitions
of voters who together will help to achieve the electoral aspirations
of the minority group."[110] Similarly, the House report that accompanied Section 5's 2006 reauthorization stated that it applies
to "[v]oting changes that leave a minority group less able to elect
a preferred candidate of choice, either directly or when coalesced
with other voters."[111] And in the lone case construing the amended
version of Section 5 in the vote-dilution context, the court explicitly ruled that "[s]ince . . . crossover districts provide minority
groups the ability to elect a preferred candidate, they must be
recognized as ability districts in a Section 5 analysis."[112] However,
the Republican-drafted Senate report contended that the provision's new language "would *not* lock into place [crossover] districts."[113]

This means, once again, that when an ability district with a
minority population below 50 percent is eliminated, there is retro-

---

[108] Id at 19.

[109] Id at 24.

[110] 539 US 461, 480 (2003); see also id at 484 (noting that "the addition or subtraction
of coalitional districts is relevant to the § 5 inquiry"); id at 492 (Souter, J, dissenting)
(agreeing that Section 5 extends to "coalition districts, in which minorities are in fact
shown to have a similar opportunity when joined by predictably supportive nonminority
voters").

[111] HR Rep No 109-478, at 71 (2006).

[112] *Texas v United States*, 831 F Supp 2d 244, 267–68 (DDC 2011); see also Guidance
Concerning Redistricting Under Section 5 of the Voting Rights Act, 76 Fed Reg 7470,
7471 (Feb 9, 2011) ("[T]he Attorney General does not rely on any predetermined or fixed
demographic percentages at any point in the [Section 5] assessment.").

[113] S Rep No 109-295, at 21 (2006).

gression under Section 5 but there (likely) is no violation of Section 2. The smaller proportion of minority members is irrelevant under Section 5—as long as it is sufficient to enable the election of their preferred candidate—but it suggests that no majority-minority district can be drawn in the area, in which case there can be no Section 2 liability. How many ability districts exist in the South that are *not* majority-minority districts is the final empirical issue that I investigate in Part II.B.

4. *Further twists.* But before turning to the empirical analysis it is important to make three more points about the relationship between Section 2 and Section 5 in the vote-dilution context. First, while until now I have stressed the provisions' distinctions, they also share a number of commonalities, including in areas where they could have been construed differently. For example, majority-minority and crossover districts do not exhaust the kinds of constituencies to which the VRA might apply. The district taxonomy also includes coalition districts, in which different minority groups join together to elect their mutually preferred candidate;[114] and influence districts, in which the minority population cannot elect the candidate of its choice, but *can* exert some sway over who is elected and what she does once in office.[115] Both Section 2 and Section 5 have been interpreted to apply to coalition districts (at least when the combined size of the minority groups is greater than 50 percent in the case of Section 2).[116] And both Section 2 and Section 5 have been interpreted not to apply to influence districts (although Section 5 did extend to them prior to its 2006 revision).[117]

Analogously, both Section 2 and Section 5 are violated when it is established that the intent underlying a district plan is racially

---

[114] See *Bartlett*, 556 US at 13.

[115] See id.

[116] See *Texas I*, 831 F Supp 2d at 268 (recognizing that under Section 5 "coalition districts are ability districts"); Katz et al, 39 U Mich J L Ref at 661 (cited in note 11) (finding that under Section 2 "[m]ost courts" regard coalition-district claims as "cognizable"). The Supreme Court has not explicitly addressed the status of coalition districts under Section 2. See *Bartlett*, 556 US at 13–14. The Republican-drafted Senate report also opposed the extension of Section 5 to coalition districts. See S Rep No 109-295, at 21 (2006).

[117] See *LULAC v Perry*, 548 US 399, 446 (2006) (holding that "the lack of [influence] districts cannot establish a § 2 violation"); *Texas I*, 831 F Supp 2d at 251 (observing that, in amending Section 5, "Congress sought to make clear that it was not enough that a redistricting plan gave minority voters 'influence'"). But see *Georgia v Ashcroft*, 539 US 461, 482–83 (2003) (holding prior to 2006 reauthorization that "a court must examine whether a new plan adds or subtracts 'influence districts'").

discriminatory. The current text of Section 5 declares outright that the provision forbids "any discriminatory purpose."[118] The role of motive in Section 2 analysis is less clear, but most lower courts have concluded that the provision is offended by *both* discriminatory intent and discriminatory results.[119] Notably, the Senate report that accompanied the 1982 amendments to Section 2 stated that "plaintiffs must either prove such intent, or, alternatively, must show" the presence of unequal effects.[120] Congress's objective in revising Section 2 was to clarify that liability could stem from disparate impact, but it had no intention of precluding claims based on invidious motivation.

Furthermore, the array of additional elements that must be demonstrated to prevail on a Section 2 claim—minority political cohesion, racial polarization in voting, the nine Senate factors, a lack of proportional representation, and the existence of a suitable policy benchmark[121]—do not meaningfully distinguish the provision from Section 5. Minority cohesion and racial polarization are not formally part of the Section 5 inquiry, but in practice they must be shown in order to prove that a minority population has the ability to elect its preferred candidate. "[A] court addressing a proposed voting plan under Section 5 must determine whether there is cohesive voting among minorities and whether minority/ White polarization is present in the jurisdiction submitting the plan."[122] Likewise, the Senate factors play no role in the Section 5 analysis, either formally or functionally, but they typically are

---

[118] 42 USC § 1973c(c); see also note 89 (explaining how this language reversed an earlier Court interpretation).

[119] See, for example, *United States v Brown*, 561 F3d 420, 432–33 (5th Cir 2009); *Cousin v McWherter*, 46 F3d 568, 572 (6th Cir 1995); *Nipper v Smith*, 39 F3d 1494, 1520 (11th Cir 1994) (en banc) ("[A] plaintiff . . . may demonstrate a [Section 2] violation by proving *either*: (1) the subjective discriminatory motive of legislators or other relevant officials; *or* (2) [discriminatory results].").

[120] S Rep No 97-417, at 107–08 (1982).

[121] See notes 78–83 and accompanying text (setting forth elements of Section 2 claim).

[122] *Texas v United States*, 831 F Supp 2d 244, 262 (DDC 2011). Moreover, even if racial polarization were relevant to Section 2 but not to Section 5, it remains rampant in most of the formerly covered jurisdictions, and thus could be established easily in most cases. See HR Rep No 109-478, at 34 (2006) (citing testimony that "the degree of racially polarized voting in the South is increasing, not decreasing" and is "in certain ways re-creating the segregated system of the Old South"); *Protecting Minority Voters* at 89–97 (cited in note 48); Stephen Ansolabehere et al, *Race, Region, and Vote Choice in the 2008 Election: Implications for the Future of the Voting Rights Act*, 123 Harv L Rev 1385, 1403, 1415–16, 1424 (2010) (reporting high and growing levels of polarization in formerly covered areas).

easy to establish in Section 2 cases in formerly covered areas. Most of the factors relate to a jurisdiction's history of discrimination, and the formerly covered areas include most of the jurisdictions with the most egregious such histories.[123]

As for a lack of proportional representation, it too is not a requirement under Section 5, but it too can be demonstrated without difficulty in a Section 2 suit. Both African Americans and Hispanics are currently underrepresented in the state legislatures and congressional delegations of every formerly covered state.[124] Lastly, a suitable benchmark with which to compare a challenged policy does not exist in certain kinds of vote-dilution cases, such as municipal annexations and objections to local governance structures.[125] But there is no benchmark problem in the redistricting context, in which the alternative district plan proposed by a Section 2 plaintiff always may be compared to the plan currently in effect.[126]

The second point about the relationship between Section 2 and Section 5 is that it is both dynamic and ambiguous. The relationship is dynamic because it shifts whenever the Court interprets the provisions, Congress amends them, or the DOJ chooses how to enforce them. For instance, the provisions' gap was smaller with respect to redistricting before the Court began limiting the scope of Section 2 in the 1990s.[127] Similarly, the gap was larger

---

[123] See Katz et al, 39 U Mich J L Ref at 696 (cited in note 11) (noting that under Section 2 "courts in Southern states assumed or outlined a long local and state history of official discrimination"); Michael J. Pitts, *Redistricting and Discriminatory Purpose*, 59 Am U L Rev 1575, 1602 (2010) (observing that "jurisdictions covered by Section 5 were subjected to the preclearance requirement in the first place because prima facie evidence of voting-related discrimination existed"); see also Adam B. Cox and Thomas J. Miles, *Judicial Ideology and the Transformation of Voting Rights*, 75 U Chi L Rev 1493, 1519–20 (2008) (describing "conventional wisdom that satisfaction of the *Gingles* factors correlates strongly with liability"); Katz et al, 39 U Mich J L Ref at 660 (cited in note 11) (finding that 57 of 68 opinions that ruled in minority group's favor as to *Gingles* preconditions also ruled in its favor as to ultimate liability).

[124] See appendix table A1; see also Nicholas O. Stephanopoulos, *Our Electoral Exceptionalism*, 80 U Chi L Rev 769, 834 (2013) (describing underrepresentation of minority groups throughout country).

[125] See *Holder v Hall*, 512 US 874, 884 (1994).

[126] See id at 880 (observing that "[i]n certain cases, the benchmark for comparison in a § 2 dilution suit is obvious"); *Thornburg v Gingles*, 478 US 30, 50 n 17 (1986) (noting that "[t]he single-member district is generally the appropriate standard" in redistricting cases).

[127] Conversely, the Court shrank the gap when it made Section 5 more difficult to violate in *Reno v Bossier Parish Sch. Bd*, 528 US 320, 328 (2000) (holding that only a retrogressive purpose violates Section 5), and *Georgia v Ashcroft*, 539 US 461, 482–85 (2003) (holding

before Congress amended Section 2 in 1982 to clarify that it could be violated by discriminatory results even in the absence of discriminatory intent.[128] The gap was smaller as well when, in the 1990s, the DOJ treated violations of Section 2 as grounds to deny preclearance under Section 5.[129] And had the Court responded to Section 5's reauthorization by construing the provision narrowly, rather than by striking it down, the gap again would have shrunk.

The relationship between the provisions also is ambiguous because their precise coverage is uncertain. A generation after its current text was adopted, it remains unclear whether Section 2 allows crossover districts to be considered as remedies, whether it extends to coalition districts, how it governs claims based solely on discriminatory intent, and how the homogeneity of minority groups is to be determined.[130] As Christopher Elmendorf has remarked, "the Supreme Court has failed to resolve basic conceptual questions about what constitutes an injury within the meaning of the statute."[131] If anything, the scope of Section 5 is even hazier. Before the 2006 amendments to the provision, the Court addressed its application to statewide redistricting only once, in a decision that Congress partially reversed just three years later.[132] Since 2006, the Court has not expounded at all on the meaning of Section 5, and only a single lower court has explored how it relates to redistricting.[133] And congressional intent on the subject is more difficult than usual to ascertain, thanks to dueling House and Sen-

---

that ability districts may be eliminated if their elimination is offset by new influence districts or other gains for minorities). See McCrary et al, *The Law of Preclearance* at 27 (cited in note 77) (describing sharp decline in preclearance denials in wake of *Bossier Parish II*); Persily, 117 Yale L J at 199–200 (cited in note 106) (same).

[128] And when Congress overturned *Bossier Parish II* and *Georgia* in 2006, it widened the gap by making Section 5 easier to violate.

[129] See Bruce E. Cain and Karin MacDonald, *Voting Rights Act Enforcement: Navigating Between High and Low Expectations*, in Epstein et al, eds, *The Future of the Voting Rights Act* 125, 132 (cited in note 8) (commenting that during this period "the distinction between section 2 and section 5 standards blurred"); see also *Reno v Bossier Parish Sch. Bd*, 520 US 471, 480–85 (1997) (*Bossier Parish I*) (rejecting this DOJ interpretation of Section 5).

[130] See Parts II.A.1–3.

[131] Christopher S. Elmendorf, *Making Sense of Section 2: Of Biased Votes, Unconstitutional Elections, and Common Law Statutes*, 160 U Pa L Rev 377, 394 (2012).

[132] This decision, of course, was *Georgia v Ashcroft*. See also Persily, 117 Yale L J at 234 (cited in note 106) (noting that "there is disagreement about what the standard [before *Georgia*] was").

[133] See *Texas v United States*, 887 F Supp 2d 133 (DDC 2012), vac'd, 133 S Ct 2885 (2013); *Texas v United States*, 831 F Supp 2d 244 (DDC 2011).

ate reports that take nearly opposite stances on the construction of key statutory terms.[134]

The final point about how Section 2 and Section 5 interrelate is that the former is not always narrower than the latter. As I have discussed above, Section 2 is less effective than Section 5 in several respects as a *shield* for existing ability districts. But, unlike Section 5, Section 2 also can be wielded as a *sword* to win the creation of additional ability districts. When plaintiffs meet the *Gingles* preconditions and show that the totality of circumstances supports their claim, their reward—which is unavailable under Section 5— is an increase in the level of minority representation.[135]

Because it can be used not just defensively but also for offense, Section 2 deserves much of the credit for the growing minority presence in the halls of power in recent years. Following the 1982 amendments to the provision, plaintiffs prevailed in many Section 2 suits throughout the country, usually obtaining as remedies new ability districts.[136] The result of this wave of litigation was "a quantum increase in minority representation" in the 1990s.[137] In the U.S. House of Representatives, for example, the number of African Americans elected from the South jumped from five to seventeen.[138] In the years since this representational spike, Section 5 has played a vital role in preserving the gains made by minorities.[139] But it was primarily Section 2, not Section 5, that made the gains possible in the first place.

---

[134] See HR Rep No 109-478 (2006); S Rep No 109-295 (2006); see also Persily, 117 Yale L J at 218 (cited in note 106) (describing how "Democrats and Republicans hold dramatically differing views as to what [the new Section 5] standard requires"); Pildes, 68 Ohio St L J at 1155 (cited in note 103) ("[T]here is a great deal of ambiguity and uncertainty about what Congress understood the renewed Act to mean.").

[135] But see note 85 (identifying certain rare circumstances in which Section 5 currently can be used for offense); note 129 and accompanying text (describing period in 1990s when DOJ treated Section 2 violations as grounds to deny preclearance, thus allowing Section 5 to be used for offense).

[136] See HR Rep No 109-478, at 52 (2006) ("In many of the [covered] jurisdictions . . . the initial gains made by minority voters were the result of Section 2 enforcement. . . ."). But see Daniel P. Tokaji, *If It's Broke, Fix It: Improving Voting Rights Preclearance*, 49 Howard L J 785, 799–803 (2006) (arguing that Section 5 also deserves credit for minorities' representation gains in 1990s).

[137] *Introduction*, in David A. Bositis, ed, *Redistricting and Minority Representation* 1, 1 (University Press, 1998).

[138] See Bernard Grofman et al, *Drawing Effective Minority Districts: A Conceptual Framework and Some Empirical Evidence*, 79 NC L Rev 1383, 1394 (2001).

[139] See Grofman and Brunell, *Extending Section 5 of the Voting Rights Act* at 312 (cited in note 8); Michael J. Pitts, *The Voting Rights Act and the Era of Maintenance*, 59 Ala L

B. EMPIRICAL GAP

The relationship between Section 2 and Section 5 thus is quite complex. But the key point for present purposes is that certain districts that used to be protected by Section 5 now may be eliminated without violating Section 2. How many such districts are there? Surprisingly, this is the first article to tackle this important question. To answer it, I first identify the existing districts that, prior to *Shelby County*, were shielded by Section 5 because their minority residents have the ability to elect the candidate of their choice. I then calculate the number of ability districts that are too noncompact or that have minority populations that are too heterogeneous or small to qualify for Section 2 coverage. These are the districts that fall into the Section 2–Section 5 gap.

1. *The Section 5 universe.* The best way to determine if minority members in a district have the ability to elect their preferred candidate—in which case the district formerly was protected by Section 5—is to examine an array of past elections.[140] Both district-specific (i.e., "endogenous") and statewide or national (i.e., "exogenous") elections ideally should be considered.[141] In combination, these elections capture the size, turnout, and political cohesion of the minority population as well as the extent of racial polarization in voting, and reveal how often the minority-preferred candidate in fact prevails.[142] Aided by a ten-day trial[143] and fourteen separate experts,[144] this was the methodology that the only court to decide a Section 5 redistricting case after the provision's 2006 reauthorization employed.

Unfortunately, the optimal methodology strained the resources of the court and litigants, and is infeasible for the entire universe of jurisdictions that previously were covered by Section 5. Exogenous data from the most recent presidential election, for ex-

---

Rev 903, 922 (2008) (observing that Section 5 "prevent[ed] any backsliding . . . of gains in descriptive representation").

[140] See *Texas v United States*, 887 F Supp 2d 133, 141–44 (DDC 2012), vac'd, 133 S Ct 2885 (2013).

[141] See id.

[142] See id at 141–42 (noting that endogenous elections in particular help "determine whether a district in the existing, or benchmark, plan has an ability to elect").

[143] See id at 139.

[144] See id at 141.

ample, are unavailable for most state legislative districts,[145] as is detailed knowledge about local political conditions. Since I was unable to carry out the first-best form of analysis, I instead took the following approach. First, I used census data[146] to find all of the congressional and state legislative districts in formerly covered states in which minorities make up more than 50 percent of the citizen voting-age population (CVAP). I included in my analysis all of the southern and southwestern states to which Section 5 previously applied in large part or in full.[147] I combined the African American and Hispanic populations in each district because these groups tend to vote cohesively (particularly in general elections).[148] I treated 50 percent as the threshold above which a constituency automatically qualifies as an ability district because the Supreme Court took the same shortcut in *Georgia*.[149] And I focused on CVAP rather than total or voting-age population because the Court also has done so and because CVAP is a superior measure of minority voting strength.[150]

Second, I used census data as well as demographic information about elected officials[151] to locate all districts with a minority CVAP above 40 percent *and* a minority representative. Political

---

[145] See *2012 Election Results by Congressional and Legislative Districts*, Daily Kos (July 9, 2013), online at http://www.dailykos.com/story/2013/07/09/1220127/-Daily-Kos-Elections-2012-election-results-by-congressional-and-legislative-districts ("*Presidential Results by State Legislative Districts*") (data unavailable for Alabama, Georgia, Louisiana, Mississippi, South Carolina, and Texas state legislative districts).

[146] See *Voting Age Population by Citizenship and Race* (*CVAP*), US Census Bureau, online at http://www.census.gov/rdo/data/voting_age_population_by_citizenship_and_race_cvap.html.

[147] These states are Alabama, Arizona, Georgia, Louisiana, Mississippi, North Carolina, South Carolina, Texas, and Virginia. See *Section 5 Covered Jurisdictions*, US Dept of Justice, online at http://www.justice.gov/crt/about/vot/sec_5/covered.php.

[148] See *Texas II*, 887 F Supp 2d at 158 n 27 ("Our calculations use the combined Black and Hispanic share of the CVAP. . . ."). Because there are rarely large black and Hispanic populations in the same districts—and rarely large Hispanic populations in any of the states I examine other than Arizona and Texas—it makes little difference whether or not the minority populations are combined. See id (obtaining same results if black and Hispanic populations are analyzed separately).

[149] See *Georgia v Ashcroft*, 539 US 461, 470–71, 487–88 (2003) (repeatedly citing number of majority-black districts in Georgia senate plan); see also *Texas II*, 887 F Supp 2d at 150 n 17 ("[C]ourts have generally presumed that success . . . in a majority-minority district is sufficient to find ability status.").

[150] See *LULAC v Perry*, 548 US 399, 423–25, 427–28, 436–38, 441, 443 (2006) (repeatedly referring to CVAP).

[151] See Joint Center for Political & Economic Studies, *National Roster of Black Elected Officials* (2013); NALEO, *Directory of Latino Elected Officials* (2013). I supplemented these data by visiting the websites of the representatives from all districts with CVAPs above 30 percent.

scientists have found that districts with CVAPs below 40 percent almost never elect minority representatives, meaning that they are highly unlikely to be ability districts.[152] Conversely, both political scientists and courts commonly have assumed that minority representatives are the preferred candidates of minority members.[153] Accordingly, when a district has a CVAP over 40 percent as well as a minority representative, it is very probable that its minority residents have the ability to elect the candidate of their choice.

Finally, I cross-checked the ability districts I identified with the limited available exogenous data in order to see whether the districts voted for Barack Obama (the minority-preferred presidential candidate) over Mitt Romney in 2012.[154] At the congressional level, twenty-four of the twenty-five districts I identified voted for Obama, and the only one that did not was a toss-up.[155] At the state level, all fifty-six of the districts I identified, and for which data were available, voted for Obama as well.[156] These results help confirm that the districts I identified indeed are ones in which minorities are able to elect the candidate of their choice.

Table A1 in the Appendix, then, lists by body and state all of the districts that formerly were protected by Section 5.[157] There are a total of 404 such districts, 25 in the U.S. House, 92 in state

---

[152] See Grofman and Brunell, *Extending Section 5 of the Voting Rights Act* at 313 (cited in note 8); Charles Cameron et al, *Do Majority-Minority Districts Maximize Substantive Black Representation in Congress?*, 90 Am Pol Sci Rev 794, 805 (1996) (finding that black population of 40.3 percent is needed in South for there to be 50 percent chance of electing black representative).

[153] See Bernard Grofman, *Operationalizing the Section 5 Retrogression Standard of the Voting Rights Act in Light of Georgia v. Ashcroft: Social Science Perspectives on Minority Influence, Opportunity, and Control*, 5 Election L J 250, 256 (2006); Katz et al, 39 U Mich J L Ref at 665–66 (cited in note 11); Persily, 117 Yale L J at 221 (cited in note 106) ("[I]t is commonplace for courts to assume that minority candidates are the minority community's candidates of choice.").

[154] See *Texas v United States*, 887 F Supp 2d 133, 142 (DDC 2012), vac'd, 133 S Ct 2885 (2013) (noting that "minority voters almost always prefer Democratic candidates" and that "minority voters lack an ability to elect in a benchmark district carried by John McCain over Barack Obama").

[155] See *Presidential Results by Congressional District for the 2012 and 2008 Elections*, Daily Kos (Nov 19, 2012), online at http://www.dailykos.com/story/2012/11/19/1163009/-Daily-Kos-Elections-presidential-results-by-congressional-district-for-the-2012–2008-elections?detail=hide. The one exception was Texas Congressional District 23, which gave Obama 48.1 percent of the vote, but which has a combined minority CVAP of 64.5 percent and elected a Hispanic Democrat in 2012.

[156] See *Presidential Results by State Legislative Districts* (cited in note 145). Data were available for state legislative districts in Arizona, North Carolina, and Virginia.

[157] See appendix table A1.

senates, and 287 in state houses. In absolute terms, Georgia has the most such districts (77) while Arizona has the least (18). As a share of all districts, Texas has the highest proportion of previously shielded districts (33.6 percent), while Virginia has the lowest (12.6 percent). The gap between the proportion of previously shielded districts and the statewide minority CVAP share is highest in Virginia (10.4 percent) and lowest in Alabama (1.4 percent). Over the whole nine-state region, the deviation from proportionality is 5.1 percent.

2. *Geographic compactness.* Which of these formerly protected districts now may be disbanded because they are too noncompact to qualify for Section 2 coverage? In a landmark 1993 study, Richard Pildes and Richard Niemi identified eleven majority-black and majority-Hispanic U.S. House districts that they believed might be in legal danger because of their odd shapes.[158] They included in their list all districts with sufficiently poor *dispersion* or *regularity* scores.[159] A district's dispersion refers to how spread out its territory is, that is, whether the district is long and narrow or essentially circular.[160] A district's regularity indicates how even its perimeter is, that is, whether the district's borders are contorted or smooth.[161] Of the eleven districts that Pildes and Niemi named, seven were struck down by the courts over the course of the ensuing decade.[162] Seven, that is, were so noncompact that they were both constitutionally suspect and beyond the scope of Section 2. This is a very impressive record that justifies my use here of the same compactness methodology.

Accordingly, I first calculated dispersion and regularity scores for all of the districts that previously were protected by Section

---

[158] See Richard H. Pildes and Richard G. Niemi, *Expressive Harms, "Bizarre Districts," and Voting Rights: Evaluating Election-District Appearance After Shaw v. Reno*, 92 Mich L Rev 483, 564 (1993). They also included seventeen other districts in their list. See id.

[159] See id (using as cutoffs dispersion score of less than or equal to 0.15 and regularity score of less than or equal to 0.05); see also id at 554 n 200, 555 n 203 (providing technical details for calculations of scores).

[160] See id at 549.

[161] See id.

[162] See *Bush v Vera*, 517 US 952 (1996) (striking down Texas Districts 18, 29, and 30); *Shaw v Hunt*, 517 US 899 (1996) (striking down North Carolina District 12); *Diaz v Silver*, 978 F Supp 96 (ED NY 1997) (striking down New York District 12); *Johnson v Mortham*, 926 F Supp 1460 (ND Fla 1996) (striking down Florida District 3); *Hays v La*, 862 F Supp 119 (WD La 1994) (striking down Louisiana District 4).

NC Congress 12   TX Congress 35

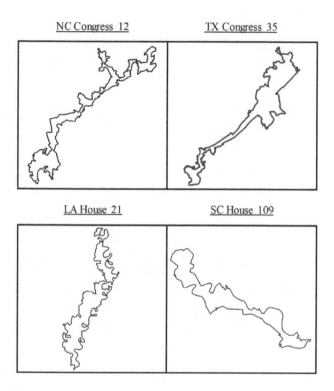

LA House 21   SC House 109

Figure 1. Ability districts with worst dispersion scores

5.[163] I then used the same cutoffs as Pildes and Niemi in order to identify the districts that are so noncompact that they likely are uncovered by Section 2.[164] As table A2 in the Appendix reveals, there are twenty-two such districts—five in Congress, four in state senates, and thirteen in state houses.[165] North Carolina and Texas account for all of the strange-looking congressional districts, while Georgia and North Carolina lead the pack at the state house level.[166] (No state is especially noteworthy at the state senate level.) Figures 1 and 2 also display maps of the formerly protected dis-

---

[163] I did so using Caliper Corporation's Maptitude for Redistricting software. I obtained congressional and state legislative district plans from *113th Congressional District TIGER/ Line Shapefiles*, US Census Bureau, online at http://www.census.gov/cgi-bin/geo/shape filesrd13/main.

[164] See note 159 (identifying cutoffs).

[165] See appendix table A2.

[166] See id.

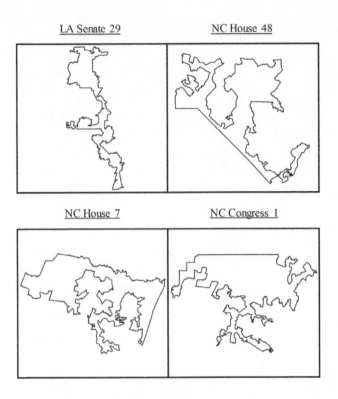

Figure 2. Ability districts with worst regularity scores

tricts with the very worst dispersion and regularity scores. North Carolina's Twelfth Congressional District, which closely resembles the constituency that gave rise to the racial gerrymandering cause of action in the 1990s,[167] has the lowest dispersion *and* regularity scores of any district in my study. North Carolina also features four of the five most irregular ability districts in the South.

But while there do exist districts that are likely beyond the legal pale, the more important point is that there are only very few such districts. If twenty-two districts are so noncompact that they might be uncovered by Section 2, then 382 districts have shapes that are unproblematic under the provision. Why are the vast

---

[167] See *Shaw v Reno*, 509 US 630 (1993). However, the district's current version is not quite as ugly as the one struck down in the 1990s. See Pildes and Niemi, 92 Mich L Rev at 564 (cited in note 158) (district formerly had dispersion score of 0.05 and regularity score of 0.01). Also, I only include the district in figure 1. The four districts in figure 2 thus are the second to fifth worst in the South with respect to regularity.

majority of ability districts sufficiently compact to qualify for Section 2 protection? The answer is probably that contemporary line-drawers have learned from the dramatic events of the 1990s, when the courts struck down bizarre-looking ability districts throughout the country. Line-drawers have found ways, that is, to continue drawing ability districts while making their shapes less aesthetically offensive.[168] Notably, there are more ability districts today than there were in the 1990s, but, at least at the congressional level, the number of highly noncompact districts (using Pildes and Niemi's cutoffs) has fallen from eleven to five.

The other significant point about these statistics is that they are not a foolproof measure of either liability under the Constitution or lack of coverage under Section 2. First, compactness scores can be misleading because they stem, to some degree, from the shape of the *states* in which districts are located. It is not entirely surprising that North Carolina performs so poorly given the contorted profile of its eastern shore.[169] Second, the constitutional definition of a racial gerrymander is a district that was created with "race [as] the predominant, overriding factor."[170] A district's strange shape is "persuasive circumstantial evidence" that race was emphasized too heavily, but it is not a "necessary element of the constitutional wrong."[171] Third, a district's strange shape also does not demonstrate conclusively that it is an invalid Section 2 remedy. As noted earlier, some uncertainty lingers as to whether *Gingles*'s compactness requirement applies to *districts* or to *minority populations*.[172] And, fourth, even if the requirement applies to districts, that a reasonably compact district was not drawn does not necessarily mean that one could not be drawn in the same area. If one could be drawn, then there indeed would be liability under Section 2 if an existing noncompact district was eliminated.

Notwithstanding these caveats, compactness scores are the best

---

[168] See Richard H. Pildes, *The Supreme Court, 2003 Term—Foreword: The Constitutionalization of Democratic Politics*, 118 Harv L Rev 28, 68 (2004) ("[L]egislators . . . internalized [the courts' rulings], not as barring them from intentionally creating [ability] districts, but as imposing general, extrinsic limits on the extent to which districts could be non-compact.").

[169] See Pildes and Niemi, 92 Mich L Rev at 565 (cited in note 158) ("One must make comparisons carefully because of the effects of state shapes.").

[170] *Miller v Johnson*, 515 US 900, 910 (1995).

[171] Id at 913.

[172] See note 96.

available proxy for both racial gerrymandering and lack of Section 2 coverage due to strange district shape. And the clear import of the scores is that very few current districts are so oddly configured that they now may be dismantled without violating Section 2. Next I consider the empirical evidence about the heterogeneity of ability districts' minority populations—the second reason why a district formerly protected by Section 5 now may be beyond the scope of Section 2.

3. *Minority heterogeneity.* In previous work of mine, I developed a technique for measuring the "spatial diversity" of districts.[173] A district is spatially diverse when its geographic subunits vary markedly with respect to a given factor. Conversely, a district is spatially homogeneous when its subunits are mostly alike with respect to the factor. Spatial diversity also can be applied to districts' minority populations (as opposed to districts in their entirety).[174] In this case, the concept indicates whether similar or dissimilar groups of minorities have been combined in a district—that is, whether similar or dissimilar minority *communities* have been merged. If dissimilar minority communities have been merged, then a district may be an unlawful racial gerrymander, and it also may be uncovered by Section 2.[175]

In my earlier work, I calculated spatial diversity scores with respect to composite factors derived from a very large set of demographic and socioeconomic data from the census.[176] I also used the census tract as the spatial subunit for my analysis, and included information about *all* of a tract's residents (rather than just its minority members).[177] Here I have refined my approach in several ways. First, I use the census block group rather than the census tract as my spatial subunit. Block groups have about one-third the population of tracts,[178] and thus allow spatial diversity to be cal-

---

[173] See Stephanopoulos, 125 Harv L Rev at 1936–41 (cited in note 102); see also Nicholas O. Stephanopoulos, *Communities and the California Commission*, 23 Stan L & Pol Rev 282, 289–93 (2012).

[174] See Stephanopoulos, 125 Harv L Rev at 1967–68 (cited in note 102).

[175] See Part II.A.2.

[176] See Stephanopoulos, 125 Harv L Rev at 1982–85 table 1 (cited in note 102) (listing nearly 100 variables used in analysis); Stephanopoulos, 23 Stan L & Pol Rev at 315–18 table 1 (cited in note 173) (same).

[177] See Stephanopoulos, 125 Harv L Rev at 1938, 1967–68 (cited in note 102).

[178] See *Geographic Terms and Concepts—Block Groups*, US Census Bureau, online at http://www.census.gov/geo/reference/gtc/gtc_bg.html.

culated more accurately, especially for smaller districts that contain relatively few tracts.[179] Second, I include only information about block groups' African American and Hispanic residents. I therefore am able to quantify the precise concept in which I am interested: the spatial diversity of ability districts' minority populations.[180] And, third, I incorporate many fewer demographic and socioeconomic variables into my analysis, because the full range of data is unavailable for minority members at the block group level. The variables that I incorporate encompass age, marital status, education, occupation, income, and housing—a broad, though not exhaustive, list.[181]

After assembling this dataset, I carried out a statistical procedure known as factor analysis, which simplifies and renders intelligible large volumes of information (see App. table A3).[182] A single composite factor emerged from the analysis, corresponding closely to socioeconomic status.[183] The factor differentiates between block groups whose minority residents live in married households, have a high household income, work in professional jobs, and own their homes; and block groups whose minority residents have the opposite attributes.[184] I then calculated factor scores for all of the block groups in the nine states included in my study. These scores indicate how the block groups' minority populations perform in terms of the newly created factor.[185] Lastly, I determined the standard deviation, with respect to the new factor, of the block groups within each congressional and state legislative district. The higher

---

[179] The use of a smaller spatial subunit also tends to increase the magnitude of the spatial diversity score. See David W. S. Wong, *Spatial Dependency of Segregation Indices*, 41 Canadian Geographer 128, 130–31 (1997).

[180] In my previous work, I was unable to quantify the concept directly because I used data about *all* residents of tracts in which minorities make up more than 40 percent of the population. See Stephanopoulos, 125 Harv L Rev at 1967–68 (cited in note 102). Here I merged the data about African American and Hispanic residents in order to produce estimates about block groups' *combined* minority populations.

[181] All data are from the 2007–11 release of the American Community Survey. See *2007–2011 ACS 5-Year Estimates*, US Census Bureau, online at http://www.census.gov/acs/www/data_documentation/2011_release.

[182] See Stephanopoulos, 125 Harv L Rev at 1938 (cited in note 102).

[183] See appendix table A3. More specifically, a single composite factor with an eigenvalue greater than two emerged. See Stephanopoulos, 125 Harv L Rev at 1938 note 179 (cited in note 102) (discussing methodology in more detail).

[184] See appendix table A3.

[185] See Stephanopoulos, 125 Harv L Rev at 1939 (cited in note 102).

the standard deviation, the more likely it is that a district merges dissimilar minority communities, and vice versa.[186]

Table A4 in the Appendix, then, lists the 146 current districts whose spatial diversity scores exceed that of the remedial district rejected by the Court in *LULAC* because it "combine[d] two far-flung segments of a racial group with disparate interests."[187] These are the districts that now may be eliminated because their minority populations are too heterogeneous to qualify for Section 2 protection. Of these districts, sixteen are in Congress,[188] forty-one are in state senates, and eighty-nine are in state houses.[189] Georgia and Texas have the largest numbers of these districts (thirty-three each), while Arizona has the fewest (just four).[190] Figure 3 also displays maps of the five worst-performing districts in the South, along with the district rebuffed in *LULAC*. The darker a block group is colored, the higher its factor score is (and thus the higher the socioeconomic status of its minority population).[191] All of the mapped districts merge dissimilar minority communities—typically disadvantaged urban areas and more affluent suburbs—and therefore are likely beyond the scope of Section 2.

The most startling aspect of these findings is the sheer number of potentially unprotected districts. The 146 districts with overly heterogeneous minority populations amount to more than *one-third* of all districts formerly shielded by Section 5. If all of these districts were disbanded, minority representation in the South would decline precipitously, thus realizing the worst fears voiced by commentators after *LULAC*.[192] Why is this segment of the Section 2–Section 5 gap so large when the compactness segment

---

[186] See id at 1939–40. Because only a single noteworthy factor emerged from the factor analysis, I did not need to compute a weighted average of the scores for different factors. See id at 1940.

[187] *LULAC v Perry*, 548 US 399, 433 (2006); see appendix table A4.

[188] Using my original methodology, I found in previous work that twenty-one congressional districts in the 2010 cycle contained minority populations that were more heterogeneous than that of the district rejected in *LULAC*. See Stephanopoulos, 125 Harv L Rev at 1978 (cited in note 102). The consistency of these findings is encouraging.

[189] See appendix table A4.

[190] See id.

[191] Data are missing for uncolored block groups, which were omitted as well from the factor analysis.

[192] See Ortiz, 105 Mich L Rev First Impressions at 50 (cited in note 103); Pildes, 68 Ohio St L J at 1146 (cited in note 103); Stephanopoulos, 125 Harv L Rev at 1978–79 (cited in note 102).

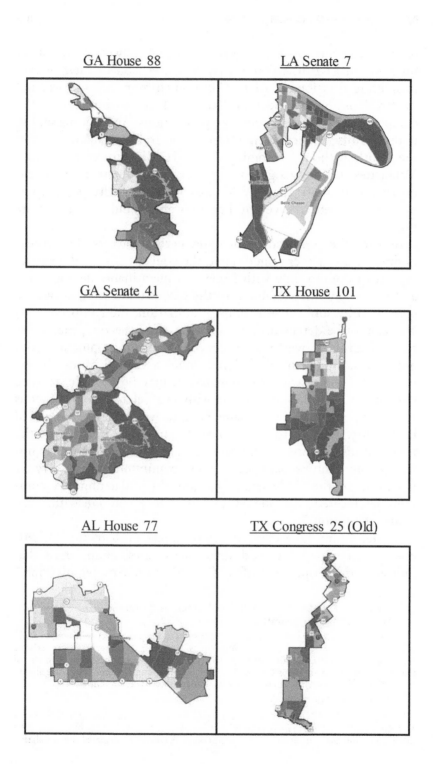

Figure 3. Ability districts with worst spatial diversity scores. Color version available as an online enhancement.

is so small? One possible answer is that line-drawers have not yet internalized *LULAC* the way they have the Court's racial gerrymandering decisions.[193] *LULAC* is a much more recent case, and to date it is the *only* Section 2 case to focus so intently on the composition of districts' minority populations. Another possibility is that ability districts simply cannot be drawn in many areas in the South without combining disparate minority communities. Minorities may be geographically distributed in such a way that districts with more spatially homogeneous minority populations cannot be created—even if line-drawers would like to create them.[194]

As with the compactness analysis, certain caveats about these findings must be mentioned. First, the concept of spatial diversity captures variation only with respect to quantifiable demographic and socioeconomic variables. To the extent that communities are generated by subjective feelings of affiliation, their improper fusion cannot be detected by a numerical score. Second, that a district contains an overly heterogeneous minority population does not necessarily mean that liability under Section 2 cannot be established if the district is eliminated. It may be possible in some circumstances to design a district with a sufficiently homogeneous minority population in the same area, in which case there would be liability. And, third, the Court declared in *LULAC* that the remedial district was invalid *both* because it joined dissimilar minority communities *and* because these communities were very far from one another.[195] Districts that join dissimilar minority communities located *near* one another therefore may fall within the ambit of Section 2.

To determine how many districts violate both of the *LULAC* criteria, I computed an additional measure of compactness that indicates the dispersion of a district's minority population.[196]

---

[193] See Pildes, 118 Harv L Rev at 68 (cited in note 168) (making internalization point in racial gerrymandering context).

[194] However, the record of Arizona, the only state in my study that relies on an independent commission to design its districts, counsels against this interpretation. Arizona has fewer ability districts with overly spatially diverse minority populations than any of the other eight states, perhaps because its independent commissioners indeed are able to create ability districts without combining dissimilar minority communities.

[195] See *LULAC*, 548 US at 435.

[196] See Richard G. Niemi et al, *Measuring Compactness and the Role of a Compactness Standard in a Test for Partisan and Racial Gerrymandering*, 52 J Pol 1155, 1165–66 (1990) (discussing population measures of compactness). Specifically, I calculated the population

When a district's minority population is highly dispersed, minority communities are likely to be far from one another (or at least to comprise a small share of the total minority population in the broader area). As table A4 in the Appendix reveals, only six ability districts contain minority populations that are both more heterogeneous and more dispersed than that of the district rejected in *LULAC*. If *LULAC* is construed narrowly, then, its impact may be much less dramatic than my analysis initially suggested. Like the compactness criterion, it may expose only a handful of unusual districts to elimination without any Section 2 recourse.

4. *Population size.* The final reason why an ability district may fall into the Section 2–Section 5 gap is that its minority population is too small to qualify for Section 2 coverage. As discussed above, Section 2 plaintiffs must demonstrate that an additional *majority-minority* district could be drawn, while under Section 5 minorities may be able to elect their preferred candidate even if they make up less than 50 percent of a district's population.[197] To determine how many ability districts in the South are not majority-minority districts, I simply counted the number of ability districts with minority CVAPs below 50 percent. As table A5 in the Appendix shows, there are seventeen such districts—zero in Congress, six in state senates, and eleven in state houses.[198] Arizona and South Carolina account for five of the six state senate districts, while Arizona, Georgia, and South Carolina account for nine of the eleven state house districts.[199]

The key point about these findings again is the scarcity of ability districts that are not majority-minority districts. If seventeen districts are beyond the scope of Section 2 because of their relatively small minority populations, then 387 districts have enough minority residents to raise no legal hackles. The explanation for the scarcity likely is twofold. First, the Supreme Court explicitly held in 2009 that there can be liability under Section 2 only if an additional majority-minority district can be drawn.[200] Risk-averse

---

circle measure of compactness, but using *minority* rather than *total* population as the input for the analysis.

[197] See Part II.A.3.

[198] See appendix table A5. In another thirty-seven ability districts, a *single* minority group does not make up a CVAP majority (though African Americans and Hispanics *combined* do).

[199] See id.

[200] See *Bartlett v Strickland*, 556 US 1, 18–19 (2009).

jurisdictions may have sought to forestall Section 2 litigation by creating majority-minority districts in almost all areas in which their creation was feasible. Second, the formation of majority-minority districts probably served the political interests of the Republicans who controlled the redistricting process in eight of the nine states in my study.[201] If ability districts must be drawn, it is preferable from the Republican perspective to make their minority populations as large as possible, thus inefficiently packing Democrats into a small number of constituencies.[202]

Some evidence for the partisan hypothesis comes from the record of Arizona, which unlike all the other states in my study relies on an independent commission to draw its district lines.[203] Arizona has less than 5 percent of the 404 formerly protected districts, but it has more than *40 percent* of the ability districts with minority CVAPs below 50 percent.[204] Because Arizona's commission did not try to enact a pro-Republican gerrymander, it had no reason to create districts with artificially inflated minority populations. The density curve in figure 4, showing the distribution of minority populations in all Republican-drawn districts in previously covered states, provides further support for the partisan hypothesis. The distribution is clearly bimodal, with one peak around 20 percent CVAP, where districts tend to be securely (but not overwhelmingly) Republican, and a smaller peak around 60 percent CVAP, where Democrats usually win by enormous margins. The distribution thus is close to optimal for maximizing the number of Republican seats while still drawing the requisite number of ability districts. Notably, there are almost no districts in the 30–50 percent CVAP range, in which Democrats are able to prevail without wasting their votes in landslide victories.[205]

Once again, a few caveats about these findings must be noted.

---

[201] See All About Redistricting, online at http://redistricting.lls.edu/ (featuring clickable map showing party in control of redistricting in each state).

[202] See Cox and Holden, 78 U Chi L Rev at 588 (cited in note 7) (noting that "packing African American voters [is] a second-best strategy" for Republicans who are compelled by VRA to create majority-minority districts).

[203] See note 194 (noting that Arizona commission also created very few districts with overly heterogeneous minority populations).

[204] See appendix table A5.

[205] See *Georgia v Ashcroft*, 539 US 461, 470, 487 (2003) (noting larger number of these districts in plan drawn by Democrats). The size of this segment of the Section 2–Section 5 gap thus depends on the partisanship of the redistricting authority. This segment of the gap is small when Republicans draw district lines and large when Democrats are in charge.

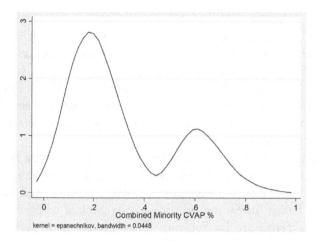

Figure 4. Distribution of Republican-drawn districts in formerly covered areas

First, because of the Supreme Court's ambiguity in *Bartlett*, it is not entirely clear that ability districts with minority CVAPs below 50 percent are beyond the scope of Section 2. These districts may be valid *remedies* even if the fact that they can be drawn cannot establish *liability*.[206] Second, even if these districts are not valid remedies, that a majority-minority district was not created does not necessarily mean that one could not be created in a given area. If one could be created, then there indeed would be liability if an existing ability district was dismantled. Lastly, the distribution of minority populations suggests, but does not quite prove, that partisan advantage was the dominant line-drawing motivation in the formerly covered states. The distribution was not very different in earlier decades when Democrats were largely responsible for redistricting, probably because the DOJ pressured states to draw majority-minority districts rather than ability districts with minority CVAPs below 50 percent.[207]

---

[206] See note 109.

[207] See Lisa Handley et al, *Electing Minority-Preferred Candidates to Legislative Office: The Relationship Between Minority Percentages in Districts and the Election of Minority-Preferred Candidates*, in Bernard Grofman, ed, *Race and Redistricting in the 1990s* 13, 32–33 (Algora, 1998) (documenting enormous 1990s decline in districts with minority proportions between 30 percent and 50 percent); Richard H. Pildes, *Is Voting-Rights Law Now at War with Itself? Social Science and Voting Rights in the 2000s*, 80 NC L Rev 1517, 1568 (2002) (same).

C. ODDS OF EXPLOITATION

There are quite a few ability districts in the South, then, that *may* be eliminated in the wake of *Shelby County*. Which of these districts in fact *will* be eliminated? It is too soon to say for certain, but I explore below the reasons why both Republican and Democratic line-drawers sometimes may wish to preserve the districts that populate the Section 2–Section 5 gap—but sometimes may wish to disband them.

To begin with, line-drawers from both parties may be unsure at times whether particular districts may or may not be jettisoned. As discussed above, the contours of both Section 2 and Section 5 are quite hazy,[208] meaning that it often is unclear whether districts previously protected by Section 5 now are covered by Section 2. Line-drawers may decide that discretion is the better part of valor, preserving districts that perhaps do not need to be preserved in order to avoid the cost and uncertainty of litigation. According to Bruce Cain and Karin MacDonald, this is precisely the course that many jurisdictions chose after earlier Court decisions that allowed ability districts to be eliminated. "[T]he legal advice that most jurisdictions [received] was . . . [p]reserve the status quo and do not attract attention."[209]

Line-drawers from both parties also may be disinclined to exploit the Section 2–Section 5 gap because they are satisfied with the status quo. Republicans, first, have found that the creation of majority-minority districts allows the enactment of district plans that tilt dramatically in their favor. By packing their opponents into majority-minority districts, they often can ensure that popular support for Democrats does not translate into a commensurate number of legislative seats.[210] Notably, when many new majority-minority districts were drawn in the 1990s, Republicans won about a dozen more congressional seats as a direct consequence,[211] while

---

[208] See notes 130–34 and accompanying text.

[209] Cain and MacDonald, *Voting Rights Act Enforcement* at 135 (cited in note 129); see also id (noting preference of incumbents to minimize alterations to existing districts); Pitts, 59 Ala L Rev at 955 (cited in note 139) ("[M]any . . . politicians . . . have a self-interest in maintaining the *status quo* with regard to minority voting rights.").

[210] See Pildes, 80 NC L Rev at 1558 (cited in note 207) ("[T]he Republican Party has come to recognize that the 'safe districting' approach of the 1990s favors its partisan interests. . . ."); Persily, 117 Yale L J at 250 (cited in note 106).

[211] See Kevin A. Hill, *Does the Creation of Majority Black Districts Aid Republicans? An Analysis of the 1992 Congressional Elections in Eight Southern States*, 57 J Pol 384, 399 (1995);

also making gains in every southern state legislature.[212] Similarly, the recently enacted plans for the 2010 cycle—all passed while Section 5 was still in effect—arm Republicans with a distinct electoral advantage. At the congressional level, the pro-Republican bias in the eight Republican-controlled states in my study averaged 9.7 percent in 2012. If Republicans had received 50 percent of the vote in these states, that is, they would have won 59.7 percent of the available seats.[213] One can see why Republicans might hesitate to upset such an auspicious political landscape.[214]

In the increasingly rare instances when they are responsible for redistricting in the South, Democrats too may have an incentive to retain the status quo. Minorities are very influential members of the Democratic coalition (especially in the South, where whites are overwhelmingly Republican), and they typically do not want existing ability districts to be eliminated. Quite understandably, minorities tend to assign a high value to descriptive representation, even if it comes at some cost to Democratic electoral prospects.[215] But just as Republicans may keep constant the number of ability districts while increasing their minority populations, Democrats may maintain their number while reducing their minority populations to the lowest level that still enables the election of the minority-preferred candidate. This, at any rate, was the approach the Democrats took in Georgia in 2000, when they still controlled the redistricting process in a state growing steadily more Republican. As the Supreme Court later recounted, Democrats did not dismantle a single majority-black district, but they did "reduce[] by five the number of districts with a black voting age population

---

David Lublin and D. Stephen Voss, *The Partisan Impact of Voting Rights Law*, 50 Stan L Rev 765, 772 (1998).

[212] See David Epstein et al, *Estimating the Effect of Redistricting on Minority Substantive Representation*, 23 J L, Econ & Org 499, 506 (2007); David Lublin and D. Stephen Voss, *Racial Redistricting and Realignment in Southern State Legislatures*, 44 Am J Pol Sci 792, 793 (2000).

[213] These data are on file with the author. See Nicholas O. Stephanopoulos, *The Consequences of Consequentialist Criteria*, 3 UC Irvine L Rev 669, 679–80, 684–85 (2013) (describing assembly of electoral database and calculation of partisan bias).

[214] And even if Republicans believe they can make gains by upsetting the landscape, the gains may not be large enough to be worth the controversy of redrawing district lines in the middle of a decade. The districts that populate the Section 2–Section 5 gap thus are likely safe until the next redistricting cycle.

[215] See *Georgia v Ashcroft*, 539 US 461, 470 (2003) (describing goal of African American legislators in Georgia to "maintain[] at least as many majority-minority districts" as prior plan).

in excess of 60 percent," and "increase[] the number of districts with a black voting age population of between 25 percent and 50 percent by four."[216]

But while there may be *favorable* strategies for both parties that are consistent with the preservation of existing ability districts, it does not follow that these strategies are *optimal*. In fact, there is good reason to think that both parties could benefit electorally by eliminating at least some current ability districts. Starting with the Republicans, they often could win even more seats by converting ability districts, which are almost always carried by Democrats, into Republican-leaning constituencies. Consider Georgia again, which has fourteen congressional districts, four of which are ability districts whose minority populations likely are too heterogeneous to qualify for Section 2 coverage.[217] Free from Section 5's constraints, Republicans easily could redraw one or more of these districts so that their minority populations no longer are large enough to elect Democrats (let alone minority-preferred candidates). The only price Republicans would pay for such revisions is a somewhat lower margin of victory for their candidates in the state's other districts.

That the Section 5 regime was not optimal for Republicans also can be inferred from Texas's actions since *Shelby County* in its ongoing redistricting litigation. The Supreme Court's decision voided a lower court's refusal to preclear Texas's district plans,[218] at which point the DOJ petitioned a different lower court to subject the state to preclearance under Section 3 of the VRA.[219] If preclearance were consistent with the most pro-Republican possible outcomes, then Texas might have been expected to accede to the DOJ's Section 3 request. But Texas did not accede, instead filing a furious memorandum in opposition to the DOJ's motion.[220] Texas's "redistricting decisions [are] designed to increase the Republican Party's electoral prospects at the expense of the Democrats," stated the memorandum—a goal that presumably can be

---

[216] Id at 470–71.

[217] See appendix table A4.

[218] See *Texas v United States*, 133 S Ct 2885 (2013).

[219] See Statement of Interest of the United States with Respect to Section 3(c) of the Voting Rights Act, *Perez v Texas* (WD Tex July 25, 2013).

[220] See Defendants' Response to Plaintiffs and the United States Regarding Section 3(C) of the Voting Rights Act, *Perez v Texas* (WD Tex Aug 5, 2013).

achieved more easily in the absence of preclearance.[221]

The status quo's nonoptimality for Republicans is further confirmed by recent theoretical work by Adam Cox and Richard Holden.[222] Cox and Holden demonstrate that the ideal strategy for maximizing a party's seats is not to "pack and crack" the opposing party's voters, but rather to "match slices" of the party's most committed supporters with slightly smaller cohorts of the opposing party's most loyal backers.[223] In southern states in which African Americans vote more reliably Democratic than any other group, the implication is that Republican line-drawers should create districts in which blacks make up slightly less than a majority and steadfast conservatives make up slightly more than a majority. The implication, in other words, is that Republican line-drawers should not create any ability districts at all. As Cox and Holden put it, "there is no plausible distribution of African American voters that would make it optimal for Republican redistricting authorities to create districts in which African Americans make up a []majority of voters."[224]

If blacks in fact are the most dependable Democratic voters in the South, then the best strategy for Democrats would be to maintain (or even increase) the number of ability districts, but to combine slim black majorities with minorities of staunch conservatives.[225] Such districts, unlike most current ability districts, would elect black Democrats by very small margins. But if there are at least some whites in the South who are as likely as blacks to vote for Democrats (in college towns, for instance), then the best Democratic strategy would be to create districts in which this liberal interracial coalition constitutes a slender majority. If the white populations of such districts are large enough, then minorities might not be able to elect the candidates of their choice. Similarly, if whites as heavily Republican as blacks are Democratic do not

---

[221] Id at 19.

[222] See Cox and Holden, 78 U Chi L Rev at 553 (cited in note 7).

[223] See id at 564–72.

[224] Id at 574. However, geographic constraints sometimes may prevent the enactment of optimal pro-Republican gerrymanders. Staunch conservatives sometimes may not live close enough to large black populations to permit their combination in the same districts. In these cases, "pack and crack" would be the best Republican strategy, and at least some ability districts would be created, albeit with overwhelming black majorities.

[225] See id at 573 (arguing that ideal tactic for Democrats is to "draw the maximum possible number of majority-minority districts in the state").

exist, or cannot be joined with black communities due to geographic constraints, then the best Democratic strategy would be
to create districts in which blacks are a minority and white voters
carry Democratic candidates to victory. Again, minorities might
not be able to elect the candidates of their choice in such districts
if their white populations are large enough.

It should come as little surprise that the pre-*Shelby County* status
quo was not optimal for either party. The point of Section 5, after
all, is to prevent the diminution of minority voting strength, not
to assure either party the most efficient possible conversion of its
popular support into legislative power. But now that Section 5
effectively has been nullified, both parties are freer than they used
to be to pursue their most electorally beneficial strategies. In at
least some cases, these strategies will entail the exploitation of the
Section 2–Section 5 gap—that is, the elimination of districts previously protected by Section 5 but now uncovered by Section 2.

III. Vote Denial

The VRA prohibits not only the *dilution* of the vote but
also its *denial*. The vote may be denied when franchise restrictions—such as photo ID requirements for voting, proof-of-citizenship requirements for registering to vote, limits on voter registration drives, cutbacks to early voting, and the like—prevent
minority members from casting ballots. After several decades in
which few were adopted, franchise restrictions have surged in pop-
ularity in recent years. In 2011 and 2012 alone, nineteen states
enacted some kind of ballot-access limitation.[226]

In this Part, then, I explore the Section 2–Section 5 gap in the
context of vote denial. I begin by describing how the provisions
diverge substantively when vote-denial claims are asserted. Under
Section 2, plaintiffs typically need to show not only that a statistical
disparity exists between minorities and whites, but also that a franchise restriction interacts with social and historical conditions to
cause the disparity. Under Section 5, on the other hand, a disparate
impact alone usually suffices to prevent a restriction from taking
effect. However, these statements of the operative standards necessarily are rather tentative. Thanks to the paucity of lower court

---

[226] See Brennan Center for Justice, *Voting Law Changes: Election Update* 1–6, 17–21
(2012).

decisions—and the lack of *any* relevant Supreme Court precedent—it remains quite unclear how either provision applies to vote denial.

Next I rely on case outcomes to estimate the magnitude of the Section 2–Section 5 gap. For instance, no plaintiff yet has prevailed in a Section 2 challenge to a photo ID law, while three such laws were blocked, at least temporarily, by Section 5. Similarly, a Florida law that curtailed early voting was denied preclearance with respect to the state's five formerly covered counties, but upheld under Section 2 with respect to the rest of the state. But too much should not be made of these few examples. Several franchise restrictions have been struck down under Section 2, and several Section 2 defeats should be attributed to poor litigation tactics rather than the provision's inherent limitations.

Lastly, I assess the likelihood that the space between Section 2 and Section 5 will be seized. Franchise restrictions commonly are thought to disadvantage Democrats, whose supporters are considered less likely to be able to comply with them. Accordingly, when Republicans are in control of state governments, their political incentives will point uniformly toward the enactment of new ballot-access limitations. Indeed, a spate of such measures already have been passed by southern states in the brief period since *Shelby County* was decided. Conversely, when Democrats are in charge, they will have no reason to try to restrict minorities' ability to vote.

A. CONCEPTUAL DIFFERENCES

Unfortunately, the Supreme Court has never decided a vote-denial case under either Section 2 or Section 5 of the VRA, likely because few franchise restrictions were adopted between the statute's enactment and the mid-2000s.[227] In order to determine how the VRA applies to vote-denial claims, it thus is necessary to turn to the case law of the lower courts—which itself is both sparse

---

[227] See *Florida v United States*, 885 F Supp 2d 299, 311 (DDC 2012) ("[T]he Court has not specifically addressed how the retrogression test applies to 'ballot access' laws."); Tokaji, 57 SC L Rev at 709 (cited in note 10) ("While *Gingles* and its progeny have generated a well-established standard for vote dilution, a satisfactory test for vote denial cases under Section 2 has yet to emerge.").

and somewhat muddled.[228] Beginning with Section 2, the lower courts are in agreement that a mere statistical disparity between minorities and whites does not suffice to establish liability. As a Florida court recently put it, "a plaintiff must demonstrate something more than disproportionate impact to establish a Section 2 violation."[229]

But the lower courts disagree as to what this "something more" actually is. Some courts require proof of proximate causation, that is, proof that the franchise restriction at issue is directly responsible for the disparity between minorities and whites.[230] If some other factor is significantly implicated—for example, lack of minority interest in the election,[231] poverty unrelated to discrimination,[232] a different electoral regulation not contested in the litigation[233]—then a Section 2 claim cannot succeed. Other courts focus on the interaction between the franchise restriction and social or historical patterns of discrimination.[234] They grant relief

---

[228] See Janai S. Nelson, *The Causal Context of Disparate Vote Denial*, 54 BC L Rev 579, 595 (2013) ("[T]he legal contours of vote denial claims remain woefully underdeveloped. . . ."); Stephen B. Pershing, *The Voting Rights Act in the Internet Age: An Equal Access Theory for Interesting Times*, 34 Loyola LA L Rev 1171, 1188–89 (2001) (noting that "through the cloud of [lower court] cases the applicable liability standard is much tougher to discern"). According to the Katz study, at most 72 out of 322 reported Section 2 cases between 1982 and 2005 involved vote denial rather than vote dilution. See Katz et al, 39 U Mich J L Ref at 656 (cited in note 11); Tokaji, 57 SC L Rev at 709 (cited in note 10).

[229] *Brown v Detzner*, 895 F Supp 2d 1236, 1249 (MD Fla 2012); see also, for example, *Smith v Salt River Project Agr Imp. & Power Dist.*, 109 F3d 586, 595 (9th Cir 1997) ("Several courts of appeal have rejected § 2 challenges based purely on a showing of some relevant statistical disparity between minorities and whites."); *Wesley v Collins*, 791 F2d 1255, 1260–61 (6th Cir1986) ("[A] showing of disproportionate racial impact alone does not establish a per se violation of the Voting Rights Act.").

[230] See, for example, *Gonzalez v Arizona*, 677 F3d 383, 405 (9th Cir 2012) (en banc) (noting that "proof of 'causal connection between the challenged voting practice and a prohibited discriminatory result' is crucial" (quoting *Smith*, 109 F3d at 595)); *Sw Voter Registration Educ. Project v Shelley*, 344 F3d 914, 918 (9th Cir 2003) (en banc); *Ortiz v City of Phila Office of City Comm'rs Voter Registration Div.*, 28 F3d 306, 312 (3d Cir 1994) ("Section 2 plaintiffs must show a causal connection between the challenged voting practice and the prohibited discriminatory result."); *Irby v Va Suite Bd of Elections*, 889 F2d 1352, 1359 (4th Cir 1989).

[231] See *Ortiz*, 28 F3d at 313.

[232] See *Smith*, 109 F3d at 595–96.

[233] See *Ortiz*, 28 F3d at 317–18.

[234] See, for example, *Gonzalez*, 677 F3d at 407 (examining whether franchise restriction, "interacting with the history of discrimination and racially polarized voting," resulted in disproportionate impact); *Stewart v Blackwell*, 444 F3d 843, 851, 879 (6th Cir 2006), superseded by 473 F3d 692 (6th Cir 2007); *Wesley*, 791 F2d at 1260; see also Nelson, 54 BC L Rev at 618 (cited in note 228) (recommending this approach); Tokaji, 57 SC L Rev at 724 (cited in note 10) (same); compare to *Thornburg v Gingles*, 478 US 30, 47 (1986)

only when the restriction's disproportionate impact occurs because of such an interaction, for example, if discrimination is responsible for minorities' lesser education, which in turn makes them more likely to misuse complicated voting machines.[235] And still other courts demand not just a statistical disparity but also the satisfaction of relevant factors from the 1982 Senate report.[236] Responsiveness to minority concerns,[237] a legacy of discrimination,[238] and socioeconomic differences[239] are the factors these courts most often have examined.

In contrast, a trio of decisions since Section 5 was reauthorized in 2006 have made clear that a disproportionate impact *does* suffice for preclearance to be denied (as long as there also is a nontrivial burden on voting). First, a court considering Florida's cutback to early voting declared that a franchise restriction is retrogressive if "(1) the individuals who will be affected by the change are disproportionately likely to be members of a protected minority group; and (2) the change imposes a burden material enough that it will likely cause some reasonable minority voters not to exercise the franchise."[240] Next, a court evaluating Texas's photo ID law denied preclearance because the law disproportionately affected the state's minority voters and these voters could not procure valid IDs "without cost or major inconvenience."[241] Lastly, a court assessing South Carolina's photo ID requirement concurred that "[a] state voting law has a discriminatory retrogressive effect if the law disproportionately and materially burdens minority voters when measured against the pre-existing state law."[242]

("The essence of a § 2 claim is that a certain electoral law . . . interacts with social and historical conditions to cause an inequality in the opportunities enjoyed by black and white voters. . . .").

[235] See *Stewart*, 444 F3d at 879.

[236] See, for example, *Johnson v Governor of State of Florida*, 405 F3d 1214, 1227 n 26 (11th Cir 2005) (en banc); *United States v Berks Cty*, 277 F Supp 2d 570, 581 (ED Pa 2003); *Roberts v Wamser*, 679 F Supp 1513, 1530 (ED Mo 1987), rev'd on other grounds, 883 F2d 617 (8th Cir 1989) ("The Court will then consider each of the [Senate] factors. . . ."); *Ct Citizen Action Group v Pugliese*, 1984 US Dist LEXIS 24869, at *12 (D Conn Sept 27, 1984).

[237] See *Pugliese*, 1984 US Dist LEXIS 24869 at *12.

[238] See *Roberts*, 679 F Supp at 1531.

[239] See *Berks Cty*, 277 F Supp 2d at 581; *Roberts*, 679 F Supp at 1531.

[240] *Florida v United States*, 885 F Supp 2d 299, 312 (DDC 2012).

[241] *Texas v Holder*, 888 F Supp 2d 113, 126, 138 (DDC 2012), vac'd, 133 S Ct 2886 (2013).

[242] *South Carolina v United States*, 898 F Supp 2d 30, 39 (DDC 2012).

The upshot of these divergent standards is that some franchise restrictions that previously would have been blocked by Section 5 now will be sustained under Section 2. Sometimes a plaintiff will be able to establish a statistical disparity between minorities and whites as well as a material burden on voting—meaning that preclearance would have been denied—but will be unable to show the "something more" required for Section 2 liability. For instance, a state might enact a nontrivial ballot-access limitation that disproportionately affects minority members. But it might be unclear that the limitation itself is directly responsible for the disparate impact, or that the limitation interacts in any meaningful way with patterns of discrimination, or that enough of the relevant Senate factors are satisfied. In this scenario, the limitation would be retrogressive, but it would not contravene Section 2.

It is important, though, not to overstate the likelihood of this scenario. If a franchise restriction disproportionately affects minorities, then it typically will be directly responsible for the disparate impact that ensues. Only if another unrelated factor intervenes will the restriction not be the proximate cause of the disparity. Similarly, the usual reason why a restriction disproportionately affects minorities is that they are poorer or less educated, and the usual reason why they are poorer or less educated is a history of discrimination. It thus will be straightforward in many cases to show that a restriction's interaction with discriminatory conditions gives rise to the disparate impact. Lastly, as noted earlier, the Senate factors generally are not difficult to establish in the mostly southern jurisdictions that formerly were covered by Section 5.[243] Accordingly, few franchise restrictions that previously would have been denied preclearance now will be upheld due to an inability to substantiate these factors.

B. EMPIRICAL GAP

The limited number of vote-denial cases not only complicates the effort to determine how Section 2 and Section 5 differ conceptually. It also makes it difficult to estimate the empirical gap between the provisions—that is, the kind and quantity of franchise restrictions that could not have withstood Section 5 review but that can survive scrutiny under Section 2. Still, it is possible to

---

[243] See note 123 and accompanying text.

reach some cautious conclusions based on both the recent spate of state-level restrictions and the much larger volume of local policies assessed under the VRA over the last generation.

Beginning with the highest-profile limitations enacted in recent years, photo ID requirements for voting, they have been sustained in both of the cases to date that addressed their validity under Section 2. First, a challenge to Georgia's photo ID law failed because of inadequate proof of a disparity in ID possession between minorities and whites. "[T]he Court simply cannot agree . . . that the evidence is sufficient to demonstrate . . . a substantial likelihood of succeeding on the merits [on a] § 2 vote denial claim."[244] Next, the Ninth Circuit, sitting en banc, rebuffed a suit against Arizona's photo ID law, again on evidentiary grounds. The court noted that the plaintiff "*alleged* that 'Latinos . . . are less likely to possess the forms of identification required under [the law] to . . . cast a ballot,' but produced no evidence *supporting* this allegation."[245]

In contrast, three photo ID requirements were denied preclearance, at least temporarily, under Section 5. In 1994, the DOJ objected to Louisiana's photo ID law because African Americans were "'four to five times less likely than white persons in the state to possess a driver's license or other picture identification card.'"[246] In 2012, a court denied preclearance to Texas's photo ID law because "the burdens associated with obtaining ID will weigh most heavily on the poor" and "racial minorities in Texas are disproportionately likely to live in poverty."[247] And also in 2012, another court denied preclearance to South Carolina's photo ID law for the next election, but allowed the measure to take effect thereafter.[248]

The fate of Florida's recent cutback to early voting also suggests that franchise restrictions are more likely to be upheld under Section 2 than under Section 5. A statewide Section 2 challenge to the cutback failed because of pledges by several counties to offer

---

[244] *Common Cause/Georgia v Billups*, 406 F Supp 2d 1326, 1375 (ND Ga 2005).

[245] *Gonzalez v Arizona*, 677 F3d 383, 407 (9th Cir 2012) (en banc) (emphasis added).

[246] Department of Justice, *Section 5 Recommendation Memorandum* 45 (Aug 25, 2005) ("*DOJ Georgia Memo*") (quoting DOJ letter to state).

[247] *Texas v Holder*, 888 F Supp 2d 113, 138 (DDC 2012), vac'd, 133 S Ct 2886 (2013). The DOJ also objected to the law prior to the judicial proceeding. See id at 117–18.

[248] See *South Carolina v United States*, 898 F Supp 2d 30, 48–51 (DDC 2012).

the largest possible number of hours of early voting (which was equal to the number required under prior law).[249] But a court denied preclearance to the cutback with respect to the five Florida counties formerly covered by Section 5, reasoning that "there is much that we do not know about how the new law will be implemented."[250] The court in the Section 2 case unsubtly hinted that it would have reached a different decision had it evaluated the cutback under Section 5. "The important distinction between a Section 5 and a Section 2 claim plays a significant role in the Court's decision in this case."[251]

Further evidence for the greater efficacy of Section 5 comes from a comparison I conducted of the DOJ's preclearance objections since 1982[252] with recorded Section 2 decisions over the same period.[253] As table A6 in the Appendix shows, the scorecard of Section 2 litigation was mixed with respect to most kinds of franchise restrictions, while several restriction types were blocked repeatedly by Section 5. For example, polling place eliminations were prevented nineteen times by Section 5, but only three successful suits and three unsuccessful suits against such actions were filed under Section 2.[254] Similarly, election date alterations were thwarted fifteen times by Section 5, but there was not a single Section 2 challenge, victorious or otherwise, to such changes.[255] And revisions to voter registration procedures were blocked ten times by Section 5, while five Section 2 cases against such amend-

---

[249] See *Brown v Detzner*, 895 F Supp 2d 1236, 1250-52 (MD Fla 2012).

[250] *Florida v United States*, 885 F Supp 2d 299, 320 (DDC 2012).

[251] *Brown*, 895 F Supp 2d at 1251.

[252] See *Section 5 Objection Determinations*, US Dept of Justice, online at http://www .justice.gov/crt/about/vot/sec_5/obj_activ.php; *Voting Rights Act: Objections and Observers*, Lawyers' Comm for Civil Rights Under Law, online at http://www.lawyerscommittee.org/ projects/section_5.

[253] I relied primarily on Katz's database of Section 2 decisions over the 1982–2005 period, but supplemented the database with searches for more recent cases. See Ellen Katz and the Voting Rights Initiative, VRI Database Master List (2006), online at http:// www.votingreport.org ("VRI Database").

[254] See appendix table A6; see also *Mark Wandering Medicine v McCulloch*, 906 F Supp 2d 1083, 1091 (D Mont 2012) (unsuccessful); *Spirit Lake Tribe v Benson Cty*, 2010 WL 4226614, at *3 (DND Oct 21, 2010) (successful); *Prescod v Bucks Cty*, 2009 WL 3617751, at *1 (ED Pa Nov 2, 2009) (successful); *Jacksonville Coalition for Voter Protection v Hood*, 351 F Supp 2d 1326, 1335 (MD Fla 2004) (unsuccessful); *Trevino v Pastrick*, 573 F Supp 806, 809 (ND Ind 1983) (unsuccessful); *Brown v Dean*, 555 F Supp 502, 505 (DRI 1982) (successful)

[255] See appendix table A6.

ments succeeded and four failed.[256] In sum, I counted seventy-three denials of preclearance to franchise restrictions, compared to eighteen successful Section 2 claims and nineteen unsuccessful claims.[257]

However, it is unclear whether these statistics should be attributed to the provisions' divergent standards for liability or to their procedural distinctions.[258] The reason why franchise restrictions often were upheld under Section 2 could be its allocation of the burden of proof to the plaintiff—not subtle distinctions between disparate impact alone and disparate impact plus "something more."[259] Likewise, the reason why the volume of blocked restrictions was higher under Section 5 could be that private parties lacked the resources to mount Section 2 challenges to all of the measures they believed to be discriminatory. Unlike in the vote-dilution context, where it can be determined with some certainty whether districts are protected under Section 2 and/or Section 5,[260] the provisions' substantive and procedural differences are almost impossible to disentangle with respect to vote denial.

In addition, neither the potency of Section 5 nor the frailty of

---

[256] See id; see also *Janis v Nelson*, 2009 WL 5216902 (DSD Dec 30, 2009) (successful); *Smith v Commonwealth of Va*, 2009 WL 2175759 at *7 (ED Va July 16, 2009) (unsuccessful); *Coleman v Board of Educ. of City of Mount Vernon*, 990 F Supp 221, 229 (SD NY 1997) (unsuccessful); *Hernandez v Woodard*, 714 F Supp 963, 969 (ND Ill 1989) (successful); *Ashe v Bd of Elec. of City of New York*, 1988 WL 95427 at *1 (ED NY Sept 8, 1988) (unsuccessful); *Central Del. Branch of NAACP v City of Dover, Del.*, 123 FRD 85, 87 (D Del 1988) (successful); *Miss State Chapter, Operation Push v Allain*, 674 F Supp 1245, 1268 (ND Miss 1987) (successful); *Ct Citizen Action Group v Pugliese*, 1984 US Dist LEXIS 24869 at *12 (D Conn Sept 27, 1984) (successful); *Trevino*, 573 F Supp at 808–09 (unsuccessful).

[257] See appendix table A6. Of the thirty-nine Section 2 challenges to "election procedures" in Katz's database, thirteen were successful. See VRI Database (cited in note 253); see also Cox and Miles, 108 Colum L Rev at 12 (cited in note 39) (finding success rate of 22 percent for "remaining catch-all category of [Section 2] challenges"). In addition to the cases mentioned above, successful Section 2 suits in the vote-denial context include *Brooks v Gant*, 2012 WL 4482984 (DSD Sept 27, 2012), *Diffenderfer v Gomez-Colon*, 587 F Supp 2d 338 (DPR 2008), vac'd as moot, 587 F3d 445 (1st Cir 2009), *Stewart v Blackwell*, 444 F3d 843 (6th Cir 2006), superseded by 473 F3d 692 (6th Cir 2007), *United States v Berks Cty*, 277 F Supp 2d 570 (ED Pa 2003), *Black v McGuffage*, 209 F Supp 2d 889 (ND Ill 2002), *Marks v Stinson*, 1994 WL 146113 (ED Pa Apr 26, 1994), *Roberts v Wamser*, 679 F Supp 1513 (ED Mo 1987), rev'd on other grounds, 883 F2d 617 (8th Cir 1989), *Campaign for a Progressive Bronx v Black*, 631 F Supp 975 (SDNY 1986), *Goodloe v Madison Cty Bd of Election Comm'rs*, 610 F Supp 240 (D Miss 1985), and *Harris v Graddick*, 593 F Supp 128 (D Ala 1984).

[258] See Part I (discussing provisions' procedural distinctions).

[259] See *Texas v Holder*, 888 F Supp 2d 113, 127 (DDC 2012), vac'd, 133 S Ct 2886 (2013) (noting that "case does not hinge *solely* on the burden of proof" (emphasis added)).

[260] See Part II (identifying and quantifying provisions' substantive differences with respect to redistricting).

Section 2 in this domain should be exaggerated. For instance, while three photo ID requirements were blocked by Section 5, at least temporarily, the DOJ did not object to several other such measures. It allowed photo ID laws passed by South Carolina in 1984, by Louisiana in 1997, by Alabama in 2002, by Arizona in 2004, by Georgia in 2005, and by New Hampshire and Virginia in 2012, all to go into effect.[261] Conversely, that past Section 2 suits against photo ID laws have failed does not mean that future actions will be doomed as well. The plaintiffs in the Arizona and Georgia cases both lost because they were unable to present evidence of a disparity in ID possession between minorities and whites.[262] But this sort of evidence has proliferated in recent years, in both academic studies[263] and Section 5 proceedings,[264] and it likely will feature prominently in future Section 2 challenges.

Analogously, a key reason why Florida's cutback to early voting was sustained under Section 2, but struck down under Section 5, is the more accurate information about counties' intentions that was available by the time of the Section 2 decision. The Section 5 court emphasized that it "ha[d] not been presented with a specific voting plan from any of the five covered counties," and thus was unaware whether, and to what degree, the counties would reduce their early voting hours.[265] In contrast, the Section 2 court received notice that "32 of Florida's 67 counties will offer the maximum number of early voting hours," and based its decision largely on these data.[266] Had the Section 5 court known about the counties' plans, "Florida would likely [have been] able to meet its burden of demonstrating that the overall effect of the changes would not

---

[261] See *DOJ Georgia Memo* at 42–47 (cited in note 246); see also *Voter Identification Requirements*, Natl Conf of State Legislatures, online at http://www.ncsl.org/legislatures-elections/elections/voter-id.aspx. Though it should be noted that these laws varied substantially in their stringency.

[262] See notes 244–45 and accompanying text; see also *Gonzalez v Arizona*, 677 F3d 383, 442 (9th Cir 2012) (en banc) (Berzon concurring) ("A different record in a future case could produce a different outcome with regard to the § 2 causation question."); Tokaji, 57 SC L Rev at 713 (cited in note 10).

[263] See Nicholas O. Stephanopoulos, *Elections and Alignment*, 113 Colum L Rev 283, 328 (2014) (summarizing academic findings about effects of photo ID laws).

[264] See *South Carolina v United States*, 898 F Supp 2d 30, 40 (DDC 2012) ("About 96% of whites and about 92–94% of African-Americans currently have one of the R54-listed photo IDs."); *Texas v Holder*, 888 F Supp 2d 113, 130–38 (DDC 2012), vac'd, 133 S Ct 2886 (2013) (discussing series of studies on disparities in ID possession).

[265] *Florida v United States*, 885 F Supp 2d 299, 312, 320 (DDC 2012).

[266] *Brown v Detzner*, 895 F Supp 2d 1236, 1250 (MD Fla 2012).

be retrogressive."[267] And had the Section 2 court *not* known about the plans, it would have concluded that the "change [would] impose a material burden on 'African-American voters' effective exercise of the electoral franchise."[268]

The figures I provided about DOJ objections and Section 2 cases since 1982 also must be taken with a grain of salt. For one thing, the number of objections is dwarfed by the number of preclearance submissions that the DOJ did *not* oppose. According to a report by the U.S. Commission on Civil Rights, between 1982 and 2004, the DOJ objected to only 0.1 percent of changes involving precincts, polling places, or absentee voting, 0.1 percent of changes involving voter registration procedures, and 0.2 percent of changes involving special elections.[269] Compared to these tiny percentages, the near-50 percent success rate I calculated for Section 2 litigation over franchise restrictions seems quite respectable.[270] Moreover, my count of Section 2 cases almost certainly is underinclusive because I, like Katz, was able to identify only recorded decisions.[271] Katz found 160 total Section 2 suits in formerly covered areas between 1982 and 2005,[272] but, including unpublished decisions, there actually were 653 successful such actions over this period.[273] The true volume of Section 2 activity in the vote-denial context therefore must be substantially higher than my data indicate.

A final caveat is that, under certain unusual circumstances, Section 2 may be *more* effective than Section 5 at invalidating franchise restrictions. In particular, when a jurisdiction loosens but does not eliminate an existing restriction, the policy change may be nonretrogressive but still in violation of Section 2. This sort of scenario unfolded in Mississippi in the 1980s, when the state partially dismantled its notorious dual registration system, which had long

---

[267] *Florida*, 885 F Supp 2d at 322.

[268] *Brown*, 895 F Supp 2d at 1252 (quoting *Florida*, 885 F Supp 2d at 329).

[269] US Commission on Civil Rights, *Voting Rights Enforcement and Reauthorization: The Department of Justice's Record of Enforcing the Temporary Voting Rights Act Provisions* 30 (2006). Of course, the vast majority of these changes were unproblematic under any standard. Section 5 objection rates thus cannot be compared directly to Section 2 success rates.

[270] See note 257.

[271] See Katz et al, 39 U Mich J L Ref at 654–55 (cited in note 11).

[272] See id at 656.

[273] See *Shelby Cty v Holder*, 679 F3d 848, 868, 872 (DC Cir 2012), rev'd, 133 S Ct 2612 (2013).

required voters to register in two different ways in order to be able to participate in all elections.[274] The amendments to the system were precleared by the DOJ because they made it easier for African Americans to register.[275] But in a subsequent Section 2 action, a court struck down the revised regime, which still required dual registration for residents of smaller towns, because of its "disparate impact on blacks . . . 'who are unable, because of disproportionate lack of transportation . . . to travel to the offices of the county registrar.'"[276] It thus was Section 2, not Section 5, that finally brought to an end one of the South's most discriminatory registration practices.

Accordingly, the empirical evidence on the size of the Section 2–Section 5 gap is mixed. On the one hand, more franchise restrictions, especially of the higher-profile sort, have been blocked by Section 5 than by Section 2. On the other hand, the available data likely understate the true performance to date of Section 2, and there is reason to think that the provision could be even more effective in the future. On balance, the safest conclusion is that there *is* substantive space between Section 2 and Section 5—but that it is not as extensive as it first might seem.

C. ODDS OF EXPLOITATION

If there indeed is space between the provisions, will it be seized now by politicians in formerly covered areas? This question is easier with respect to vote denial than it was with respect to vote dilution.[277] When Republicans are in control of jurisdictions, the answer almost certainly is yes. When Democrats are in charge, the answer most likely is no.

Franchise restrictions commonly are thought to benefit Republicans because they are more difficult for poorer and less educated voters, who lean Democratic by large margins, to comply with.[278]

---

[274] See *Miss State Chapter, Operation Push v Allain*, 674 F Supp 1245, 1248–50 (ND Miss 1987).

[275] See id at 1261–62.

[276] See id at 1264 (quoting complaint).

[277] See Part II.C (discussing odds of exploitation of Section 2–Section 5 gap in vote dilution context).

[278] See, for example, Alex Slater, *Voter ID Laws: The Republican Ruse to Disenfranchise 5 Million Americans*, Guardian (Aug 10, 2012), online at http://www.theguardian.com/commentisfree/2012/aug/10/voter-id-laws-republican-ruse-disenfranchise ("[T]hese laws

When Pennsylvania passed a photo ID requirement in 2012, for instance, the majority leader of the state house famously declared that "[v]oter ID . . . is gonna allow Governor Romney to win the state."[279] This is an area in which the conventional wisdom is correct (if somewhat overstated). According to several studies, photo ID laws reduce overall turnout by about 1 percent and produce a pro-Republican swing of 1–2 percent.[280] Other common restrictions, such as the elimination of election-day registration and felon disenfranchisement, also give rise to modest pro-Republican shifts.[281]

The political incentives of Republicans in formerly covered areas thus support the enactment of additional ballot-access limitations. By enacting such limitations, they favorably alter the composition of the electorate and make it more likely that Republican candidates will win office. Not surprisingly, southern states controlled by Republicans have passed or implemented an array of new limitations in the brief period that has elapsed between *Shelby County* and the writing of this article.[282] Photo ID laws that had been blocked in Mississippi (due to the DOJ's request for more information) and Texas (due to the court's denial of preclearance) now are on the verge of becoming operative.[283] Photo ID laws scheduled to go into effect in 2014 in Alabama and Virginia now will do so without any prior need for preclearance.[284] Florida has resumed its effort to purge noncitizens from its voter rolls.[285] And North Carolina has passed an omnibus bill that includes a photo ID requirement, a cutback to early voting, and the elimination of

---

are almost uniformly designed to disenfranchise young people and minorities—the very demographics that make up part of Obama's base.").

[279] Mackenzie Weinger, *Mike Turzai: Voter ID Helps GOP Win State*, Politico (June 25, 2012), online at http://www.politico.com/news/stories/0612/77811.html.

[280] See Stephanopoulos, 113 Colum L Rev at 329 (cited in note 263) (summarizing these studies).

[281] See id at 40.

[282] See Brief of Political Science and Law Professors as Amici Curiae in Support of Respondents at 26–30 *Shelby Cty v Holder*, 133 S Ct 2612 (No 12-96) (showing that even before *Shelby County* covered jurisdictions were more likely to enact photo ID laws, proof-of-citizenship requirements, and permanent felon disenfranchisements).

[283] See Cooper, *After Ruling, States Rush to Enact Voting Laws* (cited in note 17); *Photo Identification Requirements* (cited in note 261).

[284] See id.

[285] See Alvarez, *Ruling Revives Florida Efforts to Police Voters* (cited in note 17).

election-day registration.[286] It has not taken very long, then, for Republicans to begin exploiting the Section 2–Section 5 gap.

Conversely, Democrats have little reason to take advantage of the gap. They realize that franchise restrictions disproportionately harm their own most loyal supporters, and thus oppose the measures fiercely wherever they are proposed.[287] Were Democrats to find themselves in power in any southern state, their political calculus clearly would counsel against the adoption of any new restrictions. In fact, the optimal Democratic strategy would be to *expand* access to the polls, through policies such as longer voting hours, more flexible registration procedures, and greater absentee and early voting. This is the approach that Democrats have taken recently in states where they are in charge of the elected branches.[288] It also is the approach that Democrats would likely espouse were they to win back control of any formerly covered jurisdiction.

IV. CLOSING THE GAP

The analysis to this point has been descriptive rather than prescriptive. It has demonstrated that substantial space exists between Section 2 and Section 5, both procedurally and substantively, and that the space is likely to be seized by southern politicians. But it has not addressed how the Section 2–Section 5 gap might be *closed*, either legislatively or judicially. In this part, then, I discuss a series of steps that Congress or the Supreme Court could take in response to *Shelby County*. I explain how the steps would shrink the Section 2–Section 5 gap, while also pointing out their legal and political limitations.

But before turning to these options, it is worth considering the case for doing nothing—always the most likely scenario in our cumbersome political system. From a partisan perspective, Re-

---

[286] See Aaron Blake, *North Carolina Governor Signs Extensive Voter ID Law*, Wash Post (Aug 12, 2013), online at http://www.washingtonpost.com/blogs/post-politics/wp/2013/08/12/north-carolina-governor-signs-extensive-voter-id-law/.

[287] See, for example, *Crawford v Marion Cty Elec. Bd*, 553 US 181, 203 (2008) ("Democrats were unanimous in opposing [Indiana's photo ID law]."); *Common Cause/Georgia v Billups*, 406 F Supp 2d 1326, 1331 (ND Ga 2005) (Georgia's photo ID law voted for by just two Democrats in state house and zero in state senate).

[288] See Reid Wilson, *Democrats Push Back on Voting Rights*, Wash Post (Aug 19, 2013), online at http://www.washingtonpost.com/blogs/govbeat/wp/2013/08/19/democrats-push-back-on-voting-rights/.

publicans should cheer inactivity at the national level since it would enable them to enact more favorable district plans as well as more stringent franchise restrictions.[289] Putting aside partisan advantage, one can agree with this article's findings and still support the status quo if one does not consider the cause of minority representation to be particularly important. The interaction of politicians' incentives with the Section 2–Section 5 gap probably will give rise to policies that are electorally worse for minorities than those adopted under the prior regime. But this is a problem only if one is concerned about minorities' electoral position in the first place. If one is indifferent to their position, or more interested in other issues, then nonchalance is indeed the appropriate reaction to *Shelby County*.

A. SECTION 4

Assuming that Congress *is* concerned about minority representation, however,[290] there are several actions it could take to undo the damage inflicted by the Court's decision. First, Congress could accept the Court's invitation to "draft another formula based on current conditions."[291] Most of the metrics that commentators have suggested would result in many of the formerly covered jurisdictions once again becoming subject to preclearance, thus eliminating in one stroke the bulk of the Section 2–Section 5 gap.[292] For example, Bernard Grofman[293] and Ellen Katz[294] have proposed basing a new formula on the rate of successful Section 2 litigation

---

[289] See Parts II.C, III.C.

[290] I realize, of course, that this may not be an accurate assumption for many members of Congress.

[291] *Shelby Cty v Holder*, 133 S Ct 2612, 2631 (2013).

[292] For additional efforts to devise new coverage formulas, see Spencer Overton, *The Coverage Curve: Identifying States at the Bottom of the Class*, in Epstein et al, eds, *The Future of the Voting Rights Act* 242, 245, 252 (cited in note 8) (employing eight separate metrics and finding that all seven worst-performing states formerly were covered in part or in full), and Michael P. McDonald, *Who's Covered? Coverage Formula and Bailout*, in Epstein et al, eds, *The Future of the Voting Rights Act* 255, 262–67 (cited in note 8) (exploring how coverage would change if original formula was updated with current data on voter participation and use of tests or devices).

[293] See Bernard Grofman, *Devising a Sensible Trigger for Section 5 of the Voting Rights Act*, 12 Election L J 332, 334–35 (2013) (using cutoff of ten successful Section 2 challenges and identifying Alabama, Arkansas, Georgia, Illinois, Louisiana, Mississippi, South Carolina, Texas, and Virginia as states that would be covered).

[294] See generally Katz et al, 39 U Mich J L Ref (cited in note 11); Katz, *VRA Reauthorization* (cited in note 39).

in each state. Setting the bar at five winning cases per million residents would cause Alabama, Arkansas, Georgia, Mississippi, Montana, North Carolina, South Carolina, South Dakota, and Texas to be covered.[295] All of these states except Montana formerly were covered in part or in full by Section 4 or were bailed in under Section 3.

Similarly, Stephen Ansolabehere and others have written extensively about racial polarization in voting,[296] which "increase[s] the political vulnerability of racial and language minorities."[297] The nine states in which white and black voters diverged by at least 60 percentage points in their vote shares for Obama in 2008 were Alabama, Arkansas, Georgia, Louisiana, Mississippi, North Carolina, South Carolina, Tennessee, and Texas.[298] All of these states except Tennessee used to be covered by Section 4 or by Section 3. And Christopher Elmendorf and Douglas Spencer have focused attention on the prevalence of racially discriminatory attitudes among white voters, which may make de jure discrimination more likely. The six states that have the highest proportions of whites whose views of blacks' intelligence and work ethic are more negative than the national median are Alabama, Louisiana, Mississippi, South Carolina, Texas, and Wyoming.[299] All of these states except Wyoming previously were covered jurisdictions.

These metrics have decent hopes of being upheld by the Court because, unlike the stricken Section 4, they rely on "current data reflecting current needs."[300] The racial polarization and racial attitude figures are only a few years old, while the Section 2 statistics capture cases from the last couple decades. The metrics also are

---

[295] See *Shelby Cty v Holder*, 679 F3d 848, 876 (DC Cir 2012), rev'd, 133 S Ct 2612 (2013). This figure includes both published and unpublished Section 2 decisions from the 1982–2005 period. See id.

[296] See Ansolabehere et al, 123 Harv L Rev 1385 (cited in note 122); see also Stephen Ansolabehere et al, *Regional Differences in Racial Polarization in the 2012 Presidential Election: Implications for the Constitutionality of Section 5 of the Voting Rights Act*, 126 Harv L Rev F 205 (2013).

[297] *Shelby Cty*, 133 S Ct at 2636 (Ginsburg, J, dissenting).

[298] Exit poll data from 2008 are available at *Election Center 2008—Results*, CNNPolitics.com, online at http://www.cnn.com/ELECTION/2008/results/president/. Unfortunately, 2012 exit poll data are not available for all states.

[299] See Christopher S. Elmendorf and Douglas M. Spencer, *The Geography of Racial Stereotyping: Evidence and Implications for VRA Preclearance After Shelby County*, 102 Cal L Rev (forthcoming 2014) (manuscript at 38).

[300] *Shelby Cty*, 133 S Ct at 2629.

attractive because they would neatly close most of the Section 2–Section 5 gap. The majority of the formerly covered jurisdictions once again would be subject to preclearance, thus largely restoring the status quo ante.

However, it is unclear whether the Court is willing to countenance *any* further use of the preclearance remedy. Its opinion in *Shelby County* emphasized that preclearance can be justified only by "exceptional" conditions,[301] and observed in dicta that the claim that preclearance is now inherently invalid "ha[s] a good deal of force."[302] The probability of Congress passing a new coverage formula also is low. Any new formula would sweep in at least a few additional jurisdictions, which likely would complain vociferously about their inclusion.[303] And even formerly covered jurisdictions might object to being singled out by current data that imply that they continue to discriminate against minorities.[304]

B. SECTION 3

The second option for shrinking the Section 2–Section 5 gap is for plaintiffs to use Section 3 more aggressively to bail in jurisdictions—or, even better, for Congress to amend the provision so that it is easier to satisfy. To date, plaintiffs rarely have invoked Section 3 and courts rarely have subjected jurisdictions to preclearance pursuant to it.[305] But, in the future, plaintiffs could insert Section 3 claims into almost all of their voting rights lawsuits.[306] If they were to prevail on these claims, then a substantial number of jurisdictions would be compelled to preclear their election law changes, thus reinstating part of the regime struck down in *Shelby County*. However, even if many Section 3 claims succeeded, the

---

[301] Id at 2618, 2624, 2630–31.

[302] Id at 2625.

[303] See Persily, 117 Yale L J at 210 (cited in note 106) ("[I]t is quite another [thing] to heap a new and costly administrative scheme onto jurisdictions unaccustomed to needing federal permission for their voting laws.").

[304] See id at 211 (noting that a state's coverage under a new formula would be perceived as "a national condemnation of its recent voting rights record").

[305] See note 65 (noting that only two states, Arkansas and New Mexico, ever have been subjected to preclearance under Section 3).

[306] Notably, the DOJ already has included Section 3 claims in its challenges to Texas's photo ID law and district plans. See note 219; see also Complaint, *United States v Texas* (SD Tex Aug 22, 2013), *13. Private parties challenging North Carolina's new omnibus franchise restriction law also have filed Section 3 claims. See, for example, Complaint, *NAACP v McCrory* (MDNC Aug 12, 2013), *31–32.

result would be an odd patchwork in which coverage corresponded to litigation victories but not necessarily to actual racial discrimination in voting. And many claims probably would *not* succeed because Section 3, unlike Section 2, requires a judicial finding that a jurisdiction has engaged in intentional discrimination.[307] Courts often are reluctant to deem a jurisdiction a deliberate discriminator; indeed, this was the very reason why Section 2 was revised in 1982 to permit liability based solely on discriminatory effects.[308]

Both of these shortcomings, though, could be mitigated somewhat by congressional action. If Congress were to amend Section 3 so that preclearance applies not only to the jurisdiction found to have engaged in discrimination, but also to all of its constituent subunits, then bail-in claims would result in more geographically uniform coverage. More importantly, if Congress were to make a violation of Section 2 rather than a constitutional breach the trigger for Section 3 preclearance, then Section 3 claims would become much easier to win. As Travis Crum has commented, "[a]n effects test [for Section 3] . . . would likely result in many more jurisdictions covered," thus producing greater convergence with the former scope of Section 4.[309] However, Congress may be unable to pass any legislation on the controversial subject of preclearance as long as it remains under divided partisan control. Moreover, even a supercharged Section 3 would not result in *all* of the formerly covered jurisdictions once again becoming subject to preclearance (barring an unprecedented effusion of voting rights suits). And the Court may not look kindly on an attempt to link the Section 3 remedy of preclearance to a violation of Section 2. A garden-variety Section 2 offense may not be sufficiently "exceptional," in the Court's view, to justify preclearance.[310]

C. SECTION 2

Congress's final option for reducing the size of the Section 2–Section 5 gap—and the one that follows most directly from this article's analysis—is to amend Section 2 itself so that it more

---

[307] See 42 USC § 1973(c) (requiring constitutional violation for Section 3 to apply, which in turn requires showing of discriminatory intent).

[308] See note 120 and accompanying text.

[309] See Travis Crum, Note, *The Voting Rights Act's Secret Weapon: Pocket Trigger Litigation and Dynamic Preclearance*, 119 Yale L J 1992, 2037 (2010).

[310] See id ("But this change may also make section 3 more vulnerable to constitutional attack.").

closely resembles Section 5. On the procedural side, Congress could (1) institute a burden-shifting framework under which the onus would switch to the jurisdiction once a plaintiff makes a preliminary showing of harm; (2) increase the availability of preliminary injunctions, perhaps by authorizing their issuance whenever the preliminary showing is made; and (3) consolidate or eliminate some of the elements that must be proven to establish liability (especially the plethora of Senate factors). In combination, these steps would address all of the process-related reasons why policies that formerly would have been blocked by Section 5 now may go into effect. They would make the jurisdiction bear more of the burden of proof, they often would make suspension of a policy the default before a decision on the merits is reached, and they would reduce the cost and complexity of Section 2 litigation. Section 2 suits would not be *identical* to Section 5 preclearance proceedings, but they would be as close as possible while still retaining their character as conventional causes of action.

With respect to vote dilution, similarly, Congress could reverse the Court decisions that have made Section 2 inapplicable to districts that are bizarrely shaped or whose minority populations are overly heterogeneous or below 50 percent in size. If Congress undid these decisions, then there generally would be Section 2 liability if a constituency in which minorities were able to elect the candidate of their choice was dismantled. There generally would be Section 2 liability, that is, in the exact circumstances in which there is retrogression under Section 5. The shape of a district and the makeup and magnitude of its minority population would be immaterial under both provisions. Lastly, with respect to vote denial, Congress could make disparate impact alone the standard for a Section 2 violation (in this case without disturbing any Court precedents). The criteria for liability under Section 2 and retrogression under Section 5 then would be identical. Additional elements such as causation or interaction with patterns of discrimination would not have to be demonstrated under either provision.

These Section 2 revisions may be easier for Congress to pass than changes to Section 3 or Section 4 because they do not aim to impose preclearance on any jurisdiction. It is preclearance, with its attendant loss of state sovereignty, that always has been the most provocative feature of the VRA, and it is preclearance whose salience recently was heightened by *Shelby County*. Responses to the decision that focus on *other* aspects of the VRA therefore may be more palatable in the current political environment. In 1982, notably, a divided Congress and a Republican president managed to enact more sweeping amendments to Section 2 than those proposed here after an earlier Court case limited both constitutional and statutory claims of vote dilution.[311] Political dynamics have changed over the last generation, but this is still an auspicious precedent.

Revisions to Section 2 have the further advantage that they may be more likely to survive the Court's scrutiny than efforts to recreate the preclearance regime. There is now a decision on the books striking down the only coverage formula ever passed by Congress and casting doubt on the validity of preclearance under any circumstances. But there is no equivalently adverse decision in the Section 2 context. Individual Justices occasionally have expressed their dissatisfaction with the provision,[312] but the full Court never has implied that it is unconstitutional. Accordingly, a procedurally streamlined and substantively strengthened Section 2 would have reasonable odds of repelling a constitutional attack. None of the changes advocated here would make the provision much more legally vulnerable than it already is.

On the other hand, that Congress is *more* likely to amend Section 2 than Section 3 or Section 4 does not mean that it actually is *likely* to do so. Congressional inaction is always the safest bet in periods of divided government, especially with respect to laws that touch on highly sensitive issues of race and political power. The case for the constitutionality of a fortified Section 2 also is far from ironclad. Because it is a disparate impact provision, Section 2 already prohibits a wide range of conduct that is not motivated by invidious intent and thus is constitutionally permissible. If it were revised to prohibit even more such conduct, one could easily imagine the Court that decided *Shelby County* concluding that it too exceeds Congress's enforcement powers under the Reconstruction Amendments.[313] A reinforced Section 2 might clash

---

[311] The Court decision targeted by the 1982 amendments was *City of Mobile v Bolden*, 446 US 55 (1980), which made discriminatory intent the standard for constitutional vote dilution and construed Section 2 as mirroring the constitutional test.

[312] See, for example, *Holder v Hall*, 512 US 874, 891–945 (1994) (Thomas, J, concurring in the judgment); *Chisom v Roemer*, 501 US 380, 418 (1991) (Kennedy, J, dissenting).

[313] For an extended discussion of whether Section 2 constitutes a valid exercise of Congress's enforcement powers, see Luke P. McLoughlin, *Section 2 of the Voting Rights Act and City of Boerne: The Continuity, Proximity, and Trajectory of Vote-Dilution Standards*, 31 Vt L Rev 39 (2006).

2]   THE SOUTH AFTER SHELBY COUNTY   125

as well with the Court's ban on racial gerrymandering, which forbids race from playing too large a role in districting decisions. Indeed, Justice Kennedy warned in *Bartlett* that, "[i]f § 2 were interpreted to require crossover districts throughout the Nation, 'it would unnecessarily infuse race into virtually every redistricting, raising serious constitutional questions.'"[314]

One final (though unlikely) scenario for strengthening Section 2 also should be noted. In the event that Congress is unable to act, the Court itself could eliminate much of the Section 2–Section 5 gap by revisiting its Section 2 precedents and deciding open questions in favor of greater liability.[315] On the procedural front, the Court probably could not change the burden of proof or the availability of preliminary injunctions—which are set, respectively, by the statutory text[316] and by unrelated case law on courts' equitable powers[317]—but it could greatly simplify the elements that must be proven to establish a Section 2 violation. The profusion of these elements is squarely the fault of the Court's own decisions, not the language of Section 2,[318] meaning that doctrinal rationalization could be accomplished through judicial intervention. With respect to vote dilution, likewise, it is the Court, not the statutory text, that has produced the geographic compactness, minority heterogeneity, and minority size requirements for redistricting.[319] The Court therefore could waive these requirements even if Congress remains inactive. And with respect to vote denial, the Court has not yet specified the standard for Section 2 liability,

---

[314] *Bartlett v Strickland*, 556 US 1, 21 (2009) (quoting *LULAC v Perry*, 548 US 399, 446 (2006)). Likewise, if Section 2 were amended so as to require the construction of bizarre-looking districts or districts that merge dissimilar minority communities, the Court also might conclude that it improperly requires racial gerrymanders to be drawn. However, the recommended changes to the procedure of Section 2 litigation and the standard for vote denial liability do not seem to raise the same sorts of constitutional red flags. Congress thus may be on safer legal ground if it does not alter how Section 2 applies to vote dilution.

[315] For a recent proposal along these lines, see Christopher S. Elmendorf and Douglas M. Spencer, *Administering Section 2 of the VRA After Shelby County* (Sept 2013) (unpublished manuscript) (on file with author).

[316] See 42 USC § 1973(b) ("A violation . . . of this section is established if . . . *it is shown* . . . ." (emphasis added)).

[317] See, for example, *Prendergast v NY Tel. Co.*, 262 US 43, 50 (1923) ("It is well settled that the granting of a temporary injunction . . . is within the sound discretion of the trial court.").

[318] See notes 79–83 and accompanying text (summarizing array of judicially created elements of Section 2 claim).

[319] See Parts II.A.1–3.

and the language of the provision does not resolve the matter either.[320] The Court thus would be writing on a clean slate if it were to embrace disparate impact alone as the operative test.

Of course, there is little chance that the same Court that consistently has narrowed the scope of Section 2 over the last generation suddenly will change course. It probably would take a shift in the Court's membership for it to begin loosening the procedural and substantive limitations that it has imposed on Section 2 over the years.[321] Judicial revision of Section 2 doctrine also is complicated by the "special force" of stare decisis in the statutory interpretation context.[322] Because Congress is free to overturn statutory constructions of which it disapproves—a power it repeatedly has exercised vis-à-vis the VRA[323]—the Court tends to adhere to its rulings unless they have proven manifestly unworkable. Strikingly, there does not seem to be a single instance in which the Court explicitly has reversed one of its earlier readings of the VRA.

The upshot of this analysis is that there are no easy ways to close the Section 2–Section 5 gap. There are no options, that is, that are clearly effective from a policy perspective, passable by Congress given the current political climate, *and* likely to survive review by the Court. This conclusion should not be especially surprising. A provision as potent as Section 5 is hard to replace, a divided government typically enacts little legislation of any kind, and the Court cannot be expected to turn a blind eye to attempts to sidestep *Shelby County* when the ink on the decision is barely dry. But the conclusion also does not necessarily apply in the long run. If Democrats were to win unified control of the federal government, and if the Court's membership were to shift in a more progressive direction, then it would be quite probable that amendments to the VRA would be both passed and upheld. Accordingly, the Section 2–Section 5 gap likely will persist in the short term. But it need not endure indefinitely.

---

[320] See Part III.A.

[321] See Pildes, 68 Ohio St L J at 1140–41 (cited in note 103) (noting that "a majority of the Court has continuously sought, without interruption, to cabin and confine safe minority districting to a narrower and narrower domain").

[322] *Patterson v McLean Credit Union*, 491 US 164, 172 (1989).

[323] In 1982, Congress reversed a Court decision limiting Section 2 to liability for discriminatory intent, see note 120, and in 2006, Congress reversed Court decisions confining Section 5 to cases in which a retrogressive purpose was shown or minorities' overall political influence was diminished, see notes 127–28.

V. CONCLUSION

Everyone agrees that *Shelby County* inaugurated a new era in the South. As Heather Gerken commented on the day of the decision, the future "will look nothing like what existed at 9:59 this morning, before the Court handed down its opinion."[324] But until now there has been no systematic effort to figure out what the new era actually *will* look like—what the state of minority representation will be now that Section 5 has been struck down but Section 2 lives on. In this article, I have tried my hand at charting the contours of the unfamiliar legal and political landscape in which we now find ourselves. The conclusions of my investigation are sobering if not quite calamitous. Procedurally, Section 2 and Section 5 diverge in several major ways, all of which mean that policies that formerly would have been blocked now will go into effect. With respect to vote dilution, many districts that previously were protected now may (and probably will) be dismantled without running afoul of Section 2. And with respect to vote denial, many franchise restrictions that used to be barred now may (and probably will) be enacted with legal impunity.

To some, this new era may seem worse than the regime it replaced. But there do exist measures that could largely restore the status quo ante. A new coverage formula could be adopted, preclearance could be imposed on offending jurisdictions pursuant to a stronger bail-in provision, and Section 2 could be amended to mirror the stricken Section 5 more faithfully. However, all of these steps face serious legal and political obstacles, at least for the time being. A divided government is unlikely to pass legislation that may have uneven partisan consequences. Likewise, the current Court probably would thwart any efforts to circumvent its recent decision. Section 2 minus Section 5 thus may come to equal zero once again. But odds are it will not do so for a while.

---

[324] Heather Gerken, *Goodbye to the Crown Jewel of the Civil Rights Movement*, Slate (June 25, 2013), online at http://www.slate.com/articles/news_and_politics/jurisprudence/2013/06/supreme_court_and_the_voting_rights_act_goodbye_to_section_5.html.

Table A1

Districts Formerly Protected Under Section 5

State	Minority CVAP %	Congress: Total Districts	Congress: Section 5 Districts	State Senate: Total Districts	State Senate: Section 5 Districts	State House: Total Districts	State House: Section 5 Districts
Alabama	26.6	7	1	35	8	105	28
Arizona	22.4	9	2	30	6	60	10
Georgia	33.5	14	4	56	16	180	57
Louisiana	32.9	6	1	39	11	105	29
Mississippi	36.3	4	1	52	15	122	42
North Carolina	24.0	13	2	50	10	120	25
South Carolina	29.2	7	1	46	11	124	32
Texas	38.7	36	12	31	10	150	51
Virginia	23.0	11	1	40	5	100	13
Total	31.1	107	25	379	92	1,066	287

NOTE.—Districts formerly protected under Section 5 either (1) have a combined minority CVAP above 50 percent or (2) have a combined minority CVAP above 40 percent *and* are represented by a minority member.

Table A2

Highly Noncompact Ability Districts

District	Dispersion	Regularity
AL Senate 18	.14	.13
GA Senate 39	.14	.11
GA House 55	.15	.12
GA House 57	.14	.12
GA House 83	.14	.12
GA House 84	.13	.09
LA Senate 29	.12	.04
LA House 21	.11	.05
NC Congress 1	.29	.04
NC Congress 12	.07	.03
NC Senate 21	.34	.05
NC House 7	.28	.04
NC House 12	.12	.05
NC House 48	.23	.04
SC House 109	.11	.11
SC House 113	.12	.13
TX Congress 15	.15	.12
TX Congress 33	.23	.05
TX Congress 35	.10	.05
TX House 131	.14	.15
TX House 145	.13	.11
VA House 95	.14	.14

NOTE.—List includes all ability districts in formerly covered areas with dispersion scores less than or equal to 0.15 or regularity scores less than or equal to 0.05.

Table A3

Results of Factor Analysis

Variable	Composite Factor 1 (Socioeconomic Status)
Median age	
Married household %	.65
Nonfamily household %	−.50
High school enrollment %	
College enrollment %	
Median household income	.54
Occupation—professional %	.41
Occupation—sales %	
Occupation—construction %	
Occupation—manufacturing %	
Owner-occupied %	.90
Renter-occupied %	−.90
Variance explained (%)	35.1

NOTE.—Nine states (AL, AZ, GA, LA, MS, NC, SC, TX, VA) and 38,381 census block groups incorporated into analysis. All variables apply to combined African American and Hispanic populations. Single retained factor explains 35.1 percent of variance in data. Only loadings greater than 0.4 or less than −0.4 displayed.

Table A4

Ability Districts with Highly Spatially Diverse Minority Populations

District	Spatial Diversity	Minority Dispersion
AL Congress 7	.83	.59
AL Senate 18	.88	.33
AL Senate 19	.81	.49
AL Senate 26	.90	.81
AL House 19	.89	.51
AL House 52	.86	.39
AL House 53	.99	.50
AL House 54	.98	.25
AL House 55	.78	.24
AL House 60	.98	.27
AL House 76	.83	.47
AL House 77	1.01	.40
AL House 78	.88	.27
AL House 83	.80	.57
AZ Congress 7	.79	.72
AZ Senate 3	.82	.61
AZ House 3	.82	.61
AZ House 3	.82	.61
GA Congress 2	.80	.63
GA Congress 4	.91	.60
GA Congress 5	.86	.58
GA Congress 13	.79	.30
GA Senate 2	.83	.87

Table A4 *continued*

District	Spatial Diversity	Minority Dispersion
GA Senate 5	.89	.39
GA Senate 15	.84	.63
GA Senate 22	.89	.78
GA Senate 26	.80	.53
GA Senate 34	.90	.41
GA Senate 38	.86	.43
GA Senate 39	.88	.19
GA Senate 41	1.01	.33
GA Senate 43	.80	.61
GA House 55	**.87**	**.14**
GA House 61	.88	.19
GA House 62	**.83**	**.14**
GA House 63	**.82**	**.12**
GA House 64	.83	.21
GA House 66	.87	.51
GA House 74	.85	.38
GA House 84	**.92**	**0.11**
GA House 86	.85	.25
GA House 87	.92	.23
GA House 88	1.13	.20
GA House 91	.84	.39
GA House 100	.79	.72
GA House 132	.85	.57
GA House 136	.88	.37
GA House 142	.85	.70
GA House 153	.87	.53
GA House 162	.82	.32
GA House 163	.82	.36
LA Congress 2	.87	.59
LA Senate 3	.79	.20
LA Senate 4	.86	.46
LA Senate 7	1.04	.49
LA Senate 15	.92	.52
LA House 4	.90	.32
LA House 34	.78	.80
LA House 61	.79	.52
LA House 87	.83	.37
LA House 97	.84	.44
LA House 99	.80	.35
LA House 100	.92	.88
LA House 101	1.01	.47
LA House 102	.98	.34
MS Senate 26	.86	.21
MS Senate 29	.97	.23
MS House 45	.81	.29
MS House 55	.91	.73
MS House 57	.86	.37
MS House 66	.85	.28
MS House 69	.81	.25

Table A4 *continued*

District	Spatial Diversity	Minority Dispersion
MS House 71	.80	.40
MS House 72	.96	.22
NC Congress 12	.87	.51
NC Senate 14	.97	.69
NC Senate 20	.95	.44
NC Senate 21	.79	.54
NC Senate 28	.88	.74
NC Senate 32	.91	.88
NC Senate 38	.84	.41
NC Senate 40	.85	.60
NC House 29	.89	.72
NC House 31	.95	.54
NC House 33	.94	.57
NC House 38	.92	.57
NC House 42	.82	.48
NC House 57	.98	.57
NC House 58	.84	.44
NC House 60	.85	.59
NC House 71	.96	.59
NC House 72	.85	.71
NC House 99	.84	.57
NC House 101	.83	.48
NC House 107	.87	.30
SC Senate 7	.89	.61
SC Senate 19	.87	.58
SC Senate 21	.89	.53
SC House 12	.80	.57
SC House 73	.82	.41
SC House 76	.92	.33
SC House 111	.83	.44
TX Congress 9	.99	.43
TX Congress 16	.81	.87
TX Congress 18	.85	.41
TX Congress 20	.83	.61
TX Congress 30	.88	.58
TX Congress 33	.79	.46
TX Congress 35	.84	.35
TX Senate 6	.79	.48
TX Senate 13	.95	.36
TX Senate 15	.94	.28
TX Senate 21	.81	.20
TX Senate 23	.86	.68
TX Senate 26	.81	.60
TX House 34	.79	.59
TX House 42	.78	.80
TX House 46	.86	.46
TX House 51	.95	.68
TX House 77	.80	.69
TX House 95	.84	.43

Table A4 *continued*

District	Spatial Diversity	Minority Dispersion
TX House 100	.82	.30
TX House 101	1.01	.40
TX House 103	.85	.39
TX House 111	1.00	.33
TX House 116	.85	.30
TX House 120	.80	.65
TX House 123	.81	.34
TX House 131	**.93**	**.16**
TX House 139	.85	.28
TX House 141	.92	.28
TX House 142	.79	.24
TX House 145	.82	.20
TX House 146	.89	.26
TX House 147	.86	.24
VA Congress 3	.85	.59
VA Senate 2	.84	.49
VA Senate 5	.91	.49
VA Senate 9	.95	.29
VA Senate 16	.82	.50
VA Senate 18	.86	.25
VA House 70	.98	.33
VA House 74	**.85**	**.14**
VA House 77	.98	.24
VA House 80	.89	.46
VA House 95	.85	.35

NOTE.—List includes all ability districts in formerly covered areas with spatial diversity scores higher than remedial district rejected in *LULAC* (0.78). Spatial diversity scores computed with respect to composite factor 1 (socioeconomic status) from factor analysis. Spatial diversity and dispersion scores computed for districts' minority populations only. Districts with minority dispersion scores lower than remedial district rejected in *LULAC* (0.18) shown in bold.

Table A5

Ability Districts with Combined Minority CVAPs Below 50 Percent

District	Black CVAP %	Hispanic CVAP %	Combined Minority CVAP %
AL House 85	46.7	1.1	47.8
AZ Senate 2	4.4	42.3	46.8
AZ Senate 3	3.0	44.7	47.7
AZ Senate 30	8.1	33.9	42.0
AZ House 2	4.4	42.3	46.8
AZ House 3	3.0	44.7	47.7
AZ House 3	3.0	44.7	47.7
AZ House 4	3.5	46.2	49.7
GA House 38	40.0	6.5	46.5
GA House 66	37.5	2.8	40.3
GA House 132	42.9	1.5	44.3
NC Senate 32	45.3	4.2	49.5
SC Senate 7	46.2	2.6	48.8
SC Senate 29	46.9	.7	47.6
SC House 90	43.4	.6	44.0
SC House 116	45.1	1.3	46.4
VA House 52	31.0	12.2	43.2

NOTE.—List includes all ability districts in formerly covered areas with combined minority CVAPs below 50 percent.

Table A6

Franchise Restrictions Under Section 2 and Section 5 (1982–Present)

Policy	Section 5 Preclearance Denials	Section 2 Successful Claims	Section 2 Failed Claims
Polling place eliminations	19	3	3
Election date changes	15	0	0
Voter registration procedures	10	5	4
Bilingual election procedures	10	2	0
Voter roll purges	5	0	1
Lack of assistance to voters	4	2	2
Photo ID laws	3	0	2
Absentee voting procedures	3	2	4
Cutbacks to voting hours	2	1	1
Voting machine problems	1	3	2
Citizenship requirements for registration	1	0	0
Total	73	18	19

JENNIFER NOU

SUB-REGULATING ELECTIONS

The revelation that a federal judge was reconsidering the potentially partisan nature of voter identification laws renewed important debates about the capacity of courts to adjudicate election-related disputes.[1] Chief among them were inquiries about the ability of litigants to present reliable information in judicial forums and that of judges to draw sound inferences from the evidence proffered. How much voter fraud actually exists? To what extent do identification requirements deter fraud as opposed to disenfranchise? Many election law scholars, for their part, have long abandoned the courts as an arena for answering such questions. In their view, not only are judges limited to the cramped records presented to them, but they also remain hopelessly mired in unproductive individual rights frameworks and vain searches for manageable standards, all the while cowed by potential political questions.[2]

Jennifer Nou is Neubauer Family Assistant Professor, University of Chicago Law School.

AUTHOR'S NOTE: For helpful conversations and comments on earlier drafts, many thanks to Christopher Elmendorf, Heather Gerken, Robert Glicksman, Aziz Huq, Dennis Hutchinson, Jonathan Masur, Eric Posner, Nicholas Stephanopolous, Geoffrey Stone, Lior Strahilevitz, and to Brett Kavanaugh and the participants of a Judicial Sidebar Workshop at the University of Chicago Law School. Gabe Broughton provided excellent research assistance.

[1] See Richard A. Posner, *Reflections on Judging* 84–85 (Harvard, 2013) ("I plead guilty to having written the majority opinion (affirmed by the Supreme Court) upholding Indiana's requirement that prospective voters prove their identity with a photo ID—a type of law now widely regarded as a means of voter suppression rather than of fraud prevention.").

[2] See, for example, Heather K. Gerken, *Lost in the Political Thicket: The Court, Election Law, and the Doctrinal Interregnum*, 153 U Pa L Rev 503, 504 (2004); Samuel Issacharoff, *Gerrymandering and Political Cartels*, 116 Harv L Rev 593 (2002); Samuel Issacharoff and

Many commentators have thus turned instead to consider alternative institutions that may be better equipped to adjudicate election-related disputes.[3] In the state-level redistricting context, for example, these "new institutional" proposals include shadow line-drawing entities, advisory commissions, and independent redistricting bodies.[4] Their underlying rationales often parallel administrative law arguments in favor of delegating policy decisions to agencies over courts, whether on the grounds of superior legitimacy, accountability, or expertise. Familiar questions of institutional independence and design abound.[5] It is thus surprising that more has not been made of the intersection between election and federal administrative law, notwithstanding some already valuable inroads.[6]

Perhaps one explanation arises from the fact that administrative

---

Richard H. Pildes, *Politics as Markets: Partisan Lockups of the Democratic Process*, 50 Stan L Rev 643 (1998); Peter H. Schuck, *The Thickest Thicket: Partisan Gerrymandering and Judicial Regulation of Politics*, 87 Colum L Rev 1325, 1330 (1987).

[3] See, for example, Bruce E. Cain, *Redistricting Commissions: A Better Political Buffer?*, 121 Yale L J 1808, 1808 (2012); Heather K. Gerken and Michael S. Kang, *The Institutional Turn in Election Law Scholarship*, in Guy-Uriel E. Charles, Heather K. Gerken, and Michael S. Kang, eds, *Race, Reform, and Regulation of the Electoral Process: Recurring Puzzles in American Democracy* 17, 26 (Cambridge, 2011).

[4] "New institutional" approaches, by and large, seek to "lessen the necessity of court intervention in politically sensitive election administration matters such as redistricting by harnessing politics to fix politics." Cain, 121 Yale L J at 1808 (cited in note 3). See also Heather K. Gerken, *Getting from Here to There in Redistricting Reform*, 5 Duke J Const L & Pub Policy 1, 7–9 (2010); Christopher S. Elmendorf, *Representation Reinforcement through Advisory Commissions: The Case of Election Law*, 80 NYU L Rev 1366, 1407–12 (2005); Jeffrey C. Kubin, Note, *The Case for Redistricting Commissions*, 75 Tex L Rev 837, 849–50 (1997); Note, *A Federal Administrative Approach to Redistricting Reform*, 121 Harv L Rev 1842, 1842 (2008).

[5] Both fields, for example, search for structures and processes that can best facilitate that independence, whether through removal restrictions, salary protections, appointments qualifications, and so on. See Rachel E. Barkow, *Insulating Agencies: Avoiding Capture through Institutional Design*, 89 Tex L Rev 15 (2010).

[6] See, e.g., Adam B. Cox, *Designing Redistricting Institutions*, 5 Election L J 412, 416–17 (2006) (examining potential benefits of "centralized, federal administrative review" for partisan gerrymandering efforts); Christopher S. Elmendorf, *Election Commissions and Electoral Reform: An Overview*, 5 Election L J 425, 443–44 (2006) (identifying as a valuable research question a "larger inquiry concerning how the policy choices of nominally independent bodies are affected by, inter alia, the body's structure and powers"); Heather K. Gerken, *A Third Way for the Voting Rights Act: Section 5 and the Opt-In Approach*, 106 Colum L Rev 708, 748 (2006) (suggesting that the Department of Justice should be understood as "an agency charged with administering a statute" for Voting Rights Act purposes); Samuel Issacharoff, *Beyond the Discrimination Model on Voting*, 127 Harv L Rev 95, 121–23 (2013); Richard H. Pildes, *Voting Rights: The Next Generation*, in Charles, Gerken, and Kang, eds, *Race, Reform, and Regulation of the Electoral Process* at 17, 26 (cited in note 3); Daniel P. Tokaji, *The Future of Election Reform: From Rules to Institutions*, 28 Yale L & Policy Rev 125, 135 (2009); Saul Zipkin, *Administering Election Law*, 95 Marq L Rev 641 (2012); Note, *A Federal Administrative Approach to Redistricting Reform*, 121 Harv L Rev 1842, 1843–44 (2008).

efforts at the federal level have thus far been timid; as a result, there have been few circumstances in which to apply administrative law principles directly. Other possible explanations include the path-dependent state primacy over electoral regulation, the lack of existing federal infrastructure to monitor elections nationally, as well as the weak political will to establish robust federal electoral institutions.[7] Last Term's decision in *Arizona v Intertribal Council of Arizona*, however, helps to highlight the need for more robust theories of federal election administration.[8] A central issue in *Intertribal* was whether Arizona's attempt to require proof of citizenship for a federal voter registration form violated the National Voter Registration Act. The Act required that states "accept and use" the federal form. The Court resolved the statutory ambiguity to mean that states could not require the submission of materials beyond those listed on the form by the Election Assistance Commission (EAC). In reaching this determination, the Court ignored the EAC executive director's opinion letter concluding the same. The agency commissioners, for their part, had deadlocked on the interpretive question. In the decision's wake, Arizona, joined by Kansas, is currently engaged in litigation against the EAC under the Administrative Procedure Act (APA).[9]

While *Intertribal* can be understood as a case about federalism, constitutional, or substantive election law, this article analyzes *Intertribal* through the lens of administrative law. In doing so, it brings to the foreground an otherwise background electoral administrative agency in the case, the EAC, and uses the suit as a springboard to explore broader themes relevant to federal election administration.[10]

---

[7] See Daniel P. Tokaji, *The Birth and Rebirth of Election Administration*, 6 Election L J 118, 122–23 (2007) (reviewing Roy G. Saltman, *The History and Politics of Voting Technology: In Quest of Integrity and Public Confidence* (Palgrave, 2006)).

[8] *Arizona v Intertribal Council of Arizona, Inc.*, No 12-71, slip op (June 17, 2013), online at http://www.supremecourt.gov/opinions/12pdf/12-71_7l48.pdf.

[9] See *Kobach v United States Election Assistance Commission*, 13-cv-04095 (D Kan 2013).

[10] The sphere of election administration, as defined here, includes the administration of statutes related to the conduct of elections, including the regulation of activities leading up to an election as well as those that occur on Election Day itself—a scope that parallels that of many administrative agencies abroad. See note 47. Others have adopted narrower definitions, but usually to address a different set of issues than those pursued here. See, for example, Daniel P. Tokaji, *Teaching Election Administration*, 56 SLU L J 675, 675 (2012) (citing "voting technology, voter registration, voter identification, and the conduct of recounts" as representative election administration issues); David Schleicher, *From Here All-the-Way-Down, or How to Write a Festschrift Piece*, 48 Tulsa L Rev 401, 406 (2013) (defining "election administration" in terms of the "plumbing of the electoral system—vote counting, manning the polls, locating polling places, etc.").

In particular, it puzzles through various analytical issues that arise when courts are called upon to resolve agency deadlocks on questions of statutory interpretation, including when commissioners should be required to give reasons for their deadlock, and whose legal opinions courts should consider. In light of such deadlocks, this article proposes an institutional understanding of *Skidmore* deference to interpretive documents prepared by politically insulated actors within election-related administrative agencies.[11] Judicial deference, it posits, should give weight to the relative independence of agency staff when politically appointed officials are otherwise deadlocked. To be clear, the claim is not that staff opinions and other guidance documents would *require* deference or overrule those of appointed commissioners. Rather, the argument emphasizes that such views constitute an oft-overlooked source of expertise that would be prudent for judges to consider in electoral disputes.

This approach would help to vindicate otherwise under-enforced constitutional norms by flipping the conventional wisdom granting greater interpretive deference to more politically accountable actors—in situations where such actors have failed to resolve a statutory ambiguity themselves. In this manner, the proposal is a second-best solution for courts required to resolve a statutory ambiguity when first-best answers are unavailable due to institutional constraints and internal agency politics. As such, the proposal seeks to create greater incentives for internal agency independence in the presence of partisan deadlocks, as well as for the development of agency expertise through sub-regulatory materials—nonbinding, but informative, guidance documents such as agency manuals, advisory notices, or opinion letters.[12]

To develop these ideas, Part I critically examines *Intertribal*'s background and reasoning. Part II surveys federal election-related agencies and notes that many are structured to deadlock on partisan grounds. Part III then considers how courts should treat reviewable election agency deadlocks and, in particular, how judges can benefit from agency expertise to resolve such ties. Finally, Part IV reflects

---

[11] See *Skidmore v Swift & Co.*, 323 US 134, 140 (1944).

[12] See Mary Whisner, *Some Guidance About Agency Guidance*, 105 L Library J 385, 392 (2013) (characterizing "sub-regulatory guidance" as including "agency manuals, advisory notices, internal guidance to agency field inspectors, and letters from government officials to regulated entities.").

more broadly on how administrative law principles might be tailored to the electoral context.

I. INTERTRIBAL'S IMPASSE

In December 2005, the Arizona Secretary of State's office sent an email to the EAC with an inquiry. The year before, Arizona voters had passed a ballot initiative requiring that voting registrants provide proof of their citizenship.[13] Acceptable proof under the new state law included the applicant's birth certificate or passport, naturalization papers, or driver's license number.[14] The Secretary of State asked whether the EAC could add this new Arizona requirement to the federal mail-in registration form that the EAC had developed under the National Voter Registration Act (NVRA).[15] The federal form contained a section of state-specific instructions notifying state residents of what additional information they had to provide in order to register.[16]

The agency's executive director refused Arizona's request.[17] His letter reasoned that the NVRA mandates that states "shall accept and use the mail voter registration application prescribed by the [EAC]."[18] Accordingly, the new Arizona requirements did not alter the state's voter qualifications, but rather constituted an additional evidentiary requirement for a preexisting qualification (citizenship). Such a state-imposed requirement on the federal form would effectively result in Arizona's refusal to "accept and use" the EAC's form as required by the NVRA.[19] In the director's view, states could not condition voter registration on the submission of materials beyond those exclusively demanded by the federal form. The NVRA "regulated the area" and therefore preempted the state's conflicting requirements.[20]

Despite this opinion letter, Arizona's Secretary of State rejected the director's interpretation and continued to enforce the state law

---

[13] Ariz Rev Stat Ann § 16-166(F) (2006).

[14] Id.

[15] 42 USC § 1973gg-2(a)(2).

[16] See *National Mail Voter Registration Form*, *3–20, online at http://www.eac.gov.

[17] Letter from Executive Director Thomas Wilkey to Secretary of State Jan Brewer (Mar 6, 2006).

[18] Id.

[19] 42 USC § 1973gg-4(a)(1).

[20] Wilkey letter (cited in note 17 above).

to require the submission of proof of citizenship along with the federal form.[21] The conflict continued in both the agency and the courts. In May 2006, a consolidated group of plaintiffs, including private individuals, Indian tribes, and nonpartisan advocacy groups, filed suit in district court to enjoin various practices under the state law. The Ninth Circuit granted the plaintiffs' emergency interlocutory injunction, only to later have the injunction vacated by the Supreme Court in *Purcell v Gonzalez*.[22] In a per curiam opinion, the Court emphasized the imminence of the then-upcoming election and the failure of the Court of Appeals to defer to the findings of the district court (which had not yet issued any factual findings and, as a result, left the Supreme Court with nothing more than a "bare order" to review).[23] After further litigation,[24] a three-judge panel and the Ninth Circuit sitting en banc eventually held that the NVRA preempted Arizona's conflicting law under the Elections Clause; Arizona could not require the submission of proof of citizenship along with the federal registration form. The Supreme Court granted certiorari.[25]

As the case was winding its way to the Court, the EAC's four commissioners considered the legal matter in July 2006. Their deliberations resulted in a debilitating tie: two commissioners (Democratic nominations) voted against the change and two (Republication nominations) voted in favor.[26] Because the proposal required three votes for approval,[27] the federal form was not amended. Two of the commissioners released public statements regarding the basis

---

[21] State Petitioners' Brief on the Merits, *Arizona v Intertribal Council of Arizona, Inc.*, No 12-71, *20 (June 17, 2013).

[22] *Gonzalez v Arizona*, 485 F3d 1041, 1046 (9th Cir 2007); *Purcell v Gonzalez*, 549 US 1 (2006) (per curiam).

[23] *Gonzalez*, 549 US at 5–6.

[24] On remand, the appellate court affirmed the district court's initial denial of a preliminary injunction and held that the NVRA did not supersede Arizona's state law. 485 F3d at 1049–51. The trial court therefore granted summary judgment to Arizona.

[25] 133 S Ct 476 (2012).

[26] See Office of Representative Nancy Pelosi, Press Release, *Daschle, Pelosi Announce Nominations to Election Assistance Commission* (May 28, 2003), online at http://pelosi .house.gov/sites/pelosi.house.gov/files/pressarchives/releases/prDachlePelosiEAC052803 .htm (announcing nominations of Ray Martinez and Gracia Hillman by Democratic House and Senate leaders); US Election Assistance Commission, Certification, *In the Matter of Arizona Request for Information* (July 31, 2006), available online at http://archives.eac.gov/ voter/docs/az-tally-vote.pdf/attachment_download/file; Joint Appendix, *Arizona v Inter Tribal Council of Arizona*, 2012 WL 6198263, *222–42 (2012).

[27] 42 USC § 15328.

for their votes, underscoring the contentiousness of the outcome.[28]

After the agency's deadlocked vote, Arizona took no further action with respect to the EAC—a fact Justice Scalia later emphasized at oral argument and in his eventual majority opinion.[29] Justice Scalia agreed with the Ninth Circuit that the NVRA's "accept and use" provision precluded state-imposed registration requirements without EAC approval. On the one hand, Congress could preemptively regulate how federal elections were conducted under the Elections Clause; in this sense, the so-called presumption against preemption did not apply. Rather, Congress's power under the Elections Clause was broad. Its substantive reach extended over the "times, places, and manner" of federal elections—"comprehensive words" which "embrace authority to provide a comprehensive code for congressional elections," including regulations over federal voter registration.[30]

On the other hand, the Court also made clear that states retained the power to determine *which* voters were qualified to vote, potentially limiting previous case law regarding the scope of Congress's ability to determine voter qualifications.[31] How and where to draw this line—between a substantive qualification and a mere procedural regulation over the "manner" of federal elections subject to federal oversight—will almost surely be the subject of future litigation. One argument left open to Arizona on this question (but raised too late

---

[28] Commissioner Ray Martinez III, a Democratic nominee, argued that reversing the agency's previous legal position regarding the NVRA would create inconsistencies and confusion in other states and was, in any event, premature given the likelihood of pending judicial resolution. Finally, he worried about the EAC's institutional credibility. Until this vote, the EAC commissioners had always been able to achieve unanimity, and he feared that the outcome would be perceived as an "overly partisan federal agency that is more prone to deadlock" than to fulfilling its mission. Joint Appendix, 2012 WL 6198263 at 229–39 (cited in note 26). Commissioner Paul DeGregorio, the EAC chairman and a Republican nominee, expressed his agreement with a district court opinion considering the issue and concluded that Arizona's attempt to require proof of citizenship did not violate the NVRA. Id at 223. He cited his own personal experience as an election administrator in recounting registration applications that could not be finalized due to voters' failure to supply missing information. Thus, "leaving out key instructions on the National Voter Registration Form was likely to cause more steps for the voters and possibly keep them from being able to cast a ballot." Id at 224–25. In his view, consolidating the federal and state requirements into one form would be more efficient and increase the number of validly cast ballots.

[29] *Intertribal Council*, No 12-71, slip op at 16–17.

[30] Id.

[31] Id at 13. See, for example, *Oregon v Mitchell*, 400 US 112 (1970).

in the case) was that the state's proof-of-citizenship registration requirement was itself a qualification to vote.[32]

Justice Scalia suggested another possibility as well: that the state's authority to establish voter qualifications also included the power to demand the information required for the state's effective enforcement of its own qualifications.[33] Pointing to another NVRA provision declaring that the EAC-prescribed application "may require only such identifying information" as is "necessary" to determine "eligibility,"[34] Justice Scalia suggested that the statute might be read to require the inclusion of information essential to meaningful enforcement. In this manner, he effectively encouraged Arizona to bring suit (which it did), arguing that the EAC had a "nondiscretionary duty" to include citizenship information as "necessary" to enforce Arizona's voter qualifications.[35] EAC's inaction on or arbitrary rejection of the claim would then be subject to judicial review under the APA.[36] In a footnote, Justice Scalia further noted that the EAC lacked any active commissioners at the time, and wondered whether a court could compel agency action despite the agency's lack of leadership.[37]

For Justices Thomas and Alito, in dissent, the questions raised by *Intertribal* did not need to be resolved in administrative forums like the EAC, but rather could and should be settled in courts without bureaucratic involvement. Justice Alito, for his part, accused the majority of "send[ing] the State to traverse a veritable procedural obstacle course."[38] Justice Thomas agreed.[39] Both Justices then took pains to point out that the EAC at the time was plagued by vacancies, with the lack of a quorum rendering the commission but an "empty shell."[40]

---

[32] *Intertribal Council*, No 12-71, slip op at 15 n 9.

[33] Id at 15.

[34] Id at 12, 15–17.

[35] Id at 16–17.

[36] Id.

[37] Id at 17, n 10.

[38] Id at 6 (Alito, J, dissenting).

[39] Id at 16–17 (Thomas, J, dissenting) ("Offering a nonexistent pathway to administrative relief is an exercise in futility, not constitutional avoidance.").

[40] Id at 17 (Thomas, J, dissenting); id at 6 (Alito, J, dissenting). Concurring in the judgment, Justice Kennedy wrote separately to emphasize his view that the presumption against preemption should play no less of a role in the electoral context. Id at 1–2 (Kennedy, J, concurring). To him, the cautionary presumption played an important part when in-

Intertribal can thus be seen as an attempt by the majority to shift back to an administrative agency, rather than a court, questions it thought better suited for an initial administrative determination. Among them: What kind of scheme—attestation backed by perjury prosecutions or formal documentation—is "necessary" for legitimately establishing voter eligibility? What kind of information would properly "effectuate" a citizenship requirement? Answers to such questions would require data and evidence that agencies would be better situated to gather relative to judicial forums, subject to the constraints of administrative law.

II. ELECTION-RELATED AGENCIES

American federal elections are currently administered by a patchwork of federal agencies in collaboration with state and local governments, which still bear the bulk of administrative responsibilities on the ground.[41] While states are constitutionally charged with providing for the "times, places, and manner" of federal elections in the first instance, Congress has exercised its power to "make or alter" these regulations selectively—most notably in the areas of campaign finance,[42] anti-discrimination,[43] ballot provision,[44] vote-counting technology, and voter registration by both domestic[45] and

---

terpreting a federal statute's boundaries and the Elections Clause was no different than other enumerated powers like the commerce or bankruptcy power, where the presumption still applied. Justice Kennedy also made a pragmatic observation: States largely bear the expenses of holding federal elections, since state and federal election processes usually overlap in practice. The same voters usually use the same ballots, that is, when choosing both state and federal officials. As a result, states still maintained an important interest in federal elections given this administrative overlap. Id at 2.

[41] See Daniel P. Tokaji, *Public Rights and Private Rights of Action: The Enforcement of Federal Election Laws*, 44 Ind L Rev 113, 117 (2010) (explaining that "election administration remains mostly a matter of state law and local practice, as has been the case throughout U.S. history" and "[a]uthority is largely devolved to the fifty chief election officials in the states and to thousands of local election officials at the state and local level.").

[42] See, for example, Federal Election Campaign Act of 1971, as amended at 2 USC § 431 et seq. In *Buckley v Valeo*, 424 US 1 (1976), the Supreme Court assumed plenary congressional power over federal election campaigns and campaign finance based on the Elections Clause. *Buckley*, 424 US at 13.

[43] Voting Rights Act, 42 USC § 1973 (2011).

[44] The 1975 amendments to VRA require jurisdictions to provide ballots and instructions in language of covered language-minority groups when particular population conditions exist. A number of federal statutes concern electoral access by the disabled, including the 1982 amendment to the VRA, the Voting Accessibility for the Elderly and Handicapped Act of 1984.

[45] See National Voter Registration Act, 42 USC §§ 1973gg–1973gg-10 (2006); Help America Vote Act of 2002, 42 USC § 15301 et seq (2002).

overseas voters.[46] While these federal responsibilities are nontrivial, it is worth noting that they pale in comparison to the more comprehensive and centralized schemes of other countries.[47]

Congress, in turn, has delegated many of these election-related responsibilities to a constellation of federal administrative agencies, notable for their structural and substantive heterogeneity. Some of these agencies, for example, have traditionally independent features such as for-cause removal restrictions and multimember boards, while others are more recognizably executive in nature through at-will removal of their agency heads by the President.[48] At the fore, these agencies include the EAC involved in *Intertribal*, the Federal Election Commission, the Department of Justice (DOJ), and the Department of Defense.[49]

---

[46] Members of the uniformed services and U.S. citizens who live abroad are eligible to register and vote absentee in federal elections under the Uniformed and Overseas Citizens Absentee Voting Act of 1986 (UOCAVA, Pub L No 99-410). Since 1942, a number of federal laws have been enacted to assist these voters: the Soldier Voting Act of 1942 (Pub L No 77-712, amended in 1944), the Federal Voting Assistance Act of 1955 (Pub L No 84-296), the Overseas Citizens Voting Rights Act of 1975 (Pub L No 94-203; both the 1955 and 1975 laws were amended in 1978 to improve procedures), and the Uniformed and Overseas Citizens Absentee Voting Act of 1986.

[47] India's unitary election commission, for example, is constitutionally vested with broad authority over election-related matters. India Const, Art 324. It has used its power to promulgate a Model Code of Conduct as well as to issue robust regulations governing the disclosure of campaign expenses, election schedules, polling and counting locations, among other matters. See Elmendorf, 5 Election L J at 425, 429 (cited in note 6); Tokaji, 44 Ind L Rev at 122–23 (cited in note 41); see also Election Commission of India, *About ECI*, online at http://eci.nic.in/eci_main1/the_setup.aspx. Similarly, Canada's single national election commission has broad authority to implement and enforce electoral legislation, including campaign finance laws; maintain a national registry of electors; oversee the registration of political parties; monitor election spending and financial returns; train election administrators; and provide technical support to independent redistricting commissions. See Jean-Pierre Kingsley, *The Administration of Canada's Independent, Non-Partisan Approach*, 3 Election L J 406 (2004). The powers of the United Kingdom's Electoral Commission are similarly capacious. See Elmendorf, 5 Election L J at 425, 426–27 (cited in note 6); see also Nicholas O. Stephanopoulos, *Our Electoral Exceptionalism*, 80 U Chi L Rev 769, 780–86 (2013) (surveying non-American institutional models of election administration).

[48] See Barkow, 89 Tex L Rev at 15, 38–39 (cited in note 5).

[49] Other agencies are tangentially involved in federal election regulation, but this article focuses on the four mentioned here. The Department of Treasury, for example, oversees public funds disbursement for presidential candidates certified by the FEC as statutorily eligible, while the Internal Revenue Service reviews FEC regulations for consistency with the tax code, determines whether an organization's tax status is consistent with its political activities, as well as which political activities result in taxable income. Finally, the Federal Communications Commission also oversees broadcaster compliance with the provision of reasonable access to broadcast time for federal candidates. See Maurice C. Sheppard, *The Federal Election Commission: Policy, Politics, and Administration*, 61–63 (UPA, 2007).

A. INDEPENDENT COMMISSIONS

More specifically, the EAC and the Federal Election Commission (FEC) are both independent agencies with a distinctive design feature: both are normally headed by an even number of commissioners with staggered terms, equally split between two political parties in practice. Specifically, the EAC usually consists of four members, two of whom are Republicans and two of whom are Democrats.[50] Each serves four-year staggered terms.[51] The EAC commissioners, in turn, choose a chair and vice chair, who also cannot be from the same political party.[52] The FEC is similarly composed of six members with six-year staggered terms, no more than three of whom can be affiliated with the same political party.[53] The FEC commissioners also choose a chair and vice chair from different political parties.[54]

1. *Election Assistance Commission.* In addition to its four commissioners, the EAC is also statutorily authorized to have an executive director, a general counsel, and other professional staff.[55] The Help America Vote Act (HAVA) also created three representative advisory committees called the Technical Guidelines Development Committee, Standards Board, and the Board of Ad-

---

[50] See 42 USC § 15323(a) (specifying that members drawn from recommendations submitted by "the Majority Leader of the Senate, the Speaker of the House of Representatives, the Minority Leader of the Senate, and the Minority Leader of the House of Representatives . . . with respect to each vacancy on the Commission affiliated with the political party of the Member of Congress involved"); see also Tokaji, 28 Yale L & Policy Rev at 134 (cited in note 6) ("Bipartisan by statute, the EAC includes two commissioners from each of the major parties.").

[51] See 42 USC § 15323(b)(1).

[52] See 42 USC § 15323(c) ("The Commission shall select a chair and vice chair from among its members for a term of 1 year, except that the chair and vice chair may not be affiliated with the same political party.").

[53] See 2 USC § 437c(a)(1) (providing that "[n]o more than 3 members of the [Federal Election] Commission appointed under this paragraph may be affiliated with the same political party."); 2 USC § 437c(a)(2)(A) (2006) (specifying six FEC commissioners with six-year terms). No independent or member of a third party has ever been appointed. See Bradley A. Smith and Stephen M. Hoersting, *A Toothless Anaconda: Innovation, Impotence and Overenforcement at the Federal Election Commission*, 1 Election L J 145, 158 n 97 (2002). Interestingly, lower courts have implied for-cause protection for the FEC. See *FEC v NRA Political Victory Fund*, 6 F3d 821, 826 (DC Cir 1993).

[54] See 2 USC § 437c(a)(5) ("The Commission shall elect a chairman and a vice chairman from among its members . . . for a term of one year. . . . The chairman and the vice chairman shall not be affiliated with the same political party.").

[55] 42 USC § 15324.

visors.[56] As a substantive matter, HAVA granted the EAC the authority to disburse payments to states to replace voting systems as well as to provide guidance regarding voting system standards, testing, and certification. More generally, the statute directs the EAC to serve as a "clearinghouse" for election administration data and best practices.[57] HAVA explicitly denies the EAC authority, however, to issue any rules or regulations under the statute,[58] except in the narrow context of the mail-in voting process at issue in *Intertribal*.[59] The Attorney General, in turn, is authorized to enforce the statute and bring suits for declaratory or injunctive relief accordingly.[60]

2. *Federal Election Commission.* Apart from its six commissioners, the FEC also has a staff director and general counsel appointed by the commission, an inspector general, a chief financial officer, as well as a chief information officer.[61] Substantively, the FEC administers the Federal Election Campaign Act (FECA), which imposes caps on election spending, limits individual candidate contributions, and requires various candidate and political action committee disclosures.[62] The commission administers the provisions through both rulemaking and adjudication and facilitates enforce-

---

[56] The Technical Guidelines committee is chaired by the director of NIST and 14 other members appointed jointly by NIST and the EAC. The Standards Board has 110 members, 55 of whom are chosen by state chief election officers and the other half by local election officials. Finally, the Board of Advisors has 37 members drawn from state and local government associations, the Architectural and Transportation Barrier Compliance Board, and other federal agencies and congressional committees with election oversight responsibilities. See Election Assistance Commission, *Board of Advisors*, online at http://www.eac.gov/about_the_eac/board_of_advisors.aspx.

[57] See 42 USC §§ 15322; Vassia Gueorguieva, *Election Administration Bodies and Implementation Tools*, 13 Georgetown Pub Policy Rev 95, 103 (2008); Ray Martinez III, *Is the Election Assistance Commission Worth Keeping?*, 12 Election L J 190, 191 (2013) ("Unlike most federal independent agencies, the EAC was created as a non-regulatory body, designed primarily to serve as a national clearinghouse of election administration best practices and to distribute federal funds to state and local jurisdictions.").

[58] 42 USC § 15329 ("The Commission shall not have any authority to issue any rule, promulgate any regulation, or take any other action which imposes any requirement on any State or unit of local government, except to the extent permitted under [the mail-in voter registration form provision].").

[59] See 42 USC § 1973gg-7(a).

[60] 42 USC § 15511.

[61] See 2 USC 437c(f); Federal Election Commission, *FEC Offices*, online at http://www.fec.gov/about/offices/offices.shtml; Sheppard, *The Federal Election Commission* at 63–64 (cited in note 49).

[62] See Gueorguieva, 13 Georgetown Pub Policy Rev at 96–97 (cited in note 57); Sheppard, *The Federal Election Commission* at 60 (cited in note 49).

ment actions in conjunction with the DOJ.[63] The FEC also periodically issues advisory opinions, which are generated in response to requests by parties, candidates, and other potentially regulated entities.[64]

Formal agency action for both the EAC and FEC, in turn, normally requires the bipartisan majority approval of the agencies' commissioners. The FEC, for its part, requires a majority of commissioners to agree when making, amending, or repealing rules; issuing advisory opinions; or approving enforcement actions.[65] This requirement usually requires the assent of four of the FEC's six commissioners.[66] The EAC, in turn, requires three-member approval for its actions—typically a majority of its four commissioners.[67] When coupled with the agency's partisan balancing requirements, these voting rules help to ensure that the agencies deadlock in the absence of bipartisan agreement. Moreover, a tie vote for the FEC and EAC means that the proposed action does not proceed. By contrast, a tie vote for the International Trade Commission (one of the only other rulemaking agencies with an even-numbered, bipartisan commission structure) means that an investigation proceeds.[68] As such, both the

---

[63] 2 USC § 437d(a)(8). See Gueorguieva, 13 Georgetown Pub Policy Rev at 100 (cited in note 57).

[64] 2 USC § 437f.

[65] See 2 USC § 437c(a)(2)(c) ("All decisions of the Commission with respect to the exercise of its duties and powers under the provisions of this Act shall be made by a majority vote of the members of the [Federal Election] Commission"); see also R. Sam Garrett, *Deadlocked Votes among Members of the Federal Election Commission (FEC): Overview and Potential Considerations for Congress* 1 (Congressional Research Service, 2009), online at http://www.bradblog.com/wp-content/uploads/CRS_FEC_Deadlocks.pdf.

[66] Three commissioners may be sufficient, however, when there are vacancies, as long as the FEC fulfills its internally-mandated four-member quorum. See Rules of Procedure of the Federal Election Commission Pursuant to 2 USC § 437(c)(e), online at http://www.fec.gov/directives/directive_10.pdf.

[67] See 42 USC § 15328 (stating that "[a]ny action which the [Election Assistance] Commission is authorized to carry out under this chapter may be carried out only with the approval of at least three of its members"). This rule could require potential unanimity under the agency's informal three-member quorum requirement. See, e.g., Election Assistance Commission, *Work Continues at the EAC*, online at http://www.eac.gov/blogs/work_continues_at_the_eac (Dec 14, 2011) ("A quorum (at least three commissioners) is required to determine new EAC policies, defined as 'high level determinations, setting an overall agency goal/objective or otherwise setting rules, guidance or guidelines at the highest level.'"). This reading would be consistent with the statutory text requiring the approval of at least "three" EAC members for formal agency actions.

[68] 19 USC § 1330(d)(5). Besides the FEC and EAC, the only two other agencies that appear to have even-numbered commissions are the International Trade Commission and the Commission on Civil Rights. See 19 USC § 1330(a), (c) (2006) (six members on the

FEC and EAC are structurally biased in favor of the status quo.[69]

On the one hand, these agencies' bipartisan-vote requirements reflect lofty legislative aspirations. The FECA House Report, for example, cites the dangers of "partisan misuse" and the hope that the FEC's majority-vote requirement would help to ensure a "mature and considered judgment."[70] On the other hand, the decision rules also invite intractable impasses, particularly over significant and high-profile issues.[71] The EAC, for example, deadlocked 2–2 on *Intertribal*'s question of whether to include Arizona's proof of citizenship requirements on the federal registration form. One commenter derided the outcome as a "partisan stalemate" in the "one area" where the agency had regulatory authority.[72]

B. EXECUTIVE AGENCIES

By comparison, there are also two prominent executive agencies with single presidentially-appointed and senate-confirmed heads, the Department of Justice and the Department of Defense. While both federal agencies also regulate elections, their scope and structure differ from the FEC and EAC in important ways.

1. *Department of Justice.* The Department of Justice has been

---

International Trade Commission, not more than three of whom can be members of the same political party); 42 USC § 1975(b) (2006) (eight members on the Commission on Civil Rights, not more than four of whom can be from the same political party). The Commission on Civil Rights is primarily a fact-finding agency and periodically issues reports regarding civil rights policy and enforcement, serves as an information clearinghouse, and prepares public service announcement and advertising campaigns to discourage civil rights violations. See 42 USC § 1975a.

[69] Marian Wang, *As Political Groups Push Envelope, FEC Gridlock Gives "De Facto Green Light"* (ProPublica, Nov 7, 2011), online at http://www.propublica.org/article/as-political-donors-push-envelope-fec-gridlock-gives-de-facto-green-light/single ("Ultimately, the FEC is set up in such a way that when the commissioners deadlock, one side comes away with a de-facto win—the side seeking to preserve the status quo.").

[70] See also *Federal Election Campaign Act Amendments of 1976*, HR Rep No 94-917, 94th Cong, 2d Sess 3 (1976).

[71] See Garrett, *Deadlocked Votes* at 4 (cited in note 65) ("Those issues on which deadlocks occurred . . . featured strong disagreement among Commissioners and reflected apparently unsettled positions on some major policy questions, such as political committee status, when particular activities triggered filing requirements or other regulation, and questions related to investigations and other enforcement matters. In addition, the deadlocks that did occur always fell along partisan lines.").

[72] See Tokaji, 28 Yale L & Policy Rev at 135 (cited in note 6). See also Gueorguieva, 13 Georgetown Pub Policy Rev at 101–02 (cited in note 57); Press Release, *FEC Deadlocks on Attempted Evasion of Disclosure Laws* (Campaign Legal Center, June 14, 2012), online at http://www.campaignlegalcenter.org/index.php?option=com_content&view-article&id=1766:june-14-2012-fec-deadlocks-on-attempted-evasion-of-disclosure-laws&catid=63:legal-center-press-releases&Itemid=61.

charged with helping to enforce a number of election-related statutes, including (what is left of) the Voting Rights Act (VRA).[73]
Before *Shelby County* invalidated VRA Section 4's coverage formula,[74] the agency administered Section 5's preclearance regime
for jurisdictions covered by the formula. Those jurisdictions had
to affirmatively demonstrate that the changes would "neither
ha[ve] the purpose nor . . . the effect of denying or abridging the
right to vote on account of race or color."[75] While covered jurisdictions could submit their voting changes to the DOJ or a federal
district court in Washington, D.C., more than 99 percent of the
preclearance requests were submitted for DOJ administrative review.[76]

The current case law would make it difficult for the DOJ to
successfully claim legislative rulemaking authority under Section
5—and indeed the DOJ has not done so, explicitly treating its
regulations as guidelines.[77] Moreover, Section 5 provides that litigants can bypass the DOJ administrative process to vindicate their
claims directly in a judicial forum, further suggesting that Congress intended for the courts to play a primary interpretive role
as well; the DOJ's own regulations refer to the DOJ as a judicial
"surrogate."[78] Finally, the text of Section 5 also does not explicitly
grant DOJ rulemaking power,[79] and the Attorney General's preclearance denial letters lack precedential value.[80]

---

[73] In addition to the VRA discussed here, the Attorney General is also authorized to
bring civil actions to enforce a number of other election-related statutes, such as the
Uniformed and Overseas Citizens Absentee Voting Act, the National Voter Registration
Act, and the Help America Vote Act's provisions requiring states to provide uniform and
nondiscriminatory election technology.

[74] See *Shelby County v Holder*, 133 S Ct 2612 (2013).

[75] 42 USC § 1973c (West, 2011).

[76] See Department of Justice, Office of the Inspector General Oversight and Review
Division, *A Review of the Operations of the Voting Section of the Civil Rights Division* 13
(March 2013), online at http://www.justice.gov/oig/reports/2013/s1303.pdf (ascribing rates
to the fact that the "Department's administrative reviews are less expensive for the covered
jurisdiction and generally result in a faster outcome") (hereafter *Review of the Voting Section*).

[77] See Revisions of the Procedures for the Administration of Section 5 of the Voting
Rights Act, 75 Fed Reg 33205 (proposed June 11, 2010) (to be codified at 29 CFR pts 0
and 51), citing 5 USC § 301.

[78] 42 USC § 1973c; 28 CFR § 51.52.

[79] 42 USC § 1973c. Section 12(d) of the Act authorizes the Attorney General to file
suit to enjoin violations of Section 5.

[80] See *United States v Mead Corp.*, 533 US 218, 232 (denying *Chevron* deference to tariff
rulings on the grounds that they were not "the legislative type of activity that would
naturally bind more than the parties to the ruling"). See also J. Morgan Kousser, *The*

While Section 5 is currently a hollow shell in *Shelby County's* wake, the DOJ also enforces Section 2 of the VRA, which bans electoral structures that result in members of a class of citizens defined by race or color "hav[ing] less opportunity than other members of the electorate to participate in the political process and to elect representatives of their choice."[81] As such, Section 2 is a nationally applicable prohibition against voting practices and procedures that discriminate on the basis of race, color, or language minority group. It has been used, for example, to challenge redistricting plans and at-large election systems, poll worker hiring, and voter registration procedures. It prohibits not only election-related practices that are intended to be racially discriminatory, but also those that are shown to have a racially discriminatory impact.[82] The Act allows the Attorney General, as well as private citizens, to bring suit to obtain court-ordered remedies.[83] The provision does not explicitly provide the DOJ with binding rulemaking authority, nor does the DOJ claim any.[84]

Finally, in terms of staffing, what is striking about the DOJ is the extent to which many of the agency's election-related administrative duties are carried out by its career civil servants. The Civil Rights Division within the DOJ, for example, contains a dedicated Voting Section, which has had about thirty-five to forty career attorneys at any given time.[85] In all, the unit has about a

---

Strange, Ironic Career of Section 5 of the Voting Rights Act, 1965–2007, 86 Tex L Rev 667, 683 (2008) (characterizing DOJ as restricted to the issuance of guidelines as opposed to "rules" and noting that "its objection letters [do] not have precedential force").

[81] Pub L No 89-110, 79 Stat 437 (codified as amended at 42 USC §§ 1973–1973bb-1 (2006)).

[82] 42 USC §§ 1973–1973bb-1.

[83] 42 USC § 1973.

[84] Id. The DOJ also helps to administer other lesser-known sections of the VRA, including Sections 3 and Section 8, which grant both the federal courts and the Attorney General the authority to certify counties to allow for the assignment of federal election observers, which can include DOJ staff. 42 USC § 1973(b). Sections 203 and 4(f)(4), in turn, are the language-minority provisions of the Act, which require covered jurisdictions to provide bilingual written materials. 42 USC § 1973aa–1a(a). The DOJ has issued a guidance document to facilitate compliance. See 28 CFR 55, online at http://www.justice.gov/crt/about/vot/sec_203/28CFRPart55.pdf. Finally, Section 208 of the Act allows voters who require assistance to vote by reason of blindness, disability, or inability to read or write to receive that assistance by an individual of the voters' choosing—as long as the individual is not the voter's employer or union representative. 42 USC § 1973aa-6.

[85] See Department of Justice, *Review of the Voting Section* at 9 (cited in note 76). The number of attorneys during this time has fluctuated slightly beyond this range, with 31 attorneys in 1998 and 45 in 2010.

hundred employees, comprising attorneys, social scientists, civil rights analysts, and support personnel.[86]

2. *Department of Defense.* Like the DOJ, the Department of Defense (DOD) is another executive branch agency, with a presidentially-nominated and senate-confirmed head. The DOD has sub-delegated its election-related duties, however, to the director of the DOD's Federal Voting Assistance Program (FVAP).[87] Substantively, FVAP is charged with administering statutes related to voting by citizens and military personnel overseas.[88] The Uniformed and Overseas Citizens Absentee Voting Act, for example, provides for a federal registration application, which allows qualified citizens abroad to register to vote and request an absentee ballot simultaneously.[89] Other FVAP responsibilities include developing and implementing voter registration procedures at army recruitment offices.[90]

III. DEFERENCE AND DEADLOCKS

With independent commissions structured to deadlock and executive branch agencies largely deprived of legislative rulemaking power, the emerging portrait of federal election administration is one in which some of the most important election-related statutes are being implemented, if at all, by courts. Federal administrators, by contrast, have been relegated to the sidelines despite

---

[86] Id (cited in note 76).

[87] See Exec Order No 12,642, 53 Fed Reg 21,975 (June 8, 1988) (designating Secretary of Defense as presidential designee under Act and allowing Secretary to sub-delegate within the Department of Defense); Federal Voting Assistance Program, *About FVAP*, online at http://www.fvap.gov/info/about.

[88] 42 USC §§ 1973ff–1973ff-6 (2006) (allowing for presidential sub-delegation of duties).

[89] Pub L No 99-410.

[90] In 2009, Congress further expanded UOCAVA's protections for overseas voting through the Military and Overseas Voter Empowerment Act, which imposes a specific deadline of 45 days before election day for states to transmit validly-requested absentee ballots unless a state could show hardship. The statute also prohibits states from imposing a ballot notarization requirement. Pub L No 111-84, §§ 578–79, 123 Stat 2190, 2321–22 (2009) (codified as amended at 42 USC § 1973ff-1(a)(7)–(8) (2006 & Supp V 2012)). Pursuant to these authorities, the DOD has issued guidance establishing its polices and assigning responsibilities for implementing voter assistance offices as well as developing procedures for persons to apply to register to vote at military recruitment offices. See Department of Defense, Federal Voting Assistance Program, Instruction No 1000.04 (Sept 13, 2012), online at http://www.dtic.mil/whs/directives/corres/pdf/100004p.pdf. Other related statutes include the Soldier Voting Act of 1942, Pub L No 77-712, amended in 1944; the Federal Voting Assistance Act of 1955, Pub L No 84-296; and the 1975 Overseas Citizens Voting Rights Act, Pub L No 94-203.

their ability to collect cross-cutting data across various jurisdictions and to offer expert guidance beyond that selectively provided by self-interested litigants.

This part considers how courts should interpret election-related statutes in light of agencies' comparative expertise and structural incentives to deadlock. It suggests that deference should be calibrated to the institutional role of the actors authoring the interpretive documents and, specifically, the degree to which they are internally politically insulated. In this sense, it seeks to develop the idea of internal agency independence and, in doing so, to help foster legitimate tie-breaking considerations.

A. TIE-BREAKERS

Agency deadlocks of the kind that plagued the EAC in *Intertribal* pose an especially pernicious set of problems for election administration, and administrative law more generally. Deadlocks stymie the often swift and decisive resolution critically necessary before an impending election, especially given the risks of instability or perceived illegitimacy. Some, for example, have defended the Supreme Court's intervention in *Bush v Gore* on the grounds that, barring all else, it provided a final resolution that helped to preserve stability and order.[91] In *Intertribal*, the imminence of Arizona's impending election was cited to justify an expedited agency procedure in the hopes of providing a final resolution for various states.[92]

Administrative deadlocks also undermine the implementation of duly-enacted laws and judicial decisions. In this sense, they can foil otherwise legitimate acts through administrative impasse. Deadlocks resulting in agency inaction can also have pernicious electoral consequences. To take one extreme example, because Illinois politicians in the early 1960s deadlocked over a new redistricting plan for the state legislature in light of new census data, all 236 candidates for 177 seats ended up running together in a

---

[91] 531 US 98 (2000). See Richard H. Pildes, *Democracy and Disorder*, 68 U Chi L Rev 695, 715 (2001) (exploring *Bush v Gore* through cultural lens that "'democracy' required judicially-ensured order, stability, and certainty").

[92] Statement of EAC Chairman Paul DeGregorio, Joint Appendix, 2012 WL 6198263 at 225 ("I was also very concerned that with the August 14, 2006, voter registration deadline for the Arizona primary election fast approaching, that time was of the essence on this issue.").

single, at-large race.[93] More recently, the FEC has witnessed a
string of 3–3 votes along party lines, with some empirical evidence
suggesting a recent uptick in deadlocks for proposed enforcement
actions, audits, and rulemakings.[94] Among the most controversial
have been deadlocks preventing the FEC from promulgating
meaningful disclosure rules in response to *Citizens United*, which
upheld the statutory disclosure provisions at issue.[95] At one point,
the impasse was so protracted that the commissioners could not
even agree to accept public comments, though it eventually issued
broad questions about possible regulatory approaches.[96] A final
rule has yet to be issued.

The twin challenges for federal election administration, then,
are how to facilitate the application of high-quality information
to the development of electoral regulatory policy when interpreting ambiguous statutes, while also resolving agency impasse
in legitimate ways. While exogenous changes such as different

[93] See Adam M. Samaha, *On Law's Tiebreakers*, 77 U Chi L Rev 1661, 1684–85 (2010)
(discussing example).

[94] See Christopher Rowland, *Deadlock by Design Hobbles Election Agency*, Boston Globe
(July 7, 2013), online at http://www.bostonglobe.com/news/nation/2013/07/06/america-
campaign-finance-watchdog-rendered-nearly-toothless-its-own-appointed-commission-
ers/44zZoJwnzEHyzxTByNL2QP/story.html#share-nav (noting that the "frequency of
deadlocked votes resulting in dismissed cases . . . has shot up, to 19 percent, from less
than 1 percent"); *Roiled in Partisan Deadlock, Federal Election Commission Is Failing* (Public
Citizen, 2013), online at http://www.citizen.org/documents/fec-deadlock-statement-and-
chart-january-2013.pdf (compiling data); Garrett, *Deadlocked Votes* at 4–6 (cited in note
65) (displaying data on frequency of FEC deadlock from July 2008 to July 2009).

[95] See, for example, Bernie Becker, *Election Commission Decisions Deadlocking on Party
Lines*, NY Times A16 (Sept 27, 2009); Marian Wang, *FEC Deadlocks (Again) on Guidance
for Big-Money Super PACs* (ProPublica, Dec 2, 2011), online at http://www.propublica.org/
article/deadlocks-again-on-guidance-for-big-money-super-pacs; Kathleen Ronayne, *Federal Election Commission Deadlocks in Discussions about New Disclosure Rules for Political Ad-
vertisements*, Open Secrets Blog (June 16, 2011), online at http://www.opensecrets.org/
news/2011/06/federal-election-commission-deadlocks.html; Kenneth P. Doyle, *Bauerly:
FEC to Vote Again on Launch of Rulemaking to Adjust to Citizens United*, Daily Rep Exec
(BNA) No 11, at A-13 (June 10, 2011) ("The commissioners deadlocked 3–3 in a party-
line vote on whether to move forward with a new rulemaking proposal" to implement
disclosure rules in light of *Citizens United*.).

[96] See Trevor Potter, *How the FEC Can Stop the Tidal Wave of Secret Political Cash*, Wash
Post (Nov 16, 2012), online at http://www.washingtonpost.com/opinions/how-the-fec-
can-stop-the-tidal-wave-of-secret-political-cash/2012/11/16/966c48cc-2dae-11e2-89d4-
040c9330702a_story.html. The commission deadlocked in two 3–3 votes on draft NPRM
documents as well: 11-02, draft A, and 11-02-A, at the January 20, 2011, meeting. See
Federal Election Commission, *Minutes of an Open Meeting of the Federal Election Commission*
4–5 (Jan 20, 2011), online at http://www.fec.gov/agenda/2011/approved2011_06.pdf. See
also Federal Election Commission, *Minutes of an Open Meeting of the Federal Election
Commission* 3–4 (June 15, 2011), available online at http://www.fec.gov/agenda/2011/ap-
proved2011_39.pdf.

voting rules could be ameliorative, doctrinal innovations may be warranted when institutional reforms are unlikely.[97] One reason this approach may be prudent in the election context is that achieving legislative agreement on election reform may be difficult, if not impossible, without attached conditions such as the even-numbered bipartisan boards that lead to deadlock in the first place.

Such design choices for election-related agencies like the FEC and EAC likely reflect the congressional desire to ensure that controversial election policies do not proceed unless they serve the interests of both parties as reflected in a bipartisan majority vote. An equally plausible explanation can be couched as a legislative attempt to delay and ultimately prevent major electoral reforms by setting up such an agency structure. Under this scheme, while bipartisan consensus over how to interpret a statute would be the first-best outcome, what is a court to do when required to review the conflicting legal interpretations of split commissioners—should it determine the issue itself or defer to a particular agency actor? Answering this question requires a comparative analysis of the institutional competencies of agency and judicial actors in election-related statutory interpretation.

The situation frequently arises when the underlying statute itself provides for judicial review of a deadlocked decision or, alternatively, when the suit is brought on constitutional or APA-based grounds. Whether a court will even review an agency deadlock in the first place—as opposed to, say, characterizing it as unreviewable agency inaction—depends on a number of factors including the particular statutes governing the agency and whether courts construe them to allow for judicial review. The normally three-member Occupational Safety and Health Review Commission, for example, has frequently operated with only two members due to vacancies. When the two-member panel deadlocks, courts have split as to whether the resulting order is judicially reviewable. On the one hand, those that allow for review do so on the grounds that Congress could not have intended through its quorum and voting requirements to preclude judicial relief.[98] On the other hand, those that do not allow review usually reason that the dead-

---

[97] See Cass R. Sunstein and Thomas J. Miles, *Depoliticizing Administrative Law*, 58 Duke L J 2193, 2193–94 (2009).

[98] See, for example, *George Hyman Const. Co. v Occupational Safety and Health Review Com'n.*, 582 F2d 834, 837 (4th Cir 1978).

lock is not a final agency action under the terms of the underlying statute. Some courts further state that the agency, when fully constituted, should bring its expertise to bear on the legal issue before courts do.[99]

In this manner, Congress can determine both the voting rules necessary for agency action, as well as the ability of courts to review the results of a deadlock under those rules. In *Democratic Congressional Campaign Commission (DCCC) v FEC*, for example, the D.C. Circuit observed that the Federal Election Campaign Act explicitly allowed for judicial review of agency proceedings that resulted in the dismissal of complaints brought under the statute.[100] As background, FEC enforcement proceedings are initiated either by a complaint filed with the FEC, usually by a candidate or political party, or by the FEC itself after its review of political committee reports.[101] Once initiated, the General Counsel's office evaluates the matter and provides a recommendation to the six-member commission indicating whether there is "reason to believe" a legal violation has occurred or is about to occur. Should a majority of the commission concur with the General Counsel's finding, the FEC then attempts to reach a conciliation agreement through informal negotiation with the potential violators. If negotiation does not resolve the matter, then the commission can work with the DOJ to file suit in district court.[102]

Under this scheme, the *DCCC* plaintiffs had filed a complaint alleging that the National Republican Campaign Committee had improperly failed to allocate the cost of a mailing campaign against the relevant FECA spending cap. The complaint's validity turned on whether the mailer constituted an "electioneering message" under the statute. The FEC's General Counsel found reason to believe that it was, based on two previous commission advisory opinions interpreting the statutory term. When the FEC voted,

---

[99] See, for example, *Cox Bros., Inc. v Secretary of Labor*, 574 F2d 465, 467 (9th Cir 1978). See also *Shaw Construction, Inc. v Occupational Safety and Health Review Commission*, 534 F2d 1183, 1185–86 (5th Cir 1976).

[100] See *Democratic Congressional Campaign Committee (DCCC) v Federal Election Commission*, 831 F2d 1131 (DC Cir 1987) (noting that FECA explicitly states that "[a]ny party aggrieved by an order of the Commission dismissing a complaint filed by such party . . . or by a failure of the Commission to act on such complaint during the 120-day period beginning on the date the complaint is filed, may file a petition with the United States District Court for the District of Columbia" (citing 2 USC § 437g(a)(8)(A)).

[101] 2 USC § 437g(a)(1)–(2).

[102] 2 USC § 437g(a).

however, only three commissioners agreed. With four votes required for further action, the complaint was dismissed.[103]

In litigation, the FEC argued that the deadlock should be unreviewable since it purportedly resolved no substantive issue.[104] The court pointed out, however, that dismissals based on 5–1 or even 6–0 votes could similarly fail to resolve a decision substantively since the basis for the votes is often unclear. Perhaps the votes were the product of logrolling, legal uncertainty, or a judgment that the decision should be deferred; as a result, the court concluded, the FEC's argument rang hollow. In the alternative, the FEC argued that deadlocks were merely unreviewable exercises of prosecutorial discretion in deciding not to pursue a complaint. Again, however, the court rejected the argument on the grounds that 3–3 deadlocks could not be distinguished from 6–0 decisions to dismiss a complaint, decisions that were clearly reviewable under FECA.

As a result, the D.C. Circuit then took an intra-agency disagreement between an insulated internal actor—the General Counsel—and a split commission as reason to take a closer look at the proffered legal rationales of both sets of actors. Specifically, it held that when the FEC's General Counsel recommends an affirmative agency action but the agency's politically-appointed commissioners deadlock on the recommendation, the commissioners must provide a statement of reviewable reasons.[105] Importantly, this reason-giving requirement was justified, at least initially, only in situations when the internal staff actor disagreed with the deadlocked commission.

Without this requirement, the panel noted, it would be impossible for a court to "intelligently determine" whether the commissioners were acting contrary to law or in an arbitrary and capricious manner.[106] The FEC, that is, sent worrisome signals of arbitrariness in the form of "conflicting messages" when the FEC dismissed a complaint without a rationale, despite seemingly con-

---

[103] *DCCC*, 831 F2d at 1132.

[104] Id at 1133.

[105] See *Democratic Congressional Campaign Committee (DCCC) v Federal Election Commission*, 831 F2d 1131 (DC Cir 1987). See also *Common Cause v Federal Election Commission*, 842 F2d 436 (DC Cir 1988) (reaffirming requirement for FEC to provide reasons for deadlock when General Counsel recommends otherwise, but declining to apply requirement retroactively).

[106] Id at 1132.

trary precedents identified by the FEC's own General Counsel.[107]
A later D.C. Circuit opinion offered other policy justifications for
the requirement: it helped to ensure intra-agency reflection and
deliberation, contributed to better reasoned outcomes, and also
provided an opportunity for agency self-correction.[108] Indeed, one
way to understand this requirement is in terms of the court's
recognition that a conflict between a senior career staff member—
here, the General Counsel with a reputation for independence[109]—
and a deadlocked board merited closer review of the latter. By
imposing a reason-giving requirement, the court helped to ensure
that the agency's internal expertise could be brought to bear on
the commission's eventual resolution.

When the split commission's reasons involve contested questions of law, the next critical issue that arises, then, is *which* legal
interpretation courts should review and grant deference to, if at
all. In other words, when agencies deadlock over how to interpret
an underlying statute, courts charged with reviewing the question
of law will first have to determine which interpretation to consider
in its review, if any, given that the agency has not been able to
agree on an official one. Possibilities include the initial interpretation of the FEC's General Counsel, the separate opinions of the
commissioners, or a de novo interpretation by the court itself. Of
these, the D.C. Circuit has puzzlingly held that statements issued
by the bloc of commissioners voting against agency enforcement
should constitute the prevailing interpretation and, what is more,
that they would be entitled to *Chevron* deference—that is, deference to "permissible" interpretations of statutes that are otherwise ambiguous.[110] The court's first premise was that the com-

---

[107] Id at 1133.

[108] See *Common Cause*, 842 F2d at 449. For related discussion, see Adrian Vermeule,
The Constitution of Risk 165–85 (Cambridge, 2013).

[109] See Bob Bauer, *The Federal Election Commission and Its Choice of a General Counsel*,
More Soft Money Hard Law (June 7, 2013), at http://www.moresoftmoneyhardlaw.com
/2013/06/fec-general-counsel (noting that position "should occupy neutral ground as an
independent professional attorney unhampered by partisan loyalties or pressures in interpreting the law").

[110] See *In re Sealed Case*, 223 F3d 775, 780 (DC Cir 2000); *Federal Election Commission
v National Republican Senatorial Committee*, 966 F2d 1471 (DC Cir 1992) (applying similar
logic to the agency's interpretation of its own regulations). Agencies are currently accorded
Chevron deference to interpretations of statutes which they administer. *Chevron U.S.A.
Inc. v Natural Resources Defense Council, Inc.*, 467 US 837, 842 (1984). *Chevron's* two-part
test is a familiar one: First, the judge must ask "whether Congress has directly spoken to
the precise question at issue." If Congress's intent is "clear," then that intention governs;

missioners who voted to dismiss the complaint "constitute[d] a controlling group" and thus its "rationale necessarily states the agency's reasons for acting as it did."[111] Note, however, that the dismissing group comprised the "controlling" faction only because the decision to pursue the enforcement required a majority, which the faction was able to block.

The court further reasoned that *Chevron* deference was due since the underlying statute itself evinced a legislative intent to delegate that interpretive authority and the agency exercised that authority.[112] Such intent can ordinarily be inferred when Congress grants an agency the power to act with the force of law through formalized procedures like notice-and-comment rulemaking or formal adjudication, and the agency employed those procedures.[113] Because FECA's adjudicatory scheme was analogous to formal adjudication in essentially creating an adversarial process between the FEC's General Counsel and the respondent, the D.C. Circuit reasoned that *Chevron* applied to the controlling opinions of deadlocked decisions. The court further noted, oddly, that the "Commission is *inherently bipartisan* in that no more than three of its six voting members may be of the same political party" as further reason for deference.[114]

The D.C. Circuit's approach, however, fails to appreciate election-specific concerns amidst the structure of agencies like the FEC. Namely, it does not recognize that a deadlocked vote within an election-related agency is functionally different than a majority vote in favor of the complaint's dismissal, which would constitute an affirmative, bipartisan decision not to interpret the statute in a particular way. Whereas a majority vote in the election setting connotes agreement between parties, a deadlock suggests the converse: a vote split along party lines. Framed in this way, it becomes easier to see why courts should not grant *Chevron* deference to the deadlock coalition that successfully blocks the agency determination. As a doctrinal matter, an agency must affirmatively exercise its power to act with the force of law in order to receive

---

but if the statute is ambiguous or silent, then in step 2, courts ask whether the agency's interpretation is "permissible" and, if so, defer accordingly. Id at 842–43.

[111] See *National Republican Senatorial Committee*, 966 F2d at 1476.

[112] See *In re Sealed Case*, 223 F3d at 780.

[113] See *United States v Mead Corporation*, 533 US 218, 226–27 (2001).

[114] *In re Sealed Case*, 223 F3d at 780–81 (emphasis added), citing *Federal Election Commission v Democratic Senatorial Campaign Committee*, 454 US 27, 37 (1981).

deference.[115] To the contrary, an FEC deadlock is not an affirmative exercise of lawmaking authority according to Congress's own voting rule, but rather the result of an agency's inability to decide. As a result, the agency as a body has not brought either its collective expertise or policymaking judgment to bear on the relevant legal question, the "twin fonts" from which deference usually flows.[116] Indeed, the D.C. Circuit itself has recognized that the legal rationale adopted by the blocking coalition could not be the basis for a binding legal precedent on future cases.[117] Finally, from a dynamic perspective, granting *Chevron* deference to an agency tie also blunts the incentives of commissioners to seek bipartisan consensus; by contrast, withholding such deference until a majority is achieved is more likely to foster the cooperation across party lines that Congress desired.

B. INTERNAL INDEPENDENCE

If *Chevron* is misplaced when agencies deadlock, courts are then left to evaluate the persuasiveness of various agency interpretations for themselves, pursuant to what is known as *Skidmore* deference.[118] Under this test, courts look at a number of *Skidmore* factors such as the "thoroughness" of the agency actor's consideration, the reasoning's "validity" and "consistency," and, more generally, any factors which give an interpretation "power to persuade, if lacking power to control."[119] The analysis applies even when the agency itself is not a party, as was the case with the EAC in *Intertribal*. Because *Skidmore*, unlike *Chevron*, conceives of courts rather than agencies as the primary interpreters of statutes, some have un-

---

[115] See *Mead Corporation*, 533 US at 226–27.

[116] See *National Republican Senatorial Committee*, 966 F2d at 1476.

[117] See *Common Cause*, 842 F2d at 449 n 32 (stating that the statement of reasons provided by the blocking coalition "would not be binding legal precedent or authority for future cases" as FECA "clearly requires that for any *official* Commission decision there must be at least a 4–2 majority vote," the ignoring of which would "undermine the carefully balanced bipartisan structure which Congress has erected").

[118] See *Skidmore v Swift & Co.*, 323 US 134 (1944). *Skidmore* considered whether the time workers spent on call for a packing plant constituted "working time" due overtime pay under the Fair Labor Standards Act. In an amicus brief, the Department of Labor's Administrator of the Wage and Hour Division (who had previously issued interpretive bulletins applying the statutory provision to various hypothetical situations) opined that only some of that time could be categorized as such. While lower courts had ignored the administrator's views, the Supreme Court recognized that such views could be informed by the agency's expertise and experience.

[119] Id at 140.

derstandably questioned whether the doctrine amounts to anything more than the exercise of independent judgment in practice.[120] Limited empirical work, however, suggests that courts invoking *Skidmore* do grant deference to the agency interpretation more than when approaching the interpretive question de novo.[121] Indeed, there are sound reasons to think that requiring judges to explicitly consider the persuasiveness of particular interpretive views can sometimes result in different decisions on the margins.[122]

Given the unique concerns of federal election administration, the primary *Skidmore* factor in the electoral setting should be the extent to which the agency actor is institutionally insulated from partisan influence. Instead of blindly allowing the default controlling bloc to definitively interpret an underlying statute, that is, courts should look instead at the interpretation of the actor most likely to bring to bear the agency's expertise and administrative experience. While this approach would not necessarily modify *Skidmore*'s multifactor analysis as such, it would shift its emphasis and place the identity of the decision maker in the foreground when the agency regulates elections. Such *Skidmore* inquiries, for example, would look at indicia of political independence, such as tenure and salary protections, methods of appointment, and the degree of professionalization, among other dimensions.

Skidmore deference already applies to the myriad informal ways in which insulated agency actors attempt to provide guidance

---

[120] See, for example, Richard W. Murphy, *Judicial Deference, Agency Commitment, and Force of Law*, 66 Ohio St L J 1013, 1015 (2005) (characterizing *Skidmore* deference as requiring courts to exercise "independent judgment" subject to the "weak" requirement that they consider the agency's persuasiveness).

[121] See Kristen E. Hickman and Matthew D. Krueger, *In Search of the Modern Skidmore Standard*, 107 Colum L Rev 1235, 1275 (2007) (reporting that "*Skidmore* is relatively deferential as applied by the federal courts of appeals," as suggested by evidence that in "64 of 106, or 60.4%, of the *Skidmore* applications studied [in the paper], the courts sided with the agency"); William N. Eskridge, Jr., and Lauren E. Baer, *The Continuum of Deference: Supreme Court Treatment of Agency Statutory Interpretations from Chevron to Hamdan*, 96 Georgetown L J 1083, 1099 table 1 (2008) (reporting agency win-rate of 66% when court afforded no deference as compared to 73.5% when court invoked *Skidmore* deference). The study's dataset consisted of all cases "between 1984 and 2006 in which an agency interpretation of a statute was at issue and in which the Supreme Court produced a published opinion." Id at 1090 n 33.

[122] See Hickman and Krueger, 107 Colum L Rev at 1271 (cited in note 121) (arguing that "courts do not, on the whole, understand *Skidmore* to sanction independent judgment of a statute in the face of an administrative interpretation" but that instead "most courts [in their sample] that cite *Skidmore* believe themselves bound to afford agencies special consideration that is not due ordinary litigants").

drawn from their expertise and experience administering the statute at issue. Tailoring such deference to political insulation would
help to match *Skidmore*'s concerns to the institutional realities of
deadlocked agencies. Internally insulated expertise in such agencies, for example, is frequently generated by career staff within
them, primarily through sub-regulatory informal guidance documents or opinion letters. There are both senior career officials
who hold positions in the Senior Executive Service or otherwise
upper management General Schedule positions as well as the more
"rank-and-file career workforce."[123] In addition to career staff,
agencies also often use advisory committees to provide technical
advice or recommendations, subject to federal laws regulating the
disclosure of meetings.[124] While courts currently do not apply
formal deference doctrines to advisory committees, courts could
critically review agency rejections of expert advisory committee
opinions, especially when those opinions are required by statute.[125]

While this institutional approach could extend more broadly, it
is particularly appropriate in federal election administration given
its heightened concerns with self-dealing and partisanship. While
Skidmore speaks broadly of the "agency," treating the "agency" as
a monolithic entity makes little sense here. In Peter Strauss's
words, the "anthropomorphic tendency to treat agencies as if they
were a single human actor is particularly distracting and distorting
when one is analyzing a medium that the constituent elements of
complex institutions use to speak to each other."[126] Indeed, agen-

---

[123] See Ronald N. Johnson and Gary D. Libecap, *The Federal Civil Service System and the Problem of Bureaucracy: The Economics and Politics of Institutional Change* 7 (Chicago, 1994). The General Schedule is the basic pay schedule for federal government employees. See 5 USC § 5332. While these lines are somewhat arbitrary, another possibility for drawing the line between senior and junior career employees would follow the Supreme Court's approach in *United States v National Treasury Employees Union* engaging in a First Amendment analysis of an honoraria ban by crudely distinguishing between "high-level" and "rank-and-file" staff as those above and below General Schedule level 16 (GS-16) on the federal government's pay scale. *United States v National Treasury Employees Union*, 513 US 454, 472, 478 (1995).

[124] See, for example, Federal Advisory Committee Act (FACA), 5 USC App 2 §§ 1–16; Freedom of Information Act, 5 USC § 552(b).

[125] See, for example, *American Farm Bureau Federation v EPA*, 559 F3d 512, 521 (DC Cir 2009) ("The EPA failed adequately to explain its reason for not accepting the [Clean Air Scientific Advisory Committee]'s recommendations. . . ."); *Coalition of Battery Recyclers Association v EPA*, 604 F3d 613, 619 (DC Cir 2010) (favorably noting that the EPA had considered some of the Clean Air Scientific Advisory Committee's concerns, despite not following its precise recommendations).

[126] See Peter L. Strauss, *Publication Rules in the Rulemaking Spectrum: Assuring Proper Respect for an Essential Element*, 53 Admin L Rev 803, 810 (2001).

cies operate according to sophisticated internal decision-making processes and personnel decisions often informed by the very expertise-related factors that courts attempt to otherwise address in an institutional vacuum. One important way that judges, like ordinary individuals, evaluate the persuasiveness or credibility of an analysis is by looking at the author's identity and the related probability of bias and/or sound expertise. Expert witnesses in court, for example, are regularly called upon to disclose their conflicts of interest and related professional background.[127] For these reasons, there is great analytic value to piercing the veil of "the administrative agency,"[128] opening the black box to consider the actors inside.

The notion of looking at the institutional role of the interpretive actor when deciding whether and how to grant deference is not new. The perspective has been advanced by two current members of the Court, among others. Justice Scalia's dissent in *United States v Mead Corporation*, for example, advocated for a deference regime that would simply look to whether the interpretation is "authoritative" in the sense that it "represents the official position of the agency."[129] Because the custom letter's interpretation in *Mead* had been ratified by the General Counsel of the Treasury and the Solicitor General in briefs, in his view, *Chevron* deference was appropriate. Further developing this idea of looking at the "who" as opposed to the "how" of agency decision making, David Barron and now-Justice Elena Kagan have similarly argued that courts should give *Chevron* deference when the "congressional delegatee" identified by statute "takes personal responsibility for the decision."[130] Such an approach, they contend, would encourage more accountable and well-considered agency decision making consistent with *Chevron*'s underlying policy goals.[131]

While these proposals are *Chevron* centered, there are good reasons to extend the conceptual move to the *Skidmore* context as

---

[127] See, for example, FRCP 26(a)(2) (requiring, among other things, "a complete statement of all opinions the witness will express and the basis and reasons for them," "the facts or data considered by the witness," and "the witness's qualifications").

[128] See Richard H. Pildes, *Institutional Formalism and Realism in Constitutional and Public Law*, 2014 Supreme Court Review (in this volume).

[129] See 121 S Ct at 2187.

[130] See David J. Barron and Elena Kagan, *Chevron's Nondelegation Doctrine*, 2001 Supreme Court Review 201, 204 (2001).

[131] Id at 238.

well, particularly when the regulatory domain is that of federal election administration. Unlike *Chevron*'s grounding in hypothetical legislative intent, *Skidmore*'s foundations are prudential.[132] *Skidmore* deference recognizes that courts are well equipped to engage in statutory interpretation, but that they can also lack the experience and expertise to appreciate the consequences of alternative interpretations. As such, *Skidmore* asks judges to weigh the reasons why an interpretation is persuasive based in part on its source or "pedigree."[133] Granting *Skidmore* deference when an informal guidance document or letter is prepared and signed by an expert, insulated career staff member would privilege the myriad documents and informal guidance reviewed by the most experienced actors within an agency, while also incorporating the experiences and insights of their subordinates. Some courts already appear to be taking into account such institutional considerations.[134] To be sure, the participation of high-level political appointees bears many of these same benefits in terms of drawing upon the agency's expertise (indeed, agency heads often sign documents or interpretations that were drafted by or with the participation of career staff). But none of these benefits exist when political appointees deadlock.

Functionally, it is also important to note that the proposed tailoring in the election context would simply encourage a judicial partnership with expert, internally insulated actors. It would not call for judges to abdicate their role under *Skidmore* in reviewing such documents; they would instead continue to consider other factors such as thoroughness and consistency. Nor would this approach allow career staff to override a valid majority decision of the commissioners when they manage to secure a bipartisan consensus. Rather, the approach developed here would apply when agencies deadlock, and courts are called upon to resolve a statutory ambiguity. *Skidmore* deference simply posits that courts interpreting federal election statutes would be prudent to consider the views of actors who have more experience administering elections,

---

[132] See Hickman and Krueger, 107 Colum L Rev at 1249 (cited in note 121).

[133] Id at 1251.

[134] See, for example, *De La Mota v United.States Department of Education*, 412 F3d 71, 80 (2nd Cir 2005) ("We have shown deference to the opinions of agency officials who, though not an agency secretary or commissioner, hold substantial responsibility.").

as well as access to information about how alternative interpretations would impact elections across jurisdictions.

This interpretive approach is especially warranted given the relative institutional strengths and weaknesses of courts relative to career staff or advisory commissions in this arena. While federal judges are politically insulated by virtue of Article III tenure and salary protections, empirical evidence demonstrates that they are not immune from partisan loyalties and, to the contrary, often vote in election-related disputes in ways that favor their appointing party.[135] Moreover, most election administration litigation is fact-intensive and often arises in a procedural posture that requires courts to expedite their consideration of the claims based on incomplete records. As a result, judges must intervene without the requisite data to inform their decisions. These institutional weaknesses, coupled with the charged political nature of the cases, render courts (and particularly the Supreme Court) ill-suited to resolve election-related disputes.[136]

By contrast, career staff within administrative agencies also have various salary and tenure protections but, in addition, also possess experience and expertise in administrating federal elections. Such staff are protected, for example, by the 1978 Civil Service Reform Act, which prohibits agency personnel decisions not taken on the basis of merit.[137] They also have "strict tenure guarantees, have no expressed ties to the administration or to Congress, and by law are to be politically neutral."[138] Furthermore, civil service salaries are protected from political appropriations decisions and the wages are also fairly compressed within the federal pay structure.[139]

---

[135] See Adam B. Cox and Thomas J. Miles, *Judging the Voting Rights Act*, 108 Colum L Rev 1, 21–29 (2008) (concluding that Democratic appointees are significantly more likely than Republican ones to find violations of Section 2 of the Voting Rights Act); Randall D. Lloyd, *Separating Partisanship from Party in Judicial Research: Reapportionment in the U.S. District Courts*, 89 Am Pol Sci Rev 413, 417–18 (1995) (finding evidence that judges appointed by a party were more likely to strike down redistricting maps drawn by the other party). See also Lee Epstein, William M. Landes, and Richard A. Posner, *The Behavior of Federal Judges* 8 (Harvard, 2013) ("Justices appointed by Republican presidents vote more conservatively on average than justices appointed by Democratic ones, with the difference being most pronounced in civil rights cases.").

[136] See Daniel P. Tokaji, *Leave It to the Lower Courts: On Judicial Intervention in Election Administration*, 68 Ohio St L J 1065, 1067 (2007).

[137] Pub L No 95-454, 92 Stat 1111.

[138] See Johnson and Libecap, *The Federal Civil Service System and the Problem of Bureaucracy* (cited in note 123).

[139] See id at 5; Neal Kumar Katyal, *Internal Separation of Powers: Checking Today's Most Dangerous Branch from Within*, 115 Yale L J 2314, 2331–32 (2006).

More importantly, these internal agency actors also possess more resources, relative to judges, to gather data across jurisdictions and over longer periods of time. Indeed, it was this need for reliable information that originally spurred Congress to create a number of bureaucratic entities charged with researching cross-cutting election administration issues. In 1971, for example, Congress created the Office of Federal Elections within what is now known as the General Accountability Office.[140] The entity was moved in 1974 to the FEC where it eventually became known as the Office of Election Administration, before its staff and functions were finally later transferred to the EAC.[141] During its various evolutions, the office commissioned a number of influential election administration studies on topics such as vote-counting technology.[142] In addition, it created advisory boards and disseminated information to state and local election administrators. While housed in the EAC, the staff has formulated voluntary voting system guidelines, compiled data and reports on absentee ballots for overseas voters, as well as tested and certified voting system hardware and software.[143]

In this manner, one of the main functions of federal election-related agencies has been to aggregate, develop, and solicit information about election practices across various states and even from overseas. Election administration decisions should take into account this accumulated storehouse of information and, in the context of statutory interpretation, should consider an interpretation's persuasiveness by virtue of the experience and insulated institutional role of its author. When the role is that of making recommendations to politically-appointed commissioners based on previous experience administering the statute across a number of election cycles, then judges would be especially wise to consider those views.

---

[140] See Robert S. Montjoy and Douglas M. Chapin, *The U.S. Election Assistance Commission: What Role in the Administration of Elections?*, 35 Publius 617, 620 (2005).

[141] Id at 627.

[142] See, for example, Roy Saltman, *Effective Use of Computing Technology in Vote-Tallying* (National Bureau of Standards Project Report, 1975); Richard G. Smolka and W. Edward Weems, Jr., *A Study of Election Difficulties in Representative American Jurisdictions* (Office of Federal Elections, 1973).

[143] Id.

C. IMPLICATIONS AND OBJECTIONS

Returning now to *Intertribal*, it is useful to see how the Court's analysis might have differed when applying the institutional *Skidmore* approach developed here. Namely, this view of *Skidmore* would have drawn the Court to consider the EAC executive director's institutional role and opinion letter in light of the agency's deadlock, instead of ignoring the letter altogether as a basis for decision. Recall that, although the EAC is vested with rulemaking authority,[144] the commission split along party lines as to how to resolve the statutory ambiguity: how must states "accept and use" the federal registration form? Because it ignored the EAC executive director's opinion, the *Intertribal* Court did not explicitly consider how much weight to give the letter, though the issue was raised in the merits briefs and the Court conceded that the statute was ambiguous.[145]

Judge Kozinski, concurring in the Ninth Circuit's first panel decision below, however, did consider the question. First, he observed that the director's opinion letter lacked the "force of law" and therefore did not merit *Chevron* deference.[146] He further noted that courts did not normally grant deference to agency preemption determinations contained in informal opinion letters, but rather applied *Skidmore*.[147] While the Ninth Circuit majority acknowledged that *Skidmore* analysis could be appropriate, it declined to apply it on the grounds that the NVRA's legislative history and the EAC executive director's view were both consistent with the Ninth Circuit's holding, and the analysis was therefore unnecessary.[148] In this manner, the panel, like the Supreme Court, interpreted the NVRA independently on its own

---

[144] 42 USC § 1973gg-7(a)(1).

[145] See State Petitioners' Brief on the Merits, *Intertribal Council*, No 12-71, at *28, 44–46. *Intertribal Council*, No 12-71, slip op at 6 ("Taken in isolation, the mandate that a State 'accept and use' the Federal Form is fairly susceptible of two interpretations.").

[146] *Gonzalez*, 624 F3d at 1208 (Kozinski concurring).

[147] Id, citing *Wyeth v Levine*, 555 US 555 (2009). The *Wyeth* Court declared that "[w]hile agencies have no special authority to pronounce on pre-emption absent delegation by Congress, they do have a unique understanding of the statutes they administer . . . [thus, the] weight we accord the agency's explanation of state law's impact on the federal scheme depends on its thoroughness, consistency, and persuasiveness." *Wyeth*, 555 US at 577 (citation omitted).

[148] See *Gonzalez*, 677 F3d at 403 n 29.

and without reference to the EAC director's well-reasoned analysis.[149]

The EAC's executive director is a senior staff position with a renewable four-year appointment "responsible for implementing EAC policy and administering EAC's day-to-day operations."[150] He is appointed by a majority vote of the commission, whose members could only consider three nominations chosen from a search committee appointed by the EAC's Standards Board and Board of Advisors.[151] As such, the position requires the bipartisan vote of the commission only after nomination by expert advisory boards. The director's duties, in turn, include maintaining the federal voter registration form and answering questions regarding the application of the NVRA and HAVA consistent with EAC's guidance documents, regulations, advisories, and policy statements.[152] Though the chair of the EAC is charged with providing administrative direction to the executive director, that direction is not to be undertaken without input from each commissioner.[153]

As such, the EAC executive director has experience administering the agency's authorizing federal statutes across states and jurisdictions. Moreover, the executive director is likely to have a sound professional reputation as well as productive relationships with the state and local election officials who had nominated him.[154] Thus, there were multiple reasons to believe that norms of professionalism and expertise helped to bolster the independence of his position. In interpreting the NVRA, the Court would have benefited from considering the EAC executive director's interpretive opinion for its persuasiveness in light of the institutional position of its author.

---

[149] Among other things, the director spoke to the statutory provision's purpose—"set-[ting] the proof required to demonstrate voter qualification"—and the EAC's experience and delegated responsibility to create and administer the federal voter registration form. See Joint Appendix, *Arizona v Intertribal Council of Arizona*, 2012 WL 6198263, *184–86 (2012).

[150] See Election Assistance Commission, *The Roles and Responsibilities of the Commissioners and Executive Director of the U.S. Election Assistance Commission* 6, online at http://www.eac.gov/assets/1/workflow_staging/Page/348.PDF.

[151] 42 USC § 15324(a)(3).

[152] Id at 7.

[153] See Election Assistance Commission, *The Roles and Responsibilities of the Commissioners and Executive Director of the U.S. Election Assistance Commission* 4–5, online at http://www.eac.gov/assets/1/workflow_staging/Page/348.PDF.

[154] For details about the experience of the executive director in this case, see United States Election Assistance Commission, *Thomas R. Wilkey*, online at http://www.eac.gov/about_the_eac/thomas_r_wilkey.aspx.

While it is true that the Court's substantive conclusion happened to align with that of the director in this case, such contingencies do not warrant the lack of judicial attention to insulated agency actors in future cases.

Turning now to other implications of the *Skidmore* approach developed here, courts should conversely be more hesitant to grant deference to agency actors that lack the structural protections of the kind that existed for the EAC's executive director.[155] Indeed, the increasing sense that the DOJ—recall, an executive agency with a single, appointed agency head—had politicized its interpretations under the Voting Rights Act (VRA) may help to explain the Supreme Court's general refusal to defer to the agency.[156] Indeed, one analysis describes the Court's recent approach as one of "anti-deference" and even "hostility."[157] Helping to explain this judicial skepticism, perhaps, was the perception that the DOJ had been issuing subregulatory documents that were evolving according to the administration's partisan affiliation. In this sense, the approach proposed here may help to articulate what has already been happening as a matter of course.

To facilitate Section 5's preclearance process, for example, the DOJ first published an interpretive rule for public comment in 1971 under the Republican President Nixon.[158] The proposal initially provided that the Attorney General would object to a preclearance submission only if he or she affirmatively determined that the law would have a discriminatory effect or purpose. In practice, this required showing constituted a more onerous standard than had previously existed. The final guidelines issued a few months later, by contrast, called for the Attorney General to object even if the evidence was still indeterminate—a change prompted only by countervailing pressure from congressional and civil rights groups.[159]

---

[155] While he does not develop the insight in great depth, Christopher Elmendorf also mentions the possibility that "courts might reverse the normal presumption of deference to administrative agencies in voting cases if the agency's governing body is partisan in structure, rather than bipartisan or neutral." Christopher S. Elmendorf, *Refining the Democracy Canon*, 95 Cornell L Rev 1097 (2010).

[156] See Arpit K. Garg, *A Deference Theory of Section Five* (draft as of April 1, 2012), online at http://papers.ssrn.com/sol3/papers.cfm?abstract_id=2209636.

[157] Id at 5.

[158] See Administration of Voting Rights Act of 1965, 36 Fed Reg 9781 (May 28, 1971).

[159] See Procedures for the Administration of Section 5 of the Voting Rights Act of 1965, 36 Fed Reg 18186 (Sept 10, 1971) (codified at 28 CFR pt 51 (1972)); Kousser, 86 Tex L Rev at 667, 683 (cited in note 80) (characterizing DOJ as restricted to the issuance of

The evolution of the guidelines, with revisions in 1981 and 1987, seemingly continued to track the shifting views of the administration in power.[160] For example, in 1985, Republican President Reagan's DOJ initially proposed that it would refuse preclearance under Section 5 using Section 2's result-oriented test, that is, only if the allegations showed by "clear and convincing evidence" that the change had a discriminatory result.[161] This policy shift would have modified the previous burden of proof under Section 5 and set a new higher evidentiary standard. In response to legislative hearings and public criticism, however, the DOJ's finalized 1987 guidelines instead eliminated the burden shift and incorporated a results test with only a "clear" evidentiary standard.[162]

More recently, in 2010, Democratic President Obama's DOJ published a notice proposing amendments for public comment.[163] Among other things, the proposal sought to reflect legislative changes to Section 5, which clarified that the term "purpose" included "any discriminatory purpose" and not just those that reflected an intention to retrogress, thus potentially expanding Section 5 liability. Moreover, the regulations also clarified the nature of DOJ's "bailout" process for covered jurisdictions, including political sub-units that were now eligible to bring a declaratory judgment suit under Section 5.[164] In April 2011, the DOJ issued the final rule

---

guidelines as opposed to "rules" and noting that "its objection letters [do] not have precedential force").

[160] See generally Procedures for the Administration of Section 5 of the Voting Rights Act of 1965; Proposed Revision of Procedures, 50 Fed Reg 19,122 (proposed May 6, 1985) (to be codified at 28 CFR pt 51); Revision of Procedures for the Administration of Section 5 of the Voting Rights Act of 1965, 52 Fed Reg 486–01 (Jan 6, 1987) (codified at 28 CFR § 51.55). See also Steven F. Lawson, *In Pursuit of Power: Southern Blacks and Electoral Politics, 1965–1982* at 158–90 (Columbia, 1985); Kousser, 86 Tex L Rev at 716 (cited in note 80) ("Like the Nixon Administration a decade earlier, the Reagan Administration sought to undermine the VRA, especially Section 5, through guidelines and legal positions espoused in its briefs.").

[161] Procedures for the Administration of Section 5 of the Voting Rights Act of 1965; Proposed Revision of Procedures, 50 Fed Reg 19,122, 19,131 (proposed May 6, 1985) (to be codified at 28 CFR pt 51).

[162] Revision of Procedures for the Administration of Section 5 of the Voting Rights Act of 1965, 52 Fed Reg 486 (codified at 28 CFR § 51.55). See Kousser, 86 Tex L Rev at 718 (cited in note 80).

[163] See, for example, Revisions of the Procedures for the Administration of Section 5 of the Voting Rights Act, 75 Fed Reg 33205 (proposed June 11, 2010) (to be codified at 29 CFR pts 0 and 51).

[164] *Northwest Austin Municipal Utility District v Holder*, 557 US 193 (2009).

as an interpretive rule without major changes from the proposal.[165]

At the same time, numerous accounts have attested to the perception that the DOJ had been varying its administration of the VRA under Republican and Democratic appointees. Various reports have circulated, for instance, suggesting that Bush Administration DOJ officials had prohibited career staff attorneys from offering written recommendations in high-profile VRA determinations.[166] Not only did this new practice "mark[ ] a significant change in the procedures meant to insulate such decisions from politics," but it also followed on the heels of rare reversals by high-level political officials of career staff preclearance recommendations.[167] This dynamic of silencing or overruling internal dissent appears to have continued through the Obama Administration as well,[168] though recent DOJ officials have attempted to publicly distance themselves from such practices and profess to no longer prohibit written career staff opinions.[169] In this manner, the same executive agency which reportedly had been silencing its career attorneys had also been issuing guidance that sought to reflect the preferences of the political appointees in power. The Supreme Court's reluctance to

[165] See Revision of Voting Rights Procedures, 76 Fed Reg 21,239 (April 15, 2011); Guidance Concerning Redistricting Under Section 5 of the Voting Rights Act; Notice, 76 Fed Reg 7470 (Feb 9, 2011).

[166] See Dan Eggen, *Staff Opinions Banned in Voting Rights Cases*, Wash Post A3 (Dec 10, 2005); Edward M. Kennedy, *Restoring the Civil Rights Division*, 2 Harv L & Policy Rev 211, 218–19 (2008); Daniel P. Tokaji, *If It's Broke, Fix It: Improving Voting Rights Act Preclearance*, 49 Howard L J 785, 799 (2006) (describing criticism of DOJ's decision not to object to "Republican-backed electoral changes in Texas and Georgia against the advice of career staff"); Thomas Perez, *U.S. Department of Justice's Enforcement of the Voting Rights Act*, 64 Rutgers L Rev 939, 941 (2012) (reporting "the long-standing tradition in the Voting Section in both Republican and Democratic administrations for decades until it was changed in 2005 to exclude career attorneys and analysts from full participation in the process," including career staff who "were directed to no longer put their recommendations in writing").

[167] See Eggen, *Staff Opinions Banned in Voting Rights Cases*, Wash Post at A3 (cited in note 166); Mark Posner, *Evidence of Political Manipulation at the Justice Department: How Tom DeLay's Redistricting Plan Avoided Voting Rights Act Disapproval*, FindLaw.com (Dec 6, 2005), online at http://writ.news.findlaw.com/commentary/20051206_posner.html.

[168] See J. Christian Adams, *Internal DOJ Documents Argued for SC Voter ID Approval . . . but Obama Appointees Overruled*, PJ Media (Sept 11, 2012), online at http://pjmedia .com/jchristianadams/2012/09/11/doj-documents-argued-for-sc-voter-id-approval (President Obama's political appointees in the DOJ made the decision to object to preclearance of the South Carolina voter ID law over the recommendation of career DOJ lawyers and supervisors).

[169] See Perez, 64 Rutgers L Rev at 940–41 (cited in note 166) (as Assistant Attorney General for DOJ's Civil Rights Division, announcing that DOJ had ended the previous practice of not allowing career staff attorneys from offering written recommendations in voting rights cases).

grant deference under these circumstances, to agency actors that lacked internal mechanisms of political independence, would be consistent with the analysis developed here.

However persuasive the institutional *Skidmore* approach as an explanatory matter, one might still normatively object to it on a number of grounds. For starters, one might worry that this deference regime is somehow inconsistent with legislative intent. If Congress had wanted to create an expert, nonpartisan election administration agency with a permanent staff, it could have done so. Instead, it set up a politically appointed commission and protected against partisanship through a bipartisan voting rule. Asking judges to consider the views of career staff or other agency actors regarding questions of law somehow contravenes these conscious design choices. The piece that this objection elides, however, is that the legal issue arises whenever Congress provides for judicial review of the agency's deadlock, sometimes explicitly as in the case of FEC enforcement proceedings or implicitly through a choice not to preclude review.[170] Thus, as previously discussed, when the rationale for the agency's deadlock raises a contested legal question, courts will be called upon to resolve the statutory ambiguity. Judges, that is, will effectively have to break the tie regarding how an underlying statute should be interpreted. As such, the familiar administrative law question that arises is one of comparative institutional competence, whether such reviewable statutory ambiguities are better entrusted to a court acting alone or rather as a cooperative endeavor between courts and expert agency actors when commissioners deadlock on the issue.

Beyond concerns about subverted legislative intent are worries about partisan capture or deeper politicization that may result from the deference regime. Because courts would place a thumb on the scale for sub-regulatory guidance documents written by, say, senior career staff, general counsels, or advisory committee members, political parties would simply refocus their lobbying efforts accordingly, resulting in the heightened risk of partisan capture. By the same token, this regime could erode norms of independence over time or entrench partisanship even deeper within the agency by encouraging politicized hiring practices. Political appointees, more-

---

[170] See *Abbott Labs v Gardner*, 387 US 136, 141 (1967) (providing for a presumption of judicial review of agency action unless there was "clear and convincing" evidence that the statute precluded it).

over, may now be more likely to increase their monitoring and control of staff memoranda, or even attempt to manipulate the contents of such documents themselves. Alternatively, agency heads may simply silence or reduce the amount of otherwise useful guidance available to regulated entities.

While these objections are real and powerful, they are mitigated by a number of countervailing observations. First, as an institutional matter, there are various federal laws that limit the influence of interest groups and political parties on civil servants. The Pendleton Act, for example, prohibits agencies from making particular non-merit-based personnel actions and sends appeals of such decisions to an independent Merit Systems Protection Board.[171] The Hatch Act restricts executive branch civil servants from engaging in partisan political activity.[172] Other federal statutes and regulations also prohibit non-merit-based hiring and personnel decisions for civil servants.[173] Structurally, the ability to capture staff members would also be more difficult in multimember commissions, relative to single-headed agencies, since other commissioners (especially from the opposing party) could object to and check such efforts.

Beyond these formal buffers are informal ones as well. The reputations of election administrators, for instance, are strongly dependent on their perceived independence from special interests and adherence to professional norms.[174] Being an effective election administrator, that is, depends in large part on maintaining actual and perceived independence from parties and candidates. Thus, the incentives for partisan capture are blunted by the costs that such capture would impose on an administrator's professional reputation as well as her ongoing institutional efficacy. Perhaps one fruitful analogy here is to the Solicitor General's Office, which by many accounts draws its influence over the Supreme Court from its perceived political independence and reputation as an honest broker.[175]

---

[171] An Act to Regulate and Improve the Civil Service of the United States, Ch 27, 22 Stat 403 (1883); 5 USC §§ 2301–05 (2000); 5 USC §§ 1201–09 (2000).

[172] See 5 USC §§ 1501–08 (2012).

[173] See, for example, Pub L No 95-454, 92 Stat 1111. See generally David E. Lewis, *The Politics of Presidential Appointments: Political Control and Bureaucratic Performance* (2008).

[174] See Robert S. Montjoy, *An Ecological Approach to Election Reform*, 8 Election L J 59, 62 (2009) (favorably noting state elections director, a civil service appointee who had won "high marks from local election administrators for timely and professional advice"); Adrian Vermeule, *Conventions of Agency Independence*, 113 Colum L Rev 1163, 1212–13 (2013).

[175] See Ryan C. Black and Ryan J. Owens, *The Solicitor General and the United States*

Actions that erode either erode the power of the office itself.[176] Similarly, those who work at federal election agencies also draw their credibility from being able to resist pressures that are baldly partisan.

At a broader level are potential inter-institutional dynamics as well. Administrative agencies are the agents of multiple principals, including the President, Congress, and the courts. As such, the more an election-related agency loses its institutional credibility—say, because of capture, corruption, or a failure to incorporate new data— the more likely other institutions may be to step in to check it. This dynamic, as discussed, is one possible explanation for the Supreme Court's refusal to grant deference to what has been perceived as an increasingly politicized DOJ. A similar argument has been made to explain the Court's withholding of deference in other regulatory contexts, for example, when invalidating the EPA's refusal to regulate greenhouse gas emissions—a decision perhaps arising from the Court's perception that there had been high-level political interference with the expert, scientific judgments of EPA career staff.[177]

In terms of intra-agency dynamics, consider also that any agency heads or commissioners tempted to silence or otherwise unduly influence staff recommendations are faced with a trade-off between reaching a bipartisan decision and gaining *Chevron* deference, which favors the agency, or settling for *Skidmore* deference, which leaves interpretive authority with the courts. Faced with this choice, these appointed officials can gain more deference by securing a majority agreement among themselves, instead of leaving open the ambiguity to the uncertainties of *Skidmore* as a result of partisan deadlock. In this manner, there are relative incentives for commissioners to avoid administrative impasse and devote resources to finding bipartisan interpretations rather than micromanaging informal staff documents. Furthermore, any efforts to silence opinion letters must also be weighed against the need to provide guidance to outside regu-

---

Supreme Court: Executive Branch Influence and Judicial Decisions 136 (2012) (observing that the influence of the Solicitor General's Office on the Supreme Court likely comes from the office's "objectivity, professionalism, and independence"). This view, however, is subject to some debate. See Margaret H. Lemos, *The Solicitor General as Mediator Between Court and Agency*, 2009 Mich St L Rev 185, 187–92 (summarizing the debate).

[176] See Cornelia T. L. Pillard, *The Unfulfilled Promise of the Constitution in Executive Hands*, 103 Mich L Rev 676, 725–26 (2005).

[177] See notes 156–57 and accompanying text; Jody Freeman and Adrian Vermeule, *Massachusetts v EPA: From Politics to Expertise*, 2007 Supreme Court Review 51, 61.

lated entities. In other words, there will always be an external demand for sub-regulatory guidance despite internal pressures not to issue any.

Apart from concerns about partisan capture and interference, however, is yet another distinct worry: that greater judicial attention to the views of insulated staff members will result in commissioner deadlocks about the hiring of such staff.[178] In other words, because the stakes of appointing these internal actors now seem greater, commissioners will be more likely to disagree about who should be appointed, thus resulting in staff vacancies. While this fear is well founded, its manifestation in reality will likely depend on a number of factors, including the polarizing effects of potential candidates as well as the long-term viability of protracted staff-related deadlocks. There are also a number of practices that can help to mitigate contentious hiring disputes, some of which are already required by statute or deployed in practice in other settings such as the arbitration of deadlocked labor disputes.[179] For example, statutes underlying the Election Assistance Commission currently require the agency's executive director to be chosen from three nominations generated by a search committee, which is itself appointed by outside advisory bodies.[180] Such approaches, which constrain the number and nature of potential staff candidates as well as draw upon the involvement of external bodies, can help to ameliorate the increased potential for impasse.

IV. FEDERAL ELECTION ADMINISTRATION

Ongoing litigation regarding Arizona's proof-of-citizenship requirements, as in a recent case brought against the EAC itself, will continue to highlight the intersection between federal election and administrative law.[181] Among other issues will be the question

---

[178] Both the Federal Election Commission and Election Assistance Commission require the commission as a whole to appoint their staff directors and general counsel, likely subject to the same voting rules. See 2 USC 437c(f); 42 USC 15324(a)(3).

[179] See, for example, Thomas J. Kassin and Brian M. W. Cunningham, *Grievance Procedures: The Carrier's Perspective*, Am L Institute (Oct 11–13, 2012) (discussing selection procedures for arbitrators when boards deadlock).

[180] See 42 USC 15324(a)(3) ("When a vacancy exists in the position of the Executive Director, the Standards Board and the Board of Advisors shall each appoint a search committee to recommend at least three nominees for the position.").

[181] See *Kobach v The United States Election Assistance Commission*, 13-cv-04095 (D Kan 2013).

identified by Justice Scalia in *Intertribal*—now arising out of legislative, as opposed to administrative, deadlock: Can agencies without any appointed commissioners still act on behalf of the agency? To date, in response to a court order, the professional staff of the EAC has issued a memorandum arguing that the staff possesses the sub-delegated authority under the circumstances to resolve state requests to amend the federal form.[182] In light of recent changes to filibuster rules, the issue may soon become moot as a practical matter if Congress moves ahead on potential EAC nominations.[183] Other important issues to be resolved include whether and when the EAC's decisions can be considered final, reviewable actions under the APA.

While this article's analysis of the comparative institutional competence of insulated career staff may help to bolster the EAC's arguments going forward, this part offers some broader reflections about how administrative law may be adapted in the electoral context—themes to be more fully developed in future work. Indeed, administrative law, as traditionally conceived, is trans-substantive. It presumes principles generally applicable across a number of agencies and formulates its doctrines accordingly.[184] There are many reasons to think, however, that such doctrines should be adapted to the election administration context in ways that acknowledge the domain's unique concerns. Such shifts would resonate with broader

---

[182] Election Assistance Commission, *Memorandum of Decision Concerning State Requests to Include Additional Proof of Citizenship Instructions on the National Mail Voter Registration Form 14-20* (Jan 17, 2014), online at http://www.eac.gov/assets/1/Documents/20140117 %20EAC%20Final%20Decision%20on%20Proof%20of%20Citizenship%20Requests%20 -%20FINAL.pdf.

[183] See Committee on Rules and Administration, Election Assistance Commission Nomination Business Meeting, online at http://www.rules.senate.gov/public/index.cfm?p = CommitteeHearings%26ContentRecord_id = cebb0cf6-c060-43b3-a600-ea6eaa00693c% 26ContentType_id = 14f995b9-dfa5-407a-9d35-56cc7152a7ed%26Group_id = 1983a2a8-4fc3-4062-a50e-7997351c154b%26MonthDisplay = 2%26YearDisplay = 2014.

[184] See Richard E. Levy and Robert L. Glicksman, *Agency-Specific Precedents*, 89 Tex L Rev 499, 499–500 (2011) ("As a field of legal study and practice, administrative law rests on the premise that legal principles concerning agency structure, administrative process, and judicial review cut across multiple agencies" and noting that the "premise certainly holds true for iconic administrative law decisions like *Chenery, Overton Park, Florida East Coast Railway, Vermont Yankee, State Farm*, and *Chevron*, which are widely cited and applied") (citations omitted); Jerry L. Mashaw, *Administration and "The Democracy": Administrative Law from Jackson to Lincoln, 1829–1861*, 117 Yale L J 1568, 1688 (2008) (observing that the "jurisprudence generated through judicial review of administrative action enunciates general principles and is almost necessarily transsubstantive," which are then reinforced by "framework statutes, like the Administrative Procedure Act or the National Environmental Policy Act, and from executive orders such as those that have incrementally established the regulatory review process at the Office of Management and Budget.").

evolutions in administrative law that reflect what Richard Pildes refers to as "new 'realist' political-economy analysis of agency functioning."[185] In other words, doctrinal refinements for election-related administrative agencies would align with other judicial innovations that have similarly embraced the on-the-ground institutional realities faced by particular administrative agencies.

In recent years, judges and scholars alike have begun to recognize the potential wisdom of such tailored approaches. Richard Levy and Robert Glicksman, for example, observe a phenomenon they call "agency-specific precedents."[186] Precedents are agency-specific when a court only cites them for a particular agency in other cases involving that agency, even when the cited principles are supposedly general in nature. What is particularly striking about the practice is that courts have begun to modify these principles to accommodate particular characteristics of these agencies.[187] One traditional articulation of arbitrary-and-capricious review, for example, asks "whether the [agency] decision was based on a consideration of the relevant factors and whether there has been a clear error of judgment."[188] In the narrow contexts of the Federal Communications Commission and Federal Energy Regulatory Commission, however, Levy and Glicksman note that courts regularly invoke a different verbal formulation—simply that of "reasoned decisionmaking."[189] They argue that this alternative approach emphasizes a more rational decision-making *process*, as opposed to a focus on the substance of the decision itself. One potential explanation they offer is that the agencies at issue engage in ratemaking and licensing in regulated industries, which place a greater emphasis on procedural protections.[190]

---

[185] See Pildes, 2014 Supreme Court Review (cited in note 128) (in this volume).

[186] Levy and Glicksman, 89 Tex L Rev at 500 (cited in note 184).

[187] Id.

[188] *Citizens to Preserve Overton Park, Inc. v Volpe*, 401 US 402, 416 (1971); *Motor Vehicle Mfrs. Assn. v State Farm Mutual Automobile Insurance Co.*, 463 US 29, 59 (1983). Another common formulation asks whether the agency "relied on factors Congress has not intended it to consider, entirely failed to consider an important aspect of the problem, offered 'an explanation [for its decision] that runs counter to the evidence before the agency, or is so implausible that it could not be ascribed to a difference in view or the product of agency expertise.'" Id.

[189] Levy and Glicksman, 89 Tex L Rev at 529–34 (cited in note 184).

[190] Id at 532–33. More broadly, Levy and Glicksman posit that agency-specific precedents can be explained in part by the "silo effect" created by attorney and judicial specialization. Id at 558–59. They also acknowledge that the phenomenon derives from var-

To the extent courts are already de facto adapting administrative law principles to the shared concerns of particular agencies, a related possibility is that such customization should recognize the unique problems of federal election administration. The idea arises from the analogous argument that the exceptional nature of elections warrants particularized constitutional doctrines. In this view, the First Amendment, for example, should give some kinds of electoral speech less protection relative to nonelectoral speech in order to facilitate the heightened contest of ideas during election season.[191] The Equal Protection Clause too has received election-specific modifications. The Supreme Court's recent redistricting cases, for instance, have allowed for more race-conscious line-drawing than in other equal protection arenas, with the Court adopting a "predominant" factor rather than a "motivating" factor test for identifying impermissible racial motive.[192] One rationale is that voters voluntarily identify by race when forming political organizations, thus necessitating the recognition of legitimate group interests in the redistricting process.[193] Similarly, *Baker v Carr*'s one-person, one-vote standard is unique as one of the only contexts in which strict scrutiny is applied in the absence of a discriminatory purpose

---

iations in agency organic statutes and programs. Id at 572. Relatedly, a third explanation is likely the D.C. Circuit's familiarity with particular agencys' reputations and historical institutional concerns; indeed, the circuit is well known for its repeated experience with agency litigants and their recurring issues. See John G. Roberts, Jr., *What Makes the D.C. Circuit Different? A Historical View*, 92 Va L Rev 375, 376–77, 388–89 (2006).

[191] See Frederick Schauer and Richard H. Pildes, *Electoral Exceptionalism and the First Amendment*, 77 Tex L Rev 1803, 1806 (1999) (characterizing the "most common version of electoral exceptionalism" as permitting restrictions on communicative activity in the context of elections that would not be permitted in other contexts"). See also Richard H. Pildes, *Elections as a Distinct Sphere Under the First Amendment*, in M. Youn, ed, *Money, Politics, and the Constitution: Beyond Citizens United* 19, 19 (Century Foundation, 2011) ("Elections are distinct from the more general arena of democratic debate, both because elections serve a specific set of purposes and because those purposes can, arguably, be undermined or corrupted by actions such as the willingness of candidates or officeholders to trade their votes on issues for campaign contributions or spending."); Geoffrey R. Stone, *"Electoral Exceptionalism" and the First Amendment: A Road Paved with Good Intentions*, 35 NYU Rev L & Soc Change 665, 667 (2011).

[192] Heather K. Gerken, *Election Law Exceptionalism? A Bird's Eye View of the Symposium*, 82 BU L Rev 737, 740 (2002), citing *Easley v Cromartie*, 532 US 234, 241 (2001) ("Race must not simply have been a motivation for the drawing of a majority-minority district . . . but the predominant factor motivating the legislature's districting decision." (internal quotation marks and citation omitted)); *Miller v Johnson*, 515 US 900, 915–16 (1995) (stating that the "plaintiff's burden is to show . . . that race was the predominant factor motivating the legislature's decision to place a significant number of voters within or without a particular district").

[193] See *Baker v Carr*, 369 US 186 (1962); Pamela S. Karlan and Daryl J. Levinson, *Why Voting Is Different*, 84 Cal L Rev 1201, 1218 (1996).

or suspect classification and has "imposed a mathematical rigor on the redistricting process that no other species of equal protection law required."[194] Partisan gerrymandering doctrines too allow the state to intentionally disadvantage the otherwise constitutionally protected characteristic of political affiliation.[195]

These election-specific constitutional doctrines also have statutory analogues. Richard Hasen, for instance, identifies "democracy canons" of interpretation in state courts and advocates their use in federal settings as well.[196] Such canons generally seek to "give effect to the will of the majority" and "prevent the disenfranchisement of legal voters" when election-related statutes are otherwise ambiguous.[197] When applied, they usually counsel in favor of allowing ballots to be cast and counted and to enable candidates to appear on ballots.[198] Just as constitutional and statutory concerns might take on novel dimensions when elections are at issue, so too might administrative law's worries about nonarbitrariness, transparency, and reasoned decision making, among others. What works wholesale, that is, may need retail-level refinement.

Indeed, one of administrative law's central concerns is how to legitimate government action by an unelected bureaucracy through doctrines and procedures grounded in both political accountability and expertise. Along the first dimension, the nondelegation doctrine, for instance, requires that broad delegations of legislative power are constrained by an "intelligible principle"[199] to which legislators can be held responsible. Given Congress's broad delegations in practice, however, the President has also become an important locus of accountability, particularly through his appointment, removal, and review powers.[200] Central to these accountability-grounded accounts is the notion that federal elections can help to ensure that regulatory policies are responsive to the democratic will.

In the context of election regulation, however, the political con-

---

[194] Karlan and Levinson, 84 Cal L Rev at 1201 (cited in note 193).

[195] Id.

[196] See Richard L. Hasen, *The Democracy Canon*, 62 Stan L Rev 69, 73, 92, 106 (2009). See also Elmendorf, 95 Cornell L Rev at 1051 (cited in note 155).

[197] See Hasen, 62 Stan L Rev at 77 (cited in note 196).

[198] Id at 83–84.

[199] See *Whitman v American Trucking Associations*, 531 US 457, 472 (2001), citing *J. W. Hampton, Jr., & Co. v United States*, 276 US 394, 409 (1928).

[200] See Elena Kagan, *Presidential Administration*, 114 Harv L Rev 2245, 2328 (2001).

trol model falters. Instead of relying on elections as an exogenous check on the regulatory process, election administration influences the election outcomes themselves. As a result, there is a potential circularity: the very source of legitimacy for the agency action is a function of the agency action itself. In these circumstances, elections are a less reliable check on agency decision making when they instead reflect partisan efforts to distort signals of voter approval or disapproval.[201] Related are familiar fears of partisan entrenchment, the worry that an appointed administrator can manipulate the voting process to keep their favored party in power.[202]

Potentially more appropriate, then, is another familiar framework for justifying the delegation of policymaking authority: one grounded in the agency's superior expertise and experience. Hard-look review helps to ensure that agencies make factual and scientific judgments based on the evidence available in the record.[203] Indeed, as this article has argued, federal election administration can benefit greatly from states' experiences as well as from lessons learned from previous federal election cycles.[204] Many of the recent debates about voter identification revolve around contested facts regarding the true rates of voter fraud or racial disenfranchisement. In response, some have proposed information-forcing reforms such as electoral impact statements[205] or the application of risk-regulation principles.[206] In this manner, the legitimacy of a federal election agency

---

[201] See Zipkin, 95 Marq L Rev at 692 (cited in note 6).

[202] See Issacharoff and Pildes, 50 Stan L Rev 643 (cited in note 2).

[203] *Motor Vehicle Manufacturers' Association v State Farm*, 463 US 29, 43 (1983) (quoting *Burlington Truck Lines, Inc. v United States*, 371 US 156, 168 (1962)).

[204] In this vein, Heather Gerken has marveled at the lack of data regarding election performance indicators—including the lack of information about how many voting machines malfunctioned during an election cycle, how long voters had to stand in line, and how many ballots were discarded—and has proposed a performance index in response. See Heather K. Gerken, *The Invisible Election: Making Policy in a World without Data*, 35 Ohio N U L Rev 1013, 1024 (2009) (calling the lack of data in election administration the "mysterious outlier"); Heather K. Gerken, *The Democracy Index: Why Our Election System Is Failing and How to Fix It* (Princeton, 2009).

[205] See, for example, Issacharoff, 127 Harv L Rev at 121–23 (cited in note 6); Bruce Cain and Daniel P. Tokaji, *Promoting Equal Participation: A Voting Rights Act for the 21st Century*, Election L Blog (June 23, 2009), online at http://electionlawblog.org/archives/013914.html (proposing "'electoral impact statement,' analogous to environmental impact statements"). See also Spencer Overton, *How to Update the Voting Rights Act*, Huffington Post (June 25, 2013), online at http://www.huffingtonpost.com/spencer-overton/how-to-update-the-voting_b_3497350.html (proposing disclosure measures as means to modernize the VRA).

[206] See S. Cooper Hawley, Comment, *Applying Risk Regulation Principles to New Policy Domains: A Case Study on Voter Identification Laws*, 48 Wake Forest L Rev 515 (2013).

depends heavily on its ability to rationalize and inform electoral administration.

At the same time, purely nonpartisan rationales grounded solely in expertise may be naive in a context where administrators are appointed or hired by individuals with partisan affiliations.[207] Many election regulations also require line-drawing exercises—as in *Intertribal*'s question of how much information is "necessary" to enforce voter qualifications—which often cannot be answered by reference to pure expertise, but are rather discretionary exercises of judgment. As a result, election administration may also need other sources of legitimacy.

Perhaps one possibility suggested by this article's analysis is that of bipartisanship, the extent to which a regulatory decision has been agreed to by both political parties in a two-party system. This criteria would mirror the structural choices made by Congress for agencies like the FEC and EAC, as discussed. Relative to single-party domination, bipartisan decisions may be less suspect given the greater prospect of decisions based on the public interest rather than narrowly partisan grounds. Since they require the approval of two parties, bipartisan decisions are more likely to concern the electoral system as a whole, rather than attempts to disadvantage a particular party. Privileging bipartisan requirements may also contribute to greater stability over time since they render less likely sudden policy shifts due to contingent situations of unified government.[208]

The danger with bipartisan decisions, however, arises from the concern that political parties will collude to weaken the political process at the expense of voters. Some have argued that this danger is particularly acute in the redistricting context, though empirical evidence may suggest that such concerns are overstated.[209] Because of such worries, neither bipartisan, nor expert, nonpartisan consid-

---

[207] See Nathaniel Persily, *In Defense of Foxes Guarding Henhouses: The Case for Judicial Acquiescence to Incumbent-Protecting Gerrymanders*, 116 Harv L Rev 649, 674 (2002) (in the context of redistricting, noting that "[w]hoever draws the lines must get authority from somewhere—the person will either be appointed or elected").

[208] See Elmendorf, 95 Cornell L Rev at 1065 (cited in note 155 ("a two-party system in which the rules of electoral competition are regularly updated in a generally bipartisan fashion seems likely to be more stable than a system in which the rules remain static for long periods and are updated in partisan bursts whenever one party controls the legislative and executive branches").

[209] Compare Issacharoff, 116 Harv L Rev at 593 (cited in note 2), with Persily, 116 Harv L Rev at 649 (cited in note 207).

erations may be sufficient legitimizing rationales on their own. Rather, perhaps they must operate in tandem as proxies to guard against arbitrary regulatory policies designed to entrench. A lack of bipartisanship, for instance, might invite a heightened judicial review of the evidence-based rationale for a change in electoral regulation. Conversely, the presence of bipartisanship might warrant only ordinary arbitrary-and-capricious review of the underlying supporting data and evidence.[210]

V. CONCLUSION

Prior to last Term, election law observers had presciently predicted that the future of voting rights would shift from the VRA's antidiscrimination model toward more national, uniform approaches that "better fit" the increasingly recognized need for consistency across electoral jurisdictions.[211] Recent events such as the establishment of a presidential commission to address federal election administration further signal the potentially expanding regulatory presence in this domain.[212] As the *Intertribal* litigation suggests, a federal approach also brings with it the greater need for high-quality information and data to justify alternative regulatory approaches. This need is highlighted by the self-professed difficulties courts face in gaining this information.

To confront this challenge, this article has sought to highlight some potentially fruitful intersections between administrative and election law. Faced with deadlocks unique to the election context, the analysis developed an approach to *Skidmore* deference that would push courts to focus on the information and expertise gained by experienced institutional actors who could bring a more birds-eye view across various electoral jurisdictions. Future litigation arising

---

[210] Note that this approach is analogous to another that has been advocated by individual Justices in the context of multimember commissions, though it has not been adopted by the Court. In *FCC v Fox*, Justice Breyer joined by Justices Ginsburg, Stevens, and Souter noted that an independent "agency's comparative freedom from ballot-box control" merited a particularly searching review of the agency's policy change. In this sense, judicial and political review could serve as substitutes. See *FCC v Fox*, 556 US 502, 547 (2009). See also Randolph J. May, *Defining Deference Down: Independent Agencies and Chevron Deference*, 58 Admin L Rev 429 (2006); Randolph J. May, *Defining Deference Down, Again: Independent Agencies, Chevron Deference, and Fox*, 62 Admin L Rev 433 (2010).

[211] See Pildes, *Voting Rights: The Next Generation* at 17, 18 (cited in note 6).

[212] See Exec Order 13639, *Establishment of the Presidential Commission of Election Administration*, 78 Fed Reg 19979 (March 28, 2013), online at http://www.whitehouse.gov/the-press-office/2013/03/28/executive-order-establishment-presidential-commission-election-administr.

out of *Intertribal* will continue to test the limits of judges' abilities to sort through limited factual records. At the same time, it will rightly bring the dispute firmly back to administrative arenas with the tools and doctrines that can help to foster the legitimacy that federal election administration demands.

DALE CARPENTER

WINDSOR PRODUCTS: EQUAL
PROTECTION FROM ANIMUS

Across four decades, the concept of animus has emerged from equal protection doctrine as an independent constitutional force. In four decisions—an animus quadrilogy—the Supreme Court has struck down state and federal acts that it concluded were driven by animus toward a group of people.[1] The roots of anti-animus doctrine go

Dale Carpenter is Earl R. Larson Professor of Civil Rights & Civil Liberties Law, Distinguished University Teaching Professor, University of Minnesota Law School.

AUTHOR'S NOTE: I joined several other scholars in signing an amicus brief in *United States v Windsor*, arguing that the Defense of Marriage Act was unconstitutional under structural federalism principles. For helpful and clarifying comments, I want to thank Carlos Ball, Will Baude, Tom Berg, Brian Bix, Lackland Bloom, Mary Anne Case, Teresa Collett, Don Dripps, Dan Farber, Rick Garnett, Michael Gerhardt, Jill Hasday, Claire Hill, Jenia Iontcheva, Jeff Kahn, Orin Kerr, Heidi Kitrosser, Andy Koppelman, Mae Kuykendall, Holning Lau, Art Leonard, Brett McDonnell, Doug NeJaime, Arvid Nelsen, Michael Paulsen, Susannah Pollvogt, Mike Rappaport, Jon Rauch, Cliff Rosky, Paul Rubin, Meghan Ryan, Paul Smith, Ilya Somin, Geof Stone, Eugene Volokh, and participants in a workshop at the University of St. Thomas Law School in Minneapolis. I am indebted to Mary Bonauto for pointing me toward important aspects of the congressional debate over the Defense of Marriage Act. Special thanks go to Mae Kuykendall, who among other things inspired the title of the article. For editing, research, and cite-checking efforts, I want to thank my terrific research assistant, Samuel Light. While I would like to blame others for my remaining errors, they are of course my own.

[1] *United States v Windsor*, 133 S Ct 2675 (2013) (striking down a federal law defining marriage as the union of one man and one woman); *Romer v Evans*, 517 US 620 (1996) (striking down a state constitutional amendment barring specific legal protection from anti-gay discrimination); *City of Cleburne v Cleburne Living Center*, 473 US 432 (1985) (striking down a city's denial of a special zoning permit for housing the cognitively disabled); *Department of Agriculture v Moreno*, 413 US 528 (1973) (striking down a federal law denying food stamps to unrelated persons living in a household). This article deals with the anti-animus principle as it has developed in equal protection jurisprudence. The underlying constitutional concern about animus can also be found in other parts of the

even deeper, reaching back to political-process concerns famously articulated more than seventy years ago in *United States v Carolene Products* about how "prejudice against *discrete and insular minorities* . . . tends seriously to curtail the operation of those political processes ordinarily to be relied upon to protect minorities."[2] As a matter of constitutional law, a legislative process impelled by animus is a poisoned and poisonous one.

Nevertheless, the constitutional anti-animus principle remains an unappreciated one. There is little consensus about what animus is; about whether, why, and when it is constitutionally problematic; or about what the appropriate role of courts, if any, should be in policing it. The decisions of lower courts have been wary of relying on animus.[3] Scholars have tended to discount the doctrine.[4] Beyond

Constitution, like the First Amendment's protection of religious freedom, *Locke v Davey*, 540 US 712, 725 (2004) ("animus" against religion would be grounds to invalidate a law under the First Amendment's Free Exercise Clause), and the Constitution's clauses forbidding federal and state Bills of Attainder, see US Const, Art I, § 9, and US Const, Art I, § 10, which prevent legislatures from declaring a person guilty of a crime and stripping him of all procedural rights.

[2] *United States v Carolene Products Co.*, 304 US 144, 152–53 n 4 (1938) (emphasis added). See also John Hart Ely, *Democracy and Distrust: A Theory of Judicial Review* 76 (Harvard, 1980) (the Court should "concern itself with what majorities do to minorities").

[3] The first district court post-*Windsor* to invalidate a state ban on same-sex marriage declined to rely on the anti-animus principle because, the judge determined, "the Supreme Court has not yet delineated the contours of such an approach." *Kitchen v Herbert*, 2013 WL 6697874, *21 (D Utah). In all, within eight months after *Windsor* came down, seven district courts held that state marriage laws were at least in part unconstitutional, but none rested squarely on animus grounds. See *De Leon v Perry*, 2014 WL 715741, *1 (WD Tex) (state law denied same-sex couples their fundamental right to marry and equal protection); *Lee v Orr*, 2014 WL 683680, *1 (ND Ill) (holding based on fundamental right to marry and equal protection); *Bourke v Beshear*, 2014 WL 556729, *7 (WD Ky) ("Absent a clear showing of animus, however, the Court must still search for any rational relation to a legitimate government purpose," and then striking down state's nonrecognition of valid same-sex marriages from out of state as lacking a rational basis); *Bostic v Rainey*, 2014 WL 561978, *1, *21 (ED Va) (asserting that bans on same-sex marriage were "rooted in unlawful prejudice" but concluding that the laws lacked a rational basis); *Bishop v United States*, 2014 WL 116013, *21–23, *33 (ND Okla) (state marriage law was enacted for the purpose of excluding same-sex couples and failed rational-basis test); *Kitchen v Herbert*, 2013 WL 6697874 (D Utah) (rational-basis review); and *Obergefell v Wymyslo*, 2013 WL 7869139, *20–21 (SD Ohio). The district court decision in *Obergefell* came closest to relying upon animus. "A review of the historical background and legislative history of the Ohio laws at issue," said the court, "leads to the [] conclusion . . . that in refusing to recognize a particular type of legal out-of-state marriages *for the first time in its history*, Ohio is engaging in 'discrimination[] of an unusual character' without a rational basis for doing so." Id at *19.

[4] For scholarly treatments of the concept of animus in constitutional law, see Steven Douglas Smith, *The Jurisprudence of Denigration*, UC Davis L Rev (forthcoming, 2014); Andrew M. Koppelman, *Why Scalia Should Have Voted to Overturn DOMA* (Northwestern University Law Review Colloquy, Nov 12, 2013), available online at http://colloquy.law .northwestern.edu/main/2013/11/why-scalia-should-have-voted-to-overturn-doma.html;

uncertainty, there is strong criticism. One critique is that the doctrine is analytically empty, a conclusion clothed in argument. Another is that it calls for the kind of unprincipled judgment about subjective legislative motivation that has long been discredited in jurisprudence. A third holds that slapping the animus label on a law is an attempt to hush debate about deeply contested moral and legal controversies. On this view, it insults those who differ from the Court's majority, dismissing them as bigots—a form of constitutional name-calling. Perhaps animus doctrine is animus based.

Yet consider the simple idea that it is wrong for one person to treat another person malevolently. This sentiment so suffuses our moral and legal tradition that hardly anyone would deny it. "Of course it is our moral heritage that one should not hate any human being or class of human beings," wrote Justice Antonin Scalia in his dissent in *Romer v Evans*.[5] Animus doctrine constitutionalizes this basic precept. It asserts that just as *individuals* have a moral and sometimes legal duty not to act maliciously toward others, the *group* of people elected as representatives (or acting in some other official governmental capacity) in a liberal democracy has a moral and sometimes constitutional duty not to act maliciously toward a person or group of people.[6]

Under the anti-animus principle, the Constitution's Equal Protection guarantee is understood to "guard one part of the society

---

Daniel O. Conkle, *Evolving Values, Animus, and Same-Sex Marriage*, 89 Ind L J 27 (Winter 2014); Susannah W. Pollvogt, *Unconstitutional Animus*, 81 Fordham L Rev 887 (2012); William N. Eskridge, Jr., *Some Effects of Identity-Based Social Movements of Constitutional Law in the Twentieth Century*, 100 Mich L Rev 2062 (2002); Elizabeth S. Anderson and Richard H. Pildes, *Expressive Theories of Law: A General Restatement*, 148 U Pa L Rev 1503 (2000); Barbara J. Flagg, *"Animus" and Moral Disapproval: A Comment on Romer v. Evans*, 82 Minn L Rev 833 (1998); J. M. Balkin, *The Constitution of Status*, 106 Yale L J 2313 (1997); Ashutosh Bhagwat, *Purpose Scrutiny in Constitutional Analysis*, 85 Cal L Rev 297 (1997); Cass R. Sunstein, *Foreword: Leaving Things Undecided*, 110 Harv L Rev 4 (1996).

[5] 517 US 620, 644 (1996) (Scalia, J, dissenting). Justice Scalia went on to suggest a distinction between hatred of a person and disapproval of his conduct: "But I had thought that one could consider certain conduct reprehensible—murder, for example, or polygamy, or cruelty to animals—and could exhibit even 'animus' toward such conduct. Surely that is the only sort of 'animus' at issue here: moral disapproval of homosexual conduct. . . ." Id. Whatever remained of the status-conduct distinction in reference to homosexuality collapsed in *Lawrence v Texas*, in which, as Justice Scalia put it, the Court held that "the promotion of majoritarian sexual morality is not even a *legitimate* state interest." 539 US 558, 599 (2003) (Scalia, J, dissenting). This holding was confirmed in *Christian Legal Society v Martinez*, in which the Court declared that it would not distinguish between homosexual status and conduct—the one is intimately linked to the other. 130 S Ct 2971, 2990 (2010).

[6] Ely, *Democracy and Distrust* at 157 (cited in note 2) ("To disadvantage a group essentially out of dislike is surely to deny its members equal concern and respect, specifically by valuing their welfare negatively.").

against the injustice of the other part"[7] by checking the tendency of legislative majorities to be vindictive. The anti-animus doctrine addresses this systemic problem by scrutinizing the reasons for government action. The government acts on animus when, to a material degree, it aims *"to disparage and to injure" a person or group of people*.[8] The injury may be tangible, as in the denial of benefits and protections a group would have in the absence of animus against them. Or the injury may be intangible, as in the affront to their dignity and to the respect they deserve as equal citizens, which may be caused by their exclusion from a status they would have absent animus against them. The desire simply to reward and encourage socially beneficial behavior by one group is not by itself animus toward another group.[9] But the simple desire to harm (in a tangible and/or intangible way) one group of people is unconstitutional animus. If animus was present, moreover, it taints the law. The act is unconstitutional even if legitimate reasons might now be offered to justify it.[10]

Carolene Products would correctly predict that the targets of animus will almost always be politically unpopular minorities. Yet the anti-animus doctrine does not specify, as would formal heightened scrutiny, certain classifications that are subjected to special judicial scrutiny. It doesn't favor certain vulnerable classes. All citizens are protected from animus-based government action.[11] That is their minimal entitlement as citizens of a liberal democracy dedicated to the equal protection of the laws.

In constitutional law, the concern about animus was born in a

---

[7] Federalist 51 (Madison) in Jacob E. Cooke, ed, *The Federalist Papers* 347 (Wesleyan, 1961).

[8] *Windsor*, 133 S Ct at 2696.

[9] Whether animus is what actually drove government decision making when the government claims the benign purpose simply to encourage good conduct depends on consideration of a variety of objective factors outlined below in the introduction and in Section III.A.

[10] This raises the prospect, dreaded by some, that a law enacted for an impermissible animus-based purpose might later be reenacted for a legitimate purpose and subsequently upheld. For a response to this criticism of purpose inquiry in constitutional law, see Section II.C.3.

[11] A similar idea is described as the "pariah principle" by Dan Farber and Suzanna Sherry: "This principle, in a nutshell, forbids the government from designating any societal group as untouchable, regardless of whether the group in question is generally entitled to some special degree of judicial protection, like blacks, or to no special protection, like left-handers (or, under current doctrine, homosexuals)." Daniel Farber and Suzanna Sherry, *The Pariah Principle*, 13 Const Comm 257, 258 (1996).

time when government often acted for the purpose of harming racial minorities. The law reacted by subjecting all racial classifications to special judicial scrutiny, regardless of what motive the government might actually have had. But anti-animus principles have been sharpened and crystallized in response to the law's almost unrelenting hostility toward gay men and lesbians. For most of American history, public policy toward homosexuals was marked by fear and disgust. Homosexuals were seen as dirty, diseased, and dangerous. As a result of the long-standing mistreatment of this small minority, the Supreme Court has been schooled on the many ways that a legislative body might target a group of people for insult or injury and be literally thoughtless about their interests. For a Court unwilling to take the extraordinary step of invalidating all anti-gay legislation, the anti-animus doctrine offered a framework under which the most egregious official expressions of malice toward gays would be invalidated.

The animus quadrilogy overlaps a gay-rights trilogy that has charted the remarkable rise of respect for the dignity and rights of homosexuals. On May 20, 1996, just as Congress was beginning the process of passing the Defense of Marriage Act (DOMA) to ban any federal recognition of then-nonexistent same-sex marriages,[12] Justice Scalia cut to the heart of the question of homosexuality and the Constitution in his dissent in *Romer*. He asked, incredulously: is "the perceived social harm of homosexuality" no longer a "legitimate concern of government"?[13] Striking down a state constitutional amendment barring specific protections from anti-gay discrimination, the Court answered "yes" by concluding that Amendment 2 reflected impermissible animus against homosexuals.[14] In 2003 the Court confirmed the answer in *Lawrence v Texas*,[15] striking down a state "Homosexual Conduct" law because the state cannot "demean [the] existence" of homosexuals. It rejected the state interest in expressing moral disapproval of homosexuality.[16] Then came *United States v Windsor*,[17] striking down DOMA because

---

[12] Pub L No 104-199, 110 Stat 2419 (1996).

[13] *Romer*, 517 US at 651 (Scalia, J, dissenting).

[14] Id at 635–36.

[15] 539 US 558 (2003).

[16] Id at 564, 578 (2003).

[17] 133 S Ct 2675, 2693 (2013). When I refer in this article to "DOMA" I mean that as shorthand only for Section 3 of DOMA, the federal definition of marriage. I do not

the Court thought that by denying any federal recognition to otherwise valid same-sex marriages Congress exhibited animus against the targeted couples and their children.

These three momentous decisions involving gay rights cumulatively make it clear that the perceived social harm of homosexuality, along with simple moral disapproval of it, is no longer a proper basis on which to carve out gay people from legal protection. It is unconstitutional animus for the government to target homosexuals simply because it morally disapproves of homosexuality.[18] There must be some reasoned public-policy purpose beyond moral disapproval if state-imposed restrictions on gays are to survive anti-animus review.[19]

Windsor refined and enlarged the concept of unconstitutional animus. The decision contains three conclusions of significance for constitutional law generally and for the rights of gay men and lesbians specifically. First, in what we might call the conclusion of *principle* in *Windsor*, the opinion confirmed that legislation driven

---

mean to refer to Section 2, which purported to allow the states to disregard otherwise valid same-sex marriages from outside the state. The constitutional analysis of Section 2 would involve different considerations and justifications, like a claimed desire to prevent the "nationalization" of same-sex marriage after a single state like Hawaii recognized it. Whether Section 2 might also be unconstitutional on animus (or other constitutional) grounds is beyond the scope of the article.

[18] "[T]he desire to effectuate one's animus against homosexuals can never be a legitimate governmental purpose, [and] a state action based on that animus alone violates the Equal Protection Clause." *Davis v Prison Health Services*, 679 F3d 433, 438 (6th Cir 2012), quoting *Stemler v City of Florence*, 126 F3d 856, 873–74 (6th Cir 1997). In *Davis* a state employee claimed that "the public-works officers supervising his work crew treated him differently than other inmates, ridiculed and belittled him, and 'ma[d]e a spectacle' of him when they brought him back to the correctional facility after a public-works assignment because of his sexual orientation." Id at 436. He also claimed that "these officers did not want to strip search him because he was homosexual and would make 'under the breath' remarks when selected to do so." Id. The Sixth Circuit noted that, if true, the allegations were sufficient to find "that the officers' actions toward him were motivated by an anti-gay animus." Id at 438.

[19] The anti-animus principle is not solely concerned with protecting gay men and lesbians from malice. As discussed below, see Section II, it has also been used to strike down specific instances of discrimination against the cognitively disabled, see *Cleburne*, 473 US at 450, and "hippies," see *Moreno*, 413 US at 537, even though neither classification merited formal heightened scrutiny. As the Sixth Circuit noted in a case involving the selective arrest and prosecution of a lesbian for driving under the influence, the anti-animus principle is broader than a concern with sexual orientation. "[T]he principle would be the same if Stemler had been arrested discriminatorily based on her hair color, her college bumper sticker (perhaps supporting an out-of-state rival) or her affiliation with a disfavored sorority or company." *Stemler*, 126 F3d at 874. In this article, I will focus on the anti-animus principle as applied in the context of sexual orientation, but that should not be taken to mean that the animus doctrine is limited to a concern for anti-gay action by government. On the other hand, as discussed below in Section III.B.2.b, state action aimed at homosexuals has historically been unusually likely to reflect animus.

by animus denies the equal protection of the law guaranteed by the Constitution to every person. This constitutional principle is uncontroversial. Chief Justice Roberts, in dissent, implicitly agreed that it is unconstitutional to "codify malice," though he thought there needed to be "more convincing evidence" of that than the Court presented.[20] Nor did Justice Scalia or Justice Alito, in their separate dissents, challenge the basic premise that animus is an impermissible basis for legislation.[21] Scalia, like Roberts, simply thought a finding of animus should require "the most extraordinary evidence," which he did not think could be found in DOMA.[22] If for no other reason than that the Court has repeatedly endorsed the anti-animus principle in important decisions, it can no longer be ignored.

Second, the *institutional* conclusion of *Windsor* is that courts are competent to police unconstitutional animus. This means they must discern when legislation impermissibly arises from animus.[23] That prospect might be very troubling. To begin with, decision makers often have mixed motives and purposes, which calls for a judgment about when animus is sufficiently present in the mix of motives to justify striking down their action.[24] Further, if ferreting out animus means that courts are now self-appointed sleuths searching for the subjective motives of legislators, it is a very dubious mission.

In fact, considering the animus quadrilogy as a whole, the Court's decisions suggest that the inquiry into legislative motive—or more often, purpose—is not a subjective one. Determining whether animus materially influenced the government's act rests on a variety

---

[20] *Windsor*, 133 S Ct at 2696 (Roberts, CJ, dissenting).

[21] Id at 2697–711 (Scalia, J, dissenting); id at 2711–20 (Alito, J, dissenting). Justices Scalia and Alito also didn't explicitly *endorse* the anti-animus principle. For his part, Justice Scalia denounced the Court for suggesting that Congress and the President had "hateful hearts" in supporting DOMA. "Laying such a charge against them," he declared, "should require the most extraordinary evidence." Id at 2707 (Scalia, J, dissenting).

[22] Id at 2707 (Scalia, J, dissenting). For a discussion of the indicia supporting the animus holding, see Section III.B. Justice Alito criticized the Court for "cast[ing] all those who cling to traditional beliefs about the nature of marriage in the role of bigots or superstitious fools." Id at 2718 (Alito, J, dissenting). For a discussion of the objection that *Windsor* is constitutional name-calling, see Section II.C.4.

[23] See Ely, *Democracy and Distrust* at 103 (cited in note 2) (Judges are "in a position objectively to assess claims—though no one could suppose the evaluation won't be full of judgment calls—that . . . by acting as accessories to majority tyranny, our elected representatives are not representing the interests of those whom the system presupposes they are.").

[24] I propose that legislation reflects a constitutionally impermissible degree of animus only when it "materially influences" passage. See Section III.C.3.

of considerations that are objective in the sense that they do not depend on discovering subjective legislative intent. These include, if applicable, considerations of statutory text, context, process, impact, and the persuasiveness of any non-animus-based justifications. Animus is not merely an illegitimate purpose; it taints the government's action. The sometimes far-fetched and hypothesized rationalizations that suffice to sustain a law in ordinary rational-basis cases don't suffice once animus is detected.

The third conclusion from *Windsor*, the *substantive* one, is the most infuriating to critics. It is that DOMA itself was the product of animus. Rather than thinking of *Windsor* as a federalism opinion protecting the states' traditional authority over family relations, or as a substantive liberty decision protecting individuals from government encroachment on their marital freedom, the decision is mainly about how these two related concerns help show that DOMA maliciously targeted a small subset of married people.

This third conclusion has been the most criticized. It is the only one of the three to which the dissenting Justices explicitly objected. For them, there simply was not enough evidence of animus in DOMA. While constitutional law professors overwhelmingly believed DOMA was unconstitutional,[25] they have not overwhelmingly endorsed *Windsor*. The decision has its prominent defenders,[26] but few if any have defended its animus holding. Harsh judgments have come from those who think the Court was wrong on the merits, from those who think the Court reached the right result for the wrong reason,[27] and from those who think the decision is an indecipherable constitutional hieroglyph.[28] The most unsettling por-

---

[25] According to a 2012 survey of 485 constitutional law professors, 69 percent thought DOMA was unconstitutional. Dale Carpenter, *Constitutional Law Professors: 87% Support Same-Sex Marriage, but Only 54% Believe It Is Constitutionally Mandated*, The Volokh Conspiracy (Sept 7, 2012), online at http://www.volokh.com/2012/09/07/constitutional-law-professors-87-support-same-sex-marriage-but-only-54-believe-it-is-constitutionally-mandated.

[26] Ernest A. Young and Erin C. Blondel, *Federalism, Liberty, and Equality in United States v. Windsor*, Cato S Ct Rev 117, 119 (2012–13) (praising the opinion as "brilliant"); Ernest A. Young, *United States v. Windsor and the Role of State Law in Defining Rights Claims*, 99 Va L Rev Online 39, 40 (2013) (the opinion is not "muddled" or "vague"); Randy Barnett, *Federalism Marries Liberty in the DOMA Decision*, SCOTUSblog (June 26, 2013), online at http://www.scotusblog.com/2013/06/federalism-marries-liberty-in-the-doma-decision/.

[27] See Koppelman, *Why Scalia Should Have Voted to Overturn DOMA* (cited in note 4).

[28] Conkle, 89 Ind L J 27 (cited in note 4); Neomi Rao, *The Trouble with Dignity and Rights of Recognition*, 99 Va L Rev Online 29, 31 (2013) (criticizing the decision as "muddled" and as ungrounded in constitutional text, history, and precedent); Sandy Levinson, *A Brief Comment on Justice Kennedy's Opinion in Windsor*, Balkinization (June 26, 2013),

tion of the decision for many of its critics, especially those who oppose same-sex marriage and resent insult from the Court, is the conclusion that DOMA arose from unconstitutional animus.[29] "Kennedy's suggestion that DOMA was based on the view that gays and lesbians are inferior human beings is tendentious in the extreme," writes one critic of *Windsor*, "and demeaning to all those who for a host of non-bigoted reasons uphold the traditional understanding of marriage as an essentially heterosexual institution."[30] And that denunciation of the decision came from a *supporter* of the constitutional claim for same-sex marriage.

These criticisms are overwrought. What we have in Justice Kennedy's opinion is *Windsor* Products—an outpouring of decades of constitutional development whose fountainhead is *Carolene Products* and whose tributaries are the gay-rights and federalism streams. I will argue here that each of *Windsor*'s three central conclusions—the existence of a constitutional anti-animus principle, the assertion of institutional capacity to decide in clear cases when it is present, and the substantive holding that it was present in DOMA—was correct. Its reasoning is neither incoherent nor unprecedented. *Windsor* Products adds both meaning and modest method to the more formal and even mechanical footnote 4 approach of *Carolene Products*.

Despite what critics have said, *Windsor* did not label as bigots all supporters of opposite-sex-only marriage or reject as homophobic all reasons for hesitation on same-sex marriage. Among other possible non-animus-based rationales for limiting marriage to opposite-sex couples, policy makers might want to move slowly and incre-

---

online at http://balkin.blogspot.com/2013/06/a-brief-comment-on-justice-kennedys.html (noting "the intellectual awkwardness of [Kennedy's] opinion" and comparing it to "a camel (i.e., a horse designed by a committee)"); and Jeffrey Rosen and Michael McConnell, *Debating the Court's Gay Marriage Decisions*, New Republic (June 26, 2013), at http://www.newrepublic.com/article/113646/supreme-court-strikes-down-doma-dismisses-prop-8-debate ("[T]he DOMA decision is a logical mish-mash, portending more litigation and more instability.").

[29] See, for example, Richard W. Garnett, *Worth Worrying About?: Same-Sex Marriage & Religious Freedom*, Commonweal (Commonweal Magazine, Aug 5, 2013), online at https://www.commonwealmagazine.org/worth-worrying-about) (arguing that *Windsor* concluded that gay-marriage opponents are "backward and bigoted, unworthy of respect"); Michael J. Perry, *Right Result, Wrong Reason: Same-Sex Marriage & The Supreme Court*, Commonweal (Commonweal Magazine, Aug 5, 2013), available online at https://www.commonwealmagazine.org/right-decision-wrong-reason (calling the decision "tendentious in the extreme").

[30] Perry, *Right Result, Wrong Reason* (cited in note 29).

mentally in making important changes to social policy.[31] Finally, *Windsor* should be seen as probably the least aggressive route the Court could have taken in striking down DOMA.

Section I summarizes the legislative and judicial developments that brought the case to the Court. It discusses why *Windsor* should not be seen as a federalism decision, a substantive-liberty decision, or a *sub silentio* heightened-scrutiny case.

Section II presents the constitutional animus principle as it has developed over the last four decades, including what constitutes animus, why it offends the Constitution, and how the Supreme Court determines it is present. This section both supports the conclusion that animus offends the egalitarian principle in the Constitution and defends the limited institutional role of the Court in helping to enforce it.

Section III discusses why the Court was justified in concluding that DOMA arose from animus by looking at the textual, contextual, procedural, effectual, and pretextual factors that explain the law's passage. These considerations show why the posited non-animus-based justifications for DOMA—like a desire to boost "responsible procreation," to save federal money on benefits, or to move slowly and incrementally on matters of social policy—could not actually sustain the law. Even if such hypothesized justifications could save a marriage limitation from invalidation under ordinary rational-basis review, they cannot save it when the limitation arises from ill will. Indeed, the flimsiness of these justifications reinforces the conclusion that the law was infected with animus.

I. WINDSOR AND ITS MISINTERPRETATIONS

For many readers, simply understanding what *Windsor* held has been a challenge. The decision is peripatetic. It heads down a path toward federalism, but suddenly veers off in the direction of "liberty," looking back over its shoulder toward states' authority. Then it pivots toward equal protection, with darts toward dignity, before finally settling on animus as a destination. When we arrive— "The judgment of the Court of Appeals for the Second Circuit is

---

[31] As we shall see, the go-slow rationale does not really explain the passage of DOMA. See Section III.B.5.c. Even if a go-slow rationale might more convincingly support a state marriage law under anti-animus attack, laws excluding gay couples from marriage may have other constitutional defects.

affirmed"[32]—we may ask ourselves, "Well, how did [we] get here?"[33]

This section first summarizes the legislative steps that led to the passage of DOMA. A more detailed consideration of the legislative proceedings and how they connect to concerns about animus awaits the reader in Section III. Next, it chronicles the judicial developments that brought the case to the Supreme Court in 2013. Finally, it argues that *Windsor* should not be seen as a federalism decision, a substantive-liberty decision, or a heightened-scrutiny decision.

A. THE ACT

In the summer of 1996, responding to the possibility that the Hawaii Supreme Court might order that state to recognize same-sex marriages, Congress placed DOMA on a fast track to passage. Section 2 declared that no state could be required to recognize any other state's same-sex marriages:

> No State, territory, or possession of the United States, or Indian tribe, shall be required to give effect to any public act, record, or judicial proceeding of any other State, territory, possession, or tribe respecting a relationship between persons of the same sex that is treated as a marriage under the laws of such other State, territory, possession, or tribe, or a right or claim arising from such relationship.[34]

This permission slip to disregard marriages validly recognized in sister states was probably redundant of states' conflict-of-laws powers to reject out-of-state marriages violating their own public policy. It was also unprecedented. Congress had never before decreed, using its "effects" power under the Full Faith and Credit Clause,[35] that a state's laws and even its judicial judgments could be categorically ignored by the other forty-nine states.

Section 3, which was challenged in *Windsor*, dealt with the problem of how the federal government should treat marriages validly recognized in a state. It limited marriage for all federal purposes to the union of one man and one woman:

---

[32] *United States v Windsor*, 133 S Ct 2675, 2696 (2013).

[33] Apologies to David Byrne, Talking Heads, *Once in a Lifetime* (lyrics) (Sire Records, 1981).

[34] Defense of Marriage Act, Pub L No 104-199, 110 Stat 2419 (1996), codified at 28 USC § 1738C.

[35] "Full Faith and Credit shall be given in each State to the public Acts, Records, and judicial Proceedings of every other State. And the Congress may by general Laws prescribe the Manner in which such Acts, Records, and Proceedings shall be proved, and the Effect thereof." US Const, Art IV, § 1.

> In determining the meaning of any Act of Congress, or of any ruling, regulation, or interpretation of the various administrative bureaus and agencies of the United States, the word "marriage" means only a legal union between one man and one woman as husband and wife, and the word "spouse" refers only to a person of the opposite sex who is a husband or a wife.[36]

These sixty-five words abruptly, summarily, and comprehensively ended two centuries of federal deference to state choices about the definition and recognition of marital status.

On July 12, the House of Representatives voted for DOMA with an overwhelming and strongly bipartisan majority, 342–67.[37] With a presidential election just months away and public opinion running strongly against gay marriage, President Clinton backed the law before it was even introduced in the Senate. But his own press spokesperson labeled it election-year "gay baiting" on the very day it passed the House.[38] The Senate passed it on September 10 by a vote of 85–14, again with strong bipartisan support.[39] The president sheepishly signed it just after midnight on September 21, releasing an unusual statement urging that the law "should not, despite the fierce and at times divisive rhetoric surrounding it, be understood to provide an excuse for discrimination, violence or intimidation against any person on the basis of sexual orientation."[40]

DOMA, it was hoped, would provide a double vaccination against the spread of same-sex marriages. In 1993, the Hawaii Supreme Court announced that heightened judicial scrutiny should apply to a ban on same-sex marriage because the denial constituted sex discrimination under the state constitution.[41] It then remanded the case, originally brought by same-sex couples in 1990, back to the state trial court for a trial on the merits under the appropriate level of scrutiny. The trial court was set to take up the case again in September 1996, and the common expectation

---

[36] Defense of Marriage Act, Pub L No 104-199, 110 Stat 2419 (1996), codified at 1 USC § 7.

[37] See *Windsor*, 133 S Ct at 2696 (Roberts, CJ, dissenting).

[38] Jerry Gray, *House Passes Bar to U.S. Sanction of Gay Marriage*, NY Times A1 (July 13, 1996).

[39] See id.

[40] Chris Geidner, *Becoming Law*, Metroweekly (Sept 29, 2011), online at http://www.metroweekly.com/feature/?ak=6613.

[41] *Baehr v Lewin*, 852 P2d 44, 65 (Hawaii 1993).

was that the state's refusal to allow same-sex marriages would be struck down because the state could not show that denying marriage licenses to gay couples was closely related to any compelling state interest. On appeal, it was expected that the Hawaii Supreme Court would eventually declare the marriage law unconstitutional.

Thus, at some point in the future, there would be gay marriage in one state. DOMA would solve two perceived problems arising from that fact. First, Section 2 prevented couples around the country from traveling to Hawaii, getting married, and then demanding marital recognition in their home states. Second, Section 3 ensured that the federal government would not have to recognize even one such marriage from any state.

B. THE CHALLENGE

As it happened, DOMA had no immediate effect as there would not be a state-recognized same-sex marriage anywhere in the United States until 2004, when Massachusetts became the first state to legalize it.[42] Ironically, the very litigation that had propelled DOMA reached a dead end before the state Supreme Court could rule, when the people of Hawaii voted to strip state courts of any power to change the definition of marriage.[43]

As the number of states recognizing same-sex marriage grew, so did the number of couples denied federal benefits and legal protections to which they would otherwise have been eligible. Lawsuits challenging DOMA on constitutional grounds began to sprout. In 2009, two challenges arose from Massachusetts. *Gill v Office of Personnel Management*,[44] filed by Gay & Lesbian Advocates & Defenders (GLAD), argued that Section 3 violated equal protection principles. The second case, *Massachusetts v Department of Health and Human Services*,[45] filed by Massachusetts, claimed that Section 3 intruded on the power and sovereignty of the states and codified animus against gay people. The district court concluded

---

[42] Massachusetts began to issue marriage licenses to same-sex couples in May 2004, six months after a ruling for gay marriage by the state supreme court in *Goodridge v Department of Public Health*, 798 NE2d 941 (Mass 2003).

[43] See Hawaii Const, Art I, § 23.

[44] 682 F3d 1 (1st Cir 2012).

[45] Id.

that DOMA was indeed unconstitutional,[46] and the First Circuit agreed on equal protection grounds.[47]

The year that *Gill* and *Massachusetts* were filed was also the year that Edith Windsor's spouse, Thea Spyer, died. While the two had been married in Canada in 2007, at a time when New York did not yet permit same-sex marriages, their union was recognized in New York under state conflict-of-law principles. But where New York saw a married couple, under DOMA, the federal government saw only legal strangers. That meant Windsor had to pay the federal estate tax for her inheritance from Spyer, a tax from which a surviving opposite-sex spouse is exempt.[48]

Windsor paid $363,053 in estate tax and sued the government for a refund in the Southern District of New York. Her lawyers at the American Civil Liberties Union argued that DOMA's Section 3 violated the Fifth Amendment Due Process Clause guaranty of equal protection.[49]

The district court decided that DOMA failed the rational-basis test.[50] In October 2012, the Second Circuit applied heightened scrutiny to classifications based on sexual orientation and likewise concluded that DOMA was unconstitutional.[51] Within two months, the Supreme Court granted certiorari on the equal protection issue. The parties and their numerous amici thus directed their arguments at the equal protection question, rather than at the issue of whether there is a fundamental right of same-sex couples to marry.

C. THREE COMMON MISREADINGS OF WINDSOR

Justice Kennedy's opinion is an amalgam of federalism, liberty, and equality, and thus expresses corresponding structural, substantive, and process-based concerns. Within each of these types of concerns, moreover, there are numerous possible approaches suggested by the opinion. Below I outline some possible reasons

---

[46] *Massachusetts v United States Department of Health and Human Services*, 698 F Supp 2d 234, 253 (D Mass 2010).

[47] *Massachusetts*, 682 F3d at 9–13.

[48] *Windsor*, 133 S Ct at 2682.

[49] *Windsor v United States*, 699 F3d 169, 188 (2d Cir 2012).

[50] *Windsor v United States*, 833 F Supp 2d 394, 406 (SDNY 2012).

[51] Id at 185.

for DOMA's invalidation, all of which find some support in the decision but are ultimately unsatisfying.

Let's start with three propositions that *Windsor* might be thought to stand for:

1. The federal government's decision not to recognize state-sanctioned marriages of same-sex couples was an unconstitutional intrusion on federalism (a structural claim);
2. The federal government's decision not to recognize state-sanctioned marriages of same-sex couples was an unconstitutional infringement of a substantive right, for example, the right to marry (a liberty claim); or
3. The federal government's decision not to recognize state-sanctioned marriages of same-sex couples denied the equal protection of the law because discrimination based on sexual orientation draws heightened judicial scrutiny, and the federal government cannot satisfy that inquiry (an equal protection claim).

There are as many readings of *Windsor* as there are constitutional law scholars; in fact, there are probably many more.[52] These three are among the many plausible interpretations, but some explanations are more plausible than others. None of these adequately explains the decision.

1. *The federalism reading of Windsor.* The argument that DOMA failed as a matter of federalism, applied through the lens of equal protection, was suggested in an amicus brief that I signed with several other academics.[53] Our view, as expressed in the brief, was that Section 3 failed equal protection review for a reason quite distinct from the standard approaches relying on heightened scrutiny. We argued that whatever else may be its constitutional defects, Section 3 was not an exercise of any enumerated federal

---

[52] Will Baude has noted the openness of the opinion to a variety of interpretations. See William Baude, *Interstate Recognition of Same-Sex Marriage After Windsor*, 8 NYU J L & Lib 150 (2013).

[53] Brief of Federalism Scholars as Amici Curiae in Support of Respondent Windsor, *United States v Windsor*, No 12-307 (filed March 2013). The argument was largely the brainchild of Professor Ernest Young, who led the drafting effort, along with the superb attorneys Roy Englert, Carina Cuellar, and Erin Blondel at Robbins, Russell, Englert, Orseck, Untereiner & Sauber LLP. In addition to Professor Young and me, the other signers were Professors Jonathan Adler, Lynn Baker, Randy Barnett, and Ilya Somin. For an alternative approach to DOMA that also blends federalism and equality principles, see Mae Kuykendall, *Equality Federalism: A Solution to the Marriage Wars*, 15 U Pa J Const L 377 (2012).

power. It was also not a "necessary and proper" measure to carry into execution any of Congress's enumerated powers. Instead, it was an unprecedented expansion of federal authority into a domain traditionally controlled by the states. The federal government claimed a hitherto unknown and sweeping power to determine marital and family status.

While Congress had not prohibited states from recognizing same-sex marriages, we argued that DOMA greatly complicated and burdened their police power to do so. We acknowledged that Congress has authority to limit access to specific federal benefits otherwise available to validly married people. But Section 3, as an across-the-board enactment untethered to any specific power, was not plainly adapted to serve any "legitimate" interest of the federal government.

We asserted that the federal government can have no legitimate interest in regulating beyond its enumerated (and necessarily and properly implied) powers. And if Section 3 of DOMA did not serve any legitimate interest—indeed, if a sweeping federal determination of marital status is constitutionally prohibited—then Section 3 could not be justified under any level of scrutiny that might apply under equal protection principles.

While sounding in federalism, the argument was ultimately aimed at the equal protection analysis the Court agreed to review. It was an argument that there is, in fact, a federalism component in the equal protection principles made applicable to the federal government through the Fifth Amendment's Due Process Clause. It was thus different from the Tenth Amendment decision by the Massachusetts District Court in a similar case challenging DOMA.[54] The federalism argument did not rely on the Tenth Amendment, but on the limits on federal power that exist even without that amendment.

On the eve of oral argument in *Windsor*, Michael McConnell also endorsed federalism as a basis to hold DOMA unconstitutional:

> The leading argument *against* DOMA all along has been that the federal government lacks authority under the Constitution to create and enforce a definition of marriage different from that of the state in which a couple resides. It is hard to think of an issue more clearly reserved

---

[54] *Massachusetts*, 698 F Supp 2d at 249.

to state law under constitutional tradition than the definition of marriage.[55]

Thus, the federalism argument did not lack supporters. It was obvious in the *Windsor* oral argument that these concerns were shared by several Justices. But how did the argument fare in the actual decision?

Justice Kennedy's opinion on the merits of Section 3 opened with a discussion of how states have gradually considered and approved the extension of marriage to same-sex couples. Those states, he observed, had concluded that "[t]he limitation of lawful marriage to heterosexual couples" is "an unjust exclusion."[56] Though Congress may enact "limited federal laws that regulate the meaning of marriage in order to further federal policy" related to discrete areas like immigration and income-based criteria for Social Security, DOMA is "applicable to over 1,000 federal statutes and the whole realm of federal regulations."[57]

Justice Kennedy declared that a consideration of DOMA's intrusion on an area of traditional state authority is essential to the analysis of its constitutionality. "In order to assess the validity of that intervention," he wrote, "it is necessary to discuss the extent of the state power and authority over marriage as a matter of history and tradition."[58] His discussion of state authority set up the argument that DOMA was a significant intrusion on the "dignity and status" that comes with being married *in the same way as everyone else in the state*. Marriage had always been "uniform for all married couples within each state," but DOMA rejected that tradition. This was important, in turn, not because it violated federalism but because "discriminations of an unusual character especially suggest careful consideration . . . ."[59] That was one

---

[55] See Michael McConnell, *The Constitution and Same-Sex Marriage*, Wall Street Journal (May 21, 2013), available online at http://online.wsj.com/article/SB100014241278873242 81004578354300151597848.html. See also George F. Will, *DOMA Is an Abuse of Federalism*, Washington Post (March 20, 2013), online at http://www.washingtonpost.com/opinions/george-f-will-doma-infringes-on-states-rights/2013/03/20/fa845348-90bb-11e2-bdea-e32ad90da239_story.html; James Taranto, *Maybe Scalia Was Wrong*, Wall Street Journal (March 28, 2013), online at http://online.wsj.com/news/articles/SB10001424127 887324685104578388490905521114.

[56] *Windsor*, 133 S Ct at 2689.

[57] Id at 2690.

[58] Id at 2691.

[59] Id at 2692, quoting *Romer v Evans*, 517 US 620, 633 (1996).

important factor in the animus analysis (it explained the context[60]). The next two pages of the opinion were devoted to citations affirming state primacy over the field of family relations, the deference Congress had traditionally showed to state law, and the historical pedigree of this division of state and federal authority.[61] The Chief Justice, in dissent, had considerable justification for saying that federalism was the "dominant theme" of the majority opinion. But Chief Justice Roberts went one step further in characterizing the Court's holding: "[I]t is undeniable that its judgment is based on federalism."[62]

That was an overstatement. After discussing the interests of the states in controlling family law, Justice Kennedy expressly stated that the Court was *not* relying strictly on federalism. "Despite these considerations," he wrote, "it is unnecessary to decide whether this federal intrusion on state power is a violation of the Constitution because it disrupts the federal balance."[63]

Surely a statement in a decision declaring what it means should have some bearing on what it means. The Chief Justice, in dissent, thought federalism was nevertheless critical to the result and would help to distinguish the case from one that involved a claimed constitutional right to state recognition of same-sex marriages. He might be right about that. But the Chief Justice's explanation may have been more a hope about the limited consequences of an alternative and more aggressive *Windsor* than it was a reading of the actual *Windsor*. Either that or, as Justice Scalia would have it, Chief Justice Roberts was "fool[ed] . . . into thinking that this is a federalism opinion."[64]

2. *The substantive-liberty reading of Windsor.* As for the second proposition, that the Court upheld a substantive-liberty claim, the Court certainly mentioned liberty several times. And the context was one in which the plaintiffs claimed that "liberty" protected a right to have their marriages fully recognized by government. The Court set for itself the task of deciding "whether the resulting injury and indignity is a deprivation of . . . the liberty protected

---

[60] See discussion of the federalism context in Section III.B.1.

[61] *Windsor*, 133 S Ct at 2692–93.

[62] Id at 2697 (Roberts, CJ, dissenting).

[63] Id at 2692.

[64] Id at 2705.

by the Fifth Amendment."[65] It concluded that Congress "cannot deny the liberty protected by the Due Process Clause of the Fifth Amendment."[66]

But my sense is that reliance on the word "liberty" here was more a doctrinal formality than a substantive holding. *Windsor* was rooted in the Equal Protection component of the Fifth Amendment's Due Process Clause, which protects "liberty" against certain deprivations but makes no mention of "equal protection." "Liberty" in the Fifth Amendment has been understood to protect individuals from federal government action that denies them equal protection.[67]

Windsor arose only because the states themselves decided to recognize a substantive liberty to marry, not because the federal government had an independent constitutional obligation to recognize a fundamental right to marry.[68] If the states themselves did not recognize same-sex marriages, the federal government would not be required by *Windsor* to issue federal marriage licenses to same-sex couples. Marital recognition starts in the states, and it's hard to argue that *Windsor* held otherwise, though one could say that some liberty principle in *Windsor* (perhaps "dignity") is available for future litigation to force state recognition of such marriages.[69]

3. *The heightened-scrutiny reading of Windsor.* In *SmithKline Beecham Corporation v Abbott Laboratories*,[70] an otherwise unremarkable antitrust and unfair-trade-practices case, the Ninth Circuit concluded that heightened scrutiny should apply to classifications based on sexual orientation because *Windsor* "requires" it.[71] For that reason, the panel held that a potential juror could not be

---

[65] *Windsor*, 133 S Ct at 2692.

[66] Id at 2695.

[67] *Bolling v Sharpe*, 347 US 497, 499–500 (1954).

[68] "In *Windsor*, the Supreme Court did not clearly state that the non-recognition of marriages under Section 3 of DOMA implicated a fundamental right, much less significantly interfered with one." *Bourke v Beshear*, 2014 WL 556729, *5 (WD Ky).

[69] But see Douglas NeJaime, *Windsor's Right to Marry*, 123 Yale L J Online 219, 237–47 (2013) (arguing that principles advanced by gay-marriage advocates for a fundamental right to marry influenced the Court's decision, and may eventually lead to a successful equal protection claim against the exclusion of same-sex couples from state marriage laws).

[70] *SmithKline Beecham Corporation v Abbott Laboratories*, No 11-17357 & 11-17373, slip op (Jan 21, 2014), online at http://cdn.ca9.uscourts.gov/datastore/opinions/2014/01/24/11-17357.pdf).

[71] Id at 20.

excluded based solely on sexual orientation. Judge Stephen Reinhardt acknowledged that *Windsor* "did not expressly announce the
level of scrutiny it applied to the equal protection claim" against
DOMA.[72] That, of course, was precisely what Windsor's lawyers
and the Justice Department had urged the Court to do: treat anti-
gay discrimination as presumptively unconstitutional, requiring a
particularly strong justification and closely tailored means. But
reading between the lines in *Windsor*, the Ninth Circuit determined that the Court had indeed applied heightened scrutiny.
Among other reasons for that interpretation of *Windsor*, the panel
noted that the Court had not hypothesized possible rational bases
for DOMA, as it would do in most rational-basis cases. Instead,
the Court had evaluated only Congress's actual justifications.[73]
Reinhardt also described *Windsor* as having required Congress to
justify its unequal treatment of gays rather than indulging in the
usual presumption of constitutionality for congressional acts.[74]

   This is an aggressive and incomplete reading of *Windsor*. Justice
Kennedy's opinion didn't specify any level of scrutiny. There was
no requirement that the government's objective be "important"
or "compelling," the hallmarks of the kinds of interests required
to satisfy intermediate or strict scrutiny. There was no requirement
that the means be "closely" or "necessarily" tailored to the objective, either.

   More tellingly, the *Windsor* Court did not discuss why heightened scrutiny should be applied to sexual-orientation discrimination, a minimal analytical expectation if the Court is really about
to start down that road. There was no mention in *Windsor* of the
factors commonly associated with a heightened-scrutiny approach,
like immutability, the irrelevance of the trait to merit, or political
powerlessness.[75] The Court's decision to apply heightened scrutiny
would be a break from almost every circuit court that has considered the issue, a watershed that would ordinarily be shouted
rather than whispered, made explicit rather than implied.

   In fact, the *Windsor* court did not even characterize DOMA as

---

[72] Id at 17.

[73] Id at 20.

[74] *SmithKline Beecham Corp.*, No 11-17357 & 11-17373, slip op at 20.

[75] See factors considered in *City of Cleburne v Cleburne Living Center*, 473 US 432, 440–
42 (1985), in which the Court rejected heightened equal protection scrutiny for classifications based on cognitive disability.

discriminating on the basis of sexual orientation—the critical issue in *SmithKline Beecham Corporation*. It did not say that homosexuals per se had been disadvantaged by the exclusion from federal recognition of same-sex marriages. Instead, the Court identified the burdened class as same-sex couples who were validly married under state law.[76] It was relevant to the animus determination that these couples were gay couples, as we shall see. But the Court did not take the next logical step of declaring all anti-gay discrimination unconstitutional.[77]

It might well be that *Windsor* is a precursor to heightened scrutiny of sexual-orientation classifications, just as *Reed v Reed*[78] was a first step toward intermediate scrutiny of sex-based discrimination. But we have seen this movie before: the same prediction was made when the Court decided *Romer v Evans* using an unusually skeptical form of rational-basis review.[79] And the same speculation about heightened scrutiny arose after *Lawrence*. After two false starts, it makes sense to start looking elsewhere for an answer.

As argued in Section II below, *Windsor* stands outside the conventional tiers-of-scrutiny analysis. In cases where the Court has found animus, it does not engage in the usual equal protection review. A specialized form of review peculiar to animus cases applies. That's what ties *Windsor* to *Lawrence* and *Romer*, as well as to older cases like *Moreno*, *Cleburne*, and to *Carolene Products* itself. Like many courts and commentators, the Ninth Circuit in *SmithKline Beecham Corporation* failed to attribute any independent weight to the animus analysis. That is an error that can no longer be justified.

II. ANIMUS AND ITS AGONISTES

Instead of seeing *Windsor* as a substantive liberty or conventional equal protection decision, we should see it primarily as an animus case. That is justified by a plain reading of the decision,

---

[76] *Windsor*, 133 S Ct at 2695 ("The class to which DOMA directs its restrictions and restraints are those persons who are joined in same-sex marriages made lawful by the State.").

[77] "In *Windsor*, no clear majority of Justices stated that sexual orientation was a suspect category." *Bourke v Beshear*, 2014 WL 556729, *5 (WD Ky).

[78] 404 US 71 (1971).

[79] Farber and Sherry, 13 Const Comm at 257 (cited in note 11).

which concludes with an entire section on animus, and by the way the Court itself characterized its holding. It's also justified by the failure of other prominent readings to account for the result.

For now at least, *Windsor* is controversial. But while the federalism analysis in *Windsor* has drawn disagreement and bafflement, the animus portion of the decision has elicited outrage. Whether DOMA reflected animus is at the heart of the dispute about the result. But leaving DOMA aside for a moment, what about the antecedent question: is animus itself an unconstitutional basis for legislation? I argue below that the answer is yes, and that answer should not be controversial. The concept is a familiar one in constitutional law. It follows from the Court's precedents, from constitutional history, and from some basic constitutional-democratic theory about permissible legislative enactments.

This section explains why *Windsor* should be seen primarily as an animus decision, why that rationale for striking down legislation is justified as a matter of equal protection, and why critics of the anti-animus principle are wrong. Explaining how the Court got to its animus determination in the DOMA case first requires an examination of the Court's animus decisions in *Moreno*, *Cleburne*, and *Romer*, along with its due process holding in *Lawrence*.

A. THE ANIMUS PRECEDENTS: MORENO, CLEBURNE, AND ROMER (PLUS LAWRENCE)

Long before *Windsor*, Cass Sunstein referred to the Court's animus decisions as a trilogy.[80] It was an apt description since the Court's animus jurisprudence has been a work in progress. To these three decisions, we might add *Lawrence v Texas*, which indicated the Court's low regard for laws aimed at homosexuals and declined to accept a moral justification for a criminal sodomy law. If these cases, together with *Windsor*, are to be regarded as anything more than what Sunstein memorably called "a kind of magical trump card, a joker, hidden in the pack and used on special occasions"[81] they must be more fully linked and theorized. Each

---

[80] Cass R. Sunstein, *One Case at a Time: Judicial Minimalism on the Supreme Court* 146 (Harvard, 2001). See also Kenji Yoshino, *The New Equal Protection*, 124 Harv L Rev 747 (2011) (discussing heightened rational-basis scrutiny present in *Moreno*, *Cleburne*, and *Romer*).

[81] Sunstein, *One Case at a Time* at 148 (cited in note 80). With *Windsor*, it's now a quadrilogy.

decision added something distinctive to anti-animus methodology.

1. *United States Department of Agriculture v Moreno*. In *Moreno*, the Court invalidated a federal law denying food stamps to any household containing one or more people unrelated by blood or marriage to others in the household. In a "declaration of policy" accompanying the Food Stamp Act, Congress asserted two reasons for creating the program: ensuring adequate levels of nutrition among low-income households and strengthening the market for agriculture.[82] But these stated purposes were "irrelevant" to excluding households of unrelated people, concluded the Court, since such people had nutritional needs and since food purchases by them would equally benefit domestic agriculture.[83] Thus, even under rational-basis review, the stated justifications were insufficient.

So what was the real reason for the exclusion? The Court noted that there was little legislative history to explain the amendment, which was inserted without any committee consideration. "The legislative history that does exist," the Court noted, "indicates that that amendment was intended to prevent 'hippies' and 'hippie communes' from participating in the food stamp program."[84] Here was the heart of the problem:

> The challenged classification clearly cannot be sustained by reference to this congressional purpose. For if the constitutional conception of "equal protection of the laws" means anything, it must at the very least mean that a bare congressional desire to harm a politically unpopular group cannot constitute a legitimate governmental interest.[85]

The "purpose to discriminate against hippies cannot, in and of itself and without reference to (some independent) considerations in the public interest," justify the exclusion.[86] To be constitutional under equal protection principles, an enactment must have a public-regarding reason other than to disadvantage a group.

Every classification can be characterized negatively as "discrimination" against the group it disadvantages. Every classification can also be recast affirmatively as serving at least the good of

---

[82] *United States Department of Agriculture v Moreno*, 413 US 528, 533 (1973).

[83] Id at 534.

[84] Id.

[85] Id.

[86] Id at 534–35, quoting *Moreno v United States Department of Agriculture*, 354 F Supp 310, 314 n 11 (DDC 1972).

codifying the principle that the classification serves. In light of direct evidence in the legislative history of animus against "hippies" and "hippie communes," however, the Court refused to defer to hypothetical alternative justifications or to entertain more friendly restatements of Congress's evident animus.

Even if it were true that the exclusion bore no relationship to the stated congressional purposes of providing nutrition or spurring agricultural purchases, it might be rationally related to other hypothetical congressional purposes. The government argued early on in the litigation that excluding households of unrelated persons from the program would foster "morality,"[87] presumably by discouraging opposite-sex cohabitation. Being "pro-morality" might simply be a nicer way to say "anti-hippie." In his dissent, Justice Rehnquist asserted that Congress could decide to fund only "the family as we know it."[88] The strategy, like Justice Scalia's in *Romer*, was not to reject the animus analysis completely, but to recast the "bare desire to harm" as an effort to promote a traditional moral commitment.[89] But the district court had rejected this argument because the exclusion applied regardless of the sexes of the unrelated persons. The government subsequently abandoned the contention.[90]

Another hypothetical purpose, advanced by the government and by the dissent, was that the exclusion helped prevent fraud by "conceivably deny[ing] food stamps to members of households which have been formed solely for the purpose of taking advantage of the food stamp program."[91] Yet anti-fraud purposes did not explain why Congress needed to exclude *all* households containing unmarried persons, especially when other anti-fraud provisions in the Food Stamp Act dealt with the "voluntarily poor" who didn't want to work.[92] In an ordinary rational-basis case, the fact that the exclusion would at least minimally prevent fraud surely would have been good enough. As Justice Rehnquist noted, the fact that it would have "unfortunate and perhaps unintended consequences

---

[87] Id at 535 n 7.

[88] Id at 546 (Rehnquist, J, dissenting).

[89] Sunstein, *One Case at a Time* at 147 (cited in note 80).

[90] *Moreno*, 413 US at 535 n 7.

[91] Id at 547 (Rehnquist dissenting).

[92] Id at 535–37.

beyond [preventing fraud] does not make it unconstitutional."[93]

Yet the Court noted that the only people severed from the program as part of this "anti-fraud" rationale were those "who are so desperately in need of aid that they cannot even afford to alter their living arrangements so as to retain their eligibility" for food stamps.[94] The Court seemed to be saying that harm to a class could not be dismissed as merely incidental to the law where the means were so weakly related to purpose and where evidence of animus was otherwise present. On the slimmest justification, Congress had imposed a significant burden on a group of people.

Finally, the government speculated that perhaps anti-fraud concerns with households of unrelated persons were heightened because "such households are 'relatively unstable,' thereby increasing the difficulty of detecting such abuses." The Court noted that this rationale relied on "wholly unsubstantiated assumptions concerning the differences between 'related' and 'unrelated' households."[95]

Moreno laid the groundwork for a self-conscious anti-animus jurisprudence, ruling out a bare desire to harm a class as a permissible legislative purpose. The decision bore the political-process concerns laid down in *Carolene Products* by highlighting the fact that the affected class was "politically unpopular," and thus one for which resort to the political process was unlikely to work. It established that in such circumstances the Court was willing to examine whether the actual justifications for legislation were plausibly related to the exclusion of the class. It signaled that the Court would look into the legislative process, including the legislative history, to determine whether animus was present. Having found such evidence, the Court would then skeptically scrutinize hypothesized justifications, departing from ordinarily deferential rational-basis review. It would not accept "wholly unsubstantiated" claims about the excluded group. It would consider the harm inflicted on them by the exclusion. And it would not accept at face value that any harm done to them was excusably "incidental" to the exclusion. There are echoes of all of these themes in *Windsor*.

2. *City of Cleburne v Cleburne Living Center.* The Court next addressed animus in an Equal Protection case twelve years later

---

[93] Id at 547 (Rehnquist, J, dissenting).

[94] Id at 538.

[95] Id at 535.

in *Cleburne*, unanimously concluding that the city had unconsti-
tutionally denied a special zoning permit to a proposed group
home for the cognitively disabled.[96] The Court first rejected the
idea that classifications aimed at the cognitively disabled should
formally be subjected to heightened scrutiny even though there
had been a long history of legal discrimination against, and social
antipathy toward, the group. This sorry history had included eu-
genic marriage and sterilization laws, lifelong institutionalization,
and exclusion from public schools.[97] Among other reasons for rejecting heightened scrutiny, the Court noted that "lawmakers have
been addressing their difficulties in a manner that belies a continuing antipathy or prejudice and a corresponding need for more
intrusive oversight by the judiciary."[98] But in particular cases the
Court observed that discrimination against the group would indeed be "invidious," justifying "judicial correction under constitutional norms."[99] Quoting *Moreno*, the Court held that "some
objectives—such as 'a bare . . . desire to harm a politically unpopular group'—are not legitimate state interests."[100]

Why did the denial of a special zoning permit for a group home
constitute animus? Certainly the city of Cleburne did not concede
that it had acted simply out of desire to harm cognitively disabled
people. Instead, the city said it was responding to the "negative
attitudes of the majority of property owners" nearby and to the
"fears of elderly residents of the neighborhood."[101] "But mere negative attitudes, or fear, unsubstantiated by factors which are properly cognizable in a zoning proceeding," the Court responded, did
not justify treating a home for the cognitively disabled differently
from proposed apartments or other multiple-unit dwellings.[102]
The same fate awaited the city's worry that the home would be
located near a junior high school, whose students might harass
people living in the home. These "vague, undifferentiated fears"
by the community could not "validate what would otherwise be

---

[96] *City of Cleburne v Cleburne Living Center*, 473 US 432 (1985).

[97] Id at 461–63 (Marshall, J, concurring in part and dissenting in part).

[98] Id at 443.

[99] Id at 446.

[100] Id at 446–47 (citation omitted).

[101] Id at 448.

[102] Id.

an equal protection violation" if state officials themselves harbored such attitudes.[103]

Other asserted reasons for denying the special use permit—the fact that the home would sit on a 500-year-floodplain, doubts about who would be legally responsible if a resident caused damage, concerns about neighborhood density—did not rationally explain why the city would have allowed homes for other groups, like fraternities, nursing homes, boarding houses, or dormitories.[104] All of the city's justifications appeared to be strained efforts to allow it to act on prejudice and fears of the cognitively disabled. "The short of it," Justice White's opinion concluded, "is that requiring the permit in this case appears to us to rest on an irrational prejudice against the mentally retarded."[105]

This analysis suggests that a different fate would have befallen an oil company's complaint that a city denied a special permit to construct a gas station in the neighborhood. While we can speculate that city officials might indeed feel "animus" toward big oil companies, and nearby residents might oppose the construction of a station, a decision to deny such a permit would be plausibly explicable on safety grounds, on the desire to preserve a noncommercial zone for private residents, or even on aesthetic criteria. Such considerations would be common in a zoning decision, not out of the ordinary. The decision would be rationally related to avoiding real harm to the neighborhood quite apart from any general dislike of oil companies. Finally, the aggrieved oil company would not be the kind of politically unpopular minority that is unlikely to get its interests taken seriously in the halls of government.

Cleburne added to the animus doctrine in several respects. It clarified that even though a classification might not generally warrant heightened scrutiny, some actions taken against a class might nevertheless reflect impermissible bias. To be rational, a law must serve a "legitimate" end, and antipathy can never be a legitimate end. *Cleburne* pointed out that a departure from the usual substantive considerations governing a decision may itself raise suspicion that the decision was born of animus. An analogous concern

---

[103] Id at 449.

[104] Id at 449–50.

[105] Id at 450.

about discriminations of an unusual character arose in *Windsor*, where the government departed from its usual respect for state determinations of marital status. The Court also held that acting to assuage the animosity of constituents toward a politically unpopular class was as impermissible as acting on government officials' own personal animosity toward that class. Private citizens may carry irrational fear and hatred of a group, but government may not effectuate those feelings by discriminating against the group. Similarly, in *Windsor*, the Court noted that DOMA arose from disapproval of homosexuality itself.

3. *Romer v Evans.* Eleven years later, just as DOMA was introduced, Justice Kennedy wrote the 6–3 opinion in *Romer*.[106] In that decision, the Court struck down Colorado's Amendment 2, a broad state constitutional amendment that wiped away all existing antidiscrimination protection that specifically protected gay men and lesbians at every level and in every department of state government. Amendment 2 also forbade cities, counties, departments, and even the state legislature to pass such protections in the future. The state did this to no other identity-based group that had long been subject to invidious public and private discrimination. Amendment 2 was a backlash against the limited success of gay-rights activists in securing modest antidiscrimination protection in a few areas.[107]

The Court was concerned that Amendment 2 was almost unlimited in scope and significantly injured gay people. On the first point regarding its scope, the Court noted that Amendment 2 was "[s]weeping and comprehensive" and "far reaching" in altering the legal status of homosexuals, placing them "in a solitary class." The amendment withdrew "from homosexuals, but no others, specific legal protection from the injuries caused by discrimination."[108] It applied to "all transactions in housing, sale of real estate, insurance, health and welfare services, private education, and employment."[109] It repealed and forbade existing protection from discrimination in state government employment and at state universities, among other areas of law.[110]

---

[106] *Romer v Evans*, 517 US 620 (1996).

[107] Id at 623–25.

[108] Id at 627.

[109] Id at 629.

[110] Id at 629–30.

On the real harm this extensive enactment visited on gay people alone, the Court observed that for homosexuals, antidiscrimination protections are not mere "special rights." This put gay people in a different position from people who do not need specific protection (like blue-eyed people or lawyers) or already have such protection (like women, people of color, and religious minorities). Far from privileging gay men and lesbians, Justice Kennedy noted, antidiscrimination laws put them on an equal footing in "an almost limitless number of transactions and endeavors that constitute ordinary civic life in a free society."[111]

The Court discerned equal protection violations in two respects. The first was that the law was "at once too narrow and too broad": it withdrew civil rights protections across the board for homosexuals alone.[112] The second was that by "imposing a broad and undifferentiated disability on a single named group" it was "inexplicable by anything but animus toward the class it affects." Importantly, the Court cited previous rational-basis cases in which it had upheld laws that simply "work[ed] to the disadvantage of a particular group."[113] But those cases, involving matters like the regulation of optometry, reviewed laws in which both the justification and the burden were limited. Those contexts allow the Court to "ensure that classifications are not drawn for the purpose of disadvantaging the group burdened by the law."[114] Amendment 2 was "unprecedented" in its sweep, observed the Court, which was itself "instructive" because "[d]iscriminations of an unusual character especially suggest careful consideration to determine whether they are obnoxious to the constitutional provision."[115]

The too-broad-and-too-narrow structure of Amendment 2 "raise[s] the inevitable inference that the disadvantage imposed is

---

[111] Id at 631.

[112] Id at 633.

[113] Id at 632, citing *New Orleans v Dukes*, 427 US 297 (1976) (law favored certain pushcart vendors); *Williamson v Lee Optical of Okla, Inc.*, 348 US 483 (1955) (law favored optometrist over opticians); *Railway Express Agency, Inc. v New York*, 336 US 106 (law favored vehicles displaying ads of owner's products); and *Kotch v Board of River Pilot Commissioners for Port of New Orleans*, 330 US 552 (1947) (law favored persons related to current river boat pilots).

[114] Id at 633, citing *Railroad Retirement Board v Fritz*, 449 US 166, 181 (1980) (Stevens, J, concurring) ("If the adverse impact on the disfavored class is an apparent aim of the legislature, its impartiality would be suspect.").

[115] *Romer*, 517 US at 633, quoting *Louisville Gas and Electric Co. v Coleman*, 277 US 32, 37–38 (1928).

born of animosity toward the class of persons affected."[116] It's not that broad laws are invariably unconstitutional. They are constitutional if they "can be explained by reference to legitimate public policies which justify the *incidental* disadvantages they impose on certain persons."[117]

But the "immediate, continuing, and real injuries" inflicted by Amendment 2 were not simply incidental to the law, concluded the Court. How did the majority know that? It did not cite any of the statements made by Amendment 2 supporters during the campaign to pass it, though a plethora of false anti-gay claims could have been cited. It did not cite opinion polls showing that Coloradans disapproved homosexuals or homosexuality. Instead, it cited the objective fact that in justifying such a sweeping measure, the official rationales for Amendment 2 were very narrow: protecting the liberties of landlords and employers who object to homosexuality and conserving state government resources for fighting other kinds of discrimination. Animus was *inferred* from the unprecedented gap between an all-encompassing law and its claimed narrow purposes.

Romer introduced several themes that were further developed in *Windsor*. First, animus analysis is especially alert to laws of a broad character aimed at a particular class. Such laws inflict broad injury on a single group, raising *Carolene Products*–type concerns since the affected group will often lack allies in the political process. Second, while it's true that a law is not unconstitutional simply because it incidentally harms the interests of a class, such harm cannot be the aim of the law. Third, the Court need not have direct evidence of animus or inquire into the subjective motivations of legislators or voters. An assessment of the real aim of the law can be gleaned from objective considerations of scope and justification. Fourth, the Court will not simply accept anything the state says by way of justifying its laws. If the stated aims don't really explain the enactment, the remaining explanation is animus.

Romer left open a major question in animus doctrine. To render the law unconstitutional, must animus be the only real purpose? Is it sufficient if animus is simply the primary reason for the law, the dominant purpose among several others? Moving along the

---

[116] Id at 634.

[117] Id at 635 (emphasis added).

spectrum, is the law unconstitutional if animus is a but-for explanation, nonprimary but nonetheless necessary for its passage? Or can the law be invalidated if animus explains any part of the purpose of the law?

Whichever it was, *Romer*, handed down on May 20, 1996, foretold the death of DOMA even at the moment of the law's birth. Some members of Congress who supported DOMA realized the new scrutiny the Court was giving to anti-gay legislation and stressed that the legislation was not an effort to hurt gay people.[118] But during floor "debate"—as the prepared speeches that members of Congress deliver is called—numerous supporters made clear that they saw DOMA as a way to express disdain for homosexuals.[119]

4. *A brief detour: Lawrence v Texas.* Lurking behind the *Romer* opinion was the Court's dawning realization that gay men and lesbians are a class that might "need" the special protection of the law. This was a first in the Court's jurisprudence. While not an "animus" decision in a formal doctrinal sense, *Lawrence* nonetheless confirmed the Court's conclusion that gays were often a target for class legislation insulting their dignity. The Texas sodomy law was, after all, actually a "Homosexual Conduct" law that forbade anal and oral sex only if committed by two people of the same sex. Yet the moral interests it was said to serve came from a tradition that disfavored all nonprocreative, nonmarital sex. In a sense then, it was the mirror opposite of *Romer*. It had a much broader justification (broadly applicable moral sentiments) but a much narrower focus (selecting only the immoral activity of one group for disfavor).

Yet the harm done by the Texas law to this particular group was itself extensive. Justice Kennedy's opinion, his second in a major gay-rights case, emphasized how the Texas statute affected more than specified sexual conduct. Indeed, it "demeans the claim" of gay people to say that only sexual acts were at issue. Sodomy laws, in fact, had far-reaching "penalties and purposes" that invaded private adult sexual autonomy and did so in the most private space, the home. For those subject to the law, the Texas statute amounted to an attack on "their dignity as free persons."[120]

---

[118] See, for example, Section III.C.3.

[119] Id.

[120] *Lawrence v Texas*, 539 US 558, 567 (2003).

Under the Equal Protection Clause citizens are entitled to demand respect for constitutionally protected conduct. Sodomy laws imposed "stigma" on gay people. This stigma had a real-world effect. "When homosexual conduct is made criminal by law of the state," concluded the Court, "that declaration in and of itself is an invitation to subject homosexual persons to discrimination both in the public and in the private spheres."[121] Sodomy laws thus attacked gays' standing in their own community. *Bowers v Hardwick*, which had upheld a general anti-sodomy law applicable both to heterosexuals and homosexuals with language that made it seem appropriate for the law to target only homosexuals, had to be overruled because "[i]ts continuance as precedent demeans the lives of homosexual persons."[122] There was no justification offered by the state, including its claimed purpose to defend traditional morality, that could justify the burden imposed by the law. Then the Court summed up the problem with the Texas Homosexual Conduct law in language that could well have fit in its animus cases: "The petitioners are entitled to respect for their private lives. The State cannot demean their existence or control their destiny by making their private sexual conduct a crime."[123]

In *Lawrence*, the Court ruled that the state could not impose a majoritarian moral code on homosexuals. It could not "demean their existence or control their destiny" by driving them away from relationships. Homosexuals, the Court observed, enter relationships for the same reasons heterosexuals do: to share intimacy with a partner, to show affection and obligation, to have and raise children, to establish a place they call home and people they call family.

Lawrence was a Due Process Clause case involving a substantive-liberty claim, not an Equal Protection Clause decision demanding equal treatment for classes of citizens. But the Court noted that the equal protection argument against anti-gay laws like the Texas statute was "tenable" and that the principles are "linked." The Court wanted to be sure that neither Texas nor any other state could reenact a sodomy law applying facially to heterosexuals and homosexuals under the guise of "equality," for such a law would continue to impose stigma on homosexuals.[124]

---

[121] Id at 575.

[122] Id.

[123] Id at 578.

[124] Id at 575.

The Court's concerns about the "dignity" of gay people and their right to be respected by their government are the type of concerns at the heart of animus jurisprudence. That the law "demeaned" and stigmatized them through collateral injury without a legitimate justification is a close cousin of the concerns expressed in the animus principle. If the Court had followed the equal protection route,[125] *Lawrence* could very easily have been among the most prominent anti-animus decisions.

B. THE WINDSOR INSTALLMENT

All of this formed the jurisprudential backdrop for the demise of the Defense of Marriage Act. Forty years of case law developing a constitutional bulwark against legislative animus and a generation of greater constitutional protection for the rights of gay men and lesbians caught DOMA in a double pincers.

Windsor is primarily an equal protection decision heavily influenced by concerns about structural federalism as an important guarantor of liberty. After all, what was the "liberty" at stake under the Fifth Amendment? The Court pointed out that the government treated as "unlike" what New York treated as "alike" in a federal law that was "designed to injure" the class.[126] At least since *Bolling v Sharpe*, the liberty in the Fifth Amendment's Due Process Clause "contains within it the prohibition against denying to any person the equal protection of the laws."[127]

In *Windsor*, the Court held that dignity was denied insofar as DOMA denied equal federal recognition of same-sex and opposite-sex marriages. The Court held that "by seek[ing] to injure" married same-sex couples DOMA "violates basic due process and equal protection principles applicable to the Federal Government."[128] The very purpose of DOMA was to ensure that same-sex marriages would be treated as "second-class," said the Court, which is what raised "a most serious question under the Consti-

---

[125] In a concurring opinion, Justice O'Connor did rely on equal protection to strike down the Texas law. Id at 579 (O'Connor, J, concurring). At the same time, she suggested that traditional morality might justify a law limiting marriage to opposite-sex couples. Id at 585 (O'Connor, J, concurring).

[126] *United States v Windsor*, 133 S Ct 2675, 2692 (2013).

[127] Id at 2695, citing *Bolling v Sharpe*, 347 US 497, 499–500 (1954).

[128] Id at 2693.

tution's Fifth Amendment."[129] The effect was to "identify a subset of state-sanctioned marriages and make them unequal."[130]

The final substantive section of Justice Kennedy's opinion, Section IV, directly addressed the animus issue.[131] Quoting *Moreno*, the Court stated the basic anti-animus principle: "The Constitution's guarantee of equality 'must at the very least mean that a bare congressional desire to harm a politically unpopular group cannot' justify disparate treatment of that group."[132] The opinion devoted the next four pages to explaining why the majority believed animus was present in DOMA. The Court concluded with this statement of its holding:

> [T]he principal purpose and necessary effect of this law are to demean those persons who are in a lawful same-sex marriage. This requires the Court to hold, as it now does, that DOMA is unconstitutional as a deprivation of the liberty of the person protected by the Fifth Amendment of the Constitution.[133]

As the Court had just spent four pages explaining, a purpose to "demean" a class is a purpose to inflict a dignitary injury on them, even apart from any more concrete injury. The problem with such a purpose is that it is a species of animus. It was, for reasons the Court had just adumbrated, the principal congressional purpose driving the passage of DOMA. The equal protection principle incorporated in the Fifth Amendment's liberty guaranty, like the Fourteenth Amendment's own Equal Protection Clause, forbids such a purpose. Therefore, DOMA was unconstitutional. This was as close to a plain statement of the Court's holding in *Windsor* as can be found in the opinion. It leaves room for future development in constitutional doctrine in any number of directions, but for now its clearest import is that DOMA was found unconstitutional because it reflected impermissible animus. Justice Scalia, in dissent, agreed that "the real rationale of [the *Windsor* opinion] is that DOMA is motivated by 'bare . . . desire to harm' couples in same-

[129] Id at 2693–94.
[130] Id at 2694.
[131] Id at 2693–95.
[132] Id at 2694, quoting *Moreno*, 413 US at 528.
[133] Id at 2695.

sex marriages."[134] Lower courts have also read *Windsor* as based on a finding of unconstitutional animus.[135]

That's the comparatively easy part of understanding *Windsor*. The harder task is discovering why the Court concluded that DOMA reflected animus. Since Congress did not issue a statement of its "desires" when it passed the act, much less admit a bare desire to harm certain people, this conclusion must rest on something other than what Congress directly said about why it has passed the law. There must be circumstances where, no matter how Congress or its lawyers formulate the legislative purpose, the Court will see some purposes as malign where Congress says they are benign or as pretextual where malicious purposes are evident. When might that be?

Section IV of *Windsor* suggests several indicia of animus. The first, drawn from *Romer*, is that "'discriminations of an unusual character' especially require careful consideration."[136] A departure from the usual substantive approach toward an issue that targets a politically unpopular group "is strong evidence of a law having the purpose and effect of disapproval of that class."[137] Here is where the usual federalism-based approach to marital status played a crucial role. Against the backdrop of federal deference to state choice in family relations, DOMA was suspicious. An extraordinary and unprecedented act requires an extraordinary and unprecedented justification apart from the self-justifying desire to demean or injure a stigmatized class of people. Yet since states, not the federal government, were historically entrusted with the "defense of marriage" the desire of the federal government to "defend" it against the states' choices was anomalous.

Linked to the abandonment of deference to state marital determinations was Congress's acknowledged desire to discourage state experimentation in a field where states in fact had long been laboratories of experimentation on everything from the legal obligations of spouses to the dominance of males over females to

---

[134] Id at 2709 (Scalia, J, dissenting). Justice Scalia warned that the animus rationale would inevitably lead to the invalidation of state laws excluding same-sex couples from marriage. Id. The Federal District Court in Virginia drew upon Justice Scalia's conclusion in holding that the state marriage laws reflected "prejudice" against gay people. *Bostic v Rainey*, 2014 WL 561978, *17, *21 (ED Va).

[135] *Bishop v United States*, 2014 WL 116013, *18 (ND Okla).

[136] *Windsor*, 133 S Ct at 2693, quoting *Romer*, 517 US at 633.

[137] Id.

divorce. In none of these other profound changes in marriage had Congress acted to defend the traditional understanding of the institution. The Court approvingly quoted from the federalism-based decision by the First Circuit, which concluded that the federal goal was "to put a thumb on the scales and influence a state's decision as to how to shape its own marriage laws."[138] That is, Congress was not concerned with simply defining the limits of federal programs touching marriage but acted with the "purpose to influence or interfere with state sovereign choices about who may be married."[139] In this, Congress was partly successful, as post-*Windsor* developments have shown. Three states—New Jersey, Illinois, and Hawaii—that granted civil unions to same-sex couples but resisted marriage before *Windsor* quickly moved toward marriage in part because of persuasive arguments that civil unions had no federal status, were entitled to no federal benefits, and thus could not grant full equality.[140] None of this interference with state choice could be written off as merely the "incidental effect" of an otherwise valid law.

Second, the Court argued that the legislative history and text of DOMA demonstrated the congressional desire to interfere with the "equal dignity of same-sex marriages" conferred by the states. It then pointed to sections of the House Report that explicitly laid out the congressional purpose "to defend the institution of traditional heterosexual marriage," to prevent the "radical" redefinition of marriage to include "homosexual couples," to "express moral disapproval of homosexuality, and a moral conviction that heterosexuality better comports with traditional (especially Judeo-Christian) morality," and to emphasize "traditional moral teachings reflected in heterosexual-only marriage laws." This purpose to interfere with state choice in a matter reflecting the dignity of same-sex marriages was, the Court determined, evident in the very title of the act.[141]

Third, the Court noted that in *practice* and in principal *effect*

---

[138] Id at 2693, quoting *Massachusetts v United States Department of Health and Human Services*, 682 F3d 1, 12–13 (1st Cir 2012).

[139] Id.

[140] See Hawaii Marriage Equality Act of 2013, 2d Special Sess, 2013 Hawaii Sess Laws 1; Religious Freedom and Marriage Fairness Act, Ill Public Acts 098-0597; *Garden State Equality v Dow*, 82 A3d 336 (Superior Ct of NJ 2013).

[141] *Windsor*, 133 S Ct at 2693, citing HR Rep No 104-664, 104th Cong, 2d Sess 12–13, 16 (1996).

the act reflected animus because of its *Romer*-like scope. It was "a system-wide enactment with no identified connection to any particular area of federal law." It injected "inequality into the entire United States Code," simultaneously excluding a particular class of married couples from more than one thousand regulations and statutes governing estate taxes, Social Security, housing, criminal sanctions, copyright, veterans' benefits, access to health care, and bankruptcy protection. This broad effect, the Court concluded, could not be seen as designed to promote a non-animus-based purpose like "governmental efficiency" in the administration of federal programs.[142] Congress can enact discrete statutes that affect marital rights in order to serve limited purposes like preventing sham marriages intended to evade immigration laws.[143] But the effect of DOMA was cradle-to-grave: from increasing the cost of health care for families raising children to prohibiting couples from being buried together in veterans' cemeteries.

Fourth, there was no legitimate congressional purpose that "overcomes the purpose and effect [of DOMA] to disparage and to injure" married same-sex couples "whom the State, by its marriage laws, sought to protect in personhood and dignity."[144] That is, whatever legitimate purpose might be hypothesized for DOMA could not really explain its passage. Given the considerations the Court cited, including the devastating impact of DOMA on gay families, the best way to understand the law was as an expression of animus.

These considerations led the Court to conclude that DOMA was an assault on the dignity and social status of married same-sex couples. "The avowed purpose and practical effect of the law here in question are to impose a disadvantage, a separate status, and so a stigma upon all who enter into same-sex marriages made lawful by the unquestioned authority of the States," the Court asserted.[145]

> By this dynamic DOMA undermines both the public and private significance of state-sanctioned marriages; for it tells those couples, and all the world, that their otherwise valid marriages are unworthy of federal recognition. This places same-sex couples in an unstable po-

---

[142] Id at 2690, 2694.

[143] Id at 2690.

[144] Id at 2697.

[145] Id at 2693.

sition of being in a second-tier marriage. The differentiation demeans
the couple, whose moral and sexual choices the Constitution protects,
see *Lawrence*, and whose relationship the State has sought to dignify.[146]

Then, in perhaps the most striking passage in the entire opinion,
Justice Kennedy invoked the interests of children being raised by
same-sex couples:

> And it humiliates tens of thousands of children now being raised by
> same-sex couples. The law in question makes it even more difficult for
> the children to understand the integrity and closeness of their own
> family and its concord with other families in their community and in
> their daily lives.[147]

In 1986, in *Bowers v Hardwick*, the Court had declared that there
was no connection between homosexuality and family life.
Lawrence declared that moral condemnation of homosexuality was
no longer a legitimate state interest. In *Windsor*, the Court recognized explicitly for the first time that same-sex couples were
raising children and that their families shared values and interests
(a "concord") with more traditional families.

The use of the word "humiliates" to describe DOMA's injury
to children whose families had been excluded from the protection
of federal law was unusual and especially poignant. The humili-
ation passage calls to mind the words from *Brown v Board of Education* about the effect of public-school segregation on children:
"To separate [black schoolchildren] from others of similar age and
qualifications solely because of their race generates a feeling of
inferiority as to their status in the community that may affect their
hearts and minds in a way unlikely ever to be undone."[148] Indeed,
it is hard to find a decision apart from the racial discrimination
cases in which the Court has used such strong language to de-
nounce a law.

It is safe to assume—in fact the record shows—that Congress
gave absolutely no weight to the needs of gay couples or their
children when it passed DOMA. Until recently, the Court remarked, "many citizens had not even considered the possibility"

---

[146] Id at 2694 (citations omitted).

[147] Id.

[148] *Brown v Board of Education*, 347 US 483, 494 (1954). The analogy to racial discrimination becomes even clearer given the Court's conclusion that DOMA created "second-
class" or "second-tier marriages" (memorably termed "skim-milk marriages" by Justice
Ginsberg at oral argument).

that same-sex couples might want to be married.[149] But when states did begin seriously to consider the idea, they saw "the urgency of this issue for same-sex couples." Slowly at first and then more rapidly states realized that excluding same-sex couples from marriage was "an injustice that they had not earlier known or understood."[150] Recognizing same-sex marriages thus "reflects both the community's considered perspective on the historical roots of the institution of marriage and its evolving understanding of the meaning of equality."[151] In contrast to Congress's blunderbuss action directed at an unpopular minority, states' recognition of these marriages reflected a considered and thoughtful decision-making process.

Windsor thus further elaborated upon the anti-animus doctrine. It laid out the twin concerns of that doctrine to protect both practical and dignitary interests. It announced a series of factors that should go into the determination of whether the legislature has acted with malice toward a class, including deviations from usual substantive considerations governing a decision, the legislative history and language of a statute, the practical effect of the statute, and the comparative explanatory weakness of non-animus-based justifications for the act. An animus-based law, the Court suggested, is likely to be a product of a legislature that is hostile to the interests of a class. A more deliberative and conscientious process, one not blinded by fear and loathing, is more likely to yield new insights and increased understanding of them.

C. ANIMUS AND DEMOCRATIC-CONSTITUTIONAL THEORY

Animus is inconsistent with the premises of a well-functioning representative democracy, and violates the basic constitutional precept that every person is entitled to equal protection of the laws. Animus disserves the liberal and democratic values that undergird our constitutional system. But to accept this liberal and democratic principle is not to determine how it should be enforced. That requires some additional discussion of the appropriately limited role of courts in enforcing it. A response is also needed to critics who complain that the anti-animus doctrine disrespects those who

---

[149] *Windsor*, 133 S Ct at 2689.

[150] Id.

[151] Id at 2692–93.

believe deeply in traditional marriage without malice toward gay people.

1. *The anti-animus doctrine in principle.* The Constitution does not simply preratify all majoritarian decision making by setting up a representative process for passing legislation. Otherwise, there would be no need for provisions beyond the structural ones of democratic representation in a House and Senate and the procedural ones of bicameralism and presentment. In numerous provisions, the Constitution bounds governmental decision making by principle. Certain choices are impermissible, completely taken off the table, even if Congress thinks the reason for making that choice is compelling and even if the choice is overwhelmingly supported by the public.

The Constitution presumes that "even improvident decisions" will eventually be corrected by the democratic process.[152] But that is only a presumption. There are decisions arrived at democratically for which the opposite presumption should be indulged: the political process is not self-correcting in some kinds of cases, or at least should not be expected to be self-correcting. The mechanisms of democracy do not always work in a way that accounts for all relevant interests.[153] This is most clearly seen in cases involving race.

Legislative classifications based on race (or alienage or national origin) are presumptively unconstitutional because they are rarely relevant to legitimate (i.e., non-animus-based and nonracist) public interests. They "are deemed to reflect prejudice and antipathy— a view that those in the burdened class are not as worthy or deserving as others."[154] Such discrimination is "unlikely to be soon rectified by legislative means" precisely because the prejudice behind the classification blocks any self-correction. The very antipathy that gave birth to the classification helps to sustain it and to inhibit meaningful reexamination. The legislature is unlikely to revisit the issue because its members do not see a problem in the classification, or perhaps regard its animus-based vices as virtues.

Equal protection cases often involve legislative denials of equal dignity. In *Brown v Board of Education*,[155] the demeaning nature of

---

[152] *Cleburne*, 473 US at 440.

[153] *United States v Carolene Products Co.*, 304 US 144, 152–53 n 4 (1938).

[154] *Cleburne*, 473 US at 440.

[155] *Brown v Board of Education*, 347 US 483 (1954).

racial segregation in education informed the Court's understanding of why equal protection was important, of what was at stake in the denial. It is central to equal protection jurisprudence that the government cannot create castes of citizens because creating a second-class status is itself a harm to their dignitary interests. It would have been no answer in *Loving v Virginia* to say that the state was required to recognize a separate civil-union status for interracial couples with all the rights, but not the status, of marriage. That's because the separate recognition itself would be an unconstitutional insult to them. At the very least, the affront to their dignity more completely informed what harm they suffered in being denied equality. That harm cannot be a material purpose of the government.

A law that purposefully inflicts injury on its targets out of sheer disdain for them is the classic case of malice. Under the constitutional conception of equal protection, a deliberative democracy should restrict the reasons for which legislators pass laws to those reasons that are consistent with the recognition of other citizens as equals.[156] "To disadvantage a group essentially out of dislike is surely to deny its members equal concern and respect, specifically by valuing their welfare negatively," argued John Hart Ely.[157] As Judge Posner concluded:

> If a law is challenged as a denial of equal protection, and all that the government can come up with in defense of the law is that the people who are hurt by it happen to be irrationally hated or irrationally feared by a majority of voters, it is difficult to argue that the law is rational if "rational" in this setting is to mean anything more than democratic preference. And it must mean something more if the concept of equal protection is to operate, in accordance with its modern interpretations, as a check on majoritarianism.[158]

One might argue that legislatures pass laws out of this type of animus all the time. It is naive to suppose that it can be entirely cleansed from the legislative process. Consider some examples of

---

[156] John Rawls, *Political Liberalism* 430–31 (Columbia, 1993).

[157] Ely, *Democracy and Distrust* at 157 (cited in note 2).

[158] *Milner v Apfel*, 148 F3d 812, 817 (7th Cir 1998). To the extent Judge Posner suggested that hatred must be the sole justification in order to strike down a law based on animus, he erred. In no case has a city, state, or federal government entity conceded that animus was the sole motivation, and yet the Supreme Court has now found impermissible animus in four constitutional decisions. My suggestion, see below at Section III.C.3, is that courts should ask whether animus materially influenced the decision.

government action that might be thought to reflect animus. We create punitive sex-offender registries—perhaps because we're irrationally disturbed by sex offenders. We adopt policies that permit harsh treatment of terrorist suspects—perhaps because we hate terrorists. Partisan legislatures redistrict to disempower the other side—perhaps out of malice toward the other political party. A majority of the state legislature might pass a regulation that punishes a business that made campaign contributions to the minority—perhaps to express ill will. Yet courts do not say that these laws are unconstitutional on animus grounds. Why not?

There are several responses to this kind of objection to the anti-animus principle. Some of the acts just mentioned may transgress limits imposed by other constitutional doctrines, like the First Amendment, the Eighth Amendment, or the Due Process Clause of the Fifth or Fourteenth Amendments. In the abstract, a legislature might plausibly be thought to have acted based on animus against those targeted by a law (for example, convicted sex offenders or suspected terrorists). But whether a court should invalidate the law on that ground would depend on consideration of the objective factors laid out in Section III.A. These deal with text, context, process, effects, and pretext. Something that simply has a whiff of animus should not on that basis be invalidated. Courts can no more eradicate all spiteful and vindictive motives from legislators' minds than we can cleanse a human heart of lust or jealousy. Analysis of the objective factors is a necessary check on judicial adventurism. The constitutional anti-animus principle is actually a lot narrower than just a general prohibition on animus.

Further, some of these examples may well be defended by reasoned, public-interest justifications that do not rest principally on animus. Considering the objective factors for invalidating animus-based action, a court would need to ask whether there was a reasoned, public-regarding basis (a basis apart from blind fear, rage, or hatred) for the government's act. In most cases, there will be such a basis even though we might suspect that animus played a role. The equality tradition does not mean that everyone must always be treated the same. Felons, including sex offenders and terrorists, are an unpopular and even hated group, but they are justifiably treated differently from others. Suspected terrorists may represent an ongoing threat to life and national security. Acting

to deter and punish crime is not in itself an expression of impermissible animus.[159]

But the equality tradition does mean at least three things, even
when it comes to the way we treat reviled people. First, the state
must have non-animus-based reasons to support its measures
against the group. The broader the disability the less trustworthy
the state's asserted purpose. Second, reasons once thought to express a permissible moral judgment may, by the advance of positive
knowledge about the group, be justifiably recast as impermissible
animus. Third, exclusion of a group from common legal benefits
and protections cannot be permitted to present a threat to the
very idea of political community embodied in the precepts that
undergird a liberal democracy.

Applying these principles to the example of felons, the state has
ample justifications aside from simple spite to take measures that
disadvantage the group. The advance of positive knowledge about
felons has not exposed disapprobation of them as mere animus.
Finally, punishment of felons does not undermine the basis for
political community; such punishment defends the community
from actions by felons that would undermine it (through violence
and theft, for example).

But we cannot legitimately punish people who commit crimes
in an effort simply to injure them because we dislike them or
harbor untutored prejudices about them. Inflicting injury on a
group of people cannot be a material objective of the law. The
fact that they are hated and feared does not mean that we can do
anything we want to them. When the severity of the punishment
cannot plausibly be justified by rational penal concerns, a court
might well find a violation of equal protection (or of the Eighth
Amendment). For example, a law prohibiting sex offenders who
have paid their debt to society from ever holding a job or marrying
would seem to fit this description. These are very broad disabilities
that would be poorly connected to reasoned, public-regarding rationales. They seem based on disgust. We are grossed out by some
people. We loathe them and want to lash out against them. Such
laws would seem to violate the anti-animus doctrine, which is
rooted in the idea that the state may not deny equal protection
of the law to *any person* and instructs us that hating others, no

---

[159] *Inmates of Suffolk County Jail v Rouse*, 129 F3d 649, 660–61 (1st Cir 1997).

matter how badly they've behaved, is not a legitimate reason by itself to legislate against them.

The loathing of persons that concerns the anti-animus principal is different in kind and degree from the political and business interests often at play in politics. Legislative districting, for example, is notoriously complex and is characterized by a give-and-take among many competing political interests and concerns. Courts are hesitant to enter that thicket for good institutional reasons. But even redistricting is not immune from judicial review and is unconstitutional if it is the product of impermissible purposes under the Equal Protection Clause.[160]

Animus doctrine addresses the deeply problematic potential of a democratic republic to consistently oppress a politically unpopular minority, a concern articulated in *Carolene Products*. As Ely wrote, the political process "is undeserving of trust" when "representatives beholden to an effective majority are systematically disadvantaging some minority out of simple hostility or a prejudiced refusal to recognize commonalities of interest."[161] There are limits on what we can do to people that can be found in substantive constitutional doctrines and that, under the anti-animus principle, can be found in the very idea of equal protection.[162]

2. *The anti-animus doctrine in constitutional framing.* The anti-animus doctrine has roots in the views of the Framers, as well as in the text and history of the Fourteenth Amendment's guarantee of the "equal protection of the laws."[163] In *The Federalist*, James Madison warned against measures that limit a group's ability to

---

[160] See generally *Miller v Johnson*, 515 US 900 (1995); *Shaw v Reno*, 509 US 630 (1993).

[161] Ely, *Democracy and Distrust* at 103 (cited in note 2).

[162] Aside from malice, a second form of animus might be called "malign neglect"—a total disregard for the interests of a group of people where harm to them may not be the object of the law, but significant injury to them is the heedless by-product of the law. Such disregard fails to treat members of the group with the concern and respect that is due all citizens as equals. "[T]he duty of representation that lies at the core of our system requires more than a voice and a vote," wrote Ely. "No matter how open the process, those with most of the votes are in a position to vote themselves advantages at the expense of others, or otherwise to *refuse to take their interests into account*." Id at 135 (emphasis added). A violation of equal protection principles sometimes involves "the unconscious failure to extend to a minority the same recognition of humanity, and hence the same sympathy and care, given as a matter of course to one's own group." Paul Brest, *Foreword: In Defense of the Antidiscrimination Principle*, 90 Harv L Rev 1, 7–8 (1976), quoted in Koppelman, *Why Scalia Should Have Voted to Overturn DOMA* (cited in note 4). The idea of malign neglect as a species of animus is interesting, but ultimately beyond the scope of this article.

[163] For a fuller discussion of this idea, see Dale Carpenter, *A Conservative Defense of Romer v. Evans*, 76 Ind L J 403 (2001).

bring about change through ordinary political processes.[164] Madison worried about the development of "factions" animated by hostility.[165] Consider his comments in The Federalist No. 10:

> By a faction, I understand a number of citizens, whether amounting to a majority or a minority of the whole, who are united or actuated by some common *impulse of passion*, or of interest, adverse to the rights of other citizens, or to the permanent and aggregate interests of the community.[166]

The Constitution was intended to correct an intolerable situation that had arisen under the Articles of Confederation, Madison contended. "[M]easures are too often decided, not according to the rules of justice and the rights of the minor party, but by the superior force of an interested and overbearing majority."[167] He continued: "To secure the public good and private rights against . . . such a [majority] faction, and at the same time to preserve the spirit and the form of popular government, is then the great object to which our inquiries are directed."[168] The object of the Constitution was, in Madison's view, to render the majority "unable to concert and carry into effect schemes of oppression."[169]

On one level, Madison's definition of faction might be thought to encompass virtually all democratic decision making, since every decision is necessarily the product of a legislative (or voting) majority motivated sufficiently to act in some fashion. Often, the democratic result will be detrimental to the interests of an identifiable group within the polity.

But ordinary democratic decision making cannot have been Madison's principal concern since the Framers wanted to make self-government possible and lasting. Rather, Madison focused on the idea that the faction is driven by a "passion," or an "impulse," to such an extent that it becomes "overbearing" and seeks to enforce "schemes of oppression." Madison was concerned about nondeliberative decision making, a characteristic of animus-based leg-

---

[164] Federalist 51 (Madison) in Roy P. Fairfield, ed, *The Federalist Papers* 161–62 (2d ed 1966).

[165] Federalist 10 (Madison) in Roy P. Fairfield, ed, *The Federalist Papers* 16–20 (2d ed 1966).

[166] Id at 17 (emphasis added).

[167] Id at 16.

[168] Id at 19–20.

[169] Id at 20.

islation. That is, he was concerned with decisions that result from a pure desire to oppress, an unreasoned backlash against a group, produced not by any studied weighing of alternatives and interests but by demagoguery and invective.

Madison's views were echoed across the Atlantic in the work of Edmund Burke. Burke, writing roughly contemporaneously with the Framers, also warned of the dangers of majoritarian power in a democracy. "Of this I am certain," he wrote, "that in a democracy the majority of the citizens is capable of exercising the most cruel oppressions upon the minority whenever strong divisions prevail in that kind of polity, as they often must. . . ."[170] Minorities so targeted by a majority "are deprived of all external consolation," he observed.[171] "They seem deserted by mankind, overpowered by a conspiracy of their whole species."[172]

Like Madison, Burke believed that representative government was not merely the exercise of raw power. It was also not simply the expression of popular will. Rather, he saw representative government as a matter requiring the interaction of the popular will and the legislators' own independent judgment. As he explained to his Bristol constituents in his acceptance speech upon election to Parliament in October 1774: "If government were a matter of will upon any side, yours, without question, ought to be superior. But government and legislation are matters of reason and judgment, and not of inclination. . . ."[173] Further, Burke posited the existence of a general welfare upon which representatives had a duty to act. He therefore shared Madison's disdain for faction-dominated politics.[174] In his acceptance speech, Burke characterized his vision of the deliberative role of government in a fashion that Madison would have understood and approved:

Parliament is not a congress of ambassadors from different and hostile

---

[170] Edmund Burke, *Reflections on the Revolution in France* 143–44 (ed Thomas H. D. Mahoney) (Bobbs-Merrill Educational Publishing, 1981).

[171] Id at 144.

[172] Id.

[173] *Letter from Edmund Burke to John Farr and John Harris, Esqrs. Sheriffs of the City of Bristol on the Affairs of America* at 187 ("*Letter to the Sheriffs*") (April 3, 1777), in *Edmund Burke: Selected Writings and Speeches* 186, 205 (ed Peter J. Stanlis 1963).

[174] Madison and Burke would likely have disagreed on how to discourage unreasoned factionalism. Burke was an early advocate of political parties, which Madison distrusted. For his part, Burke would have been dubious of Madison's mechanistic system of checks and balances. I am indebted to Ernest Young for pointing out these differences.

interests, which interests each must maintain, as an agent and advocate, against other agents and advocates; but Parliament is a deliberative assembly of one nation, with one interest, that of the whole—where not local purposes, not local prejudices, ought to guide, but the general good, resulting from the general reason of the whole.[175]

Burke objected most vehemently to Parliament's partial suspension of the Habeas Corpus Act because it operated only against some citizens, those who had been out of the realm for a prescribed time, rather than against all. Presaging the rationale for the structural protections of minorities built into the Fourteenth Amendment, Burke wrote:

> [I]t is never the faction of the predominant power that is in danger: for no tyranny chastises its own instruments. It is the obnoxious and suspected who want the protection of the law; and there is nothing to bridle the partial violence of state factions but this—"that, whenever an act is made for a cessation of law and justice, the whole people should be universally subjected to the same suspension of their franchises."[176]

The problem, as Burke saw it, was that under the selective provisions of the act "the lawful magistrate may see particular men with a malignant eye."[177]

By the middle of the nineteenth century it was clear that the original constitutional design had failed to prevent the majority from effecting "schemes of oppression" against minorities, especially the enslaved black population in the South. The Civil War, and the constitutional amendments that followed it, arose partly from a desire to correct this abuse of power.

Addressing the concerns of Madison and others about the abuse of power by aroused majorities, the Fourteenth Amendment explicitly forbade states to "deny to any person . . . the equal protection of the laws."[178] In a proposed joint resolution for the Fourteenth Amendment, Charles Sumner argued that the amendment would abolish "oligarchy, aristocracy, caste, or monopoly with particular privileges and powers."[179] Senator Howard (R-MI), floor

---

[175] Edmund Burke, *Speech to the Electors of Bristol* (Nov 3, 1774), online at http://press-pubs.uchicago.edu/founders/documents/v1ch13s7.html.

[176] Burke, *Letter to the Sheriffs* at 191 (cited in note 173).

[177] Id.

[178] US Const, Amend XIV, § 1.

[179] Balkin, 106 Yale L J at 2313, 2348 (cited in note 4), quoting Cong Globe, 39th Cong, 1st Sess 674 (1866).

manager of the Fourteenth Amendment, argued that it would
"abolis[h] all class legislation . . . . and [do] away with the injustice
of subjecting one caste of persons to a code not applicable to
another."[180]

The men who wrote and ratified the Fourteenth Amendment
could not have anticipated that their work would one day be used
to invalidate legislation excluding same-sex couples from marriage.
But the text they wrote and adopted expresses a broad protection
of "any person" and impliedly incorporates a norm of respect for
all individuals in government decision making. To respect that
norm, legislation must have some substantial justification beyond
"we don't like you," "we couldn't care less about you," or "we just
want it that way."

3. *Limited judicial role.* One could accept the anti-animus principle as a good rule for legislatures and other governmental decision makers without accepting that courts should have any role
in enforcing it. Indeed, under anti-animus doctrine, courts have
only a limited role in policing legislative actions.

Animus has been the minimalist alternative to more substantive
decisions in each of the Supreme Court cases in which it has been
found. It does not rely on adventurous theories of constitutional
substance, like the existence of some hitherto undeclared fundamental right or special scrutiny of judicially selected classifications.
These substantive approaches assume a great deal more constitutional certainty about the ultimate ends of law than is often
warranted by the facts of given cases. Anti-animus doctrine is more
concerned with legislative process than with legislative results. It
allows the legislature more freedom to pursue chosen ends in ways
that it deems appropriate, but seeks to ensure that democratic
bodies choose those ends and means in a way that seriously and
nonmaliciously accounts for relevant interests.

Consider that *Moreno* did not declare a fundamental right to
food stamps, or protect a right of unrelated people to live together,
or expand the nebulous unconstitutional conditions doctrine, or
recognize a new category of besieged minorities (hippies) for
whom special judicial solicitude is always required. It just said that
Congress cannot do whatever it wants to do to them in order to

---

[180] Id, quoting Cong Globe, 39th Cong, 1st Sess 2766 (1866). For a more complete
discussion of the history of the Fourteenth Amendment, see Andrew Kull, *The Color-Blind
Constitution* 74–75 (Harvard, 1992).

hurt them. *Cleburne*, similarly, was limited in its reach. It did not elevate judicial scrutiny of classifications based on cognitive disability, an alternative holding that would have led to judicial supervision of virtually all mental health laws and restrictions. It simply said that a city must have better reasons to single out cognitively disabled people than the mere fact that others in the community fear and dislike them. *Romer* did not mandate that states and cities must protect gay men and lesbians from discrimination or declare that classifications based on sexual orientation always warrant heightened scrutiny, a holding that would immediately have called into question all marriage laws and the ban on military service by openly gay people codified under "Don't Ask, Don't Tell."[181]

Windsor, too, should be seen as comparatively minimalist. It was perhaps the least aggressive or theoretically ambitious route the Court could have taken in striking down DOMA. The other main contending arguments for the Court's attention—heightened scrutiny under equal protection doctrine or under fundamental-rights analysis, or the kind of rational-basis-with-bite review employed by several district courts post-*Windsor*[182]—would have left the Court no principled choice but to invalidate the laws of thirty-seven states that had failed to recognize same-sex marriages. That is not to say these alternative arguments for a constitutional resolution are groundless. It is only to say that if there is any room left for democratic evolution on the issue of same-sex marriage, an animus holding offers a better chance of that than any of the leading alternatives would have.

The doctrine is not concerned as much with the legislature's substantive conclusion (limiting marriage to one man and one woman) as it is with the kinds of considerations (desire to harm the disadvantaged group) that materially influenced the outcome. Even evidence that some legislators harbored and acted upon animus in supporting or sponsoring legislation would not, by itself, be enough to invalidate the law. It is likely that any legislative body, and certainly an electorate the size of California's, would act with a multitude of purposes in mind. Some of these might involve animus, but others might not. It is also possible that a

---

[181] Don't Ask, Don't Tell, 10 USC § 654, repealed by Don't Ask, Don't Tell Repeal Act of 2010, Pub L 111-321, 124 Stat 3515, 3516, 3517.

[182] See, for example, *Kitchen v Herbert*, 2013 WL 6697874 (D Utah).

marriage law might be defended as rationally advancing some minimally legitimate purpose. These questions remain after *Windsor*.

The mere fact that a group has repeatedly lost in the political
arena would not be enough to show that it was the target of hateful
purposes in a particular challenge. The anti-animus principle
should be used sparingly, and only in extraordinary cases, where
analysis of the objective factors leaves little doubt that the outcome
reached by the democratic decision maker (for example, a zoning
board, a legislature, or voters) was the product of animus.

There remains the question, which the Court has not squarely
addressed, of the degree to which animus must be found to have
played a role before governmental action should be invalidated.
The Court's rhetoric has at times suggested that it will strike down
an act where expressing animus was the government's sole purpose
("a bare . . . desire to harm . . . .").[183] At other times, as in *Windsor*,
it has suggested that animus need only be the principal (primary)
reason for the act ("the principal purpose and the necessary effect
of this law are to demean . . . .").[184] At yet other moments, the
Court has suggested that a weighing of purposes should be performed ("no legitimate purpose *overcomes* the purpose and effect
to disparage and to injure.").[185]

A quantitative approach is not practical. If the equal protection
interests in recognizing individual worth and in ensuring that governmental acts have some substantial justification grounded in reason explain why we have an anti-animus principle, it should be
enough to show that animus materially influenced the outcome.[186]
That means that an impermissible degree of animus would be
found when it was a substantial factor in passage, rather than the
sole factor. But it must also be more than simply one of the things
that might have motivated some members of the legislature or
other governmental actor.

Even with these limitations, three objections against judicial
oversight of legislative animus might still arise. One would note

---

[183] *Moreno*, 413 US at 534.

[184] *Windsor*, 133 S Ct at 2695.

[185] Id at 2696 (emphasis added).

[186] The "material influence" standard is suggested by John Hart Ely. Ely, *Democracy and
Distrust* at 138 (cited in note 2). Under this standard, animus does not have to be the sole
or primary purpose of the law to violate the anti-animus principle. It's enough that animus
was a substantial factor in the outcome.

that the kind of multifactored inquiry called for by anti-animus doctrine is prone to judicial abuse, is difficult to apply even when not abused, and is indeterminate even when faithfully applied. These are substantial concerns. But judgments of the kind called for by the doctrine are also endemic to constitutional law, neither more nor less beyond the capacity of federal courts than deciding whether a case is justiciable,[187] whether a regulation constitutes a taking of private property, whether particular commercial speech can be regulated, and indeed, in equal protection jurisprudence, whether a classification should be subject to strict scrutiny requiring that the means be sufficiently "narrowly tailored" to achieve "compelling" ends. What are these if not hybrids of legal and policy determinations, indeterminate but not unbounded? Commentators who need certainty are in a Sisyphean struggle against all of constitutional law. Constitutional law is painting a picture, not doing a sum.[188]

A second concern would object to any judicial inquiry into legislative purpose. Criticism of purposive approaches to statutory and constitutional law is common,[189] and justifies caution by courts. But it's untrue that the Court never considers, or ought never to consider, legislative purpose in constitutional cases. In fact, it has repeatedly done so, especially in equal protection cases, where the government's decision to select people for deprivations is based on race, religion, or even simply dislike.[190] If—based on

---

[187] Indeed, difficult justiciability questions of standing and genuine adverseness were raised in the two same-sex marriage cases the Court decided the same day, with results that were not obviously consistent. Compare *Windsor*, 133 S Ct at 2688–89 (controversy over DOMA is justiciable even though the parties agreed on the merits and on the remedy), with *Hollingsworth v Perry*, 133 S Ct 2652, 2667–68 (2013) (controversy over state constitutional amendment is not justiciable where the parties agreed on the merits and on the remedy).

[188] "Life is painting a picture, not doing a sum." Oliver Wendell Holmes, Jr., *Address to the Harvard Alumni Association to the Class of '61*, in Oliver Wendell Holmes, *Speeches* 96 (1913).

[189] *Palmer v Thompson*, 403 US 217, 224–25 (1971) (asserting the difficulty and "futility" of judicial inquiry into legislative motive).

[190] Ely, *Democracy and Distrust* at 137 (cited in note 2); Paul Brest, *Palmer v. Thompson: An Approach to the Problem of Unconstitutional Legislative Motive*, 1971 Supreme Court Review 95 (answering criticisms of difficulty, futility, and impropriety in judicial inquiry into governmental motive). Equal protection cases authorizing judicial inquiry into legislative purpose or motive include *Personnel Administrator of Mass v Feeney*, 442 US 256 (1979) (decision maker cannot choose course of action because of, rather than despite, adverse discriminatory impact); *Village of Arlington Heights v Metropolitan Housing Corp.*, 429 US 252, 266–67 (1977) (listing factors for determining presence of a racially discriminatory purpose); *Washington v Davis*, 426 US 229 (1976) (racially discriminatory

textual, contextual, procedural, and effectual considerations—animus appears materially to have influenced the government's act, the purpose is an unconstitutional one. Add to that the absence of a plausible alternative explanation (as opposed to a pretextual one), and the animus motivation is both obvious and constitutionally fatal.

A third concern about judicial inquiry into possible animus-based purposes is that it is ineffective. The Court has occasionally noted a seeming oddity in purpose-based constitutional analysis.

> [T]here is an element of futility in a judicial attempt to invalidate a law because of the bad motives of its supporters. If the law is struck down for this reason, rather than because of its facial content or effect, it would presumably be valid as soon as the legislature or relevant governing body repassed it for different reasons.[191]

Despite this criticism, the Court continues to inquire into governmental purpose in a host of constitutional fields. The objection to purpose-based constitutional analysis is not unique to the animus doctrine.

The fact that the government might subsequently act for a constitutionally permissible purpose after having acted for an impermissible one is not a decisive objection to purpose analysis. It's possible that a legislature, after being told that it acted for an impermissible purpose, will refuse to vote for reenactment. If a law is invalidated by a court, the legislature will often fail even to

---

purpose would invalidate facially neutral law); *Yick Wo v Hopkins*, 118 US 356 (1886) (stark racially disparate effect showed racially discriminatory purpose). In the Establishment Clause context, the Court has held that a law passed to promote fundamentalist Christianity was unconstitutional, *Epperson v Arkansas*, 393 US 97, 107–09 (1968) (invalidating a state law that forbade teaching evolution in public schools), that a law requiring "equal time" for the teaching of creation science and evolution in public schools had an improper purpose to advance religion, *Edwards v Aguillard*, 482 US 578, 588 n 7 (1987), and that legislative history could be reviewed to find an unconstitutional preferentialist purpose in a case involving a "religious gerrymander" targeting practitioners of the Santeria faith, *Church of the Lukumi Babalu Aye v City of Hialeah*, 508 US 520, 535 (1993). Under the Dormant Commerce Clause, the Court has held that states may not act with a protectionist purpose in regulating businesses, see, for example, *Bacchus Imports Ltd. v Dias*, 468 US 263, 276–77 (1984) (invalidating state tax law on imports that had a protectionist purpose). A facially neutral law is unconstitutional if the Court nevertheless discerns a protectionist purpose—one that discriminates against out-of-state interests. Indeed, even a law that could be reenacted today for a permissible purpose has been held unconstitutional because it was originally motivated by an unconstitutional purpose. *Hunter v Underwood*, 471 US 222, 233 (1985) (invalidating 1901 state constitutional provision disenfranchising felons that had been motivated by a desire to disenfranchise blacks, even though felons could be denied the right to vote for some other purpose today).

[191] *Palmer v Thompson*, 403 US 217 (1971).

consider the issue again. The passage of time, by itself, may allow the legislature to consider new evidence or to reevaluate what it previously did in haste. In fact, "judicial action on the basis of motive results in an effective, not a futile, invalidation."[192] So let the legislature find a reason other than disempowering black voters for drawing a city's boundaries as a twenty-eight-sided figure.[193] Let the school board close down all of its schools again for some purpose other than separating black and white schoolchildren.[194] For that matter, let the zoning commission find some reason other than animus against the cognitively disabled for uniquely denying them a home. Let the Congress cleanse the legislative record of vindictiveness against nontraditional families in order to deny them assistance to buy food.

In many cases, there simply won't be an alternative legitimate explanation for the challenged action.[195] The reasons that led a court to conclude that the initial action was based on animus will "rightly make it somewhat skeptical of claims of a subsequent change of heart."[196] The existence of a legitimate justification will also likely have been considered in the initial judicial review. The fact that animus was nevertheless found will make it less likely that the non-animus-based justification might save it after reenactment. The more plausible objection to purpose inquiry is not that it is futile, but that it may be far too censorious and thus far too *effective* as a tool for invalidating government action.

Beyond the practical concern about futility, there is nothing unusual or wrong *in principle* about declaring that an act properly done for one reason may be impermissible if done for another reason. Ely observes:

> [S]uppose from time to time an action previously invalidated for unconstitutional motivation is retaken and upheld: so what? We don't regard the system as having failed when a person whose conviction was reversed because the jury was biased is reconvicted by a jury on remand: indeed we regard it as vindicated.[197]

[192] Theodore Eisenberg, *Disproportionate Impact and Illicit Motive: Theories of Constitutional Adjudication*, 52 NYU L Rev 36, 116 (1977).

[193] *Gomillion v Lightfoot*, 364 US 339, 340 (1960).

[194] *Griffin v County School Board of Prince Edward County*, 377 US 218 (1964).

[195] Ely, *Democracy and Distrust* at 138 (cited in note 2).

[196] Id.

[197] Id at 139.

When it comes to fears of excessive judicial intrusion, the upshot is that very few litigants will successfully use the animus doctrine. Most laws can plausibly be explained as reasonably related to legitimate objectives, with little or no indication that spite materially produced the act. The Eighth Circuit, for example, appropriately rejected an animus attack on a city ordinance prohibiting outdoor smoking on public property.[198] The public-regarding health justifications for such an ordinance were plausible even if not a slam dunk; the law was not the product of a bare desire to harm smokers. The Sixth Circuit was right to reject an animus challenge to a Kentucky law that accelerated the date at which the issuers of travelers' checks were required to remit unclaimed funds to the state.[199] The Eleventh Circuit correctly held that Congress's decision to deny food stamps and supplemental security income benefits to some classes of aliens, but not others, could plausibly be explained by factors other than animus: the need to save money, the desire to reward aliens who had been working for a long time in the United States, the need to assist those who were particularly vulnerable to poverty (like the blind and disabled), and the desire to help refugees seeking to escape catastrophic political and economic conditions.[200] Judge Posner, writing for a panel of the Seventh Circuit, justifiably rejected an animus attack on a federal law that denied social security disability benefits to persons who had been confined to mental health facilities after being acquitted of a crime by reason of insanity.[201] They did not need the money and were already "subsisting at the state's expense," he reasoned.[202] None of these cases implicated the basic concern of the anti-animus principle that a governmental decision maker should have reasoned justifications, and should not act based on ill will toward a group of people.

4. *Animus and the morality of homosexuality.* Numerous academic and nonacademic critics, especially, but not only, opponents of same-sex marriage, have excoriated the Court for allegedly insulting those who supported DOMA. These critics have protested

---

[198] *Gallagher v City of Clayton*, 699 F3d 1013, 1020–21 (8th Cir 2012).

[199] *American Express Travel Related Services Co. v Kentucky*, 641 F3d 685, 691–92 (6th Cir 2011).

[200] *Rodriguez v United States*, 169 F3d 1342, 1351–53 (11th Cir 1999).

[201] *Milner v Apfel*, 148 F3d 812, 816–17 (7th Cir 1998).

[202] Id at 817.

that they are not anti-gay bigots and that a moral belief in marriage as an opposite-sex-only institution should not be equated with hatred of homosexuals. These criticisms miss the mark when it comes to *Windsor*, which is more complicated on the subject of morality-as-animus than they suggest.

a) Windsor as insult. After *Windsor*, Professor Hadley Arkes described the opinion as "hate speech" in the *National Review*. For Justice Kennedy, Arkes wrote, "the defense of marriage was simply another way of disparaging and 'denigrating' gays and lesbians, and denying dignity to their 'relationships.'" Plausible justifications for marriage as the union of one man and one woman were to be viewed as "so much cover for malice and blind hatred."[203] Echoing Chief Justice Roberts's dissent, Professor John Yoo lamented in the *National Review* that the Court had damned 342 members of the House, 85 Senators, and President Bill Clinton as "all guilty of antigay bias in 1996, when DOMA was enacted."[204]

Writing in *Commonweal*, Professor Richard Garnett warned that the animus rationale threatened religious freedom:

> We should be concerned that the characterization by the majority in *Windsor* of DOMA's purpose and of the motives of the overwhelming and bipartisan majority of legislators that supported it reflects a view that those states—and religious communities—that reject the redefinition of marriage are best regarded as backward and bigoted, unworthy of respect. Such a view is not likely to generate compromise or accommodation and so it poses a serious challenge to religious freedom.[205]

Professor Patrick Lee wrote that "[the] strident campaign to redefine marriage will only become more intense in the next few years.

---

[203] Hadley Arkes, *Worse Than It Sounds, and It Cannot Be Cabined*, Bench Memos (National Review Online, June 26, 2013), online at http://www.nationalreview.com/bench-memos/352114/worse-it-sounds-and-it-cannot-be-cabined-hadley-arkes. Longtime anti-gay activist Robert Knight agreed that "[b]y accusing backers of traditional marriage of being motivated only by animus against homosexuals, the U.S. Supreme Court has become the most prominent hate group in the country." Robert Knight, *The High Court Gleefully Defamed Christians*, GOPUSA (Washington Times (DC), July 2, 2013), online at http://www.gopusa.com/freshink/2013/07/02/the-high-court-gleefully-defamed-christians/.

[204] John Yoo, *Windsor: Tarring "the Political Branches with Bigotry,"* The Corner (National Review Online, June 26, 2013), online at http://www.nationalreview.com/corner/352098/windsor-tarring-political-branches-bigotry-john-yoo. Justices Scalia and Alito first sounded this alarm about *Windsor* in their respective dissenting opinions. *Windsor*, 133 S Ct at 2707 (Scalia, J, dissenting); id at 2718 (Alito, J, dissenting).

[205] Garnett, *Worth Worrying About?* (cited in note 29).

Catholics will be increasingly labeled as bigots and hate mongers."[206] From now on, warned Rod Dreher in *The American Conservative*, "the Court has declared open season on religious and social conservatives and their institutions." The decision should "put fear into the hearts of anyone who does not share the belief that homosexuality is morally neutral, or morally good. The Supreme Court says we are haters, full stop."[207]

Similar criticisms could have been leveled at the Court for using the anti-animus rationale to strike down food-stamp limitations in *Moreno*. That law, too, was defended as reinforcing the normative value of traditional families. The denial of a permit for a home for the cognitively disabled in *Cleburne* was based on neighbors' fears. For that matter, the prohibition on all civil rights protections for homosexuals in *Romer* was defended as a measure to stave off the piecemeal deterioration of traditional sexual morality.

Windsor does not actually label DOMA supporters bigots. It does not even claim that any particular legislator harbored animus against gays, although malice toward homosexuals was a significant driver. Can this be? Professor Michael Greve, calling *Windsor* "transparently absurd," scoffed at the idea that DOMA was "a product of an 'animus' that no one may have had but that, like a devilish spirit, worked behind the legislators' backs to produce DOMA[]."[208] That leads to a consideration of the relationship of morality and animus.

b) Morality and animus. It is true that *Windsor* declared, for the third time in seventeen years, that moral disapproval of homosexuality is an illegitimate basis for legislation fencing out homosexuals. Supporters of DOMA claimed that morals legislation is good for people, that homosexual acts are immoral, and that nobody is better off when people engage in homosexual acts. That is not a bare desire to harm anyone, they say; it is a desire to make

---

[206] Patrick Lee, *Is Marriage Bigoted and Discriminatory?*, The Catholic World Report (July 20, 2013), online at http://www.catholicworldreport.com/Item/2431/is_marriage_bigoted_and_discriminatory.aspx.

[207] Rod Dreher, *Scalia: "Open Season on Marriage Traditionalists,"* The American Conservative (June 26, 2013), online at http://www.theamericanconservative.com/dreher/scalia-doma-open-season/. Another commentator opined that "Christians who speak out and stand up for traditional marriage are more likely than ever to be persecuted and even prosecuted for it." Paul Strand, *Open Season on Christians after Pro-Gay Rulings*, CBN News (July 30, 2013), online at http://www.cbn.com/cbnnews/us/2013/July/Open-Season-on-Christians-after-Pro-Gay-Rulings/.

[208] Michael S. Greve, *Windsor: A Dia-Tribe*, Library of Law and Liberty (June 27, 2013), online at http://www.libertylawsite.org/2013/06/27/windsor-a-dia-tribe/.

men moral,[209] which makes them good, which helps them. A sodomy law criminalizing homosexual acts might even be good *for homosexuals*, on this account.

This argument has not fared well in the animus decisions. Colorado defended Amendment 2 on moral grounds. Texas defended its Homosexual Conduct Law on moral grounds. Congress defended DOMA on moral grounds. Yet all three laws were held unconstitutional. One's views enforced in law do not get a constitutional pass simply because one affixes a "morals" or "natural law" tag on the product. Decorating it further with one's interpretation of biblical passages cannot save it from review. To conclude otherwise is to say that a law is constitutional as long as a majority wants it that way and expresses its desire as based on morality.

It's also the case that animus doctrine, like much of constitutional law, has a normative component. It expresses the normative principle, implicit in equal protection and in the postulates of a liberal democracy, that every individual has dignity and is worthy of respect. It offers the observation that unreasoning prejudice against persons expressed in law is inconsistent with the commitment to the equal protection of the law. Government must not act maliciously to injure or disparage them and must not act as if their interests are unworthy of any consideration.

What we call morality is guided by experience. Morals reflect human learning and history. They evolve. They adjust. They are critiqued and revised. Experience and empirical learning about murderers have not taught that we should not condemn murder or fear the murderer's potential for future harm. Moral judgments often arise from an unstated and complicated calculation about harm. Not every law prohibiting or limiting some activity for what are said to be moral reasons reflects animus against the people who engage in it. One might condemn as immoral the possession of guns, or running a casino, or using marijuana. That doesn't make every effort to ban guns, to prohibit gambling, or to criminalize drug usage a product of animus against gun owners, gamblers, or drug users. Each of these enactments would have a plausible connection to concern about harm independent of ill will toward the people who engage in these acts. None of these pro-

---

[209] See generally Robert P. George, *Making Men Moral: Civil Liberties and Public Morality* (Clarendon, 1995).

hibitions would run a serious risk that they were simply expressions of spite against the people who engage in the prohibited behavior.

When experience and empirical learning demonstrate that the feared harm undergirding a "moral" view is baseless, a continued moral condemnation expressed in law is likely to be an animus-based act. It is a *prejudice*, an unthinking and anachronistic hold-over from an earlier time. Such unfounded negative prejudgments cannot be a permissible basis for government action if we really mean what we say about respecting individual worth and dignity. To take a person's citizenship seriously entails a willingness to learn about him, to adapt our attitudes, and to modify our treatment of him as we learn.

The moral condemnation of homosexuality has typically rested on hysterical claims about homosexuality—claims rife in the congressional debate over DOMA—that have turned out to be baseless. Experience and empirical learning have demonstrated that hoary myths about homosexuals as sick, maladjusted, contagious, subhuman, dangerous, and predatory were baseless. Same-sex couples have the same capacities and desires for love, affection, and commitment as opposite-sex couples. At the same time, laws aimed at homosexual "conduct"—whether that conduct is intimate sexual activity or the formation of relationships—are inseparable from laws aimed at homosexual status.[210] The same can't be said of laws that prohibit, on moral grounds, the conduct of gun possession, gambling, and drug usage. To condemn homosexual conduct *is to condemn homosexual people* in a way that, say, prohibiting slot machines is not a condemnation of people who overestimate their chances of winning a game designed to profit from their gullibility.

To say that the *moral* condemnation of homosexuality enacted in a broad and unprecedented law like DOMA is impermissible animus is not the same as saying that *all* reasons for rejecting same-sex marriage are animus-based. A legislature may decline to pass same-sex marriage legislation in circumstances that genuinely demonstrate no ill will toward gay people, but that instead reflect uncertainty about the consequences of change to a social and legal practice as important as marriage. The legislature may prefer to take things slowly. A general preference for incremental change,

---

[210] *Christian Legal Society v Martinez*, 130 S Ct 2971, 2990 (2010); see generally Dale Carpenter, *Flagrant Conduct: The Story of Lawrence v. Texas* ch 8 (W. W. Norton, 2012).

when other indicia of animus are not present,[211] is surely not animus. The converse is also true: merely reciting a preference for slow change (or morality) when other indicia of animus are present can't exempt a law from constitutional attack.

To say that DOMA reflected animus is also not to say that those who hew closely to the traditional religious understanding of marriage in their own lives and within their own faith traditions are themselves hateful. Good people can do bad things for what they think are good reasons. The focus of animus doctrine is not on the bad nature of the person who supports legislation. The focus is on the inadmissibility of the reasons offered for supporting the legislation in a republic committed to the concept of equal protection for every citizen. The issue in *Windsor* is not whether a belief in marriage as only the union of one man and one woman is bigoted. It is whether, in context, the affirmative decision by Congress in 1996 to select one class of potential future marriages for second-class status reflected animus against the persons entering those marriages.

This characterization of the *Windsor* holding may not ease the hurt feelings or quiet the indignation of traditional-marriage supporters, of course. The insult to them, if an insult at all, is not unique to an animus holding, however. An alternative holding based on heightened scrutiny of sexual-orientation classifications would have informed them that traditional sexual morality is akin to race-based discrimination. A rational-basis holding resting on the irrelevance of the means (denying federal recognition to married same-sex couples) to the stated ends (inter alia, encouraging responsible procreation) would have suggested that they suffered a serious cognitive failure verging on insanity when they urged passage of DOMA. There is no nice way to tell people that policies they have fervently supported are unconstitutional. Nor would these alternative routes to eliminating DOMA be more solicitous of religious beliefs.

The animus portion of Justice Kennedy's opinion in *Windsor* played into a calculated strategy by gay-marriage opponents to claim the status of victims in the debate over the issue. The leading anti-gay-marriage advocacy group, the National Organization for Marriage, has even urged that gay-marriage supporters be baited

---

[211] See Section III.

into calling opponents "bigots" in order to split the coalition of gays and blacks who work together on other causes.

> The strategic goal of this project is to drive a wedge between gays and blacks—two key Democratic constituencies. Find, equip, energize and connect African-American spokespeople for marriage, develop a media campaign around their objections to gay marriage as a civil right, provoke the gay marriage base into responding by denouncing these spokesmen and women as bigots. No politician wants to take up and push an issue that splits the base of the party.[212]

It should be no surprise, then, that the immediate reaction of DOMA supporters to *Windsor* was to claim that they had been unfairly called bigots by the Court. Supporters of Colorado's Amendment 2 similarly cried foul when the Court in *Romer* struck down that patently anti-gay enactment because it reflected animus. They were simply "tolerant Coloradans" who didn't hate gay people but wanted to halt the "piecemeal deterioration" of traditional sexual morality, protested Justice Scalia.[213] The Court held otherwise. The fact is that opponents of the Court's decision in *Windsor* would have objected strenuously to *any* basis for striking down DOMA. Their real complaint about *Windsor* lies in its substantive conclusion, not in its supposed disrespect toward Congress, President Clinton, and the millions of Americans who backed the law. It is to that substantive conclusion that we now turn.

III. DOMA and Its Animus

Critics of *Windsor* have charged that the Court found animus in DOMA "without any evidence on the matter."[214] The criticism seems to be that Justice Kennedy magically divined animus in the decision to pass DOMA. Or perhaps he simply believed that there was no conceivable rational basis to define marriage solely as the union of a man and a woman, and thus "found" animus as the only remaining explanation for why the law passed. At first glance, only bald assertion rather than reasoned analysis or "evidence" is used to reach the result.

---

[212] Kevin Nix, *Breaking: Previously Confidential Documents Shed Light on NOM Strategy*, Human Rights Campaign (March 26, 2012), online at http://www.hrc.org/nomexposed/entry/must-read#.UvUeyPldWSo.

[213] *Romer*, 517 US at 636, 653 (Scalia, J, dissenting).

[214] Sven Wilson, *We're All Haters Now*, Pileus (June 27, 2013), online at http://pileus-blog.wordpress.com/2013/06/27/were-all-haters-now/.

But as a close reading of *Windsor* and its predecessor animus decisions indicates, a variety of objective factors should be considered to determine whether animus infected governmental decision making. These include considerations of text, context, legislative procedure and history, actual effects, and pretext.

This section lays out the basic components of the Court's methodology in animus cases. It then applies that methodology to the Defense of Marriage Act, concluding that the Court correctly held that DOMA reflected animus.

A. ANIMUS METHODOLOGY

In equal protection cases, the Court has teased out impermissible purposes where governmental decision makers (including legislatures) have claimed permissible ones. In race cases, the impermissible purpose is the purpose to discriminate on the basis of race. In animus cases, the impermissible purpose is the purpose to inflict injury or indignity. While the Court hasn't systematically laid out its methodology, based on the racial-purpose cases and the animus quadrilogy we can discern an approach for determining when an unconstitutional purpose has materially driven governmental decision making despite the government's argument that it hasn't.

Consider the Court's equal protection methodology in racial discrimination cases. "Necessarily," the Court has held, "an invidious discriminatory purpose may often be inferred from the totality of the relevant facts, including the fact, if it is true, that the law bears more heavily on one race than another."[215] A law's disproportionate racial effect is relevant, but usually not sufficient, to show a racially discriminatory purpose. There is no requirement that the discriminatory purpose be the only conceivable one. "Rarely can it be said that a legislature or administrative body operating under a broad mandate made a decision motivated solely by a single concern, or even that a particular purpose was the 'dominant' or 'primary' one."[216] The racial purpose need only be "a motivating factor in the decision" to support the conclusion that the action is unconstitutional.[217]

---

[215] *Washington v Davis*, 426 US 229, 242 (1976).

[216] *Arlington Heights v Metropolitan Housing Corp.*, 429 US 252, 265 (1977).

[217] Id at 266.

Whether an invidious purpose was "a motivating factor" can be inferred from "such circumstantial and direct evidence of intent as may be available."[218] This indirect evidence may include consideration of the "impact" of the official action, the historical background of the decision, the "specific sequence of events leading up to the challenged decision," departure from normal procedures for making a decision, departures from substantive considerations that would usually drive the result, and "the legislative or administrative history," including "contemporary statements by members of the decisionmaking body, minutes of its meetings, or reports."[219] Once there is a threshold showing of an impermissible purpose, the burden shifts to the government to "establish[] that the same decision would have resulted even had the impermissible purpose not been considered."[220]

The Court has repeatedly struck down laws that were facially neutral on the grounds that they reflected a racially discriminatory purpose. It invalidated a state law redrawing the boundaries of a city by altering the shape "from a square to an uncouth twenty-eight sided figure," removing all but five black voters from the city's election rolls while keeping all white voters within city boundaries.[221] A decision by a school board to close all of the public schools was struck down on the grounds that the purpose of the closure was to prevent blacks and whites from going to school together, even though the district might have been able to close the schools for other reasons.[222] It struck down an at-large election system that had effectively prevented any blacks from being elected in a Georgia county where 53.6 percent of the population was black.[223] It also struck down a facially neutral law that disenfranchised all persons convicted of crimes involving moral turpitude.[224] Under this law, adopted as part of the Alabama Constitution in 1901, ten times more blacks than whites had lost the right to vote. The constitutional convention had purposefully "selected such crimes as vagrancy, living in adultery, and wife beating

---

[218] Id.

[219] Id at 267–68.

[220] Id at 270 n 21.

[221] *Gomillion v Lightfoot*, 364 US 339, 340 (1960).

[222] *Griffin v County School Board of Prince Edward County*, 377 US 218 (1964).

[223] *Rogers v Lodge*, 458 US 613 (1982).

[224] *Hunter v Underwood*, 471 US 222, 233 (1985).

that were thought to be more commonly committed by blacks."[225] None of these laws created classifications based on race, but all were unconstitutional because of their impermissible racial purposes.

In the past four decades, an analogous methodology has gradually developed in animus cases. In these cases, the invidious and unconstitutional purpose is not racial, but animus-based. Animus is a desire to disparage and to injure a person or group of people. As in the race cases, the government rarely concedes that it acted because of animus against a person or group of people—indeed, such a purpose is disclaimed. Instead, the government often characterizes the harm done to one class as merely an effort to benefit a different class. Or the government justifies the harm inflicted as an effort to encourage socially optimal behavior while not encouraging, or perhaps even discouraging, suboptimal or harmful behavior. In a given case, which characterization of the government's purpose, the government's own benign characterization or the challenger's malign one, should the Court credit?

Under the anti-animus doctrine, the Court need not accept either characterization as the sole or dominant explanation for the government's act. It is possible that the government's act could be characterized accurately as involving both benign and malign purposes. But that mix does not save it from unconstitutionality. As in the race cases, the impermissible animus-based purpose need not be the "sole" or "dominant" one. It need only be a "motivating factor," or as I propose, a "material influence" in the decision. As in the race cases, the impermissible purpose may be gleaned from circumstantial and direct evidence.

The inference that animus was a material influence in the government's decision is drawn from a totality of the evidence rather than from a mechanical rule. A number of factors should be considered in making this inference. The animus decisions, especially *Windsor*, taken together with the racial-purpose decisions, suggest that these factors include consideration of:

1. the statutory text (textual);[226]
2. the political and legal context of passage, including a historical background demonstrating past discriminatory acts, and a de-

---

[225] Id at 232.

[226] See *Romer*, 517 US at 624; *Windsor*, 133 S Ct at 2693.

parture from the usual substantive considerations governing the decision, especially if the considerations usually relied upon by the decision maker strongly favor a decision contrary to the one reached (contextual);[227]

3. the legislative proceedings, including evidence of animus that can be gleaned from the sequence of events that led to passage, the legislative procedure, and the legislative history accompanying passage (procedural);[228]

4. the law's harsh real-world impact or effects, including injury to the tangible or dignitary interests of the disadvantaged group (effectual);[229] and

5. the utter failure of alternative explanations to offer legitimate ends along with means that really advance those ends (pretextual).[230]

From a consideration of these factors, an animus-based purpose may be inferred even where it is not admitted. The Court's animus cases show that no single one of these factors must be present in order to make the inference. The factors may be used to evaluate decisions made by a legislature,[231] by a popular vote,[232] by an ad-

---

[227] See *Moreno*, 413 US at 537–38; *Cleburne*, 473 US at 448; *Romer*, 517 US at 623–24; *Windsor*, 133 S Ct at 2693–94; see also *Arlington Heights*, 429 US at 257–59.

[228] See *Moreno*, 413 US at 536–57; *Windsor*, 133 S Ct at 2694–95. Citing *Windsor* and the other animus decisions, a Michigan district court relied on legislative history to conclude that the state's denial of benefits to same-sex domestic partners was rooted in animus. *Bassett v Snyder*, 951 F Supp 2d 939, 968 (ED Mich 2013) ("The historical background and legislative history of the Act demonstrate that it was motivated by animus against gay men and lesbians."). See also *Arlington Heights*, 429 US at 268 (inquiring into legislative history to find racial purpose).

[229] See *Romer*, 517 US at 627–28; *Windsor*, 133 S Ct at 2693–95. See also *Washington*, 426 US at 242 (consideration of law's disparate impact). The Court has not explained why a law's harmful impact is a sign that animus motivated its passage. It may be that the Court believes the Congress is likely to have intended the tangible and dignitary damage the law actually inflicted. This may or may not be true in a given case. Congress might not have foreseen or given any thought to the negative impact. But in the case of DOMA, which purposefully affected thousands of provisions in the United States Code, the idea that Congress couldn't have foreseen any consequences is hard to credit. Congress at the very least had constructive knowledge of the consequences. In the case of DOMA, evidence of impact is thus the kind of evidence from which an inference about purpose and motivation can be drawn.

[230] See *Moreno*, 413 US at 537; *Cleburne*, 473 US at 449–50; *Romer*, 517 US at 635; *Windsor*, 133 S Ct at 2693–94. Concern about using pretext to justify an unconstitutional act is as old as *McCulloch v Maryland*, 17 US 316, 423 (1819) (Congress may not accomplish an unconstitutional objective under the pretext of using its constitutional powers).

[231] *Moreno*, 413 US at 529 (evaluating a federal statute); *Windsor*, 113 S Ct 2682 (evaluating a federal statute).

[232] *Romer*, 517 US 620 (evaluating a statewide referendum).

ministrative body,[233] or by any other governmental official or entity.[234] The animus-based purpose may be found in government acts that are very broad[235] or very narrow.[236]

The fifth factor—consideration of the government's non-animus-based justification for the act—deserves special attention. In the race cases, the fifth factor comes into play as a burden-shifting exercise: when a prima facie case of impermissible racial purpose is made the burden shifts to the government to explain its decision on nonracial grounds.[237] In the animus cases, this factor has played out somewhat differently: consideration of the strength of the government's non-animus-based justification is a part of what goes into the ultimate determination of whether animus was a materially motivating purpose behind the government's act.

When other indicia of animus are present, the fifth factor is more demanding and operates differently than traditional rational-basis review. If a mere "rational" relationship to a "legitimate" purpose were all that was required in animus cases, each of the four animus decisions would have come out the other way because the government's act in each could be justified on some far-fetched and hypothetical ground. In *Moreno*, the desire to save money could have rationally explained the denial of food stamps to hippies. In *Cleburne*, concerns about 500-year floods could have justified the denial of a zoning variance for a home for the cognitively disabled. In *Romer*, an attempt to conserve state resources for combatting other forms of discrimination could have saved Amendment 2. And in *Windsor*, Congress's asserted preference for moving slowly on social change or its efforts to control its own spending programs would have prevailed in a challenge to DOMA. But they didn't.

Ordinarily, a poor fit between means and ends could be explained by many things other than animus: bad information, stupidity, or excessive caution. But it's obvious that the Court is not

---

[233] *Cleburne*, 473 US 436–37 (evaluating the decision of a city zoning board).

[234] *Davis v Prison Health Services*, 679 F3d 433, 438 (6th Cir 2012) (government acting as employer); *Stemler v City of Florence*, 126 F3d 856, 873–74 (6th Cir 1997) (government as prosecutor).

[235] *Romer*, 517 US at 624 (denial of all civil rights protections); *Windsor*, 113 S Ct at 2682–83 (exclusion from status and all benefits of marriage under federal law).

[236] *Moreno*, 413 US at 529 (denial of food stamps); *Cleburne*, 473 US at 435 (denial of special use permit for housing).

[237] *Washington*, 426 US at 241; *Arlington Heights*, 429 US at 270 n 21.

always willing to indulge the presumption that Congress was merely incompetent rather than hateful. And it's not willing to tolerate wildly over- or underinclusive laws once animus is detected. That's because, for the Court, the presence of animus has what we might call a tainting effect. In animus cases, the Court does not simply declare that a discovered malicious purpose is "illegitimate" and that Congress must find an alternative "legitimate" one. It does not just take one proffered justification off the table and then ask the government, "What else have you got?" The discovery of animus is instead an affirmative reason to invalidate an otherwise constitutional law.

By the time the Court reaches consideration of possible pretext—the relationship between the asserted (non-animus-based) objective and the means used to serve that objective—it has already been alerted to the strong possibility that the permissible explanation is makeweight or pretextual. The fact that proffered innocuous rationales in the animus quadrilogy failed suggests that the usual presumption of constitutionality was no longer operative. *Windsor* Products thus draws from *Carolene Products*, in which the Court concluded that the presumption of constitutionality should not apply where the political process could not be trusted to deal fairly with unpopular minorities.

B. INDICIA OF ANIMUS IN DOMA

We come at last to the application of anti-animus doctrine and methodology to DOMA. Each of the factors the Court has considered in its decisions, when applied to DOMA, indicate that animus materially influenced Congress's act. The Court's decision in *Windsor* did not fully flesh out the arguments that might have been made to support its conclusion, but the skeleton of the argument is there.

1. *Text.* The text of a given statute is a starting point for identifying its objective purpose or purposes. *Windsor* concluded that the very text of DOMA indicated animus,[238] though it is a bit puzzling why the text alone should be thought to indicate that. Perhaps it was the breezy combination of breadth and brevity in the act that suggested a congressional inattention to serious class interests or any consideration of narrower means for achieving

---

[238] *Windsor*, 133 S Ct at 2693.

non-animus-based congressional objectives, like cost savings or discouraging judicial activism.

The text of the act did lay bare its scope and purpose. Though not challenged in the *Windsor* litigation, Section 2 of the act might get the suspicion of animus started. Section 2 dealt with the possibility that married same-sex couples might some day in the future demand interstate recognition. It declared that no state could be required to recognize any other state's same-sex marriages.[239] It was the first time Congress had ever made such a declaration about the effect of one state's laws in the other states, which itself represents a departure from the usual substantive approach governing full faith and credit practices. Why the exception to recognition for the first time here?

Section 3, which was challenged, declared that Congress would not recognize otherwise valid same-sex marriages. It limited marriage for all federal purposes to the union of one man and one woman.[240] It brushed away any possible morsel of federal recognition or regard for any future marriage validly entered between two men or two women under state law.

Beyond the sweeping text, the title of the law, the "Defense of Marriage Act," immediately raises three questions. First, against what or whom is the law a "defense"? What is the threat and how has it been generated? Second, assuming there is a hypothetical future invader armed with weaponry capable of bringing down the entire institution of marriage, why must the "defense" be a Great Wall running up and down the continent rather than a moat around a specific and vulnerable fortification? Third, since when is the Congress charged with "defending" marriage? That has been the states' responsibility, with Congress acting only interstitially or at the margins. The text cannot answer these questions, but it at least introduces the problem.

Under this analysis, the suspicion of animus would grow as the text of the law itself broadens and as it points away from usual areas of congressional concern. A law defining marriage as the union of one man and one woman for a much more limited purpose identifiable in the text, like determining household eligibility

---

[239] Defense of Marriage Act, Pub L No 104-199, 110 Stat 2419 (1996), codified at 28 USC § 1738C.

[240] Defense of Marriage Act, Pub L No 104-199, 110 Stat 2419 (1996), codified at 1 USC § 7.

for food stamps, would not generate quite the same degree of concern that a shotgun law like DOMA generated.

A similar lesson might be applicable to state limits on marriage. For example, state constitutional amendments regarding marriage that have been passed since the late 1990s lie along a spectrum from (1) enactments empowering the legislature to decide the definition of marriage without intrusion by state courts,[241] to (2) bans on the status of marriage for same-sex couples but that leave open the possibility of benefits and rights for same-sex couples through an alternative status like civil union or domestic partnership,[242] to (3) bans on any status "identical" to or even "similar to" marriage for same-sex couples, denying them any marriage-like benefits.[243] The text of some state marriage amendments, like the one in Virginia, even suggest the possibility that private contracts and benefits conferring rights on same-sex couples might be unenforceable.[244] Not coincidentally, the broader the textual sweep of the marriage limitation, the more burdensome the law is likely to be in effect.

2. *Context.* The political and legal context in which the government acts may suggest an animus-based purpose. DOMA was both a departure from the nation's substantive adherence to federalism and the latest in a series of governmental acts discriminating against gay men and lesbians. It departed from the usual presumption of federalism that allows states to control basic family relations, including the recognition of marital status. It also departed from historic practice under which the federal government plays a minimal, distinctly secondary, and derivative role in family policy. Departures from the usual substantive considerations in decision making indicate possible animus, especially when the usual substantive considerations would likely have produced a different result. *Windsor* reaffirmed what is now a venerable principle of constitutional law by emphasizing that discrimination of an

---

[241] See Hawaii Const, Art I, § 23. Note that the Hawaii state legislature had denied marriage to same-sex couples in 1994, see Section 3 of Act 217, Reg Sess, 1994 Hawaii Sess Laws 531, but later decided to extend marriage to same-sex couples. See Hawaii Marriage Equality Act of 2013, 2d Special Sess, 2013 Hawaii Sess Laws 1.

[242] See, for example, Ariz Const, Art XXX, § 1; Miss Const, Art XIV, § 263-A; Mo Const, Art I, § 33.

[243] See, for example, Neb Const, Art I, § 29; Okla Const, Art II, § 35; Tex Const, Art 1, § 32; Utah Const, Art I, § 29.

[244] Va Const, Art I, § 15-A.

unusual sort raises judicial suspicion that some impermissible purpose was afoot.[245]

But DOMA was also the perpetuation of a different and largely
discredited historical practice: the tradition of treating gay people,
and in this case specifically gay relationships, as at best unworthy
of serious consideration and, at worst, as a threat from which the
country and its institutions must be "defended."

a) **Departure from usual substantive considerations:
federalism.** The *Windsor* decision placed heavy emphasis on the
fact that DOMA was a departure from the usual practice of federalism in family law, and especially in the recognition of marital
status.[246] The classic statement of federalism in family law, quoted
many times since by the Court, came in 1890: "The whole subject
of the domestic relations of husband and wife, parent and child,
belongs to the laws of the states, and not to the laws of the United
States."[247] It's not that Congress has never legislated on the subject
of family law. It has done so in numerous ways, including the more
than one thousand rights and benefits that were denied in
DOMA.[248] And it's true that Congress did require states like Utah
to reject polygamy as a condition for entry into the union in the
late nineteenth century.[249] But the authority of the states to define
marriage, and to have this definition respected and relied upon by
the federal government even in the provision of federal rights and
benefits, is unquestioned. There had never before DOMA been a
single, across-the-board federal definition of marriage. Even the
nineteenth-century polygamy restriction did not purport to con-

---

[245] *Windsor*, 133 S Ct at 2693; *Romer v Evans*, 517 US 620, 633 (1996).

[246] *Windsor*, 133 S Ct at 2692. For a discussion of *Windsor*'s use of federalism, see
Courtney G. Joslin, *Windsor, Federalism, and Family Equality*, Columbia Law Review Sidebar (Colum L Rev, Oct 2013), online at http://columbialawreview.org/windsor-federalism-
and-family-equality/. States may similarly enact legislation or enforce policies that suspiciously depart from the usual substantive rules. After *Windsor*, a district court invalidated
Ohio's refusal to recognize the plaintiffs' Maryland same-sex marriage for purposes of
issuing a state death certificate, noting that Ohio had never before refused to recognize
a valid marriage from a sister state. *Obergefell v Wymyslo*, 2013 WL 6726688, *2, *23 (SD
Ohio). This reflected a substantive departure from the state's own historic practice of
recognizing valid foreign marriages even if those marriages could not have been entered
in Ohio, suggesting the possibility of animus.

[247] *In re Burrus*, 136 US 586, 593–94 (1890), quoted with approval in *Ankenbrandt v
Richards*, 504 US 689, 703 (1992).

[248] For a detailed discussion of family law and federalism, see Jill Elaine Hasday, *Family
Law Reimagined* ch 1 (forthcoming 2014).

[249] See Federal Enabling Act, Pub L No 112, 28 Stat 107 (1894).

strain the states already admitted to the union. As discussed in Section II.B above, DOMA's sharp departure from this substantive tradition was a major consideration in the Court's analysis of whether there was animus behind the law. It is now accepted in constitutional law that departures from substantive principles ordinarily guiding decision makers indicate a possible impermissible purpose.[250]

Two points are worth emphasizing here. The Court did not declare that unconstitutional animus will be found anytime Congress departs from traditional federalism. Unless the legislation is beyond Congress's enumerated and necessarily implied powers,[251] or otherwise invades some core aspect of state sovereignty,[252] or violates some other provision like those protecting individual rights,[253] the limits on its powers to legislate are political rather than constitutional.

While the Court acknowledged the existence of substantial federalism concerns in *Windsor*, its holding did not squarely rest on that ground.[254] The anti-animus principle is not another source of support for state power against federal intrusion. Rather, the departure from the usual respect for federalism engendered suspicion about why Congress acted as it did. It was another indicator, but not a proof, of animus.

The second and related point is that the departure was from the usual posture of deference by the *federal* government to the states. Though other factors might point toward animus in a *state* ban on same-sex marriages, this particular consideration would not. It is the states, after all, that have historically exercised the power to define marriage.

b) Historical background indicating past discrimination: anti-gay public policy. To identify an invidious purpose in government action, the Court has looked at historical practices in-

---

[250] See *Windsor*, 133 S Ct at 2697 (Roberts, CJ, dissenting); *Arlington Heights*, 429 US at 267.

[251] See, for example, *United States v Morrison*, 529 US 598, 607 (2000); *United States v Lopez*, 514 US 549, 567 (1995).

[252] See, for example, *Printz v United States*, 521 US 898, 932 (1997); *New York v United States*, 505 US 144, 177, 188 (1992).

[253] See, for example, *District of Columbia v Heller*, 554 US 570, 622 (2008).

[254] See discussion in Section I.

dicating discrimination against the group.[255] The sorry history of this country's legalized discrimination against homosexuals is striking for the absence of reasoned justifications, for arbitrary lines between conduct allowed and conduct forbidden, and for a tendency to use the asserted immorality of homosexual acts to justify widespread opprobrium of homosexual persons. That history suggests an unreasoning prejudice or aversion that lies beneath the surface of laws shutting out gay people. Even if the Court has not yet recognized that such a history justifies formal heightened scrutiny of all classifications based on sexual orientation, at least it raises a yellow flag alerting the Court to the increased risk of animus.

Through the nineteenth and into the twentieth centuries, every state had laws prohibiting anal sex, often called in state statutes "crimes against nature," "sodomy," or "buggery."[256] In the late nineteenth and early twentieth century, states also began specifically prohibiting oral sex. Prior to the late 1960s, sodomy laws applied regardless of the sex of the participants in the act and regardless of whether the couple was married. A husband and wife who engaged in oral sex were potentially as guilty as two men who had anal sex. However, there was little enforcement of the laws against private sex between consenting adults; and what occasional enforcement there was fell most harshly on homosexuals.

After the Civil War, cities and states began more aggressively regulating sexuality.[257] Some of the laws enacted during the early to mid-twentieth century were especially draconian. A 1911 Massachusetts law allowed the state to incarcerate "degenerates" (including homosexuals) and other "mental defectives" for indefinite periods of time in state mental institutions. More commonly, state laws called for sterilization or castration of moral degenerates and sexual perverts, usually for homosexual behavior. In an effort to "treat" homosexuals, hospitals performed prefrontal lobotomies,

---

[255] Much of the discussion in the section is drawn from Carpenter, *Flagrant Conduct* chs 1–2 (cited in note 210). Other sources for a review of the history of anti-gay laws and social stigma are William N. Eskridge, Jr., *Gaylaw: Challenging the Apartheid of the Closet* 328–37 (Harvard, 1999); Michael J. Klarman, *From the Closet to the Altar: Courts, Backlash, and the Struggle for Same-Sex Marriage* (Oxford, 2012); and Andrew Koppelman, *The Gay Rights Question in Contemporary American Law* (Chicago, 2002).

[256] Eskridge, *Gaylaw* at 328–37 (cited in note 255) (App. A1: listing dates of first sodomy laws for each state, starting in 1610).

[257] Id at 27–34.

injected massive doses of male hormones, and administered electric shock and other aversion therapy.[258]

Federal authorities also suppressed homosexuality. They seized and destroyed obscene publications, excluded immigrants convicted of sexual crimes, and barred military service by "degenerates,"[259] a ban not completely lifted until 2010. U.S. Customs censored or seized novels depicting homosexuality in a positive way, including the 1886 edition of *The Arabian Nights*. Authorities censored homosexual content from films.[260]

Immediately following World War II, American society and government became increasingly alarmed by the spread of Communism, which was linked in the public mind to deviant sexuality. Between 1946 and 1961 alone, when arrests for violation of sodomy laws reached historic highs, the state "imposed criminal punishments on as many as a million lesbians and gay men engaged in consensual adult intercourse, dancing, kissing, or holding hands."[261] Officials often worried that homosexuals, like Communists, were infiltrating and undermining government agencies. Senator Joseph McCarthy (R-WI) was on the lookout for government officials who tolerated "flagrant homosexuals."[262] The "sexual perverts," warned one politico, were "just as dangerous as the actual Communists." In the space of seven months in 1950, President Harry Truman's administration investigated the alleged sexual perversion of 382 civil servants, most of whom subsequently resigned. A government report warned that "[o]ne homosexual can pollute an entire office." In fact, more State Department employees were fired for homosexuality than for alleged Communist sympathies in 1951 and 1952, the height of McCarthy-era red-hunting.[263]

At the same time, states were also cracking down on homosexuals. State and municipal laws were enforced to suppress homosexual association, including groups formed to advocate liberalization of sex regulations. States also used professional licensing

---

[258] Id at 42.

[259] Id at 34–37 (cited in note 255).

[260] Id at 47–48.

[261] Id at 60.

[262] David K. Johnson, *The Lavender Scare: The Cold War Persecution of Gays and Lesbians in the Federal Government* 26 (Chicago, 2004).

[263] Eskridge, *Gaylaw* at 69 (cited in note 255).

laws to prevent homosexuals from becoming doctors, dentists, pharmacists, embalmers, guardians, lawyers, teachers, and other professionals.[264]

State authorities used both direct and indirect methods to shut down gay bars. Liquor license laws requiring holders to be of "good character" were used both to prevent gay bars from opening and to shut them down when they slipped through the system. States and municipalities closed gay bars through business and liquor license schemes. A 1954 Miami ordinance, for example, made it illegal for a bar owner "to knowingly allow two or more persons who are homosexuals, lesbians or perverts to congregate or remain in his place of business." This one-homo-per-bar rule resulted in the closing of all of Miami's gay bars by the late 1950s.[265] New York's State Liquor Authority, among others, prohibited bars from serving prostitutes and homosexuals.

Law enforcement authorities aggressively used police stakeouts at suspected gay bars, decoy operations, and police raids to arrest large numbers of socializing homosexuals. For example, a 1960 raid on a San Francisco bar resulted in the disorderly conduct arrests of 103 people for same-sex dancing. Remarkably, when a serial killer targeted homosexuals in Santa Monica in 1956, police used details of the killer's confession to start an anti-gay cleanup of the city.[266]

Gays reacted to this crusade in part by attempting to organize politically. Two fledgling gay-rights groups, the Mattachine Society (mostly men) and the Daughters of Bilitis (women), formed in the 1950s. Mattachine emerged in Los Angeles in 1950; DOB, in San Francisco in 1955.[267] The FBI closely monitored their activities, beginning an internal security investigation of Mattachine in 1953 and of DOB in 1959. Neither group, of course, represented a credible national security threat. "Nonetheless," William Eskridge writes, "FBI agents infiltrated both organizations, archived their declarations and publications, reported their meetings and activities, recruited informants, compiled lists of members

---

[264] Id at 72–74.

[265] Id at 78–80.

[266] Id at 63–65.

[267] John D'Emilio, *Gay Politics and Community in San Francisco Since World War II*, in Martin Duberman, Martha Vicinus, and George Chauncey, Jr., eds, *Hidden From History: Reclaiming the Gay & Lesbian Past* 460 (Meridian, 1990).

whom they could identify, and speculated on the organizations' influence and future activities." Agents interviewed the staff of the Mattachine's publication, *One*, and notified their employers. Group members met in secret and resorted to using pseudonyms to protect their identity. Similar monitoring and harassment of gay groups by state and federal authorities occurred throughout the country. Police harassment and spying on gay organizations continued into the 1970s.[268] Police raids on gay bars and other forms of harassment of homosexuals continued well into the 1990s in some places, including the Lone Star State of Texas.

The case of Texas is illustrative. The state banned gay sex in 1973 in a so-called "homosexual conduct" law, but in the very same year it legalized heterosexual sodomy, adultery, and even bestiality. This was nonsense to one Texas appeals court judge, a Republican and self-described "country lawyer," who had no familiarity with gay-rights causes. In an interview about the *Lawrence* case, he reported that when the litigation reached his court he wondered how the state could justify a surgically precise ban on gay sex. "I kept thinking that if they decriminalized all those things that one would normally say are immoral, then why did they leave this one in? There had to be a reason," he recalled thinking, obviously still baffled. "And nobody could explain to me why."[269]

The Court seemed to acknowledge the history of anti-gay laws in *Romer*, when it suggested that homosexuals "needed" the protection of specific antidiscrimination laws and for that reason concluded that such laws did not extend "special rights" to gays.[270] Laws forbidding anti-gay discrimination guaranteed equal rights. In *Windsor* itself, Justice Kennedy noted that most Americans had never given a thought to the possibility of marriage between two people of the same sex—a literal thoughtlessness, the lack of thought, about the needs of a class of people.[271]

DOMA was adopted at a time when gay sex was still illegal in more than a dozen states, when gays and lesbians were barred from serving openly in the military, when federal law and all but a handful of states permitted gays to be fired or denied housing because of sexual orientation, when a solid majority of Americans

---

[268] Eskridge, *Gaylaw* at 75–76, 114 (cited in note 255).

[269] Carpenter, *Flagrant Conduct* at 167 (cited in note 210).

[270] *Romer v Evans*, 517 US 620, 631 (1996).

[271] *Windsor*, 133 S Ct at 2689.

believed homosexual relations were immoral, and when there were—despite the "defense" asserted in the title of the act—no homosexual marriages or even civil unions to defend against. While significant progress toward equality under the law had been made by 1996, that progress was subject to constant and strident backlash, like the voters' decision to bar all civil rights protections for gays in Colorado's Amendment 2.

These considerations alone support the view that gays and lesbians have historically been the target of systemic and legalized discrimination at the state and federal levels. No federal appeals court has denied that fact, even though most appeals courts have refused to treat sexual-orientation discrimination as suspect. Any legislative or electoral act excluding gays from benefits and protections available to others comes to the courts with at least this indicator that animus might be afoot. The fact of such discrimination is not enough by itself to invalidate the exclusion under the anti-animus doctrine, for that would turn the doctrine into simply a stand-in for heightened scrutiny. But it does mean that every enactment excluding gays faces additional scrutiny because it carries a large risk that it was materially driven by animus.

DOMA, as a law intentionally excluding gay couples from common benefits and protections, came to the Court with at least this factor leaning against it. This is true even before examining the other factors that, taken together, decisively show animus in DOMA's passage. This factor would also weigh against a state constitutional amendment banning same-sex marriages.

3. *Procedure.* The process by which legislation is adopted can also offer clues about whether its adoption was driven by animus. Evidence of animus in DOMA can be found in the sequence of events that led to passage, the legislative procedure Congress used to pass it, and the legislative history accompanying its passage. It helps answer the question whether decision makers were lashing out at an unpopular group. It reveals that legislators gave no serious consideration to a more limited imposition on the affected class. And evidence from the legislative history, including numerous statements by members of Congress, exposes the deeply malevolent attitudes upon which legislators acted against gay couples. These considerations support the conclusion that DOMA arose from unconstitutional animus.

a) **Expedited passage.** From introduction to final passage,

DOMA was pending for just four months, and much of that ab-
breviated period was consumed by congressional vacation time. It
was moved into committee hearings with just thirty legislative days
left before the 104th Congress adjourned for the fall campaign.[272]
Why the haste? No state or nation had yet recognized gay marriage. There was no impending federal court decision mandating
nationwide recognition of gay marriage. No federal suit had even
been filed, which should not be surprising: *Bowers v Hardwick* was
still good law, allowing homosexual acts to be criminalized. Only
the Hawaii litigation had even been filed. The trial court had not
begun hearing testimony when DOMA was introduced. A final
decision from the Hawaii Supreme Court was probably at least
two years away.[273] The rush to block same-sex couples from the
altar cannot be explained by an actual rush of same-sex couples
to the altar.

There was one impending event for which the hasty passage of
DOMA was exquisitely timed: the election of 1996. This fact was
noted frequently in press reports and during the congressional
debate by Democrats.[274] Republicans denied any such political motivation, but did so in a way that hinted at their desire not even
to think about the issue. "Political? I wish I'd never heard of this
issue. This is a miserable, uncomfortable, queasy issue. There's
no political gain, but there is a moral issue. . . . [S]ome of us think
same-sex unions legitimated by the Government trivialize marriage and condone public immorality, and the politics of that are
miserable."[275]

The unusual speed of Congress's action on DOMA, and its
refusal to study the law's effects or possible alternatives to it, might

---

[272] *Defense of Marriage Act, Hearing Before the Subcommittee on the Constitution of the House Judiciary Committee*, 104th Cong, 2d Sess 37 (1996) (statement of Representative Conyers) ("*May 15, 1996 Hearing*").

[273] This point was made repeatedly by opponents of DOMA, see, for example, Defense of Marriage Act, 104th Cong, 2d Sess, in 142 Cong Rec H7491 (July 12, 1996) (statement of Representative Skaggs) ("*July 12, 1996 Debate*"), and was not refuted by supporters.

[274] See, for example, id at H7482 (statement of Representative Frank); *Defense of Marriage Act*, 104th Cong, 2d Sess, in 142 Cong Rec S10101 (Sept 10, 1996) (statement of Senator Kennedy) ("*Sept 10, 1996 Debate*"). Another large round of marriage bans, this time at the state level, came during the election season of 2004. See Sarah Kershaw, *Gay Marriage Bans Gain Wide Support in 10 States*, NY Times (Nov 3, 2004), online at http:/ /www.nytimes.com/2004/11/03/politics/campaign/03gay.html.

[275] *Markup Session on H.R. 3396, The Defense of Marriage Act, Subcommittee on the Constitution of the House Judiciary Committee*, 104th Cong, 2d Sess 53–54 (May 30, 1996) (statement of Representative Hyde) ("*Markup Session*").

be defended as a show of unusual efficiency rather than unseemly purpose. Nobody wants Congress to plod along where it need not do so. But DOMA's reach was so broad and its implications for the targeted group so momentous that a more thoughtful and thorough consideration was called for.

b) Rejection of proposals for study and more limited application. It's not that leaders in Congress were not presented with ideas for further study, or for some substantive limit on the reach of DOMA. Some supporters claimed that DOMA was needed to limit federal payments to spouses.[276] "We have enough problems financing our Social Security trust funds," claimed DOMA sponsor Jim Sensenbrenner. If DOMA was not enacted, he warned, "there will be a huge expansion of the number of people eligible to receive Medicare survivor benefits."[277] Another House member said that failure to pass DOMA would "take money out of the pockets of working families across America" and use that money to support same-sex marriages, ignoring that same-sex couples were also part of working families.[278] All Americans would be "paying for benefits for homosexual marriages."[279] Yet another wondered whether same-sex marriage might "have an enormous financial impact on our country."[280]

But nobody had any idea how much federal recognition of same-sex marriage would cost, or even whether recognition might save the federal government money in the long run because more spouses would be providing care to each other rather than relying on government services.[281] The cost of providing benefits to mar-

---

[276] *Providing for Consideration of H.R. 3396, Defense of Marriage Act*, 104th Cong, 2d Sess, in 142 Cong Rec H7276 (July 11, 1996) (statement of Representative Largent) (*"July 11, 1996 Debate I"*).

[277] *July 12, 1996 Debate*, 142 Cong Rec at H7484 (cited in note 273) (statement of Representative Sensenbrenner).

[278] Id at H7493 (statement of Representative Weldon).

[279] Id at H7495 (statement of Representative Lipinski).

[280] *Sept 10, 1996 Debate*, 142 Cong Rec at S10116 (cited in note 274) (statement of Senator Burns).

[281] In fact, in 2004 the Congressional Budget Office estimated that federal recognition of same-sex marriage would *save* the federal government a modest amount of money: in some cases, recognizing same-sex marriages would increase outlays and revenues; in other cases, it would have the opposite effect. The Congressional Budget Office (CBO) estimates that on net, those impacts would improve the budget's bottom line to a small extent: by less than $1 billion in each of the next 10 years (CBO's usual estimating period). That result assumed that same-sex marriages were legalized in all 50 states and recognized by the federal government. Letter and Report from Douglas Holtz-Eakin, Director, Con-

ried same-sex couples was repeatedly cited in the congressional debate as a justification for DOMA, but that cost was never examined, verified, or even estimated. Supporters acknowledged that they simply did not know what the recognition of same-sex marriage in one or more states might cost the federal government in benefits to spouses, but they assumed the worst.[282] Senator Phil Gramm speculated that there might be "hundreds of thousands" of beneficiaries created under federal and state law if same-sex marriage were permitted, but "no one knows what the number would be."[283] No one knew what *any* of the numbers would be. Senator Byrd asked the relevant questions, but had no answers:

> I urge my colleagues to think of the potential cost involved here. How much is it going to cost the Federal Government if the definition of "spouse" is changed? . . . What is the added cost in Medicare and Medicaid benefits if a new meaning is suddenly given to these terms? I know I do not have any reliable estimates of what such a change would mean, but then, I do not know of anyone who does. That is the point—nobody knows for sure.[284]

In other words, Byrd's colleagues were to think about something in the absence of any knowledge or study of it.

One proposal was that, before it was voted upon, DOMA's costs and benefits should be reviewed and studied in the regular committee process.[285] This proposal was summarily dismissed. It seems that the mere possibility that same-sex relationships might draw to some extent from public funds at some date in the future was enough to justify denying them more than one thousand public benefits—even ones that cost nothing. The interests of same-sex couples simply did not merit any consideration by Congress.

---

gressional Budget Office, to Honorable Steve Chabot, Chairman, Subcomm on the Constitution, Comm on the Judiciary 2 (June 21, 2004), online at http://www.cbo.gov/sites/default/files/cbofiles/ftpdocs/55xx/doc5559/06-21-samesexmarriage.pdf.

[282] *July 11, 1996 Debate I*, 142 Cong Rec at H7274 (cited in note 276) (statement of Representative McInnis).

[283] *Sept 10, 1996 Debate*, 142 Cong Rec at S10106 (cited in note 274) (statement of Senator Gramm).

[284] Id at S10111 (statement of Senator Byrd). He then speculated about the cost: "I do not think, though, that it is inconceivable that the costs associated with such a change could amount to hundreds of millions of dollars, if not billions—if not billions—of Federal taxpayer dollars." Id. The closest anyone came to an estimate of added cost was Senator Bob Kerrey (D-NE), who calculated that nationwide recognition of same-sex marriage would add at most 2 percent to the number of marriages in the country. Id at S10124 (statement of Senator Kerrey).

[285] *July 11, 1996 Debate I*, 142 Cong Rec at H7272 (cited in note 276) (statement of Representative Moakley).

An undecided House Republican offered to vote for DOMA if it were amended to require that the Government Accountability Office study the ability of same-sex couples to provide for their families and protect their relationships. The study was to be completed by October 1997 and would provide some empirical grounding for possible further legislative action. While the idea was initially embraced by DOMA sponsor Representative Henry Hyde (R-IL), it was rejected in the House Rules Committee and never made it to the floor. The Congress that gave the nation DOMA had no interest in studying the real-world hardships faced by gay families.[286]

Another idea was that, to the extent the concern was judicial activism, DOMA could be limited to contexts in which a state court (rather than the state legislature or the people through a referendum) had ordered the state to recognize gay marriages.[287] Yet congressional leaders were undeterred, revealing that concerns about judicial overreaching were largely makeweight arguments for something else.

Even as DOMA was justified by a stated desire to defend "traditional marriage," other proposals to protect lifelong monogamous marriage were summarily rejected. Representative Patricia Schroeder (D-CO), for example, proposed that the federal definition of marriage should exclude any subsequent marriage unless the first marriage was terminated on fault grounds.[288] This would have seriously eroded the no-fault divorce revolution that marriage traditionalists had long said was undermining the institution. It might also save the federal government a lot of money in benefits payments. But several sponsors of DOMA were living in their second or third marriages.[289] They would have lost federal recognition under the proposal. Large numbers of their heterosexual constituents, too, would have lost their own benefits. The idea was dismissed as a "diversion."[290] Sponsors of DOMA were es-

---

[286] *July 12, 1996 Debate*, 142 Cong Rec at H7492–93 (cited in note 273) (statement of Representative Gunderson).

[287] Id at H7487 (statement of Representative Frank).

[288] See *July 11, 1996 Debate I*, 142 Cong Rec at H7272 (cited in note 276) (statement of Representative Moakley); id at H7273 (statement of Representative Schroeder).

[289] Id at H7274 (statement of Representative Abercrombie) ("Because I understand some of the people sponsoring this bill are on their second or third marriages. I wonder which one they are defending.").

[290] Id at H7273 (statement of Representative McInnis).

sentially saying to gay couples: "Traditional marriage restrictions for thee, but not for me."

c) Legislative history. The Court has been willing to consult evidence from legislative history to determine whether a law arose from unconstitutional animus. It did so in *Moreno*, observing that members of Congress had openly targeted "hippies" and "hippie communes" for exclusion from the food stamp program. In his opinion for the Court in *Windsor*, Justice Kennedy famously cited evidence from the legislative history of DOMA to show that it reflected impermissible animus.[291] This history, he wrote, showed that denying the "equal dignity" of same-sex marriages was "more than an incidental effect of DOMA." It was the "essence" of DOMA, its core purpose.

> The House Report announced its conclusion that "it is both appropriate and necessary for Congress to do what it can to defend the institution of traditional heterosexual marriage. . . . H.R. 3396 is appropriately entitled the 'Defense of Marriage Act.' The effort to redefine 'marriage' to extend to homosexual couples is a truly radical proposal that would fundamentally alter the institution of marriage." H.R. Rep. No. 104-664, pp. 12–13 (1996). The House concluded that DOMA expresses "both moral disapproval of homosexuality, and a moral conviction that heterosexuality better comports with traditional (especially Judeo-Christian) morality. *Id.*, at 16 (footnote deleted). The stated purpose of the law was to promote an "interest in protecting the traditional moral teachings reflected in heterosexual-only marriage laws." *Ibid.*[292]

In *Windsor*, the House Report was the smoking gun of animus. Former Solicitor General Paul Clement, representing the Bipartisan Legal Advisory Group, did not try to defend the conclusions or statements in the committee report, but suggested that such evidence should not be enough for the Court to strike down a statute.[293]

But the fact is that the House Report only scratched the surface of a large mass of similar, and even more hysterical, denunciations

---

[291] Following *Windsor*, one district court struck down a denial of benefits to same-sex domestic partners, relying in part on the legislative history of the Michigan law being challenged. *Bassett v Snyder*, 951 F Supp 2d 939, 968–69 (E D Mich 2013). Among other scholarly treatments of animus in the legislative history of DOMA, see Mark Strasser, *DOMA, the Constitution, and the Promotion of Good Public Policy*, 5 Albany Gov't L Rev 613, 617–19 (2012).

[292] *Windsor*, 133 S Ct at 2693.

[293] Oral Argument Transcript, *United States v Windsor*, No 12-307, *74 (March 27, 2013), at http://www.supremecourt.gov/oral_arguments/argument_transcripts/12-307_jnt1.pdf.

of homosexuals and homosexuality in the proceedings to pass
DOMA in the House and Senate. It was the tip of an animus
iceberg. The legislative history leading to passage of DOMA indicated both that many members of Congress were motivated by
deep hostility toward homosexuality and that many others were
completely unconcerned about their interests.[294]

One can, of course, glean many purposes from the legislative
record. Supporters of DOMA, mindful of the need to argue that
it was not an act of malice against homosexuals, have often con-
jured a sanitized version of the congressional purposes behind the
law. In this narrative, DOMA was not the result of hatred, but of
a prudent caution toward important social change; not a dispar-
agement of gay relationships, but a reaffirmation of the superiority
of moms and dads; not a condemnation of gays at all, but a mild
expression of traditional religious views about sexuality and marriage. Does this happy tale hold up?

According to the legislative record, DOMA's exclusion in 1996
of all married same-sex couples from all federal marital protections
and obligations was intended to:

1. "defend[] and nurtur[e] the institution of traditional, heterosexual marriage,"
2. "promot[e] heterosexuality,"
3. "encourag[e] responsible procreation and child-rearing,"
4. "protect[] . . . democratic self-governance,"
5. "preserve scarce government resources" by preventing marital
   benefits from "hav[ing] to be made available to homosexual
   couples and surviving spouses of homosexual marriages," and
6. express "moral disapproval of homosexuality, and a moral conviction that heterosexuality better comports with traditional
   (especially Judeo-Christian) morality."[295]

Of these, the first, second, and sixth were more or less explicit
condemnations of homosexuality. ("Promoting heterosexuality" is
only a nicer way of condemning homosexuality.) These will be
discussed in more detail immediately below. The third was not

---

[294] For catalogs of some of this legislative history, see generally Mae Kuykendall, *Essay:
On Defined Terms and Cultural Consensus*, 13 J L & Pol 199 (1997); and Note, *Litigating
the Defense of Marriage Act: The Next Battleground for Same-Sex Marriage*, 117 Harv L Rev
2684, 2701–04 (2004).

[295] *Defense of Marriage Act*, HR Rep No 104-664, 104th Cong, 2d Sess 12–13, 15, 17–
18 (1996).

necessarily anti-gay, but was so flimsily served by DOMA that it is fairly understood as a pretext for underlying hostility. It will be discussed in Section III.B.5.b below. The fourth was not homophobic but could have been served by a much narrower and less burdensome law like the proposed alternative, discussed above in Section III.B.2, denying federal recognition only from states where same-sex marriage was judicially imposed. The fifth was not homophobic, but as noted in Section III.B.2, was unstudied by Congress and was unsupported in any empirical evidence. The failure to consider any alternative to DOMA that might be less injurious to married gay couples, or to study the law's actual budgetary effects, strongly suggests that these avowed congressional purposes were makeweight arguments.

Knowing that the Court had just decided *Romer*, one of the primary authors of DOMA tried to inoculate it against constitutional challenge.

> [S]aying that marriage means today what it has meant through our entire history is certainly not a novel idea. . . . [T]here are very clear legitimate government interests in this legislation. It is not motivated by animus, but rather a reaction to deliberate efforts by opponents of heterosexual marriages, being the legal basis for the building block of our society . . . .[296]

This was in fact the very defense offered against animus claims in the *Windsor* litigation. But pro forma statements in Congress could not mask the reality of what happened as the congressional debate heated up. What follows is a very incomplete catalogue of some examples of this hostility.

i) Active malice: From the time of its introduction in the House of Representatives on May 7, 1996, the defense of the Defense of Marriage Act was characterized by inflammatory rhetoric directed at gay people and their relationships. Numerous statements by members of Congress during committee hearings and floor debates evidenced deep hostility.

Many DOMA supporters, in both floor speeches and legislative hearings, described the effects of same-sex marriage in apocalyptic and paranoid terms. Allowing same-sex marriage would be a "disastrous policy," warned the chairman of the House Subcommittee

---

[296] *Markup Session*, 104th Cong, 2d Sess at 41 (cited in note 275) (statement of Representative Bob Barr).

on the Constitution.[297] Admitting "my bias" for "traditional heterosexual marriage," a sponsor asserted without explanation that
same-sex marriage would "derogate it."[298] Same-sex marriage was
an attempt to eliminate the distinction between "what is right and
wrong."[299] It was a "frontal attack on the institution of marriage."[300] It would "abolish thousands of years of legal tradition"
and "destroy every other State's laws regulating marriage."[301] The
country "cannot survive" the "destruction of the family unit" that
gay marriage would cause.[302] It was nothing less than an "assault
on America's families and the sacred institution of marriage."[303]
It would "destroy thousands of years of tradition."[304] These denunciations exploited unsubstantiated fears and stereotypes of gay
people as immoral, subversive, and disproportionately influential
enemies of the country's history and its institutions.

Supporters of DOMA repeatedly condemned homosexual relationships. In many speeches this condemnation was expressed as
an affirmation of "nature," morality, and tradition. "What is at
stake in this controversy?" asked DOMA sponsor Representative
Charles Canady (R-FL) as debate on the House floor opened.
"Nothing less than our collective moral understanding—as expressed in the law—of the essential nature of the family—the fundamental building block of society."[305] Only opposite-sex marriage
"comports with nature and our Judeo-Christian moral heritage."
At other times the condemnation of gay relationships was more
explicit. Law "should not treat homosexual relationships as the
moral equivalent of heterosexual relationships on which the family
is based. That is why we are here today."[306] Same-sex marriages

---

[297] *May 15, 1996 Hearing*, 104th Cong, 2d Sess at 2 (cited in note 272) (statement of
Representative Canady).

[298] Id at 32–33 (statement of Representative Sensenbrenner).

[299] Id at 36 (statement of Representative Inglis).

[300] Id at 37 (statement of Representative Barr).

[301] Id at 75 (statement of Representative Whyman).

[302] *Defense of Marriage Act*, 104th Cong, 2d Sess, in 142 Cong Rec H7442 (July 11,
1996) (statement of Representative Hutchinson) (*"July 11, 1996 Debate II"*).

[303] Id at H7449 (statement of Representative Packard).

[304] *July 12, 1996 Debate*, 142 Cong Rec at H7495 (cited in note 273) (statement of
Representative Lipinski).

[305] *July 11, 1996 Debate II*, 142 Cong Rec at H7411 (cited in note 302) (statement of
Representative Canady).

[306] Id.

would "demean" and "trivialize" everyone else's marriages.[307] Gay marriage threatened "the moral fiber that keeps this Nation together" and "the future of families."[308] It would be "the final straw."[309] Such condemnations of homosexuals and homosexuality, once understood as a profound and positive moral commitment, are now constitutionally illegitimate as justifications for excluding gay people from rights and recognition freely given to others.

A debate formally about federal recognition of same-sex marriages easily slipped into open expression of a general disgust toward homosexuality itself, reflecting the underlying animus. Gay people were described as sick, perverted, and dangerous. "Homosexuality has been discouraged in all cultures because it is inherently wrong and harmful to individuals, families, and societies," declared a House member.[310] Same-sex marriages not only demeaned marriage, another argued, but "[t]hey legitimize unnatural and immoral behavior."[311] Senator Jesse Helms (R-NC) thundered that gays "seek to force their agenda upon the vast majority of the American people who reject the homosexual lifestyle."[312] DOMA, in Helms's view, was needed to protect marriage and families against "those who seek to destroy them and who are willing to tear apart America's moral fabric in the process."[313] Members rejected the idea that tolerance should play a role in the debate. "Tolerance does not require us to say that all lifestyles are morally equal. It doesn't require us to weaken our social ideals. . . . And it should not require special recognition for those who have rejected that standard."[314]

One representative seized on the argument that homosexual orientation is not consciously chosen as an admission that "it is

---

[307] *Markup Session*, 104th Cong, 2d Sess at 53–54 (cited in note 275) (statement of Representative Hyde).

[308] *July 12, 1996 Debate*, 142 Cong Rec at H7488 (cited in note 273) (statement of Representative Stearns).

[309] Id at H7495 (statement of Representative Lipinski).

[310] Id at H7487 (statement of Representative Funderburk).

[311] Id at H7494 (statement of Representative Smith).

[312] *The Defense of Marriage Act*, 104th Cong, 2d Sess, in 142 Cong Rec S10068 (Sept 9, 1996) (statement of Senator Helms) ("*Helms's Remarks*").

[313] Id.

[314] *Sept 10, 1996 Debate*, 142 Cong Rec at S10114 (cited in note 274) (statement of Senator Coats).

not a desirable lifestyle, and there's something wrong with it."[315] He wanted gays to be "rescued" and "returned to where they can have a happy lifestyle, because I think it's inherently destructive."[316] Supporters read into the Congressional Record an especially odd denunciation of acceptance for homosexuals: "Overcome by miasmic gases of diversity and inclusion wafting from the Nineties swamp, we have turned into the Punchdrunk kid, a twitching lummox with cauliflower ears who mumbles 'Sure, Jake, sure' to everybody."[317]

Senator Nickles (R-OK) invoked stereotypes of gay couples as sex-obsessed, threatening traditional families by their presence in polite society so much that landlords should be able to deny them housing.

> [I]f you are saying if a person had 10 apartment complexes and he or she had rented those out to—I'm going to say traditional families, and you had a couple of vacancies and you had two homosexual couples come in with T-shirts that said, "I'm gay and proud of it. Let's make love," would I want that person to be able to deny renting those two units? Yes, I think they should have the right to do that. . . .[318]

Representative Tom Coburn (R-OK) took the gloves off, making it clear that the real objective was to condemn homosexuality:

> We have heard a lot tonight. We heard a lot in the debate on the rule about discrimination. We just heard about family values. I do not think it is about any of those things. *The real debate is about homosexuality and whether or not we sanction homosexuality in this country.*[319]

Representative Canady, a chief sponsor, agreed. "That is what is at stake here: Should the law express its neutrality between heterosexual and homosexual relationships? Should the law elevate homosexual unions to the same status as the heterosexual relationships on which the traditional family is based? . . ."[320] Citing

---

[315] *May 15, 1996 Hearing*, 104th Cong, 2d Sess at 236 (cited in note 272) (statement of Representative Inglis).

[316] Id at 236–27 (statement of Representative Inglis).

[317] *July 12, 1996 Debate*, 142 Cong Rec at H7494 (cited in note 273) (reprinting of Florence King, *The Misanthrope's Corner*, National Review, June 3, 1996).

[318] *The Defense of Marriage Act: Hearing Before the Committee on the Judiciary on S 1740*, 104th Cong, 2d Sess 12–13 (1996) (statement of Senator Nickles) ("*July 11, 1996 Hearing*").

[319] *July 11, 1996 Debate II*, 142 Cong Rec at H7444 (cited in note 302) (statement of Representative Coburn) (emphasis added).

[320] Id at H7447 (statement of Representative Canady).

the work of the Family Research Council, one House member asserted that all cultures discourage homosexuality "because it is inherently wrong and harmful to individuals, families, and societies."[321] Another said that same-sex marriage would "legitimize unnatural and immoral behavior."[322] "[T]wo men loving each other does not hurt anybody else's marriage," said Representative Hyde, "but it demeans, it lowers the concept of marriage by making it something that it should not be and is not, celebrating conduct that is not approved by the majority of the people."[323]

Representative Coburn reported his constituents' views on homosexuality, which he said derived from biblical sources:

> I come from a district in Oklahoma who [sic] has very profound beliefs that homosexuality is wrong. I represent that district. They base that belief on what they believe God says about homosexuality. . . . What they believe is, is that homosexuality is based on perversion, that it is based on lust . . . it is discrimination towards the [homosexual] act, not toward the [homosexual] individuals.[324]

As *Cleburne* made clear, the government cannot act to satisfy constituents' animosity toward a group. Their irrational fears, stereotypes, and unsubstantiated assertions are no more permissible grounds for inflicting injury on a group than is legislators' own personal malice toward the group.

The distinction between the "act" and the "individual" cited by DOMA supporters is a common refrain in condemnations of homosexuality, and was echoed in Justice Scalia's dissent in *Romer*. But the distinction fuels general condemnations of homosexual persons, just as *Lawrence* recognized that a homosexual conduct law stimulates prejudice in the public and private spheres toward homosexual persons. Coburn alluded to "studies" that he said found that 43 percent of all homosexuals had more than 500 sexual partners during their lives. Yet the studies reporting hyper-prom-

---

[321] *July 12, 1996 Debate*, 142 Cong Rec at H7487 (cited in note 273) (statement of Representative Funderburk).

[322] Id at H7494 (statement of Representative Smith).

[323] Id at H7501 (statement of Representative Hyde).

[324] *July 11, 1996 Debate II*, 142 Cong Rec at H7444 (cited in note 302) (statement of Representative Coburn).

iscuity among gay men have been debunked as junk science,[325] and at any rate do not even purport to make claims about the sexual practices of lesbians.

In a debate ostensibly about federal recognition of marriage, homosexual sex was never far from the congressional mind. "The homosexual movement has been very successful in intimidating the psychiatric profession. Now people who object to sodomy, to two men penetrating each other are homophobic," said Representative Hyde. "They have the phobia, not the people doing this act. That is a magnificent accomplishment for public relations."[326]

Members openly and cavalierly disparaged gay parents and their families. Gay couples were not good parents, many members suggested, and "do not make strong families. . . . No society has ever granted same-sex unions the same kind of official recognition granted to marriages, and for good reason."[327] "If same-sex marriage is accepted," said Senator Robert Byrd (D-WV), "America will have said that children do not need a mother and a father, two mothers or two fathers will be just as good. This would be a catastrophe."[328] Not content to be the Senate's self-appointed historian, Byrd also took on the mantle of Senate sociologist by asserting that in gay relationships "emotional bonding oftentimes does not take place."[329] There was absolutely no basis for this bald assertion and insult to same-sex couples. Nor did Byrd even attempt to offer one. Senator Trent Lott (R-MI) suggested that gay relationships were not valuable to society, but were merely "a living arrangement of two persons of the same sex."[330] This unfounded characterization demeaned the committed relationships of same-

---

[325] Eugene Volokh, *The Myth of the Median Hyper-Promiscuous Gay Male*, The Volokh Conspiracy (May 22, 2003), online at http://www.volokh.com/2003_05_18_volokh_archive.html#200329250. Even if the myth were fact, it's not clear why gay-male promiscuity would be relevant to whether same-sex marriages should be permitted, especially for lesbian couples. See Dale Carpenter, *The Traditionalist Case: The Contagious-Promiscuity Argument*, The Volokh Conspiracy (Nov 2, 2005), available online at http://www.volokh.com/posts/1130971386.shtml.

[326] *July 12, 1996 Debate*, 142 Cong Rec at H7501 (cited in note 273) (statement of Representative Hyde).

[327] *Sept 10, 1996 Debate*, 142 Cong Rec at S10117 (cited in note 274) (statement of Senator Faircloth).

[328] Id at S10111 (statement of Senator Byrd).

[329] Id at S10108 (statement of Senator Byrd).

[330] Id at S10101 (statement of Senator Lott).

sex couples. Reliance on unsubstantiated fears and stereotypes is evidence of animus.

Members of Congress all but claimed that God himself demanded the passage of DOMA because they said the Bible condemned homosexuality.[331] "Permit me to be theological and philosophical, for a moment," said one. "I believe that as a people, as a people [sic], as a God-fearing people, at times, that there are what are viewed, what I believe are called depraved judgments by people in our society," he observed. "They come in all forms of sin." Momentarily lapsing into King James English, he intoned that "God breatheth light into the face of chaos" and "shineth the light into our face." He continued:

> We as legislators and leaders for the country are in the midst of a chaos, an attack upon God's principles. God laid down that one man and one woman is a legal union. That is marriage, known for thousands of years. That God-given principle is under attack. It is under attack. There are those in our society that try to shift us away from a society based on religious principles to humanistic principles; that the human being can do whatever they want, as long as it feels good and does not hurt others.[332]

Representatives repeated the baseless historical claim that homosexuality had destroyed any society that tolerated it:

> We hear about diversity, but we do not hear about perversity, and I think that we should not be afraid to talk about the very issues that are at the core of this. . . . The fact is, no society that has lived through the transition to homosexuality and the perversion which it lives and what it brought forth.[333]

Another representative concurred that "no culture that has ever embraced homosexuality has ever survived."[334] Representative Bob Barr (R-GA) was especially florid in his depiction of modern-day America as a place where "Rome burned, Nero fiddled":

---

[331] "Let us defend the oldest institution, the institution of marriage between male and female, as set forth in the Holy Bible." *Sept 10, 1996 Debate*, 142 Cong Rec at S10111 (cited in note 274) (statement of Senator Byrd). Whether sentiments of this kind might in some circumstances offend Establishment Clause principles is beyond the scope of this article.

[332] *July 12, 1996 Debate*, 142 Cong Rec at H7486 (cited in note 273) (statement of Representative Buyer).

[333] *July 11, 1996 Debate II*, 142 Cong Rec at H7444 (cited in note 302) (statement of Representative Coburn).

[334] *July 11, 1996 Debate I*, 142 Cong Rec at H7278 (cited in note 276) (statement of Representative Largent).

> The very foundations of our society are in danger of being burned. The flames of hedonism, the flames of narcissism, the flames of self-centered morality are licking at the very foundations of our society: the family unit. . . . What more does it take, my colleagues, to wake up and see that this is an issue being shouted at us by extremists intent, bent on forcing a tortured view of morality on the rest of the country?[335]

Senator Byrd drew similar lessons from ancient Greece and Rome, which he said were societies that declined because they had "waxed casual" about the uniqueness and importance of marriage.[336] He then chronicled the same-sex loves of the ancients, including Achilles and Patroclus, Catiline and his male lover, Julius Caesar and King Nicomedes, Nero and Sporus. Nero took Sporus to resorts in Greece and Italy, he remarked, "many a time, sweetly kissing him."[337] All of this was to note that same-sex marriage "make[s] a mockery" of marriage.[338]

Demonizing a group of people is a classic indication of animus against them. Gay-marriage advocates were condemned as "homosexual extremists" forming "[e]xtremist homosexual groups" and pushing "bizarre social experimentation upon unwilling participants."[339] Gay marriage was the product of "a radical element, a homosexual agenda that wants to redefine what marriage is," said Representative Steve Largent (R-OK).[340] Advocates' desire to formalize their love and commitment to each other was dismissed: "To them marriage means just two people living together alone. Is that not sweet? In other words, it means absolutely nothing."[341] Senator Helms claimed that "inch by inch, little by little, the homosexual lobby has chipped away at the moral stamina of some of America's courts and some legislators."[342] Senator Byrd agreed. "The drive for same-sex marriage is, in effect, an effort to make a sneak attack on society by encoding this aberrant behavior in

---

[335] *July 12, 1996 Debate*, 142 Cong Rec at H7482 (cited in note 273) (statement of Representative Barr).

[336] *Sept 10, 1996 Debate*, 142 Cong Rec at S10109 (cited in note 274) (statement of Senator Byrd).

[337] Id.

[338] Id at S10110.

[339] *May 15, 1996 Hearing*, 104th Cong, 2d Sess at 74–75 (cited in note 272) (statement of Representative Whyman).

[340] *July 11, 1996 Debate II*, 142 Cong Rec at H7443 (cited in note 302) (statement of Representative Largent).

[341] Id at H7445 (statement of Representative Barr).

[342] *Helms's Remarks*, 142 Cong Rec at S10068 (cited in note 312).

legal form before society itself has decided it should be legal," he warned.[343]

Overblown assertions about wealthy and privileged homosexuals also infected the debate. The efforts of gays for equal rights could not be compared to black civil rights struggles, one representative averred, because "homosexuals, by most studies that I'm aware of, have a higher standard of living than heterosexuals."[344] He did not mention what "studies" he had in mind. Without support, he also asserted that "it is obviously a choice to be homosexual."[345]

A particular fear of DOMA supporters was the effect that recognition might have on children and what they are taught in schools. The subtext was the blood libel of anti-gay rhetoric that homosexuals molest and "recruit" children. "I can't even imagine all the ramifications that that would have," said one state representative from Colorado. "What about the education of our children? What about health education? What about Madison Avenue? What about advertising?" she continued, as if gay advocates were going to convert children through slick marketing campaigns.[346] Representative Canady wondered whether children should be taught that it doesn't matter whether "they establish families with a partner of the opposite sex or cohabit with someone of the same sex," that "there is no moral difference between homosexual relationships and heterosexual relationships," and that "the parties to a homosexual union" are entitled to equal "rights and benefits and privileges"?[347] The implication was that, given a slight nudge, children might decide to be homosexual.[348]

Relatedly, another representative claimed that the same activists supporting gay marriage were also suing the Boy Scouts for discrimination under laws granting homosexuals "special rights." They wanted to "place young boys under homosexual men on

---

[343] *Sept 10, 1996 Debate*, 142 Cong Rec at S10110 (cited in note 274) (statement of Senator Byrd).

[344] *May 15, 1996 Hearing*, 104th Cong, 2d Sess at 236 (cited in note 272) (statement of Representative Inglis).

[345] Id.

[346] Id at 61 (statement of Representative Musgrave).

[347] *July 11, 1996 Debate II*, 142 Cong Rec at H7447 (cited in note 302) (statement of Representative Canady).

[348] For a discussion of the constitutional implications of these fears, particularly in the context of DOMA, see Clifford J. Rosky, *Fear of a Queer Child*, 61 Buff L Rev 607, 608 (2013); and Clifford J. Rosky, *No Promo Hetero: Children's Right to Be Queer*, 35 Cardozo L Rev 425, 448 (2013).

camping trips."[349] The image was a dog whistle evoking the outrageous and baseless stereotype of gay men as child predators.

Slippery-slope arguments were deployed to warn that the legal
recognition of same-sex relationships would lead to legalizing in-
cest and bestiality, among other things. The effect was dehuman-
izing. The redefinition of marriage "does not even have to be
limited to human beings, by the way. I mean it could be anything."[350] "How could we stop" at the recognition of same-sex
marriages "and say it should not also include two men and one
woman, or three men, four men, or an adult and a child?"[351] Representative Bob Dornan (R-CA) was incredulous that "we would
ever be discussing homosexuals have the same rights as the sac-
rament of holy matrimony." He predicted that "within 3 or 4 years
we are going to be discussing pedophilia only for males."[352]

ii) Passive malice: Beyond the numerous expressions of active
malice, there was evidence of what might be called passive malice
in the debate over DOMA. Congress failed even to consider the
interests of future married gay couples when it passed DOMA. It
conducted no study of these effects. No supporter of DOMA even
mentioned a possible impact on gay couples. As Koppelman notes:
"Congress was not thinking about solving a policy problem at all,
and it certainly was not thinking about the actual human beings
whom this law was going to injure. It lashed out at gay people for
the sake of pure political posturing."[353] DOMA "reflects the fan-
tasy, unfortunately quite common, that gay people can be wished
out of existence."[354] The failure to consider the needs of a group
burdened by the law was a serious failure of the political process
that should have been expected given the subject matter—marriage
and homosexuality.

It's not that *nobody* in Congress saw the extensive denial of rights

---

[349] *July 12, 1996 Debate*, 142 Cong Rec at H7487 (cited in note 273) (statement of
Representative Funderburk).

[350] *July 11, 1996 Debate II*, 142 Cong Rec at H7443 (cited in note 302) (statement of
Representative Largent).

[351] *July 11, 1996 Debate I*, 142 Cong Rec at H7276 (cited in note 276) (statement of
Representative Largent).

[352] *July 12, 1996 Debate*, 142 Cong Rec at H7489 (cited in note 273) (statement of
Representative Dornan).

[353] Koppelman, *Why Scalia Should Have Voted to Overturn DOMA* at 143 (cited in note
4).

[354] Id at 145.

and benefits that would be denied validly married couples. Opponents of DOMA noted that gay couples would lose

> Federal retirement benefits, health benefits under Federal programs, Federal housing benefits, burial rights, privilege against testifying against [a] partner in Federal trials, visitation rights at hospitals by partners, rights to family and medical leave to care for a partner, and many more programs which allow special rights to spouses.[355]

Representative Steve Gunderson (R-WI) cited letters from constituents who, among other deprivations and indignities, had been denied access to their partners dying in federally funded hospitals. He recounted the story of a friend who had recently lost his partner of sixteen years to AIDS. While the hospital allowed him to visit the dying partner, the funeral home refused to allow him to sign the formal documents or make funeral arrangements. "The debate fails to recognize the painful reality thrown on many innocent people who happen to be in long-term relationships outside of marriage," Representative Gunderson said.[356] Others cited similar practical problems faced by same-sex couples.[357] Nobody responded.

In fact, the striking thing about the entire congressional debate is that supporters of DOMA did not respond at all to these concerns. It's as if the concerns did not register as real human needs. To the extent legislators mentioned federal rights and benefits at all, it was only to complain that married gay couples were going to cost the government some unspecified and unstudied amount of money.[358] One representative remarked that his constituents were "outraged that their tax money could be spent paying veteran's benefits or Social Security based on the recognition of same-sex marriages."[359] A House co-sponsor said it would be irresponsible "to throw open the doors of the U.S. Treasury to be raided by the homosexual movement."[360]

---

[355] *July 12, 1996 Debate*, 142 Cong Rec at H7481 (cited in note 273) (statement of Representative Mink).

[356] Id at H7492 (statement of Representative Gunderson).

[357] *July 11, 1996 Hearing*, 104th Cong, 2d Sess at 11 (cited in note 318) (statement of Senator Simon).

[358] *July 12, 1996 Debate*, 142 Cong Rec at H7484 (cited in note 273) (statement of Representative Sensenbrenner).

[359] Id at H7487 (statement of Representative Funderburk).

[360] Id at H7488 (statement of Representative Barr).

Some members seemed annoyed at even having to consider the issue. "It is amazing to me . . . and disturbing that this debate should even be necessary,"[361] said Senator Coats. Right before the vote, Senator Nickles declared it was "almost absurd" that Congress would have to act.[362] He was even perturbed that gay spouses might be entitled to take time off to care for each other under the Family and Medical Leave Act of 1993.[363] The best course, sponsors said, was to legislate now and study the problem later. "It seems to me that the wise and prudent thing to do . . . is to keep the law the way it is now, and if there are any changes that are necessary . . . let the Congress deal with it legislatively, after hearings, where we know what we're doing and we know the financial impact it will have."[364] Congress was advised it should act before it knew what it was doing. Like the Queen of Hearts in *Alice in Wonderland*, Congress would have the "sentence first, verdict afterwards."

The House rejection of any attempt to study or consider the needs of gay families led Representative Gunderson to the following conclusion:

> Unfortunately, this action exposes those who advance this legislation for their real goals. There is no sincere attempt to simply reaffirm marriage. There is certainly no attempt to respond to legitimate and real issues facing many Americans in 1996. There is, unfortunately, every attempt to pursue a mean, political-wedge issue at the expense of the gay and lesbian community in this country.[365]

iii) Other motives: Not all of the stated aims of DOMA sounded in animus against gay couples. Indeed, the vast majority of members who spoke in committees and on the floor of the House and Senate cited several reasons for supporting DOMA. Some sponsors of the bill, for example, saw Section 2 of DOMA as a defense of states' rights to determine their own marriage policy—that is,

---

[361] *Sept 10, 1996 Debate*, 142 Cong Rec at S10114 (cited in note 274) (statement of Senator Coats).

[362] *Defense of Marriage Act—Rollcall Vote No 280 Leg*, 104th Cong, 2d Sess, in 142 Cong Rec S10129 (1996) (statement of Senator Nickles).

[363] *Sept 10, 1996 Debate*, 142 Cong Rec at S10103 (cited in note 274) (statement of Senator Nickles).

[364] *Markup Session*, 104th Cong, 2d Sess at 40 (cited in note 275) (statement of Representative Sensenbrenner).

[365] *July 12, 1996 Debate*, 142 Cong Rec at H7493 (cited in note 273) (statement of Representative Gunderson).

to prevent the "nationalization" of same-sex marriage.[366] But others asserted that while states should have their own power over marriage, "[t]he larger issue" was protecting "traditional family values."[367] Appeals to "tradition" were common,[368] as were condemnations of judicial activism. Many members celebrated the superior skills of opposite-sex parents. "Children do best in a family with a mom and a dad," asserted Representative Tom DeLay (R-TX),[369] although neither he nor others offered a plausible account of how federal recognition of valid same-sex marriages would make opposite-sex parents less successful.

It is far from clear that *every* legislator who voted for DOMA did so as a way to injure gay couples, or that every legislator was unconcerned that such injury would be the necessary by-product of the law. Senator Nancy Kassebaum (R-KS), who supported DOMA mainly as a way to protect states' power to decide the issue for themselves, was a notable exception to the rule of malignity. Her speech on the Senate floor was pained and humane:

> [N]o purpose is served by abandoning civility and a respect for differing viewpoints in the process. Nor should we forget that at the heart of the debate over homosexuality are individual Americans. An abstract subject takes on different dimensions when given the face of a friend, a family member, a coworker. The things we all hold dear—family, friendships, a job, a home—present a unique set of challenges for the gay community. It should come as little surprise that, like anyone else, gay men and women would like to live their lives without being defined only by their sexual orientation.[370]

She seemed implicitly to rebuke her colleagues for their strident tone:

> Congress is not the ideal forum for the resolution of these issues, nor will any piece of legislation settle them. However, the tone we set in our deliberations is one which will be echoed around kitchen tables and worksites throughout the Nation. Let that tone be one which hon-

---

[366] *May 15, 1996 Hearing*, 104th Cong, 2d Sess at 32 (cited in note 272) (statement of Representative Sensenbrenner).

[367] *July 11, 1996 Debate II*, 142 Cong Rec at H7449 (cited in note 302) (statement of Representative Packard).

[368] *July 12, 1996 Debate*, 142 Cong Rec at H7485 (cited in note 273) (statement of Representative Seastrand).

[369] Id at H7487 (statement of Representative DeLay).

[370] *Sept 10, 1996 Debate*, 142 Cong Rec at S10119 (cited in note 274) (statement of Senator Kassebaum).

4]   **WINDSOR PRODUCTS**   277

ors our democratic traditions of reasoned debate, responsible decision-making, and respect for all individuals.[371]

Senator Bill Bradley (D-NJ), who voted for DOMA, expressed anguish. "I wish I did not have to deal with this issue," he said. "It makes me feel uncomfortable. I feel I'm on ground full of quicksand."[372] He explained that he supported civil rights for gay people in housing and employment, and that he did not believe homosexual orientation was chosen. But given that marriage was so heavily intertwined with religious belief, he advised "we need to proceed cautiously." He believed there should be some way to accommodate the legitimate needs of gay couples, but marriage should not be redefined "at this time."[373] Perhaps Senator Bradley and others who wanted a "go slow" approach were overly cautious, and DOMA was a massive overreaction even if caution was warranted, but caution alone is not malice.

In fact, as usual, most legislators said nothing in hearings or on the floor. No doubt many of them sat glumly, assenting silently to passage of DOMA not out of anti-gay bias but because they feared a "no" vote would imperil their political careers. In fact, the evidence suggests that some legislators privately opposed DOMA but voted for it anyway for fear of the political consequences.[374] This may be cowardice, but cowardice is not animus.

Yet the anti-animus doctrine does not permit legislators to hide behind the prejudices of constituents. They may not be able to control private prejudices but neither may they give them effect.[375] That much was made explicit in *Cleburne*, which denied the power of a zoning commission to decide variances based on the unreasoning fears and prejudices of a neighborhood.[376]

It is not the case that every legislator who backed DOMA did so for essentially bigoted reasons, much less that every pro-DOMA

---

[371] Id.

[372] Id at S10124 (statement of Senator Bradley).

[373] Id at S10125.

[374] Senator Chuck Robb (D-VA) revealed that some of his colleagues had told him they were uncomfortable with DOMA but voted for it because "the political consequences are too great to oppose it." *Sept 10, 1996 Debate*, 142 Cong Rec at S10122 (cited in note 274). Others, he added, had told him "that they intend to discriminate, but they believe that discrimination here is acceptable" because they believe "homosexuality is morally wrong." Id.

[375] *Palmore v Sidoti*, 466 US 429, 433 (1984).

[376] See Section II.A.2.

legislator was an anti-gay bigot. But unanimity of malicious purpose is not, and cannot be, the standard for finding unconstitutional animus. It is enough that animus materially influenced the
result. Enough has been said to demonstrate that animus—in both
its active and more passive forms—materially influenced the passage of this major legislative reform.

Investigating legislative history is a hazardous business. It's possible simply to cherry-pick the evidence that supports one's conclusion (in this case, the conclusion that animus was a material
influence in passage of the law) and ignore or downplay the rest.
The mere presence of fear or "negative attitudes" among some
legislators is not reason enough to strike down a law, the Court
has held.[377] As Judge Posner has written, "scattered comments of
a vindictive nature in a legislative history" do not prove animus.[378]

But the expressions of outrage and hysterical fear that accompanied Congress's consideration of DOMA were not isolated ut-
terances. They dominated the debate. At the very least, they demonstrate that animus (as the Court defines it) materially influenced
the passage of DOMA. Finding this evidence is not picking out
thorns in a field of strawberries. On DOMA, the Congressional
Record is a field of thorns. No wonder President Clinton, at the
very moment he signed DOMA, urged citizens not to use it as a
justification for violence and discrimination against gay people.[379]
In the view of DOMA's supporters, gay marriage was a hedonistic,
self-centered, Sybaritic indulgence. In their view, it was championed by the depraved, dangerous to innocent children, damned
by God, and causing chaos in the land. It served no worthwhile
purpose. It had nothing to do with love, commitment, or responsibility. It was not a response to human needs for understanding
and family. It destroyed nations, ancient institutions, and whole
moral codes.

Caroline Products recognized that prejudice toward a group of
people tends to deform the political process that can ordinarily
be relied upon to protect their interests and rights. It inhibits
rational thought and deliberation. As the campaign to pass DOMA

---

[377] *Board of Trustees of the University of Alabama v Garrett*, 531 US 356, 357 (2001).

[378] *Milner v Apfel*, 148 F3d 812, 817 (7th Cir 1998).

[379] Geidner, *Becoming Law* (cited in note 40).

amply demonstrated, gay couples were sinners in the hands of an angry legislature.

4. *Effects.* If all that we had as evidence of animus was statements by intemperate members of Congress aroused by the passions of a passing moment, the Court should resist invalidating legislation on the grounds that it reflected impermissible animus. Anti-animus doctrine is a not a rule of good manners and decorum for congressional debate. It does not police politeness. The Court has been clear that evidence of animus must also be found in the actual injury (tangible or dignitary) inflicted on the targets of malice. In the case of DOMA, that evidence is abundant. Indeed, no knowledgeable observer can deny the massive effects of the law. Like Amendment 2 in *Romer*, the consequences of DOMA were far-reaching. To supporters of both measures, that effect was the very point.

Congress's failure to consider the interests of married same-sex couples is especially glaring in light of the broad impact the law threatened. As noted, DOMA imposed cradle-to-grave harm on gay families: from humiliating the children of married gay couples to the denial of shared cemetery plots. The broad scope of the law was not denied by anyone on either side of the debate. Supporters of DOMA acknowledged that the word "marriage" appeared approximately 800 times in the United States Code and that the word "spouse" appeared more than three thousand times.[380] Andrew Koppelman summarized some of the major effects of DOMA on married same-sex couples:

> Same-sex spouses could not file joint tax returns. Pretax dollars could not be used to pay for health insurance or healthcare expenses for a same-sex spouse or that spouse's dependent children. Same-sex spouses' debts incurred under divorce decrees or separation agreements were dischargeable in bankruptcy. Same-sex spouses of federal employees were excluded from the Federal Employees Health Benefits Program, the Federal Employees' Group Life Insurance Program, and the Federal Employees' Compensation Act, which compensates the widow or widower of an employee killed in the performance of duty. Same-sex spouses were the only surviving widows and widowers who would not have automatic ownership rights in a copyrighted work after the author's death. Same-sex spouses were denied preferential treatment under immigration law and, therefore, were the only legally married

---

[380] *May 15, 1996 Hearing*, 104th Cong, 2d Sess at 32 (cited in note 272) (statement of Representative Sensenbrenner).

spouses of American citizens who faced deportation. It is a federal crime
to assault, kidnap, or kill a member of the immediate family of a federal
official in order to influence or retaliate against that official—but it was
not if you did that to a same-sex spouse. With the end of the exclusion
of gay people from the military, DOMA made it official policy to withhold any survivor's benefits from the surviving spouse of a soldier killed
in the line of duty.[381]

Even this list does not begin to exhaust the over one thousand
disabilities placed on valid same-sex marriages.[382] The impact was
so massive and inescapable that injury to married same-sex couples
was not merely incidental to DOMA; it was the object of the law.
The fact that the injury was not merely incidental is another indicator that animus was present.

It should be noted that in some ways DOMA actually benefited
married same-sex couples in comparison to their married opposite-
sex friends. Marriage imposes legal responsibilities in addition to
conferring benefits and protections. Under DOMA, married gay
couples could evade the federal "marriage penalty" under which
some of them would have had to pay higher income taxes. Their
income tax burden was actually lower than similarly situated opposite-sex couples. Federal employees could also avoid ethics rules
dealing with spousal financial interests and gifts to a spouse. They
could qualify for more federal student aid because a spouse's income would not count toward eligibility. The Court itself noted
some of these unanticipated consequences of DOMA.[383]

It's clear that Congress was not trying to help gay couples in
any way. And the net effect, in both practical and dignitary terms,
was overwhelmingly to hurt gay families united in marriage. But
Congress did alleviate some of the responsibilities that same-sex
couples "would be honored to accept were DOMA not in force."[384]
In its blind effort to strike at gay couples, Congress actually disfavored opposite-sex marriages in some ways and impaired federal
interests. The expressive animus in DOMA overwhelmed practical

[381] Koppelman, *Why Scalia Should Have Voted to Overturn DOMA* at 139 (cited in note 4).

[382] In the animus section of its opinion, the Court offered its own partial list of the disadvantages that DOMA imposed on same-sex marriages. *Windsor*, 133 S Ct at 2694–95 (listing Social Security, housing, taxes, criminal sanctions, copyright, veterans' benefits, healthcare, and bankruptcy). From this, it concluded that the "principal purpose was to impose inequality, not for other reasons like governmental efficiency." Id at 2694.

[383] *Windsor*, 133 S Ct at 2695.

[384] Id.

considerations. That, too, suggests a legislative process driven substantially by animus.[385]

5. *Pretext.* Even extraordinary and far-reaching laws can be justified by the ultimate objectives they serve. But a law that poorly serves its stated objectives, or that is wildly over- or underinclusive in relation to that objective, is open to the suspicion that claimed objectives are a mere pretext for animus against those injured by the law. That was the case in *Moreno*, where Congress's purposes in the Food Stamp Act were not at all served by the exclusion of nontraditional family-living arrangements. It was true in *Cleburne*, where claimed concern about legal liability, parking, the possibility of a 500-year flood, and so on, were not sufficient reasons for rejecting a home for the cognitively disabled while allowing multiunit dwellings for nursing homes, fraternities, and sororities. Given the stated concerns of the zoning board, the discrimination against the group was underinclusive. And it was true in *Romer*, where solicitude for the liberties of individual landlords and small businesses could not justify a sweeping denial of antidiscrimination protection for homosexuals in every facet of life. Given the state's claimed interests, the discrimination against gay people was overinclusive.

DOMA suffered all three defects: it did not appear to serve some of Congress's stated objectives at all; it was overinclusive by denying married gay couples all benefits rather than those that could be tied to a specific legitimate purpose; and it was underinclusive because it treated married gay couples differently from others who could not or would not meet the traditional expectations of procreation, child-rearing, and lifelong marriage. These defects were in addition to the constitutionally impermissible objective of condemning homosexuality on moral grounds,[386] which was either express or implied in several stated aims of DOMA.

The flimsiness of Congress's justifications for Section 3 of DOMA have been reviewed repeatedly and at length elsewhere and won't be repeated here.[387] Three examples should suffice to

---

[385] I am grateful to Mary Anne Case for making this observation.

[386] *Windsor*, 133 S Ct at 2694; *Lawrence v Texas*, 539 US 558, 583 (2003).

[387] For a consideration of DOMA's means-ends defects, see Note, 117 Harv L Rev at 2696–2700 (cited in note 294); Jon-Peter Kelly, *Act of Infidelity: Why the Defense of Marriage Act Is Unfaithful to the Constitution*, 7 Cornell J L & Pub Policy 203, 247–49 (1997); Kevin H. Lewis, Note, *Equal Protection After Romer v. Evans: Implications for the Defense of Marriage Act and Other Laws*, 49 Hastings L J 175, 204–14 (1997).

show how mightily Congress and later the lawyers for BLAG strove to create the appearance of constitutionally permissible purposes.

a) Fiscal impact. First, as we have seen,[388] there was no empirical basis for concern about the fiscal impact of failing to prohibit federal recognition of same-sex marriages recognized by the states. Such marriages might even have produced a small financial benefit for the federal government.[389] But since Congress refused to review the potential costs and benefits, it is hard to know what the fiscal impact would have been. This was makeweight material.

b) Responsible procreation. A second justification for DOMA—encouraging "responsible procreation"—had no basis in reason, experience, or evidence. While legislators like Senator Byrd invoked the biblical injunction to "be fruitful and multiply,"[390] nobody explained why it should be thought that federal recognition of already valid same-sex marriages would affect fertility among heterosexual couples. Nor could anyone begin to explain why the denial of most of the rights associated with marriage—like burial next to a spouse in a veterans' cemetery—would have any relationship at all to heterosexuals' willingness to procreate.

Perhaps the emphasis should be placed on "responsible" in "responsible procreation." Perhaps legislators thought that if the federal understanding of marriage encompassed same-sex marriages validated in the states, heterosexuals might take marriage less seriously, be less likely to marry, and might begin to procreate even more than they do now outside of marriage. Illegitimacy rates might rise, with harmful consequences for children. Married homosexual couples might spoil marriage for everyone else. They might contaminate it. As Representative Barney Frank (D-MA) put it during the DOMA debate: "Is there some emanation that is given off [from gay marriage] that ruins it for you? Gee, Hawaii is pretty far away. Will not the ocean stop it?"[391]

To believe that the federal recognition of same-sex marriages

---

[388] See Section III.B.3.b.

[389] See *Letter and Report from Douglas Holtz-Eakin* (cited in note 281).

[390] *Sept 10, 1996 Debate*, 142 Cong Rec at S10109 (cited in note 274) (statement of Senator Byrd).

[391] *July 12, 1996 Debate*, 142 Cong Rec at H7482 (cited in note 273) (statement of Representative Frank).

(which the federal government was not banning) would destroy the institution of marriage was to believe that homosexuals had a superhuman corrosive power. It was a power far beyond their paltry numbers. It was to indulge stereotypes that gay men and lesbians ruin everything they touch or might be allowed to participate in, whether it was federal employment, the military, the church, or marriage. The fear was so far-fetched, so baseless, and ultimately so hysterical, that it was in fact another expression of malice.

c) **Cautious and incremental reform.** A third reason for enacting DOMA might be that society should move slowly and incrementally in accepting a change in the understanding of something as important as marriage. Perhaps we should await evidence of the effects of allowing same-sex couples to wed before fully endorsing the change. Congress did not stop states from experimenting with marriage, it simply applied the brakes to national acceptance of it. In general, a preference for slow and incremental reform is not animus-based. It is a matter of prudence.

Nevertheless, the asserted go-slow purpose does not save DOMA from invalidation. To begin with, in our federal system, it is not traditionally Congress's role to decide whether and at what pace to experiment with marital-status determinations. DOMA did not, and Congress could not, stop the states from moving at whatever pace they deemed appropriate for recognizing same-sex marriages. To the extent that Congress was trying to apply the brakes to *state* determinations of marital status, its action departed from the tradition of federalism in family law. To the extent Congress was trying to slow down *federal* acceptance of same-sex marriage, it must be asked why it decided to move slowly on this change in marriage rather than on one of the many other fundamental changes to marriage enacted by the states over the past century. This was a selectively cautious Congress.

Also, Congress did not allow for incremental, partial, or cautious changes in federal recognition of same-sex marriages. It denied all federal recognition for all purposes, without any consideration of a special need to move slowly in specific contexts. Whatever else may be said of the process that produced DOMA in the summer of 1996, caution and careful deliberation were not evident.

Finally, even if a preference for moving cautiously on marital reform was genuinely one purpose behind DOMA, that does not preclude a determination that animus was also a purpose behind the law. Given the many indicia of animus in DOMA, a desire to injure and disparage married same-sex couples materially influenced passage regardless of whether prudence might also have been a motivation.

If legislators had to advert to justifications about financial savings, responsible procreation, and "caution," they were scrounging for reasons that might make DOMA sound benevolent.

IV. Conclusion

Animus analysis is successfully doing the work that arguments for heightened scrutiny have failed to do in equal protection cases challenging anti-gay discrimination. Historical experience, and now two major Supreme Court decisions, support the inference that anti-gay discrimination will often be animus-based. But the Court's decision does not necessarily condemn all laws limiting marriage to opposite-sex couples. The animus holding in *Windsor* is so closely tied to federalism concerns that it is not obvious the Court would come to the same conclusion about a *state* law defining marriage as one man and one woman.[392]

As the Court argued in the important concluding section of the opinion, there was unconstitutional "animus" behind DOMA, which itself is an impermissible legislative purpose and a breach of the government's duty to treat every individual as though he possessed some worth represented by the word "dignity." The government failed even to consider the interests of future married gay couples when it passed DOMA; to the extent it did so, it acted to disparage and injure their marriages. And federalism principles, by assisting the states in protecting the substantive liberties of their own citizens, by limiting the reach and substance of federal legislation frustrating the implementation of state policy on family relations, and by confirming a historical practice from which DOMA dramatically and suspiciously departed, supported the conclusion that equal protection was denied. As Justice Jackson once wrote, equality structurally protects liberty because it means

---

[392] The district court in *Kitchen v Herbert*, 2013 WL 6697874, *24, *30 (D Utah), holding the Utah ban on same-sex marriage unconstitutional, expressly declined to rely on animus. In *Jackson v Abercrombie*, 884 F Supp 2d 1065, 1092 (D Hawaii 2012), the district court held that Hawaii's marriage law could be justified as a way to protect tradition, which is not the same as animus.

that the majority can't impose on some what it would not impose upon itself.[393] *Windsor Products* is what happened when *Carolene Products*, the advance of gay rights, and the federalism revolution converged.

Rather than relying on formal tiers of scrutiny, verbal formulations that measure the strength of state interests and narrowness of means, and tests for what constitutes a discrete and insular minority, *Windsor* Products is a guide to the underlying constitutional legitimacy of governmental decision making. It is agnostic about who might next benefit from judicial policing of animus-based action. There is no single, predetermined list of groups that benefit from its judicial vigilance. The beneficiaries of judicial protection have been food-stamp users, disabled persons, gay men and lesbians, and married couples.

Our constitutional tradition holds that we're better off in a republic where there are some things a majority can't do to a person, including treat the person maliciously, and where the government knows there will be someone occasionally enforcing the idea that there are some things it cannot do to a person. Under *Windsor* Products, this salutary possibility of correction extends as much to a decision-making process driven by animus as it does to substantive outcomes denying constitutional rights.

---

[393] *Railway Express Agency v New York*, 336 US 106, 466–67 (Jackson, J, concurring).

LEE ANNE FENNELL AND
EDUARDO M. PEÑALVER

EXACTIONS CREEP

Imagine you are a Supreme Court Justice who cares deeply about property rights. You worry that landowners are too easily exploited by governmental entities, and you believe that the Constitution must protect their prerogatives as owners. You recognize, however, that a panoply of zoning restrictions, building codes, and other laws and ordinances often preserve and enhance the value and security of landownership. The idea that property must be both protected *from* state power and *with* state power resonates with you, but it presents a doctrinal challenge. How can the Constitution protect landowners from the government without disabling the machinery that protects ownership itself? The Supreme Court's exactions jurisprudence can be understood as an attempt to confront this chal-

Lee Anne Fennell is Max Pam Professor of Law and Herbert and Marjorie Fried Research Scholar, University of Chicago Law School. Eduardo M. Peñalver is John P. Wilson Professor of Law, University of Chicago Law School.

AUTHORS' NOTE: During Lee Anne Fennell's tenure as associate counsel at the State and Local Legal Center, she worked on an amicus brief filed in *Dolan v City of Tigard* on behalf of the National Association of Counties et al. Her academic work on the topic of exactions began several years later and has always reflected only her own views. She is grateful to the Stuart C. and JoAnn Nathan Faculty Fund for financial support. Eduardo M. Peñalver is grateful to the Roger Levin Faculty Fund for its support of this research. Both authors appreciate the helpful comments on earlier drafts provided by Hanoch Dagan, John Echeverria, Mark Fenster, Paul Gowder, Alexander Reinert, Stewert Sterk, Lior Strahilevitz, and David Strauss, and by participants in the Colloquium on the Public Purpose Requirement in Expropriation, hosted by the University of Groningngen in the Netherlands, and in faculty workshops at Cardozo School of Law and the University of Iowa. They also thank Kristin Czubkowski and Monica Ghosh for excellent research assistance.

lenge.[1] The Court has sought to subject some local land use actions to heightened scrutiny as a matter of federal constitutional law[2] while leaving the superstructure of zoning, permitting, and taxation in place.[3] The difficulties with this approach became apparent in *Koontz v St. Johns River Water Management District*.[4] *That* the Supreme Court has failed in this difficult balancing act is no surprise. *How* it has failed, and why it may continue to fail, is an interesting question and the impetus for this article.

The Court's exactions jurisprudence, set forth in *Nollan v California Coastal Commission*,[5] *Dolan v City of Tigard*,[6] and now *Koontz*, requires the government to satisfy demanding criteria for certain bargains—or proposed bargains—implicating the use of land. But the Court has left the domain of this heightened scrutiny wholly undefined. Indeed, the *Koontz* majority eschewed any boundary principle that would hive off its exactions jurisprudence from its land use jurisprudence more generally. By beating back one form of exactions creep—the possibility that local governments will circumvent a too narrowly drawn circle of heightened scrutiny—the Court has left land use regulation vulnerable to the creeping expansion of heightened scrutiny under the auspices of its exactions jurisprudence.

At first blush, the fact that exactions always involve actual or proposed land use "bargains" might seem to mark out a clear and well-defined arena for heightened scrutiny. But in fact, virtually

---

[1] We do not mean to suggest that all or even any of the Justices would frame the enterprise in quite this way, only that the pattern of decided cases reflects a struggle prompted by these competing goals.

[2] The Court has grounded this selectively intensified scrutiny in the unconstitutional conditions doctrine—a foundation that is notoriously unstable. See notes 33–35 and accompanying text.

[3] Even if most of the garden-variety land use regulations and taxes falling into this latter category could ultimately survive heightened scrutiny, the exercise of applying such scrutiny would be undesirably costly for both courts and local governments.

[4] 133 S Ct 2586 (2013). In the short time since the decision, *Koontz* has generated numerous and varied academic responses, some of which we engage in more detail below. Papers forthcoming or under development include, for example, Steven J. Eagle, *Koontz in the Mansion and the Gatehouse*, 61 Urban Lawyer (forthcoming 2014), online at http://papers.ssrn.com/sol3/papers.cfm?abstract_id=2354617; John D. Echeverria, *Koontz: The Very Worst Takings Decision Ever?* (Vermont Law School Research Paper No 28-13, Dec 2013), online at http://ssrn.com/abstract=2316406; Mark Fenster, *Substantive Due Process by Another Name: Koontz, Exactions, and the Regulatory Takings Doctrine*, Touro L Rev (forthcoming 2014) (on file with authors).

[5] 483 US 825 (1987).

[6] 512 US 374 (1994).

every restriction, fee, or tax associated with the ownership or use of land can be cast as a bargain.[7] To retain its commitment to heightened scrutiny for a subset (and only a subset) of land use controls, the Court must construct some stopping point. Ideally, a boundary principle would be relatively easy to apply and would track relevant normative considerations reasonably well. In the exactions context, however, markers that can even minimally approximate these criteria are in short supply—and the Court thinned its options further in *Koontz*.

The difficulty the Court has experienced and will continue to experience in constructing a logically coherent, administrable, and normatively appealing way to bound heightened scrutiny should, we suggest, lead it to rethink its exactions jurisprudence, and especially its grounding in the Takings Clause, rather than in the Due Process Clause. Choosing an approach going forward requires examining not only the impact of heightened scrutiny on land use bargains but also the collateral damage that the rule in question may do to takings law and other constitutional doctrines, including the broader doctrine of unconstitutional conditions.

This article proceeds in six parts. Part I lays out the doctrinal terrain and shows where the *Koontz* case fits in. Part II demonstrates the potential boundlessness of the domain to which heightened scrutiny applies under the Court's recently revamped exactions jurisprudence. To maintain land use law as we know it, limits must be somehow derived or constructed. Part III approaches this question by asking what normative principles might underlie the sort of skepticism about bargaining reflected in exactions jurisprudence. After considering several possibilities, we suggest that the most plausible answer is found in rule-of-law concerns implicated by land use deal making. Part IV tries to divine the limits that the *Koontz* majority might have had in mind, given the way that its holdings intersect with prior doctrine. This sets the stage for Part V, which considers a series of alternatives that would attempt to reconcile the Court's twin interests in restraining governmental power over property owners and in keeping the gears of ordinary land use

---

[7] The point is not limited to land use law. Virtually all governmental restrictions and impositions, head taxes aside, can be cast in conditional terms, as they are premised upon choosing to sell, earn, employ, and so on. See Richard A. Epstein, *Bargaining with the State* 11 (Princeton, 1993).

regulation running in ways that protect the property interests of those owners. Part VI concludes our analysis.

I. Takings, Due Process, and Exactions

Koontz arose out of a conflict between Coy Koontz, a Florida landowner, and the St. Johns River Water Management District ("District"), a regional water authority. Koontz had purchased a 14.9-acre tract of land near Orlando in 1972. The land was mostly wetlands, though it also contained some forested uplands. Florida law required Koontz to obtain permission from the District before filling any wetlands. In 1994, Koontz applied for a permit from the District to develop the northern 3.7 acres of his parcel, virtually all of which were wetlands.[8] He offered to dedicate a conservation easement covering the remaining 11 acres. In the past, the District had required owners seeking permission to fill wetlands to preserve 10 acres of wetland for every acre they filled.[9] In keeping with this general practice, the District proposed that Koontz either reduce the size of his development to a single acre (dedicating a conservation easement for the remainder of the property) or, alternatively, that he develop the 3.7 acres as he proposed, but pay to improve the drainage on additional, District-owned land.[10] The District also indicated that it was willing to entertain "equivalent" alternative proposals from Koontz.[11]

Koontz rejected the District's proposal, and the District denied the permit. Rather than go back to the bargaining table, Koontz filed a lawsuit in state court. He claimed that the conditions for permit approval contained in the District's proposal violated the Takings Clause.[12] Among other things, Koontz challenged the District's suggested swap of development approval for wetlands protection or mitigation as an unlawful "exaction." This exactions claim is different from a claim that the permit denial itself took Koontz's

---

[8] *St. Johns River Water Management District v Koontz*, 77 S3d 1220, 1224 (Fla 2011).

[9] See Echeverria, *Koontz: The Very Worst* at *4 (cited in note 4) (citing Brief for Respondent, *Koontz v St. Johns Water Management District*, No 11-1447, *12 (filed Dec 21, 2012) (available on Westlaw at 2012 WL 6694053)).

[10] *Koontz*, 133 S Ct at 2593.

[11] Id.

[12] Koontz sued under Fla Stat § 373.617(2), which provides a cause of action for damages if a state action is "an unreasonable exercise of the state's police power constituting a taking without just compensation."

property. Instead of challenging the regulatory burden that a denial would impose, Koontz's exaction theory contested the legality of the bargain the District was trying to strike. In order to understand how the mere attempt to bargain with a property owner—without any property changing hands—might violate the Takings Clause, we must briefly explore the contours of the Supreme Court's regulatory takings jurisprudence.

A. TAKINGS AND DUE PROCESS

In considering whether a regulation of land constitutes a taking of property requiring just compensation, the Supreme Court usually adheres to the analysis laid out in *Penn Central Transportation Co. v New York City.*[13] The *Penn Central* factors include the "economic impact of the regulation on the claimant," "the extent to which the regulation has interfered with distinct investment-backed expectations," and "the character of the governmental action."[14] The focus of this default regulatory takings inquiry, as the Court made clear in *Lingle v Chevron USA, Inc.,*[15] is the severity of the burden the regulation imposes on the property owner.[16] The unanimous Court in *Lingle* contrasted this burden-focused inquiry with a means-ends style inquiry into the rationality of government regulation. The latter, the Court said, falls within the province of the Due Process Clause and, in undertaking it, courts should be highly deferential to the elected branches.[17]

The Court has carved out from its default *Penn Central* takings analysis two per se rules governing discrete categories of regulation. First, in *Loretto v Teleprompter Manhattan CATV Corp.,* the Court held that a permanent physical invasion of property authorized by the government necessarily constitutes a taking.[18] In

---

[13] 438 US 104 (1978).

[14] Id at 124.

[15] 544 US 528 (2005).

[16] As the *Lingle* Court explains, "severity of the burden" represents a common thread running through all of its regulatory takings jurisprudence, one that can be used to test how closely a given governmental act approximates a physical appropriation, and to assess the distributive fairness of the imposition. Id at 539; see id at 539–40, 542–43.

[17] Id at 543–45. The inquiries serve different purposes as well. A violation of the Due Process Clause leads to the invalidation of the enactment, whereas a Takings Clause violation represents an otherwise legitimate governmental act that can be fully validated by the payment of just compensation. Id at 543.

[18] 458 US 419, 441 (1982).

subsequent cases, the Court has characterized the state appropriation of discrete pools of money, such as the interest from a specific account, as *Loretto*-type takings.[19]

The Court created a second per se regulatory takings rule in *Lucas v South Carolina Coastal Council*.[20] In that case, the Court held that a regulation is a per se taking (and not subject to the *Penn Central* analysis) when it permanently deprives an owner of all economically viable use of her property—unless the rule does no more than codify limitations on owners' rights already built into "background principles" of state property law, such as nuisance.[21] The *Loretto* and *Lucas* exceptions to *Penn Central* are consistent with the Court's characterization of the takings inquiry in *Lingle*: Their focus is on the burden a government action imposes on owners.

The Court's takings framework is not a model of clarity or coherence. It can be (and has been) assailed on normative, logical, and administrability grounds. We will not delve into those criticisms here, but will instead accept these principles as given for purposes of addressing one particularly problematic corner of the doctrinal picture: exactions.

B. ENTER EXACTIONS

Sitting uncomfortably with *Lingle*'s takings/due-process typology is the Court's treatment of claims that the government has conditioned development approval on exactions of constitutionally protected property rights from the landowner. In *Nollan v California Coastal Commission*,[22] the plaintiffs owned a small beachfront home in California. They wanted to demolish the existing home and build a new, larger home on their lot. California law required them to obtain permission from the Coastal Commission before they could undertake their project. The Commission refused to grant the Nollans permission to build unless they would give the state a lateral easement allowing the public to cross over the por-

---

[19] See, for example, *Brown v Legal Foundation of Washington*, 538 US 216, 235 (2003). Cases finding the appropriation of interest from specific accounts to be takings predate *Loretto*. See, for example, *Webb's Fabulous Pharmacies, Inc. v Beckwith*, 449 US 155, 159, 164 (1980) (applying this principle and citing cases).

[20] 505 US 1003 (1992).

[21] Id at 1027–31.

[22] 483 US 825 (1987).

tion of their property adjacent to the mean high tide line.[23] The
Supreme Court concluded that the exaction was unconstitutional.[24] It held that the demanded easement did not share an
"essential nexus" with the goal the Commission would have (legitimately) advanced by simply denying the requested permission
to expand the house.

In *Dolan v City of Tigard*,[25] the Court added to *Nollan*'s "essential
nexus" inquiry the requirement that the burden of the condition
imposed upon development permission be roughly proportional
to the harm that would be caused by permitting the development
to go forward.[26] The plaintiff in *Dolan* owned a small hardware
store. When she applied for a permit to expand the store and pave
her parking lot, the city conditioned approval of her application
on her dedication of a piece of her property to the city for use as
a flood plain (subject to a recreational easement) and bicycle path.[27]
The Court conceded the existence of a nexus between the city's
demands and the impacts of the plaintiff's expanded use of her
property on storm-water runoff and traffic. But it nonetheless held
that the city had violated the Takings Clause because it had failed
to establish that its exaction was sufficiently proportional to the
impacts the plaintiff's proposed expansion would cause.[28]

The "essential nexus" and "rough proportionality" tests established in *Nollan* and *Dolan* together produced an inquiry, ostensibly
operating under the Takings Clause, that is noteworthy in two
respects. First, it scrutinizes the fit between means (the condition
imposed by the government) and ends (mitigation of the harm
caused by the proposed development). Importantly, it does not
evaluate the burden imposed on the landowner by the underlying
regulatory regime from which she is seeking relief. This would
appear to place the test in the domain that the Court identified

---

[23] Id at 827–29.

[24] See id at 837–42.

[25] 512 US 374 (1994).

[26] Id at 391.

[27] See id at 379–81, 393–94.

[28] See id at 388, 394–95. The Court left ambiguous whether it is the harm eliminated
by the exaction that must be proportional to the harm the development causes or whether
it is the burden of the exaction (to the landowner) that must be proportional to those
harms.

in *Lingle* with the Due Process Clause, not the Takings Clause.[29] Second, the exactions inquiry involves a level of scrutiny of the proffered ends and chosen means that would be highly unusual in the due process context.[30] The court in *Dolan* specifically opted for the "rough proportionality" language in order to make clear that the inquiry was to be more searching than the usual "rational basis" review.[31] Moreover, it placed the burden of establishing compliance with the exactions test squarely on the government's shoulders, thereby inverting the traditional presumption of constitutionality of properly enacted regulations.[32]

The Court has characterized its exactions jurisprudence as an application of the unconstitutional conditions doctrine.[33] That

---

[29] See *Lingle*, 544 US at 542–43. This is not to say that the determination that an owner has been singled out to bear an unfair burden—an inquiry that that Court in *Lingle* identified with the Takings Clause—does not involve any questions of fit. After all, to determine that a given burden is unfairly placed on a landowner, we need to know something about the reasons why the government has imposed it. A landowner whose use constitutes the equivalent of a nuisance, for example, might fairly be required to bear burdens that would not be appropriate for another landowner—a point the Court made explicit in *Lucas v South Carolina Coastal Council*:

> The "total taking" inquiry we require today will ordinarily entail (as the application of state nuisance law ordinarily entails) analysis of, among other things, the degree of harm to public lands and resources, or adjacent private property, posed by the claimant's proposed activities, the social value of the claimant's activities and their suitability to the locality in question, and the relative ease with which the alleged harm can be avoided through measures taken by the claimant and the government (or adjacent private landowners) alike.

505 US 1003, 1030–31 (1992) (citations omitted). Similarly, some of the *Penn Central* factors arguably reach considerations that relate to matters of fit or that otherwise seem to sound in due process. See, for example, Mark Fenster, *The Stubborn Incoherence of Regulatory Takings*, 28 Stan Envtl L J 525, 529 (2009); Lee Anne Fennell, *Picturing Takings*, 88 Notre Dame L Rev 57, 85 & n 87, 88 (2012). Nonetheless, *Lingle* marks out a basic division of labor between the clauses based on the dominant inquiry involved in a given cause of action. The fact that exactions analysis involves no examination of the magnitude of the initial regulatory burden from which the landowner seeks relief, but rather begins the inquiry by examining the terms of a proposed exchange involving that burden, would seem to locate it in the realm of due process by the Court's own account.

[30] Governmental acts directed at social and economic goals receive rational basis review unless they implicate fundamental rights or involve suspect classifications. Such review requires only that the act be rationally related to a legitimate governmental purpose (see, for example, *Schweiker v Wilson*, 450 US 221, 230 (1981)). While a governmental act that "fails to serve any legitimate governmental objective may be so arbitrary or irrational that it runs afoul of the Due Process Clause," *Lingle*, 544 US at 542, the test is a deferential one that does not put the government to its proof in establishing how well, or even if, the legislation serves particular goals.

[31] 512 US at 391.

[32] See id at 394–96; id at 405–11 (Stevens, J, dissenting); id at 413–14 (Souter, J, dissenting).

[33] *Dolan*, 512 US at 385; *Koontz*, 133 S Ct at 2594–95; *Lingle*, 544 US at 547.

doctrine limits the ability of the government to condition its grant of a discretionary benefit to a claimant on the claimant's waiver of some constitutional right that the government would not be entitled simply to override.[34] For example, the government cannot condition its grant of employment—something it is entitled under normal circumstances to withhold—on an applicant's waiver of his First Amendment right to choose his own religion. In the exactions context, the constitutional right at issue has been located in the Takings Clause. As the Court put it in *Koontz*, by conditioning development approval on the landowner's conveyance of some property interest to the government, "the government can pressure an owner into voluntarily giving up property for which the Fifth Amendment would otherwise require just compensation."[35]

C. THE SCOPE OF SCRUTINY

Nollan and *Dolan* sparked two axes of disagreement among the lower courts about the reach of the exactions doctrine.[36] First, courts split over whether *Nollan/Dolan* heightened scrutiny applied to exactions in which the government demands a cash payment rather than a dedication of an interest in land in exchange for development permission.[37] Second, they divided over whether the

---

[34] The unconstitutional conditions doctrine has spawned considerable scholarly output. Influential treatments include, for example, Richard A. Epstein, *Bargaining with the State* (1993); Vicki Been, *"Exit" as a Constraint on Land Use Exactions: Rethinking the Unconstitutional Conditions Doctrine*, 91 Colum L Rev 473 (1991); Kathleen M. Sullivan, *Unconstitutional Conditions*, 102 Harv L Rev 1413 (1989); Seth F. Kreimer, *Allocational Sanctions: The Problem of Negative Rights in a Positive State*, 132 U Pa L Rev 1293 (1984). Despite the *Dolan* Court's characterization of the doctrine as "well-settled," 512 US at 385, it has so thoroughly eluded attempts to reduce it to a workable formula that some scholars have urged abandonment of it altogether. See generally Frederick Schauer, *Too Hard: Unconstitutional Conditions and the Chimera of Constitutional Consistency*, 72 Denver U L Rev 989 (1995); Cass R. Sunstein, *Why the Unconstitutional Conditions Doctrine is an Anachronism with Particular Reference to Religion, Speech and Abortion*, 70 BU L Rev 593 (1990). Theoretical work on the doctrine continues, nonetheless. Notable recent works include, for example, Philip Hamburger, *Unconstitutional Conditions: The Irrelevance of Consent*, 98 Va L Rev 479 (2012); Mitchell N. Berman, *Coercion without Baselines: Unconstitutional Conditions in Three Dimensions*, 90 Georgetown L J 1 (2001).

[35] *Koontz*, 133 S Ct at 2594.

[36] Another unresolved issue, addressed in *Koontz*, was the status of "failed exactions"— exactions proposed to a landowner but not accepted or implemented. See generally Mark Fenster, *Failed Exactions*, 36 Vt L Rev 623 (2012); Timothy M. Mulvaney, *Proposed Exactions*, 26 J Land Use & Envir L 277 (2011).

[37] See Ann E. Carlson and Daniel Pollak, *Takings on the Ground: How the Supreme Court's Takings Jurisprudence Affects Local Land Use Decisions*, 35 UC Davis L Rev 103, 137–38 (2001) (suggesting that *Nollan* and *Dolan* may encourage use of impact fees and discourage physical land exactions); David A. Dana, *Land Use Regulation in an Age of Heightened*

exactions doctrine applies only to so-called "ad hoc" or "adjudi-cated" exactions, that is, exactions whose terms are worked out on a case-by-case basis in negotiations with landowners. Courts and commentators usually contrast adjudicative exactions with exactions that are more "legislative" in character.[38] A legislative exaction is one in which the state's conditions on development are spelled out in advance in a generally applicable formula or schedule.

Before *Koontz*, the Supreme Court had not intervened to decisively resolve either debate. On at least two occasions, however, it had used dicta to describe its exactions cases as having involved ad hoc state demands that owners turn over tangible interests in land. In *City of Monterey v Del Monte Dunes at Monterey Ltd.*,[39] the Court defined "exactions" as "land-use decisions conditioning approval of development on the dedication of property to public use."[40] Later, in *Lingle*, the Court suggested that the reach of *Nollan/Dolan* scrutiny was limited to "adjudicative land-use exactions," in which the state demands—in exchange for development permission—that the property owner hand over an interest in land that, if imposed directly, "would have been a *per se* physical taking."[41] This dicta in *Lingle* appeared to put the Court in the camp

---

Scrutiny, 75 NC L Rev 1243, 1259–60 (1997) (considering the varying interpretations of *Dolan*'s application to monetary exactions); see also *Dudek v Umatilla County*, 69 P3d 751, 757–58 (Or Ct App 2003) (discussing the split among courts over the question of whether *Dolan* applies to monetary exactions). Cases holding that *Nollan* and *Dolan* do not apply to monetary exactions include *McClung v City of Sumner*, 548 F3d 1219, 1228 (9th Cir 2008); *Smith v Town of Mendon*, 4 NY3d 1, 12 (2004); *Home Builders Association v City of Scottsdale*, 930 P2d 993, 999–1000 (Ariz 1997); *West Linn Corporate Park, L.L.C. v City of West Linn*, 240 P3d 29, 45–46 (Or 2010); *City of Olympia v Drebick*, 126 P3d 802, 808 (Wash 2006). Cases holding that monetary exactions are subject to *Nollan/Dolan* scrutiny include *Town of Flower Mound v Stafford Estates Ltd Partnership*, 135 SW3d 620, 635–40 (Tex 2004); *Home Builders Association of Dayton and the Miami Valley v City of Beavercreek*, 89 Ohio St 3d 121, 128 (2000); *Ehrlich v City of Culver City*, 911 P2d 429, 433 (Cal 1996); *Northern Illinois Home Builders Association v County of DuPage*, 165 Ill 2d 25, 32–35 (1995).

[38] Cases holding that *Nollan* and *Dolan* do not apply to "legislative" exactions include *McClung v City of Sumner*, 548 F3d 1219, 1227–28 (9th Cir 2008); *St. Clair County Home Builders Association v City of Pell City*, 61 S3d 992, 1007 (Ala 2010); *Greater Atlanta Home-builders Association v DeKalb County*, 588 SE3d 694, 697 (Ga 2003); *San Remo Hotel v City and County of San Francisco*, 27 Cal 4th 643, 671–72 (2002); *Krupp v Breckenridge Sanitation District*, 19 P3d 687, 695–96 (Colo 2001); *Curtis v Town of South Tomaston*, 708 A2d 657, 659–60 (Me 1998); *Parking Association of Ga., Inc. v City of Atlanta*, 450 SE2d 200, 203 n 3 (Ga 1994). In *Town of Flower Mound*, 135 SW3d at 640–42, in contrast, the Texas Supreme Court applied *Nollan* and *Dolan* to a legislative exaction.

[39] 526 US 687 (1999).

[40] Id at 702.

[41] 544 US at 546.

of the lower courts that had declined to apply *Nollan* and *Dolan* to so-called "legislative" exactions (exactions that operate according to a predetermined formula or schedule) and on the side of those lower courts that had declined to apply *Nollan* and *Dolan* to exactions of money.[42]

D. THE KOONTZ DECISION

In *Koontz*, the Supreme Court definitively rejected the notion—hinted at in *Del Monte Dunes* and *Lingle*—that the *Nollan/Dolan* test applies only to exactions of physical interests in land. *Koontz* had prevailed in the state trial court and intermediate appellate court on an exactions theory, but the Florida Supreme Court had reversed, finding *Nollan* and *Dolan* inapplicable based on its interpretation of the scope of the Supreme Court's exactions doctrine. Relying on the limiting language in *Del Monte Dunes* and *Lingle*, the Florida Supreme Court concluded that *Nollan* and *Dolan* do not apply to exactions of money and, in addition, do not apply when an agency denies the requested permit (as opposed to granting the permit subject to certain conditions).[43]

The U.S. Supreme Court rejected both of these limits on *Nollan* and *Dolan*. All of the Justices agreed that, contrary to the Florida Supreme Court's holding, permit denials as well as conditional permit grants are subject to exactions scrutiny. In the majority's words,

> [a] contrary rule would be especially untenable . . . because it would enable the government to evade the limitations of *Nollan* and *Dolan* simply by phrasing its demands for property as conditions precedent to permit approval. Under the Florida Supreme Court's approach, a government order stating that a permit is "approved if" the owner turns over that property would be subject to *Nollan* and *Dolan*, but an identical order that uses the words "denied until" would not.[44]

The Justices split over the question whether a demand for money fell within the boundaries of *Nollan* and *Dolan*. The five-Justice majority opinion by Justice Samuel Alito held that the Court's exactions jurisprudence reached demands for money. The

---

[42] See *McClung*, 548 F3d at 1226–28 (relying on *Lingle* to limit *Nollan* and *Dolan* analysis to adjudicated land use exactions); *Wisconsin Builders' Association v Wisconsin Department of Transportation*, 702 NW2d 433, 446–48 (Wis App 2005) (same).

[43] See *St. Johns River Management District v Koontz*, 77 S3d 1220, 1230 (Fla 2011).

[44] *Koontz*, 133 S Ct at 2595–96. The dissent agreed. See id at 2603 (Kagan, J, dissenting).

dissenters, led by Justice Elena Kagan, rejected this position.

In reaching its conclusion, the *Koontz* majority had to navigate around the Court's 1998 decision in *Eastern Enterprises v Apfel*.[45] In *Eastern Enterprises*, a plurality of the Court had concluded that retroactively imposing liability on a former coal operator for retired coal miners' medical benefits violated the Takings Clause.[46] However, the four dissenters in *Eastern Enterprises*, along with Justice Anthony Kennedy (who concurred in the judgment on due process grounds), took the position that the Takings Clause did not apply at all when government imposes general obligations to pay money.[47] As Justice Kennedy put it, "the Government's imposition of an obligation . . . must relate to a specific property interest to implicate the Takings Clause."[48] Kennedy thereby distinguished cases like *Brown v Legal Foundation of Washington*,[49] in which the government had seized interest earned on specific accounts.

The concern with applying the Takings Clause to more generalized obligations to pay money was, as Justice Stephen Breyer noted in his dissenting opinion, the difficulty of distinguishing such obligations from taxes, which have long been understood to lie beyond takings scrutiny.[50] "If the Clause applies when the government simply orders A to pay B," he asked, "why does it not apply when the government simply orders A to pay the government, *i.e.*, when it assesses a tax?"[51]

---

[45] 524 US 498 (1998).

[46] Significantly, the plurality did not conclude that the imposition of retroactive liability constituted a per se regulatory taking under *Loretto* or *Lucas*. Instead, it found a taking only after applying the multifactor *Penn Central* analysis. *Eastern Enterprises*, 524 US at 529–37.

[47] Id at 554–58 (Breyer, J, dissenting); id at 543–45 (Kennedy, J, concurring in the judgment and dissenting in part).

[48] Id at 544 (Kennedy, J, concurring in the judgment and dissenting in part).

[49] 538 US 216 (2003).

[50] *Eastern Enterprises*, 524 US at 556 (Breyer, J, dissenting). Although Richard Epstein has famously argued that takings analysis *should* apply to taxes, this approach has not been pursued by the judiciary or political branches. See Richard A. Epstein, *Takings: Private Property and the Power of Eminent Domain* 95 (Harvard, 1985) (casting all regulations, taxes, and changes in liability rules as "takings of private property prima facie compensable by the state"); id at 283 ("The proposition that all taxes are subject to scrutiny under the eminent domain clause receives not a whisper of current support."); see also Eduardo M. Peñalver, *Regulatory Takings*, 104 Colum L Rev 2182, 2185–86 (2004) ("Whatever influence Epstein's theory has had on discussions of takings law generally, few have accepted his invitation to turn their backs on the unqualified power to tax.").

[51] *Eastern Enterprises*, 524 US at 556 (Breyer, J, dissenting).

Courts and commentators alike have read *Eastern Enterprises* to mean that general obligations to pay money do not fall within the ambit of "private property" protected by the Takings Clause.[52] In *Koontz*, the majority did not reject this reading of *Eastern Enterprises*—unsurprising, given that Justice Kennedy joined the *Koontz* majority. Instead, Justice Alito seized on Justice Kennedy's specific language in *Eastern Enterprises* to argue that, unlike in *Eastern Enterprises*, "the demand for money at issue [in *Koontz*] did 'operate upon . . . an identified property interest' by directing the owner of a particular piece of property to make a monetary payment."[53] As a consequence, the majority argued, "the demand for money burdened petitioner's ownership of a specific parcel of land"[54] and takings scrutiny was appropriate.

II. EXACTIONS UNBOUND

Having described the relevant legal terrain, let us return to our hypothetical Supreme Court Justice worried about both protecting private property rights from government abuse and safeguarding the ability of government to protect property expectations through tools like zoning law. Applying heightened means-ends scrutiny to land use regulation across the board would seem to tip the scales too far in the direction of limiting government power.[55] Even if the bulk of existing land use regulation could survive such scrutiny (a proposition that is by no means clear), subjecting every decision on zoning, taxation, and permits in tens of thousands of municipalities across the country to such searching review would generate prohibitive costs for local gov-

---

[52] See, for example, Thomas W. Merrill, *The Landscape of Constitutional Property*, 86 Va L Rev 885, 903–07 (2000); *Koontz*, 133 S Ct at 2605–07 (Kagan, J, dissenting).

[53] *Koontz*, 133 S Ct at 2599, quoting *Eastern Enterprises v Apfel*, 524 US 498, 554–56 (1998).

[54] *Koontz*, 133 S Ct at 2599.

[55] The *Koontz* majority presumably shares this view, although the opinion leaves some room for doubt. After noting the need for exactions jurisprudence to accommodate both externality control and control of governmental overreaching, Justice Alito suggests that the *Nollan/Dolan* test can serve both functions by ensuring that landowners can be required to cover their own externalities, but nothing more. *Koontz*, 133 S Ct at 2594–95. If land use regulation is only legitimate to the extent that it actually controls quantifiable landowner-caused externalities, as this passage almost implies, extending tests of nexus and proportionality to the whole of land use regulation might seem unproblematic. But that line of reasoning would ignore the very real costs of applying the scrutiny itself. It would also be at odds with the Court's prior pronouncements and analysis, including that in *Euclid* (which Justice Alito cites in this very passage).

ernments and courts.[56] Such widely applied scrutiny would upend the established expectations of the very landowners that our Justice means to protect. And so a doctrine like *Nollan/Dolan* nexus and proportionality review must be kept within limits.

At first blush, the Court's exactions jurisprudence seems to occupy a well-bounded territory: Heightened scrutiny only applies when the government attempts to bargain with a landowner over the grant of a permit (or some other land use privilege). But this apparently straightforward means of firewalling off the domain of *Nollan* and *Dolan* depends on a doubtful proposition: that land use "bargains" (understood broadly as land use regulations that are somehow conditional in their application to particular landowners) can be readily picked out from land use controls more generally. For several reasons, including some exacerbated by *Koontz* itself, deal spotting is not so simple. As a consequence, defining the Court's exactions test in terms of bargaining alone risks allowing the test to slip its bonds and become the basis for wide-ranging heightened judicial scrutiny of land use regulation generally.

A. THE UBIQUITY OF DEAL MAKING IN LAND USE LAW

Discretionary, conditional, or negotiated applications of land use laws are not aberrations that stand out against a backdrop of well-ordered, prospectively announced, and uniformly imposed land use regulations. Instead, land use control typically proceeds in a piecemeal fashion.[57] Land use deal making frequently takes the form embodied in the Court's exactions cases: regulators have discretion to block a project or permit it to go forward, and they bargain with the landowner over the terms on which they will approve the project. As a consequence, the exactions test already potentially covers a large portion of land use regulation. But even in the absence of such explicit bargaining, most if not all land use law can be framed as deal making given that the laws are conditional in nature and subject to frequent and fine-grained revision.[58]

---

[56] For further discussion of extending heightened scrutiny in this manner, see Part V.D.

[57] See, for example, Carol M. Rose, *Planning and Dealing: Piecemeal Land Controls as a Problem of Local Legitimacy*, 71 Cal L Rev 837, 841 (1983) (describing piecemeal changes as "the everyday fare of local land regulations").

[58] Jurisdictions vary in their approaches to piecemeal changes as well as to the enterprise (and indeed necessity) of comprehensive land use planning. See text accompanying notes 187, 200–203. Nonetheless, all jurisdictions incorporate some flexibility into their land

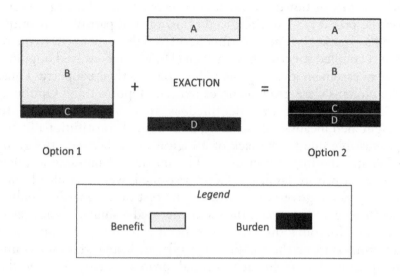

Figure 1. The exaction

To see why the fluid and highly individualized nature of land use regulation makes it difficult to isolate the phenomenon of bargaining, consider Figure 1's stylized depiction of an exaction. At its essence, an exaction pairs some desired land use benefit with some land use burden. We will defer for the moment the question of *which* burdens are sufficient to trigger scrutiny as an exaction, and assume that the burden depicted is of this nature.

An exaction, as envisioned by *Nollan* and *Dolan*, offers a bundled choice to a landowner. Option 1 in Figure 1 represents the status quo land use package, which includes benefits B and burdens C. In the prototypical exaction, the state offers the landowner the paired set of benefit A and burden D, which when added to the existing land use package comprises Option 2. For a concrete example, consider the facts in *Nollan*. The Nollans began with a land use package that gave them certain rights (B), including the right to maintain and use the existing residential structure on their beachfront property. This package also came with certain burdens (C), such as complying with zoning and building codes, not creating a nuisance, paying property taxes, and so on. The Nollans

---

use control regimes, and hence afford some degree of discretion to local decision-making bodies.

wished to tear down the existing cottage and build a larger home on the property. The right to do this was not part of their initial land use package. The government offered this benefit (A) to them, but it coupled it with a new burden (D), which consisted of granting an easement allowing the public to cross their property. Thus, the Nollans were given a choice between Option 1 and Option 2.

This choice set was identified as an exaction, subjected to heightened means-ends scrutiny, and deemed constitutionally impermissible due to the lack of a logical nexus between the grant of A and the imposition of D. The impacts of building a larger house on private land, the Court reasoned, were completely unrelated to the government's stated interest in safeguarding public beach access.[59] In *Dolan*, the Court deemed a similar choice set—between forgoing the right to expand a hardware business and granting land of the public for a bike path and greenway—impermissible due to the lack of rough proportionality between the impact of expanding the store and the value of the property interests demanded by the state.[60] In both cases, the Court assumed for the sake of argument that the government had no duty to supply benefit A at all, but could instead leave the landowners with Option 1, their initial mix of burdens and benefits.[61] What the Court held that the government could not constitutionally do was condition the grant of benefit A on the concession of burden D—unless the deal passed the tests of nexus and rough proportionality.

Suppose, however, there were no other burden of interest to the government that would meet the *Nollan* and *Dolan* tests—or that the government did not want to bear the high cost of proving that it was in compliance with those tests. In that case, the government would be put to the following choice: leave the landowner with Option 1 or provide an alternative (Option 3) in which it simply grants benefit A without any additional burden. This is shown in Figure 2.

---

[59] *Nollan*, 483 US at 837–38.

[60] See *Dolan*, 512 US at 392–96.

[61] See *Nollan*, 438 US at 835–36 (assuming without deciding that preventing blockage of the beach is a legitimate public purpose, "in which case the Commission unquestionably would be able to deny the Nollans their permit outright if their new house . . . would substantially impede these purposes, unless the denial would interfere so drastically with the Nollans' use of their property as to constitute a taking."); *Dolan*, 512 US at 387 ("Undoubtedly, the prevention of flooding along Fanno Creek and the reduction of traffic congestion in the Central Business District qualify as the type of legitimate public purposes we have upheld").

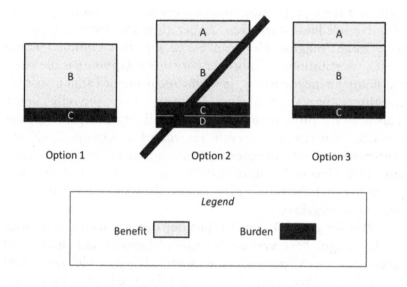

Figure 2. The government's choice set sans exaction

Why might the government choose Option 3 over Option 1? It would do so if it actually expected the additional development allowed by granting the landowner benefit A to be valuable on net for the community (due, say, to an enriched property tax base, new local employment opportunities, or otherwise).[62] Of course, there are also plenty of reasons a local government might just stick with Option 1—even if both it and the landowner would prefer the now unavailable Option 2.[63]

B. HIDDEN BARGAINS

Already, we can see how the category of exactions threatens to

[62] See Epstein, *Bargaining* at 183 (cited in note 7) (referencing the "empirical guess" in the *Nollan* situation that the government will choose not to deny the permit outright, since doing so "necessarily deprives the community of the increased taxes generated by a new residence which probably will not increase the demands on public facilities by the same amount").

[63] A number of scholars have focused on the possibility that restrictions on exactions will block efficient bargains. See, for example, Mark Fenster, *Takings Formalism and Regulatory Formulas: Exactions and the Consequences of Clarity*, 92 Cal L Rev 609, 661–65 (2004); Lee Anne Fennell, *Hard Bargains and Real Steals: Land Use Exactions Revisited*, 86 Iowa L Rev 1, 28–33 (2000); William A. Fischel, *The Economics of Land Use Exactions: A Property Rights Analysis*, 50 L & Contemp Probs 101, 104–06 (1987).

swallow a large proportion of land use control.[64] But the problem of unboundedness goes even deeper than the discussion to this point might suggest: How can we be sure that Option 1 is not itself a constitutionally improper bargain? If Option 1 is the starting point for negotiations, it might seem like it cannot possibly constitute a bargain itself. But Option 1 is never the only choice. This is so for three reasons: (1) the possibility that past bargains produced the law as presently incarnated in Option 1, (2) the existence of as-yet-unchosen options and trade-offs intentionally built into Option 1 (embedded bargains), and (3) the pervasive possibility that the existing law can be changed in the future (hypothetical bargains).

1. *Past bargains.* Option 1 is just one of many forms into which the law might have crafted the mix of benefits and burdens of landownership in a particular jurisdiction. It is possible, and indeed likely, that the law reached its present form only after lawmakers engaged in a great deal of bargaining with affected landowners, bundling burdens with benefits in ways that look very much like the paradigmatic exaction shown in Figure 1. For example, Lynne Sagalyn describes how, in the 1980s, New York City consulted with private developers, civic groups, and nonprofit foundations as it attempted to facilitate the redevelopment of Times Square.[65] As Sagalyn put it, "the political problem of rebuilding West 42nd Street involved an extraordinarily delicate act of balancing the city and state's aggressive plan for large-scale ground-up development . . . with its other goals for preserving the historic midblock theaters and their symbolic sense of place . . . while accommodating the intense community and business concerns of Clinton and the Garment District. . . ."[66] To be sure, these negotiations—and the kinds of changes in New York's zoning laws that grew out of them—happened at some point in the past. But this would not necessarily put them beyond the reach of constitutional scrutiny.

---

[64] Not all governmental actions that count as exactions must necessarily be subjected to heightened scrutiny. It may be possible to identify some characteristic of the burden in question, or some distinguishing feature of the way in which the burden and benefit are paired or presented to the landowner, that pares down the category that will receive *Nollan/Dolan* review, even if the term "exactions" sweeps more broadly. See Parts III and IV.

[65] Lynne B. Sagalyn, *Times Square Roulette: Remaking the City Icon* 91–102 (MIT, 2001).

[66] Id at 101.

The Court held in *Palazzolo v Rhode Island*[67] that the mere fact
that a law was enacted in the past does not prevent a landowner
from challenging it as a taking. As Justice Kennedy put it in his
opinion for the *Palazzolo* Court, some "enactments are unreasonable and do not become less so through the passage of time or
title."[68] It is not obvious why similar logic would not apply to past
bargains between landowners and the state that violated the requirements of *Nollan* and *Dolan*.

2. *Embedded bargains.* In addition, some versions of Option 1
will include what we might call "embedded bargains"—as yet un-
realized bargains between the state and the landowner built into
the very structure of the law. For instance, a "floor area ratio"
(FAR) that is used to regulate building bulk invites landowners to
make a kind of trade-off. Unlike traditional setbacks and height
limits, floor area ratios control bulk by limiting the total internal
square footage of a structure as compared with the square footage
of the parcel as a whole. For example, if someone owns a 10,000-
square-foot lot, assigning that lot a FAR of 0.5 means that the
owner can build a 5,000-square-foot structure on the lot. How
she uses that 5,000 square feet is up to her (within whatever other
limits the state imposes). Thus, she could comply with the FAR
by building a structure with a single floor of 5,000 square feet,
with two floors of 2,500 square feet each, three floors of 1,667
square feet, and so on. In effect, the law constitutes an offer to
the owner to trade the benefit of greater height for the burden
of preserving more open space around the building, or the benefit
of smaller setbacks for the burden of lower height.

Conditional use permits are another example of this kind of
built-in bargain. Conditional uses are presumptively permissible
under a zoning law provided that the landowner complies with
the conditions specified in the zoning law. For example, the zoning
code might permit a day-care business in a residential district if
the owner (1) keeps off-street parking to the rear of the building,
(2) operates only during certain hours, (3) installs a landscaping
buffer between her business and neighboring owners, etc. So-
called "incentive zoning," in which landowners obtain permission
to exceed zoning limits in exchange for providing various public

---

[67] 533 US 606 (2001).

[68] Id at 627.

goods (such as low-income housing or public space), similarly embeds bargains, but allows a broader divergence between the impacts of the landowner's development and the specified conditions.[69]

In these examples, the state's position on the terms of any bargain is spelled out in advance and available to all on the same basis. Thus, the law embeds a take-it-or-leave-it offer, not an invitation to haggle.[70] For instance, depending on the level of specificity of the conditions, obtaining a permit to engage in a conditional use can be a fairly ministerial act without any interaction with the state that we might characterize as bargaining. However, land use ordinances can also embed conditional elements that leave significant discretion to local governmental actors, whether explicitly or through the use of open-textured terms subject to official interpretation.[71]

3. *Hypothetical bargains.* Finally, as we have already observed, the highly individualized revision of land use law is a pervasive phenomenon. For any given pattern of land use benefits and burdens (Option 1), there is almost always some other package (call it Option X) that would be acceptable to the government. This alternative package, let us suppose, would vary from the existing law that applies to an owner's parcel by increments corresponding to Benefit Y and Burden Z, as shown in Figure 3.

If Benefit Y and Burden Z are actually paired together by the government and offered to the landowner, the situation is that of the prototypical exaction. But what if Benefit Y and Burden Z are simply "in the air," so to speak? The government may know very well that the landowner wants Benefit Y, or something like Benefit Y. Perhaps the landowner has asked for it, or it is the sort of benefit that anyone in the landowner's position would want. The landowner may also be aware that the government would like to impose Burden Z, or something like Burden Z. Perhaps the landowner looks around and sees other landowners who currently have

---

[69] For an example of incentive zoning, see Barry D. Yatt, *Cracking the Codes: An Architect's Guide to Building Regulations* 154 (John Wiley, 1998) (describing incentive zoning in Seattle).

[70] See Epstein, *Bargaining* at 11 (cited in note 7) (observing that a wide variety of government regulations and taxes might be characterized "as take-it-or-leave-it offers that are extended by the government to all individuals").

[71] See text accompanying note 182.

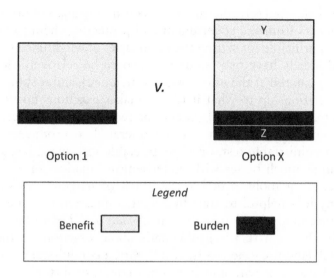

Figure 3. Option X

Option X and prefers their situation over her own, and voices a preference for this alternative.

How much must be said about Option X, and by whom, and in what way, in order for the situation to amount to "bargaining" (and therefore potentially an impermissible exaction)? Here it becomes important that, after *Koontz*, an exaction need not take the form of an explicit condition placed on permit approval in order to receive heightened scrutiny and be found unconstitutional. Instead, a demand made prior to a permit denial should, according to the Court, receive the exact same treatment.[72] But when do ambient discussions about an Option X (of which there may be innumerable versions) coalesce into a "failed exaction" that receives *Nollan/Dolan* review?

III. LOOKING FOR NORMATIVE FOUNDATIONS

The discussion above establishes only that the domain of exactions is not self-limiting as a conceptual or practical matter—not that it cannot be somehow limited. The difficulty lies in finding a coherent way to identify what is in and what is out of the

---

[72] See *Koontz*, 133 S Ct at 2595–96.

realm of elevated scrutiny, given the conflicting goals of protecting landowners from the government and protecting them from each other. A principle for setting the boundaries of heightened scrutiny should ideally have two features: it should be relatively clear (so that one can tell at the outset what is included), and it should bear some relationship to what it is that makes exactions normatively problematic.[73] Trade-offs between the two goals may be necessary; a less good normative fit may be tolerated to produce a much more administrable test, or a less tractable test might be selected if it aligns much better with underlying normative concerns.

In crafting tools to define the reach of heightened exactions scrutiny it is helpful to start by asking a question that the Court in *Koontz* (and, for that matter, in *Nollan* and *Dolan*) largely ignored: what is it that is problematic about exactions in the first place? A land use exaction is, at its heart, a conditional regulation of land use. But why and how does conditionality raise constitutional worries? The question takes us back to the doctrine of unconstitutional conditions.

A. UNCONSTITUTIONAL CONDITIONS IN LAND USE

In a previous article, one of us identified three possible problems with the conditional grant of governmental benefits: (1) "receiving forbidden goods," in which the government uses the leverage provided by conditionally applicable laws to obtain legal entitlements that it is not authorized to receive; (2) "bargaining with the opponent's chips," in which the government confiscates entitlements belonging to an individual for the sole purpose of selling them back to that individual; and (3) "appropriations from third parties," in which the government obtains desired benefits by trading away entitlements belonging to third parties whose interests are not represented in the negotiation.[74]

---

[73] These two criteria echo in some measure Frank Michelman's pairing of "settlement costs" and "demoralization costs" in his analysis of compensable takings. Frank I. Michelman, *Property, Utility, and Fairness: Comments on the Ethical Foundations of "Just Compensation" Law*, 80 Harv L Rev 1165, 1214–15 (1967). Just as bright-line rules that mark out distinctive, easily identified cases help to limit the costs of settling up over compensable takings, so too would a clearly articulated boundary around heightened scrutiny reduce the costs of administering the system. And just as one would wish for the cases identified for compensation to track normative concerns like demoralization, so too would one wish for the region of heightened scrutiny to align with relevant normative criteria.

[74] The discussion in this section draws on Fennell, 86 Iowa L Rev at 42–56 (cited in note 63).

The first problem (receiving forbidden goods) can be illustrated by a governmentally initiated bargain that would require a person to change her religion in order to receive government benefits. A commitment to change one's religion is not something the government is authorized to receive from any citizen. This problem, however, is not really implicated by individually negotiated, conditional land use laws. We do not normally think of it as improper to sell or give *property* to the government. Indeed, unlike other contexts in which the unconstitutional conditions doctrine might apply, the Constitution itself explicitly envisions property rights as subject to (involuntary) alienation to the state for public use upon the payment of just compensation.

The second potential problem (bargaining with the opponent's chips) is readily illustrated by a gunman who threatens "your money or your life"—entitlements that both belonged to the victim before the gunman came along. Translated into the land use context, this concern about illicit appropriations can be more directly addressed by applying a standard takings analysis to the regulation that keeps the landowner from being able to develop as of right. The *Nollan/Dolan* analysis, however, like unconstitutional conditions doctrine generally, typically proceeds on the assumption that the government can lawfully decline to waive the land use restriction in question.[75] If this is so, then there has been no preliminary grab of entitlements, but rather only a legitimate governmental act in restricting development. Moreover, even if there *had* been an illegitimate confiscation of land use rights, nexus and proportionality review would hardly solve the problem.[76]

Only the third problem (third-party effects) is arguably addressed by the nexus and proportionality doctrine. In theory, these limits could ensure that the actual costs of development are properly remediated through connected and commensurate concessions, rather than left to fall on third parties while the government reaps (or confers on others) unrelated benefits. But this is not the typical exactions case. Exactions claims under *Nollan* and *Dolan* are brought by regulated landowners, not by neighbors who were

---

[75] See *Nollan*, 438 US at 835–36.

[76] See, for example, Fennell, 86 Iowa L Rev at 53 (cited in note 63) (observing that the fact that a misappropriated good can only be swapped for connected and proportionate benefits does not do anything to address the initial misappropriation).

unrepresented in the negotiations and who object to the bargain that was struck.[77]

There is a fourth possibility, which we might understand as straddling the boundary between the second and third categories: that conditional regulations are objectionable because of the potential they create for government favoritism or even outright corruption. The prototypical exaction—the government's demand for a payment or other concession from a landowner in exchange for regulatory relief—is structurally very similar to the prototypical bribe. The key distinction between the two is the end to which the regulator directs the payment or concession from the landowner. If the regulator directs the payment toward the pursuit of a legitimate public purpose, demanding it does not amount to soliciting a bribe. If the regulator directs the demanded payment to her own (or some favored third party's) private benefit, then it becomes "corruption."[78]

As with the "bargaining with the opponent's chips" scenario, improper government favoritism requires the existence of legal roadblocks in order to thrive. Roadblocks generate the possibility for government favoritism and corruption when removing them is both highly discretionary and privately beneficial.[79] And, as with the "appropriations from third parties" scenario, government favoritism and corruption have harmful effects on disfavored third

---

[77] This presumably follows from the nature of the alleged constitutional violation, which is premised on some property of the landowner being taken (or proposed to be taken) without just compensation. A neighbor or other third party would not be able to claim that specific constitutional injury. See Fenster, 92 Cal L Rev at 655 n 228 (cited in note 63) ("It is the expropriation of the property owner's land, not effects on anyone else's land, that leads the Court to apply the Takings Clause in *Nollan* and *Dolan*."). However, neighbors and third parties can and do bring claims that land use bargaining practices, including incentive and contract zoning, violate other principles of law. See, for example, *Municipal Art Society of New York v City of New York*, 522 NYS2d 800, 803–04 (NY Sup Ct 1987) (striking down incentive zoning plan following challenge from third party, on the ground it amounted to an improper sale of zoning); *Hartnett v Austin*, 93 So2d 86, 89–90 (Fla 1956) (allowing a neighboring third party to challenge a zoning amendment that embedded a collateral contract requirement). See also Fenster, 92 Cal L Rev at 655 n 228 (cited in note 63) (discussing and collecting cites on possible bases for third-party challenges).

[78] See, for example, Susan Rose-Ackerman, ed, *International Handbook on the Economics of Corruption* xvii (Edward Elgar, 2006) ("In the most common [corrupt] transaction a private individual or firm makes a payment to a public official in return for a benefit.").

[79] See Edward L. Glaeser and Raven E. Saks, *Corruption in America*, 90 J Pub Econ 1053, 1055 (2006) ("The benefits of corruption come from government actors being able to allocate resources, including the right to bypass certain regulations, to private individuals.").

parties. The two scenarios come together in the following way: the government places roadblocks in front of landowners that it fully expects to remove at some price, but the price that it charges any particular landowner will determine whether that landowner foots more or less than her share of the costs associated with development.[80] The focus of this objection, however, is not only on distributive consequences, but also on the nature of the government action.

The structural similarity between exactions and corruption is the marker of a larger problem, one that exactions may raise even in the absence of any evidence of government corruption or favoritism. The problem stems from the very flexibility that the exactions device is designed to create, which may operate in tension with principles of rule of law.

B. RULE OF LAW

Theorists working in divergent political and philosophical traditions have emphasized the importance of the rule of law.[81] The most influential accounts focus on several distinctive features deemed vital to law's ability to sustain a society of free and equal persons. The rule of law fosters freedom by increasing the predictability and intelligibility of the regulatory landscape within which the citizen operates and by constraining officials from exercising unfettered discretion.[82] John Rawls argues that the rule of law "constitute[s] grounds upon which persons can rely on one another and rightly object when their expectations are not fulfilled.

---

[80] The question of what constitutes a party's proper share is itself subject to debate. See, for example, Joseph L. Sax, *The Property Rights Sweepstakes: Has Anyone Held the Winning Ticket?* 34 Vt L Rev 157, 163–65 (2009) (examining the different fairness intuitions that follow from a resource-allocation rule based on space, rather than time).

[81] See, for example, F. A. Hayek, *The Constitution of Liberty* 133–61 (Chicago, 1960) (discussing the ability of the state, under certain conditions, to prevent coercion through law by creating a "private sphere" for the individual); John Rawls, *A Theory of Justice* 235–43 (Belknap, 1971) (discussing the rule of law and its connection to equality and individual autonomy); Richard A. Epstein, *Beyond the Rule of Law: Civic Virtue and Constitutional Structure*, 56 Geo Wash L Rev 149, 149–52 (1987) ("There is no question that the rule of law is a necessary condition for a sane and just society . . . [I]t is a very different question to ask whether it is *sufficient* to achieve that result."); Jeremy Waldron, *The Rule of Law and the Importance of Procedure*, in James E. Fleming, ed, *NOMOS L: Getting to the Rule of Law* 3, 14–16 (NYU 2011) (discussing the importance of procedure, particularly in adjudicative settings, for administering the rule of law).

[82] See Scott J. Shapiro, *Legality* 395–96 (Belknap, 2011); see also Hanoch Dagan, *Reconstructing American Legal Realism and Rethinking Private Law Theory* ch 9 (Oxford, 2013).

If the bases of these claims are unsure, so are the boundaries of men's liberties."[83] Scott Shapiro summarizes this line of thought nicely when he says that the rule of law "enables members of the community to predict official activity and hence to plan their lives effectively," and, at the same time, "constrains official behavior and hence protects citizens from arbitrary and discriminatory actions by officials."[84]

In addition to asserting its intrinsic connection to equality and liberty, theorists have posited that adherence to the rule of law generates a number of consequential benefits. Some have argued, for example, that excessive disregard of the forms of legality has a corrosive effect on citizens' respect for the law and on their willingness to follow it.[85] Others have argued that the rule of law fosters the kind of stability and predictability necessary for economic development.[86]

Lon Fuller's discussion of the "inner morality of law" is typical in terms of the formal features it identifies as crucial to the rule of law.[87] Fuller identifies eight ways that state action may deviate from the rule of law. Those are: (1) a failure to generate generally applicable rules ("generality"), "so that every issue must be decided on an ad hoc basis"; (2) a failure to publicize the law; (3) excessive use of retroactive legislation; (4) the use of rules that are not intelligible; (5) the enactment of rules that contradict one another; (6) use of rules that are beyond the power of the regulated party to follow; (7) changing rules too frequently; and (8) permitting "a failure of congruence between the rules as announced and their actual administration."[88]

---

[83] Rawls, *A Theory* at 235 (cited in note 81).

[84] Shapiro, *Legality* at 395–96 (cited in note 82).

[85] See, for example, Lon L. Fuller, *The Morality of Law* 39–40 (Yale, rev ed 1969).

[86] See, for example, Kenneth W. Dam, *The Law-Growth Nexus: The Rule of Law and Economic Development*, chs 1, 10 (Brookings, 2006).

[87] See Fuller, *The Morality* at 39–43 (cited in note 85). This is not to suggest that Fuller's are the only possible requirements for satisfaction of the requirements of the rule of law, or that the only requirements are formal (as opposed to substantive). See generally Paul Gowder, *Equal Law in an Unequal World*, Iowa L Rev (forthcoming 2014), online at http://papers.ssrn.com/sol3/papers.cfm?abstract_id=2203735 (arguing against a conception of the rule of law as exclusively formal). Jeremy Waldron similarly points out that, in addition to the formal features Fuller identifies, rule of law is also associated with procedural principles, such as "[a] right to hear reasons" for a decision, and substantive principles, such as "[r]espect for private property." See Waldron, *Procedure* at 5–7 (cited in note 81).

[88] Fuller, *The Morality* at 39 (cited in note 85). Fuller's list is perhaps the best known

Several of these deviations are present in the exactions context, particularly where the terms of exactions are not spelled out in advance or, in other words, where they are negotiated with land-owners on a case-by-case basis. To the extent that different de-velopers are offered different deals in exchange for regulatory re-lief, there is a failure of generality. When the terms on which the state actor is willing to grant regulatory relief are communicated to different developers privately, there is a failure of publicity. To the extent that exactions rely on frequent changes in the applicable zoning law, there may be excessive instability. And, where devel-opers are frequently offered regulatory relief on an ad hoc basis, there can be a pervasive failure of congruence between the rules on the books and way the rules are actually applied.[89]

Understanding heightened scrutiny for exactions through the lens of a concern with the rule of law has the virtue of tying the third-party appropriations threatened by land use regulatory bar-gains to the landowners most likely to become actual *Nollan/Dolan* claimants: relatively inexperienced developers who feel abused by the land use process.[90] Their objection, on this view, is not to land use regulations as such, but to the degree of regulatory discretion surrounding land use bargains. Excessive discretion renders the law opaque to the unsophisticated and permits officials to strike vastly different deals with different landowners, demanding much less from favored landowners in exchange for the waiver of reg-ulatory burdens.[91] This differential treatment smacks of arbitrar-

---

of the "laundry lists" of principles generated to capture formal requirements of the rule of law. See Waldron, *Procedure* at 5–6 (cited in note 81).

[89] There is also a form of retroactivity at work in exactions, insofar as changes in conditions or requirements deviate from what was required at earlier points, when the property was purchased or when expectations were formed. To some extent this is an inherent feature of the need to apply law that is responsive to changing conditions to an enduring asset; it is not unique to the exactions context. However, the concerns associated with retroactivity gather added force in the exactions context if the rules for obtaining a permit can be unexpectedly changed in ways that are known (and indeed designed) to disadvantage particular parties based on their past conduct (here, investments in land).

[90] For a discussion of the types of plaintiffs who have appeared in (and who might be expected to appear in) exactions cases, see, for example, Eagle, *Koontz in the Mansion* at *15–17 (cited in note 4).

[91] Note, however, that the facts in *Nollan* itself do not fully square with this interpre-tation, insofar as the same lateral easement condition was consistently required of other landowners along the same stretch of beachfront. See *Nollan*, 483 US at 829 (observing that the Commission reported similarly conditioning "43 out of 60 coastal development permits along the same tract of land"; of the others, "14 had been approved when the Commission did not have administrative regulations in place allowing imposition of the condition, and the remaining 3 had not involved shorefront property").

iness and can easily shade into favoritism and corruption. Lurking in the background is the possibility that favored landowners may have become so for improper reasons. Even when nefarious behavior is absent, the existence of bargaining around the law on the books may create the impression among outsiders that mischief is at work.

By imposing the limits of nexus and proportionality in its exactions cases, the Court might be understood as attempting to structure bargaining between governments and developers in ways that increase the conformity of that bargaining to the formal requirements of the rule of law. On this account, the exactions criteria impose (admittedly broad) outer limits on the relative disadvantage that favorable land use deals (which are obviously not going to be challenged by the favored developers) can inflict on disfavored landowners. The exactions test might thereby act as a crude price cap on the waiver of discretionary land use regulations.[92] Arguably, this cap attacks both the corruption problem (by reducing the value of the bargained-for discretionary override) and the horizontal equity problem (by limiting the potential gaps in burdens the state can impose on permit applicants).

This rule-of-law account of the exactions jurisprudence mirrors discussions of eminent domain's public use requirement, especially following *Kelo v City of New London*.[93] Arguments about public use in the economic redevelopment context have frequently cited the danger of governmental favoritism toward powerful and well-connected private interests to justify limiting the scope of eminent

---

[92] The "rough proportionality" portion of the test seems most plausibly related to this equalizing function, but the "essential nexus" requirement could also make regulatory burdens easier to evaluate by limiting the complexity, reach, and heterogeneity of deal making in a given context.

[93] 545 US 469 (2005). In *Kelo*, a group of property owners challenged New London, Connecticut's use of eminent domain as part of an economic redevelopment scheme. See id at 473–76. The property owners argued that taking property that was not blighted to give to private developers for the purpose of economic development was not a valid "public use." See id at 475–76. The Supreme Court rejected the challenge, affirming prior cases holding the Takings Clause's "public use" requirement to permit the state to pursue through the use of eminent domain any public purpose (including economic development) that it could legitimately pursue through other means. See id at 483–84. See also *Hawaii Housing Authority v Midkiff*, 467 US 229, 240–43 (1984); *Berman v Parker*, 348 US 26, 33–36 (1954). As Justice Sandra Day O'Connor put it for the unanimous Court in *Midkiff*, "[t]he 'public use' requirement is thus coterminous with the scope of a sovereign's police powers." 467 US at 240.

domain.[94] This focus is also consistent with the general thrust of substantive due process review, which aims to root out situations in which the government acts arbitrarily and in ways that cannot be justified (even minimally) by reference to permissible government purposes. The Court has employed a similar approach in its equal protection jurisprudence.[95] A conclusion that government policy or distinction is not rationally related to a permissible government purpose, like a finding of no public use in eminent domain, often implies that government is impermissibly serving some private agenda (such as corruption or animus) at the expense of the public good.[96]

C. SOME WRINKLES AND QUALIFICATIONS

Rule-of-law concerns, broadly construed, seem to offer a theoretically grounded normative explanation for the *Nollan/Dolan* inquiry. But it is not entirely clear that these concerns map well onto the way that inquiry has been structured. Moreover, certain features associated with rule of law may clash with normatively

---

[94] For example, in a summary of the anti-*Kelo* backlash five years after the case was decided, the property-rights litigators at the Institute for Justice framed the conflict in terms of unequal political influence:

> The parties who gain from eminent domain abuse—in particular, local government officials and financially powerful private business interests—have disproportionate influence in the political arena. Not surprisingly, those groups have fought hard against eminent domain reform in virtually every state where it has been proposed. Given their tremendous influence, as well as the fact that ordinary home and business owners do not have lobbyists or special access, the question that the critics should be asking is: "How on earth did the *Kelo* backlash meet with such success?"

Five Years After Kelo: The Sweeping Backlash Against One of the Supreme Court's Most-Despised Decisions *5 (Institute for Justice, 2010), online at http://www.ij.org/images/pdf_folder/ private_property/kelo/kelo5year_ann-white_paper.pdf.

[95] The similarity—both in terms of normative underpinnings and legal content—between the substantive due process and equal protection inquiries is most apparent in the so-called "class of one" equal protection cases, where the claimant alleges she has been singled out arbitrarily for adverse treatment. See, for example, *Village of Willowbrook v Olech*, 528 US 562, 564 (2000) ("[T]he purpose of the equal protection clause of the Fourteenth Amendment is to secure every person within the State's jurisdiction against intentional and arbitrary discrimination" (quoting *Sioux City Bridge Co. v Dakota County*, 260 US 441, 445 (1927)). But see *Engquist v Oregon Dept. of Agr.*, 553 US 591 (2008) (refusing to apply a "class of one" analysis to situations in which government action is necessarily "subjective and individualized" as in the context of public employment).

[96] See Jeremy Waldron, *The Concept and the Rule of Law*, 43 Ga L Rev 1, 31–32 (2008) (suggesting that an "orientation to the public good" is a necessary feature of law; thus, "we might say that nothing is law unless it *purports* to promote the public good" even if it does not always manage to do so).

valuable aspects of the way that land use control is carried out—
or indeed with other rule-of-law principles. The sections below
explore these issues.

1. *The problem of favoritism.* The *Nollan/Dolan* inquiry does not
target favoritism directly. It does not engage in the sort of comparative analysis that one would expect from an inquiry motivated
by horizontal equity. Instead, in considering challenges by disfavored developers, the *Nollan/Dolan* analysis focuses on nexus and
proportionality within the challenged deal only.[97] Moreover, even
if nexus and proportionality would produce a general tendency
toward more equal deal making when consistently applied to all
development-related deals, there is reason to doubt such consistency will actually obtain. Significantly, the kinds of developers
who seem most likely to be *Nollan/Dolan* claimants are relatively
inexperienced, one-time players, not the kinds of sophisticated
repeat actors interested in maintaining favorable relationships with
local governments.

Here it becomes important to underscore the difference between the allocation of proof burdens within the *Nollan/Dolan*
framework and in other contexts that present concerns about favoritism. In the areas of substantive due process, equal protection,
and eminent domain, courts approach their inquiries with a great
deal of deference and with the burden of proof squarely on the
shoulders of the party challenging the government's bona fides.
In the exactions context, however, the presumption is reversed. A
primary effect of designating such a domain of heightened scrutiny
is to induce governmental avoidance of litigation within that domain. This might occur either openly, by causing governments to
shift toward forms of regulation that lie outside the realm of intensified scrutiny,[98] or covertly, by steering their bargaining efforts
toward parties who can be trusted not to sue.[99]

---

[97] Arguably, evidence about other, more favorable deals might come in as part of the consideration of the proportionality prong of the test.

[98] An analogous point has been made about heightened standards for public use in the eminent domain context, given that governments have the capacity to select alternative ways of achieving their objectives. See, for example, Abraham Bell and Gideon Parcho-movsky, *The Uselessness of Public Use*, 106 Colum L Rev 1412, 1416 (2006) ("The Achilles heel of the anti-*Kelo* movement is its failure to consider the place of the public use doctrine within the full arsenal of government regulatory powers over property.").

[99] See Dana, 75 NC L Rev at 1286–99 (cited in note 37) (suggesting that *Nollan/Dolan* restrictions can be circumvented through local governments' reliance on repeat-play de-velopers who can be trusted not to bring legal challenges).

The *Nollan/Dolan* framework therefore generates the costs of heightened scrutiny while leaving a great deal of space for back-room deals. Indeed, the test (particularly if it extends too widely) may well exacerbate the problem of horizontal inequity by making land use regulators reluctant to propose horse trading with anyone but those least likely to turn to the courts for redress: repeat-play developers.[100] Expansive *Nollan/Dolan* scrutiny, as currently formulated, might well have the effect of driving bargaining underground, which in turn may convert publicly motivated bargaining over regulatory burdens into a furtive act that does more (and not less) to undermine the rule of law.[101]

We might imagine courts using rule-of-law considerations to construct safe harbors (or domains of less intense scrutiny) into which local governments would be encouraged to channel their regulatory activity. In the eminent domain context, for example, the Court has treated the connection of a land use decision to a lengthy and public planning process as a reason for judicial deference.[102] The Court's exactions jurisprudence does not currently incorporate this consideration—either in the substantive nexus and proportionality analysis, or in setting boundaries for the application of *Nollan/Dolan* scrutiny. Nonetheless, it is possible that planning (or other procedures thought to undercut favoritism) could be used to help distinguish the realm within which the usual deferential stance should govern from the one in which heightened scrutiny prevails.[103]

2. *Overreaching against landowners generally.* So far, our description of the rule-of-law account of exactions jurisprudence might create the misimpression that the only axis of conflict is between different would-be developers. But characterizing exactions conflicts in this way would disregard the potential for conflict between a political majority and all those who stand to gain by developing

---

[100] See id.

[101] See Rose-Ackerman, ed, *International Handbook* at xviii (cited in note 78) (discussing the role governmental discretion plays in generating low-level corruption).

[102] See *Kelo*, 545 US at 483–84 (emphasizing that the government's condemnation of land was undertaken pursuant to a lengthy and public planning process as a reason for finding the use to be sufficiently public). See also Nicole Stelle Garnett, *Planning as Public Use?* 34 Ecology L Q 443, 448 (2007) ("[I]n both regulatory takings and public use cases, the Court often has cited governmental planning efforts to bolster the case for judicial deference.").

[103] See Shapiro, *Legality* at 195, 394–95 (cited in note 82) (discussing the conceptual links between planning, legality, and the rule of law).

land. Fears that majoritarian interests will overburden property owners lie at the heart of the Takings Clause's protections, and concern about governmental overreaching (as opposed to differential reaching) is evident in the Court's exactions jurisprudence. Thus, some Justices may locate the normative considerations underlying the exactions cases not (just) in concerns about the rule of law posed by the government's offers of disparate deals for different landowners, but (also) in the more straightforward potential for the government to abuse landowners (whether en masse or individually) through excessively burdensome land use regulation.[104]

For reasons already suggested in the "bargaining with the opponent's chips" critique, restrictions on exactions are not especially well suited to deal with the problem of regulatory excess. Significantly, constraining governmental deal making is not the same as decreasing the average or total regulatory burden. It is certainly possible that constraining the government's ability to bargain away restrictions would make the government less interested in imposing the restrictions in the first place.[105] But it is equally plausible that governments prohibited from bargaining will impose burdens on owners that are (on balance) the same, or perhaps even greater, than they would impose if they were able to negotiate customized packages of benefits and burdens with individual landowners. This is particularly true for local governments motivated, as William Fischel has hypothesized, by voters' risk aversion about the value of their homes.[106] Thus, the possibility of tyranny by a local antidevelopment majority, which Fischel has argued is par-

---

[104] For example, Justice Clarence Thomas asserted in dissent from the denial of certiorari in *Parking Association of Georgia v City of Atlanta*, 450 SE2d 200 (Ga 1994), that "the general applicability of the ordinance should not be relevant in a takings analysis," and illustrated his point by observing it would clearly be a taking "if Atlanta had seized several hundred homes in order to build a freeway." 515 US 1116, 1118 (1995) (Thomas, J, dissenting).

[105] Alienability limits have sometimes been proposed as a way to address strategic behavior by private actors, by removing the incentive to acquire an entitlement for leverage purposes only. For example, see generally Lee Anne Fennell, *Adjusting Alienability*, 122 Harv L Rev 1403 (2009); Ian Ayres and Kristin Madison, *Threatening Inefficient Performance of Injunctions and Contracts*, 148 U Pa L Rev 45 (1999). Governmental bodies may enact land use restrictions, including inefficient ones, for a variety of reasons other than gaining bargaining leverage. See text accompanying notes 62–63. See also Fennell, 122 Harv L Rev at 1455 (discussing and critiquing the use of alienability limits to address insincere lawmaking in the land use context).

[106] William A. Fischel, *The Homevoter Hypothesis* 8–10 (Harvard, 2001).

ticularly salient in locally enacted land use law,[107] would not justify singling out exactions (as opposed to local land use law generally) for special scrutiny.

While a standard takings analysis of the burdens placed on landowners may offer a more direct and fruitful way to approach this problem, bargains may muddy the waters in ways that could call for special scrutiny. Consider, for example, the rise of community benefit agreements. These are private agreements between developers and community groups that promise community stakeholders specific benefits, such as jobs or local amenities, in exchange for their acquiescence in the development plan.[108] While governments may view these agreements as a politically attractive way of collaboratively addressing community concerns, the very involvement by government produces risks. If channeling benefits directly to third parties becomes a de facto requirement of development approval, bargains can generate burdens (and not just benefits) for developers that are not apparent from an examination of regulatory impositions alone.[109] Such opaque burdens raise many of the same concerns that we have already discussed.

Here it becomes helpful to separate two inquiries that can become entangled in evaluating land use bargains. The first, which standard takings analysis is well equipped to handle, is the severity of the burden that is imposed on a given landowner or group of landowners. The second is whether the government's overall dealings with landowners are consistent with the rule of law. This inquiry goes to the fit between the procedural and substantive framework the government has established and the legitimate goals of the governmental entity. By the Court's own doctrinal lights, this is the kind of inquiry that sounds in due process: whether the government is acting properly. The connection between the burden-severity and rule-of-law questions emerges in takings cases in the following way: one of the ways in which rule of law might be undermined is through bargaining processes that make it too difficult to answer the burden-severity question ac-

---

[107] See William A. Fischel, *Regulatory Takings* 276–88 (Harvard, 1995).

[108] See, for example, Vicki Been, *Community Benefits Agreements: A New Local Government Tool or Another Variation on the Exactions Theme?* 77 U Chi L Rev 5, 5–6 (2010).

[109] See, for example, id at 27–28 (discussing the possibility that approval by community groups might be an implicit requirement for development approval, and the associated legal implications).

curately and that therefore make it impossible for courts to protect landowners from excessive regulatory burdens.

But the *Nollan/Dolan* criteria do not really address this problem. Their brand of heightened scrutiny is anchored in an application of the unconstitutional conditions doctrine that requires first identifying some governmental act that would qualify as an uncompensated taking if divorced from the bargaining context.[110] The concerns associated with rule of law, including the concern that impermissibly severe uncompensated burdens will be obscured by the bargaining apparatus, do not depend on first identifying such an uncompensated taking.[111] Conversely, the distinctions in the underlying takings doctrine that are considered critical to the question of burden severity—such as *Loretto*'s carve-out for physical takings—have no bearing on whether the government is acting *improperly* in its dealings with landowners. Instead, those distinctions go only to the compensability or noncompensability of the burdens imposed by governmental actors engaged in otherwise legitimate governmental acts.

There is therefore a fundamental mismatch between the *Nollan/Dolan* goals of ferreting out bad government behavior (that, among other things, might allow it to take from owners in a tricky or sneaky manner) and the presumption of the Takings Clause that the governmental conduct in question is otherwise legitimate but burdensome enough to require compensation.[112] Because bad behavior is notoriously shape-shifting and opportunistic, the tools for addressing it cannot be found in a toolkit devoted to categorizing and evaluating burdens for compensation purposes. What is required instead are principles that can channel governmental

---

[110] See Part IV.A.3.

[111] Conversely, identifying an act that would be a taking if viewed in isolation outside of the bargaining context does not necessarily establish the existence of a constitutionally impermissible burden, since the bargain itself may supply the just compensation. See Part IV.A.4.

[112] Of course, an *uncompensated* regulatory taking implicates concerns that we might characterize as related to the rule of law. That is, a taking without compensation would be a kind of lawless act. But it is one anticipated by the Takings Clause itself, which provides for compensation that (once provided) fully legitimates the governmental act itself. To be sure, the Court's rhetoric in regulatory takings cases sometimes conveys outrage at what are perceived as attempts on the part of governmental entities to take without paying. But the underlying aims and methods of the governmental body are not in question in these cases, apart from the isolated issue of whether compensation is required—a question that, for all of its problems, the burden-focused regulatory takings inquiry has been crafted to address.

behavior along lines that reduce problems like obfuscation and corruption—problems that lie outside the domain of the Takings Clause.[113]

3. *The cost of reducing flexibility.* Perhaps the largest concern with using a rule-of-law approach to mark out the edges of heightened scrutiny is its potential tendency to swallow the entire field of land use control. We have already shown how bargains permeate the whole of land use regulation, and we have emphasized the conditionality and tentativeness inherent in the state's approach to a resource as unique, enduring, and essential as land.

If conditionality and bargaining are pervasive in land use law, and if such conditionality raises significant rule-of-law concerns, why not just say so much the worse for land use regulation? That is, why not just extend exactions scrutiny to land use regulation across the board? Taken to the extreme, doing so could make land use regulation prohibitively costly—a bad result for landowners and government alike. A more modest approach, some incarnations of which we will consider below, would attempt to bleed the discretion out of the land use process by applying elevated scrutiny only to those land use regulations that fail to satisfy rule-of-law criteria like generalizability and publicity—that is, actions that are ad hoc rather than legislative in character. The effect of applying heightened exactions scrutiny in this way would not be an unmitigated good, however. A likely result would be a net decrease in the flexibility and customizability of local land use laws, as compared to existing practices.

Efforts to specify and address all variations and contingencies in advance can make lawmaking unnecessarily cumbersome and costly. At the same time, inflexibly applying a single set of land use rules to every parcel would itself undermine the rule of law by treating differently situated people the same.[114] Moreover, as

---

[113] We will suggest below that the Due Process Clause offers the most suitable home for this inquiry See Part V.E.1.

[114] See Gowder, *Equal Law* at *11–14 (cited in note 87). Of course, this possibility focuses our attention on the question of how to identify the sorts of differences that the law can appropriately take into account when justifying differential treatment. For instance, it would seem appropriate for the law to treat two parcels differently because of their drainage characteristics, but not because of the racial makeup of the residents of the neighborhood. See id. Identifying policy-relevant differences requires adopting or developing a theory of the kinds of "public reasons" on the basis of which the state is entitled to act. Such an undertaking, which in turn requires grappling with competing accounts of what is entailed by state rationality and nonarbitrariness, is beyond the scope of this article. Related ques-

even Fuller recognized, blanket rules that are a poor fit for individualized conditions can spur frequent amendments (instability) or encourage gaps between the law on the books and law as applied (incongruence).[115] Fuller's account of rule of law also suggests a crucial and robust role for market institutions and exchange—one in which heterogeneity of interests makes possible gains from trade.[116] The inefficiencies that may be associated with blocked bargains between landowners and governments can threaten rule-of-law values by generating pressure (in the form of unexploited surplus) for illicit deals.

Reducing discretion can also interfere with the ability of governments to appropriately price land use impacts—including positive ones. This consideration becomes increasingly important as the nation's population becomes overwhelmingly urbanized. Agglomeration benefits and congestion costs make the relative spatial placement of people, buildings, and uses—especially within cities—crucially important.[117] As John Logan and Harvey Molotch put it in their classic work on the political economy of land use, "[e]very parcel of land is unique in the idiosyncratic access it provides to other parcels and uses. . . . In economists' language, each property use 'spills over' to other parcels and, as part of these 'externality effects,' crucially determines what every other property will be."[118] A local government intent on maximizing positive synergies within cities will not want to charge everyone the same regulatory "price" to locate or develop in a given place.[119] Applying

---

tions often arise in tax policy discussions. See Liam Murphy and Thomas Nagel, *The Myth of Ownership: Taxes and Justice* 12 (Oxford, 2002) (referencing "the principle that like-situated persons must be burdened equally and relevantly unlike persons unequally").

[115] See Fuller, *The Morality* at 39 (cited in note 85).

[116] Id at 22–24.

[117] The benefits of agglomeration (including transportation savings, knowledge spillovers, and specialization gains) have long been recognized. See, for example, Alfred Marshall, *Principles of Economics* 328–29 (Macmillan, 1890); J. Vernon Henderson, *Urban Scale Economies*, in Ronan Paddison, ed, *Handbook of Urban Studies* 243, 243–48 (Sage, 2001). For recent discussions of trade-offs between agglomeration benefits and congestion costs in city formation and growth, see generally Luís M. A. Bettencourt, *The Origins of Scaling in Cities*, 340 Science 1438 (2013); Jeffrey C. Brinkman, *Congestion, Agglomeration, and the Structure of Cities* (Federal Reserve Bank of Philadelphia Working Paper No 13-25, May 2013), online at http://ssrn.com/abstract=2272049. For a discussion connecting agglomeration effects to the law and economics of cities, see generally David Schleicher, *The City as a Law and Economic Subject*, 2010 U Ill L Rev 1507 (2010).

[118] John R. Logan and Harvey L. Molotch, *Urban Fortunes: The Political Economy of Place* 23–24 (University of California, 20th ann ed 2007).

[119] This is because parties differ in the agglomeration benefits they contribute to urban

heightened exactions scrutiny too broadly could thus reduce local governments' ability to use forms of differential pricing—carried out through individualized bargaining and other flexibility-enhancing devices—to manage agglomeration effects.[120]

As this discussion suggests, rule-of-law considerations in the abstract cannot tell us where to strike the balance between flexibility and predictability.[121] But these considerations can tell us what *sort* of inquiry is required. This, in turn, can help us identify the best doctrinal hook for the analysis and, as important, can point up the shortcomings of existing approaches.

It is noteworthy that many state courts, years before the Supreme Court entered the fray, perceived the need to police bargaining in the land use context.[122] Like *Nollan/Dolan*, these state law exactions tests typically took the form of an evaluation of the fit between the conditions imposed and the impact of the proposed land use.[123] To be sure, many of these tests did not burden local governments with levels of scrutiny as demanding as those established in *Nollan* and *Dolan*.[124] Yet despite their differences, the existence of state-law exactions doctrine suggests a widespread

environments (and may have differential effects on congestion as well). See, for example, Gideon Parchomovsky and Peter Siegelman, *Cities, Property, and Positive Externalities*, 54 Wm & Mary L Rev 211, 215–16, 241–43 (2012) (noting the asymmetry in positive externalities bestowed by larger businesses on their smaller neighbors); see also id at 241–45 (explaining how shopping malls adjust rents to reflect the relative contributions of "anchor stores" and smaller shops). Differential pricing is likewise used in a variety of other contexts where the mix of users or customers impacts the product or experience produced. See, for example, Michael Rothschild and Lawrence J. White, *The Analytics of the Pricing of Higher Education and Other Services in Which the Customers Are Inputs*, 103 J Pol Econ 573, 575–76 (1995).

[120] See Ronit Levine-Schnur, *Koontz, Bargained Land Development, and the Rationales of Land Use Law* *47–52 (unpublished article, Apr 2013), online at http://law.huji.ac.il/upload/KoontzBargained.pdf (proposing an approach to exactions jurisprudence that would take into account differential contributions to and draws from urban surpluses). For reflections on how land use regulations influence and structure the "location market" within cities, see generally Daniel B. Rodriguez and David Schleicher, *The Location Market*, 19 Geo Mason L Rev 637 (2012).

[121] Shapiro, *Legality* at 398 (cited in note 82) ("Legal systems have no choice but to decide how to balance the needs for guidance, predictability, and constraint on the one hand against the benefits of flexibility, spontaneity, and discretion on the other. Legal systems, therefore, not only must heed the Rule of Law but also must have views about how the Rule of Law itself is best heeded.").

[122] See *Dolan*, 512 US at 389–91 (discussing state law exactions scrutiny).

[123] See id.

[124] See, for example, *Jenad, Inc. v Village of Scarsdale*, 218 NE2d 673, 676 (NY 1966) (partial abrogation by *Dolan* recognized in *Twin Lakes Development Corp. v Town of Monroe*, 801 NE2d 821, 826 (NY 2003)).

perception that land use regulatory deal making constitutes a discrete and problematic identifiable category of governmental action in need of judicial oversight. We have suggested that this perception may find normative footing in rule-of-law concerns. While those normative roots fit imperfectly with exactions jurisprudence as it has developed, they may nonetheless offer useful guidance going forward.

IV. Searching for Limits Within Koontz

Having surveyed the normative terrain, we can return to the hard question of how the Court might cabin its exactions jurisprudence given its dual goals of protecting meaningful land use regulation and restraining local land use power. In this part, we turn explicitly to the *Koontz* decision for insight into the limiting principles that remain open to the Court, as well as the ones that it seems to have foreclosed.

Before *Koontz*, the unconstitutional conditions doctrine and substantive takings law seemed to embed constraints on the reach of *Nollan* and *Dolan*. A claimant seeking heightened means-ends exactions scrutiny would first need to clear two preliminary hurdles. For starters, she would need to show that the government was attempting to bargain—expressly offering to release the landowner from a discretionary regulatory burden in exchange for some valuable concession by the landowner. Second, she would have to show that the concession sought by the government was one that would, on its own, violate the Takings Clause if simply imposed by the state.

Lingle and *Del Monte Dunes* further hinted that only those land use interactions that cleared these two hurdles in the clearest and most prototypical way—bargains initiated *through an ad hoc or adjudicative process* to appropriate *tangible interests in real property*—would trigger *Nollan/Dolan* scrutiny.[125] The ad hoc element would have limited the exactions doctrine to the most unambiguous of bargains: those that were available only to particular landowners on an individually negotiated, case-by-case basis. Limiting the doctrine to demands for physical interests in real property would have reserved heightened exactions scrutiny for bargains involving the clearest, most easily identifiable type of takings: per se *Loretto*

---

[125] See Part I.C.

takings, which the Court has deemed so uniquely intrusive as to justify categorical treatment.[126]

In *Koontz*, however, the Court jettisoned the requirement of a physical exaction and remained conspicuously silent (despite prodding from the dissent) about where it stood on the legislative/adjudicative distinction.[127] With one limit clearly off the table and the second deferred to another day, what can we discern from the *Koontz* opinion about the boundary principles it meant to apply? Such limits might relate either to the nature of the concession or burden the government demands, or to the nature of the interaction or bargain between the government and the landowner. The sections below examine the Court's treatment of each of these dimensions.

A. BURDEN-RELATED LIMITS

The *Koontz* majority decisively rejected the distinction between physical exactions of land and monetary exactions. It also indicated that it viewed at least some subset of monetary impositions connected to identifiable land as per se takings. But it left several crucial questions unanswered that will have profound implications for the scope of heightened exactions scrutiny and for takings analysis more generally. First, what distinguishes the monetary obligations that trigger exactions scrutiny from those that do not? Second, what is the status, for purposes of exactions analysis, of in-kind regulatory burdens that are neither physical appropriations of land nor monetary impositions? Third, and closely related, is it still necessary for a burden to constitute a "taking on its own" in order to trigger heightened scrutiny under *Nollan* and *Dolan*— and if so, what does "on its own" mean? Fourth, what role, if any, does in-kind compensation play in thinking about the constitutional foundations of exactions analysis?

1. *Which monetary obligations?* The *Koontz* majority held that

---

[126] See *Lingle v Chevron*, 544 US 528, 538 (2005) ("The Court has held that physical takings require compensation because of the unique burden they impose . . . ."). Although limiting qualifying burdens to physical takings might seem arbitrary, it tracks a quirk in the underlying takings jurisprudence: the categorical treatment that permanent physical occupations receive under *Loretto*, which diverges dramatically from the *Penn Central* treatment that usually governs regulatory takings inquiries, as well as from the treatment that most monetary burdens had received prior to *Koontz*. See Part I.A.

[127] We will take up below the possibility that the Court might ultimately adopt the legislative/adjudicative distinction it dodged in *Koontz*. See Part V.A.

conditioning development on a monetary obligation triggers heightened scrutiny under *Nollan* and *Dolan*. But which monetary obligations qualify for this treatment? Because there is no clear indication that the Court meant to jettison the requirement that the burden in question constitute a taking on its own—a point we will revisit below—we might start by supposing that only those monetary impositions that constitute per se takings will trigger heightened scrutiny. This approach gets us little traction, however.

Until *Koontz*, monetary impositions were not thought to constitute takings at all, much less per se takings, outside of very limited contexts. The relatively narrow exception articulated in *Brown v Legal Foundation of Washington*[128] involved situations in which the government seized some discrete pool of money (in *Brown*, the interest earned by a particular trust account). The basis for this exception has never fully been fleshed out by the Court, but its scope was typically understood to be self-limiting.[129] Even the plurality in *Eastern Enterprises* only concluded that the monetary obligation in that case worked a taking after going through the full *Penn Central* analysis.[130]

Koontz thus moved into uncharted waters by suggesting that generalized monetary obligations tied to identifiable land (or some not-fully-specified subset of such monetary impositions) count as per se takings. Justice Alito's opinion for the majority expressly refers to the petitioner's case as being premised on a per se taking of money, citing *Brown*.[131] Later, he states that "any such demand [for a monetary expenditure linked to land] would amount to a per se taking similar to the taking of an easement or a lien."[132] But all monetary obligations imposed on land holdings, including such ubiquitous tools as property taxes, special assessments, and permitting fees, share this connection to ownership of specific parcels of land.[133] And the *Koontz* majority insists that it does not mean to sweep all of these impositions into the compass of exactions scrutiny.

We know, then, that some subset (and only some subset) of

---

[128] 538 US 216 (2003).

[129] See Merrill, 86 Va L Rev at 903–07 (cited in note 52).

[130] See *Eastern Enterprises*, 524 US at 522–23.

[131] *Koontz*, 133 S Ct at 2600.

[132] Id.

[133] See id at 2606–07 (Kagan, J, dissenting).

monetary impositions tied to land now qualify as per se takings that will trigger exactions analysis. But the *Koontz* majority does not articulate any principle that would distinguish the routine impositions it means to exempt from heightened scrutiny from the sorts of land-related monetary obligations it intended to subject to heightened scrutiny. Justice Alito's opinion instead points to the Court's distinction between takings and taxes in *Brown* as proof that such a distinction is possible—without acknowledging the sea change in the coverage of *Brown* that the *Koontz* opinion itself seems to work.

The majority also finds reassurance in state court cases defining "taxes."[134] But these cases typically involve judicial efforts to interpret state-law restrictions on local governments' power to tax, restrictions generally understood not to reach things like "fees."[135] The *Koontz* Court apparently meant to shield both taxes *and* fees (at least routine user fees) from heightened scrutiny.[136] The boundaries of state delegations of revenue-raising power to local governments seem entirely orthogonal to the meaning of a federal constitutional provision focused on the relationship between individual property owners and the state. It is not impossible, however, that state law procedural prerequisites for taxes, such as the requirement that they be enacted by the legislature, could provide a back-door way for the Court to import something like the legislative/adjudicative distinction that it studiously avoided drawing in *Koontz*.[137]

A different (if somewhat recursive) way of defining the subset

---

[134] See *Koontz*, 133 S Ct at 2602 n 3.

[135] See, for example, *Elizabeth River Crossings OPCO v Meeks*, 749 SE2d 176 (Va 2013) (distinguishing "taxes" from "user fees" and rejecting a claim that the Virginia legislature had improperly delegated taxing power to a transportation authority responsible for operating a tunnel between Portsmouth and Norfolk); *Silva v City of Attleboro*, 908 NE2d 722 (Mass 2009) (reviewing the standards for distinguishing taxes from fees for state law purposes and finding that a charge for a burial permit falls in the latter category and hence was lawfully imposed by the city).

[136] 133 S Ct at 2600–01 ("It is beyond dispute that '[t]axes and user fees . . . are not "takings."' . . . . This case therefore does not affect the ability of governments to impose property taxes, user fees, and similar laws and regulations that may impose financial burdens on property owners.") (quoting *Brown*, 538 US at 243 n 2) (Scalia, J, dissenting)).

[137] Suggestive in this regard is the Court's explanation of why the monetary imposition in *Brown* could not have been a tax, due to state law: "in Washington, taxes are levied by the legislature, not the courts." *Koontz*, 133 S Ct at 2601. Although the point is not developed further, it is likely that the Court will eventually have to confront the question of whether heightened exactions scrutiny exempts some or all legislative enactments. See Parts V.A and V.B.

of monetary impositions subject to heightened scrutiny would make the imposition's appearance in a bargaining context relevant to the question. The idea might be that the government's choice to isolate a particular burden by demanding it as a quid pro quo fundamentally alters the way the burden is understood. Thus, money demanded in exchange for development permission is viewed as different than money demanded unconditionally—with only the former, and not the latter, potentially amounting to a per se taking.

One piece of evidence for this interpretation is Justice Alito's puzzling statement that Koontz's claim—that a monetary imposition tied to land is a per se taking—is "more limited" than would be a claim that such a monetary imposition triggered a *Penn Central* inquiry.[138] How could declaring a wide swath of monetary impositions to be per se takings be "more limited" than applying the much more forgiving *Penn Central* standard to them? The answer could be that Justice Alito viewed his *Koontz* pronouncements about per se takings as somehow limited to the exactions context rather than applying to the larger realm of takings law. This way of viewing the case would confine the effects of *Koontz* to exactions cases, but it would put increased pressure on the problem of determining which interactions count as exactions.

The Court in *Koontz* clearly wanted to treat monetary exactions just like physical exactions to keep local governments from using the former as a substitute for the latter. The problem, however, is that physical appropriations had up until *Koontz* been treated differently under takings law than most monetary impositions. To maintain the symmetry between in-kind exactions and in-lieu payments by treating both as per se takings, the Court may have significantly widened the domain of takings law as it applies to monetary obligations.

2. *What about regulatory burdens?* Although *Koontz*'s treatment of monetary impositions has received the lion's share of scholarly attention, the case leaves unanswered another question with far-reaching implications: what about the wide range of regulatory burdens that are accepted (or proposed) in exchange for development permission? Many conditions do not take the form of monetary impositions and also do not amount to physical appro-

---

[138] See *Koontz*, 133 S Ct at 2600.

priations of property. Such in-kind regulatory conditions on development are ubiquitous, including set-back requirements, parking and landscaping requirements, limits on hours of operation,
and many more. None of these would be a taking on its own under
standard takings analysis. The post-*Koontz* treatment of regulatory
burdens, then, depends crucially on another question that the
Court left unanswered in *Koontz*—the status of the "taking on its
own" requirement.

3. *A taking on its own.* The unconstitutional conditions doctrine
is premised on the notion that the government is asking the claimant to trade away a constitutionally protected right in order to
receive a discretionary government benefit.[139] Accordingly, it
seems to require a burden that would constitute a taking on its
own if imposed outright. And, indeed, in *Nollan* and *Dolan* the
Supreme Court's application of heightened scrutiny proceeded on
the assumption that the government had conditioned development
approval on the conveyance by the claimant of an interest in property that the government could not simply have taken on its own
without triggering the duty to pay just compensation under the
Takings Clause.[140] As Justice Kagan put it in her *Koontz* dissent,
Nollan and *Dolan* "apply only if the demand would have constituted
a taking when executed *outside* the permitting process."[141]

Despite the dearth of substantive takings analysis in the majority
opinion, there is no clear indication that the *Koontz* Court intended
to do away with the requirement that the state's demand—if uni-
laterally imposed—constitute a taking on its own. On the contrary,
the majority considered the monetary obligation imposed by the
state to be the sort of state action that would count as a per se
taking if imposed by the state. But retaining the "taking on its

---

[139] See, for example, Sullivan, 102 Harv L Rev at 1415 (cited in note 34) ("The doctrine
of unconstitutional conditions holds that government may not grant a benefit on the
condition that the beneficiary surrender a constitutional right, even if the government
may withhold that benefit altogether.").

[140] See *Nollan* 483 US at 831 ("Had California simply required the Nollans to make an
easement across their beachfront available to the public on a permanent basis in order to
increase public access to the beach . . . we have no doubt there would have been a taking.");
Dolan, 512 US at 384 (1994) ("Without question, had the city simply required petitioner
to dedicate a strip of land along Fanno Creek for public use, rather than conditioning the
grant of her permit to redevelop her property on such a dedication, a taking would have
occurred."); see also *Lingle*, 544 US at 546 ("In each case [*Nollan* and *Dolan*], the Court
began with the premise that, had the government simply appropriated the easement in
question, this would have been a *per se* physical taking.").

[141] 133 S Ct at 2607 (Kagan, J, dissenting).

own" prerequisite raises the question of how the idea of "on its own" should be interpreted outside of the specific facts in *Koontz*. Interestingly, the Court did not have to confront this question as long as it limited heightened scrutiny to physical exactions. The Court's carve-out in *Loretto* makes any permanent physical appropriation—no matter how small, no matter how insignificant in proportion to the rest of the parcel—a taking on its own. The presence of a physical *Loretto* taking has the interesting effect of making the overall context in which the imposition occurs irrelevant—one can combine a permanent physical occupation with any other property elements one likes, and it is still a taking.

By contrast, context is tremendously relevant for the rest of takings analysis. *Penn Central*'s framework uses a "parcel as a whole" approach to determine whether landowners have been saddled with burdens that should instead be spread across society.[142] The infamous "denominator problem" arises in both *Penn Central* and *Lucas* analyses precisely because it is necessary to consider impositions in a context larger than the regulatory burden itself.[143] If every small regulatory act were treated as a *Loretto* taking, regardless of how it were situated within the overall framework of benefits and burdens, "government hardly could go on."[144]

---

[142] *Penn Central*, 438 US at 130–31.

[143] A central inquiry in takings analysis is the degree of diminution in value (or, at the extreme, deprivation of all economically viable use). To determine how much the value of a piece of property has diminished or whether all economically viable use has been eliminated, one must first establish the base against which the diminution is to be measured: the denominator. For example, a ten-acre plot might be subject to a regulation that destroys entirely the value of one acre. How much the plot's value has diminished depends on whether each acre is considered separately, or whether the whole plot is considered together. See *Lucas v South Carolina Coastal Council*, 505 US 1003, 1016–17 n 7 (1992) (discussing this difficulty using a similar example and observing that "uncertainty regarding the composition of the denominator in our 'deprivation' fraction has produced inconsistent pronouncements by the Court"). The Court has, however, rejected "conceptual severance" that would enable a landowner to define the property interest by reference to the scope of the regulation itself. See *Tahoe-Sierra Preservation Council, Inc. v Tahoe Regional Planning Agency*, 535 US 302, 326–27, 331 (2002); see also Margaret Jane Radin, *The Liberal Conception of Property: Cross Currents in the Jurisprudence of Takings*, 88 Colum L Rev 1667, 1674–79 (1988) (coining the term "conceptual severance" and discussing how the concept had been treated in past takings cases).

[144] *Pennsylvania Coal v Mahon*, 260 US 393, 413 (1922) (Holmes, J). Oregon's ill-fated experiment with Measure 37 demonstrates the unworkability of a compensation requirement that attaches to even the smallest diminutions in value. Before being largely gutted through the subsequent adoption of Measure 49, Measure 37 required local governments to either lift restrictions that reduced property values or compensate for them. Perhaps unsurprisingly, local governments overwhelmingly elected the former alternative, essentially making the regulation of land use impossible to carry on. See Bethany R. Berger, *What Owners Want and Governments Do: Evidence from the Oregon Experiment*, 78 Fordham

This is even more true where monetary impositions are concerned. Before *Koontz*, these had never even been treated as subject to takings analysis outside of the narrow context of specifically designated funds, liens placed on specific property, and the like. It is not workable or logically cohesive to treat all monetary obligations relating to land as *Loretto* takings. Yet to put some obligations outside the *Loretto* box while leaving others inside requires a preliminary sorting task that inevitably draws on the surrounding context and purpose of particular monetary obligations.[145]

The reason is simple. Very few governmental burdens—including taxes and fees—would survive even the most deferential constitutional review if they were examined in isolation from their wider contexts. If the government summarily ordered you to hand over a certain sum of money, or to undertake certain costly tasks, this surely would look like some sort of constitutional violation. But if the sum of money involved were your property tax liability, or if the task involved simply remediating harmful conditions on your property, the apparent infirmity would disappear—at least in the absence of some extraordinary facts not given here. The difficulty is in determining which aspects of the surrounding context can be taken into account in deciding whether there is a constitutional right up for trade that would trigger *Nollan/Dolan* analysis.

Now that the Court has unmoored *Brown* from its prior grounding in specific funds, monetary *Loretto* takings can no longer be identified in a context-free way. Yet the *Koontz* Court was adamant that no *Penn Central* analysis was necessary.[146] So it would seem that the Court has in mind some impressionistic initial step, conducted outside of ordinary takings doctrine, in which it classifies some monetary impositions related to land as *Loretto* takings that trigger *Nollan/Dolan* analysis, and some monetary impositions as taxes or fees that are wholly exempt from takings analysis.

Whether the Court has in mind a similar preliminary assessment

---

L Rev 1281, 1284 (2009) ("In only one claim, out of the over 7000 Measure 37 claims filed, did the state or municipality choose to compensate the property owners rather than waive the regulation.").

[145] To be clear, consideration of the surrounding context is built into the nexus and proportionality requirements used to assess the permissibility of a given exaction, after it is initially flagged for heightened scrutiny. The discussion in the text goes to an antecedent question: when and how will the surrounding context be used to decide *whether* heightened scrutiny applies in the first place?

[146] *Koontz*, 133 S Ct at 2600.

of conditional regulatory burdens that fall short of permanent physical occupations is unclear. The same circumvention concerns that led the Court to reject the distinction between monetary and physical exactions could lead the Court to reject an interpretation that would immunize non-*Loretto* regulatory burdens from exactions scrutiny. Here too, the Court's desire for consistency in the exactions arena may clash with distinctions that have been hammered out in the underlying takings doctrines, potentially putting pressure on those doctrines.

In *Koontz*, a nonphysical regulatory alternative was offered to the landowner: preserving more of the property in an undeveloped state under a conservation easement. Because that alternative would have apparently allowed Koontz to make viable use of his property, and because it would not have compromised his right to exclude as did the access easements at issue in *Nollan* and *Dolan*, it seems inconceivable that it would amount to a per se taking under existing doctrine.[147] And the Court never says that it does.[148] Curiously, though, Justice Alito's opinion implies that *every* alternative offered to Koontz was a potential *Nollan/Dolan* violation: the majority states that even one valid alternative would be sufficient to save the proposed bargain from unconstitutionality.[149]

We think the most plausible interpretation that emerges from the Court's discussion is that it reframed the regulatory alternative offered to Koontz in a way that effectively tainted it with the monetary exaction and thereby denied it status as a stand-alone alternative.[150] If this is so, then nothing in *Koontz* reads directly

---

[147] But see Ilya Somin, *Two Steps Forward for the "Poor Relation" of Constitutional Law: Koontz, Arkansas Game & Fish, and the Future of the Takings Clause*, 2012–13 Cato S Ct Rev 215, 236 (2013) (observing in connection with the conservation easement condition in *Koontz* that "[f]orcing a property owner to allow an easement surely would be a taking even outside the permitting process"). The easement at issue in *Koontz* was a negative easement that restricted development (just as zoning codes do ubiquitously), not an affirmative easement that granted access to the property like the ones at issue in *Nollan* and *Dolan*. While Somin is aware of this distinction, see id at 237, he does not appear to fully appreciate its potential significance under takings law.

[148] Had it engaged in a takings analysis of the restriction on development, the Court would have needed to proceed under *Penn Central* or (more implausibly) *Lucas*; there is no basis for claiming that such a restriction amounts to a *Loretto* physical taking.

[149] 133 S Ct at 2598 ("We agree with respondent that, so long as a permitting authority offers the landowner at least one alternative that would satisfy *Nollan* and *Dolan*, the landowner has not been subjected to an unconstitutional condition.").

[150] In brief, because the regulatory burden could be avoided by paying money, and because paying money was framed as a per se taking, the regulatory avoidance opportunity was seemingly framed as just another way in which the District tried to "extort" money from the individual. See id. This interpretation is explored in Part V.C.2.

on the status of purely in-kind regulatory conditions (conditions, that is, that are not paired with a monetary alternative). The question remains, however, whether the usual rules of takings analysis—ones that examine the surrounding context to determine whether a burden rises to the level requiring just compensation—continue to apply after *Koontz* to limit the class of impositions that will trigger heightened exactions scrutiny.

The problem the Court confronts is not limited to takings jurisprudence; similar questions of bundling and framing run through the unconstitutional conditions doctrine more generally.[151] The Fourth Amendment challenge in *Wyman v James*[152] illustrates the problem well. There, receipt of welfare benefits under the Aid to Families with Dependent Children (AFDC) program was conditioned on a visit to the recipient's home. Considered on its own, the mandatory visit would seem to be plainly unconstitutional: a government agent cannot simply force her way into the home of a random citizen for a friendly chat. But the Court held that the AFDC home visit was not a search at all within the meaning of the Fourth Amendment, much less an unreasonable one, given the level of intrusion involved and the governmental interest in determining eligibility for benefits.[153] That is, the Court used the very benefit for which the burden was being traded to conclude that the burden did not implicate a constitutional right.

As this example shows, a key reason that the unconstitutional conditions doctrine is so disordered is that it is never quite clear when the benefit that is granted in exchange for ostensibly giving up a constitutional right is relevant to the question *whether* one is being asked to give up a constitutional right.[154] The problem is exacerbated in the takings context not only by the muddy and

---

[151] See generally Adam B. Cox and Adam M. Samaha, *Unconstitutional Conditions Questions Everywhere: The Implications of Exit and Sorting for Constitutional Law and Theory*, 5 J Legal Analysis 61 (2013); Daryl J. Levinson, *Framing Transactions in Constitutional Law*, 111 Yale L J 1311 (2002).

[152] 400 US 309 (1971).

[153] The Court first found that there was no search in the Fourth Amendment sense. Id at 317–18. The Court went on to opine in the alternative that even if there were a search, it would be a reasonable one, given its nature and purpose. Id at 318–24.

[154] A somewhat parallel issue arose in *Penn Central* with respect to the treatment of transfer development rights (TDRs). In the majority's view, the fact that the restrictions associated with historic landmark status were accompanied by TDRs counted as a point in favor of finding those restrictions not to work a taking. 438 US 136–37. The dissent argued that TDRs should enter the analysis only in order to determine whether they constituted just compensation for the taking. Id at 150–52 (Rehnquist, J, dissenting).

context-specific nature of the underlying takings analysis, but also by the fact that one type of exchange—property for just compensation—can be constitutionally unproblematic even when it is involuntary.

4. *The role of compensation.* Substantive takings law contains a unique feature: the payment of just compensation removes the constitutional infirmity associated with an involuntary taking for public use. Only a broken bundle—a taking for public use *without* just compensation—presents a constitutional violation.[155] The takings context thus differs from other contexts in which parties may be asked to waive their constitutional rights in exchange for benefits. Where the waiver of a right must be voluntary to be effective, it is capable of being improperly coerced. However, there is no possibility of improperly coercing a property owner to accept just compensation in exchange for her property since her consent is not required at all; the government has every right to simply compel the exchange when it does so for public use.

How should this background fact change our assessment of the (ostensibly) *voluntary* interactions in which landowners and governments engage over development rights? In a sense, we can understand the parties to be bargaining in the shadow of eminent domain. This is not thought to be problematic in the actual context of eminent domain: the government can (indeed typically must) first attempt a voluntary purchase before resorting to condemnation, and if the landowner agrees to it, there is no claim that she has been coerced to give up her right to just compensation.[156]

Exactions present a similar scenario: a landowner's acceptance of an in-kind regulatory benefit (development permission) in exchange for a taking for which she could have otherwise received just compensation. The landowner's acceptance might suggest that the in-kind benefit was preferred to just compensation.[157] No less

---

[155] Although the Takings Clause is the focus of the Court's exactions analysis, it is possible that monetary or regulatory impositions could implicate another constitutional provision, such as the Due Process Clause. See Eduardo Peñalver, *A Few More Thoughts About Koontz*, PrawfsBlawg (June 26, 2013), online at http://prawfsblawg.blogs.com/prawfsblawg/2013/06/takings-and-taxes-after-koontz.html (observing that "there is no reason why the underlying constitutional violation has to be a taking—it could be a first amendment violation, a violation of the due process clause, etc.").

[156] See, for example, NY Eminent Domain Procedure Law § 303.

[157] Perhaps some landowners are not fully informed about their rights and would not understand that just compensation would be available for a given concession, if it were demanded in isolation. But it would be possible to offer just compensation as an explicit

of a property rights proponent than Richard Epstein has suggested that just compensation can be provided in kind as well as in cash.[158] If it is permissible for just compensation to be provided in kind, and if an individual prefers an in-kind benefit to monetary just compensation, hasn't just compensation then been provided?[159] Justice Alito's discussion of the constitutional problem with exactions in his majority opinion in *Koontz* provides an emphatic negative answer:

> By conditioning a building permit on the owner's deeding over a public right-of-way, for example, the government can pressure an owner into voluntarily giving up property for which the Fifth Amendment would otherwise require just compensation. . . . So long as the building permit is more valuable than any just compensation the owner could hope to receive for the right-of-way, the owner is likely to accede to the government's demand, no matter how unreasonable. Extortionate demands of this sort frustrate the Fifth Amendment right to just compensation, and the unconstitutional conditions doctrine prohibits them.[160]

This argument has implications for substantive takings law that are both puzzling and troubling. Why would providing something that the landowner herself deems *more valuable* than just compensation "frustrate the Fifth Amendment right to just compensation"? The implicit claim must be that the government has somehow acted wrongly in failing to provide the desired benefit for free. But nothing in the Court's analysis supplies the basis for this assertion.

The mystery only deepens when monetary exactions are considered. Here, the property that is being taken is *money*. What just compensation would a person be entitled to for a taking of money? Presumably, the money back again. But if every payment made to the government in connection with land will be evaluated in isolation and marked as a per se taking, and if nothing other than

---

alternative to the regulatory benefit in question. Douglas Kendall and James Ryan proposed just such an approach, although they admitted some doubts about its constitutionality. Douglas T. Kendall and James E. Ryan, *"Paying" for the Change: Using Eminent Domain to Secure Exactions and Sidestep Nollan and Dolan*, 81 Va L Rev 1801, 1803–04 (1995).

[158] See Epstein, *Takings* at 195 (cited in note 50) ("The Constitution speaks only of 'just' compensation, not of the form it must take."); id at 195–215 (developing the idea of implicit in-kind compensation).

[159] See Kendall and Ryan, 81 Va L Rev at 1843–44 (cited in note 157) (suggesting that disallowing the waiver of monetary just compensation in favor of in-kind compensation would be inconsistent with the property-protection rationale underlying the just compensation requirement).

[160] *Koontz*, 133 S Ct at 2594–95 (internal citations omitted).

monetary just compensation will cure this constitutional infirmity, then the analysis spelled out in *Koontz* would appear to broadly disable local governments from collecting land-related monetary payments.[161] Even if—indeed, especially if—the benefits provided in exchange appeared much more attractive to the landowner than the monetary payment, nothing but having the money itself back would apparently suffice under the majority's reading of the just compensation requirement. The Court's expansion of exactions doctrine thus throws into doubt all manner of fees and assessments.

Clearly this is not what the Court had in mind. It obviously wanted to leave intact all monetary impositions related to land *except extortionate ones*. But sifting through every imposition to identify the bad ones is no trivial exercise; it involves a significant recalibration of the relationship between federal courts and other government actors. Courts need some principle for defining at the outset the boundaries separating heightened exactions scrutiny from its more traditional, deferential analysis. But, apart from rejecting the Florida Supreme Court's use of the distinction between monetary and in-kind exactions, the Court in *Koontz* offers few clues for identifying those boundaries.

B. BARGAIN-RELATED LIMITS

The distinction between ordinary land use restrictions and land use regulatory bargains is extremely unstable, for reasons that we

---

[161] The difficulty stems from two facets of the Court's analysis. First, in counting monetary impositions as an appropriate predicate for exactions scrutiny, the majority appears to be saying that as a matter of substantive takings law, some subset of monetary impositions linked to identifiable land will now count as per se *Loretto* takings. This on its own creates grave difficulties, ones that the majority tries to minimize by emphasizing that *of course* they do not mean for this new rule to reach ordinary taxes and fees, which have never been considered takings. The Court, however, does not offer a principled basis for its distinction between the different categories of monetary impositions. In addition, the problem reenters the analysis at a second point. Exactions analysis by its very nature separates out what is demanded from what is provided in return, and applies heightened scrutiny to interrogate the relationship between those elements. To exempt taxes and fees from this analysis means that in some category of cases courts will not undertake this separate-and-interrogate move at all. Yet the reason can never be, as Justice Alito's analysis makes clear, that the implicit or explicit consent of the landowner to the payment arrangement pulls it out of the domain of constitutional concern. Something else—something not specified by the Court—must do so. To be sure, it is fully in alignment with unconstitutional conditions analysis to disregard a citizen's consent to cede her constitutional rights. See generally Hamburger, 98 Va L Rev 479 (cited in note 34). What makes applying the principle so problematic here is that (unlike in any other context) the Court seems to be disabling landowners from consenting *to pay money* to the government, regardless of how highly they value what they receive in exchange.

have already discussed in Part II. The Court tiptoed around this instability in *Del Monte Dunes* and *Lingle*. But it plowed headlong into it in *Koontz*. Not only did it speak unclearly about the nature of the burden that qualifies for heightened scrutiny, it also disavowed some potential markers relating to the nature of qualifying bargains.

All of the Justices rejected as excessively formalistic the distinction the Florida Supreme Court had drawn between an exaction that takes the form of a condition precedent (denial of a permit "until condition X is satisfied") and one that takes the form of a condition subsequent (issuance of a permit "subject to condition X"). Thus, "failed exactions," as Mark Fenster has called them,[162] also receive *Nollan/Dolan* scrutiny. But failed exactions are far more heterogeneous than completed exactions, as Justice Kagan's dissent underscores.[163] When a permit is actually issued with a burden attached to it, the link between the benefit proffered and the burden demanded is clear, as is the demand itself. When a permit is denied, however, the reasons may be opaque, multiple, or contested. The Court does not mean to second-guess all permit denials, presumably. But how is it possible to pick out which denials receive heightened scrutiny?

One possibility would be to examine the factual record for evidence that the local government explicitly demanded the burden in question prior to denying the permit, effectively linking the unmet demand to the denied permit. But determining whether a demand has been made is itself problematic, as *Koontz* illustrates. The dissent in *Koontz* disagreed that there was any such demand,[164] while the majority declined to address whether the District's "demands for property were too indefinite to give rise to liability."[165] This ambiguity about the existence and nature of the demand is unsurprising. The fluid and often informal nature of discussions between landowners and land use regulators make the identification of "demands" a difficult proposition, as our earlier discussion of Option X emphasized. In light of *Koontz*, we might expect more guarded and ambiguous conversations and less reason-giving

---

[162] Fenster, 36 Vt L Rev 623 (cited in note 36).

[163] See *Koontz*, 133 S Ct at 2610–11 (Kagan, J, dissenting); see also Fenster, *Substantive Due Process* at *8 (cited in note 4).

[164] 133 S Ct at 2609–11 (Kagan, J, dissenting).

[165] Id at 2598.

associated with permit denial if an explicit demand were a pre-requisite to an exactions challenge.[166] This will have the effect of making it even harder to determine the existence of demands in the future.

While formalistic when considered on its own terms, the Florida Supreme Court's position had the virtue of providing a clear boundary principle for determining which demands would be subjected to the exactions test. Given *Koontz*'s rejection of it, what other boundaries might be constructed to hive off the kinds of interactions that will trigger *Nollan/Dolan* analysis?

C. TAKING STOCK

To appreciate where *Koontz* leaves us, it is helpful to briefly revisit the two dimensions along which boundaries on the scope of heightened scrutiny might be constructed: (1) the nature of the concession or burden that the government asks the landowner to accept, and (2) the nature of the interaction or bargain between the government and the landowner.

As Figure 4 illustrates, burdens can be arrayed along a spectrum that runs from general obligations (a requirement to pay or spend money) to the taking of specific assets (e.g., taking over an access easement).[167] Bargains can be arrayed along a spectrum from individualized (ad hoc deals) to formulaic (e.g., tax schedules). The facts of *Nollan* and *Dolan* fall in Cell I in this schematic; they involved exactions that would otherwise be per se takings of land, and were carried out through an individualized administrative or adjudicative process. The Court in *Koontz* expressly extended the reach of heightened scrutiny into (at least) Cell II by making a general obligation to spend or pay money, when tied to land, a qualifying burden type.[168] The *Koontz* majority also indicated that

---

[166] Justice Kagan sensibly raises a concern about chilling communications between landowners and local governments if unequivocal demands are *not* required. See id at 2610 (Kagan, J, dissenting) ("If a local government risked a lawsuit every time it made a suggestion to an applicant about how to meet permitting criteria, it would cease to do so; indeed, the government might desist altogether from communicating with applicants."). But if explicit demands *are* required, communication is still likely to change in ways that may not improve the administration of land use.

[167] There are other ways in which burdens might be differentiated. See Part V.C.

[168] See *Koontz*, 133 S Ct at 2598–2603. Significantly, the facts of *Koontz* suggest that the monetary impositions at issue might well be categorized as falling within Cell IV, and not Cell II. After all, the District's demands were based on policies it had implemented in negotiations with other landowners seeking permission to fill wetlands. See note 9 and

Bargain Type

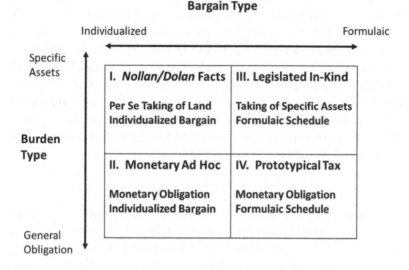

Figure 4. Burdens and bargains

it did not mean to extend heightened scrutiny fully into Cell IV, the domain of ordinary taxes.[169] But because it did not explain why, it is uncertain whether all formulaic monetary impositions would be exempt from *Nollan/Dolan* analysis. The status of Cell III—formulaic applications that burden specific assets—also remains unclear after *Koontz*.[170]

V. A WAY FORWARD?

Koontz left the Court's exactions and takings jurisprudence in a confused and unsustainable state that will demand further elaboration (or amendment) in coming Terms. What path can, will, or should the Court take? The framework presented in Figure

accompanying text. Moreover, although the Court clearly treated the remediation conditions set by the District as monetary in nature, the fact that they involved spending money on discrete projects rather than paying it to the government could move the case closer to Figure 4's top row.

[169] *Koontz*, 133 S Ct at 2600–02.

[170] An example would be a legislative enactment that dictates the dedication of a certain portion of property for public use. See, for example, *Parking Ass'n of Georgia v City of Atlanta*, 450 SE2d 200 (Ga 1994), cert denied, 515 US 1116 (1995) (Atlanta City ordinance requiring owners of surface parking lots to set aside 10% of the area for landscaping and provide one tree for every eight parking spaces).

4 above can help to structure the inquiry. The Court might keep in place its existing pattern of decisions and construct boundaries around the domain of heightened scrutiny that would exempt all legislative enactments (Cells III and IV) or just formulaic monetary impositions (Cell IV). Or it might draw lines along different dimensions and split up one or more of Figure 4's cells. More radical (and much less likely) alternatives would involve the Court overruling past decisions to bring all of the quadrants in Figure 4 either inside or outside the domain of heightened scrutiny.[171] The sections below explore these possibilities.

A. THE LEGISLATIVE/ADJUDICATIVE DISTINCTION

Discussed by the dissent and adopted by a number of states, one possible distinction the Court might adopt would limit exactions scrutiny to burdens that are imposed on a discretionary, piecemeal (i.e., adjudicative) basis.[172] This approach would omit from heightened scrutiny any exactions or conditions that are imposed through a broad, prospective (i.e., legislative) enactment. The *Koontz* majority, perhaps unsurprisingly, did not focus on this distinction between so-called legislative and adjudicative exactions. Addressing the distinction was not strictly necessary to resolve the case, and doing so would have likely made it impossible for Justice Alito to hold together a majority.[173] But a newly constituted majority (perhaps containing some of the *Koontz* dissenters) might well choose the clarity and relative boundedness of this alternative over the morass of uncertainty left behind in *Koontz*. Although the distinction involves difficulties of its own (as we will see), some sort of legislative/adjudicative distinction might keep *Nollan* and *Dolan* from becoming the basis for completely open-ended heightened scrutiny.

1. *The distinction's traction.* The distinction between legislative and adjudicative state action is an appealing one for a number of reasons. First, it is well established in both the case law and legal

---

[171] Domains exempted from heightened exactions scrutiny would not, of course, be exempted from all review. Rather, they would remain subject to due process and takings challenges, as well as to challenges based on other constitutional provisions.

[172] See 133 S Ct at 2608 (Kagan, J, dissenting).

[173] Justice Thomas, part of the five-Justice *Koontz* majority, had previously suggested in a dissent from a denial of certiorari that he viewed the legislative-adjudicative distinction as constitutionally irrelevant. See *Parking Ass'n of Georgia v City of Atlanta*, 450 SE2d 200 (Ga 1994), cert denied, 515 US 1116, 1118 (1995) (Thomas, J, dissenting).

commentary.[174] In a well-functioning democratic system, extensive political checks attend legislative enactments, and these arguably make it less necessary (and indeed, inappropriate) to add intrusive judicial checks. This is the usual explanation for why legislative enactments not burdening fundamental rights or employing suspect classifications are afforded the most deferential standards of judicial review.[175] The same justifications for judicial deference would seem to apply in the exactions context.[176] In *San Remo Hotel v San Francisco*, the California Supreme Court argued that

> [a] city council that charged extortionate fees for all property development, unjustifiable by mitigation needs, would likely face widespread and well-financed opposition in the next election. Ad hoc individual monetary exactions deserve special judicial scrutiny mainly because, affecting fewer citizens and evading systematic assessment, they are more likely to escape such political controls.[177]

As we have discussed, the line between broadly applicable, legislative acts and more individualized, adjudicative land use bargains also coheres with what seems normatively problematic about some exactions. Although legislative acts often emerge from bargains between landowners (or coalitions of landowners) and government actors, the result appears to be (at least at first glance) a generally applicable law that similarly situated landowners will be able to enjoy (or under which they would chafe) equally. Such legislatively enacted bargains do not implicate concerns with the rule of law to the same degree as bargains that are available only to specifically favored (or disfavored) landowners. To return to Fuller's criteria, exactions promulgated through a legislative process meet the requirements of generality, publicity, prospectivity, and congruence.

---

[174] See note 38 and accompanying text.

[175] See *Bi-Metallic Investment Co. v State Bd. of Equalization*, 239 US 441 (1915) (contrasting broadly applicable legislation, where reliance on political checks is appropriate, with case-by-case, adjudicative decisions).

[176] See, for example, *McClung v City of Sumner*, 548 F3d 1219, 1228 (9th Cir 2008) (arguing that the concerns raised by legislative exactions are better addressed through the "ordinary restraints of the democratic process" (internal quotation marks omitted), quoting *San Remo Hotel v City and County of San Francisco*, 27 Cal 4th 643, 671 (2002). Although the Supreme Court expressly cited *McClung*'s refusal to extend exactions scrutiny to monetary exactions with disapproval in *Koontz*, see 133 S Ct 2586, at 2594, the Ninth Circuit's decision was also grounded in its distinction between legislative and adjudicative exactions. Because the Supreme Court did not address the adjudicative/legislative distinction in *Koontz*, the latter ground for the *McClung* holding appears to remain intact after *Koontz*.

[177] *San Remo Hotel L.P. v San Francisco*, 27 Cal 4th 643, 671 (2002).

And, as long as the law is not amended too frequently, they may satisfy the requirement of stability as well.

More pragmatically, drawing the line between legislative and adjudicative exactions would successfully immunize taxes, broadly applicable fees, and many aspects of zoning from heightened scrutiny. Thus, if the distinction is judicially administrable, it could help stave off the concern that *Koontz* has so expanded the exactions doctrine that every land-related decision has become susceptible to heightened judicial scrutiny. And it would do so in a manner broadly consistent with the decided cases to date.[178]

2. *Caveats and complications.* There are some problems with the legislative/adjudicative distinction, however. Perhaps most importantly, the boundary between the categories of legislative and adjudicative is not nearly as clear-cut in the local government arena as it may be in other contexts.[179] It is far from clear on the facts of *Koontz* itself, for example, whether the exaction in that case was legislative or ad hoc in character.[180] The fluidity between the categories may spark concerns about gamesmanship by local governments.

Consider the typical zoning code, which most people would treat as a legislative enactment. In the usual Euclidean zoning law, the kind at work in virtually every community in the United States, the municipality divides its land up into various zones. These can vary in number, from as few as three or four to well over a hundred. Within each zone, certain uses are permitted as of right, certain uses are prohibited, and others are permitted with special approval, provided certain conditions are met.

In one sense, the zoning law operates through generally applicable provisions: all those who fall within the same zoning category are subject to the same regulations. But the higher the number of zones, the more that uniformity claim breaks down. (Imagine a city with a different zoning classification for each parcel.) And, of

---

[178] Arguably, it is not fully consistent with *Nollan*, which seemed to involve a policy of requiring lateral easements from all beachfront owners in a particular area. See 483 US at 829. However, the facts in *Nollan* are susceptible to an interpretation in which the exaction in that case is individualized, notwithstanding some degree of standardization across property owners. Certainly this is the way the case was characterized by the Court in *Lingle*. See 544 US at 546 ("Both *Nollan* and *Dolan* involved Fifth Amendment takings challenges to adjudicative land-use exactions[.]") .

[179] See Carol M. Rose, *New Models for Local Land Use Decisions*, 79 Nw U L Rev 1155, 1158–59 (1985).

[180] See note 168.

course, along the boundaries between zones, the lawmaker has to make highly individualized judgment calls about which individual parcels to include within which classification in a way that puts enormous pressure on the distinction between legislation and adjudication.

Even setting aside the problem of placing parcels into one or another of the possible zoning classifications, bargaining and discretion are built into most zoning and land use laws. Consider the three categories of bargains we introduced above in Part II:

Past bargains. The complexity of zoning laws makes them almost infinitely customizable. During a comprehensive rewriting of a zoning law, property owners can lobby lawmakers to place their parcel in one zone or another. They can also lobby lawmakers to include some borderline use in the category in which their land is ultimately placed. A landowner may lose the fight to have her property designated as commercial but convince zoning officials to include convenience stores as a conditional use in a high-density residential zone. Neighbors may insist that convenience stores in residential neighborhoods operate under strict limits on size and business hours. The negotiations can go on and on. In the end, they will be memorialized in generally applicable packages of benefits and burdens.

Despite the messiness and complexity of zoning code writing, it arguably still makes sense to place these past bargains in the legislative box. After all, the bargains built into the code are in some sense prospectively available to all similarly situated landowners. The mere fact that a particular zoning provision might have been crafted through a process of individualized horse trading is not so different from the way legislation is written in other areas. Rather than fixating on the fact of past horse trading, a concern with the rule of law would seem to argue in favor of considering the substance of zoning provisions on their own terms. That is, instead of asking whether a zoning provision is based on past bargaining, the question would be whether the lines it draws are unfair or arbitrary or leave excessive room for administrative discretion. These are questions that courts have typically (at least in recent years) answered by applying the most deferential standards of review.[181]

---

[181] See, for example, *Hernandez v City of Hanford*, 159 P3d 33 (Cal 2007) (applying rational basis review in assessing an equal protection challenge to a zoning provision that

Embedded bargains. Embedded bargains are pervasive in zoning codes. As long as the conditions they impose are defined with sufficient precision, these need not present too much of a problem for the legislative/adjudicative distinction. Like past bargains embedded in existing law, formulaic trade-offs that are available on equal terms to all similarly situated landowners do not present the favoritism and rule-of-law concerns that seem to be the most plausible justifications for heightened exactions scrutiny.

Some embedded bargains, however, include conditions that place a great deal of discretion in the hands of land use regulators. The zoning code for the city of Puyallup, Washington, for example, is not unusual in specifying that, in considering an application for any conditional use, "[t]he hearing examiner shall have the authority to impose conditions and safeguards as he/she deems necessary to protect and enhance the health, safety and welfare of the surrounding area."[182] Although formally embodied in a legislative work product, such a scheme clearly contemplates case-by-case, ad hoc judgments.[183]

In contrast, incentive zoning normally operates through schedules of the burdens the developer must undertake in exchange for the specified regulatory relief. The available regulatory benefits—and their "prices"—are typically spelled out in advance in a great deal of detail and publicly available to all prospective developers on equal terms. For example, under Seattle's incentive zoning scheme, developers can exceed height restrictions by a specified amount if their building is LEED certified and they pay a certain amount of money per additional square foot into an affordable housing fund.[184]

---

prohibited stand-alone furniture stores outside of the downtown commercial district while allowing the sale of furniture in large department stores in those areas).

[182] Puyallup Municipal Code, 20.80.015.

[183] Interestingly, the code goes on to say that "[n]o conditional use permit shall require as a condition the dedication of land for any purpose not reasonably related to the use of property for which the conditional use permit is requested, nor posting of a bond to guarantee installation of public improvements not reasonably related to the use of property for which the conditional use permit is requested." Id. In effect, it incorporates a modified exactions analysis into the code itself in an attempt to structure the discretion of decision makers in tacking customized conditions onto embedded bargains. In so doing, it seems to invite a kind of means-ends scrutiny by a court tasked with evaluating the legality (under the municipal code) of a particular condition that a hearing examiner attaches to a conditional use permit. This approach is consistent with the idea that the need for robust review increases as discretion grows.

[184] See Seattle Planning Commission, Incentive Zoning in Seattle, 3 (2007), online at http://www.seattle.gov/planningcommission/docs/SPC_IncZon.pdf.

Where embedded bargains put broad discretion in the hands of regulators, and where regulators use that discretion to impose one-off exactions on landowners on a case-by-case basis, the mere fact that they do so pursuant to the language of a zoning code would not justify treating their impositions as "legislative." Particularly in the state courts, judges have shown a willingness to scrutinize legislative enactments that place unbridled discretion in the hands of land use administrators.[185] But where the embedded bargains employ publicly available terms that are spelled out in detail and broadly available—as in incentive zoning—the scheme seems far more legislative in nature and the case for judicial scrutiny is weaker.[186]

Hypothetical bargains. Finally, hypothetical bargains reflect the reality that land use decision making often occurs through piecemeal modification of the zoning law. Even inchoate or unsuccessful efforts by landowners to revise the mix of burdens and benefits embodied in an existing zoning code present the same opportunities for favoritism and corruption that are present in the classic exactions cases. To be sure, if the negotiations break down because of a landowner's objection to burdens the municipality proposes to write into the modified zoning law itself (burdens that would therefore be generally applicable to all similarly situated landowners), the adjudicative/legislative distinction would counsel against treating the hypothetical bargain as an exaction that calls for heightened scrutiny. But where a local government declines to modify the zoning code because of an owner's refusal to accede to the municipality's demands that the owner accept some customized burden, the refusal to rezone looks structurally identical

---

[185] See, for example, *Anderson v City of Issaquah*, 851 P2d 744 (Wash App 1993) (finding a municipal regulation of aesthetic standards to be void for vagueness); *Kosalka v Town of Georgetown*, 752 A2d 183, 187 (Maine 2000) (holding that a regulation that is "totally lacking in cognizable, quantitative standards . . . violate[s] the due process clause.").

[186] Scholars have pointed to the potential for abuse in incentive zoning, sometimes noting its structural similarity to bribery. See Eagle, *Koontz in the Mansion* at *12–13, *21–23 (cited in note 4) (citing Jerold Kayden, *Zoning for Dollars: New Rules for an Old Game?* 39 Wash U J Urb & Contemp L 3 (1991)); see also Nestor M. Davidson, *Values and Value Creation in Public-Private Transactions*, 94 Iowa L Rev 937, 954 n 56 (2009) (describing but not endorsing the position that "'selling' regulatory privileges in exchange for public benefits" may create "skewed regulatory priorities and the potential for outright corruption"). To the extent that critics think that the generality and transparency of incentive zoning are insufficient safeguards to justify deferential rational-basis review, the question arises whether their distrust of incentive zoning reflects a broader distrust of land use regulation more generally and a desire to see heightened judicial scrutiny of land use regulation across the board.

to the exaction at issue in *Koontz*. Heightened exactions scrutiny for individualized hypothetical deals would operate almost like a penalty on (attempted) contract zoning.

Not all states treat piecemeal zoning modifications as legitimate legislative acts. Some, such as Maryland, apply a kind of heightened scrutiny to such changes under the so-called "change-mistake" doctrine. Under that doctrine, piecemeal zoning changes, as opposed to comprehensive rezonings, must be justified as necessary to either fix a mistake in the original code or to respond to some change in circumstances since the code was comprehensively (re)written.[187] Applying heightened exactions scrutiny to some failed negotiations over zoning amendments would seem to push municipalities in the direction of states like Maryland. Indeed, in states where piecemeal rezoning is discouraged by doctrines like the change-mistake rule, the category of hypothetical bargains may largely disappear.

B. EVERYTHING BUT TAXES AND FEES

There is another way that the Court could keep its commitment to elevated scrutiny for most exactions without endangering taxes and fees. It could construct a test that effectively immunizes from heightened scrutiny only conditional burdens that fall within Cell IV of Figure 4: those that use a formulaic schedule to impose purely monetary burdens on landowners. To trigger heightened scrutiny, then, a landowner could show *either* that the government was engaging in an individualized deal with her (involving any sort of concession) *or* that it was requiring some in-kind concession (whether through a legislative or adjudicative process).

Such an approach would not exempt the sorts of Cell III legislative enactments at issue in *Parking Association of Georgia v City of Atlanta*[188]—a city ordinance that required surface parking lot owners to provide a specified quantum of landscaping.[189] It would,

---

[187] See *Clayman v Prince George's County*, 292 A2d 689 (Md 1972).

[188] 450 SE2d 200 (Ga 1994), cert denied, 515 US 1116 (1995).

[189] It is possible, however, that such burdens might be deemed insufficient to trigger *Nollan/Dolan* analysis for another reason: that they do not amount to takings on their own. While it is true that the ordinance in *Parking Association of Georgia* required physically placing one tree for every eight parking spaces, it would seem that landscaping requirements, including the placement of privately owned trees, would be no different from the requirement of a smoke alarm that the *Loretto* Court suggested would not be a taking. See *Loretto*, 458 US at 440.

however, exempt property taxes, standardized permitting fees, and
so on. This would help to address some of the concerns that the
Koontz decision introduced. But what should remain problematic
from the Court's perspective is the extension of scrutiny into the
Cell III box. Virtually all of zoning law resides there (to the extent
it is not captured in Cell I). Heightened scrutiny applied to everything but taxes would upend the generally deferential treatment
that land use controls receive, unless it were coupled with some
other boundary principle. The Court resisted such an open-ended
extension of heightened scrutiny in *Del Monte Dunes*.[190]

Expanding heightened scrutiny to reach in-kind regulatory burdens that are legislatively applied would also have the interesting
consequence of encouraging price schedules to stand in for con-
textualized, qualitative evaluations and in-kind adjustments. Thus,
if a side-yard requirement would receive heightened scrutiny under this approach (because it conditions permission to build on
leaving an area unbuilt, albeit legislatively), a local government
could instead put a price on the right to build closer to the lot
line. This could effectively make zoning more alienable by re-
placing property rules with liability rules—a result many law and
economics scholars would find attractive, but that others might
view with concern.[191] By extending heightened scrutiny so deeply
into the heartland of land use, the Court could prompt changes—
perhaps unintended ones—in the way that land use control is
carried out.

C. OTHER LIMITS

The Court need not approach each of our cells in Figure 4 as
an all-or-nothing proposition, of course. There are any number
of ways that the spectrums of concessions and interactions could
be divided up, and features other than the ones emphasized in the
figure—between specific assets and general obligations, and between individualized and particularized bargains—could play a
role in marking out the exactions that would trigger *Nollan/Dolan*
scrutiny.

1. *Burden sorting.* We have already suggested one way of iden-

---

[190] 526 US 687, 702 (1999).

[191] For an argument in support of the extensive use of development taxes instead of land
use regulation, see Stewart E. Sterk, *Exploring Taxation as a Substitute for Overregulation
in the Development Process*, 78 Brooklyn L Rev 417 (2013).

tifying those concessions that will trigger heightened scrutiny: the existence of a burden that would constitute a taking on its own. It is unclear how the Court will ultimately square its claim in *Koontz* that some general monetary obligations are *Loretto* takings with the rest of takings jurisprudence. However, it is possible that some category of regulatory actions and financial obligations will be safeguarded against heightened scrutiny on the grounds that they would not constitute takings on their own. Although the Court seems to have doomed itself (and lower courts) to struggle with which land-related financial obligations will now constitute *Loretto* takings, it is still possible for it to apply this principle of a "taking on its own" to exempt from heightened scrutiny regulatory exactions that do not rise to the level of permanent physical occupations.

Setbacks, landscaping requirements, and all manner of ordinary zoning tools (such as conditional use permitting requirements) could be kept clear of the *Nollan/Dolan* framework through this expedient alone, even without drawing a distinction between legislative and adjudicative acts. This restriction on eligible burdens could also be combined with the exemption of formulaic monetary impositions (the Cell IV cases). In combination, these approaches would salvage most of what the Court likely wishes to protect from heightened scrutiny, while allowing it to keep *Nollan*, *Dolan*, and *Koontz* in place.

There are other possible ways to slice and dice the universe of concessions. Requirements to spend money could be distinguished from payments directly to the government.[192] Expenditures to bring one's own property into compliance with particular requirements could be distinguished from off-site expenditures. Concessions that reduce the value of one's property without benefiting identifiable people directly (such as by placing certain areas under a conservation easement) could be distinguished from concessions that are undertaken for the benefit of specific neighbors or third parties. All such alternatives must be assessed with an eye to the impact on administrability, the collateral effects on takings doctrine more generally, and the degree of fit with whatever normative goals are supposed to be served by heightening scrutiny in the exactions area.

---

[192] See Justin R. Pidot, *Fees, Expenditures, and the Takings Clause* (working paper 2013), online at http://ssrn.com/abstract=2298307.

2. *Multiple-choice tests.* The practical reach of exactions scrutiny could also be limited through the treatment of multiple-option governmental offers. *Koontz* itself involved a landowner who could develop his parcel if he did enough to mitigate the effects on the wetlands. The District gave him at least two choices that it considered sufficient: cutting back the amount of developed land to one acre (that is, placing a larger amount under a conservation easement than he had initially contemplated), or providing funds necessary to carry out wetlands mitigation on another parcel. The Court found this to be a potentially extortionate choice set. Although Justice Alito suggested that the exaction would pass muster if even one of the alternatives were acceptable, this is not how his analysis played out. Because the monetary exaction was offered as an alternative to giving up the use of a greater proportion of the parcel, the majority opinion framed the monetary imposition as a charge for getting to use more of the parcel, which in its view collapsed the District's multiple-choice offering to a single extortionate demand.

In fact, the Court appears to be saying that, if money is offered as an alternative way to fulfill the landowner's obligation, all other choices will be viewed as tainted. The constitutional hook would be that the demand for money, if viewed in isolation, counts as a per se taking (although this had never been the law before *Koontz*). If so, the monetary choice might seem to dangle before the landowner the possibility of reducing regulatory burdens (including the burdens of the other available alternatives offered to the landowner) by giving up the right to just compensation for what in the *Koontz* majority's view amounts to a per se taking (i.e., the money itself). As actually carried out in *Koontz*, then, the addition of alternatives does nothing to avoid heightened scrutiny—as long as one of the choices is monetary in nature. On the contrary, adding a monetary choice seemingly subjects the entire enterprise to *Nollan/Dolan* analysis.

There are other ways the analysis could have proceeded, however. If Justice Alito had taken seriously his point about any valid alternative validating the exaction, then the ability of Koontz to glean viable economic use from his property without being required to cede anything that remotely resembled a per se taking should have been sufficient to keep the negotiation out of the realm of *Nollan* and *Dolan* scrutiny. Yet it is easy enough to see why the *Koontz* majority proceeded as it did. The alternative that allowed development of a portion of the property without ceding anything that would count as a taking on its own simply became, in the Court's mind, part of the baseline against which a new bargain—this one involving money—was offered. And the same will always be true whenever money is allowed to stand in for other regulatory alternatives—even one that is presented as another conditional option.

But what if the governmental entity does not offer a monetary alternative at all, and also does not propose a physical taking? Suppose, to take the facts of *Koontz*, that the owner were simply told that he could develop one acre of his land if he placed another portion of the parcel under a conservation easement, or allowed it to be downzoned to a less intensive development classification. Would this constrained choice set avoid triggering heightened scrutiny? Seemingly yes, at least if the *Koontz* majority meant to retain the "taking on its own" requirement. What is being asked in exchange for development rights is the sort of concession that would not count as a taking under *Loretto*, nor under *Lucas* or *Penn Central*. This analysis suggests that by removing options, heightened scrutiny may be dodged, and by adding them, it may be triggered. Such a result might not seem surprising in the context of the unconstitutional conditions doctrine. After all, the doctrine of unconstitutional conditions is puzzling precisely because it frowns on governments adding, rather than removing, choices.

Is there a way to structure a menu of choices so that it reduces rather than exacerbates the normative concerns behind exactions? One possibility might involve offering landowners a choice between a fee generated by a formula or schedule and an individualized in-kind regulatory concession. The presence of the former, offered as a take-it-or-leave-it offer available on equal terms to all, could address worries about the rule of law and horizontal inequity, while the latter might allow mutually beneficial adjustments to be made from that baseline.

An obvious objection would be that the monetary schedule might be set artificially high, so that no one would elect it. All the real action would then occur within the individualized regulatory deals. But if this were so, then the monetary schedule would not actually serve the sort of illegitimate leveraging purpose that troubled the *Koontz* Court. An option that no one actually chooses (and cannot be forced to choose) cannot plausibly constitute a form of extortion. It is true, however, that less powerful developers might find themselves limited to the monetary schedule, while the government offered favored developers lighter regulatory alternatives. Some of the regulatory alternatives offered by the government might also be problematically burdensome in their own right, even if they were insufficient to amount to takings on their own. The existence of a fixed menu of choices would not by itself ensure perfect equity or safeguard rule-of-law values. But it would be possible to reinterpret the significance of multiple alternatives in a manner that is more conducive to the efforts of local governments to arrive at alternatives that offset development impacts in the least costly manner.

D. SCRUTINY ALL AROUND

The impetus for our effort to craft a boundary principle for *Nollan/Dolan* analysis has been the need to maintain the two fixed points created by past takings cases: deferential review of most land use regulations and the carve-out of heightened judicial scrutiny for certain "exactions." If, however, we were liberated from these two fixed points, the pressure to precisely define the domain of exactions scrutiny would diminish. In that situation, what direction should the law take? It is worth thinking about two very different scenarios. In the first, taken up in this section, courts would jettison the long-standing deference afforded to land use regulation since *Euclid*. Instead of deferring, courts would employ something like heightened exactions scrutiny to all land use regulations. This would be a kind of Lochnerism, but one reserved for the context of land use law. In the second, taken up in Section E, courts would broaden the domain of *Euclid* deference to exactions, abandoning the island of heightened scrutiny it has created under *Nollan* and *Dolan*.

It would certainly be (conceptually) possible to subject all or most land use controls to heightened scrutiny. The disadvantages of this approach are obvious. Although many land use regulations would withstand judicial scrutiny, the costs of adjudicating the legitimacy of those regulations would be enormous. Small local governments are particularly poorly situated to bear those costs. Rather than risk being hauled into court, local governments would be more likely to simply scale back their regulation. This might superficially seem like a desirable outcome for a certain brand of naive libertarianism. But it would have the perverse effect of depriving local governments of their principal tools for protecting landowners against threats to the use and enjoyment of their property. Oregon's unhappy experience with Measure 37 suggests that, once they confront the unpredictability of unregulated land use, owners quickly come to realize the mutually protective value of at least some land use regulation.[193]

On the other hand, enhanced judicial scrutiny of land use regulation would have some silver linings. Although zoning is a crucial tool for protecting owners from the unpredictability of neighboring land uses, it is also a vehicle by which local governments give the force of law to those owners' prejudices and narrowly framed self-interest. From its inception, the story of zoning has been as much about exclusion, free-riding, and sprawl as it has been about the thoughtful coordination of conflicting land uses. Key among the benefits of extending the domain of heightened judicial scrutiny in the domain of land use regulation would be its ability to lay bare the thin justifications for many types of zoning restrictions.

While it is interesting to consider the implications of such a move, we view it as too unlikely to carry the day and too disruptive of settled expectations to warrant a full exploration here. Nor is it likely to be, all things considered, the most attractive or useful tack for addressing problems like exclusionary zoning. Nonetheless, it is helpful to bear in mind the nature of the constraints the Court faces as it seeks to avoid this outcome.

E. RELOCATE EXACTIONS

An alternative to extending the reach of heightened exactions scrutiny would be to give up on the exactions project, at least as understood as part of takings jurisprudence. It would be possible to revert to rational basis style means-ends review for all land use controls, including those that are packaged into bargains or that involve concessions that would otherwise be takings. This suggestion is less radical than it appears. The Supreme Court's exactions cases are of relatively recent vintage. And reverting to deferential review as a matter of federal constitutional law would

---

[193] See Berger, 78 Fordham L Rev at 1281 (cited in note 144).

not mean abandoning all checks on governmental power. Takings analysis under *Penn Central, Lucas,* and *Loretto* would provide a continuing avenue for landowners seeking relief from the most onerous regulatory burdens. In addition, landowners would be able to seek judicial review of arbitrary and irrational regulation through the Due Process Clause. Further, any of a number of special purpose state-law doctrines constrain bargaining in various ways to protect landowners and third parties. We will discuss these last two options in turn.

1. *The Due Process Clause.* Courts can already review local land use bargains for basic fairness and rationality using the tools of substantive due process, and they could continue to do so in the absence of any federal exactions doctrine located within the Takings Clause.[194] Relying on due process review to police improper bargains would fit better with the Court's prior pronouncements about the division of labor between the Takings Clause and the Due Process Clause.[195] As the Court made clear in *Lingle,* the Takings Clause is focused on protecting owners from bearing excessive burdens. Scrutiny of the fit between the public ends served by a land use regulation and the means chosen is not a takings question, but one of substantive due process.

This distinction between due process questions and takings questions is not an empty formalism. The remedy for a violation of the Takings Clause is payment of just compensation. The remedy for a violation of due process is invalidation of the government action. This is because the wrong associated with the Takings Clause is simply the failure to structure a legitimate government

---

[194] Many of the claims that would be amenable to due process scrutiny could just as easily be evaluated under an equal protection analysis. As we have already discussed, see text accompanying notes 93–96, the means-end inquiry at work in the substantive due process context closely resembles similar inquiries courts have used in both the due process and public use contexts. That similarity is likely generated by a common normative foundation in rule-of-law concerns about the dangers of arbitrary government action. And the fundamental exactions complaint in its most attractive form—that the government has treated the landowner arbitrarily—is largely the same under both theories. For an examination of how equal protection analysis might even address concerns that are currently treated as regulatory takings issues, see generally Nestor M. Davidson, *The Problem of Equality in Takings,* 102 Nw U L Rev 1 (2008).

[195] We are not alone in making this suggestion. See, for example, Echeverria, *Koontz: The Very Worst* at *26–28 (cited in note 4). Indeed, Mark Fenster has suggested that the Court effectively adopted a substantive due process approach to exactions in *Koontz,* and that the majority's reliance on the unconstitutional conditions doctrine served to remove exactions from the realm of takings law altogether. See Fenster, *Substantive Due Process* at *13–14 (cited in note 4).

354 THE SUPREME COURT REVIEW [2013

action in a way that avoids putting an excessive burden on a particular property owner. This wrong is fixed by the payment of
compensation. The wrong associated with a violation of substantive due process is more grave: a failure of the government to act
according to basic rationality or to act in pursuit of legitimate
ends.[196] And so the remedy is to block the government action in
a more categorical way.

The rule-of-law harms that exactions doctrine seems designed
to capture—favoritism and corruption—are much closer in their
nature and seriousness to the harms encompassed by the Due
Process Clause than they are to those that form the subject of
protection against uncompensated takings. In recent years, Justice
Kennedy has championed a more vigorous use of rational basis
due process review to address problems ranging from "judicial
takings"[197] to general obligations to pay money.[198] He has also
connected due process concerns to the public use requirement
within takings law.[199] Consistent with this approach, the Court
should consider extending meaningful due process review into the
domain of the kinds of adjudicative land use bargains we have been
discussing. Grounding this inquiry in due process would eliminate
the need for an anomalously heightened means-ends exactions
review within the takings doctrine. At the same time, focusing it
narrowly on the category of bargains most likely to provide opportunities for government favoritism and abuse would limit the
danger of an ever-expanding domain of heightened judicial scrutiny in the land use context.

We do not mean to suggest that moving the exactions inquiry
into the due process arena will automatically resolve all difficulties.
Appropriate doctrines must be crafted or adapted to achieve rule-
of-law ends. Our discussion has suggested that this undertaking
will involve difficult trade-offs between flexibility and stability,
uniformity and customization. Whatever tests are crafted—and we
do not undertake to specify them here—will be imperfect and

[196] See Eduardo M. Peñalver and Lior Jacob Strahilevitz, *Judicial Takings or Due Process?*
97 Cornell L Rev 305, 323–24 (2012).

[197] *Stop the Beach Renourishment, Inc. v Fla Department of Environmental Protection*, 130
S Ct 2592, 2614 (2010) (Kennedy, J, concurring in part and concurring in the judgment).

[198] *Eastern Enterprises v Apfel*, 524 US 498, 446–50 (1998) (Kennedy, J, concurring in
the judgment and dissenting in part).

[199] *Kelo v City of New London*, 545 US 469, 490 (2005) (Kennedy, J, concurring).

subject to criticism. But they should at least be addressed to the right sort of inquiry. What makes grounding exactions doctrine in the Takings Clause so problematic is that it requires piggybacking on a set of substantive doctrines that are asking an entirely different question (whether burdens should be borne without compensation) than the one to which exactions concerns are most plausibly addressed (has the government abused its power). Moving exactions doctrine into the Due Process Clause would produce conceptual congruence between the doctrinal foundation and the concerns that exactions generate. It would free the Court from the futile and destructive task of attempting to shoehorn its worries about government misbehavior into categories created to address compensable (but otherwise proper) governmental burdens. And it would reduce the risk that such shoehorning will (in the process) distort both exactions and takings doctrine.

2. *State law.* Apart from federal due process review, it is important to remember that state courts have developed a number of state-law doctrines to address the issues raised by bargaining and discretion in the land use context. These include (1) restrictions on contract and spot zoning;[200] (2) state law exactions doctrines;[201] (3) limitations on the ability to engage in piecemeal rezonings, such as the change-mistake rule;[202] and (4) standards of due process review that exceed those imposed by federal constitutional norms.[203] All of these doctrines work either to constrain the sort of discretion necessary to get land use bargains off the ground or to police those bargains once they are made.

An advantage of relying on state law is broader state court exposure to land use conflicts and more permissive standing doctrines in state courts that would permit a (potentially) all-encompassing approach to bargains. "Exactions" as a problem of federal constitutional law seems concerned only with landowners being

---

[200] See *Little v Winborn*, 518 NW2d 384, 387–89 (Iowa 1994) (scrutinizing spot zoning); *Dacy v Village of Ruidoso*, 845 P2d 793, 796–98 (NM 1992) (discussing judicial scrutiny of contract zoning).

[201] See *Dolan v City of Tigard*, 512 US 374, 389–91 (1994) (surveying state-law exactions doctrines). Some state law limits on development conditions do not expressly use the term "exaction" or may find doctrinal footing outside the Takings Clause. See, for example, *Rosen v Village of Downers Grove*, 167 NE2d 230 (Ill 1960).

[202] See note 187 and accompanying text.

[203] See, for example, *Johnson v City of Peducah*, 512 SW2d 514 (Ky 1974) (striking down a local land use ordinance as violating Section 2 of the Kentucky Constitution, which prohibits "arbitrary" state action).

exploited, and that is the pattern that exactions claims have invariably taken: a landowner challenges the conditions imposed on her in exchange for development approval. But land use bargains raise important questions of fairness to third parties not included in the negotiations. Neighbors may have cause to challenge land use bargains that exact too little from developers in exchange for permission to develop land in ways that harm others. Having a layer of federal protection that applies only to a subset of the overall issue of improper bargains arguably impedes coherent state law solutions.

Another advantage to leaving (more) exactions review to the states is that state courts are well equipped to tailor solutions to the ways in which deals are typically accomplished in the particular jurisdiction. Most land use law is state law. State courts are far more familiar with the dynamics of land use regulation in their jurisdictions than federal courts can realistically hope to become.[204]

One concern of the *Koontz* dissent is that—if heightened review extends too broadly—communications between landowners and government will be inhibited. This is not necessarily a bad thing, if we examine some of the strategic implications of placing one party or the other into the position of making a take-it-or-leave-it offer.[205] Changing the way lines of communication work can be useful, but there is no reason to think that federal courts are best able to fine-tune these changes. Even if there is some best way to reduce leverage, experimentation at the state level seems more likely to arrive at it than occasional Supreme Court pronouncements.

---

[204] See Stewart E. Sterk, *The Federalism Dimension of Takings Jurisprudence*, 114 Yale L J 203, 226–28 (2004) (discussing the difficulty that federal courts have in assessing land use laws for constitutional validity and arguing that state courts are better situated to undertake that role); Rick Hills, *Bill Fischel on Koontz: Why Federalism Should Limit Enforcement of the Takings Doctrine*, Prawfsblawg, Aug 16, 2013, 12:50 pm, http://prawfsblawg.blogs.com/prawfsblawg/2013/08/bill-fischel-on-koontz-why-federalism-should-limit-enforcement-of-takings-doctrine.html (making a case for using state law as the primary mechanism for policing exactions and quoting Fischel for the point that a more localized perspective dominates "the view from Olympus."). See also Robert C. Ellickson, *Federalism and Kelo: A Question for Richard Epstein*, 44 Tulsa L Rev 751, 762 (2009) (maintaining that "state courts, not federal courts, should be centrally responsible for limiting eminent domain abuses by state and local agencies").

[205] See, for example, Ian Ayres and Eric Talley, *Solomonic Bargaining: Dividing a Legal Entitlement to Facilitate Coasean Trade*, 104 Yale L J 1027, 1049–50 (1995) (discussing the bargaining advantages associated with take-it-or-leave-it offers).

VI. Conclusion

In *Nollan* and *Dolan*, the Court started down a path that, if followed beyond a certain point, cannot be reconciled with broad judicial deference to garden-variety land use controls. When a particular fact pattern is placed in the *Nollan/Dolan* box, it receives astonishing treatment: the government must prove that the burdens it has imposed are logically related to and proportionate to the costs of the permitted development. Applying this approach to all of land use would mean that zoning and much else would either disappear or become prohibitively expensive to administer. This presumably would be unacceptable to the Court and to most property owners. Yet *Koontz* heedlessly lurched toward this unwanted endpoint, knocking over barriers that it found logically unconvincing, unaccountably confident that its exactions jurisprudence would obviously and automatically spare all "good" land use regulations.

The result is a doctrinally disordered decision. It is entirely possible, perhaps even likely, that some of the worst on-the-ground impacts will be significantly buffered. For example, Rick Hills has suggested that the *Koontz* Court's failure to specify damages offers courts a viable "exit strategy."[206] Anemic remedies or procedural blockades may keep many of the problems foreseen by the dissent from coming about, or from taking their most catastrophic

---

[206] See Rick Hills, *Koontz's Unintelligible Takings Rule: Can Remedial Equivocation Save the Court from a Doctrinal Quagmire?* Prawfsblawg, June 25, 2013, 3:41 pm, http://prawfs-blawg.blogs.com/prawfsblawg/2013/06/koontzs-unintelligible-takings-rule-can-remedial-equivocation-make-up-for-an-incoherent-substantive-.html ("*Koontz* carefully preserves a convenient albeit disingenuous 'remedial' exit strategy that should insure that the decision is a dead letter."). Hills focuses on the following line from the majority opinion: "Because petitioner brought his claim pursuant to a state law cause of action, the Court has no occasion to discuss what remedies might be available for a *Nollan/Dolan* unconstitutional conditions violation either here or in other cases." *Koontz*, 133 S Ct at 2597 (quoted in Hills). If Hills's prognosis is correct, *Koontz* might never cash out in a meaningful way for landowners, echoing the outcomes in cases like *Loretto* and *Brown*. In *Loretto*, the Supreme Court remanded on the question of just compensation and the New York Court of Appeals upheld the power of the Commission on Cable Television to set the compensation rate. *Loretto v Teleprompter Manhattan CATV Corp.*, 446 NE2d 428 (NY 1983). This rate had been set by the Commission at $1 as a general matter. See *Loretto v Teleprompter Manhattan CATV Corp.*, 423 NE2d 320, 325 (NY 1981). In *Brown*, the Court held that the transfer of interest from specific accounts could be a per se taking, but found that the compensation due in the case at hand would be zero, as the owners of the principal did not suffer any net loss. 538 US at 240. Expanding the range of exactions scrutiny, like extending the scope of per se takings, may thus have the effect of pushing contextual inquiries, such as those involving in-kind compensation, later in the analysis rather than suppressing them altogether. The threat of litigation and uncertainty over remedies could remain quite costly for local governments, however, at least in the short run.

forms.[207] Repeat-play developers may acquiesce with local governments in legally questionable but mutually beneficial deals.[208] In this sense, *Koontz* may turn out to be much ado about nothing. But in another sense, *Koontz* embodies a tension that the Court cannot ultimately avoid addressing—one over the best way to reconcile fundamentally inconsistent strands of property rights protection. We hope that by conveying something of this tension here, we have added to an understanding of the contradictory dictates of property protection itself—whether or not the Court manages to address them in a satisfying way.

---

[207] It is even possible that procedural and remedial developments will inform courts' future understanding of the underlying exactions doctrine. See Fenster, *Substantive Due Process* at *13–14 (cited in note 4) (reading into the *Koontz* Court's remedial ambivalence an understanding of exactions doctrine that would pull it out of the Takings Clause and permit remedies like invalidation that fit instead with substantive due process).

[208] See Dana, 75 NC L Rev at 1286–99 (cited in note 37). Doctrines of standing play a role here, including whether (and on what grounds) third parties such as neighbors are allowed to challenge deals that affect their interests. See note 77.

TRACEY MACLIN

MARYLAND v KING: TERRY v OHIO
REDUX

Forty years ago, the Supreme Court's search incident to arrest doctrine was settled and relatively clear: as a routine matter, police
could, without any particularized suspicion, search an arrestee for
weapons and any evidence in his possession that the arrestee might
try to conceal or destroy. The twin rationales justifying a search
incident to arrest—officer safety and evidence preservation—
marked the outer boundaries of police authority. In *Schmerber v
California*, the Court explained that these two justifications "have
little applicability with respect to searches involving intrusions beyond the body's surface."[1] According to *Schmerber*, "the interests in
human dignity and privacy which the Fourth Amendment protects
forbid any such intrusions on the mere chance that desired evidence
might be obtained."[2] Thus, *Schmerber* required either a judicial warrant or some emergency that justified an exemption from the warrant requirement for the police to invade an arrestee's body.[3]

Tracey Maclin is Professor of Law, Boston University School of Law.

Author's note: I would like to thank Sarah Bidinger and Colleen Laffin for their
excellent research and editing assistance.

[1] *Schmerber v California*, 384 US 757, 769 (1966).

[2] Id at 769–70.

[3] As Professor Wayne LaFave has explained: "[I]t seems clear from the *Schmerber* case
that a more demanding test must be met when the search incident to the arrest involves
the taking of a blood sample or the making of some similar intrusion into the body."
Wayne R. LaFave, 3 *Search and Seizure: A Treatise on the Fourth Amendment* § 5.3(c) at
220–21 (West, 5th ed 2012) (footnote omitted).

Despite the apparent clarity of search incident to arrest doctrine, Justice Lewis Powell suggested in a concurring opinion in *United States v Robinson* that such searches should not be limited to the objectives of police safety and evidence preservation.[4] In *Robinson*, a police officer looked inside a cigarette package found in the coat pocket of a person arrested for driving with a revoked license. The Court, in an opinion by then-Justice William Rehnquist, held that this was a valid search incident to arrest. Rehnquist explained that "in the case of a lawful custodial arrest a full search of the person is not only an exception to the warrant requirement of the Fourth Amendment, but is also a 'reasonable' search under that Amendment."[5] Although stated in expansive terms, the holding in *Robinson* was consistent with the rationale of the search incident to arrest doctrine.[6] Although the police officer did not find any evidence or fruits of the offense for which Robinson was arrested, the search of the cigarette package was "reasonable" because it ensured that Robinson did not possess a weapon that might be used to harm the arresting officer. The Court was unwilling to qualify an officer's "general authority" to search incident to arrest on the "rather speculative judgment" that persons arrested for traffic offenses "are less likely to possess dangerous weapons than are those arrested for other crimes."[7]

Although joining Rehnquist's opinion, Justice Powell wrote separately that "an individual lawfully subjected to a custodial arrest retains no significant Fourth Amendment interest in the privacy of his person."[8] According to Powell, once a lawful arrest occurs, any privacy interest protected by the Fourth Amendment "is subordinated to a legitimate and overriding governmental concern."[9] Going beyond then-existing doctrine, Powell argued that "a valid arrest justifies a full search of the person, even if that search is not narrowly limited by the twin rationales of seizing evidence and disarming the

---

[4] *United States v Robinson*, 414 US 218, 237 (1973) (Powell, J, concurring).

[5] Id at 235 (1973).

[6] Existing precedents confined police authority to search the arrestee for weapons and for "any evidence on the arrestee's person in order to prevent its concealment or destruction." *Chimel v California*, 395 US 752, 763 (1969).

[7] *Robinson*, 414 US at 234 (footnote omitted).

[8] Id at 237 (Powell, J, concurring).

[9] Id.

arrestee."[10] Powell reasoned that search incident to arrest is "reasonable" because an arrestee's privacy "is legitimately abated by the fact of arrest."[11]

Powell's views on this issue were not embraced by the Court for forty years—until *Maryland v King*.[12] At issue in *King* was whether a Maryland law requiring forensic testing of DNA samples taken from persons arrested for violent crimes violated the Fourth Amendment. The purpose behind the statute, like other DNA collection laws, seemed obvious: collecting and analyzing DNA samples advances the capacity of law enforcement to solve both "cold cases" and future crimes when the government has evidence of the perpetrator's DNA from the crime scene. Maryland did not contend that the DNA statute promoted either officer safety or evidence preservation. The Maryland Court of Appeals held the statute was unconstitutional because the government interests promoted by the law did not outweigh King's right to privacy.[13] In a 5–4 decision, the Court, in an opinion by Justice Anthony Kennedy, upheld the Maryland law—and presumably the similar laws of twenty-seven other states and the federal government.[14]

On the day *King* was decided, Orin Kerr, a respected criminal procedure scholar, described *King* as "hugely important as a practical matter, but it's not very interesting from a theoretical or academic standpoint."[15] I disagree; *King* is a significant ruling in terms of our

[10] Id (footnote omitted). In a footnote, Powell quotes a Ninth Circuit ruling, *Charles v United States*, 278 F2d 386, 388–89 (1960), which included the following statement: "Once the body of the accused is validly subjected to the physical dominion of the law, inspections of his person, regardless of purpose, cannot be deemed unlawful, unless they violate the dictates of reason either because of their number or their manner of perpetration." *Robinson*, 414 US at 237 n 1 (Powell, J, concurring).

[11] *Robinson*, 414 US at 238 (footnote omitted) (Powell, J, concurring).

[12] *Maryland v King*, 133 S Ct 1958 (2013).

[13] *King v State*, 42 A3d 549, 555–56 (Md 2012).

[14] According to a study by the Urban Institute, published shortly before *King* was announced, "about half [of the twenty-eight states that have enacted laws authorizing DNA collection from arrestees] align their collection practices with convicted offender laws and authorize collection from persons arrested for any felony crime. The other half of states limits collection to a subset of felonies, typically involving violence, sexual assault, or serious property crimes. Seven arrestee DNA states also collect from individuals arrested or charged with select misdemeanor crimes. Broader than any of the state laws, federal law authorizes collection from all arrestees and non-US citizens detained by the US government." Julie E. Samuels et al, *Collecting DNA at Arrest: Policies, Practices, and Implications, Final Technical Report* 25–26 (Urban Institute, May 2013).

[15] Orin Kerr, *A Few Thoughts on Maryland v King* (The Volokh Conspiracy June 3, 2013), online at http://www.volokh.com/2013/06/03/a-few-thoughts-on-maryland-v-king-2/.

understanding of Fourth Amendment law.[16] Individuals and organizations who rarely agree on constitutional issues criticized the
decision. Conservative Republican Senators Rand Paul and Ted
Cruz, the *New York Times* editorial pages, the *American Prospect*, and
the American Civil Liberties Union all condemned *King*.[17] Moreover, Justice Samuel Alito, a former federal prosecutor, acknowledged during the oral argument that *King* "is perhaps the most
important criminal procedure case that this Court has heard in
decades."[18] The result in *King* was so important—and so controversial—that retired Justice John Paul Stevens publicly endorsed
the Court's ruling.[19]

Although Justice Kennedy's opinion in *King* suggests otherwise,
King has the potential to fundamentally alter Fourth Amendment
law. Indeed, it is analogous to *Terry v Ohio*.[20] Before *Terry* was
decided in 1968, the Court had never authorized police to detain
or search a suspicious person without probable cause to arrest. Although police officers frequently performed "investigative stops,"
car searches, and weapons frisks on evidence short of probable cause,
the Court had never approved such tactics.[21] Indeed, as Justice Wil-

---

[16] See also Erin Murphy, *License, Registration, Cheek Swab: DNA Testing and the Divided
Court*, 127 Harv L Rev 161, 161 (2013) (describing *King* as "no ordinary Fourth Amendment case," and noting that it "represents a watershed moment in the evolution of Fourth
Amendment doctrine and an important signal for the future of biotechnologies and policing.").

[17] See Rand Paul, *Big Brother Says "Open Your Mouth!"*, American Conservative (June
10, 2012), online at http://www.theamericanconservative.com/articles/big-brother-says-
open-your-mouth/; Senator Ted Cruz, press release, *Statement on SCOTUS Decision in
Maryland v. King* (June 3, 2012), online at http://www.cruz.senate.gov/record.cfm?id =
342973&&; Editorial, *DNA and Suspicionless Searches*, NY Times (June 3, 2013), online
at   http://www.nytimes.com/2013/06/04/opinion/the-supreme-court-rules-on-dna-and-
suspicionless-searches.html?_r=0; Scott Lemieux, *Scalia Gets It Right*, American Prospect
(June 3, 2013), online at http://prospect.org/article/scalia-gets-it-right; ACLU, press release, *Comment on Supreme Court DNA Swab Ruling (Maryland v. King)* (June 3, 2013),
online at https://www.aclu.org/criminal-law-reform/aclu-comment-maryland-v-king-de-
cision.

[18] Transcript of Oral Argument, *Maryland v King*, No 12-207, 35 (Feb 27, 2013), online
at http://www.supremecourt.gov/oral_arguments/argument_transcripts/12-207-lp23.pdf.

[19] Justice John Paul Stevens (Ret), speech to American Constitution Society Convention,
Capital Hilton Hotel, Washington, DC (June 14, 2013) (while admitting that he had not
read the briefs in *King*, Justice Stevens stated, "I think I would have voted with the majority
if I were still on the Court.").

[20] *Terry v Ohio*, 392 US 1 (1968).

[21] In the classic article on the subject, Professor LaFave characterizes stop-and-frisk
techniques as "a time-honored police procedure [where] officers . . . stop suspicious persons
for questioning and, occasionally, . . . search these persons for dangerous weapons." Wayne
R. LaFave, *"Street Encounters" and the Constitution: Terry, Sibron, Peters, and Beyond*, 67

liam Douglas emphasized in his dissenting opinion in *Terry*, the Court had ruled "precisely the opposite over and over again."[22] By departing from those precedents and embracing an open-ended balancing formula, *Terry* held that a frisk for weapons is permissible when an officer has reasonable grounds to believe that a suspect is currently armed and dangerous, even if the officer lacks probable cause to arrest that person. When it was announced, *Terry* could be narrowly read: a frisk for weapons is permissible only when an officer's safety is threatened. The Court explained in *Terry* that the decision did not address "the constitutional propriety of an investigative 'seizure' for purposes of 'detention' and/or interrogation."[23] As Justice Douglas predicted, however, the "hydraulic pressures" exerted on the Court "to water down constitutional guarantees and give the police the upper hand,"[24] combined with a balancing analysis, eventually persuaded the Court to enlarge police search-and-seizure powers in a wide swath of cases, many of which had nothing to do with police safety.

Like *Terry*, *King* alters the "rules of game" and significantly expands the government's authority to search persons subject to custodial arrest. Just as a balancing analysis made it easy for the Court to extend *Terry*'s rationale to different scenarios between police and suspicious persons, *King*'s reasoning can be used to support collection and analysis of DNA samples from other persons subjected to governmental restraint (such as persons arrested for misdemeanors or traffic offenses or detained for investigative stops), or from those who possess diminished privacy interests vis-à-vis the government (such as public school students, driver's license applicants, and lawyers). Indeed, because *King* approved suspicionless searches of persons under a free-form balancing analysis, it will be difficult to cabin the Court's logic when government officials seek innovative search

---

Mich L Rev 39, 42 (1968). Stop-and-frisk procedures were a staple of police procedure long before *Terry* sanctioned the practice. See Lawrence P. Tiffany et al, *Detection of Crime* at 10–17 (Little, Brown, 1967) (distinguishing stop-and-frisk practices, like "field interrogation" and "aggressive patrol," from traditional police procedures involving arrest or search incident to arrest); id at 15 (noting that "[m]inor traffic infractions are [ ] often used by the police to justify stopping for questioning or searching."). According to one 1967 study of the practice, although police regularly "stop and question suspects on the street when there are insufficient grounds to make an arrest, . . . this important law enforcement practice has been either ignored or treated ambiguously by courts and legislatures." Id at 6.

[22] *Terry*, 392 US at 36 (Douglas, J, dissenting) (footnote omitted).

[23] Id at 19, n 16.

[24] Id at 39 (Douglas, J, dissenting).

powers in other contexts in which individuals arguably possess diminished privacy interests. As Professor Barry Friedman commented shortly after the decision, *King* "will have ramifications far beyond DNA testing, affecting much of policing in the 21st century."[25]

This article explains in more detail why *King* is so important. Part I summarizes Justice Kennedy's opinion and Justice Antonin Scalia's dissent, and offers some criticism of the Court's opinion. Part II explains why the Court's precedents do not support the decision. Part III addresses the implications of *King*'s reasoning, and explains why the holding will not be confined to persons arrested for violent felonies. Finally, Part IV explores the similarities (as well as one important difference) between the judicial styles exhibited by the Court in *King* and *Terry*.

I. THE COURT'S REASONING IN KING

DNA testing in the United States began in 1987. It has had a significant impact on the criminal justice system.[26] Initially, DNA databases included only "those classes of offenders with a high recidivism rate, such as sex offenders and violent felons."[27] Today, every state and the federal government collects and analyzes DNA from all persons convicted of felonies. Lower federal and state courts have uniformly upheld DNA collection from convicts. In light of the investigative capabilities provided by DNA technology, "the collection of DNA samples from individuals arrested for criminal misconduct has been advocated by police officials and endorsed by

---

[25] Barry Friedman, *The Supreme Court Fails the Fourth Amendment Test*, Slate Magazine (June 5, 2013), online at http://www.slate.com/articles/news_and_politics/jurisprudence/2013/06/dna_collection_in_maryland_v_king_the_supreme_court_fails_on_the_fourth .html.

[26] Michelle Hibbert, *DNA Databanks: Law Enforcement's Greatest Surveillance Tool?*, 34 Wake Forest L Rev 767, 768 (1999); compare Brandon L. Garrett, *Convicting the Innocent: Where Criminal Prosecutions Go Wrong* at 5–6 (Harvard, 2011) (explaining that "[s]ince DNA testing became available in the late 1980s, more than 250 innocent people have been exonerated by postconviction DNA testing," and that "DNA exonerations have changed the face of criminal justice in the United States by revealing that wrongful convictions do occur and, in the process, altering how judges, lawyers, legislators, the public, and scholars perceive the system's accuracy."); Erin Murphy, *A Tale of Two Sciences*, 110 Mich L Rev 909, 926 (2012) (observing that "news sources are full of stories about some new mind-boggling scientific development" involving DNA typing. "Sadly, however, revelations of laboratory malfeasance, errors, or sloppy mistakes are as common as stories about the use of forensic science to convict a dangerous criminal or exonerate an innocent accused.").

[27] Hibbert, 34 Wake Forest L Rev at 769 (cited in note 26).

politicians."[28] Therefore, it was no surprise when states began to extend DNA collection procedures to arrestees. In 2002, Virginia became the first state to collect DNA from convicts and arrestees when it passed a law requiring that DNA samples be taken from those arrested for violent felonies. The Virginia Attorney General explained that "[i]t's no secret that an enhanced database increases the chances of solving crimes,"[29] and that database expansion "will help us solve cases much quicker and ensure public safety by making sure somebody's not released back into the general public who has committed a string of crimes."[30] Three years later, Congress enacted a statute requiring that DNA samples be collected from *all* persons arrested by federal officers, regardless of the nature of the crime for which they are arrested.[31] A year later, Congress made funding available to the states to collect and analyze DNA samples obtained from arrested individuals. In 2008, Maryland enacted the law at issue in *King*, requiring the collection and testing of DNA from persons arrested for serious felonies. Thus, when the Court agreed to review the constitutionality of the Maryland statute, the case attracted widespread attention. Twenty-four amicus briefs were filed with the Court.

A. JUSTICE KENNEDY'S MAJORITY OPINION

Alonzo King was arrested for assault on April 10, 2009, after menacing a group of people with a shotgun. As a routine part of the arrest procedure for a serious offense, Maryland law required that a DNA sample be taken by applying a cotton swab to the inside of King's cheek.[32] Under the law, a DNA sample may not

---

[28] D. H. Kaye, *Who Needs Special Needs? On the Constitutionality of Collecting DNA and Other Biometric Data from Arrestees*, 34 J L Med & Ethics 188 (2006); see generally D. H. Kaye, *The Constitutionality of DNA Sampling on Arrest*, 10 Cornell J L & Pub Policy 455 (2001).

[29] Ellen Sorokin, *Attorney General Hopefuls Favor More DNA Collection*, Washington Times C1 (Aug 7, 2001).

[30] Francis X. Clines, *Virginia May Collect DNA in Every Arrest for a Felony*, NY Times 22 (Feb 17, 2002).

[31] 42 USC § 14135a (a)(1)(A).

[32] As Justice Kennedy noted, the statute authorizes collecting DNA samples from "'an individual who is charged with . . . a crime of violence or an attempt to commit a crime of violence; or . . . burglary or an attempt to commit burglary.'" *King*, 133 S Ct at 1967, quoting Md Pub Saf Code Ann § 2-504(a)(3)(i). The charge of first-degree assault was eventually dismissed. King entered a plea pursuant to *North Carolina v Alford*, 400 US 25 (1970) (a defendant's refusal to admit to guilt and professed belief in his innocence does not bar a trial judge from accepting a guilty plea, particularly when the record provides

be processed or placed in a database before the individual is arraigned. King's first court appearance was three days after his arrest. King's DNA sample was received by the Maryland State Police's Forensic Division two weeks after his arrest, on April 23, 2009. Several months later, on August 4, 2009, King's DNA profile was found to match the DNA discovered from an unsolved rape committed in another Maryland city in 2003. After being charged with that rape, King argued that the collection of his DNA after his arrest for assault was an unreasonable search, and that the evidence was therefore inadmissible in the rape trial. The trial court rejected King's suppression motion; he was convicted of rape and sentenced to life in prison without the possibility of parole. The Maryland Court of Appeals reversed, and the Supreme Court decided to weigh in.

Justice Kennedy began his analysis in *King* by observing that "the framework for deciding the issue is well established."[33] According to Kennedy, the procedure constituted a Fourth Amendment search, because the DNA sample taken from King entailed the use of a buccal swab on the inner tissues of his cheek. Kennedy explained that "[v]irtually any" intrusion into the body by state officials triggers constitutional scrutiny.[34] Kennedy then added, however, that a "buccal swab is a far more gentle process than a venipuncture to draw blood."[35] The "negligible" nature of the intrusion, according to Kennedy, "is of central relevance to determining the reasonableness" of the search.[36]

Kennedy explained that reasonableness in Fourth Amendment cases depends on the circumstances of each case. For example, warrants are required in some situations, but not in others. Individualized suspicion of wrongdoing is generally "preferred" before police conduct a search, but there is no per se prohibition of suspicionless intrusions.[37] A search's constitutionality is determined by evaluating law enforcement goals, the nature and magnitude of the privacy interests at stake, the standardized nature of

a strong factual basis for the plea) and was convicted of second-degree assault, a misdemeanor offense.

[33] *King*, 133 S Ct at 1968.
[34] Id at 1969.
[35] Id.
[36] Id.
[37] Id.

the search or seizure, and the extent of the intrusion on individual privacy and dignity.[38] Because the Maryland DNA collection law applies to "all arrestees charged with serious crimes," and because police have no discretion when deciding whom to search, Kennedy concluded that the buccal swab used to collect King's DNA fell within the "category of cases" calling for a balancing analysis— weighing "the privacy-related and law enforcement-related concerns to determine if the intrusion was reasonable."[39]

Turning first to the government's side of the balance, Kennedy argued that the government interest in *King* was the time-honored need for police to "process and identify the persons and possessions they must take into custody."[40] Kennedy argued that DNA identification serves several governmental interests. In order of importance, these interests include identifying the arrestee, protecting the safety and integrity of the detention facility that will house the arrestee, ensuring that the arrestee will be available for trial, enabling sound decisions about whether the arrestee should be released on bail, and "freeing a person wrongfully imprisoned for the same offense."[41] Although the Court listed five interests served by DNA testing, only the first interest—identifying the arrestee—is important for constitutional purposes. Indeed, the Court did not place significant weight on the other four interests, and for good reason. DNA testing takes at least several weeks to perform. The time lag between the DNA search and test and the receipt of matches prevents the arrestee's sample from serving any of the other interests identified by Justice Kennedy. An arrestee's DNA test is of no use to the state's interests in protecting jailhouse security and making accurate bail determinations, because these matters arise long before an arrestee's DNA results are available. As Justice Scalia noted in his dissent, "DNA testing does not even begin until after arraignment and bail decisions are already made. The samples sit in storage for months, and take weeks to test."[42]

---

[38] Id.

[39] Id at 1970, quoting *Illinois v McArthur*, 531 US 326, 331 (2001).

[40] *King*, 133 S Ct at 1970.

[41] Id at 1970–74.

[42] Id at 1986 (Scalia, J, dissenting). In an exchange between counsel for King and Chief Justice Roberts during the oral argument, the Chief Justice seems to recognize the weakness of the argument that DNA searches advance the state's interest in accurate bail determinations: "Now, your brief says, well, the only interest here is the law enforcement interest. And I found that persuasive because of the concern that it's going to take months

Moreover, it is hardly self-evident that taking an arrestee's DNA deters flight before trial. Kennedy argued that if DNA is not taken upon arrest, a "defendant who had committed a prior sexual assault might be inclined to flee on a burglary charge, knowing that in every State a DNA sample would be taken from him after his conviction on the burglary charge that would tie him to the more serious charge of rape,"[43] but if a DNA sample is taken upon arrest, the arrestee has little to gain by flight, because the police already have his DNA. This logic is flawed, however, because an arrestee who has his DNA taken upon arrest might also conclude he has nothing to lose by flight, because he knows the government will link him to the sexual assault. If anything, taking the DNA at the time of arrest may actually *increase* the likelihood of flight.

Finally, the interest in exonerating those who have been wrongfully accused or convicted is mere window dressing for the majority's argument. This is so because collecting DNA from arrestees cannot help vindicate the innocent.[44] As Justice Scalia observed in dissent in *King*, mandating collection of DNA from arrestees for analysis against the FBI database cannot assist in freeing wrongfully convicted persons, because the FBI database includes DNA only from *unsolved* crimes. As Scalia sarcastically noted: "I know of no indication (and the Court cites none) that [the FBI database] also includes DNA from all—or even any— crimes whose perpetrators have already been convicted."[45]

---

to get the DNA back anyway, so they are going to have to release him or not before they know it." Oral Argument in *King*, at 42–43 (cited in note 18).

[43] *King*, 133 S Ct at 1973.

[44] In fact, *Osborne v District Attorney's Office*, 557 US 52 (2009), "rejected a freestanding due process right for prisoners to obtain DNA tests that might prove their innocence." Brandon. L. Garrett, *Criminal Justice and the Court's Past Term*, Harvard University Press Blog (Harvard University Press, Aug 2, 2013), online at http://harvardpress.typepad.com/ hup_publicity/2013/08/criminal-justice-and-the-courts-past-term-brandon-garrett.html. To say the least, *Osborne* "is a striking contrast" to *King*'s "warm embrace of essentially unlimited law enforcement use of DNA from mere arrestees." Id. Professor Garrett also states that "[n]o DNA exonerations have ever resulted from DNA collected from unconvicted arrestees, while many whose convictions were overturned have benefited from DNA matches with serious convicts."

[45] *King*, 133 S Ct at 1984, n 2 (Scalia, J, dissenting). Compare Samuels et al, *Collecting DNA at Arrest* at 8, n 8 (cited in note 14), quoting *National DNA Database Submission to the Home Affairs Committee* at 2, Gene Watch UK (Jan 2010), online at http:// www.genewatch.org/uploads/f03c6d66a9b354535738483c1c3d49e4/GWsub_Jan10.doc: "'although DNA can undoubtedly be useful to exonerate the innocent, a database of individual DNA profiles (as opposed to crime scene profiles) is never necessary to exonerate an innocent person, since this can always be done by comparing the DNA of the innocent suspect directly with the crime scene DNA profile.'"). After *King* was announced, Barry

With respect to the issue of identification, Justice Kennedy reasoned that law enforcement officials must know whom they have arrested. "An individual's identity is more than just his name or Social Security number, and the government's interest in identification goes beyond ensuring that the proper name is typed on the indictment."[46] Kennedy observed that the identification process includes "searching the public and police records based on the identifying information provided by the arrestee to see what is already known about him."[47] To this effect, an arrestee's "criminal history is a critical part of his identification that officers should know when processing him for detention."[48] Moreover, DNA is "an irrefutable identification"[49] of the arrestee, and is even more reliable as a type of identification than a photograph, social security number, or fingerprint. Kennedy therefore analogized taking a DNA sample to the practices and procedures police have traditionally used in processing arrestees. It is similar to matching an arrestee's face to a photo of a previously unidentified suspect, or "comparing tattoos to known gang symbols to reveal a criminal affiliation; or matching the arrestee's fingerprints to those recovered from a crime scene."[50] Kennedy argued that "[j]ust as fingerprinting was constitutional for generations prior to the introduction of [the FBI's automated fingerprint identification system], DNA identification of arrestees is a permissible tool of law enforcement today."[51] In Kennedy's view, it makes no difference that DNA analysis takes weeks or months to complete: "The question of how long it takes to process identifying information obtained from a valid search goes only to the efficacy of the search for its purpose of prompt identification, not the constitutionality of the search."[52] Kennedy therefore concluded that taking the DNA sam-

---

Scheck, a cofounder of the Innocence Project, told the *New York Times* that Justice Scalia's comment "goes too far." Adam Liptak, *Cited by a Justice, but Feeling Less Than Honored*, NY Times (June 10, 2013), available at http://www.nytimes.com/2013/06/11/us/cited-by-a-justice-but-feeling-less-than-honored.html?_r = 0. Scheck told the *Times* that "there had been times when prisoners had been exonerated through the testing of DNA in closed cases." Id.

[46] *King*, 133 S Ct at 1971.

[47] Id at 1972.

[48] Id at 1971.

[49] Id.

[50] Id.

[51] Id at 1977.

[52] Id at 1976 (citation omitted).

ple served a legitimate and important law enforcement goal.

On the other side of the balance—King's privacy interests—Kennedy emphasized that the intrusion is "minimal" and that an arrestee's privacy expectations are curtailed by his lawful custody.[53] Kennedy reasoned that DNA testing "differs from the sort of programmatic searches of either the public at large or a particular class of regulated but otherwise law-abiding citizens that the Court has previously labeled as 'special needs' searches."[54] Although the special needs cases "do not have a direct bearing on the issues presented in" *King* because the taking of DNA from an arrestee does not fall within that doctrine, Kennedy noted that searches authorized by the Court's special needs doctrine "intrude upon substantial expectations of privacy."[55] Kennedy then stated, rather curiously, that the Court's special needs cases support his position in *King* "because unlike the search of a citizen who has not been suspected of a wrong, a detainee has a reduced expectation of privacy."[56]

Finally, Justice Kennedy argued that the manner of the search itself raised no constitutional problems. The DNA obtained and tested does not reveal the arrestee's genetic traits, and even if the DNA could provide some private genetic information, the state analyzes the DNA sample for the sole purpose of generating a unique identifying number against which future samples may be matched. Kennedy left open whether law enforcement analysis of samples to determine an arrestee's predisposition for a particular disease or other hereditary factor would be constitutional.[57]

B. JUSTICE SCALIA'S DISSENTING OPINION

Justice Scalia's acerbic dissent begins with a categorical rule: "The Fourth Amendment forbids searching a person for evidence of a crime when there is no basis for believing the person is guilty of the crime or is in possession of incriminating evidence."[58] This per se rule, according to Scalia, "lies at the very heart of the Fourth

---

[53] Id at 1977–78.

[54] Id at 1978.

[55] Id.

[56] Id.

[57] Id at 1979.

[58] Id at 1980.

Amendment."[59] Suspicionless searches, in Scalia's view, are permissible only when the government is motivated by a concern beyond the needs of ordinary law enforcement. Because the state of Maryland had no basis for intruding into King's body, the buccal swab, no matter how brief and minimally intrusive, violated the Fourth Amendment.

Regarding the government interest in identifying arrestees, Scalia remarked that the Court's "assertion that DNA is being taken, not to solve crimes, but to *identify* those in the State's custody, taxes the credulity of the credulous."[60] The Court's definition of "identifying" is obviously wrong—"unless what one means by 'identifying' someone is 'searching for evidence that he has committed crimes unrelated to the crime of his arrest.'"[61] This form of identification, according to Scalia, "is indistinguishable from the ordinary law-enforcement aims that have never been thought to justify a suspicionless search."[62] He observed sardonically that searching cars of lawfully stopped drivers might reveal information about unsolved crimes committed by the driver, "but no one would say that such a search was aimed at 'identifying' him, and no court would hold such a search lawful."[63]

Moreover, Scalia explained why the collection and testing of King's DNA was not intended to *identify* him. After King's DNA was taken by the police, it was eventually shipped to the FBI's DNA database. The FBI database contains two types of DNA collections: DNA samples taken from *known* convicts and arrestees, and DNA samples found at crime scenes belonging to *unknown* persons or perpetrators. At the FBI laboratory, King's DNA profile was compared with the DNA profiles of the second group. The purpose of this comparison was not to determine King's identity, but to determine whether King's DNA profile matched any of the DNA profiles found at scenes of unsolved crimes, such as the 2003 rape. If Maryland had wanted to *identify* King, "the logical thing to do" would have been to compare his DNA against the first group—*known* convicts and arrestees.[64] As Scalia observed, Mary-

---

[59] Id.
[60] Id.
[61] Id at 1983.
[62] Id.
[63] Id.
[64] Id at 1985.

land did not do this, because it already knew who King was and "because this search had nothing to with identification."[65]

Finally, Scalia pointed out that Maryland's DNA law itself does not support the "identification" purpose attributed to it by the Court. According to Scalia, the relevant section of the statute specifies the purpose behind the DNA searches: samples are tested "'as part of an official investigation into a crime.'"[66] By contrast, another section of the statute permits testing for identification purposes: "'to help identify *human* remains,'" and "'to help identify *missing* individuals.'"[67] No section of the statute authorizes DNA testing for the purpose of identifying *arrestees*. Moreover, another section of the law expressly prohibits using DNA samples "for any purposes other than those specified" in the statute.[68]

Justice Scalia was not persuaded by the Court's claim that DNA testing is indistinguishable from traditional procedures used to process and identify arrestees. Scalia noted that photographing an arrestee does not trigger Fourth Amendment scrutiny because taking a photograph is not a physical intrusion, nor does it implicate a legitimate expectation of privacy. Additionally, Scalia observed that the Court's precedents "provide no ready answer" as to whether fingerprinting constitutes a search.[69] But even assuming that fingerprinting is a search, "[f]ingerprints of arrestees are taken primarily to identify them (though that process sometimes solves crimes); the DNA of arrestees is taken to solve crimes (and nothing else)."[70] Regarding the constitutional status of fingerprinting, Scalia rightly noted that the Court's claim that fingerprinting has been "constitutional for generations" is "bereft of citation to authority because there is none for it."[71] Scalia observed that the fact that many Americans have apparently accepted fingerprinting in various contexts is not the equivalent of the Court's imprimatur. In his view, it is "wrong" to imply that fingerprinting has always been "uncontroversial," or to suggest "that this Court blessed uni-

---

[65] Id.

[66] Id, quoting Md Pub Saf Code Ann § 2-505(a)(2).

[67] *King*, 133 S Ct at 1986, quoting Md Pub Saf Code Ann § 2-505(a)(3) & (a)(4) (emphasis in original).

[68] *King*, 133 S Ct at 1986, quoting Md Pub Saf Code Ann § 2-505 (b)(2).

[69] *King*, 133 S Ct at 1987.

[70] Id.

[71] Id at 1988.

versal fingerprinting for 'generations' before it was possible to use it effectively for identification."[72]

Scalia might have added that fingerprinting arrestees has not always received the approval of the judiciary. As Professor Wayne Logan has explained, fingerprinting gained prominence in the early part of the twentieth century, "and by the 1930s fingerprinting was the nation's criminal-identification method of choice."[73] The judiciary, however, imposed limits on the use of fingerprints, especially when prints were obtained from persons not convicted of crimes.[74] A crucial change in the judiciary's acceptance of the routine use of fingerprinting occurred in *United States v Kelly*, when the United States Court of Appeals for the Second Circuit rejected a challenge to the use of fingerprints to confirm a suspect's identity.[75] *Kelly*'s holding, however, was "predicated on the need to verify identity, and was decided well before the forensic investigative heyday of prints, allowing for digitized matches to 'latent' prints found at a crime scene or stored in databases."[76] Even with *Kelly* on the books, "the constitutional propriety of identity verification methods at the pre-conviction stage has always merely been 'assume[d].'"[77]

Comparing fingerprinting to DNA profiling is problematic for another reason. Fingerprints are "useful only as a form of identification."[78] They cannot be analyzed, for example, "to determine whether two individuals are related."[79] By contrast, "[e]ven noncoding regions of the DNA transmit more information than a standard fingerprint."[80] Although the noncoding regions of DNA used to create DNA identification profiles "may never be found to have highly sensitive direct coding functions, they may very

---

[72] Id.

[73] Wayne A. Logan, *Policing Identity*, 92 BU L Rev 1561, 1574 (2012) (footnote omitted).

[74] Id at 1583 (fingerprints were "as a general rule, collected and stored only in the event of conviction").

[75] *United States v Kelly*, 55 F2d 67 (2d Cir 1932).

[76] Logan, 92 BU L Rev at 1583 (footnotes omitted) (cited in note 73).

[77] Id at 1584 (footnote omitted; bracket in original).

[78] Sheldon Krimsky and Tania Simoncelli, *Genetic Justice: DNA Data Banks, Criminal Investigations, and Civil Liberties* 235 (Columbia, 2011).

[79] Id.

[80] Id at 236.

well be found to *correlate* with things we may care about and deem private."[81]

Scalia also criticized the Court's willingness to accept the claim that the government is developing technology that will analyze DNA samples in "mere minutes."[82] Although conceding that there may come a day when it is possible to analyze DNA samples instantaneously, Scalia correctly observed that "[t]he issue before us is not whether DNA can *some day* be used for identification; nor even whether it can *today* be used for identification; but whether it *was used for identification here.*"[83]

Finally, Scalia predicted that the search approved in *King* will not be confined to those arrested for violent felonies. "I cannot imagine what principle could possibly justify this limitation, and the Court does not attempt to suggest any."[84] Thus, Scalia envisions a future where every person's DNA will be taken and tested upon arrest, whether they are arrested for a traffic violation or an illegal political protest. "If one believes that DNA will 'identify' someone arrested for assault, he must believe that it will 'identify' someone arrested for a traffic offense. This Court does not base its judgments on senseless distinctions."[85] Tellingly, Justice Kennedy offered no reply to Justice Scalia's dissent.[86]

---

[81] Id.

[82] *King*, 133 S Ct at 1988.

[83] Id at 1988–89. There may soon come a day when technology allows the police to instantaneously analyze an arrestee's DNA sample and determine whether it matches the DNA found at the crime scene of an unresolved murder or rape. Under Justice Kennedy's analysis in *King*, however, the speed of obtaining test results "goes only to the efficacy of the search . . . , not the constitutionality of the search." Id at 1976. In any event, instantaneous analysis should not change the Fourth Amendment judgment. Even if police obtain immediate results from a DNA test, this test still occurs by means of a physical intrusion, conducted without suspicion of criminal wrongdoing, and motivated by law enforcement interests. The only difference between the situation in *King* and a case involving instantaneous analysis is the speed with which police have access to the fruit of their search. If future technology gives the police the ability to instantaneously discover the contents of a home, contraband and noncontraband items alike, the search remains unreasonable even when the results are instantaneous. See *Kyllo v United States*, 533 US 27, 34 (2001) ("We think that obtaining by sense-enhancing technology any information regarding the interior of the home that could not otherwise have been obtained without physical 'intrusion into a constitutionally protected area' constitutes a search—at least where (as here) the technology in question is not in general public use."). The same logic applies when the search involves a person.

[84] *King*, 133 S Ct at 1989.

[85] Id.

[86] See also Lyle Denniston, *Opinion Recap: Solving "Cold Cases" Made Easier*, SCOTUSblog (June 3, 2013), available at http://www.scotusblog.com/2013/06/opinion-recap-solving-cold-cases-made-easier/ ("The Kennedy and Scalia opinions were almost totally at

II. A Decision Without Precedent

As one chronicler of the Court has observed, Justice Kennedy's opinion in *King* "sought to make it appear that the outcome was easily reached and involved no real alteration of existing constitutional norms."[87] In fact, the Court's most relevant precedents support the opposite conclusion.[88]

A. DNA SAMPLING CANNOT BE JUSTIFIED AS A SEARCH INCIDENT TO ARREST

Certainly, the Court's search incident to arrest precedents do not support the decision in *King*. During the oral argument, Justice Kennedy compared taking a DNA sample to the search of an arrestee's coat pocket, the type of search upheld in *United States v Robinson*.[89] But the Court's search incident to arrest rulings do not come close to authorizing a search *into an arrestee's body*.[90] Although Kennedy quoted *Robinson*[91] and *Florence v Board of Chosen Freeholders*[92] for the proposition that "[a] search of the detainee's person when he is booked into custody may 'involve a relatively extensive exploration,' including 'requir[ing] at least some detainees to lift their genitals or cough in a squatting position,'"[93] Justice

odds with each other, in tone and in substance. . . . [Kennedy] also made no effort to respond to the dissenting opinion.").

[87] Id.

[88] Although Justice Kennedy would not concede the point in his opinion, Deputy Solicitor General Michael Dreeben acknowledged during oral argument that "there is no case on my side that decides the case" for the government, while quickly adding "there's no case that—on [King's] side that decides the case for him." Oral Argument in *King*, at 24–25 (cited in note 18). The Chief Deputy Attorney General for Maryland made a similar concession: ". . . [T]here's no—there's no case in this Court's jurisprudence that's exactly like this." Id at 12.

[89] Id at 26. Kennedy noted: "Just—just like taking the pockets out and—seeing what's in the person's overcoat and so forth is a search incident to arrest."

[90] Justice Rehnquist recognized in *Robinson* that "virtually all of the statements of this Court affirming the existence of an unqualified authority to search incident to a lawful arrest are dicta." *Robinson*, 414 US at 230. See also LaFave, 3 *Search and Seizure* § 5.2(b) at 136 (cited in note 3) (noting that "neither the prior decisions of the Supreme Court nor the 'original understanding' evidence [regarding the Fourth Amendment] conclusively establishes whether the 'general authority' to search the person incident to arrest is 'unqualified.'").

[91] "'The validity of the search of a person incident to a lawful arrest has been regarded as settled from its first enunciation, and has remained virtually unchallenged.'" *King*, 133 S Ct at 1970–71, quoting *Robinson*, 414 US at 224.

[92] *Florence v Board of Chosen Freeholders of County of Burlington*, 132 S Ct 1510 (2012).

[93] *King*, 133 S Ct at 1978, quoting *Robinson*, 414 US at 227, and *Florence*, 132 S Ct at 1520.

Scalia correctly responded that "[t]he objects of a search incident to arrest must be either (1) weapons or evidence that might easily be destroyed, or (2) evidence relevant to the crime of arrest. Neither is the object of the search at issue here."[94] Indeed, none of the Court's search incident to arrest rulings since *Chimel v California*[95] permit a suspicionless search for ordinary crime-solving or identification purposes.[96] *Robinson* certainly did not approve such a search, because a weapon such as a razor blade might have been inside the cigarette package. Moreover, none of the Court's decisions, old or new, have ever authorized suspicionless searches *into* the bodies of arrestees. To the contrary, the Court in *Schmerber* expressly foreclosed such searches when it explained that the rationale of search incident to arrest has "little applicability with respect to searches involving intrusions beyond the body's surface."[97]

Perhaps Kennedy cited *Robinson* and other search incident to arrest rulings merely to establish that arrestees possess a diminished expectation of privacy while in custody. Kennedy conceded that a warrant would be required to perform surgery on King or to search his home, notwithstanding his diminished privacy interests as an arrestee. As the Court noted in *Schmerber*, logic dictates that "absent an emergency, no less could be required where intrusions into the human body are concerned."[98] Put simply, the Court's search incident to arrest precedents do not authorize bodily intrusions. Because there was no emergency, judicial authori-

---

[94] *King*, 133 S Ct at 1982 (Scalia, J, dissenting) (citations omitted).

[95] *Chimel*, 395 US 752.

[96] Compare Brandon L. Garrett and Erin Murphy, *Supreme Court 2013: Collecting DNA from People Who Are Arrested Won't Solve More Crimes*, Slate Magazine (Feb 12, 2013), available at http://www.slate.com/articles/news_and_politics/jurisprudence/2013/02/dna_collection_at_the_supreme_court_maryland_v_king.html ("the Supreme Court has never held that if police have probable cause to arrest, they can also search a suspect for evidence of past or future crimes"); Sandra J. Carnahan, *The Supreme Court's Primary Purpose Test: A Roadblock to the National Law Enforcement DNA Database*, 83 Neb L Rev 1, 35 (2004) ("The Supreme Court has never approved a suspicionless search involving bodily intrusion for a law enforcement purpose, and to do so [for a national law enforcement DNA database for convicts] would be a substantial departure from traditional Fourth Amendment principles."). But compare Kerr, *A Few Thoughts* (cited in note 15) ("in light of the broad language of *Robinson*'s holding, "it seems wrong, based on current law, to say that a suspicionless search is never allowed incident to arrest for purposes of ordinary crime-solving.")

[97] *Schmerber*, 384 US at 769.

[98] Id at 770.

zation, or probable cause for the search, the buccal swab was an "unreasonable" search.

The Court's precedents also suggest that a second search occurred when King's DNA was subjected to forensic analysis. In *Ferguson v Charleston*, the Court found that "urine tests conducted by [state actors] were indisputably searches within the meaning of the Fourth Amendment."[99] *Ferguson*'s conclusion rested on the legal principle established twelve years earlier in Justice Kennedy's opinion for the Court in *Skinner v Railway Labor Executives' Association*.[100] *Skinner* addressed whether obtaining and testing blood and breath samples from railroad personnel who were involved in train accidents, or who violated certain safety rules, constituted searches. After concluding that collecting the samples was a search, the Court added that chemical analysis of the samples "to obtain physiological data is a further invasion of the tested employee's privacy interests."[101] *Skinner* explained that, although collecting and testing urine samples does not require a bodily intrusion, "chemical analysis of urine, like that of blood, can reveal a host of private medical facts about an employee, including whether she is epileptic, pregnant, or diabetic."[102]

In *King*, Justice Kennedy rejected the claim that the processing of King's DNA sample violated the Constitution, arguing that, because "the CODIS loci come from noncoding parts of the DNA that do not reveal the genetic traits of the arrestee,"[103] it was "open to dispute" whether "the testing . . . in this case reveals any private medical information."[104] The implication is that analysis of DNA samples does not infringe any privacy interest. This conclusion also means that when police obtain a DNA sample without a per-

---

[99] *Ferguson v Charleston*, 532 US 67, 76 (2001). Justice Scalia's dissent in *Ferguson* questioned whether obtaining and testing urine samples of hospital patients triggered Fourth Amendment scrutiny. "There is only one act that could conceivably be regarded as a search of petitioners in the present case: the *taking* of the urine sample. I suppose the *testing* of that urine for traces of unlawful drugs could be considered a search of sorts, but the Fourth Amendment protects only against searches of citizens' 'persons, houses, papers and effects'; and it is entirely unrealistic to regard urine as one of the 'effects' (i.e., part of the property) of the person who has passed and abandoned it."). Id at 92 (Scalia, J, dissenting).

[100] *Skinner v Railway Labor Executives' Assn*, 489 US 602 (1989).

[101] Id at 616.

[102] Id at 617. Thus, collecting and testing urine also "must be deemed searches under the Fourth Amendment." Id.

[103] *King*, 133 S Ct at 1979.

[104] Id.

son's knowledge, say, from a discarded cigarette butt or water bottle, analysis of the sample does not trigger the Fourth Amendment at all.[105] This understanding is predicated on the assumption that the end product of analysis—the DNA profile—does not reveal genetic information about the individual. However, this assumption ignores the real threat to privacy posed by DNA data banking: "[T]he chance for government officials to surpass their [statutory] authority and use our DNA samples, containing our full genome and a 'treasure map' of our sensitive genetic information, for nefarious purposes."[106]

In addition to emphasizing the arrestee's diminished expectation of privacy, Justice Kennedy also stressed the trifling nature of the cheek swab. This description of King's constitutional interest is "especially problematic; King complained about the information taken from him, not the Q-tip in his mouth."[107] More importantly, Kennedy ignored the Court's precedents. The minimal character of the intrusion should not matter. In *Arizona v Hicks*, police entered Hicks's home in response to a call that a gun had been fired through Hicks's apartment floor, injuring a man in the unit below.[108] While police were lawfully in the apartment searching for the shooter and any other victims, they noticed two sets of stereo equipment they suspected were stolen.[109] The police recorded the serial numbers, which required moving some of the equipment, and seized the equipment after learning that it had been stolen.[110] The Court found that police action (i.e., slightly moving stereo equipment to see the serial number) unrelated to the objectives of the lawful search constituted a separate and distinct invasion of the suspect's privacy that was unjustified by the exigency of the lawful police entry. *Hicks* explained:

---

[105] For an excellent discussion of some of the legal issues surrounding the government's collection of "abandoned DNA," see Elizabeth E. Joh, *Reclaiming "Abandoned" DNA: The Fourth Amendment and Genetic Privacy*, 100 Nw U L Rev 857 (2006).

[106] Andrea Roth, *Maryland v. King and the Wonderful, Horrible DNA Revolution in Law Enforcement*, 11 Ohio St J Crim L 295, 303 (2013). See also Krimsky and Simoncelli, *Genetic Justice* at 235–36 (cited in note 78) ("DNA samples, which are stored indefinitely by forensic laboratories . . . have the potential to reveal almost unlimited information" about individuals.).

[107] Elizabeth E. Joh, *Maryland v. King: Policing and Genetic Privacy*, 11 Ohio St J Crim L 281, 287 (2013).

[108] *Arizona v Hicks*, 480 US 321 (1987).

[109] Id at 323.

[110] Id at 323–24.

> It matters not that the search uncovered nothing of any great personal
> value to [the suspect]—serial numbers rather than (what might con-
> ceivably have been hidden behind or under the equipment) letters or
> photographs. A search is a search, even if it happens to disclose nothing
> but the bottom of a turntable.[111]

If moving a turntable a few inches requires probable cause under
the Court's precedents, so should a compelled police entry into a
person's mouth.

Moreover, the Court in *Schmerber* described extraction of blood
samples as a "common-place" procedure that "involves virtually
no risk, trauma, or pain."[112] Since then, many courts have described
a compelled blood extraction as a painless, routine procedure.[113]
In fact, Justice Kennedy cited *Schmerber* and other precedents in
a 1989 ruling to confirm "'society's judgment that blood tests do
not constitute an unduly extensive imposition on an individual's
privacy and bodily integrity.'"[114] Nonetheless, the Court has never
disavowed *Schmerber*'s judgment regarding the need for a warrant
when the police want to draw blood from an arrestee. Indeed, in
Missouri v McNeely, decided only six weeks before *King*, the Court
reaffirmed *Schmerber* and rejected the state's call for a per se rule
allowing warrantless blood testing in drunk-driving cases.[115] Put
simply, bodily intrusions by the police, no matter how painless or
commonplace, have always required a showing of probable cause
and a warrant.

B. DNA SAMPLING CANNOT BE JUSTIFIED UNDER THE SPECIAL
   NEEDS EXCEPTION

Justice Kennedy's opinion in *King* appears to draw on the
Court's special needs cases. For example, Kennedy invoked *Veronia
School District 47J v Acton* to support the balancing analysis he
employs,[116] *Treasury Employees v Von Raab* to bolster his conclusion

---

[111] Id at 325.

[112] *Schmerber*, 384 US at 771.

[113] See, for example, *United States v Amerson*, 483 F3d 73, 84 (2d Cir 2007) (noting that
the Court "has long maintained that the intrusion effected by taking a blood sample . . .
is minimal."), quoting *Nicholas v Goord*, 432 F3d 652, 659 (2d Cir 2005).

[114] *Skinner v Ry. Labor Executives' Assn*, 489 US 602, 625 (1989), quoting *Winston v Lee*,
470 US 753, 762 (1985).

[115] *Missouri v McNeely*, 133 S Ct 1552, 1554 (2013).

[116] *King*, 133 S Ct at 1969, quoting *Vernonia School Dist. 47J v Acton*, 515 US 646, 652
(1995) ("As the text of the Fourth Amendment indicates, the ultimate measure of the
constitutionality of a governmental search is 'reasonableness'").

that warrants are not required "when the search involves no discretion that could be properly limited by the 'interpo[lation of] a neutral magistrate between the citizen and the law enforcement officer,'"[117] and several other special needs cases to support the proposition that an arrestee's privacy interests must be assessed in light of his "'legal relationship with the State.'"[118] In these cases, the Court has permitted suspicionless searches of individuals

---

[117] *King*, 133 S Ct at 1969–70, quoting *Treasury Employees v Von Raab*, 489 US 656, 667 (1989). Of course, the assertion that collecting DNA from arrestees involves "no [police] discretion" is ridiculous. Professor Erin Murphy rightly notes that the "notion that arrestee testing invites no law enforcement discretion makes sense only if one believes that the police lack discretion in making decisions about arrest." Murphy, 127 Harv L Rev at 189 (cited in note 16) (footnote omitted). Even the Court knows this isn't true. See *Town of Castle Rock, Colorado v Gonzales*, 545 US 748, 760 (2005) ("A well-established tradition of police discretion has long coexisted with apparently mandatory arrest statutes."). Many scholars have shown that the decision to arrest can be highly discretionary. See, for example, Wayne R. LaFave, *Arrest: The Decision to Take a Suspect into Custody* 60 (Brown, 1965) ("It is not common to arrest a person unless he is at least suspected of having engaged in criminal conduct. It is common for some persons not to be arrested even though it can easily be proved that they have engaged in criminal conduct."); id at 155 ("A decision not to arrest in a specific case does not ordinarily come to the attention of members of the community. . . . In most situations, the decision is known only to those who know of the crime and to the police officer who decides not to arrest."); Michael K. Brown, *Working the Street: Police Discretion and the Dilemmas of Reform* at 152 (Rose Sage Foundation, 1988) (stating that "felonies are the least interesting of discretionary incidents, for these violations are usually enforced. Refusal to arrest a person who has committed a felony not only counters the police code, but many policemen believe they have no discretion where a felony is concerned. This does not mean that every person who commits a felony will be arrested, since the determination of whether or not a felony has been committed is often a matter of interpretation."). Police exercise even greater discretion regarding misdemeanor arrests. See Alexandra Natapoff, *Misdemeanors*, 85 S Cal L Rev 1313, 1331–37 (2012) ("police arrest people for a variety of reasons that may or may not involve probable cause"); id at 1337 ("while we do not know how many people are arrested for petty offenses without evidence, we know the practice is ingrained in phenomena like urban loitering and trespass policies, zero tolerance policing, and routine urban street control. . . . Because misdemeanor arrests are low profile, unlikely to be litigated, and staples of police control tactics, they can easily be driven not by evidence, but by other police aims and goals."); see also Logan, 92 BU L Rev 1561 at 1589–90 (cited in note 73) (discussing the discretion police have when making arrests). Thus, even Professor David Kaye, an advocate for universal DNA testing, recognizes that "making arrest the threshold for inclusion in law enforcement DNA databases reflects a naïve view of what it means to be arrested. . . . Indeed, probable cause to arrest is spread thick and wide through the populace, attaching to the innocent-in-fact as well as to those guilty of the crime for which probable cause exists. Probable cause is thus an extremely low threshold, and a poor shield against the government taking and profiling our DNA—and against abuse of that power." D. H. Kaye and Michael E. Smith, *DNA Identification Databases: Legality, Legitimacy, and the Case for Population-Wide Coverage*, 2003 Wis L Rev 413, 458 n 153 (2003). See also Joh, 11 Ohio St J Crim L at 285 (cited in note 107) ("What *King* fails to acknowledge is that the very existence of a DNA database gives the police incentives to turn every encounter into an arrest. . . . While it is true that database laws give the police few choices at the literal moment of sample collection, little reins in the police in their decision about whom to target, when, and why" (footnotes omitted).

[118] *King*, 133 S Ct at 1978, quoting *Vernonia*, 515 US at 654.

"when 'special needs, beyond the normal need for law enforcement, make the warrant and probable cause requirement impracticable.'"[119] A synthesis of the cases shows that three factors are important to the Court when it decides whether a challenged search falls within the special needs doctrine: the purpose of the search, whether law enforcement officials will have access to the fruits of the search, and the extent of police involvement in conducting the search.[120]

Several lower courts have upheld DNA testing of arrestees on the theory that the testing is reasonable both for immediate identification purposes *and* for "maintaining a permanent record to solve other past and future crimes."[121] This reasoning, however, cannot be squared with legal principles announced in the Court's most recent special needs case, *Ferguson v City of Charleston*.[122] In *Ferguson*, the Court invalidated a public hospital's policy of conducting urine tests of pregnant women suspected of drug use and disclosing the results to law enforcement officials. Writing for the Court, Justice Stevens explained that the urine tests were designed to obtain incriminating information that would be revealed to police and prosecutors. Because the urine tests' central purpose "was to use the threat of arrest and prosecution in order to force women into treatment, and given the extensive involvement of law enforcement officials at every stage of the policy,"[123] the Court found that "this case simply does not fit within the closely guarded category of 'special needs.'"[124] Stevens explained that the "fact that positive test results were turned over to the police does not merely provide a basis for distinguishing" the special needs cases, it "also provides an affirmative reason for enforcing the strictures of the Fourth Amendment."[125] Stevens added that, "[w]hile the ultimate goal of the policy may well have been to get [women] into sub-

---

[119] *Griffin v Wisconsin*, 483 US 868, 873 (1987), quoting *New Jersey v T.L.O.*, 469 US 325, 351 (1985) (Blackmun, J, concurring).

[120] See Tracey Maclin, *Is Obtaining an Arrestee's DNA a Valid Special Needs Search Under the Fourth Amendment? What Should (and Will) the Supreme Court Do?* 33 J L Med & Ethics 102, 108–15 (2005).

[121] *Anderson v Commonwealth*, 634 SE2d 372, 375 (Va App 2006), quoting *Jones v Murray*, 962 F2d 302, 306 (4th Cir 1992).

[122] *Ferguson v City of Charleston*, 532 US 67 (2001).

[123] Id at 84.

[124] Id (footnote omitted).

[125] Id.

stance abuse treatment and off of drugs, the immediate objective of the searches was to generate evidence for law enforcement purposes in order to reach that goal."[126] For that reason, the special needs doctrine was inapplicable.

In light of *Ferguson*, it is difficult to conclude that DNA testing of an arrestee is a valid special needs search. Although the government has legitimate interests in knowing the identity of arrestees and in accurately identifying arrestees in a manner superior to fingerprinting or photography, it does not follow that DNA testing falls within the special needs doctrine because the government's interests in this context are directly related to law enforcement.[127] Further, police are thoroughly involved in conducting and using the results of DNA searches. As Justice Kennedy observed in his concurring opinion in *Ferguson*, "[n]one of our special needs precedents has sanctioned the routine inclusion of law enforcement . . . to implement the system designed for the special needs objectives."[128]

It might be argued that because the police are permitted to fingerprint arrestees for administrative purposes related to "identification" and to use those fingerprints for investigative purposes, the same should be true for DNA searches. This is a false analogy, however. As David Kaye, a well-known proponent of universal DNA testing, noted in the aftermath of *Ferguson*, it is "extremely implausible" that taking DNA samples from arrestees can be justified on the theory that the search's primary purpose is to ascertain an arrestee's true identity.[129] Rather, "[t]he legislative interest in DNA databases has not been primarily to supplement or supplant fingerprints as markers of true identity; it has always been to generate investigative leads."[130] For all these reasons, DNA

---

[126] Id at 82–83 (footnotes omitted).

[127] Compare Kaye and Smith, 2003 Wis L Rev at 434 (cited in note 117) ("'Normal law enforcement' would appear to be the primary purpose of a program requiring arrestees to provide DNA samples, typing those samples at standard forensic loci, and including the profiles in an identification database that can be searched for a profile matching DNA recovered in connection with unsolved past or future crime.").

[128] *Ferguson*, 532 US at 88 (Kennedy, J, concurring).

[129] D. H. Kaye, *Two Fallacies About DNA Data Banks for Law Enforcement*, 67 Brooklyn L Rev 176, 203 (2001).

[130] Id; compare Kaye, 34 J L Med & Ethics at 192 (cited in note 28) (stating that the reasoning of *Ferguson* "has pulled the rug out from under special-needs balancing for DNA databanks. The convicted-offender databases exist primarily to facilitate the identification of the perpetrators of sexual assaults, murders, and many other crimes, . . . criminal investigation is their *raison d'etre*.").

testing of arrestees does not fit within the category of special needs cases.

C. DNA SAMPLING CANNOT BE JUSTIFIED UNDER THE SAMSON/ KNIGHTS PRINCIPLE

If DNA testing is justified neither as a search incident to arrest nor as a special needs search, how can it be squared with the Fourth Amendment? As one federal appellate court has observed, the "Supreme Court has never applied a general balancing test"[131] in the context of searches designed to investigate ordinary criminal conduct. Indeed, as Justice Scalia emphasized in his dissenting opinion in *King*, the Court has generally embraced a "categorical" rule that the Fourth Amendment bars "searching a person for evidence of a crime when there is no basis for believing the person is guilty of the crime or is in possession of incriminating evidence."[132]

The "categorical" rule was jostled a bit, however, in *United States v Knights*[133] and *Samson v California*.[134] Both cases cast doubt on this "rule." In 2001, the Court in *Knights* upheld a warrantless police search of a probationer's home based on reasonable suspicion that criminal evidence would be discovered. *Knights* did not rely upon the special needs doctrine, because the search was directly related to law enforcement purposes and conducted by police. Additionally, there was no exigency justifying the warrantless search of Knights's home. The Court held that the search was "reasonable under our general Fourth Amendment approach of 'examining the totality of the circumstances.'"[135] The Court emphasized that Knights had signed a probation order that permitted suspicionless searches of his person, property, and effects "at anytime."[136] This agreement, although not determinative of Knights's Fourth Amendment rights, "significantly diminished" his "reasonable expectation of privacy."[137] The Court concluded that the

---

[131] *Nicholas v Goord*, 430 F3d at 666.

[132] *King*, 133 S Ct at 1980.

[133] *United States v Knights*, 534 US 112 (2001). Professor LaFave is quite critical of *Knights*. See LaFave, 5 *Search and Seizure* § 10.10(c) at 542–46 (cited in note 3).

[134] *Samson v California*, 547 US 843 (2006).

[135] *Knights*, 534 US at 118.

[136] Id at 114.

[137] Id at 120 (footnote omitted). Although *Knights*'s holding incorporates the reasonable suspicion the police had for searching Knights, the statute governing the search permitted

warrantless search of Knights's home advanced the government's "justified" concern in protecting the community from criminal acts committed by a probationer, who "will be more likely to engage in criminal conduct than an ordinary member of the community."[138]

Samson went a step further and upheld a suspicionless police search of a known parolee seen walking down the street with a woman and a child. The officer testified that he searched Samson's person for the "sole reason . . . that defendant was 'on parole,'" and noted that he "does not search all parolees 'all the time,' but does conduct parole searches 'on a regular basis' unless he has 'other work to do' or already 'dealt with' the parolee."[139] Like Knights, Samson had signed a release condition which permitted suspicionless searches at any time of the day or night. According to the Court, the issue in *Samson* was whether the condition of parole can so diminish a parolee's reasonable expectation of privacy that a suspicionless search by police does not violate the Fourth Amendment. In a 6–3 ruling (with Justice Scalia in the majority), the Court held that the search was "reasonable," once again suggesting the propriety of an open-ended type of balancing. The Court emphasized that Samson had signed a search condition that diminished any reasonable expectation of privacy he might otherwise harbor. For good measure, the Court added that probationers and parolees are on a "'continuum' of state-imposed punishments" and that "[o]n this continuum, parolees have fewer expectations of privacy than probationers, because parole is more akin to imprisonment than probation is to imprisonment."[140] The Court found that the suspicionless search served several state interests, including reducing recidivism of parolees, supervising parolees, and protecting the public from criminal acts by reoffenders. In practical effect, *Samson* eliminated Fourth Amendment protec-

---

suspicionless searches of probationers, a fact not lost on the *Knights* majority. Id at 120, n 6. Indeed, the Court seemed to plant the seeds for the result in *Samson* in *Knights* when it explicitly left open "whether [a] probation condition so diminished, or *completely eliminated*, Knights' reasonable expectation of privacy . . . that a search by a law enforcement officer without any individualized suspicion would have satisfied the reasonableness requirement of the Fourth Amendment." Id (emphasis added).

[138] *Knights*, 534 US at 121.

[139] *Samson*, 547 US at 843.

[140] Id.

tion for parolees, though the Court denied this result.[141]

According to Professor Wayne LaFave, *Samson* is the most relevant precedent in assessing the constitutionality of arrestee DNA testing.[142] It is, indeed, the only modern precedent in which the Court has upheld a suspicionless search for investigative purposes under a standardless balancing analysis.[143] Interestingly, though Justice Kennedy could have cited *Knights* and *Samson* as direct support for the result in *King*, he did not.[144] Perhaps Kennedy avoided relying upon either *Knights* or *Samson* because *Knights* and *Samson* apply only to searches of persons who have already been convicted of crime. During the oral argument, Kennedy seemed

---

[141] Justice Thomas's majority ruling in *Samson* denied the charge in Justice Stevens's dissent that the result in *Samson* permitted arbitrary, capricious, or harassing searches of parolees. According to Thomas, a statutory prohibition against these types of searches prevented that result. *Samson*, 547 US at 856. Justice Thomas's statement is unconvincing. If the statutory prohibition had any teeth, why wasn't the search of Samson deemed "arbitrary"? Is there much difference "between a search made without suspicion (and without adherence to any neutral criteria) and one made in an arbitrary or capricious manner?" Yale Kamisar et al, *Modern Criminal Procedure* 451 (West, 13th ed 2012). The officer's testimony—he searched Samson for the "sole reason . . . that defendant was 'on parole'"—suggested that the search was arbitrary. In any event, when the result in *Samson* is paired with the holding in *Pa Bd of Probation and Parole v Scott*, 524 US 357 (1998) (Fourth Amendment's exclusionary rule does not apply in a state parole hearing to suppress the fruit of an unconstitutional search conducted against a parolee), Fourth Amendment protection for parolees seems nonexistent.

[142] According to LaFave, none of the Justices in *King* measured DNA testing of arrestees by the "one and only suspicionless-search/no-special-needs/balancing-of-interests precedent, *Samson v. California*." Wayne R. LaFave, 3 *Search and Seizure: A Treatise on the Fourth Amendment* § 5.4(c) (forthcoming, West, 5th ed supp 2013–14).

[143] Compare Charles J. Nerko, Note, *Assessing Fourth Amendment Challenges to DNA Extraction Statutes After Samson v California*, 77 Fordham L Rev 917, 945 (2008) (noting that although the *Samson* Court "described its decision as 'far from remarkable,' never before had the Court approbated a search devoid of a warrant or individualized suspicion by invoking the totality of the circumstances test."); id at 945 (stating that "*Samson* provides courts with a *new* Fourth Amendment approach to justify the monumental governmental interests" that DNA testing of convicts furthers) (emphasis added); see also LaFave, 3 *Search and Seizure* § 5.4(c) (supp 2013–14) (cited in note 142) ("What makes *King* so disappointing is neither opinion comes to grips with the real issue in the case"—namely, "whether on a balancing-of-interests analysis a standardized procedure—consisting of a suspicionless minimal search by way of a cheek swab to obtain DNA for the primary purpose of identifying the perpetrators of otherwise unsolved past and future crimes— may constitutionally be applied to all persons lawfully arrested and then held pursuant to a valid charge of a serious offense, in light of the reduced expectation of privacy of those detainees.").

[144] See LaFave, 3 *Search and Seizure* § 5.4(c) (supp 2013–14) (cited in note 142) (noting that the result in *King*, as intimated by the Court majority, comes from a "process of balancing privacy and law enforcement interests in cases where there exists a lesser-expectation-of-privacy than is normally the case, which the majority could have specified (but didn't) as having been accepted by a majority of the Court" in *Knights* and *Samson*).

to accept that position.[145] Because parolees and probationers could be in prison and thus subject to frequent and suspicionless searches,[146] it might seem reasonable for the government to release them on the condition that they remain subject to similar searches.[147] On this view, arrestees are distinguishable, because they have not been placed on a "'continuum' of state-imposed punishments."[148]

In sum, then, Justice Kennedy's opinion in *King* cannot persuasively be explained in terms of the *Knights/Samson* principle, the search incident to arrest doctrine, or the special needs concept. What, then, explains *King*'s holding? In the end, *King* appears to rest on the Fourth Amendment jurisprudence of open-ended interest balancing, and this will likely portend how *King* will be read in the future. As *Terry v Ohio* and its progeny have shown, such an approach is an open invitation to expansive police powers.

III. Implications of King

King's application in future cases depends on how one reads Justice Kennedy's opinion. *King* can be read narrowly to apply only to persons arrested on felony or other serious charges. Kennedy himself framed the issue in that way, asking only whether the Fourth Amendment bars DNA testing from "persons arrested . . . on felony charges."[149] As Justice Scalia noted in dissent, at

---

[145] When counsel for King noted his strong disagreement with Maryland and the federal government's argument to use the "rationale of *Samson v. California* and essentially extend that rationale to the point of arrest," Justice Kennedy responded: "I think—I think there is some merit to your argument in that regard. In *Samson*, he was a parolee, and he actually, as I recall, signed a—a consent form as part of the probation." Oral Argument in *King* at 30 (cited in note 18).

[146] *Hudson v Palmer*, 468 US 517 (1984) (ruling that the Fourth Amendment does not provide protection for claims that a convicted prisoner has a privacy interest in his cell or possessory interest in his effects therein).

[147] Compare Oral Argument in *King* at 11 (cited in note 18) (Justice Sotomayor: "As I read *Samson*, it was the special relationship between the parolee or the probationary person, that line of cases, and the assumption being that they're out in the world, I think, by the largesse of the State. So the State has a right to search their home, just as it would their cell, essentially."); id at 24 (Chief Justice Roberts: "According to *Samson* and *Knights*, you're dealing with people who are still subject to the—criminal sentence."). See also Murphy, 127 Harv L Rev at 185 (cited in note 16) (stating that "*Samson* is not an iconic case describing the core of the Fourth Amendment," rather, "[i]t was, until *King*, an outlier" permitting suspicionless searches for law enforcement purposes. *Samson* was "explicable only as a reflection of the all but extinguished privacy expectations of those [under] conditional liberty.") (footnote omitted).

[148] *Samson*, 547 US at 843.

[149] *King*, 133 S Ct at 1966.

several places Kennedy's opinion appeared to confine the analysis to those arrested for serious offenses. Indeed, Kennedy stated in the last sentence of his opinion: "When officers make an arrest supported by probable cause to hold for a *serious offense* and they bring the suspect to the station to be detained in custody, taking and analyzing a cheek swab of the arrestee's DNA is, like fingerprinting and photographing, a legitimate police booking procedure that is reasonable under the Fourth Amendment."[150]

On the other hand, a few passages in the opinion indicate that the Court's analysis might apply to *all* arrestees. For example, Kennedy noted that Maryland's law is similar to laws enacted by other states and the federal government that authorize "the collection of DNA from . . . *all* arrestees."[151] Moreover, the logic of *King* would seem to extend to all arrestees. Indeed, in his dissenting opinion, Justice Scalia directly challenged the proposition that *King* will apply only to persons arrested for serious crimes:

> I cannot imagine what principle could possibly justify [limiting *King*'s holding to serious offenses], and the Court does not attempt to suggest any. If one believes that DNA will 'identify' someone arrested for assault, he must believe that it will 'identify' someone arrested for a traffic offense. This Court does not base its judgments on senseless distinctions. At the end of the day, *logic will out*. . . . Make no mistake about it: As an entirely predictable consequence of today's decision, your DNA can be taken and entered into a national DNA database if you are ever arrested, rightly or wrongly, and for whatever reason.[152]

Tellingly, Justice Kennedy did not respond to Scalia's challenge. Although the only issue before the Court in *King* concerned DNA testing of persons arrested for violent offenses, the federal government takes DNA samples from *all* arrestees, and seven states collect DNA samples from a subset of misdemeanor arrestees.[153] Moreover "a growing number of local law enforcement agencies across the country" now take DNA samples from anyone arrested

---

[150] Id at 1980 (emphasis added).

[151] Id at 1968 (emphasis added).

[152] Id at 1989 (Scalia, J, dissenting).

[153] 42 USC A § 14135(a). Alabama, Ala Code Ann § 36-18-25 (2013); Arizona, Ariz Rev Stat Ann § 13-610(L) (2013); Kansas, Kan Stat Ann § 21-2511 (2013); Louisiana, La Rev Stat Ann § 609 (2013); Minnesota, Minn Stat Ann § 299C105 (2013); South Carolina, SC Code Ann § 23-3-620 (2009); and South Dakota, SD Cod Laws § 23-5A-16.

for minor offenses.[154] This phenomenon will no doubt "accelerate" after *King*.[155] This trend is not surprising, for many law enforcement officials insist that "the crime-solving benefits of local databases are dramatic."[156]

When lower courts are confronted with constitutional challenges to DNA testing of persons arrested for minor offenses, they will naturally look to the Court for guidance. Because Justice Kennedy offered no reply to Scalia, lower court judges will have to decide how to interpret *King*, and in light of that exchange, most judges are likely to uphold DNA testing for all arrestees. It is, after all, a familiar adage that silence can be seen as assent.

Another issue is whether the police can use DNA testing on persons stopped for investigative detention.[157] One week after *King* was decided, the *New York Times* reported that some local police departments were "taking DNA from people on the mere suspicion of a crime, long before any arrest, and holding on to it regardless of the outcome."[158] Indeed, the police have been taking

---

[154] Joseph Goldstein, *Police Agencies Are Assembling Records of DNA*, NY Times (June 12, 2013), online at http://www.nytimes.com/2013/06/13/us/police-agencies-are-assembling-records-of-dna.html?pagewanted = all; see also Tami Abdollah, *Arrested in O.C.? A DNA Sample Could Buy Freedom*, LA Times (Sept 17, 2009), online at http://articles.latimes.com/2009/sep/17/local/me-oc-dna17 (describing a policy instituted by the Orange County, California District Attorney "offering a deal to some people who have only been arrested: give a DNA sample and have your charges dropped. . . . The [policy] applies to people arrested for nonviolent misdemeanors, including petty theft, trespassing and low-level drug-possession felonies.").

[155] Goldstein, *Police Agencies* (cited in note 154). The public safety director of Bensalem Township, Pennsylvania, read *King* in just this manner: "In light of the Supreme Court decision, more and more organizations are going to be [expanding DNA collection]." Id. See also *King*, 133 S Ct at 1989 (Scalia, J, dissenting). Professor Erin Murphy agrees. According to Murphy, "*King* is a green light" to conduct more DNA testing. "It's a ringing endorsement of DNA testing, and many law enforcement agencies would see this as a dramatic opportunity to expand DNA collection." Goldstein, *Police Agencies* (cited in note 154).

[156] Goldstein, id.

[157] The federal government already obtains DNA samples from noncitizens detained by federal officers. See 42 USC § 14135(a). This section permits, as prescribed by the Attorney General's regulations, collecting "DNA samples from . . . non-United States persons who are *detained* under the authority of the United States" (emphasis added). To be sure, the word "detained" is ambiguous in this context. Neither the statute nor the Attorney General's regulations define the term. The sponsor of the DNA Fingerprint Act stated, "the word 'detained' covers a wide spectrum of circumstances. The dictionary definition of 'detained' is to keep from proceeding or to keep in custody or temporary confinement." Statement of Senator Kyle, 151 Cong Rec S13757 (daily ed, Dec 16, 2005). Perhaps, "detained" means persons held in custody, but does not apply to persons temporarily seized for investigation as occurs during a *Terry* stop.

[158] Goldstein, *Police Agencies* (cited in note 154). According to the *New York Times*, "New York City has amassed a database with the profiles of 11,000 crime suspects. In Orange

forensic evidence from persons suspected, but not yet arrested, for many years. Not only is the Court aware of the practice, but it has signaled its approval.

The Court first confronted the practice of taking forensic evidence prior to arrest a year after *Terry*. In *Davis v Mississippi*,[159] the police brought Davis to a police station for fingerprinting and questioning in the course of a rape investigation. Davis's fingerprints matched those found at the crime scene and he was therefore convicted of rape. The Court held the detention unconstitutional because it had not been authorized by a judicial warrant, and it therefore suppressed the fingerprint evidence. The Court suggested, however, that it might approve a different type of fingerprinting detention. Speaking for the Court, Justice William Brennan wrote that, "because of the unique nature of the fingerprinting process, such detentions might be valid, under narrowly defined circumstances, even though there is no probable cause in the traditional sense."[160] Brennan explained that fingerprinting is less intrusive than other types of searches; it does not require the type of probing into a suspect's private life or thoughts that is associated with interrogation; it is inherently more reliable than eyewitness identifications or confessions; it is not subject to police manipulation; and because fingerprints cannot be destroyed, the detention can be planned by the police and authorized by a judicial warrant.[161]

County, California, the district attorney's office has 90,000 profiles, many obtained from low-level defendants who give DNA as part of a plea bargain or in return for having the charges against them dropped. . . . Others want to compile DNA profiles from suspects or low-level offenders long before their DNA might be captured by the state or national databases, which typically require conviction or arrest."

[159] *Davis v Mississippi* 394 US 721 (1969).

[160] Id at 727.

[161] Id. In a concurring opinion, Justice John Harlan made clear his view that, under a different set of facts than those presented in *Davis*, a "compelled submission to fingerprinting would not amount to a Fourth Amendment violation even in the absence of a warrant." Harlan felt that question should be left open. Id at 728–29 (Harlan, J, concurring). "The *Davis* dictum has had considerable impact." LaFave, 4 *Search and Seizure* § 9.8(b) at 975–76 (cited in note 3) (noting that laws have been enacted authorizing detention at a police station on less than probable cause for certain identification procedures, and that courts have "consistently" upheld such laws and such procedures even in the absence of an authorizing statute or court rule). Professor Kaye believes that the dicta from *Davis* "suggest[s] that the Supreme Court would uphold compulsory acquisition of biometric data from a person when the process is not physically or mentally invasive, when the data are useful primarily to link individuals to crime scenes or to establish the true identity of a given individual, and when the data are valid, reliable, and effective for this purpose." Kaye, 34 J L Med & Ethics at 193 (cited in note 28) (footnote omitted).

The door *Davis* opened for possible forensic detentions was opened still wider in *Hayes v Florida*.[162] The issue in *Hayes* was whether the Fourth Amendment permits the police to transport a suspect to a police station for fingerprinting without his consent and absent probable cause or a warrant. Relying on *Davis*, the Court held that the police cannot constitutionally seize an individual and transport him to a police station for investigative detention. The Court implied, however, that *street detentions* for fingerprinting might be consistent with the Fourth Amendment. Speaking for the Court, Justice White suggested "that a brief detention in the field for the purpose of fingerprinting, where there is only reasonable suspicion not amounting to probable cause," might be constitutional.[163] Noting that *Terry* and similar decisions had held that a brief detention of a suspicious person is permissible "in order to determine his identity,"[164] "to pose questions to the person, or to detain the person briefly while attempting to obtain further information,"[165] White concluded that the Fourth Amendment might

> permit seizures for the purpose of fingerprinting, if there is reasonable suspicion that the suspect has committed a criminal act, if there is a reasonable basis for believing that fingerprinting will establish or negate the suspect's connection with that crime, and if the procedure is carried out with dispatch.[166]

If, as *Hayes* suggests, the police can fingerprint a suspect during a *Terry* stop, can they also obtain a DNA sample during the stop, as long as they have reasonable grounds to believe that the suspect has committed a crime and that DNA analysis might either establish or negate the suspect's guilt? Is taking a DNA sample different from taking a fingerprint? Perhaps. *King* established that obtaining a DNA sample via a cheek swab is a "search." The Court has never decided, however, whether fingerprinting is a search. Indeed, on at least one occasion, it has suggested that fingerprinting might not constitute a search because it involves "mere 'phys-

---

[162] *Hayes v Florida*, 470 US 811 (1985).

[163] Id at 816.

[164] *Adams v Williams*, 407 US 143, 146 (1972).

[165] *United States v Hensley*, 469 US 221, 232 (1985).

[166] *Hayes*, 470 US at 817.

ical characteristics . . . constantly exposed to the public.'"[167] Because the Court has never held that there is a "search-for-evidence
counterpart to the *Terry* weapons search,"[168] it might permit fingerprinting during an investigatory stop, if fingerprinting is not
a search, but not DNA testing, which *is* a search. On the other
hand, it is possible to read *King* as authorizing compelled DNA
samples during investigative stops by employing the same type of
balancing analysis utilized in *King* and concluding that the government's interest in identifying a suspected criminal outweighs
the minimal intrusion involved in obtaining a DNA sample, even
if it is a search.[169]

Moreover, although the Court has never extended *Terry* to allow
"investigative identification search[es]" incident to a stop, the Wisconsin Supreme Court has upheld such searches during lawful
investigative detentions,[170] and federal prosecutors have urged
lower courts to recognize such an exception.[171] In light of these
developments, courts might increasingly be persuaded after *King*
to uphold "investigative identification search[es]" by combining
the logic of *King* with the reasoning of *Hiibel v Sixth Judicial
District Court*,[172] which was also authored by Justice Kennedy.

In *King*, Justice Kennedy emphasized that accurate identification
of an arrestee includes knowing more than the arrestee's name:
police also need to know "what is already known about him."[173]
According to Kennedy, a "suspect's criminal history is a critical

---

[167] *Cupp v Murphy*, 412 US 291, 295 (1973), quoting *United States v Dionisio*, 410 US
1, 14 (1973).

[168] LaFave, 4 *Search and Seizure* § 9.6(g) at 941 (cited in note 3) (footnote omitted).

[169] In a pre-*King* ruling, four judges of the District of Columbia Court of Appeals
endorsed this reasoning. *Askew*, 529 F3d at 1156–63 (Kavanaugh dissenting) (concluding
that police may conduct a search—unzipping a suspect's jacket—during a *Terry* stop to
facilitate a victim's identification of the suspect).

[170] *State v Flynn*, 285 NW2d 710 (Wis 1979). *Flynn* explained that to accept the notion
that a suspect properly detained for investigation can refuse an officer's request for identification "would reduce the authority of the officer granted by [the state stop and identify
statute] and recognized by the United States Supreme Court in *Adams v Williams*, 407
US 143 (1972) to identify a person lawfully stopped by him to a mere fiction." Id at 717–
18. While *Flynn* applied a balancing analysis, according to Professor LaFave, no other
court has embraced this result and recognized an identification search. See LaFave, 4
Search and Seizure § 9.6(g) at 943 (cited in note 3).

[171] In *Askew*, 529 F3d at 1134, the government urged the court to approve an "identification" search during a *Terry* investigation.

[172] *Hiibel v Sixth Judicial District*, 542 US 177 (2004).

[173] *King*, 133 S Ct at 1972.

part of his identity."[174] Kennedy observed that persons stopped for traffic offenses are often dangerous criminals, noting that Timothy McVeigh was stopped for driving without a license plate only hours after the Oklahoma City bombing, and that one of the terrorists involved in the September 11 attacks was ticketed for speeding two days before the attacks.[175] Kennedy explained that DNA is a "metric of identification used to connect the arrestee with his or her public persona, as reflected in records of his or her actions that are available to the police."[176] Accordingly, police may link an arrestee to "a variety of relevant forms of identification" possessed by the government, which "are checked as a routine matter to produce a more comprehensive record of the suspect's complete identity."[177]

If these government interests are sufficient to justify DNA searches of arrestees, it arguably follows that similar interests justify DNA searches during *Terry* stops. *Hiibel* might be viewed as a first step in that direction. Hiibel was detained and questioned about a reported domestic dispute. After he refused to identify himself, he was arrested and later convicted of violating Nevada's "stop and identify" law, which requires a person subject to a lawful investigative detention to provide police with his identity. Relying on prior rulings, Hiibel argued that he had a right not to identify himself during a *Terry* stop. The Court, in an opinion by Justice Kennedy, disagreed. Kennedy explained that the Court had made "clear that questions concerning a suspect's identity are a routine and accepted part of many *Terry* stops."[178] He noted that the Court had recognized that the authority to detain, ask questions, and check identification, even without probable cause to arrest, "promotes the strong government interest in solving crimes and bringing offenders to justice."[179] Applying a balancing analysis, Kennedy found that learning a suspect's identity "may inform an officer that a suspect is wanted for another offense, or has a record of violence or mental disorder."[180] Moreover, he added, identity is

---

[174] Id.

[175] Id.

[176] Id.

[177] Id.

[178] *Hiibel*, 542 US at 186.

[179] Id.

[180] Id.

particularly important in domestic violence cases, because police "need to know whom they are dealing with in order to assess the situation, the threat to their own safety, and possible danger to the potential victim."[181] Kennedy added that the "request for identity has an immediate relation to the purpose, rationale, and practical demands of a *Terry* stop."[182] Finally, and importantly, Nevada's identification requirement does not change the duration or location of the stop. Taking all this into account, Kennedy upheld the law.

Although Wayne LaFave believes that *Hiibel* "does not lend much support" for an investigative identification search,[183] that proposition is not so clear after *King*. Relying on the government interests identified in *King* and *Hiibel*, and *Hayes's* procedural framework for obtaining fingerprints from a suspect during an investigative stop, a court could easily find that the government's interest in accurately identifying persons subject to *Terry* stops outweighs the minor intrusion of taking a DNA sample.[184] Courts have already approved warrant and criminal background checks for persons detained for traffic offenses, even though such procedures can take thirty minutes to complete.[185] In *Illinois v Caballes*, the Court impliedly conferred approval on these investigative procedures, provided that they do not unduly prolong the length of the stop.[186] If there is reasonable suspicion that a suspect has committed a crime, the state has a strong interest in obtaining an accurate identification of the suspect, similar to its interest in obtaining fingerprints. A court might therefore conclude that "the only difference between DNA analysis and the accepted use of

[181] Id.

[182] Id at 188.

[183] See LaFave, 4 *Search and Seizure* § 9.6(g) at 947 (cited in note 3).

[184] See *Askew*, 529 F3d at 1161 (Kavanaugh dissenting) (four judges, relying upon *Hiibel* and other cases, stating: "Identification procedures constituting searches are permitted during *Terry* stops so long as procedures are reasonable under the circumstances.").

[185] See, for example, Wayne R. LaFave, *The Routine Traffic Stop from Start to Finish: Too Much "Routine" and Not Enough Fourth Amendment*, 102 Mich L Rev 1843, 1876–78 (2004); Tracey Maclin, *Police Interrogation During Traffic Stops: More Questions Than Answers*, 31 Champion 34, 37 n 64 (Nov 2007).

[186] *Illinois v Caballes* 543 US 405, 408 (2005). In *Caballes*, police conducted a warrant check and a criminal background check before having a drug-detection dog sniff Caballes's car. *People v Caballes*, 802 NE2d 202, 203 (Ill 2003). Although these facts were not mentioned in Justice Stevens's majority opinion in *Caballes*, he did state that the "duration of the stop in this case was entirely justified by the traffic offense and the ordinary inquiries incident to such a stop." *Caballes*, 543 US at 408.

fingerprint databases is the unparalleled accuracy DNA provides."[187]

Furthermore, a court might believe that a *Terry* "suspect's criminal history is a critical part of his identity that officers should
know when" conducting an investigative detention.[188] The same
government interests in accurate identification that are served by
obtaining a suspect's fingerprints are also promoted by obtaining
a DNA sample. If the police may obtain a suspect's fingerprints
during a *Terry* stop, as *Hayes* seems to suggest, then it would seem
to follow that they may take a DNA swab for the same purpose.[189]
Although obtaining a DNA sample constitutes a separate and additional search, a court could decide that taking the sample "does
not alter the nature of the stop itself: it does not change its duration, or its location."[190] Borrowing from the analysis of *King*, a
court could find that "the additional intrusion upon the [suspect's]
privacy beyond that associated with fingerprinting is not significant," and thus justifies this minor intrusion.[191]

To be sure, the Court has not yet endorsed an investigative
search for identification under *Terry*. However, the Court had not
approved a suspicionless search of the body for identification be-

---

[187] *King*, 133 S Ct at 1972.

[188] Id. See also Joh, 11 Ohio St J Crim L at 291–92 (cited in note 107). ("If 'knowledge
of identity' has long been an acceptable objective in the *Terry* context, and a DNA profile
is a part of the individual's identity for Fourth Amendment purposes, its collection would
seem appropriate even in circumstances short of arrest.") (footnotes omitted).

[189] In *Askew*, four judges of the District of Columbia Court of Appeals argued that
prohibiting identification procedures that amount to searches during *Terry* stops would
"lead to absurd and dangerous results." *Askew*, 529 F3d at 1162 (Kavanaugh dissenting)
(observing that such a rule would mean police could not "remove a suspect's gloves to
perform the fingerprinting that *Hayes* expressly allows," "lift a rape suspect's sleeve to view
a tattoo on the suspect's forearm, even though the rape victim said the perpetrator had
a distinctive tattoo on his forearm," "take fingernail scrapings or a saliva swab from a
murder suspect in a case where the victim was killed in a violent struggle."). According
to these judges, barring identification searches during investigative detentions "would mean
that a large number of state statutes, rules, and decisions permitting identification procedures on less than probable cause—which have been on the books for decades—are all
unconstitutional and wrongly decided." Id.

[190] *Hiibel*, 542 US at 178 (internal citations omitted). During the oral argument in *King*,
Chief Justice Roberts asked counsel for Maryland about taking DNA samples during traffic
stops: "But there's no reason you couldn't, right? I gather it's not hard. Police officers
who give Breathalyzer tests, they can also take a Q-tip or whatever and get a DNA sample,
right?" After counsel noted that the Court's cases presume that traffic stops be brief, the
Chief Justice suggested that taking a DNA sample would not take much time: "Well, how
long does it take to—to undergo the procedure? You know, you say, ah, and then—you
know." Oral Argument in *King* at 7 (cited in note 18).

[191] *King*, 133 S Ct at 1976.

fore *King*. Prior to *King*, the Court had permitted *Terry* searches only for weapons. Nonetheless, after *King*, lower courts might find that a DNA search during a *Terry* stop is constitutional. One might argue, for example, that taking DNA during a stop is designed not to discover *evidence*, but rather, as *King* found, to produce an *accurate identification*. Moreover, the intrusion on privacy is no greater than the intrusion authorized in *King*, and is not significantly more intrusive than fingerprinting,[192] which the Court has already said is permissible in these circumstances. Put differently, just as *King* invoked a balancing process similar to that used in *Terry* to assess "the reasonableness of the government adding a very little search (this kind of cheek swabbing) to the booking process,"[193] a judge in a future case could take the next step and approve the same type of search in the context of an investigative detention.[194]

---

[192] Compare id at 1976 (describing the intrusion on privacy of taking a DNA sample: "The additional intrusion upon the arrestee's privacy beyond that associated with fingerprinting is not significant . . .").

[193] E-mail from John Q. Barrett to crimprof@chicagokent.kentlaw.edu (June 6, 2013 at 6:48 pm) (explaining that *King* "is a *Terry*/balancing decision about the Fourth Amendment reasonableness of the government adding a very little search (this kind of cheek swabbing) to the booking process for . . . these kinds of 'serious' crime arrestees.").

[194] Although this is not the place for a detailed analysis of the issue, the reasoning of *King* can also be extended to persons not suspected of criminal conduct. For a long time, mandatory fingerprinting has been associated with criminal investigations. "With technological advances, however, the criminal stigma has somewhat lessened as fingerprinting has become a more common form of identification utilized outside of the criminal justice system." Christina Buschmann, *Mandatory Fingerprinting of Public School Teachers: Facilitating Background Checks or Infringing on Individuals' Constitutional Rights?*, 11 Wm & Mary Bill Rts J 1273, 1279–80 (2003). Many states require applicants to certain professions to provide fingerprints for identification purposes and criminal background checks, including individuals applying to be lawyers, doctors, nurses, public school teachers, bankers, and pawnbrokers. Some states require welfare recipients to provide fingerprints as a condition for receiving benefits. See Recent Legislation, *Welfare Policy—Fraud Prevention—New York Requires Finger Imaging for Welfare Recipients*, 109 Harv L Rev 1168 (1996). Six states require fingerprints to obtain a driver's license. Although the statutes vary in form, the purpose behind most mandatory fingerprinting requirements is to verify the identification of the applicant and to facilitate criminal background checks. For example, California's fingerprint requirement for the bar exam serves two purposes: "to establish the identity of the applicant and in order to determine whether the applicant . . . has a record of criminal conviction in this state or in other states." Cal Bus & Prof Code § 6054 (West 2013). Similarly, the California Supreme Court, in upholding California's fingerprint requirement for driver's licenses, explained that the state legislature had found that "'the driver's license and identification card issued by the Department of Motor Vehicles are the basic identification documents in this state and that the state has a compelling interest in insuring the accuracy and integrity of this identification system.'" *Perkey v Dept of Motor Vehicles*, 721 P2d 50, 51 (Cal 1986) (citation omitted).

If states can require potential school teachers and applicants for a driver's license to provide fingerprints, can states also require applicants to provide a DNA sample for iden-

IV. Is KING ANOTHER TERRY?

Near the conclusion of oral argument in *King*, Justice Kennedy asked King's counsel a series of questions that, for Kennedy, encapsulated the heart of the case:

> [A] person has been arrested for a felony and is in custody, do the police—does the justice system have an interest in knowing whether that person committed other crimes?[195]

> My question is whether or not the police, who have John Doe in custody for a felony, have an interest in knowing, at the outset or within a few weeks' time, whether or not that person has committed other crimes?[196]

> And my—my question is, do they have an interest—a legitimate interest in knowing if that person has committed other crimes?[197]

Counsel did not provide the answers Kennedy sought; therefore, Kennedy answered his own questions: Yes, Justice Kennedy concluded in *King*, the state does have a legitimate interest in knowing

---

tification purposes? After all, "[i]f the Constitution allows the police to keep a fingerprint or a photograph as a biometric identifier, as many courts have held, then it is hard to see why they cannot keep a DNA profile if it is properly limited to 'vacuous' loci." Kaye and Smith, 2003 Wis L Rev at 432 (cited in note 117). And as *King* observed in the context of identifying arrestees, "the only difference between DNA analysis and the accepted use of fingerprint databases is the unparalleled accuracy DNA provides." *King*, 133 S Ct at 1972. Indeed, "if DNA collection is also okay because DNA is just a 21st century fingerprint, and all that it tells us is just a part of 'identity,' then it is hard to read [*King*] as rejecting collection of DNA in any case where collection of fingerprints is already allowed." Murphy, 127 Harv L Rev at 178 (cited in note 16).

As noted above, the Court has not found that fingerprinting is a search for constitutional purposes, while *King* establishes compelling a DNA sample via a buccal swab is a search. Nevertheless, a lower court might decide, using a balancing analysis and the reasoning of *King*, that although obtaining a DNA sample constitutes a search, the state's compelling interest in accurately identifying applicants for particular professions outweighs the minimal nature of the intrusion in obtaining the sample. *King* described a DNA search as a "negligible" intrusion, "a far more gentle process" than a blood draw and a "minimally invasive search." *King*, 133 S Ct at 1969 & 1977. Moreover, while it is a debatable proposition, an argument can be made that because of extensive regulation by the state, members of certain professions, for example, doctors and lawyers, possess a diminished or no-privacy interest concerning their identity. In a similar vein, the Court has ruled that suspicionless and random urinalysis drug testing of public school students does not violate the Fourth Amendment. In two separate cases, the Court concluded that the collection of urine, which is considered a search, was reasonable because students have diminished privacy interests due to the state's "'custodial and tutelary responsibility for children'" and the collection of a urine sample was relatively unobtrusive, and thus the privacy interests compromised were "negligible." *Bd of Ed of Pottawatomie City v Earls*, 536 US 822, 830 (2002) (citation omitted); *Vernonia Sch Dist*, 515 US 646, 658 (1995).

[195] Oral Argument in *King* at 41 (cited in note 18).

[196] Id.

[197] Id at 42.

whether an arrestee has committed other crimes. A DNA search obviously advances that interest. Moreover, a DNA search also promotes the state's interest in being able to identify the arrestee if he commits a future crime and his DNA is found at the scene. As Scalia put the point in *King*, "[w]hat DNA adds—what makes it a valuable weapon in the law enforcement arsenal—is the ability to solve unsolved crimes, by matching old crime-scene evidence against the profiles of people whose identities are already known."[198] Indeed, the Justices in the majority envisioned arrestee DNA searches as "an indispensable tool in the fight against crime."[199] This understanding no doubt prompted Justice Alito's comment that *King* "is perhaps the most important criminal procedure case that this Court has heard in decades."[200]

To act on this understanding, Justice Kennedy had to deal with the Court's existing doctrine. Because the Court's precedents offered no support for Kennedy's position, he had to create an expansive and novel definition of "identity" in order to uphold DNA searches of arrestees.[201] The felt necessity to uphold DNA searches explains Kennedy's unconvincing assertion that the purpose of the DNA search was to "identify" King. As they say, necessity is the mother of invention.[202]

Both *King* and *Terry v Ohio* upheld unprecedented police searches, using reasoning motivated by a sense of necessity. In *Terry*, the Court confronted a controversial and pressing issue: the authority of police officers to stop and frisk a suspicious person absent probable cause to believe that he has committed a crime. While patrolling in plain clothes on the afternoon of October 31, 1963, Cleveland police detective Martin McFadden observed two men peer into a store window roughly twenty-four times. The two men then left the scene and joined a third man. The officer

---

[198] *King*, 133 S Ct at 1989 (Scalia, J, dissenting).

[199] Murphy, 127 Harv L Rev at 181 (cited in note 16) (footnote omitted).

[200] Oral Argument in *King* at 35 (cited in note 18).

[201] See also Murphy, 127 Harv L Rev at 177 (cited in note 16) ("The most radical aspect of *King* is its reimagination of the idea of 'identity' to include criminal history and other information beyond 'name and social security number.'").

[202] See *The New Oxford American Dictionary* 1135 (2d ed, 2005) ("*proverb*, when the need for something becomes imperative, you are forced to find ways of getting or achieving it."). *Cambridge Dictionaries Online* (Cambridge University Press, 2007), online at http://dictionary.cambridge.org (select "American English"; search "necessity is the mother of invention") ("if someone really needs to do something, (s)he will think of a way of doing it.").

suspected the men of "'casing a job, a stick-up'" and worried that
"'they may have a gun.'"[203] After approaching the men and not
receiving a satisfactory explanation of their behavior, the officer
grabbed one of the men, John Terry, spun him around and patted
down the outside of his clothing. The officer felt a gun in Terry's
overcoat pocket. The officer removed another gun from the second man's overcoat.

The Court's precedents required probable cause to believe that
criminal conduct was afoot before the police could seize or search
a person. The trial court in *Terry* stated that it "'would be stretch-
ing the facts beyond reasonable comprehension' to find that Officer McFadden had had probable cause to arrest the men before
he patted them down for weapons."[204] None of the Justices questioned this conclusion. Yet, because of the "necessity" of the situation, the Court voted 8–1 to uphold the search of Terry. Speaking for the Court, Chief Justice Earl Warren stated: "we cannot
blind ourselves to the need for law enforcement officers to protect
themselves and other prospective victims of violence in situations
where they lack probable cause for an arrest."[205] Thus, the Court
ruled that where an officer reasonably believes that a suspicious
person under investigation is armed and presently dangerous, the
officer may frisk the person "to determine whether the person is
in fact carrying a weapon and to neutralize the threat of physical
harm."[206]

Prior to *Terry*, New York's highest court, the Court of Appeals,
tried to reconcile stop-and-frisk authority with the Court's precedents by concluding that the procedure did not involve either a
seizure or a search, and thus did not trigger Fourth Amendment
protection.[207] *Terry* dismissed that conclusion as implausible.[208] At

---

[203] *Terry*, 392 US at 6.

[204] Id at 7–8.

[205] Id at 24.

[206] Id.

[207] In *People v Rivera*, 201 NE2d 32, 35 (NY 1964), the Court of Appeals explained that
the physical intrusion involved during a frisk "is not very far different from the sense of
sight or hearing—senses upon which police customarily act."

[208] *Terry*, 392 US at 16. ("It is quite plain that the Fourth Amendment governs 'seizures'
of the person which do not eventuate in a trip to the station house and prosecution for
crime—'arrests' in traditional terminology. . . . And it is nothing less than sheer torture
of the English language to suggest that a careful exploration of the outer surfaces of a
person's clothing all over his body or her body in an attempt to find weapons is not a
'search.'").

the same time, the Court had to abandon the Fourth Amendment's presumptive procedural safeguards of a warrant and probable cause, because no precedent authorized a frisk for a weapon. The Court therefore improvised and explained that "the conduct involved in this case must be tested by the Fourth Amendment's general proscription against unreasonable searches and seizures."[209] Tellingly, this and similar statements[210] in *Terry* lacked any citation to precedent. Soon, the Court extended the open-ended balancing analysis embraced in *Terry* to other cases far removed from the "necessity" in *Terry*. As a member of the *Terry* majority later said: "It seems that the delicate balance that *Terry* struck was simply too delicate, too susceptible to the 'hydraulic pressures' of the day. As a result of today's decision, the balance struck in *Terry* is now heavily weighted in favor of the government."[211] Over time, the balancing analysis adopted in *Terry* eventually became the "touchstone of modern Fourth Amendment jurisprudence."[212]

The Court's reasoning in *Terry* and *King* was motivated by the perceived necessity of upholding the challenged searches. Each case involved a controversial search that the state argued was vital to law enforcement. Although the Court's prior rulings did not authorize the respective searches, that fact did not prevent the Court from reaching its desired outcome. In *Terry*, the Court gave its approval to a police procedure that the Court recognized generated "strong resentment" in black urban communities.[213] In *King*, the Court sanctioned a suspicionless search unlike other procedures approved by the Court, implying unpersuasively that it was simply following the Court's precedents. There is, however, one important difference between *Terry* and *King*. In *Terry*, the Court acknowledged that it was constructing a new legal landscape in

---

[209] Id at 20 (footnote omitted).

[210] See, for example, *Terry*, 392 US at 19 ("The distinctions of classical 'stop-and-frisk' theory thus serve to divert attention from the central inquiry under the Fourth Amendment—the reasonableness in all the circumstances of the particular governmental invasion of a citizen's personal security.").

[211] *Adams v Williams*, 407 US 143, 162 (1972) (Marshall, J, dissenting).

[212] John Q. Barrett, *Deciding the Stop and Frisk Cases: A Look Inside the Supreme Court's Conference*, 72 St John's L Rev 749, 753 (1998).

[213] *Terry*, 392 US at 17. Stop-and-frisk practices continue to generate anger in certain minority neighborhoods. See *Floyd v City of New York*, 2013 WL 4046209 (SDNY) (concluding that the stop-and-frisk practices of the New York City Police Department violate the Fourth Amendment and the Equal Protection Clause of the Fourteenth Amendment).

authorizing searches of the person on less than probable cause. The first sentence of Chief Justice Warren's opinion recognized the "serious questions" presented by the case.[214] A few pages later, Warren observed: "We would be less than candid if we did not acknowledge that this [case] thrusts to the fore difficult and troublesome issues regarding a sensitive area of police activity—issues which have never before been squarely presented to this Court."[215] Justice Harlan's concurrence was more direct; he stated in no uncertain terms that *Terry* announced an "important new field of law."[216]

By contrast, Justice Kennedy's opinion in *King* proceeds as if the Court was merely applying settled principle to a new set of facts. DNA collection from arrestees serves a state interest "that is well established: the need for law enforcement officers in a safe and accurate way to process and identify the persons and possessions they must take into custody."[217] Obtaining and analyzing an arrestee's DNA sample is just like taking an arrestee's fingerprints. "[T]he only difference between DNA analysis and the accepted use of fingerprint databases is the unparalleled accuracy DNA provides."[218] Comparing an arrestee's DNA profile to the DNA profiles in unsolved cases "uses a different form of identification than a name or fingerprint, but its function is the same."[219] Finally, Kennedy declared that the privacy interests at stake are a close equivalent to the privacy interests invaded by fingerprinting. "The additional intrusion upon the arrestee's privacy beyond that associated with fingerprinting is not significant, and DNA is a markedly more accurate form of identifying arrestees."[220]

Chief Justice Warren wanted to confine the police power newly approved in *Terry* to cases where police safety was threatened,[221] but *Terry*'s "reasonableness" analysis was soon extended to give

---

[214] *Terry*, 392 US at 4.

[215] Id at 9.

[216] Id at 31 (Harlan, J, concurring).

[217] *King*, 133 S Ct at 1970.

[218] Id at 1972.

[219] Id.

[220] Id at 1976.

[221] Barrett, 72 St John's L Rev at 794 (cited in note 212) ("*Terry* would be, as Warren saw things, a decision that gave the Court's limited approval solely to Detective McFadden's frisks of the three men.").

the police additional authority to detain suspicious persons in contexts presenting no danger to the police.[222] *Terry*, in other words, fundamentally changed Fourth Amendment law and diminished Fourth Amendment protections. It is too early to assert that *King* will inevitably alter search and seizure jurisprudence.[223] Eight years ago, I predicted that the Court would not invalidate a DNA arrestee statute "on Fourth Amendment or any other constitutional grounds."[224] Now, I predict that *King* will follow in *Terry*'s footsteps and chart a path that similarly narrows Fourth Amendment liberties.[225]

---

[222] See, for example, *United States v Montoya de Hernandez*, 473 US 531 (1985) (*Terry* analysis used, in part, to uphold a sixteen-hour border detention of a person suspected of alimentary canal smuggling); *United States v Place*, 462 US 696 (1983) (*Terry* analysis used to validate detention of luggage for investigation); *Florida v Royer*, 460 US 491 (1983) (*Terry* analysis supports detaining a person suspected of narcotics smuggling); *Michigan v Summers*, 452 US 692 (1981) (*Terry* analysis used to uphold detention of occupants found on premises subject to a search warrant for contraband).

[223] Compare Murphy, 127 Harv L Rev at 196 (cited in note 16) ("Whether [*King*] marks the beginning of a new era, however, only time will tell.").

[224] Maclin, 33 J L Med & Ethics at 118 n 261 (cited in note 120).

[225] It is worth noting that the Obama administration cites *King* to defend the constitutionality of a program whereby the Foreign Intelligence Surveillance Court directs telecommunications companies to provide telephone "metadata" in bulk to the National Security Agency ("NSA"). Under this program, analysts from the NSA have access to telephone metadata from almost every telephone call made "within the United States and between the United States and foreign countries." Federal Government, *Administration White Paper: Bulk Collection of Telephony Metadata Under Section 215 of the USA Patriot Act* at 1 (Aug 8, 2013). By the government's account, telephone metadata "includes information about what telephone numbers were used to make and receive the calls, when the calls took place, and how long the calls lasted." The phone companies do not report any information about the content of calls. Id.

The Obama administration contends that even if the collection of telephone metadata constitutes a search under the Fourth Amendment, the Court's reasonableness standard "authoriz[es] the Government to conduct large-scale, but minimally intrusive, suspicionless searches." Id at 21. The administration cites *King*'s balancing test to conclude that a balancing analysis "overwhelmingly favors the Government in this context." Id. The administration argues that telephone metadata collection results only in a "minimal" intrusion on privacy interests, the program does not collect or disclose the content of calls, and data may be accessed only when the government has a reasonable suspicion that a particular phone number is associated with a specific foreign terrorist organization. The government emphasizes that "only an exceedingly small fraction of the data collected has ever been seen," and claims that this "weighs heavily in the Fourth Amendment calculus." Id (citing *King*, 133 S Ct at 1979, for the proposition that intrusions on privacy interests are limited when DNA analysis is used to provide identification information alone).

As this article goes to press, two federal district courts have split on the constitutionality of the NSA's telephone surveillance program. See *Klayman v Obama*, 2013 WL 6571596, *2 (DDC 2013); *ACLU v Clapper*, 2013 WL 6819708, *21 (SDNY 2013).

Although this is not the place to closely examine whether the government action to collect and review phone records is constitutional, it is interesting to note the similarities between DNA registries and the NSA telephone surveillance program. Both intrusions involve collecting and storing vast amounts of personal information, and are executed

Forty years ago, Justice Powell bluntly stated that an arrestee retains no privacy interest in his person in the face of "a legitimate and overriding government concern."[226] He saw no reason to frustrate law enforcement goals by requiring that every search incident to arrest be justified by the twin rationales of seizing evidence or weapons; searches could serve other government interests as well—like solving crimes. "The search incident to arrest is reasonable under the Fourth Amendment because the privacy interest protected by that constitutional guarantee is legitimately abated by the fact of arrest."[227]

I believe the result in *King* is best explained as a search incident to arrest. Taking DNA samples from arrestees may help close unsolved crimes.[228] It certainly accelerated the identification of King as the perpetrator of an unresolved rape. But the search incident to arrest doctrine does not allow DNA searches. Rather than openly confront this obstacle and expand the boundaries of permissible searches incident to arrest, Justice Kennedy's opinion in *King* fashioned a definition of "identification" that allowed the Court to elude settled doctrine. More troubling, *King* invites law

---

without individualized suspicion of wrongdoing. Both intrusions also yield potential fruits that facilitate law enforcement interests.

While many are alarmed that the government collects and warehouses massive amounts of information about individuals, extensive surveillance and data mining do not necessarily amount to a Fourth Amendment violation. Indeed, when confronted with comparable intrusions in prior cases, the Court has not ruled that collecting and stockpiling large amounts of information publicly disclosed or revealed to third parties constitutes a search under the Fourth Amendment. The Court most recently considered collection of informational data in *United States v Jones*, 132 S Ct 945 (2012). *Jones* held that a search occurred when the government attached a global positioning system (GPS) tracking device to a vehicle and used that device to monitor the vehicle's movements on the streets for twenty-eight days. However, the result in *Jones* did not turn on the amount of data revealed and retained through government surveillance, but on the *trespass* associated with the attachment of the GPS device. Thus, *Jones* did not decide whether obtaining extensive location data is a search, let alone an unreasonable search. Compare id at 955 (Sotomayor, J, concurring) (observing that "GPS monitoring generates a precise, comprehensive record of a person's public movements that reflects a wealth of detail about her familial, political, professional, religious, and sexual associations.").

At first glance, the result and reasoning of *King* seem to be miles away from the broad data mining involved with the NSA's telephone surveillance program. Yet, it is telling that the government views *King* as support for collecting and analyzing the nation's telephone metadata.

[226] *Robinson*, 414 US at 237 (Powell, J, concurring).

[227] Id at 237–38 (footnote omitted).

[228] Although some law enforcement officials and scholars argue that expanding DNA databases will help solve more cold cases and deter future crimes, Professors Brandon Garrett and Erin Murphy contend that "[r]esearch shows that bigger is only better if DNA databases grow in the right way: by entering more samples from *crime scenes*, not samples from arrestees." Garrett and Murphy, *Supreme Court 2013* (cited in note 96).

enforcement officials to extend DNA searches to persons arrested for any offense and even to persons merely detained by the police. Justice Scalia may be right that "most Members of the Court" are not quite ready to "just come out and say that any suspicionless search of an arrestee is allowed if it will be useful to solve crimes."[229] More time is needed before the Court will openly embrace that result. That conclusion is coming, and *King*'s balancing analysis provides the template for achieving that goal.

---

[229] *King*, 133 S Ct at 1982 n 1 (Scalia, J, dissenting).

FREDERICK SCHAUER

ANALOGY IN THE SUPREME COURT: LOZMAN v CITY OF RIVIERA BEACH, FLORIDA

Is a houseboat a house or a boat? This may sound like a trick question, but it is not. Or it may sound like an SAT question, but it is not that either. Nor is it even the kind of question to which the thoughtful and intelligent answer is that a houseboat has attributes of a house and attributes of a boat, and nothing further need be or can be said. Rather, the question whether a houseboat is a house or a boat is precisely the question the Supreme Court was required to answer in *Lozman v City of Riviera Beach, Florida*.[1] And, importantly, the Court was required to give an answer different from the thoughtful and intelligent one just described. The thoughtful and intelligent answer, it turns out, is typically ineligible in law, precisely because legal decision making, in its archetypal mode, is bivalent.[2] In many legal contexts "some of this and some

Frederick Schauer is David and Mary Harrison Distinguished Professor of Law, University of Virginia School of Law.

AUTHOR'S NOTE: I am grateful to George Rutherglen for valuable assistance with the law of admiralty, to Caleb Nelson for useful discussions about statutory interpretation, and especially to Bobbie Spellman for countless conversations about analogical reasoning, most of which she will likely find unreflected or misunderstood in the pages of this article.

[1] 133 S Ct 735 (2013).

[2] The phenomenon has been noted before. See Ronald Dworkin, *A Matter of Principle*, 119–45 (Harvard, 1985); Timothy Endicott, *Vagueness in Law* 72–74 (Oxford, 2000); Leo Katz, *Why Law Is So Perverse* 137–81 (Chicago, 2011); Frederick Schauer, *Profiles, Probabilities, and Stereotypes* 87–92 (Harvard, 2003); Larry Alexander, *Scalar Properties, Binary*

of that" is not a permissible legal answer, however reasonable such an answer might be in most nonlegal domains. Just as defendants in criminal cases cannot ordinarily find themselves adjudged a little bit guilty and a little bit innocent,[3] however true such a characterization might be, and just as juries in civil cases are not, at least officially, permitted to reach compromise or expected value or split-the-difference verdicts,[4] so too do many legal problems, especially those arising in the application of statutes and regulations, require the judge or jury to determine whether some act or event or thing is or is not within the statutory language, however much the reality may be that the item or action in question is in some respects in and in some respects out.

Lozman was an admiralty case. The central question was whether what most people would perceive as a houseboat was a "vessel" for purposes of the Rules of Construction Act, the statute that, among other things, defines "vessel" for the purposes of almost all of admiralty law.[5] If a houseboat is determined to be a vessel, then most legal proceedings involving it would lie within the exclusive domain of federal admiralty jurisdiction.[6] More particularly, and most relevantly in the context of the *Lozman* case, if a houseboat is a vessel, but only if it is a vessel, it becomes vulnerable to an *in rem* action in admiralty against the vessel itself. In thus forcing on the courts a consequential either/or decision about whether a particular houseboat, one that had some attributes of a house and other attributes of a boat, was or was not a vessel, *Lozman* presented a perfect case study in law's bivalence.

Judgments, 25 J Applied Phil 85 (2008); Saul Levmore, *Public Choice and Law's Either/Or Inclination*, 79 U Chi L Rev 1663 (2012) (book review).

[3] Scotland does allow the verdict of "not proven," but a defendant who receives such a verdict suffers no judicial punishment. See Samuel Bray, Comment, *Not Proven: Introducing a Third Verdict*, 72 U Chi L Rev 1299 (2005).

[4] See *Mitchell v Port Authority of New York and New Jersey*, 885 NYS2d 489 (App Div 2009) (invalidating compromise verdict); Michael Abramowicz, *A Compromise Approach to Compromise Verdicts*, 89 Cal L Rev 231 (2001); John E. Coons, *Compromise as Precise Justice*, 68 Cal L Rev 250 (1980); John E. Coons, *Approaches to Court Imposed Compromise—The Uses of Doubt and Reason*, 58 Nw U L Rev 750 (1964); Elizabeth A. Faulkner, *Using the Special Verdict to Manage Complex Cases and Avoid Compromise Verdicts*, 29 Ariz St L J 297 (1989). The best-known exception is the occasional willingness of courts to allocate damages in mass tort cases on the basis of market share. *Sindell v Abbott Laboratories*, 607 P2d 924 (Cal 1980). And the traditional aversion to compromise verdicts is applicable to criminal as well as civil cases. See Allison Orr Larsen, *Bargaining Inside the Black Box*, 99 Georgetown L J 1567, 1602–12 (2011).

[5] 1 USC § 3 (2010) (defining "vessel").

[6] *Chamber of Commerce v Whiting*, 131 S Ct 1968, 1983 (2011); *United States v Locke*, 529 US 89, 99–100 (2000).

Although *Lozman* provides us with an example of the bivalent nature of so much of legal decision making, the case turns out to be even more interesting than that. For by looking at the way in which the Supreme Court approached the question whether the houseboat was a house or a boat, we can see the case as an important window through which to examine the Court's approach to analogical reasoning. It has long been argued that reasoning by analogy—which is often claimed to be central to human thought generally[7]—is at the core of legal reasoning, legal interpretation, and legal decision making.[8] Sometimes the argument is based on the fact that judges must often determine whether some act or event or thing that does not fall easily within or without a statutory term is close enough to the prototype implicit in the statute to be included within the statute. Judges are thus called upon, so it is said, to decide whether the contested item—a bicycle, in H. L. A. Hart's famous example[9]—is analogous to the noncontested item—the standard automobile. Even more commonly, the argument for analogical reasoning's centrality in legal decision making is based on the way in which judges are frequently required to decide whether some act or event or thing is analogous to the members of one line of precedent or instead to the members of another line.[10] But in both the

---

[7] See Dedre Gentner, Keith J. Holyoak, and Boris N. Kokinov, eds, *The Analogical Mind: Perspectives from Cognitive Science* (Cambridge, 2001); Keith J. Holyoak and Paul Thagard, *Mental Leaps: Analogy in Creative Thought* (Cambridge, 1995); Dedre Gentner et al, *Analogy Just Looks Like High Level Perception: Why a Domain General Approach to Analogical Mapping Is Right*, 10 J Experimental & Theoretical Artificial Intelligence 231 (1998); Keith J. Holyoak, *Analogy*, in Keith J. Holyoak and Robert G. Morrison, eds, *The Cambridge Handbook of Thinking and Reasoning* 117 (Cambridge, 2005).

[8] See especially Edward H. Levi, *An Introduction to Legal Reasoning* (Chicago, 2d ed 2013). See also Melvin Aron Eisenberg, *The Nature of the Common Law* 83–96 (Harvard, 1988); Kent Greenawalt, *Statutory and Common Law Interpretation* 187–88, 217–44 (Oxford, 2013); Neil MacCormick, *Legal Reasoning and Legal Theory* 155–63, 180–92; Lloyd L. Weinreb, *Legal Reason: The Use of Analogy in Legal Argument* (Cambridge, 2005); James R. Murray, *The Role of Analogy in Legal Reasoning*, 29 UCLA L Rev 833 (1982); Cass R. Sunstein, *On Analogical Reasoning*, 106 Harv L Rev 741 (1993). See also Norberto Bobbio, *The Science of Law and the Analysis of Language*, in Anna Pintore and Mario Jori, eds, *Law and Language: The Italian Analytical School* 21, 44 (Deborah Charles, 1997) (arguing that analogical extension is a necessary part of legal discourse but not "a creative act").

[9] H. L. A. Hart, *Positivism and the Separation of Law and Morals*, 71 Harv L Rev 593, 606–15 (1958), and then H. L. A. Hart, *The Concept of Law* 125–27 (Oxford/Clarendon, 3d ed, 2012).

[10] See Levi, *Introduction to Legal Reasoning* (cited in note 8). See also Hart, *The Concept of Law* at 274 (cited in note 9); Christopher J. Peters, *A Matter of Dispute: Morality, Democracy, and Law* 164 (Oxford, 2011); Neil MacCormick, *H. L. A. Hart* 161 (Stanford, 2d ed 2008); Dan Hunter, *Reason Is Too Large: Analogy and Precedent in Law*, 50 Emory L J 1197 (1997); Jefferson White, *Analogical Reasoning*, in Dennis Patterson, ed, *A Companion to Philosophy of Law and Legal Theory* 583 (Blackwell, 1996).

statutory interpretation and competing lines of precedent versions the claim is that reasoning by analogy is a vital component of legal argument and legal decision making. It is thus worth noting that one of the more famous decisions in the analogical reasoning in law canon turns out to have posed a question quite similar to the one presented in *Lozman*. In the 1896 case of *Adams v New Jersey Steamboat Company*,[11] the New York Court of Appeals was required to decide whether a sleeping cabin on a steamboat was like a room in an inn or instead like a sleeping compartment on a train. In deciding that the sleeping cabin was more like a room in an inn than a railroad berth, the Court of Appeals seemingly[12] engaged in a process of analogical reasoning, which is often said to be ubiquitous in law and legal interpretation.[13]

The view that cases like *Adams* exemplify analogical reasoning in law has been subject to strong and influential challenges. In one form or another, Larry Alexander,[14] Richard Posner,[15] Peter Westen,[16] and others[17] have argued that what the traditional view understands as analogical reasoning in law is nothing (or not much) more than (or less than) rule creation or rule application, with the only difference being that sometimes judges are less than transparent about which rule they are applying or which rule they are

---

[11] 45 NE 369 (NY 1896).

[12] See below, text at notes 75–77.

[13] Phoebe Ellsworth, *Legal Reasoning*, in Holyoak and Morrison, *Cambridge Handbook* at 685 (cited in note 7); Gerald J. Postema, *A similibus ad similia: Analogical Thinking in Law*, in Douglas E. Edlin, ed, *Common Law Theory* 102 (Cambridge, 2007); Barbara A. Spellman, *Reflections of a Recovering Lawyer: How Becoming a Cognitive Psychologist—and (in Particular) Studying Analogical and Causal Reasoning—Changed My Views about the Field of Law and Psychology*, 79 Chi Kent L Rev 1187 (2004).

[14] Larry Alexander, *Bad Beginnings*, 145 U Penn L Rev 57 (1996). See also Larry Alexander and Emily Sherwin, *The Rule of Rules: Morality, Rules, and the Dilemmas of Law* 128–35 (Duke, 2001); Larry Alexander, *The Banality of Legal Reasoning*, 73 Notre Dame L Rev 517 (1998); Larry Alexander, *Incomplete Theorizing*, 72 Notre Dame L Rev 531 (1997) (book review).

[15] Richard A. Posner, *Reasoning by Analogy*, 71 Cornell L Rev 761 (2006) (book review). See also Richard A. Posner, *The Problems of Jurisprudence* 86–92 (Harvard, 1990); Richard A. Posner, *Overcoming Law* 518–22 (Harvard, 1995).

[16] Peter Westen, *On "Confusing Ideas": Reply*, 91 Yale L J 1153 (1982).

[17] Kent Greenawalt, *Law and Objectivity* 200 (1992) ("[R]easoning by analogy is not sharply divided from reasoning in terms of general propositions"); Richard Warner, Note, *Three Theories of Legal Reasoning*, 62 S Cal L Rev 1523, 1552–55 (1989). A somewhat different challenge, and one whose importance lies largely in its use of the idea (from formal logic) of *abduction* to explain the practice, is Scott Brewer, *Exemplary Reasoning: Semantics, Pragmatics, and the Rational Force of Legal Argument by Analogy*, 109 Harv L Rev 923 (1996).

creating. By thus acting as if the current decision was based on a preexisting analogy rather than the application of a newly-created but hidden rule, so the argument goes, judges purporting to rely on an analogy are able to mask the extent to which they are in reality making policy decisions, making new rules, and making new law.

The dialectic about analogical reasoning in law does not end at this point, however. For although there is a certain logical appeal to the idea that judges engaging in analogical reasoning are actually making policy decisions and applying rules, many cognitive scientists would claim that the arguments (and prescriptions) of Alexander, Posner, Westen, and others are unfaithful to the reality of human thinking and reasoning. People often do not (and perhaps often cannot) consciously or deliberately reason from particular to general and back to particular, they say, but often go from particular to particular without the conscious mediation of a generalization including both the past instance and the one now under consideration.[18] When judges engage in analogical reasoning, therefore, they are not so much hiding the reality of judicial rule creation and rule application as simply doing what ordinary nonjudicial people do all of the time in the process of thinking and reasoning. Or so it is said.

Lozman thus presents an ideal vehicle not only to note briefly law's bivalence, but also to examine at greater length the even larger topic of analogical reasoning in law. Perhaps the case itself is of little import as a matter of doctrine except to admiralty lawyers and scholars of a small corner of property law. Yet what *Lozman* reveals about the nature of legal reasoning is of considerably more pervasive importance. Indeed, the fact that *Lozman* comes only eight years after the decision in *Stewart v Dutra Construction Company*,[19] in which the Supreme Court decided that an enormous dredge called the "Super Scoop" was to be considered a vessel for purposes of maritime law liability, shows that such questions are very much the stuff of even Supreme Court decision making.[20] How and why this

---

[18] See Holyoak and Thagard, *Mental Leaps* (cited in note 7), whose title phrase of "mental leaps" captures the idea nicely. See also Isabel Blanchette and Keith Dunbar, *How Analogies Are Generated: The Roles of Structure and Superficial Similarity*, 28 Memory & Cognition 108 (2001).

[19] 543 US 481 (2005).

[20] I say "even" because it would be plausible to suppose that by virtue of the selection effect (George L. Priest and William Klein, *The Selection of Disputes for Litigation*, 13 J

is so, and what we should make of it, will constitute the principal focus of this article.

I. The Case

In many respects *Lozman* seems to those of us who are not admiralty specialists like a small case,[21] although it was clearly not so for Fane Lozman. In 2002 he bought a 60-foot by 12-foot houseboat.[22] Over the next four years he lived in the houseboat in four different locations, the craft being towed from one location to another. Finally Lozman and the houseboat wound up in Riviera Beach, Florida, where the houseboat was then docked, and where the events that led to the litigation ensued. A series of disputes between Lozman and the city took place,[23] eventually culminating

Legal Stud 1 (1984)), the Supreme Court's docket would contain few or no cases in which analogical argument from previous cases would be of much value. See Frederick Schauer, *Judging in a Corner of the Law*, 61 S Cal L Rev 1717 (1988). But *Lozman* shows that such a conclusion might be too strong.

[21] On the significance of the case within admiralty law, see Lindsey C. Brock III, *The Practical Effects of Lozman*, 38 Tulane Maritime L J 89 (2013). See also David W. Robertson and Michael F. Sturley, *Vessel Status in Maritime Law: Does Lozman Set a New Course?* 44 J Maritime L & Commerce 393 (2013).

[22] Justice Breyer's majority opinion, about which much more will be said presently, is an interesting exercise in judicial rhetoric. As early as the fifth line of the opinion, Justice Breyer describes the houseboat as a "floating home," 133 S Ct at 739, and proceeds to note immediately thereafter that it is "not self-propelled." Id. Even at that point it should be clear to the reader of the opinion that the Court is going to find the houseboat to be a house and not a boat. And it is likely that had the Court used the term "houseboat," which seems to connote a sort of boat and not a sort of house (just as "boathouse" describes a sort of house and not a sort of boat), there would have been a similar rhetorical effect, but with the opposite conclusion. Indeed, Lozman himself, perhaps as part of his litigation strategy and perhaps not, has always been quite insistent that his residence is a floating home and not a houseboat. See Matt Krantz, *High Court to Hear Trader's Floating Home Case*, USA Today (Oct 1, 2012), available at http://www.usatoday.com/story/money/personalfinance/2012/09/30/eminent-domain-houseboat/1580789//.

[23] The primary dispute revolved around Lozman's efforts to stop a commercial development at the marina where his craft was moored. See Deirdra Funcheon, *After Winning Supreme Court Houseboat Case, Fane Lozman Scores Another Win Against Riviera Beach*, Broward/Palm Beach New Times (March 21, 2013), available at http://www.blogs.browardpalmbeach.com/pulp/2013/03/riviera_beach_amendment_marina_fane_lozman.php. But it is also likely that Lozman was (or was at least perceived by the city as) a litigious gadfly whose persistence, backed by his own personal wealth, eventually got under the city's skin. See *Lozman v Putnam*, 884 NE2d 756 (Ill App, 1st Dist, 2008), leave to appeal denied, 897 NE2d 253 (Ill 2008); *Blue Water Partners, Inc. v Edwin D. Mason, Foley & Lardner*, 975 NE2d 284 (Ill App, 1st Dist, 2012); *Lozman v City of Riviera Beach*, 995 So2d 1027 (Fla App, 4th Dist, 2008), aff'd, 46 So3d 573 (table) (Fla App, 4th Dist, 2010), aff'd, 79 So3d 36 (Fla All, 4th Dist, 2012). See also *City of Riviera Beach v That Certain Unnamed Gray, Two-Story Vessel Approximately Fifty-Seven Feet in Length*, 649 F3d 1259, 1262 n 2 (11th Cir 2011). And see further *City of Riviera Beach v That Certain Unnamed Gray, Two-Story Vessel Approximately Fifty-Seven Feet in Length*, 527 Fed Appx 841 (11th Cir 2013); *Lozman v City of Riviera Beach*, 713 F3d 1066 (11th Cir 2013).

in the city's attempt to evict Lozman and recover dockage fees by instituting an *in rem* admiralty action in federal district court against the houseboat.

The *in rem* action against a vessel is a standard proceeding in admiralty,[24] but the availability of that remedy turns, as it did here, entirely on whether the action was properly considered an admiralty case. If the houseboat was determined to be a vessel, as that term is defined in the Rules of Construction Act,[25] then admiralty jurisdiction would be appropriate (and, indeed, necessary), and the *in rem* remedy sought by the city more or less routine. But if the houseboat was determined to be not a vessel but a house, then there would be no basis for admiralty jurisdiction, no basis for an *in rem* proceeding, and, on the facts of this case, no basis for federal jurisdiction on any other ground. The propriety of the case being in federal court and the availability of the remedy sought by the city therefore turned completely on whether Lozman's houseboat was a boat, and thus a vessel, and thus within admiralty jurisdiction, or whether instead it was a house, and thus not a vessel, and thus not properly the subject of federal jurisdiction or the *in rem* action pursued by the city.

Lozman moved to dismiss the city's action on just these grounds, claiming that his houseboat was a house and not a boat, and therefore not a vessel, making admiralty jurisdiction impermissible. And in addition to advancing the broader claim that his houseboat was principally a house, he relied on the exact statutory language in the Rules of Construction Act, language that included in the definition of a vessel a "watercraft or other artificial contrivance used, or capable of being used, as a means of transportation on water."[26] In particular, Lozman argued that his houseboat, which contained no means of propulsion and which drew its power and utilities from land-based sources, was not "capable of being used" for water-based transportation.

Lozman's efforts to have the suit dismissed for want of admiralty jurisdiction were unsuccessful in the district court, and, after a bench trial in which the city was awarded slightly over three thousand

---

[24] See Steven F. Friedell, 1 *Benedict on Admiralty* §§ 22, 114, 122 (LexisNexis, 7th rev ed 2010); Thomas J. Schoenbaum, *Admiralty and Maritime Law* 894–904 (West, 5th ed 2012).

[25] 1 USC § 3 (2010).

[26] Id.

dollars for dockage fees, Lozman appealed to the Eleventh Circuit. Again he failed in his jurisdictional arguments, the Court of Appeals holding that as long as the houseboat was capable of movement over water it was to be considered a vessel, Lozman's subjective intent to have the boat permanently moored in one place notwithstanding.[27] Because of a split among the circuits on the exact question pressed by Lozman,[28] the Supreme Court granted certiorari.

With Justice Breyer writing for a 7–2 majority, the Supreme Court reversed the Eleventh Circuit and sided with Lozman, holding that his houseboat was not a vessel and that there was consequently no basis for admiralty jurisdiction or an *in rem* action. Rejecting as overinclusive an "anything that floats" understanding of what was to count as a vessel,[29] Justice Breyer and the Court focused on the statutory requirement that the floating "contrivance," to use the language of the statute, must be one, as the statute also put it, "capable of being used . . . as a means of transportation on water." And in then seeking to define and operationalize *this* phrase, the Court held that a floating structure would qualify as being capable of being used as a means of transportation on water only if "a reasonable observer, looking at the home's physical characteristics and activities, would consider it designed to a practical degree for carrying people or things over water."[30]

Justice Breyer and the Court found the application of this newly-created test to Lozman's houseboat a relatively straightforward matter:

> But for the fact that it floats, nothing about Lozman's home suggests that it was designed to any practical degree to transport persons or things

---

[27] *Riviera Beach v That Certain Unnamed Gray, Two-Story Vessel Approximately Fifty-Seven Feet in Length*, 649 F3d 1259 (11th Cir 2011).

[28] Compare *De La Rosa v St. Charles Gaming Co.*, 474 F3d 185, 187 (5th Cir 2006) (holding that a structure is not a vessel where its ability to sail is theoretical and not real, and where the owner intends indefinite mooring in one place), with *Board of Comm'rs of Orleans Leveee District v M/V Belle of Orleans*, 535 F3d 1299, 1311–12 (11th Cir 2008) (structure capable of moving under tow on water is a vessel, regardless of intent to moor indefinitely).

[29] 133 S Ct at 743. See Brock, 38 Tulane Maritime L J at 94, 101 (cited in note 21).

[30] 133 S Ct at 741. Although the subjectivity of the reasonable-observer standard was the principal concern of Justice Sotomayor's dissent, 133 S Ct at 751–52 (Sotomayor, J, dissenting), it is worth noting that the Court did set out an actual test, even if one hardly capable of mechanical application. Still, the Court's willingness to provide a test, rather than issue a fact-specific decision unhelpful to lower courts in future cases, is both unusual (these days) and commendable. See Frederick Schauer, *Abandoning the Guidance Function: Morse v Frederick*, 2007 Supreme Court Review 316.

over water. It had no rudder or other steering mechanism. Its hull was unraked, and it had a rectangular bottom 10 inches below the water. It had no special capacity to generate or store electricity but could obtain that utility only through ongoing connections with the land. Its small rooms looked like ordinary nonmaritime living quarters. And those inside those rooms looked out upon the world, not through watertight port-holes, but through French doors or ordinary windows. [And] [a]lthough lack of self-propulsion is not dispositive, it may be a relevant physical characteristic. And Lozman's home differs significantly from an ordinary houseboat in that it has no ability to propel itself.[31]

The Court's decision attracted two dissenting votes. Writing for herself and Justice Kennedy,[32] Justice Sotomayor objected to the majority's new "reasonable observer" test as unnecessarily subjec-tive. Likening the test to Justice Stewart's memorable "I know it when I see it" understanding of hard core pornography,[33] Justice Sotomayor objected that the test allowed the majority to "import" various "esthetic criteria" into the analysis of what would count as a vessel, and that a more straightforward application of a "practical capacity" for "maritime transport" standard would be far less mal-leable than the majority's "reasonable observer" standard, with se-rious consequences for the predictability of admiralty jurisdiction, consequences that themselves would generate even more conse-quential uncertainties in related areas, for example, the commercial financing of vessels.[34]

Although Justice Sotomayor objected to what she perceived to be a new test, she remained uncertain about the result that would have been produced either by that test or by the older test that she

---

[31] 133 S Ct at 741.

[32] Id at 748 (Sotomayor, J, dissenting).

[33] Id at 752 (Sotomayor, J, dissenting), quoting *Jacobellis v Ohio*, 378 US 184, 197 (1964) (Stewart, J, concurring). Justice Stewart's observation has unfortunately become a common laugh line in academic and popular commentary, but a charitable understanding of what he said would first recognize that he offered the observation as an understanding of the idea of hard core pornography, and *not* as an understanding or definition or test of the legally operative term "obscenity." And a similar charitable understanding would also appreciate that conclusions that cannot be fully explained or justified are often viewed with favor in a not inconsiderable amount of legal, moral, and political theory. To give one prominent example, the particular judgments that serve an important role in the Rawlsian search for a reflective equilibrium are not that different from "I know it when I see it" judgments. Moreover, "I know it when I see it" is not far removed from the view that people can often agree on outcomes even if they cannot agree on the reasons for those outcomes. Cass R. Sunstein, *One Case at a Time: Judicial Minimalism on the Supreme Court* (Harvard, 1999); Cass R. Sunstein, *Legal Reasoning and Political Conflict* (Oxford, 1996); Cass R. Sunstein, *Incompletely Theorized Agreements*, 108 Harv L Rev 1733 (1995).

[34] 133 S Ct at 755 n 6.

understood to be largely a matter of settled law produced by "long-standing admiralty precedent."[35] As a result, she concluded her dissent with a futile plea to remand the case for further proceedings, taking issue not only with the majority's allegedly new test, but also with the fact that the majority proceeded to apply that test itself rather than have it applied in the first instance by a trial court.[36]

II. The Analogical Process

The majority opinion in *Lozman* takes the reader on a Grand Tour of many (perhaps most) of the various contemporary sources of guidance in the interpretation of statutes. Justice Breyer draws heavily on the plain meaning of the words in the text of the Rules of Construction Act,[37] makes use of dictionary definitions of the words in the statute,[38] concludes that the outcome is consistent with the purpose of the statute,[39] finds that the Court's conclusion is compatible with the precedents on the issue,[40] interprets the statute so as to be consistent with other statutes dealing with the same or similar subject matters,[41] and makes what is largely a policy decision[42] when he concludes that an "anything that floats" understand-

---

[35] Id at 755.

[36] Id.

[37] Id at 740, 741–42. See *Perrin v United States*, 444 US 37, 42 (1979) (ordinary meaning is the "fundamental canon" in the interpretation of statutes); *Burns v Alcala*, 420 US 575, 581–82 (1975) (starting with ordinary meaning in interpreting statute); Caleb Nelson, *Statutory Interpretation* 83–84 (Foundation, 2011); Frederick Schauer, *Statutory Construction and the Coordinating Function of Plain Meaning*, 1990 Supreme Court Review 231.

[38] 133 S Ct at 741. See *Ernst & Ernst v Hochfelder*, 425 US 185, 199 nn 20–21 (1976); James J. Brudney and Lawrence Baum, *Oasis or Mirage: The Supreme Court's Thirst for Dictionaries in the Rehnquist and Roberts Eras*, 55 Wm & Mary L Rev 483 (2013); Philip A. Rubin, Note, *War of the Words: How the Courts Can Use Dictionaries in Accordance with Textualist Principles*, 60 Duke L J 167 (2010).

[39] 133 S Ct at 743–44. See *Harbison v Bell*, 556 US 180, 187 n 6 (2009); *United States v Fausto*, 484 US 439, 444 (1988). On the distinction between statutory purpose and actual legislative intent, see especially Felix Frankfurter, *Some Reflections on the Reading of Statutes*, 47 Colum L Rev 527 (1947).

[40] 133 S Ct at 742–43. See *Randall v Sorrell*, 548 US 230, 244 (2006); *Patterson v McLean Credit Union*, 491 US 164 (1989); Nelson, *Statutory Interpretation* at 418–85 (cited in note 37).

[41] 133 S Ct at 744. See *Carlsbad Technology v HIF Bio, Inc.*, 556 US 635, 638 (2009); *Erlenbaugh v United States*, 409 US 239, 243 (1972); Antonin Scalia and Bryan A. Garner, *Reading Law: The Interpretation of Legal Texts* § 39 (Thomson West, 2012).

[42] Antonin Scalia, *Judicial Deference to Administrative Interpretations of Law*, 1989 Duke L J 511, 515 ("[p]olicy evaluation . . . is part of the traditional judicial tool-kit"), as quoted in Nelson, *Statutory Interpretation* at 946 (cited in note 37). See also John Bell, *Policy Arguments in Judicial Decisions* (Oxford/Clarendon, 1983).

ing of a vessel would produce unfortunate applications in other and future cases.[43]

Although Justice Breyer buttresses his conclusion that Lozman's contrivance is a house and not a boat with this wide array of (unweighted and unprioritized[44]) interpretive sources and principles, it remains difficult to escape the conclusion, as the quotation above shows, that the Court's result is actually driven by an analogical process, and one that is based largely on what is almost a counting up of the most obvious features of Lozman's residence and what the Court understands as a typical vessel. That is, the Court appears largely to have reached its conclusion on the basis of a perception of what cognitive psychologists label a "surface similarity"[45] between Lozman's contrivance and a house and a perception of a surface *dis*similarity between it and a boat. In the final analysis, Lozman's residence simply looked more to the Court like a house than a boat. Thus the Court observes, tellingly, that "[b]ut for the fact that it floats, nothing about Lozman's home suggests that it was designed to any practical degree to transport persons or things over water."[46] Yet the "[b]ut for the fact that it floats" phrase is revealing. After all, but for the fact that it flies, an airplane is little more than a bus. Both airplanes and buses are long narrow enclosures with metal on all sides, on front and back, and on top and bottom. Both airplanes and buses have many seats designed to transport, principally, paying

---

[43] 133 S Ct at 744.

[44] For a similar concern about the inability of factors or "general observations" to provide useful guidance to lower courts, see *Daubert v Merrell Dow Pharmaceuticals, Inc.*, 509 US 579, 598–99 (1993) (Rehnquist, J, concurring in part and dissenting in part).

[45] Blanchette and Dunbar, 28 Memory & Cognition (cited in note 18); Dedre Gentner and Cecile Toupin, *Systematicity and Surface Similarity in the Development of Analogy*, 10 Cognitive Science 277 (1986); Keith J. Holyoak and Kyunghee Koh, *Surface and Structural Similarity in Analogical Transfer*, 15 Memory & Cognition 332 (1987). To the same effect, other psychologists distinguish between "featural" and other (and deeper or more structural) forms of similarity. Robert L. Goldstone and Ji Yun Son, *Similarity*, in Holyoak and Morrison, *Cambridge Handbook* at 155 (cited in note 7). And it is plainly the featural similarity between Lozman's houseboat and a house that most heavily influences the Court. This is as good a place as any to note that although cognitive psychologists pay considerable attention to analogical reasoning, they also treat *categorization* and *similarity* as related but different domains of research. In the context of legal decision making, however, what lawyers often think of as analogical reasoning in law partakes of issues of categorization and of similarity as well as of analogical reasoning in the narrower sense. Indeed, although analogical reasoning in law and genuine constraint by precedent are different, see Frederick Schauer, *Why Precedent in Law (and Elsewhere) is Not Totally (or Even Substantially) About Analogy*, 3 Perspectives on Psych Sci 454 (2008), the confluence of questions about categorization and similarity exists for both.

[46] 133 S Ct at 741.

customers from one place to another. And both airplanes and buses have fuel-driven motors designed to produce speeds considerably greater than what can be achieved by walking or on horseback. But for the fact that airplanes fly, there is little to distinguish airplanes from buses.

The purpose of the foregoing *reductio* is to emphasize that any two items have a potentially infinite number of points of similarity and points of difference. When we engage in analogical reasoning, we decide that some of the similarities (or differences) are important and others are not. We perceive a blue car to be more like a red car than like a blue suit because we think that in the standard instance car-ness and suit-ness are more important than blue-ness. Were it otherwise we would think it odd to believe that cars of different colors were similar, just as in most contexts we now think it odd to believe that cars of different colors are not importantly similar, or that cars with the same color as other things are similar to those other things just because of a shared color.

It is at exactly this point that the issue is joined between the majority and the dissent in *Lozman*. The majority believes that floating is just one attribute among many, and that the ability to float is less important than a combination of self-propulsion, style of windows, shape of the hull, and what appears to be primary use. The dissent believes that floating is really important in the definition of a vessel, and that something that floats has at least established a presumptive claim to be a vessel, notwithstanding the lack of self-propulsion, notwithstanding the utility connections to the shore, and notwithstanding the presence of an unconventional (for a ship or boat) shape of hull and style of interior fittings.

In discounting the importance of floating, the majority appears troubled by the overinclusiveness of that criterion. There are things that float but that are not vessels, the majority rightly observes,[47] and from this entirely correct observation then concludes, far more debatably, that floating is just not that important. More precisely, the majority appears to believe that any attribute that is necessary but not sufficient should immediately be downgraded to the category of simply being one among many attributes. But this move is a mistake. Identifying analogies or disanalogies between or among multi-attribute items is not just a matter of counting attributes when

[47] Id at 740, noting that wooden washtubs, plastic dishpans, and doors off their hinges, among others, can float and carry things, but are plainly not vessels in the relevant sense.

none of the attributes is strictly necessary. Some of attributes are simply more important than others. Like floating for vessels. Floating may not be sufficient for vessel-ness, but it is almost certainly necessary, in a way that the presence of portholes or a raked hull are not. Or, to put it differently, floating thus occupies a centrality in the paradigm or prototype case of a vessel that is not occupied by any of the other attributes that the majority identifies as collectively sufficient to render Lozman's home a nonvessel.[48]

The issue of which attributes to feature in determining the extent to which a nonstandard item will still count as sufficiently analogous to the prototypical item is highlighted by contrasting *Lozman* with the Court's relatively recent confrontation with the highly similar question presented in *Stewart v Dutra Constriction Co.*[49] As in *Lozman*, the question in *Stewart* was whether a nontypical floating contrivance was or was not a vessel for purposes of admiralty law. In *Stewart* the contrivance in question was an enormous dredge called the "Super Scoop," which was being used to dredge out part of Boston Harbor as part of the so-called Big Dig highway, tunnel, and harbor construction project. Stewart was a worker injured while employed on the Super Scoop. If the Super Scoop was found to be a vessel, then Stewart would, if he could prove negligence, have a range of tortlike remedies in state or federal court under the Jones Act, and would be entitled to a jury trial.[50] But if the Super Scoop was not a vessel, then Stewart would be deemed a longshoreman or a harbor worker, limited in his relief to the worker's compen-

---

[48] On prototypes, see especially Eleanor Rosch, *Principles of Categorization*, in Eleanor Rosch and Barbara B. Lloyd, eds, *Cognition and Categorization* 27 (Erlbaum, 1978). See also Hans Kamp and Barbara Partee, *Prototype Theory of Compositionality* 57 Cognition 129 (1975); Lance J. Rips, Edward E. Smith, and Douglas L. Medin, *Concepts and Categories: Memory, Meaning, and Metaphysics*, in Holyoak and Morrison, *Cambridge Handbook* at 177, 183–85 (cited in note 7). There is an increasing convergence between psychological and philosophical perspectives. See Dirk Geeraerts, *On Necessary and Sufficient Conditions*, 5 J Semantics 275 (1986); William Ramsey, *Prototypes and Conceptual Analysis*, 11 Topoi 59 (1992). It is clear that the majority and dissent in *Lozman* have different prototypes of vessels in mind, but it is not clear just what those prototypes are. But in thinking that the absence of portholes was a factor in making Lozman's home less of a vessel, it seems at least plain that the majority had in mind a prototype other than a modern cruise ship. And on the related possibility that analogical reasoning in law is best understood as an attempt to engage in a weighted averaging of the attributes of the source and target examples, see Joshua C. Teitelbaum, *Analogical Legal Reasoning: Theory and Evidence*, Georgetown Public Law and Legal Theory Research Paper No 12-131, http://ssrn.com/abstract=2145478.

[49] 543 US 481 (2005).

[50] 46 USC § 688(a) (2010).

sation-like remedies under the Longshore and Harbor Workers Compensation Act.[51]

In unanimously concluding that the Super Scoop was a vessel, the Supreme Court in *Stewart*, with Justice Thomas writing the sole opinion, seemed largely unconcerned with the Super Scoop's limited capacity for self-propulsion, nor with the fact that in few respects did the enormous dredge resemble the prototypical vessel, whatever prototype one has in mind. Rather, the fact that the employees who worked on the Super Scoop were designated as captain and crew, and functioned in such a capacity, appeared to the Court to be relevant,[52] as did the fact that the Super Scoop actually moved workers and equipment while working, albeit only at the rate of thirty to fifty feet every two hours.[53] Like Lozman's houseboat, the Super Scoop rarely moved great distances, had no raked hull, had no portholes, and was not designed to carry goods or passengers from one place to another. In fact the Super Scoop looks like a steam shovel on a flat platform, which is basically what it is. Except that the platform floats. But although the various attributes just noted seemed important to the Court in concluding that Lozman's houseboat was not a vessel, those same attributes seemed relatively unimportant to the *Stewart* Court when it concluded that the Super Scoop was indeed a vessel.[54]

So how are we to understand the difference in outcome between the two decisions? The *Lozman* Court did recognize the basic similarity between the cases, but it distinguished *Lozman* from *Stewart* primarily on the grounds that the Super Scoop had the function of transporting "machinery, equipment, and crew over water."[55] Yet although the Super Scoop did move thirty to fifty feet every few

---

[51] 33 USC §§ 901 et seq. The description in the text truncates a rather more complicated doctrinal issue, in part because the Jones Act is keyed to whether the injured worker is a "seaman," a determination that, through a tortuous doctrinal path, requires determination of whether the craft on which he worked was a "vessel." But for present purposes the oversimplification in the text will suffice.

[52] 543 US at 484.

[53] Id.

[54] It is of some interest that the Court's opinion in *Lozman* includes a photograph of the craft at issue, 133 S Ct at 748, but that the opinion in *Stewart* does not. Given that neither Lozman's floating home nor the Super Scoop look very much like what most people think of as a boat, a ship, or any other sort of water-going vessel, including the photograph in the *Lozman* opinion reinforces the Court's conclusion, just as excluding a photograph from the *Stewart* opinion reinforces the conclusion in that case.

[55] *Stewart*, 543 US at 492, cited in *Lozman*, 133 S Ct at 743–44.

hours, the actual digging was a stationary activity, and the members of the crew were presumably[56] conveyed from their land-based residences to the Super Scoop on a daily basis by a boat—that is, by something far closer to a prototypical vessel than the Super Scoop itself. Indeed, we suspect that when Lozman's houseboat was towed from one location to another, as it had been four times in the previous seven years, Lozman himself was actually on board, or at least could have been,[57] but that when the Super Scoop moved from harbor to harbor the crew followed after it in an entirely different mode of transportation. It is thus plausible to conclude that both Lozman's houseboat and the Super Scoop were plainly designed to *hold* people over water, but that neither was designed to *carry* people over water, at least under any ordinary understanding of the difference between "hold" and "carry."

All of this is to suggest that whatever the Court was doing in *Lozman*, it was not simply following the *Stewart* precedent. Of course the existence of multiple attributes made it possible for the Court to show that its result was not inconsistent with *Stewart*, but it could have as easily done that with the opposite result in the latter case. Plainly the Court felt a need to distinguish *Stewart*, given the similarity of the issues, but given the ease with which any competent lawyer could have identified points of similarity and dissimilarity between the Super Scoop and Lozman's houseboat the conclusion remains that something else seems to have been doing the work in *Lozman*.

It is at this point in the analysis that the Court's reference in *Lozman* to the "reasonable observer" comes to the fore. It is far from clear who the reasonable observer is in the Court's test. Ordinary people, after all, simply do not spend very much time observing either houseboats or waterborne dredges. If one were to ask the person on the street—or the "man on the Clapham omnibus," as the English quaintly put it—whether Lozman's houseboat was "designed to a practical degree for carrying people or things over water," she might well answer in the negative, but we suspect she would answer in the negative for a large number of other things

---

[56] None of the opinions in the case makes reference to cabins or sleeping quarters, although the First Circuit decision below (230 F2d 461, 464 (1st Cir 2000)) notes the existence of a dining area. The most plausible inference is that the Super Scoop contained a lunchroom for the crew but no other living quarters.

[57] That Lozman was apparently quite wealthy, see note 23 above and references therein, might suggest that he had other ways of getting from city to city.

that have been found to be vessels for purposes of admiralty law, including, of course, the Super Scoop, which the reasonable observer might think was designed to a practical degree for digging out harbors and not for carrying people or things.

Thus, the Court's reasonable observer test, especially when its application in this case is seen to rely heavily on an unstructured list of the most overt features of Lozman's craft, seems little more than a substitute for some variety of holistic, intuitive, and largely surface perception of whether something is or is not a vessel. But to the extent that that is so, then *Lozman* can be understood as providing evidence for the traditional view of analogical reasoning, and against the skeptics, for reasons that now warrant closer inspection.

III. The Debate about Analogical Reasoning in Law

As noted above,[58] there exists a genuine debate about the nature of analogical reasoning in law. Against the claims of a long line of theorists and common law celebrants who perceive analogy as central to legal decision making, especially in common law contexts, there are skeptics who see claims about the importance of analogical reasoning in law as little more than attempts to disguise the process of policy making or rule application under an unarticulated or newly-created rule. And one of the features of the debate that makes it both interesting and important is that the skeptics appear to have a certain logic on their side,[59] while the traditionalists, perhaps unknown to many of them,[60] appear to have a considerable amount of cognitive psychology and other forms of cognitive science on theirs. Ordinary people often do think and reason from particular to particular (Piaget labeled it "transduction"[61]), the

---

[58] Text accompanying notes 7–18.

[59] I say "a certain logic" rather than "logic" in part because John Stuart Mill, famously, described inductive logic as the process of moving from particular to particular. John Stuart Mill, *A System of Logic Ratiocinative and Inductive, Being a Connected View of the Principles of Evidence and the Methods of Scientific Investigation* bk 2, ch 3 (Routledge, 1974). See Biaggio G. Tassone, *From Psychology to Phenomenology* 272 (Palgrave Macmillan, 2012).

[60] But not all. The psychological literature is extensively acknowledged in Sunstein, 106 Harv L Rev (cited in note 8), and Weinreb, *Legal Reason* (cited in note 8).

[61] Jean Piaget, *Play, Dreams, and Imitation in Childhood* 231–32 (Norton, 1962). For Piaget (whose experimental methods seem to have consisted largely of observing his own children), but not necessarily for others, moving from particular to particular was a characteristic of early or childhood development. It is thus implicit in Piaget's account that reasoning from particular to particular is something undeveloped, and something that

science appears to say,[62] and often do base their assessment of similarity and difference on the surface rather than structural features of the compared or analogized particulars.[63] And ordinary people frequently do this without the mediation of at least a consciously understood rule.[64] The scientists do not deny that some rule or generalization is necessary in order to determine which similarities and differences are relevant and which not, and in that sense the scientists agree with the skeptics. But the scientists nevertheless reject the notion that what I have called the rule of relevance[65] is consciously understood in many or even most cases of analogical reasoning. Rather, the scientists say, the similarities are frequently perceived as primary, reflecting a deeper rule of relevance, but not a rule that is part of the conscious reasoning process. The rule is still a contingent one, nonuniversally based on the experiences and goals and much else of the analogizer, but it is most often experienced as being just there, rather than as being deliberately or consciously chosen. When people perceive the blue car as similar to the red car but not to the blue dress, for example, they are reflecting a world—or at least their world—in which car-ness is ordinarily more salient than blue-ness and thus comes across to them as immediately and unreflectively obvious.

The foregoing paragraph is embarrassingly truncated, but for present purposes probably sufficient to establish the basic point, which is that ordinary people making ordinary decisions frequently

---

normal people grow out of. Similar claims have been presented in the context of moral development by Piaget's follower Lawrence Kohlberg. See Lawrence Kohlberg, *Essays on Moral Development* (Harper and Row, 1981). Especially but not only in the context of moral development, the view that particularized reasoning is less developed and abstract reasoning more so is highly controversial, both normatively and descriptively. See, for example, Dennis L. Krebs and Kathy Denton, *Toward a More Pragmatic Approach to Morality: A Critical Evaluation of Kohlberg's Model,* 112 Psych Rev 629 (2005). These debates are important, but for present purposes all that we need is the idea that a particular-to-particular reasoning process is possible, without necessarily locating it in any particular stage of development or level of sophistication.

[62] See Lawrence W. Barsalou, *Perceptual Symbol Systems,* 22 Behavioral & Brain Sciences 577 (1999); Robert L. Goldstone and Lawrence Barsalou, *Reuniting Perception and Cognition,* in Steven A. Sloman and Lance J. Rips, eds, *Similarity and Symbols in Human Thinking* 145 (MIT, 1998).

[63] Miriam Bassok, *Analogical Transfer in Problem Solving,* in Janet E. Davidson and Robert J. Sternberg, *The Psychology of Problem Solving* 343 (Cambridge, 2003).

[64] See Arthur B. Markman and Dedre Gentner, *Nonintentional Similarity Processing,* in Ran R. Hassin, John A. Bargh, and James S. Uleman, eds, *The New Unconscious* 107 (Oxford, 2005).

[65] See Frederick Schauer, *Playing by the Rules: A Philosophical Examination of Rule-Based Decision-Making in Law and in Life* 106 (Clarendon/Oxford, 1991).

see similarity and difference, and thus analogy and disanalogy, as primary, or fundamental, or basic. And more importantly, they draw their analogies and reject their disanalogies often without ever going to or even seeing the level of abstraction or generalization that, as a logical matter, undergirds their judgments of similarity and difference.

When we attempt to translate these findings about ordinary people to the thinking, reasoning, decision-making, and analogizing behavior of judges, two important differences need to be noted. First, judges (and lawyers) bring to the process of judging and analogizing a range of knowledge and experiences different from those of the man on the Clapham omnibus.[66] If the ordinary person—perhaps Justice Breyer's "reasonable observer"—is asked whether Nazis, puppy torturers, and members of the Ku Klux Klan are similar to the Jehovah's Witnesses, *The New York Times*, and the leaders of the civil rights movement, we suspect their answer would be no, perhaps coupled with wonderment about how anyone could conceivably think otherwise. But if we ask the same question to someone steeped in the history, theory, and doctrine of the First Amendment, the similarity is obvious.[67] And if we ask our same ordinary person about the similarity among cases of Scotch whisky, racehorses, orange groves, life insurance, and shares of IBM stock, we are likely to receive the same negative response, even though most practitioners of securities law will more or less instantly recognize that all of these seemingly diverse items are (or can be) examples of securities[68] for purposes of registration under the Securities Act of 1933.[69]

Second, judges operate in a world in which they are ordinarily expected both to reflect on their decisions and to justify those decisions with reasons, typically in writing. Judges cannot *say* that they have relied on their hunches or intuitions or immediate reactions,

---

[66] See Barbara A. Spellman, *Judges, Expertise, and Analogy*, in David Klein and Gregory Mitchell, eds, *The Psychology of Judicial Decision Making* 149 (Oxford, 2010).

[67] See, in the order noted above, *Collin v Smith*, 578 F2d 1197 (7th Cir 1978); *United States v Stevens*, 559 US 460 (2010); *Brandenburg v Ohio*, 395 US 444 (1969); *Schneider v Irvington*, 308 US 147 (1939); *New York Times Co. v United States*, 403 US 713 (1971); *Shuttlesworth v Birmingham*, 394 US 147 (1969).

[68] See, in the order noted above, *Glen-Arden Commodities, Inc. v Costantino*, 493 F2d 1027 (2d Cir 1974); *Sheets v Dziabis*, 738 F Supp 307 (ND Ind 1990); *S.E.C. v W.J. Howey Co.*, 328 US 293 (1946); *Wuliger v Eberle*, 414 F Supp 2d 814 (ND Ohio 2006); Securities Act of 1933, § 2(a)(1), 15 USC § 77b (2010).

[69] 15 USC § 77b (2010).

and insofar as they have them we expect at the very least that the requirement of reflection and written justification will weed out those hunches and intuitions and immediate reactions that cannot support a reasoned justification.[70] And so although the traditionalists may have much of contemporary cognitive science on their side in believing that going from particular to particular is possible, the skeptics are also on sound footing in observing that there is a rule of relevance lying behind all analogies, even if it is not consciously perceived as such. And the skeptics are also justified in their seeming belief that, as a normative matter, it is the job of the judge, even if not the job of the experimental subject or the ordinary person in everyday life, to search for, to explain, and to justify just what it is about some feature of the instant case that makes the instant case similar to some previous case, or that, as in *Lozman*, makes the instant case similar to an uncontroversial prototype of the category under discussion.

The existence of a debate between the so-called traditionalists and the so-called skeptics may thus reflect a disagreement that is far more normatively philosophical and jurisprudential than it is psychological and scientific. The skeptics do not typically deny that particular-to-particular reasoning is possible, but argue that, in the context of legal decision making, it is important to go deeper and identify the rules of relevance that make some particulars similar to others.[71] And the traditionalists, who if pressed would recognize the role played by contingent rules of relevance, do not stop simply by claiming that judicial particular-to-particular analogizing is possible and frequent, but also typically go further and treat this process as the occasion for some celebration. Insofar as the more particularized reasoning we associate with analogical reasoning in law necessarily leaves more open, then it brings familiar advantages of flexibility, and with the familiar costs to certainty, predictability, and constraint on decision makers.[72] Conversely, the skeptics are right

---

[70] Although expressed in different terms, the sentence in the text is compatible with the argument in Brewer, 109 Harv L Rev (cited in note 17), drawing on the logical idea of *abduction* to explain legal analogical reasoning in terms of a process that starts with a particular observation, but then uses that observation to construct the explanation that makes the analogy a seemingly sound one. Also useful in thinking about analogy in this way is Peter Lipton, *Inference to the Best Explanation* (Routledge, 2d ed 2004).

[71] See Larry Alexander and Emily Sherwin, *Demystifying Legal Reasoning* 68–76 (Cambridge, 2008).

[72] And thus the debate about analogical reasoning may reflect and travel with the familiar debates about rules versus standards, formalism versus instrumentalism, judicial discretion

to point out the existence of contingent rules of relevance lying behind all analogies, but they too can be seen as making ultimately normative arguments in urging that such rules of relevance be recognized for what they are, and, often brought to the surface for closer inspection. But doing so, like all reason giving, is constraining,[73] and it should be recognized that leaving an analogy unjustified may facilitate a strategy of leaving options open and retaining flexibility to deal with a rapidly changing world, a strategy that may underlie, contingently and controversially, the very idea of the common law itself.

IV. LOZMAN AGAIN, AND SOME ADDITIONAL APPLICATIONS

Understanding the debate between the traditionalists and the skeptics in the way just described allows us to see the issues in *Lozman* in a new light. In relying on the reasonable observer, and in seemingly permitting their initial reaction to the "Is a houseboat a house or a boat?" question to drive almost all of the analysis and conclusion, Justice Breyer and the Court appear to be doing what the cognitive scientists have identified as possible, frequent, and arguably even typical. They are identifying surface similarity and difference without very much delving into the rule or rules of relevance that would produce the similarities and differences, and without exploring those structural similarities and differences that might make surface analogies disanalogous, and surface disanalogies analogous. If the skeptics are understood as saying that moving from particular to particular without consciously identifying a rule of relevance is impossible, or that all rules of relevance are based on nonsurface structural and relational similarities, then the skeptical position appears to be descriptively in error, both for ordinary people and for judges. And that is why it is both more charitable and simply better not to understand the skeptics as denying the possibility of particular-to-particular reasoning,[74] but rather to under-

---

versus judicial constraint, and civil law versus common law models of legal institutional design.

[73] See Frederick Schauer, *Giving Reasons*, 47 Stan L Rev 633 (1995). The constraint is a function of the necessary generality of reasons, such that giving a reason is potentially committing of outcomes in other and future cases. Id. See also Greenawalt, *Law and Objectivity* at 199–200 (cited in note 17).

[74] Thus, Alexander and Sherwin, *Demystifying Legal Reasoning* at 72–74 (cited in note 71), acknowledge that such intuitive or particular-to-particular judgments of similarity are widespread, but would withhold the term "reasoning" as a description of the process.

stand them as arguing on normative grounds for why such a process ought to be deemed, at least in law, as the occasion for further and deeper analysis.

Once we see the skeptics as offering arguments that are substantially normative rather than descriptive, the issue takes on a different cast. If the skeptics are understood to be contending that in the legal and judicial context it is the responsibility of the judge (and of the lawyer arguing to a judge) to dig beneath the surface analogy in order to identify, explain, and justify the rule of relevance, then the skeptics are on sound logical ground in criticizing the Court for failing to engage in the process that we should, they would say, expect of judges even if we do not always expect it of ordinary people and do not expect it of reasonable observers.

This contrast between the descriptive accuracy of the possibility of going from particular to particular and the argued normative desirability, at least for judges, of trying not to do so is hardly restricted to houseboats, dredges, vessels, or admiralty law. Indeed, a useful contrast to *Lozman* may be *Adams v New Jersey Steamboat Company*,[75] noted above, nowadays one of the most prominent cases discussed in the literature on analogical reasoning in law.[76] For although the problem in *Adams*—Is a sleeping cabin on a steamboat like a room in an inn or like a berth in a railroad sleeping car?— is certainly susceptible to a particular-to-particular form of analysis, in fact the New York Court of Appeals did what the skeptics would wish it to do. The judges in *Adams* recognized that the sleeping cabin on the steamboat had attributes of both. It was on an instrumentality of transportation and thus in some respects like the berth on a railroad sleeping car, but it was also a more or less regular room with a lockable door, and thus in some respects like a room in an inn. Recognizing this, the Court of Appeals proceeded to examine the policy considerations underlying the rule of strict liability of innkeepers and those applicable to the requirement of a showing of negligence to recover against a railroad, concluding that those policy arguments militated in favor of strict liability in the

---

[75] 45 NE 369 (NY 1896).

[76] See Weinreb, *Legal Reason* at 41–45, 111–15 (cited in note 8); Alexander, *Bad Beginnings* (cited in note 14); Brewer, 109 Harv L Rev (cited in note 17); Hunter, 50 Emory L J (cited in note 10); Posner, *Reasoning by Analogy* (cited in note 15); Danny Priel, Book Review, 57 J Legal Ed 579 (2007). The first to use *Adams* to analyze the idea of analogical reasoning in law was apparently Martin Golding, *Legal Reasoning* 104 (Knopf, 1984, reissued, Broadview, 2001).

steamboat case. In effect, the Court of Appeals identified an admittedly complex and goal-oriented rule of relevance and applied it, the result of which was to say that the similarities between the sleeping cabin and the inn were legally relevant and the similarities between the sleeping cabin and the berth were not. Rather than being a prime example of analogical reasoning in law, *Adams* on close inspection appears to be Exhibit A for the skeptics.

Much the same conclusion follows if we examine some of the issues arising under the Fourth Amendment. The Fourth Amendment by its words covers "persons, houses, papers, and effects," and we might imagine that application of the amendment would involve the frequent analogical comparison between something searched— an automobile,[77] say, or a telephone conversation,[78] or the cardboard shelter of a homeless person[79]—and the items stated in the text. What has actually happened, however, is that rather than trying to determine whether the particular item is or is not like a house, say, a rule of greater generality has been substituted for the more particular textual specification. The rule of greater generality—the requirement of a "reasonable expectation of privacy"[80]—is then applied to the less clear items. The reasonable lay observer might see an automobile as different from a house, but judges developing a principle underlying the prototype case—the house—can then apply it to other and less clear instances.

Or consider the development of equal protection doctrine. In considering whether discrimination on the basis of gender should be treated in a way similar to discrimination on the basis of race, the Court could have noted the ways in which the two are similar and the ways in which they are different, proceeding then to announce that the similarities were more important than the differences. This would have been more or less the method of *Lozman*. Instead, however, the Court, in the line of cases starting with *Reed v Reed*[81] and continuing with *Frontiero v Richardson*[82] and then on

---

[77] See *California v Acevedo*, 500 US 565 (1991).

[78] See *Katz v United States*, 389 US 347 (1967).

[79] See *State v Mooney*, 588 A2d 145 (Conn 1991).

[80] *Katz* (cited in note 78) at 361 (Harlan, J, concurring). The phrase was incorporated by a majority of the Supreme Court first in *Terry v Ohio*, 392 US 1, 9 (1968), and then in *Alderman v United States*, 394 US 165, 178 n 11 (1969).

[81] 404 US 71 (1971).

[82] 411 US 677 (1973).

to *Craig v Boren*[83] and *Mississippi University for Women v Hogan*,[84] attempted to identify the underlying goals of the Equal Protection Clause itself, and the principles underlying the prototype case of racial discrimination, and, having done so, went on to apply those goals to a form of classification other than race. Indeed, that was the method as well in *Massachusetts Board of Retirement v Murgia*,[85] concluding that discrimination on the basis of age did *not* justify any form of heightened scrutiny.

The current debates about same-sex marriage often seem on the surface to be analogical, but again the surface impression may be misleading. The question of same-sex marriage is in some respects like the question of interracial marriage addressed in *Loving v Virginia*,[86] and in some respects it is different.[87] In public debate the analogical appeal appears to predominate, as proponents of same-sex marriage ask their audiences simply to grasp the similarity, but in judicial (and, often, academic) context we see advocates trying to explain why the similarities are relevant and the differences not.[88] And when they do so, they are offering a theory of equality, or a theory of equal protection, which can then be applied so as to encompass some inequalities and exclude others.

Indeed, a more charitable reading of *Lozman* than I have offered (or than the majority opinion may fully justify) could see the case in much the same way. Justice Breyer does make reference to the purpose of actions *in rem* in admiralty, which is to prevent a major asset, one that may often be the only way to satisfy a judgment, from quickly departing the jurisdiction. The arrest (yes, that is the proper term of art in admiralty law[89]) of the ship emerges as the principal way of preventing this occurrence. Justice Breyer describes this rationale, and then applies it to Lozman's houseboat, conclud-

---

[83] 429 US 190 (1976).

[84] 458 US 718 (1982).

[85] 427 US 307 (1976).

[86] 388 US 1 (1967).

[87] See Stephen Clark, *Same-Sex but Equal: Reformulating the Miscegenation Analogy*, 34 Rutgers L J 107 (2002).

[88] With reference to public policy debates, where again the surface appeals to analogy may reflect deeper differences about goals and rules of relevance, see Barbara A. Spellman and Keith J. Holyoak, *If Saddam Is Hitler then Who Is George Bush? Analogical Mapping Between Systems of Social Roles*, 62 J Personality & Social Psych 307 (1992).

[89] Indeed, one of the charming aspects of admiralty law is its quaint symbolism (the silver oar) and language (not only the "arrest" of a ship, but also, among others, the fact that lawyers who are certified specialists in maritime law are called "proctors in admiralty").

ing that the lack of self-propulsion makes this rationale less applicable here. The Court's application of the rationale seems dubious—we suspect that the houseboat could be towed away in scarcely
more time than the towing vessel could itself depart the jurisdiction—but that is beside the main point here, which is that the Court
does make some effort to give a rule of relevance explaining why
some similarities—the ability to float—and differences—non-self-
propulsion—between Lozman's houseboat and the prototypical vessel are relevant while others are not.[90] Unfortunately, the effect of
this is undercut by an identification of other differences—what Justice Sotomayor calls the "esthetics," for example—that are used to
support a more superficial analogical comparison without an explanation of why they are relevant and why others are not.

On the uncharitable—but seemingly more accurate—reading of
Lozman, then, the case really is an example of analogical reasoning
in the Supreme Court. It is an example of movement from particular
to particular (or from prototype to contested application) without
a substantial explanation of an underlying rationale or rule of relevance explaining which features of the source and which of the
target are relevant and which are not. The argument of the skeptics
is in an interesting way like the ladder in Wittgenstein's *Tractatus*.[91]
Just as we need a ladder to reach a certain height but can discard
it once we have gotten there (putting aside a possible desire to come
back down!), the particulars according to the skeptics may be necessary to help us locate the rule of relevance, but once we have
done so we are applying that rule directly, just as we would apply
any other rule.

The nonadmiralty examples described in this section are only a
small group, and are certainly open to the charge of biased selection.
But insofar as they are representative of a process that can and often
does take place, the examples suggest that true analogical reasoning
in the Supreme Court, and maybe in courts in general, is not nearly
as common as the traditionalists or celebrants would have us believe.
Such true analogical or particular-to-particular reasoning is indeed
possible, as the uncharitable but arguably more accurate reading of

---

[90] On the role of perceived goals in drawing analogies, see Barbara A. Spellman and
Keith J. Holyoak, *Pragmatics in Analogical Mapping*, 31 Cognitive Psych 307 (1996).

[91] Ludwig Wittgenstein, *Tractatus Logico-Philosophicus* 6.54 (Routledge, 1974). See Ly-
nette Reid, *Wittgenstein's Ladder: The Tractatus and Nonsense*, 21 Philosophical Investigations 99 (1998).

Lozman suggests, but a broader survey of examples in which analogical reasoning might have taken place suggests that more often,
at least in courts, the process looks much as the skeptics would have
it, resembling more straightforward instances of rule application.
A charitable reading of the skeptics would not see them as denying
the possibility of particular-to-particular thinking, and thus not as
denying what the cognitive science literature strongly suggests is a
widespread phenomenon. But insofar as the skeptics are advancing
a normative argument about what courts, and not ordinary people,
ought to do, especially when what they do has implications for other
and future cases, it may well be that the reality turns out to be
closer to what the skeptics prefer than even the skeptics tend to
have believed.

V. The Realist Challenge

One of the several attractive features of *Lozman* as a vehicle
for exploring larger themes is that it appears difficult to sympathize
with Lozman himself. Under most understandings of the central
claims of legal realism, judges reach their decisions on largely nonlegal grounds prior to searching for the legal justifications that
would best legally support an outcome generated for nonlegal reasons.[92] And under the version of this claim most commonly attributed to Joseph Hutcheson[93] and Jerome Frank,[94] the nonlegal impetus for the outcome is a hunch, and often a hunch based on the
judge's idiosyncratic reaction to the particular litigants, their lawyers, or the very particular facts of the case.

Lozman may well be an exception to a more general trend in the
opposite direction, but at the very least it is hard to explain this
outcome in Hutcheson-Frank terms. Lozman seems to be a wealthy
and somewhat persistent litigator of sometimes legally dubious
causes,[95] and although such individuals may serve valuable social

---

[92] See generally, on this understanding of realism's central claims, Brian Leiter, *Natu-
ralizing Jurisprudence* (Oxford, 2007); Frederick Schauer, *Thinking Like a Lawyer: A New
Introduction to Legal Reasoning* 124–47 (Harvard, 2009); Frederick Schauer, *Legal Realism
Untamed*, 91 Texas L Rev 749 (2013).

[93] Joseph C. Hutcheson, Jr., *The Judgment Intuitive: The Function of the "Hunch" in Judicial
Decision*, 14 Cornell L J 274 (1929).

[94] Jerome Frank, *Law and the Modern Mind* (Brentano's, 1930).

[95] Including his claim, post-Supreme Court victory, that the very court that he had
argued successfully lacked the jurisdiction to hear the case nevertheless had the jurisdiction
to award him costs against the City of Riviera Beach. *City of Riviera Beach v That Certain*

functions at times, and although Lozman's campaign against commercial development in the Riviera Beach marina might well attract some sympathy, it is unlikely that the full portfolio of Lozman's characteristics and litigation history would show him as someone deserving of the benefit of the doubt, at least as perceived by the typical judge. It is thus difficult to imagine that any of the Justices, on their first encounter with the record, perceived this as a case in which it would constitute a nonlegal good for Lozman to prevail.

Under the less particularistic versions of realism associated with Karl Llewellyn and most of the other realists,[96] Lozman's own case and his own characteristics become less important. Under these versions of realism, the judges are seen as pursuing largely nonlegal policy or moral or ideological goals, with the particular attributes of the particular litigants or even the particular case being of lesser importance.[97] That account would indeed render substantially irrelevant anything about Lozman himself, but in reality there is scant indication that any of the Justices were overly concerned about the larger policy implications of the decision. The very fact that *Lozman* and *Stewart* reached different conclusions about different quasi-vessels suggests the absence of a concern about uniformity across the corpus of admiralty law. And the fact that even the treatment of houseboats, let alone possibly faux houseboats like Lozman's, may be a minor policy matter[98] appears to indicate that the Justices did not have a strong sense of the policy or ideological implications of a decision one way or another. *Lozman* seems simply a case of the Justices applying the law *qua* law as best they saw it, and, insofar as that explanation is sound, *Lozman*, although only one case, stands as somewhat of a counterexample to realist claims about the nature

---

Unnamed Gray, Two-Story Vessel Approximately Fifty-Seven Feet in Length, 527 Fed Appx 841 (11th Cir 2013); *Lozman v City of Riviera Beach*, 713 F3d 1066 (11th Cir 2013).

[96] See William Twining, *Karl Llewellyn and the Realist Movement* (Routledge, 1973); Karl N. Llewellyn, *The Theory of Rules* (Chicago, 2011); Karl N. Llewellyn, *Some Realism about Realism—Responding to Dean Pound*, 44 Harv L Rev 1222 (1931); Karl N. Llewellyn, *A Realistic Jurisprudence: The Next Step*, 30 Colum L Rev 431 (1930). On the even more concrete policy focus of later realism, see Laura Kalman, *Legal Realism at Yale, 1927–1960* at 176–87 (North Carolina, 1986).

[97] Even the policy-focused realists tended to identify and promote more fact- and context-specific legal rules, see Leiter, *Naturalizing Jurisprudence* at 91 (cited in note 92), but these were still rules broader than the particular characteristics of particular litigants.

[98] Although it would be otherwise if *Lozman* turned out to be important for issues involving floating but moored casinos, floating but permanently moored hotels, and the like. See *Lozman*, Brief of the American Gaming Association as Amicus Curiae in Support of the Petitioner, 2012 WL 1773028. See also Brock, 38 Tulane Maritime L J (cited in note 21).

of judicial decisions in general, and about the ideological motivations for Supreme Court decisions in particular.[99]

This conclusion, even if just about one case, is especially important in the context of analogical reasoning in the courts. Once we see that there is no logical or even empirical error in observing that a blue car is in some respects like a blue coat and in those respects unlike a red car, the door is open for a realist understanding of the role of analogical reasoning in judicial decisions. For if any two items are always similar in some respects and different in others, the determined judge with nonlegal goals will always be able to justify the non-legally-generated outcome in terms of a legally appearing analogy. Indeed, that explanation is not that far from that of Edward Levi, whose defense of analogical reasoning in law is often and correctly understood to be an important manifestation of realist thought.[100]

Lozman, however, suggests that even when judges do engage in genuine analogical thinking and reasoning, they may do so without a particular outcome in mind. Rather, like ordinary people in their ordinary thinking processes, they may simply see certain things as similar and other things as different without any view as to whether what follows from that judgment is desirable or not. The analogical reasoning in *Lozman* may be less pervasive than many of the celebrants of analogical reasoning in law suppose, but it may also support the view that the presence of analogical reasoning in law is less supportive of realist arguments than many of the sympathizers (whether descriptively or normatively) with realism have tended to believe.

VI. Conclusion

Lozman is not an important case. It may not even be an

---

[99] Because of the ideological character of much of constitutional litigation, and because the Supreme Court's choice to decide roughly eighty cases a year out of the eight thousand presented to it displays the selection effect in the extreme, so-called attitudinal explanations of judicial behavior seem most justified in the context of the Supreme Court. See, for example, Jeffrey J. Segal and Harold J. Spaeth, *The Supreme Court and the Attitudinal Model Revisited* (Cambridge, 2004). And although it is always a mistake to take a single counterexample as falsifying or even challenging a statistical or probabilistic claim, it is still worth noting that attitudinal explanations appear to do little or no work in explaining *Lozman*.

[100] See Frederick Schauer, *Foreword*, in Levi, *An Introduction to Legal Reasoning* at v (cited in note 8).

important admiralty case.[101] But often the least important cases are the ones that are the most instructive. *Lozman*, after all, resembles not only the issue in *Stewart*, but also the question whether a bicycle or roller skates or a baby carriage or a toy car is a vehicle for purposes of the "no vehicles in the park" rule.[102] H. L. A. Hart came up with that example[103] not because he thought it important, and not even because he thought the real case on which it was probably based was important,[104] but because he believed it was representative of a ubiquitous form of legal decision making.

So too with *Lozman*. But what *Lozman* shows us is not only that the forced choice between something that is some of this and some of that is a pervasive feature of legal decision making, and not only that characterizing debated fringe or penumbral cases around an agreed central core is everywhere in law, but also that many of these cases can be decided analogically or not. That *Lozman* seems to have been decided analogically shows that analogical reasoning in law—going from particular to particular and largely on the basis of surface similarities, without deep consideration of the larger rationales that I have referred to as rules of relevance—is possible. But looking carefully at *Lozman* helps us also to see that analogical reasoning in law may be less common than is often imagined, and that it may also be less desirable than is frequently believed.

---

[101] But see Brock, 38 Tulane Maritime L J (cited in note 21); Robertson and Sturley, 44 J Maritime L & Commerce (cited in note 21).

[102] See Frederick Schauer, *A Critical Guide to Vehicles in the Park*, 83 NYU L Rev 1109 (2008).

[103] Hart, 71 Harv L Rev at 606–15 (cited in note 9).

[104] *McBoyle v United States*, 283 US 25 (1931).

CASS R. SUNSTEIN

CONSTITUTIONAL PERSONAE

Debates over constitutional law familiarly explore competing theories of interpretation. Should judges follow the original understanding of the Constitution,[1] or attempt to reinforce democratic processes,[2] or offer moral readings?[3] The differences among competing theories are of course fundamental. But if we investigate the arc of constitutional history, we will discover another set of differences. They involve disparate *Constitutional Personae*—judicial roles and self-presentations that sharply separate judges (as well as academic commentators). The leading Personae are Heroes, Soldiers, Burkeans, and Mutes. Broadly speaking, Heroes are willing to invoke the Constitution to invalidate state and federal legislation; Soldiers defer to the actions of the political branches; Burkeans favor only incremental change; and Mutes prefer not to decide difficult questions.

Cass R. Sunstein is Robert Walmsley University Professor, Harvard University.

Author's note: I am grateful to Bruce Ackerman, Jack Balkin, Martha Nussbaum, Eric Posner, Geoffrey Stone, David Strauss, Mark Tushnet, and Adrian Vermeule for exceedingly valuable comments on an earlier draft. Daniel Kanter also provided excellent comments and valuable research assistance.

[1] See Antonin Scalia, *A Matter of Interpretation: Federal Courts and the Law* (Princeton, 1998).

[2] See John Hart Ely, *Democracy and Distrust: A Theory of Judicial Review* (Harvard, 1980). The core of the theory can be found in *United States v Carolene Products*, 304 US 144, 153 n 4 (1938).

[3] Ronald Dworkin, *Freedom's Law: The Moral Reading of the American Constitution* (Harvard, 1997).

The four Personae[4] help to define not only internal disputes on the Court but also famous cases and entire eras of Supreme Court history. Countless past and present constitutional disputes involve contests among Constitutional Personae. Consider, for example, recent disputes over same-sex marriage,[5] the Affordable Care Act,[6] the Voting Rights Act,[7] and affirmative action.[8] In all these disputes, and many more, each of the four Personae play important roles (while also cutting across standard ideological and methodological divisions).[9] We can also identify periods of Supreme Court heroism, soldiering, and Burkeanism (though not muteness), certainly with respect to particular constitutional clauses, and sometimes with respect to the Court in general.

An understanding of the Personae cannot, of course, displace standard theories of constitutional interpretation. On the contrary, the choice of Persona is dependent on the selection of some such theory, certainly as a matter of logic. A particular theory (say, originalism) might lead a judge to be heroic, soldierly, Burkean, or mute, as the controversy and the occasion demand. I shall devote considerable attention to this point and hence to the relationship between the Personae and competing constitutional theories. Nonetheless, an understanding of the Personae provides a novel and illuminating perspective on recurring constitutional debates (or so I shall attempt to show).

It is important to emphasize that the Personae are both abstract and stylized, and no real-world judge "is" one or another of them. To be sure, particular judges can be associated with particular Personae, but any such association is best taken to mean only that on especially prominent occasions, the judge has assumed that Persona, or that the judge shows a tendency to adopt that Persona in the most important and challenging cases. Over the course of a career or even a year, many real-world judges will adopt each of the Personae. Some judges switch their Persona from case to case fre-

---

[4] Cicero also spoke of four personae, but in a quite different context and for quite different purposes. See Christopher Gill, *Personhood and Personality: The Four-Personae Theory in Cicero, De Officiis I*, in 6 *Oxford Studies in Ancient Philosophy* 169 (Oxford, 1988).

[5] *United States v Windsor*, 133 S Ct 2675 (2013).

[6] *National Federation of Independent Business v Sebelius*, 132 S Ct 2566 (2012).

[7] *Shelby County v Holder*, 133 S Ct 2612 (2013).

[8] *Fisher v University of Texas*, 133 S Ct 2411 (2013).

[9] See below.

quently, because their preferred theory of interpretation calls for such switching. Other judges have a more or less consistent Persona because their preferred theory calls for it. Still other judges change their stance for strategic or other reasons.

It is important to see that adoption of a Persona need not be opportunistic or manipulative. It is generally an authentic reflection of the role that "falls out" of the judge's preferred theory of interpretation. Nonetheless, it cannot be denied that a judge might adopt a Persona for strategic reasons. For example, a judge might prefer in the abstract to be a Hero, but in light of relevant constraints (such as precedent, internal dynamics on a multimember court, or anticipated public reaction), she might write as a Burkean—with the hope that the Burkean path might eventually produce the same result that heroism would dictate. Muteness might also be strategic, a form of biding one's time until the time is right.[10]

As we shall also see, a Persona might be a reflection of a judge's actual thinking or instead a judge's preferred self-presentation. A judge might, for example, write and present herself as a Burkean even though her actual conception of the judicial role is heroic. Few judges are likely to say or think, "I am a Burkean," but a judge might well have an explicit or implicit account of the judicial role that leads to Burkean votes and opinions. Such a judge would be likely to have a Burkean self-presentation.

No judge self-identifies as a Mute, but all judges think that on occasion, silence is appropriate, and when they do, they are self-conscious Mutes. Most judges do have a soldierly conception of their role, at least on certain occasions. And while no judge will announce, "I am a Hero," many judges do believe that the Constitution sets out ambitious principles of one or another kind, and that it is appropriate for judges to invoke those principles even if the result is to invalidate legislation. In especially interesting cases, a judge might present himself as a Soldier, and that presentation might even reflect his self-understanding—but the judge might be taken as a Hero in the relevant community. As we will see, a Persona might also reflect not a judge's self-understanding or self-presen-

---

[10] While the focus throughout is on American constitutional law, the four Personae can be found in countless legal systems. For example, the Israeli judge Aharon Barak is a well-known Hero, see Aharon Barak, *The Judge in a Democracy* (Princeton, 2008), and the South African Constitutional Court has often been heroic, see Theunis Roux, *The Politics of Principle: The First South African Constitutional Court, 1995–2005* (Cambridge, 2013).

tation, but how a judge is received by some, many, or all members of the community.

The remainder of this essay is organized as follows. Part I describes the four Personae. Part II sets out stylized conflicts among the Personae, describing their standard positions and conflicts. Part III investigates how different theories of interpretation can lead to different Personae. Part IV discusses the relationship between Personae and what is sometimes described as "judicial ideology." Part V discusses how to choose a Persona, with an emphasis on the logical priority of the appropriate theory of interpretation.

I. Heroes, Soldiers, Burkeans, and Mutes

A. heroes

Because of its importance and social salience, the heroic Persona may be the most familiar. The defining characteristic of Heroes is that they are entirely willing to invoke an ambitious understanding of the Constitution to invalidate the decisions of the federal government and the states. Heroes come in many varieties, but whatever their favored approach to constitutional interpretation, Heroes believe in an imperial and potentially transformative role for the federal judiciary in the Constitution's name.

Within the categories of Heroes and heroism, we can find significant differences of degree, from relatively modest Heroes who are willing to strike down acts of Congress without having major reformist aims, to more far-reaching Heroes (Superheroes?) who have large-scale visions and are willing (and perhaps even eager) to embark on significant projects of social change. To sharpen the category, I will generally understand Heroes to have a high degree of theoretical ambition, with an acknowledgment that their ambition may stem from disparate theories of constitutional interpretation. Both originalists and nonoriginalists can be Heroes; we could imagine Second Amendment Heroes, or Equal Protection Heroes, who draw either on their preferred account of the original understanding or on a moral reading of both provisions.

All Heroes can be considered "activist" in the distinctive sense that they are willing to use the Constitution to strike down acts of Congress and of state legislatures.[11] It is important to see that

---

[11] For this definition of activism, see Lee Epstein, William M. Landes, and Richard A.

as used here, the term "heroic" should not be taken to be one of approval; it is merely a descriptive term. In ordinary language, soldiers can of course be heroes as well, and while I aim to distinguish them here, we shall encounter some interesting alliances and antagonisms between the Hero and the Soldier.

Brown v Board of Education[12] is the iconic heroic decision, and its author, Chief Justice Earl Warren, is the iconic heroic judge.[13] The Warren Court was the Court's iconic heroic era, helping to define a conception of the federal judiciary for a generation and more.[14] But other eras have been heroic too, and many judges have been heroic, at least on prominent occasions. John Marshall was the original judicial Hero,[15] especially insofar as *Marbury v Madison*[16] established the institution of judicial review.[17] The *Dred Scott* decision[18] is an important part of the constitutional anticanon,[19] and even if it is egregiously wrong, it reflects a large-scale vision of the constitutional settlement, and so is unquestionably heroic in the sense in which I use that term. The *Lochner* era had many heroic moments (even if some of the Justices on the *Lochner* Court understood and presented themselves as Soldiers or Burkeans).[20] For decades, William Brennan[21] and Thurgood Marshall[22] counted as exemplary Heroes.

Posner, *The Behavior of Federal Judges: A Theoretical and Empirical Study of Rational Choice* (Harvard, 2013).

[12] 347 US 483 (1984).

[13] See Jim Newton, *Justice for All: Earl Warren and the Nation He Made* (Riverhead, 2007).

[14] See Morton Horwitz, *The Warren Court and the Pursuit of Justice: A Critical Issue* (Hill and Wang, 1994).

[15] See in this vein Jean Edward Smith, *John Marshall: Definer of a Nation* (Owl, 1998).

[16] 5 US 137 (1803).

[17] Chief Justice Marshall was also a complex Hero in the sense that many of his decisions did not involve invalidation of the actions of the political branches, but instead gave the national government room to maneuver and thus count as soldierly (in the sense in which I am using that term). See Smith, *John Marshall: Definer of a Nation* (cited in note 15). *McCulloch v Maryland*, 17 US 316 (1819), is of course the most famous decision in this vein. A more soldierly decision is *Gibbons v Ogden*, 22 US 1 (1824).

[18] *Dred Scott v Sandford*, 60 US 393 (1857).

[19] See Jamal Greene, *The Anticanon*, 125 Harv L Rev 379, 406–12 (2011).

[20] For different perspectives, see Howard Gillman, *The Constitution Besieged: The Rise and Demise of Lochner Era Police Powers Jurisprudence* (Duke, 1992); Paul Kens, *Lochner v. New York: Economic Regulation on Trial* (Kansas, 1998); David E. Bernstein, *Rehabilitating Lochner: Defending Individual Rights against Progressive Reform* (Chicago, reprint ed 2012).

[21] See, for example, *New York Times v Sullivan*, 376 US 254 (1964).

[22] See, for example, *San Antonio School District v Rodriguez*, 411 US 1, 70 (1973) (Marshall, J, dissenting).

With his willingness to offer large pronouncements about values such as liberty and dignity,[23] Justice Anthony Kennedy may well be the most heroic member of the current Court,[24] though Antonin Scalia[25] and Clarence Thomas have heroic moments and tendencies.[26] In recent years, heroic judges have voted to invalidate the Affordable Care Act[27] and university affirmative action programs.[28]

Disparate constitutional provisions provide the occasions for heroism, and Heroes qualify as such with respect to particular provisions, not the Constitution as a whole. (General heroism, as I am understanding it here, would be difficult to imagine, because it fits with no recognizable theory of constitutional interpretation.) There are Free Speech Heroes,[29] Equal Protection Heroes,[30] Due Process Heroes,[31] Religious Liberty Heroes,[32] Commerce Clause Heroes,[33] Second Amendment Heroes,[34] Executive Power Heroes,[35] Takings Heroes,[36] Standing Heroes,[37] and many more. A judge might endorse heroism with respect to one provision but firmly reject it with respect to others. Indeed, that pattern is common. When the Court as a whole is heroic for certain periods, its heroism can be found in connection with particular provisions— with, for example, the Warren Court using the First Amendment and the Equal Protection Clause,[38] and the *Lochner* Court invoking the Commerce Clause and the Due Process Clause.[39]

---

[23] See, for example, *Windsor*, 133 S Ct 2675.

[24] See, for example, *Romer v Evans*, 517 US 620 (1996); *Lawrence v Texas*, 539 US 558 (2003); *Windsor*, 133 S Ct 2675. For a general account, see Frank J. Colucci, *Justice Kennedy's Jurisprudence: The Full and Necessary Meaning of Liberty* (Kansas, 2009).

[25] *District of Columbia v Heller*, 554 US 570 (2008).

[26] *Fisher*, 133 S Ct at 2422 (Thomas, J, concurring)

[27] See *National Federation of Independent Business*, 132 S Ct at 2642 (2012) (Scalia, Kennedy, Thomas, and Alito, JJ, dissenting).

[28] See *Fisher*, 133 S Ct at 2422 (2013) (Thomas, J, concurring).

[29] See, for example, *Sullivan*, 376 US 254.

[30] *Brown v Board of Education*, 347 US 483 (1954).

[31] *Roe v Wade*, 410 US 113 (1973).

[32] *Engel v Vitale*, 370 US 421 (1962).

[33] See *United States v Morrison*, 529 US 598 (2000).

[34] *Heller*, 554 US 570 (2008).

[35] See *Myers v United States*, 272 US 52 (1926).

[36] See *Lucas v South Carolina Coastal Council*, 505 US 1003 (1992).

[37] *Lujan v Defenders of Wildlife*, 504 US 555 (1992).

[38] See notes 12–14 and accompanying text.

[39] See note 20 and accompanying text.

Heroism has enthusiastic academic defenders,[40] and academic commentators are often inclined to lionize judicial Heroes and to argue for more in the way of heroism.[41] But it is important to see that heroism's academic defenders are highly diverse in both their ideological orientation and their theory of interpretation. In the aftermath of the era that *Brown* helped to define, many academic commentators saw that decision as establishing the appropriate judicial role, and they hoped for many *Brown*s, vindicating large-scale conceptions of liberty or equality, and reforming society accordingly.[42]

Ronald Dworkin's discussion of Hercules, rendering moral judgments, is the most sustained academic elaboration of the heroic judicial Persona.[43] Emphasizing the heroic role of judges in promoting democratic self-government, John Hart Ely dedicates his influential book to Earl Warren, specifically observing that "you don't need many heroes if you choose carefully."[44] Those who embrace Ely's democracy-reinforcing theory of judicial review are likely to support heroism, at least some of the time.

More recently, those with a libertarian conception of the Constitution, like Randy Barnett[45] and Richard Epstein,[46] are seeking to promote judicial heroism through aggressive use of certain constitutional provisions in the interest of a particular conception of liberty. Efforts to promote a broad understanding of the Takings Clause are meant to produce a form of heroism.[47] Contracts Clause heroism has also been vigorously defended.[48] Consider too recent efforts to understand the Commerce Clause and the Necessary and Proper Clause in such a way as to impose serious restrictions

---

[40] See Ronald Dworkin, *Justice in Robes* (Belknap, 2008).

[41] See Laurence H. Tribe and Michael C. Dorf, *On Reading the Constitution* (Harvard, 1991).

[42] See, for example, Frank Michelman, *The Supreme Court, 1968 Term, Foreword: On Protecting the Poor through the Fourteenth Amendment*, 83 Harv L Rev 7 (1969) (arguing for constitutional welfare rights).

[43] See Ronald Dworkin, *Law's Empire* 238–75 (Belknap, 1986).

[44] Ely, *Democracy and Distrust* at v (cited in note 2).

[45] See Randy Barnett, *Restoring the Lost Constitution: The Presumption of Liberty* (Princeton, 2005).

[46] See Richard A. Epstein, *Takings: Private Property and the Power of Eminent Domain* (Harvard, 1985).

[47] See id.

[48] See Richard A. Epstein, *Toward a Revitalization of the Contract Clause*, 51 U Chi L Rev 703 (1984).

on congressional authority.[49] As we shall shortly see, originalists can certainly be Heroes, and there are Burkean Heroes as well (though their Burkeanism severely qualifies their heroism).

B. SOLDIERS

At the opposite pole from Heroes are Soldiers, who argue in favor of following orders. The defining feature of the judicial Soldier is a willingness to defer to the will of his superiors, typically understood as the political branches of government.[50] In ordinary language, of course, the idea of the soldier can be understood in many different ways. As I understand them here, Soldiers are deferential, and they understand or portray themselves to be subordinates, essentially doing what others have told them to do. (Originalists, who also portray themselves as Soldiers, provide an important wrinkle, to which I will turn in due course.)

Justice Oliver Wendell Holmes is a hero to many, and he may well deserve the label. But in terms of Personae, he was largely a Soldier, as reflected in his famous suggestion, "If my fellow citizens want to go to Hell I will help them. It's my job."[51] With his famous dissenting words in *Lochner*, Holmes helped to define the Persona of the Soldier for more than a century: "a constitution is not intended to embody a particular economic theory, whether of paternalism and the organic relation of the citizen to the state or of *laissez faire*. It is made for people of fundamentally differing views, and the accident of our finding certain opinions natural and familiar, or novel, and even shocking, ought not to conclude our judgment upon the question whether statutes embodying them conflict with the Constitution of the United States."[52] To the extent that he favored protection of freedom of speech,[53] Holmes was a Hero, not a Soldier, but his heroism was limited to that context.

There are many distinguished academic defenses of the Sol-

---

[49] See Richard A. Epstein, *How Progressives Rewrote the Constitution* (Cato, 2006).

[50] This is a familiar theme in the area of statutory interpretation. See Frank H. Easterbrook, *Judges as Honest Agents*, 33 Harv J L & Pub Pol 915 (2010).

[51] Letter from Oliver Wendell Holmes Jr., to Harold J. Laski (March 4, 1920), reprinted in Mark DeWolfe, ed, 1 *Holmes-Laski Letters* 248, 249 (Harvard, 1953).

[52] *Lochner v New York*, 198 US 45, 75–76 (1905) (Holmes, J, dissenting).

[53] See, for example, *Abrams v United States*, 250 US 616, 630 (1919) (Holmes, J, dissenting).

dier.[54] James Bradley Thayer, the great advocate of judicial deference to the outcomes of political processes, is the most important early expositor of the soldierly conception of the judicial role.[55] Adrian Vermeule is its most sophisticated contemporary proponent, offering a careful justification of judicial deference to the outcomes of political processes.[56] Those who embrace populist accounts of constitutional law, who challenge judicial review, or who stress the sovereignty of We the People are likely to endorse the role of the Soldier.[57] To some people, Soldiers are heroes, because they adopt the proper role, and respect the limited place of, the judiciary in the constitutional system. While Soldiers can be seen as heroes, they are emphatically not Heroes.

As with heroism, so with soldiering: there are Equal Protection Soldiers,[58] Due Process Soldiers,[59] Commerce Clause Soldiers,[60] Second Amendment Soldiers,[61] Article II, section 1 Soldiers,[62] Takings Soldiers,[63] Standing Soldiers,[64] and many more. A judge might endorse soldiering with respect to one provision but reject it with respect to others, and again this pattern is common. If a judge or a court embraces heroism in some domains, it is likely to embrace soldiering in others. There is no logical necessity here,[65] but the phenomenon is unmistakable, with (for example) the Warren Court and the *Lochner* Court showing the familiar pattern of selective heroism and soldiering.

[54] See, for example, J. Harvie Wilkinson III, *Cosmic Constitutional Theory: Why Americans Are Losing Their Inalienable Right to Self-Governance* (Oxford, 2012).

[55] James B. Thayer, *The Origin and Scope of the American Doctrine of Constitutional Law*, 7 Harv L Rev 129 (1893).

[56] See Adrian Vermeule, *Judging under Uncertainty: An Institutional Theory of Legal Interpretation* (Harvard, 2006).

[57] See, for example, Larry Kramer, *The People Themselves: Popular Constitutionalism and Judicial Review* (Oxford, 2005); Mark Tushnet, *Taking the Constitution Away from the Courts* (Princeton, 2000).

[58] *Massachusetts v Murgia*, 427 US 307 (1976).

[59] *Roe*, 410 US at 171 (Rehnquist, J, dissenting).

[60] See *Morrison*, 529 US 598 (Breyer, J, dissenting).

[61] *Heller*, 554 US at 636 (Stevens, J, dissenting).

[62] See *Humphrey's Executor v United States*, 295 US 602 (1935).

[63] See *Lucas*, 505 US 1003 (Stevens, J, dissenting).

[64] *Lujan*, 504 US 555 (Blackmun, J, dissenting).

[65] Across-the-board soldering is certainly possible and in some respects appealing, see Vermeule, *Judging under Uncertainty*, cited in note 56, and across-the-board heroism is not unimaginable (though it would be difficult, and it is not easy to see how it might be defended).

To this general account of the Soldier, there is an important qualification. While soldiering as I understand it is associated with judicial deference to the political process, and while I am treating Holmes as the iconic Soldier, other judges, with positions distinctly different from that of Holmes, can claim the mantle of Soldier as well. Insofar as originalists, such as Justice Antonin Scalia and Justice Hugo Black,[66] seek to speak for We the People,[67] they can plausibly be described as Soldiers. Indeed, a form of soldiering is built into their self-presentation, and it is a large part of what gives originalism its intuitive appeal.[68] They too contend that they are simply following orders, not offering moral readings or venturing their own personal accounts of what the Constitution requires. But these kinds of Soldiers are entirely willing to invalidate the actions of the federal government or of the states. To the extent that this is so, it is because they are Soldiers, not in spite of that fact.[69]

We should therefore distinguish between first-order Soldiers, who defer to the judgments of the political process, and second-order Soldiers, who can in a sense count as Hero-Soldiers, willing to trump those judgments when the original public meaning of the Constitution so requires.[70] In fact, many judges present themselves as second-order Soldiers, even if they reject originalism. They contend that they are merely following the Constitution, and adhering to its mandates, even if the result is to strike down legislation. We can go further. Soldiering is the most fundamental and enduring part of the judicial self-presentation and even of judges' self-understanding.[71] In referring to Soldiers, I shall be

[66] See *Adamson v California*, 332 US 46, 68 (1947) (Black, J, dissenting); *Griswold v Connecticut*, 381 US 479, 507 (1965) (Black, J, dissenting).

[67] See Scalia, *A Matter of Interpretation* (cited in note 1).

[68] Id.; Steven G. Calabresi, ed, *Originalism* (Regnery, 2007). For an illuminating and skeptical empirical study, see Frank Cross, *The Failed Promise of Originalism* (Stanford, 2013).

[69] See *Heller*, 554 US at 634–35 ("Constitutional rights are enshrined with the scope they were understood to have when the people adopted them, whether or not future legislatures or (yes) even future judges think that scope too broad").

[70] See, for example, id.

[71] "Formalism," in the pejorative sense, consists of claiming to follow orders, and hence to be soldierly, when some kind of discretionary judgment is being made. See H. L. A. Hart, *The Concept of Law* (Oxford, 1961). Some purported soldiering is a species of formalism in that sense ("faux soldiering"). It follows that a judge may be a Hero but present herself as a second-order Soldier.

speaking of the first-order variety unless otherwise indicated.

C. BURKEANS

Some judges are neither Heroes nor Soldiers but Burkeans,[72] in the sense that they favor small, cautious steps, building incrementally on the decisions and practices of the past.[73] Unlike Heroes, who celebrate ambitious accounts of liberty and equality or of the Constitution's structural provisions, those who adopt the Burkean Persona emphasize the limits of large-scale theories.

In dealing with cases involving basic rights, Burkeans do not want to embrace any kind of foundational theory. They argue for careful attention not to abstractions but to traditions, understood at a level of concreteness. Consider Burke's own words, challenging the primacy of abstract theories: "And first of all, the science of jurisprudence, the pride of the human intellect, which, with all its defects, redundancies, and errors, is the collected reason of ages, combining the principles of original justice with the infinite variety of human concerns, as a heap of old exploded errors, would no longer be studied. Personal self-sufficiency and arrogance (the certain attendants upon all those who have never experienced a wisdom greater than their own) would usurp the tribunal."[74]

Burkeans also prefer narrow rulings, focused on the facts of particular cases. When sitting on the court of appeals, Chief Justice Roberts captured this preference with an aphoristic summary of the Burkean position in constitutional law: "[I]f it is not necessary to decide more, it is necessary not to decide more."[75] Committed Burkeans will choose Burkeanism in all or most contexts, but some judges might be more cautious (and in a sense Burkean) with respect to Burkeanism itself, insisting that the decision whether to be Burkean is best resolved case by case. And in arguing against theoretical ambition and in favor of narrowness, a judge might

---

[72] The classic source is Edmund Burke, *Reflections on the Revolution in France*, in Isaac Kramnick, ed, *The Portable Edmund Burke* 416 (Penguin, 1999).

[73] See Cass R. Sunstein, *Burkean Minimalism*, 105 Mich L Rev 353 (2006); see also Cass R. Sunstein, *One Case at a Time: Judicial Minimalism on the Supreme Court* (Harvard, 1999).

[74] Burke, *Reflections on the Revolution* at 456–57 (cited in note 72).

[75] The "cardinal principle of judicial restraint" is that "if it is not necessary to decide more, it is necessary not to decide more." *PDK Laboratories, Inc. v United States Drug Enforcement Administration*, 362 F3d 786, 799 (DC Cir 2004) (Roberts concurring in part and concurring in judgment).

endorse Burkeanism with respect to one provision but reject it with respect to others.[76]

With their modesty and humility, Burkeans might seem to be close cousins of those Soldiers who are reluctant to invalidate legislation, and alliances are certainly possible between the two Personae. But the two are fundamentally different breeds. Burkeans do not purport to be following anyone's orders or will. They acknowledge and even insist that judges exercise discretion, and to Burkeans, that fact poses a serious problem. Burkeans claim that it is best for judges to exercise their discretion in a way that brackets foundational questions and that ensures small, incremental steps from the status quo. They believe that it is important for judges to speak softly and to carry a small stick.[77]

Notwithstanding this point, some Heroes present themselves as Burkeans, contending that a heroic decision is merely an incremental step.[78] We can certainly imagine at least mildly heroic Burkeans, who are genuinely committed to incrementalism, and who reject the largest theories, but who are nonetheless willing to wield judicial power so as to invalidate legislation. On some occasions, Burkeans might be counted as Heroes as I have used the term, though of a relatively modest variety.

Because of his enthusiasm for tradition,[79] his commitment to case-by-case judgment,[80] and his skepticism about large-scale theories,[81] Justice Felix Frankfurter can be seen as an iconic Burkean. Justice John Marshall Harlan falls in the same category, and in some ways, he may be the most Burkean Justice of all.[82] Justice Sandra Day O'Connor showed strong Burkean inclinations, especially insofar as she liked to focus narrowly on the facts of particular cases.[83] Chief Justice Roberts has written a number of

---

[76] See Sunstein, *Burkean Minimalism* (cited in note 73).

[77] A closely related Persona, not discussed here, is that of the Trimmer, who attempts to steer between the poles. See Cass R. Sunstein, *Trimming*, 122 Harv L Rev 1049 (2009).

[78] *Morrison*, 529 US 598 (2000), is a plausible example.

[79] See, for example, *Youngstown Sheet & Tube Co. v Sawyer*, 343 US 579, 589 (1952) (Frankfurter, J, concurring).

[80] See *Rochin v California*, 342 US 16 (1952).

[81] See *Youngstown*, 343 US at 589 (1952) (Frankfurter, J, concurring).

[82] See Tinsley E. Yarbrough, *John Marshall Harlan: Great Dissenter of the Warren Court* (Oxford, 1992).

[83] See, for example, *Grutter v Bollinger*, 539 US 306 (2003). For a popular account, see Joan Biskupic, *Sandra Day O'Connor: How the First Woman on the Supreme Court Became Its Most Influential Justice* (Harper, 2006).

Burkean opinions,[84] and hence on prominent occasions, he seems to write as a self-conscious Burkean. Justice Ruth Bader Ginsburg can also be counted as a Burkean, in the sense that she emphasizes the need to focus carefully on both facts and precedents.[85] From this catalogue, it should be clear that no less than Heroes and Soldiers, Burkeans come in different shapes and sizes. All of them prize narrow, theoretically unambitious rulings, but they may well disagree with one another.

D. MUTES

While Burkeans favor narrow and unambitious rulings, the Mute prefers to say nothing at all. Of course no judge can be a consistent or frequent mute, and for that reason, Mutes are infrequent players in the constitutional drama. No member of the Court, past or present, can be characterized as a Mute, and for obvious reasons. But when fundamental issues are at stake, the persona of the Mute will have its attractions. Constitutional avoidance is a preferred strategy of the Mute;[86] so too with doctrines of justiciability. With his emphasis on "the passive virtues," through which the Court declines to rule, Alexander Bickel is of course the great theorist of constitutional muteness.[87]

Bickel's own approach emphasizes the strategic and prudential importance of silence, especially on large questions on which the nation is divided. In his account, premature judicial engagement could have a range of harmful consequences for both the nation and the Court.[88] But others favor muteness on nonstrategic grounds, emphasizing what they regard as the restrictions of Article III.[89] We can even identify Mute Soldiers, who maintain silence not for prudential reasons, but because of what they see as the commands of the Constitution itself.

---

[84] See *Windsor*, 133 S Ct at 2696 (Roberts, CJ, dissenting).

[85] See *Shelby County*, 133 S Ct at 2632 (Ginsburg, J, dissenting); *Fisher*, 133 S Ct at 2432 (Ginsburg, J, dissenting).

[86] See, for example, *Kent v Dulles*, 357 US 116 (1958); Anthony Vitarelli, Comment, *Constitutional Avoidance Step Zero*, 119 Yale L J 837 (2009).

[87] See Alexander M. Bickel, *The Least Dangerous Branch: The Supreme Court at the Bar of Politics* (Bobbs-Merrill, 1962).

[88] See id.

[89] See Antonin Scalia, *The Doctrine of Standing as an Essential Element of the Separation of Powers*, 17 Suffolk U L Rev 881 (1983).

Naim v Naim,[90] declining to pronounce on the constitutionality of restrictions on racial intermarriage, is the most prominent example of muteness in action. *Poe v Ulman*,[91] declining to review a Connecticut law forbidding the sale and use of contraceptives, is another prominent illustration. *Hollingsworth v Perry*,[92] invoking standing to dismiss a challenge to a California law banning recognition of same-sex marriage, is the most recent example; it might well turn out to be this generation's *Naim v Naim*. Here yet again, a judge might endorse muteness with respect to one provision (or even controversy), but reject it with respect to others.

II. Dueling Personae

It is easy to find examples of the Personae in action. Many constitutional disputes pit them directly against each other. Such disputes are often illuminatingly seen as stylized debates among the four Personae, with one or another judge assuming a particular role, depending on the issue and the context.

A. IN THE ABSTRACT

In those disputes, the Hero might invoke a large-scale understanding of equality or liberty, or perhaps of the limits on federal power under Article I. The Soldier responds that courts should defer to the outcomes of the political process unless the constitutional infirmity is quite clear—and concludes that it is not. In this way, the Soldier accuses the Hero of arrogance or hubris.[93] The Hero responds, implicitly or explicitly, that the Soldier is willing to disregard clear constitutional constraints on government power, and even to disparage the power of judicial review, usually because of what the Hero sees as the Soldier's unduly narrow conception of liberty or equality.

The Burkean rejects both positions. Like the Soldier, he accuses the Hero of hubris, but he contends that the Soldier is arrogant in his own way, insofar as he adopts a large-scale posture of def-

---

[90] 350 US 891 (1955).

[91] 367 US 497 (1961).

[92] 133 S Ct 2652 (2013).

[93] See, for example, *Lochner*, 198 US at 60 (Holmes, J, dissenting); *Adkins v Children's Hospital*, 261 US 525 (1923) (Holmes, J, dissenting); *Sullivan*, 376 US 254 (White, J, dissenting); *Windsor*, 133 S Ct at 2697 (2013) (Scalia, J, dissenting).

erence (which the Burkean regards as grounded in a theory or abstraction of some kind). Against both the Hero and the Soldier, the Burkean insists on the importance of avoiding large pronouncements and the value of engaging carefully with the particular facts.[94]

The Hero might not respond to the Burkean at all, but if he does, he will insist that the Constitution identifies a general principle and that clarity in the law is far preferable to case-by-case obscurantism.[95] The subtext of the heroic response will be that the Burkean is a coward. The Soldier will regard the Burkean as a temporizer, unwilling to show the proper respect for the democratic branches and leaving a degree of chaos for lower courts to sort out. Where the Burkean sees prudence, the Soldier sees a distinctive kind of arrogance, alongside an inexplicable focus on isolated cases.

The Mute will object to the Hero and the Soldier on grounds similar to those invoked by the Burkean. To the Mute, the proper course is to allow the democratic process to play itself out. Judges ought not to be taking sides. Both invalidation and validation are unacceptable. For the Mute, invalidation is worst of all, because it disables self-government, but validation is also troublesome in light of its legitimating effect in the very domain that people are actively debating.[96] The Mute is more sympathetic to the Burkean, but she believes that it is simpler and cleaner to stay out of the area entirely than to take an incremental step.

Of course the Hero has no patience for the Mute, who (in the Hero's view) is abdicating the judicial role and allowing the Constitution to be ignored in the process. The Soldier insists that the Mute is wrong to stay silent when judges might instead clarify that the issue is for the political process to resolve. The Burkean and the Mute have overlapping concerns, but the Burkean might well believe that a small, incremental step is highly desirable, because it moves the ball in the preferred direction. In the Burkean's view, the Mute is too coy by half.

---

[94] *Chicago v Morales*, 527 US 41, 64 (1999) (O'Connor, J, concurring).

[95] For relevant discussion, see Antonin Scalia, *The Rule of Law as a Law of Rules*, 56 U Chi L Rev 1175 (1989).

[96] See Bickel, *The Least Dangerous Branch* (cited in note 87).

B. ON THE GROUND

For the most vivid recent illustration of these kinds of disputes, consider academic and judicial debates over the constitutionality of restrictions on same-sex marriage.[97] Heroes would want to insist that such restrictions are unacceptable; they would enlist the Equal Protection Clause in support of that conclusion. Citing the example of *Brown*, and even more the heroic decision in *Loving v Virginia*,[98] many academic observers have argued in this direction.[99] By contrast, Soldiers would defer to the political process, saying, in Justice Scalia's words, "the Constitution neither requires nor forbids our society to approve of same-sex marriage, much as it neither requires nor forbids us to approve of no-fault divorce, polygamy, or the consumption of alcohol."[100]

At least if they are not prepared to defer to traditions, Burkeans would favor narrow, incompletely theorized decisions, leaving the most fundamental questions for another day. For example, the Department of Justice urged a broadly Burkean approach to the constitutional challenge to California's Proposition 9, contending that the Court should decline to resolve the largest questions and rule more narrowly that those states that have recognized same-sex civil unions cannot be permitted to deny those unions the label of "marriage."[101] Under this approach, the Court would bracket the question whether states could refuse to recognize same-sex marriages altogether. For their part, Mutes would use doctrines of justiciability to stay entirely out of this domain, and indeed the Court's use of standing in *Hollingsworth* is a conspicuous example of the triumph of the Persona of the Mute.[102]

We can find the same Personae in many other constitutional disputes. *Roe v Wade* is heroic, and those who think the decision

---

[97] See *Windsor*, 133 S Ct 2675; Adam Liptak, *To Have and Uphold: The Supreme Court and the Battle for Same-Sex Marriage*, NY Times (2013).

[98] 388 US 1 (1967).

[99] See, for example, Andrew Koppelman, *Why Discrimination against Lesbians and Gay Men Is Sex Discrimination*, 69 NYU L Rev 197 (1994).

[100] Id.

[101] Brief for the United States as Amicus Curiae Supporting Respondents, *Hollingsworth v Perry*, No 12-144 (filed Feb 28, 2013), see also John Schwartz and Adam Liptak, *U.S. Asks Justices to Reject California's Ban on Gay Marriage*, NY Times (Feb 28, 2013), online at http://www.nytimes.com/2013/03/01/us/politics/administration-to-urge-justices-to-overturn-a-gay-marriage-ban.html.

[102] 113 S Ct 2652, 2659 (2013).

was wrong tend to claim the mantle of Soldiers, while Burkeans wish that the *Roe* Court had ruled narrowly,[103] and of course Mutes would try not to speak at all. *Citizens United*[104] is an emphatically heroic decision, and the three nonheroic Personae can easily be found in debates over campaign finance legislation.[105] Heroes would like to invalidate the Affordable Care Act,[106] while Soldiers would like to uphold it.[107] Here yet again, Mutes would avoid the question, and Burkeans would seek to rule as narrowly as possible.

C. THE LESSONS OF HISTORY (OF ICONS AND ANTI-ICONS)

Some of these disagreements are influenced by a reading of history and by an understanding of the lesson of canonical examples and counterexamples.[108] I have noted that Heroes tend to invoke *Brown*, seeing it as iconic; above all, they do not want to be on the wrong side of history. For such Heroes, *New York Times v Sullivan*[109] and *Reynolds v Sims*[110] are also iconic. For many Heroes, *Lawrence v Texas*[111] is a recent exemplar of an iconic decision (though it can also be characterized as Burkean insofar as it is relatively narrow).

For many Heroes, prominent anti-icons include *Plessy v Ferguson*,[112] *Korematsu v United States*,[113] and *Bowers v Hardwick*,[114] upholding a criminal ban on same-sex marriage. Heroes do not want to write or join another *Plessy*, and they do not want to replicate the experience in *Korematsu* or *Bowers*. Concerned about

---

[103] See Ruth Bader Ginsburg, *Some Thoughts on Autonomy and Equality in Relation to Roe v. Wade*, 63 NC L Rev 375 (1985).

[104] *Citizens United v Federal Election Commission*, 558 US 310 (2010).

[105] For example, Heroes, Soldiers, and Burkeans can be found in *Buckley v Valeo*, 424 US 1 (1976).

[106] See *National Federation of Independent Business*, 132 S Ct at 2642 (Scalia, Kennedy, Thomas, Alito, JJ, dissenting).

[107] Id at 2609 (Ginsburg, J, concurring in part and dissenting in part).

[108] On counterexamples, see Jamal Greene, *The Anticanon*, 125 Harv L Rev 379 (2011). Authors of counterexamples, and architects of the anticanon, might be regarded as Villains. No judge, of course, seeks to assume the Persona of the Villain, and so I do not discuss Villains independently here.

[109] 376 US 254 (1964).

[110] 377 US 533 (1964).

[111] 539 US 558 (2003).

[112] 163 US 537 (1896).

[113] 323 US 214 (1944).

[114] 478 US 186 (1986).

what they see as judicial abdication during wartime,[115] many Heroes see *Korematsu* in particular as an example of what can go wrong when judges operate as Soldiers. Other Heroes regard *Wickard v Filburn*[116] as an anti-icon insofar as it seemed to stretch the meaning of the Commerce Clause in such a way as to give Congress something akin to general police power. Some Heroes are skeptical of *NFIB v Sebelius*[117] and *United States v Carolene Products*[118] insofar as those decisions suggest a degree of deference to legislation that is, in their view, invalid. And for those who believe that Article III imposes sharp limits on standing, *United States v SCRAP* is an anti-icon.[119]

For their part, Soldiers tend to see *West Coast Hotel v Parrish*,[120] with its emphasis on judicial deference, as iconic. They think the same for *Wickard*, because of its deferential approach to the Commerce Clause, and also *Katzenbach v Morgan*, with its endorsement of broad deference to congressional power under the Fourteenth Amendment.[121] For Soldiers, *Dred Scott*[122] tends to be the worst decision in the anticanon; they also focus on *Lochner v New York*. They are acutely aware of Justice Holmes's cautionary notes about the hazards of reading any particular moral or political theory into the Constitution. Many Soldiers believe that *Roe v Wade* is a more recent incarnation of *Lochner*—and they invoke *Roe* as a reason for deference to political processes.[123] Some Soldiers also object to *Miranda v Arizona*,[124] which they regard as a form of lawless heroism.

It is important to acknowledge, however, that second-order Soldiers understand *Lochner, Roe,* and *Miranda* as wrong not merely or even mostly because they invalidated the outcomes of democratic processes, but because they did so without a warrant in the

---

[115] See William H. Rehnquist, *All The Laws But One: Civil Liberties in Wartime* (Vintage, 2000).

[116] 317 US 111 (1942).

[117] 132 S Ct 2566 (2012).

[118] 304 US 144 (1938)

[119] 412 US 669 (1973).

[120] 300 US 179 (1937).

[121] 384 US 641 (1966).

[122] See *Dred Scott v Sanford*, 60 US 393 (1857).

[123] See Ely, *Democracy and Distrust* (cited in note 2). Ely did not, of course, consistently defend soldiering, but he did so in this context.

[124] 384 US 436 (1966).

Constitution. Hero-Soldiers reject *Lochner* and *Roe*, but they are perfectly willing to strike down limits on the individual right to possess firearms,[125] to invoke the limited nature of the Commerce Power to strike down the Affordable Care Act,[126] and generally to reinvigorate restrictions on national power.

Some Burkeans might approve of the Court's sex discrimination cases, in which the Court did not rule broadly all at once, but instead proceeded narrowly and cautiously.[127] For those Burkeans, the sex discrimination cases are iconic. Burkeans tend to see *Roe* as objectionable not because it took steps to protect the right to choose, but because of its heroism, embodied in a broad, ambitious ruling, going well beyond what was necessary to decide the case.[128] In this sense, *Roe* is a Burkean anti-icon. As noted, *Naim v Naim* occupies pride of place in the canon of muteness—and the 5–4 decision in *Hollingsworth v Perry*,[129] understood as an exercise of the passive virtues, promises to join it.

D. PERSONAE AS LITERARY DEVICES

One way to understand the Personae is as rhetorical or literary devices. On this understanding, the Soldier (for example) has a characteristic rhetorical strategy, which is to say, "I am compelled to do X, even though I might like to do Y." This strategy might be, and is, used both by first-order and second-order Soldiers. Something similar could be said about Burkeans, who like to say that they are building narrowly on precedent, even if what they are doing is a novelty or a substantial departure, or plausibly characterized as a form of heroism. To be sure, it is not possible to disguise or feign muteness, but a judge might adopt the Persona of the Mute not because of a commitment to soldiering (as in the view that Article III requires muteness) but as a rhetorical gambit designed as part of "the long game." On this view, the analysis of Constitutional Personae might properly be regarded as belonging to the study of judicial politics or even law and literature.[130]

---

[125] See *Heller*, 554 US 570.

[126] See *National Federation of Independent Business*, 132 S Ct at 2642 (Scalia, Kennedy, Thomas, Alito, JJ, dissenting).

[127] See, for example, *Reed v Reed*, 404 US 71 (1971).

[128] See Ginsburg, 63 NC L Rev 375 (cited in note 103).

[129] 133 S Ct 2652 (2013).

[130] I am indebted to Adrian Vermeule for making this suggestion.

This view is not exactly wrong, and much can be learned by examining the Constitutional Personae in this light. But I am understanding them quite differently here. We might well see the Personae not as a matter of judicial politics or rhetoric, but instead as a product of how different judges actually understand their jobs, and of how they perform those jobs in different contexts. When scholars defend the moral reading of the Constitution,[131] they are not adopting a mere rhetorical stance,[132] and the same is true of judges who essentially attempt moral readings.[133] And when judges operate as Soldiers, it may well be because that Persona captures their understanding of their appropriate role. These points bring us directly to the relationship between theories of interpretation and the Personae.

III. Personae and Theories of Interpretation

It is natural to wonder about the relationship between the Constitutional Personae and standard theories of constitutional interpretation. We can already glimpse the basic answer, which is that the standard theories can lead to adoption of one or another of the Personae, depending on the occasion. The words "depending on the occasion" are important. As we shall see, any one of the Personae can fall out of a given theory of interpretation. What matters is exactly when it does so, and here the relevant theory is critical.

A. THEORIES FIRST, PERSONA SECOND?

Suppose that judges embrace originalism. Such judges would be Mutes when the original understanding of Article III so requires, but they would be Hero-Soldiers if (say) the original understanding of the Commerce Clause or the Fourteenth Amendment calls for invalidation of the Affordable Care Act or affirmative action programs, and they would become Soldiers if the original understanding of the Fourteenth Amendment requires them to uphold restrictions on same-sex marriage. If, by contrast, judges believe in democracy-reinforcement, they might be Heroes on voting

---

[131] See Dworkin, *Freedom's Law* (cited in note 3).

[132] At least they are not adopting a rhetorical stance by virtue of defending a moral reading, though of course rhetoric will play a role in their arguments.

[133] See, for example, *Lawrence*, 539 US 558.

rights but Soldiers in the context of abortion rights.[134] And if judges endorse a moral reading of the Constitution, they might be Heroes with respect to same-sex marriage but Soldiers with respect to economic rights (or vice versa, depending on their preferred moral theory).[135]

From these examples, it seems clear that many judges will adopt a Persona in accordance with their own theory of constitutional interpretation, whether or not that theory is made explicit. Of course it is true that judges may lack a simple or unitary theory, and they may adopt a Persona on the basis of a collection of considerations that cannot be captured in any kind of theory or "ism."

There are some important (if speculative) qualifications. We have seen that judges may adopt a Persona for strategic reasons. They may speak as Burkeans even though their own theory is Heroic, and the same is true for second-order Soldiers. They may act as Mutes even though they would like to be Heroes (and plan to be). Some judges are undoubtedly drawn to a Persona for social or psychological reasons, and as a matter of causation, the Persona might well antedate their adoption of the relevant constitutional theory. Some judges' self-understanding draws them to the idea of the Soldier, whereas others are led to Burkeanism or to enthusiasm for the Hero. Before they even begin to engage with questions of theory, some people greatly admire the idea of heroic judging (as elaborated, for example, by Dworkin[136] or Ely[137]), whereas to others, that idea seems anathema or a form of hubris. In my view, these social or psychological motivations are important and even foundational, but that claim is highly speculative.

B. CONTEXT

We should also be able to see that different judges may well adopt different Personae in different situations, perhaps because of their preferred approach to constitutional interpretation, perhaps because of contextual considerations. Judges need not be inconsistent or flighty if they are Heroes on one day and Mutes

---

[134] See John Hart Ely, *The Wages of Crying Wolf*, 82 Yale L J 920 (1973).

[135] See Ronald Dworkin, *Taking Rights Seriously* (Harvard, 1977).

[136] See Dworkin, *Law's Empire* (cited in note 43).

[137] See Ely, *Democracy and Distrust* (cited in note 2).

on the next. Whatever their approach, most judges are likely to believe that there is a place for "the passive virtues."[138] When the nation is sharply divided, they might therefore choose to be Burkean or Mute even if they would choose Heroism if a national consensus authorized it.

For example, someone who believes in moral readings (as did Bickel, emphatically[139]) might also believe in prudence, and for that reason might believe that silence is golden if courts seek to preserve their own political capital. In the words of Gerald Gunther, Bickel believed that courts should be "100 percent principled, 20 percent of the time."[140] Gunther was a critic of Bickel, but a believer in the passive virtues could easily embrace the basic idea. A judge who believes in democracy-reinforcement could similarly agree that there is a time and a place for muteness.

IV. PERSONAE AND IDEOLOGY

Commentators often divide judges along political lines, and reasonably so. A great deal of empirical work shows that in ideologically contested cases, Republican appointees vote differently from Democratic appointees, and Republican appointees differ from one another, as do Democratic appointees.[141] We should now be able to see that a central division, not involving ideology as such, is among Personae. As noted, Justice Kennedy is often a Hero while Chief Justice Roberts is often a Burkean, and Justice Antonin Scalia is frequently a Hero-Soldier. Consider, for example, Justice Scalia's opinion for the Court in *Heller*,[142] invoking the original understanding in support of the view that the Second Amendment creates an individual right.

During and after the *Lochner* era, the great liberal judges were Soldiers.[143] Rejecting the heroism of judicial decisions invalidating minimum wage and maximum hour legislation, celebrated Soldiers

---

[138] Bickel, *The Least Dangerous Branch* (cited in note 87).

[139] See id.

[140] See Gerald Gunther, *The Subtle Vices of the "Passive Virtues,"* 64 Colum L Rev 1, 3 (1964).

[141] See Epstein, Landes, and Posner, *The Behavior of Federal Judges* (cited in note 11).

[142] *Heller*, 554 US 570.

[143] See *West Coast Hotel*, 300 US 379; *National Labor Relations Board v Jones & Loughlin Steel Co.*, 301 US 1 (1937).

(above all Justice Holmes[144]) argued in favor of judicial deference to legislation. During the Warren Court, by contrast, conservatives assumed the mantle of the Soldier.[145] They treated the heroic Warren Court decisions of the 1950s and 1960s as a form of hubris. And indeed, a judge can be heroic on a Tuesday (for example, by voting to invalidate a provision of the Voting Rights Act[146]) and a Soldier on Wednesday (for example, by voting to uphold the Defense of Marriage Act[147]). The rapid switch from Hero to Soldier might seem to be a form of inconsistency, even hypocrisy, but the appearance may well be misleading, for it need not be anything of the kind. The shift might be an artifact of the judge's theory of interpretation.

Edmund Burke is known of course as one of history's great conservatives,[148] and to qualify as such, all Burkeans are conservative in the sense that they seek to build incrementally on the past. But some Burkeans (as I am understanding them) build incrementally in a liberal direction, whereas others build incrementally to the right. In many areas, Byron White was a liberal Burkean,[149] while Chief Justice Roberts is a conservative one, as was Sandra Day O'Connor.[150]

There are multiple theories of constitutional muteness, and they need have no political valence. We have seen that some judges embrace an account of Article III, grounded in text and history, that forbids courts from issuing advisory opinions or hearing generalized grievances.[151] That account would produce a number of Mute decisions. But we have also seen that by emphasizing "the passive virtues," Bickel meant to draw attention to, and to embrace, quite pragmatic and strategic uses of silence, designed to limit the occasions for judicial intervention into the political domain.[152]

---

[144] *Lochner*, 198 US at 65 (Holmes, J, dissenting).

[145] See, for example, *Frontiero v Richardson*, 411 US 677, 690 (1973) (Rehnquist, J, dissenting); *Roe*, 410 US at 171 (Rehnquist, J, dissenting).

[146] See *Shelby County*, 133 S Ct 2612.

[147] See *Windsor*, 133 S Ct at 2697 (Scalia, J, dissenting).

[148] See Jesse Norman, *Edmund Burke: The First Conservative* (Basic, 2013).

[149] See Dennis J. Hutchinson, *The Man Who Once Was Whizzer White: A Portrait of Justice Byron R. White* (Free Press, 1998).

[150] See Sunstein, *One Case at a Time* (cited in note 73), for references.

[151] See, for example, Scalia, 17 Suffolk U L Rev (cited in note 89).

[152] See Bickel, *The Least Dangerous Branch* (cited in note 87).

Bickel did not contend that his own account was required by the text of Article III; his emphasis was on prudence.

On one view, muteness is an extreme point on the same continuum with Burkeanism, reflecting a form of judicial statesmanship, and Mutes are Burkeans with less courage (or more prudence). What is clear is that the passive virtues can be enlisted in the service of either conservative or progressive goals.

V. Choosing a Persona

Which Persona is best? Is it possible to offer criteria by which to answer that question?

A. THE RIGHT THEORY

I have suggested that the answer lies in the identification of the right theory of constitutional interpretation. If originalism is the right theory, the appropriate Persona will be an artifact of that theory. So too with judges who embrace a democracy-reinforcing approach to judicial review, or who insist on a moral reading. The correct theory is logically prior to the choice among the Constitutional Personae, who may well appear as they do because of the theory that lies in the background.[153]

This is particularly easy to see for Heroes and Soldiers; both of these Personae will "fall out" of the prevailing theory of interpretation. Which Persona falls out of any particular theory will depend on the nature of the particular question. The same is true for Burkeans and Mutes. We could have a Burkean theory of interpretation, seeing constitutional law as closely akin to the common law.[154] Even if a judge believes that a Burkean theory is only part of the picture, and unlikely to be complete, Burkean considerations, counseling prudence, might make Burkeans out of those who also have enthusiasm for some other theory of interpretation. If an originalist believes in the claims of precedent, he might sound like a Burkean, and to the extent that he is willing to abandon the original understanding to protect precedent, he might even turn out to be a Burkean, at least in particular cases.[155] We have seen

---

[153] I have noted, however, that a Persona may be adopted for strategic reasons.

[154] See David A. Strauss, *The Living Constitution* (Oxford, 2010).

[155] See Antonin Scalia, *Originalism: The Lesser Evil*, 57 U Cin L Rev 849, 861–64 (1989) (embracing "faint-hearted originalism" in light of the claims of precedent).

that muteness may be a product of originalism, but it might also be part of an account of interpretation that allows a place for silence.

It would be possible to end simply by insisting that the choice of Personae must be parasitic on the choice of a theory of interpretation (bracketing psychological or strategic factors that may lead a judge to favor a particular Persona). But that claim leaves open the question about how to make that choice.[156] On that question, a few remarks will be in order.

B. WHAT'S INTERPRETATION?

Some people insist that the very idea of interpretation leads to a particular account of what judges must do to claim that they are engaged in the interpretive enterprise. Perhaps interpretation, to qualify as such, entails a search for the original "intent"[157] or the original public meaning,[158] or instead for a judgment that puts the existing legal materials in the best constructive light.[159] If so, the idea of interpretation generates the appropriate theory, which in turn produces the relevant Persona.

It is true that some activities cannot be counted as interpretation at all. If a judge disregards the constitutional text and rules however he sees fit, he is not engaged in interpretation. But it is false to say that the idea of interpretation, as such, makes the choice among competing approaches. A judge who is committed to interpretation might nonetheless choose to disregard the original intent in favor of the original understanding—or vice versa. Such a judge might emphasize specific and concrete understandings or instead understandings that are more abstract and general[160]—or vice versa. Such a judge may or may not favor moral readings.

---

[156] See Adrian Vermeule, *Interpretive Choice*, 75 NYU L Rev 74 (2000).

[157] See Walter Benn Michaels, *In Defense of Old Originalism*, 31 W New Eng L Rev 21 (2009), and in particular this suggestion: "[Y]ou can't do textual interpretation without some appeal to authorial intention and, perhaps more controversially, you can't (coherently and non-arbitrarily) think of yourself as still doing textual interpretation as soon as you appeal to something beyond authorial intention—for example, the original public meaning or evolving principles of justice." Id at 21.

[158] Saikrishna Prakash, *Radicals in Tweed Jackets: Why Extreme Left-Wing Law Professors Are Wrong for America*, 106 Colum L Rev 2207 (2006).

[159] See Dworkin, *Law's Empire* (cited in note 43) (contending that interpretation involves tasks of "fit" and "justification").

[160] See Jack M. Balkin, *Living Originalism* (Belknap, 2011).

There is nothing in the idea of interpretation that resolves real debates among competing theories or about competing Personae.

C. ERRORS

As a first approximation, the choice is an inescapably pragmatic one, and it turns mostly on the magnitude and number of errors ("error costs").[161] Suppose that Heroes move society in the right direction, because they have the right conception of liberty and equality. If so, it would seem to follow that judges should be heroic.[162] But suppose that judicial Heroes are error-prone and that Burkeans would do far better, in the sense that they would make fewer and less damaging mistakes. If so, Burkeanism is preferable, because it is safer insofar as it minimizes the seriousness of errors.

However simple, these points suggest the need for a comparative assessment, involving the judgments of judges and of those whom they would displace.[163] In a world in which judges systematically err and in which democratic processes do well, the argument for Soldiers would be very strong. In a world in which judges are excellent at correcting for democratic deficits—for example, by safeguarding rights that are indispensable to well-functioning political process—a democracy-reinforcing conception of review, overseen by Heroes, would be difficult to contest. The argument for such Heroes would be weakened if judges are unable or unwilling to undertake that task. There is no acontextual argument on behalf of Heroes or Soldiers, and nothing in the idea of interpretation can settle the choice.

An evident complication is that to know whether we have error costs, we need an account by which to identify error. Suppose that democratic self-government is one of the rights to which people are entitled. If so, the arguments for Soldiers are strengthened. Those who reject soldiering might respond that the ideal of self-government has its own internal morality,[164] and that an imperfectly democratic process, or a process that fails to respect basic

---

[161] To the same general effect, see Vermeule, *Judging under Uncertainty* (cited in note 56).

[162] I am bracketing the question whether self-government is one of the rights that people have and whether and when Heroism is objectionable for that reason.

[163] See Vermeule, *Judging under Uncertainty* (cited in note 56).

[164] See Dworkin, *Law's Empire* (cited in note 43).

rights, calls for heroism not in opposition to democracy but in its name.[165] Originalists might want to insist that to be worthy of the name, Soldiers do not merely implement legislative will. They must follow the will of We the People as well, and that approach will call for invalidation of democratic outcomes, and indeed for decisions that might be mistaken for heroism.[166] Hero-Soldiers— they will insist—are Soldiers, not Heroes at all.[167]

An independent complication involves the level of generality at which judges are choosing among Personae. It is hard to make an across-the-board judgment in favor of heroism or muteness, but a judge might be confronted with a decision whether to be a Soldier in general or only in particular cases, and the same decision might be made by a judge contemplating Burkeanism. A judge could plausibly conclude that some provisions and some occasions call for soldiering, but that others do not, and that no categorical judgment for or against soldiering would make sense.

To be sure, some advocates of soldiering argue vigorously on behalf of a categorical or general choice in favor of the Soldier.[168] They may be correct, but an evaluation of their view, and of whether a general commitment to soldiering is preferable to a case-by-case judgment about whether soldiering makes sense in the circumstances, requires an assessment of the magnitude and number of errors associated with the competing approaches.[169] The same can be said for Burkeans. Perhaps a Burkean approach makes sense for the Due Process Clause but not for the Equal Protection Clause,[170] or perhaps such an approach is best for the Constitution as a whole. Here too an assessment of error costs is inescapable.

VI. CONCLUSION

Constitutional law is populated by Four Personae, who argue with one another in a wide variety of periods and contexts.

---

[165] Id.

[166] See Scalia, 57 U Cin L Rev 849 (cited in note 155).

[167] For an empirical test, see Cross, *The Failed Promise of Originalism* (cited in note 68).

[168] See Vermeule, *Judging under Uncertainty* (cited in note 56).

[169] This is a version of the familiar choice between rules and standards. See Louis Kaplow, *Rules Versus Standards: An Economic Analysis*, 42 Duke L J 557 (1992).

[170] See Cass R. Sunstein, *Sexual Orientation and the Constitution: A Note on the Relationship Between Due Process and Equal Protection*, 55 U Chi L Rev 1611 (1988).

For example, we can find debates between Heroes and Soldiers in disputes over substantive due process,[171] free speech,[172] and property rights;[173] Heroes and Mutes are often in conflict.[174] Because the arguments of the four Personae are easily identifiable, at least in the abstract, an understanding of those arguments, and of their characteristic features, helps to illuminate the enduring nature of constitutional disagreement.

Different theories of constitutional interpretation can lead judges to adopt one or another of the Personae, depending on the controversy. Hence it should be no surprise, and no cause for embarrassment, if a judge turns out to be a Hero on Monday and a Soldier on Tuesday. We can also find incompletely theorized agreements[175] in favor of heroism, soldiering, Burkeanism, or muteness—as, for example, when judges with different methodological commitments converge on silence.[176] And while I have contended that a theory of constitutional interpretation is logically prior to the choice of a Persona, it is not at all unreasonable to speculate that a Persona might be adopted for strategic reasons, or that a Persona might have special appeal for psychological reasons.

No judgment about the role of the courts, or about Constitutional Personae, can sensibly be made in the abstract, or independently of concrete judgments about what can be counted as a mistake, and about who is likely to be trustworthy. In some imaginable worlds, Heroes are heroes; in others, they are hardly that, and they may even be villains. In some imaginable worlds, Soldiers respect democracy without jeopardizing anything of importance; in others, they leave fundamental rights vulnerable to unreliable majorities. In some imaginable worlds, Burkeans strike the proper balance between self-government and other values; in others, they are far too cautious, and their incrementalism is a vice. In some imaginable worlds, Mutes make silence golden; in others, they capitulate to the worst forms of injustice and overreaching. The right Persona depends on the plot of the play.

---

[171] See *Roe*, 410 US 113.

[172] See *Sullivan*, 376 US 254.

[173] See *Lucas*, 505 US 1003.

[174] See, for example, *Windsor*, 113 S Ct 2675.

[175] See Cass R. Sunstein, *Incompletely Theorized Agreements*, 108 Harv L Rev 1733 (1995).

[176] See *Perry*, 113 S Ct 2652.